THE OXFORD F

WOMEN AND GENDER IN MEDIEVAL EUROPE

The *Oxford Handbook of Women and Gender in Medieval Europe* provides a comprehensive overview of the gender rules encountered in Europe in the period between approximately 500 and 1500 C.E. The essays collected in this volume speak to interpretative challenges common to all fields of women's and gender history—that is, how best to uncover the experiences of ordinary people from archives formed mainly by and about elite males, and how to combine social histories of lived experiences with cultural histories of gendered discourses and identities. The collection focuses on Western Europe in the Middle Ages but offers some consideration of medieval Islam and Byzantium.

The *Handbook* is structured into seven sections: Christian, Jewish, and Muslim thought; law in theory and practice; domestic life and material culture; labour, land, and economy; bodies and sexualities; gender and holiness; and the interplay of continuity and change throughout the medieval period. It contains material from some of the foremost scholars in this field, and it not only serves as the major reference text in medieval and gender studies, but also provides an agenda for future new research.

Judith M. Bennett taught women's history and medieval history at the University of Southern California. She is the author of a number of books and articles on medieval women and on the feminist practice of history, as well as a popular textbook on medieval European history. She is a former president of the Coordinating Council for Women in History.

Ruth Mazo Karras teaches history at the University of Minnesota. She is the author of five books and numerous articles in medieval history and the history of gender and sexuality. She is General Editor of the Middle Ages Series at the University of Pennsylvania Press, and a former president of the Berkshire Conference of Women Historians.

THE OXFORD HANDBOOK OF

WOMEN AND GENDER IN MEDIEVAL EUROPE

Edited by

JUDITH M. BENNETT

and

RUTH MAZO KARRAS

OXFORD

UNIVERSITY PRESS

OXFORD
UNIVERSITY PRESS

Great Clarendon Street, Oxford, OX2 6DP,
United Kingdom

Oxford University Press is a department of the University of Oxford.
It furthers the University's objective of excellence in research, scholarship,
and education by publishing worldwide. Oxford is a registered trade mark of
Oxford University Press in the UK and in certain other countries

© Oxford University Press 2013

The moral rights of the authors have been asserted

First published 2013
First published in paperback 2016

Published in the United States of America by Oxford University Press
198 Madison Avenue, New York, NY 10016, United States of America

British Library Cataloguing in Publication Data
Data available

Library of Congress Cataloging in Publication Data
Data available

ISBN 978-0-19-958217-4 (Hbk.)
ISBN 978-0-19-877938-4 (Pbk.)

Acknowledgments

The editors and authors thank our colleagues who commented on drafts, our families who endured our distractions, and Cameron Bradley for the good humor, efficiency, and care with which he helped the volume take final shape.

Contents

PART V BODIES, PLEASURES, DESIRES

PART VI ENGENDERING CHRISTIAN HOLINESS

PART VII TURNING POINTS AND PLACES

List of Illustrations

LIST OF CONTRIBUTORS

John H. Arnold is Professor of Medieval History at Birkbeck College, University of London.

Kathleen Ashley is Professor of English at the University of Southern Maine.

Judith R. Baskin is Philip H. Knight Professor of Humanities at the University of Oregon.

Elisheva Baumgarten is Associate Professor of Jewish History and History at the Hebrew University, Jerusalem.

Judith M. Bennett is John R. Hubbard Professor of History at the University of Southern California.

Jonathan P. Berkey is James B. Duke Professor of International Studies and Professor of History at Davidson College.

Constance H. Berman is Professor of History and Collegiate Fellow in Liberal Arts and Science at the University of Iowa.

Lisa M. Bitel is Professor of History and Religion at the University of Southern California.

E. Jane Burns is Druscilla French Distinguished Professor of Women's and Gender Studies at the University of North Carolina.

Kate Cooper is Professor of Ancient History at the University of Manchester.

Jennifer Kolpacoff Deane is Associate Professor of History at the University of Minnesota at Morris.

Albrecht Diem is Associate Professor of History at the Maxwell School of Syracuse University.

Joanna H. Drell is Associate Professor of History at the University of Richmond.

Dyan Elliott is Peter B. Ritzma Professor of the Humanities in the Department of History at Northwestern University.

Amalie Fößel is Professor of Medieval History at the University of Duisburg-Essen.

Katherine L. French is J. Frederick Hoffman Professor of History at the University of Michigan.

Monica H. Green is Professor of History at Arizona State University.

Fiona J. Griffiths is Associate Professor of History at New York University.

Martha C. Howell is Miriam Champion Professor of History at Columbia University.

Ruth Mazo Karras is Professor of History at the University of Minnesota.

Marie A. Kelleher is Associate Professor of Medieval History at California State University.

Maryanne Kowaleski is Joseph Fitzpatrick SJ Distinguished Professor of History at Fordham University.

Roberta L. Krueger is Burgess Professor of French at Hamilton College.

Carol Lansing is Professor of Medieval European History at the University of California, Santa Barbara.

Sara McDougall is Associate Professor of History at John Jay College of Criminal Justice, CUNY.

Sally McKee is Professor of European History at the University of California, Davis.

Anneke B. Mulder-Bakker is Senior Lecturer Emerita in History and Medieval Studies at the University of Groningen.

Janet L. Nelson is Emeritus Professor of Medieval History at King's College London.

Katharine Park is Samuel Zemurray, Jr and Doris Zemurray Stone Radcliffe Professor of the History of Science at Harvard University.

Helmut Puff is Professor of History and German at the University of Michigan.

Sarah Rees Jones is Senior Lecturer in the Department of History at the University of York.

Kathryn Reyerson is Professor of History at the University of Minnesota.

Kathryn M. Ringrose is Professor of History at the University of California, San Diego.

Alice Rio is Lecturer in Medieval European History at King's College London.

Miri Rubin is Professor of Medieval and Early Modern History at Queen Mary University of London.

Laura Stokes is Assistant Professor of History at Stanford University.

Rachel Stone is Postdoctoral Research Associate in History at King's College London.

Susan Mosher Stuard is Professor of History Emerita at Haverford College.

Jane Whittle is Professor of History at the University of Exeter.

CHAPTER 1

....

WOMEN, GENDER, AND MEDIEVAL HISTORIANS

....

JUDITH M. BENNETT AND RUTH MAZO KARRAS

MEDIEVAL people considered "man" the human standard and "woman" peculiarly capable of both extraordinary good, as with the Virgin Mary, and evil, as exemplified by Eve. For many centuries after the close of the Middle Ages, historians echoed these assumptions, treating medieval women as *the* marked gender—as opposed to men whose gender went unnoticed—and characterizing women as both revered (ladies on pedestals) and maligned (witches at the stake). But no longer. Since the 1970s, historians of medieval women have written more often about variety and opportunity than pedestals or stakes, and since the 1990s, gender historians have unpacked the many genders and gendered languages of medieval Europe.

This volume grows from these new understandings of medieval women, men, and gender. On the one hand, the essays collected here continue the ongoing task of creating fully peopled histories of the Middle Ages, and to that end, the volume focuses more on women than men. Some authors highlight women's agency and creativity (see chapters by Fiona Griffiths and Anneke Mulder-Bakker). Others focus on how women's lives varied across social, regional, religious, and temporal contexts (see chapters by Elisheva Baumgarten, Sarah Rees Jones, and Martha Howell). Still others argue that women were central actors in the unfolding of medieval history (see chapters by Albrecht Diem and Constance Berman). On the other hand, this volume also explores the many meanings of gender in the Middle Ages. The chapters by Kathryn Ringrose, E. Jane Burns, and Helmut Puff evoke a rich history of medieval gender benders and diverse masculinities and femininities. Some women seemed manly in their devotion; some men seemed feminine in their subjection to God; and gendered ideas flowed so freely that scholars can now argue that medieval people sometimes made room for three or more genders.[1]

Gender shaped the life options of medieval women and men; it also shaped how medieval people thought about their world. Gendered language described institutions—Christians saw their church, for example, as a bride of Christ—shaped views of nature, often imagined as a sort of goddess, and even worked to malign minorities;

Christians saw Muslim men as sodomitical and Jewish men as effeminate. Gendered metaphors—God as a father; Mercy as a female; Jesus (or in Jewish mysticism, God) as a mother—were everywhere in medieval Europe. Even biblical stories opened up multiple possibilities, as discussions of the figures of Mary and Martha by Kate Cooper (for the early Middle Ages) and Jennifer Deane (for later) show.

As the editors of this collection, we are acutely aware of the boundaries we set, especially our focus on the medieval west, and the gaps that remain, especially our slight coverage of medieval masculinities. We also hope that our new histories will not drown out the old. The stereotypes of pedestal and stake seem hopelessly dichotomous today, but they contain some truth. Medieval thinkers both respected *and* denigrated women; women themselves were both restricted *and* resourceful, as has been true, it seems, in virtually all human societies. Despite all the flexibilities of medieval genders, the pervasive notion of a God-given hierarchical gender binary—"man" as more perfectly human than "woman"—constrained medieval ideas about both sexual difference and the agency of women. Thus, although Christians, Jews, and Muslims disagreed on many issues, they agreed that "woman" was less than "man," a necessary but weaker divergence from the male (human) standard (see chapters by Dyan Elliott, Jonathan Berkey, Judith Baskin, and Katharine Park). Yes, some extraordinary medieval women achieved a great deal—more than even most men—and some were even deemed man-like, for better or worse. But these viragoes had first to transcend their lesser femaleness by virtue of wealth, privileged birth, personality, or spiritual power. At any given level of medieval society and in any medieval century, a girl—and the woman she became—had fewer choices and opportunities than did her brother.

BACK STORIES

Stories about women and gender helped to create the very idea of the "Middle Ages." Some of the earliest stories were remarkably silly yet long-enduring. In the "Renaissance" (from the fourteenth century in Italy, the sixteenth century farther north), when Europeans were beginning to construct a medieval dark age between the glories of ancient Rome and their own self-perceived glory, they concocted barbaric gender customs for that medieval past: aristocratic lords who by right took the maidenheads of peasant brides; crusaders who clasped hideous chastity belts on their wives; and a cross-dressed woman who became pope and died in public procession, after going into labor and giving birth. The burden of these myths echoes even today, in brides threatened with legal violation as in the film *Braveheart*, in pornographic "reconstructions" of chastity belts, and in a Pope Joan reimagined as a feminist heroine.[2]

In early modern Europe, these stories did what cross-cultural comparisons of women and gender have often done: they elevated one civilization and denigrated another. It is no accident that the earliest stories about the "right of the first night" were set not just in a medieval past but also in the wilds of Scotland and Ireland, or that the story of

Pope Joan was gleefully repeated by Protestant critics of Catholicism. These early stories tell more about the interpretive creation of a maligned "Middle Ages" than about actual medieval women and genders.

When nineteenth-century European intellectuals settled on a three-part past of ancient, medieval, and modern, stories about women and gender remained powerfully determinative of "medieval." In France, a heated public debate raged for decades about whether lords had, indeed, once claimed the virginity of serf brides (and if so, the church's complicity in the practice). In England, a gothic revival reimagined the Middle Ages as a glorious age of unquestioned faith, chivalrous knights, and honored ladies. The Lady of Shalott—celebrated in poetry by Alfred Lord Tennyson (1833) and in painting by John William Waterhouse (1888)—epitomized the feminine in Victorian medievalism: loosely lifted from Arthurian legend, she was young, beautiful, pure, and tragic. In the United States, Henry Adams's *Mont-Saint-Michel and Chartres* (1904), addressed to his nieces and based largely on a reimagination of the Virgin Mary, introduced Americans to this romantic, touching, and forever-lost Middle Ages.

This is not to say that much serious study was given to medieval women and gender during the nineteenth century. The first professional medievalists—all men—told stories about kings and state-building, popes and religious institutions. They systematically doubted the authenticity of female authors: they dubbed Dhuoda's handbook the product of a household priest, Hrosvit of Gandersheim's plays a clever hoax, Hildegard of Bingen's writings the work of male secretaries, and Heloise's letters the creation of Peter Abelard. Medievalists are still undoing this mischief today.[3]

By the early twentieth century, however, a few female medievalists had found secure footing, mostly at women's colleges and mostly in technical fields (especially legal and economic history) that signaled their non-amateur status. A few, emboldened by the emerging politics of feminism, began to study medieval women as a subject in their own right. Like male historians interested in state-building kings and reforming popes, these female medievalists focused on elites and told stories that spoke to the aspirations of their day; they found in the Middle Ages a rough-and-ready equality of women and men. Their foundational studies were full of insight, archival discoveries, and admirable women—confident nuns, hard-working wives, and intrepid queens.

When feminism waned in the middle decades of the twentieth century, so too did interest in medieval women and gender, and the few studies then produced usually offered more downbeat evaluations. In 1955, Betty Bandel traced a negative trajectory for women, arguing that a powerful ruler like Æthelflæd of Mercia (r. 911–918) was discussed matter-of-factly in the tenth century, considered disturbingly man-like by the twelfth century, and trivialized as a troublesome wife soon thereafter. When medieval women's history revived in the 1970s, the mid-century gap was so profound that Eileen Power's half-century-old essays were repackaged as a new and authoritative survey.[4]

The 1970s and 1980s created the study of medieval women as a vibrant field. Susan Mosher Stuard edited an early collection of essays (1976); Shulamith Shahar produced the first textbook (1981); feminist medievalists started a journal (1986), now the *Medieval Feminist Forum*; and the Society for Medieval Feminist Scholarship was established

(1992).[5] These were heady decades of fact-finding, when feminist historians scoured archives, accumulated data, and crunched numbers, all with an eye to recovering the lost history of women. David Herlihy, often working with Christiane Klapisch-Zuber, told about women's restricted land-holding, their improved life expectancy after 1000, their ages at marriage and family sizes.[6] His use of quantitative data provided a new evidentiary base, but the data and their meanings, once seemingly so secure and transparent, are now much debated, as Maryanne Kowaleski shows in her chapter. Caroline Bynum traced how female mystics reshaped Christian spirituality and how they and others played with gender by, for example, imagining Jesus as a maternal figure.[7] Some now question the extent of a specifically female spirituality, but Bynum's pioneering work encouraged extensive feminist interrogation of the texts and artifacts of medieval piety, reflected here especially in the chapters by Deane, Miri Rubin, Kathleen Ashley, and Mulder-Bakker. Herlihy and Bynum, just two among the scores of feminist historians who published in these decades, also lent their substantial credibility—as presidents of both the Medieval Academy of America and the American Historical Association—to this emerging field.

Some historians of medieval women also began at this time to expand on a narrative of decline. Among social historians, Georges Duby argued that early medieval aristocratic families had been relatively egalitarian, but that this changed from the eleventh century, when women's options narrowed, thanks to the growing importance of patrimonial property, primogeniture, and public office. Among feminist historians, Marion Facinger (who argued in 1968 that early Capetian queens enjoyed powers later queens lacked) and Jo Ann McNamara and Suzanne Wemple (who traced in 1973 the "power of women through the family" in early medieval Europe) also saw ever-lessening options for medieval women. These narratives accorded well with Joan Kelly's electrifying thesis (in 1977) that women tended to lose opportunity precisely when male opportunity was expanding.[8] Timing the decline earlier than Kelly (who located it in the Renaissance), medievalists suggested that there might have been no "High" Middle Ages for women, that this triumphal era of religious reform, state-building, universities, and cathedrals was, for women, an era of waning opportunity.

This neat chronology is no longer quite so compelling. Duby's thesis has been substantively undermined by archival studies, as Joanna Drell's chapter indicates. The circumstances of women in early medieval Europe are now understood as more limited than McNamara and Wemple allowed (chapters by Lisa Bitel, Janet Nelson and Alice Rio, and Rachel Stone capture the wide range of these circumstances). Continuities in women's lives can seem more striking than changes (see, for example, Jane Whittle's chapter on rural economies). And historians now understand medieval women as much fuller participants in the developments that enhanced European life from the eleventh century (see, for example, the chapters by Griffiths, Berman, and Kathryn Reyerson). But the notion of ever fewer opportunities for women remains a quiet backbeat in many feminist histories; readers will discern it, for example, in Stuard's discussion of marital assigns and Howell's treatment of the gendered meanings of mercantile capitalism.

By 1993, when the Medieval Academy of America devoted an issue of *Speculum* to "Studying Medieval Women: Sex, Gender, Feminism," the field was securely established.[9] It was also changing rapidly, influenced especially by postmodernism and third-wave feminism. "Women" no longer constituted a secure, transparent category; differences among women took on new importance; grand chronologies seemed newly suspicious; historians more openly acknowledged the interpretative processes that give meaning to seemingly transparent facts; and "gender" took center stage. From the 1970s, feminists had understood biological "sex" as distinct from the social construction of "gender." By the 1990s, this sex/gender distinction was less secure, particularly under the force of the argument that even biological sex differences were, in fact, socially created—thus, all "sex" was "gender."[10] Joan Scott's path-breaking article on "Gender: A Useful Category of Historical Analysis" (1986) inspired a plethora of studies that delved more deeply than before into discursive constructions of genders and sexualities.[11]

This collection shows how much feminist medievalists today draw on—and move beyond—these varied traditions. We strive to juggle both women's history and gender history. We tussle about the possibility of women's changing status over time—whether within the Middle Ages or at the junctures of ancient/medieval and medieval/modern. The essays collected here are most certainly not the fruit of a single methodology, a single chronological vision, or a single judgment as to women's status, and we do not aim in this introduction to wrestle these many voices into a univocal synthesis. Using the seven categories into which we have grouped our chapters, we review the ways in which feminist medievalists are now—armed with new sources, new methods, and new questions—rewriting yet again the many histories of medieval women and gender.

GENDERED THINKING

Every era has its own beliefs about what constitutes "women," "men," and their proper interrelationship; in the Middle Ages these assumptions accorded rather more authority to religion and less, for example, to science. Thinking on gender was rooted in the three religions of the time, Christianity, Judaism, and Islam; in scientific teachings; and in political traditions. Each constituted an authoritative literate discourse, and together they spoke about women and gender in a remarkably coherent chorus. Women were understood as less than men, female attributes as less good than male ones, and gender relations as properly characterized by womanly submission and manly governance. Theology had pride of place in these discussions not only because so much medieval learning was produced in religious contexts but also because religious inquiry then included almost all knowledge. For example, natural philosophy, which we today call science, explained God's creation, and political theory taught how humans should operate within God's rules. Gender rules were similarly God-given, and the submission of women to men paralleled the submission of all humanity to God.

There was much variation and change, of course. Elliott shows how Christian teach-ings on marriage and virginity developed over time, albeit from a core of patristic texts; Berkey traces the many elements—Arab, Roman, and Sassanid contexts, as well as Qur'anic teachings—that comprised Islamic traditions; and Baskin stresses that restrictions on Jewish women were more acute in religious ritual than economic prac-tice. Scholars once favored hierarchical histories of these three intertwined traditions, usually telling how Jewish women were best off, Muslim women least so, and Christian women somewhere in between. Now, historians more often depict women in all three traditions as swimming against patriarchal tides that varied by time, place, and faith. Many also now see women as moving more readily than men across confessional divides—in market places, childbearing, domestic service, and, indeed, even slavery (see chapters by Baumgarten and Sally McKee).

We are only beginning to appreciate how much Latin, Hebrew, and Arabic cul-tures learned from each other. Thus, for example, whether finding piety in celibacy (Christians) or marriage (Jews and Muslims), theologians in all three traditions con-structed female sexuality as a disruptive and polluting worry. Medical theories, as Katharine Park shows, traveled across these cultures, as each adapted classical texts (especially Aristotelian ones) in distinctive but similar ways. Medieval misogyny was not, then, solely a nefarious construct of sexually repressed Christians, nor a mere offshoot of Christian misogamy (anti-marriage polemic). Denigration of women was vicious, powerful, and cross-cultural; it was also sometimes little more than a learned game in which, as Alcuin Blamires has put it, authors could "show off their literary paces."[12]

Medieval Europe was by no means unusual in assuming male dominance; nor was it unique in articulating this assumption inconsistently and applying it ambivalently. Medieval thinkers were quite capable of holding, at one and the same time, contradic-tory ideas about women and gender. This is perhaps nowhere clearer than in political theory as enacted in coronation rituals, where, as Amalie Foessel shows, rule by women was at once intolerable and tolerated.

In the fifteenth century, anti-woman discourses were both magnified and challenged. Beliefs about women as sorcerers became more prominent, growing alongside a con-tinuing tradition of learned magic as a male preserve; from this development, among others, would emerge the witch crazes of early modern Europe (see chapter by Laura Stokes). As some strands of anti-woman discourse deepened, explicit refutations also developed. Christine de Pizan initiated in 1405 a debate about the misogynous ideas so deeply embedded in literature and theology, and her determined writings mark one ori-gin of feminist thought in Europe (see chapter by Roberta Krueger).

Learned traditions—articulated mostly by men working in major intellectual insti-tutions—speak to only some parts of the gendered thinking of medieval people. Imaginative literatures move away from universities, yeshivas, and madrasas into the more lay, albeit still elite, worlds of medieval courts and townhouses. There, medi-evalists now discern considerable pleasure in stories that dwell on gender trouble—in women who act like men, men who act like women, and a wide array of sexual desires.

Thomas Aquinas and other scholastics prescribed how women and men *should* be; the poems and romances produced by Chrétien de Troyes and others imagined how women and men *might* be. Yes, husbands should govern their wives, just as theologians taught; yes, it was fun to laugh at tales of disobedient wives, such as Alison in Chaucer's *Miller's Tale*; in practice, most people expected wives to behave as competent but lesser partners to their husbands. As Berkey notes in relation to Islamic practices, the rich were particularly able to adhere to learned gender ideals. Most medieval people were poor, very poor. Ordinary folk certainly imbibed some learned ideas from clergy and elites, but they had their own traditions too, visible rarely, only partially, and mostly for the last medieval centuries.

LOOKING THROUGH THE LAW

Law provides some of the best source material for medieval gender rules as applied to ordinary people. Prescriptive law reveals how lawyers, judges, and legislators understood gender differences; it broadly echoes the story told in other learned traditions. Documents of legal practice, such as court records, notarial registers, and charters, tell something else; they provide valuable evidence for the actual lives of humble women and men. These records of legal process did not mirror social reality, for only certain matters merited legal attention and court procedures determined how those matters were reported. But for historians today, medieval law, as both prescribed and practiced, constitutes an exceedingly important source of information about women and non-elites.

In its own time, medieval law also provided durable frameworks, especially with regard to women and gender. Legal categories regularly differentiated women and men, thereby solidifying gender as a critical determinant of status and thus, of identity. Specific laws about women's legal status and participation in court proceedings varied by jurisdiction, but the terms of the debate proved remarkably consistent across legal systems and across time. Questions of women's rights with regard to the ownership, control, and transmission of property—both landed and liquid—long endured. So, too, did moral regulation, which in the Middle Ages especially focused around the sexual behaviors of women and their implications for family formation and inheritance.

Medieval societies had such a bewildering variety of jurisdictions, each with its own procedures, that it is difficult to compare gendered legal statuses. Roman law remained crucially important throughout the Middle Ages, not so much as a body of specific enactments but as a set of procedures and a way of thinking about the world. Civic law drew on it extensively, as did the canon law of the church, and as Marie Kelleher's chapter suggests, local customs interacted with Roman law to create new ways of thinking about women and gender. Germanic law (already codified within a Romanized context by the time the first sources survive) and local customary law (at first unwritten, but then codified) also entered the medieval mix, although as Nelson and Rio show, the surviving sources for the "barbarian" law codes can be very difficult to interpret. Individual concepts from these various legal systems, such as the Roman *dos* (roughly, dowry), were recast to suit changing socio-economic conditions; as Stone and Stuard discuss, these reinterpretations not only shaped medieval family structures but also stimulated economic development.

Law strictly prescribed women's disability, but practice was often more forgiving. In late medieval Mediterranean towns (which are exceptionally rich in legal records), women negotiated, with or without men's help, their own legal and business affairs (see chapters by Reyerson and Carol Lansing). Even in canon law, a jurisprudence studied and applied across Christian Europe, litigants still had considerable room to maneuver (as shown in chapters by Kelleher and Sara McDougall). Feminist historians today look both *at* the law—its bewildering uniformity and diversity, in both theory and practice— and *through* it to discern what its records might tell about otherwise undocumented women and men.

DOMESTIC LIVES

Modern English obfuscates the realities of domestic labor in the Middle Ages. "Lady" suggests a refined femininity far from the authoritative ladies of the medieval aristocracy; "housewife" has lost much of its original, medieval emphasis on work; and "servant" evokes the parlor more than the field or workshop. Our understandings are further clouded by all-too-ready biological assumptions—that, for example, it was the fate of medieval women to produce streams of children in quick succession, or that it was somehow natural for women take on more domestic tasks than men (see critiques in chapters by Kowaleski, Whittle, and Rees Jones).

Historians of the early Middle Ages, working mostly with sparse evidence for the aristocracy, have built narratives of change—marriage (once multiple and weak) becoming a single, permanent bond, and lineage narrowing from bilateral to patrilineal. McNamara and Wemple once characterized this half-millennium as a time of extraordinary opportunity for elite women. Nelson and Rio now read law codes as more contingent, but at the same time less positive for women. Stone sees Carolingian women as ideologically more "moral" and more "private" than their Merovingian counterparts. And Drell doubts that the first five hundred years of the Middle Ages did, in fact, produce a halcyon age for aristocratic women.

From 1000, several different general patterns of European domesticity emerge. As Kowaleski notes, one cuts Europe south and north, with women in Mediterranean Europe marrying younger, more often, and to older husbands than did women in the north—and thus, more likely to be dependent on their husbands at first and widowed later. Another trend cuts Europe by class, with aristocratic women throughout Europe marrying in high numbers and at young ages, as Drell shows. Yet another distinction cuts by religion, for, as Baumgarten argues, Jews throughout Europe tended to marry early and universally. To these must be added at least three more domestic situations: those of never-married singlewomen, accounting for as much as one third of adult women in the north; those of nuns; and of course, those of widows. Some experiences transcended these variations; throughout Europe, for example, clerks identified men by such public characteristics as occupation or rank and women by family ties.[13]

By the later Middle Ages, three themes—middle-class domesticity, gendered space, and domestic piety—loom large.[14] The development of the European middle class, long a preoccupation of modern historians, now seems critical to understanding late medieval domesticity. Wealthy burghers possessed many more things than ever before: better houses, more furnishings, and more fashionable clothes. The management of these goods, as Katharine French shows in her chapter, quickly became a female responsibility and a source of female agency, and as Howell argues, a new bourgeois ideology of gender emerged whereby women were to be good housewives, busy at home, and men were to be good citizens, busy in public work.[15] Slowly but steadily, in Rees Jones's view, these changes spread to other social groups. Once burghers' wives adopted a new definition of female honesty rooted in their own domestic roles, the age-old public work of more humble women became newly suspect.

As Rees Jones also stresses, medieval spaces did not always divide neatly into public (masculine) and private (feminine). Markets, streets, and guildhalls provided common spaces and public spheres; designs of late medieval castles, townhouses, and cottages promoted the privatization and engendering of domestic spaces; and housewifery, challenged by the abounding possessions of late medieval households, was redefined to better accommodate to an emerging consumer economy.

Medieval households were also deeply embedded in faith. This was always obvious for Jewish households (see Baumgarten), but in the 1970s and 1980s, the study of medieval Christian life focused on the public and institutional, and the study of female piety was accordingly a study of nuns. Now, however, nunneries look more domestic,[16] and lay households, as Deane argues, seem holy, equipped with chapels and chaplains (if rich), psalters (if middling), and rosaries (if poor). Mulder-Bakker shows how sanctity also changed, with more wives and widows recognized for exceptional holiness in the later Middle Ages, and with more holy women, like Catherine of Siena, pursuing their devotions at home.

LAND, LABOR, ECONOMY

When medieval women's history took firm shape in the 1970s and 1980s, economic history was a natural ally, providing a developed feminist historiography buttressed by Marxist scholarship. From these foundations grew robust investigations of women's work that revolved around two primary issues. The first focused on clothmaking, urbanization, and a chronology that stretched across the medieval millennium. As set out in David Herlihy's *Opera Muliebria* (1990), the cloth industry exemplified how women's work outside the home slowly became less important: cloth was usually made by women before 1000, men became more active in clothmaking during the central Middle Ages, and by 1500, men executed all but the craft's most menial tasks. Herlihy's core insight—that women and clothmaking were critical to the medieval economy—remains strong. Thus, Berman has linked economic growth c.1000 to the spread of wind and water mills, which freed women from laborious hand-milling and sent them into the cloth industry.[17]

The second issue focused on the medieval/modern divide, particularly in England. Was there a 150-year "golden age" for working women during the labor shortage that followed the plague of 1347–1349 that was eventually snuffed out by population growth and a surge towards capitalism c.1500? This question produced a plethora of new facts and a variety of answers—yes, no, and maybe just a little bit.[18] Today, feminist research focuses less on work and more on wealth: women's bodies as wealth; women and the production of wealth; and women's control of wealth.

Women were, themselves, a sort of wealth, for their reproductive work—both biological and social—was highly valued in medieval family economies. Men needed women to produce their heirs and run their households (as Whittle and Drell explore). Women were also valued for the wealth they could bring in marriage, whether to plowmen, knights, merchants, or artisans.[19] Women's bodies were even assessed and sold more directly: prices for enslaved women depended, as McKee shows, on their suitability for sexual service, and prostitution also represented a direct purchase of women's bodies.[20]

Women labored, as did men, in the production of food, goods, and services. As Reyerson and Whittle argue, the sexual division of productive labor was clear but highly flexible. Women worked in fields and forests, in markets and shops, for themselves and for employers. They tended, more than men, to juggle many occupations. They were especially prominent in poorly remunerated trades—minor food trades, spinning, small-scale marketing. They worked for wages much lower than those paid to men. Medieval women, in short, worked hard, but they were rarely empowered by their work. The same could be said for many working men in medieval villages and towns, but hard, unrewarding work was especially women's lot.

Medieval women were more often carriers of wealth to husbands or children—wealth in the form of goods, land, or coin—than creators or managers of it. Women possessed relatively little wealth: women's wages and work produced less income, and women received less from parents, in either gifts or inheritance. Rich or poor, women held, at best, about one fifth of all feudal and peasant tenures; both proportions fell by the later Middle Ages (see Drell and Whittle, respectively). Women also had less control over what little they held. Guardians oversaw the assets of unmarried heiresses; husbands managed dowries, dowers, and other properties; and many widows enjoyed only usufruct of conjugal lands. These patterns were not hard rules. Sometimes law or custom allowed women full control of wealth; sometimes rules were circumvented or ignored; and sometimes (especially when husbands were absent) wives directly managed family assets.

BODIES, PLEASURES, DESIRES

Bodies and sexualities have always been inextricably linked to women and gender. Studies of medieval sexual behavior exploded after the 1976 publication of the first volume of Michel Foucault's *History of Sexuality*.[21] Foucault discussed sexuality as a field of discourse rather than a set of behaviors, and he argued that "sexuality" did not really exist before the advent of bourgeois capitalism. Although Foucault tended to equate male sexuality with human sexuality, his ideas complemented those of feminist historians who argued that it was language and culture, rather than nature, that dictated the reproductive destiny of women, the permeability of the female body, and beliefs about gender. Foucault's interest in male homosexuality, which he argued did not exist as an identity before the nineteenth century, also stimulated new research. John Boswell's *Christianity, Social Tolerance, and Homosexuality* (1980) argued that gay identity was as old as the Middle Ages and so, too, was tolerance of gay lifestyles. In the extensive debates that followed, male same-sex relations—whether socially "constructed" or biologically "essentialist"—briefly became *the* central category in the history of medieval sexuality.[22]

Scholars now question whether "homosexuality" is even a relevant concept in the Middle Ages. As Puff shows in this volume, medieval texts reveal a variety of affectionate and erotic relationships among same-sex couples that do not readily map onto modern categories. Medieval people seem not to have thought, for example, that sex-of-partner determined gender identity. Dominance was gendered male and passivity female. Thus, in the few extant court cases that treat female same-sex relations before 1500, the dominant (penetrating) partner is figured as man-like and abominable, the other (passive) partner as woman-like and forgivable.[23] Sex without penetration was unimaginable in medieval law, and as a result, some sexual practices were ignored, reinterpreted, or reconfigured as gender transgressions.

Sorting out the affectionate from the erotic—or put another way, determining what kinds of desires medieval people felt—has proven difficult. Insofar as medieval people wrote about desire, they mostly wrote about God. Imaginative literature was a bit more down to earth. Courtly ideals, expressed particularly in love lyrics and Arthurian romances, shaped aristocratic culture and practice, and they were remarkably playful about gender and sex. As Burns shows, men were not always manly, women were not always passive, and desire did not always move along a male–female axis. Indeed, medieval bodies seem to have been malleable and negotiable. Differences between male and female bodies were certainly an important way of organizing medical knowledge; as discussed by Park, the male body was taken as standard, and the female body assessed against it. But the interplay of body and gender in the Middle Ages was not just an either/or proposition. The thirteenth-century *Roman de Silence* explicitly explored some of the possibilities. Its heroine is born female but raised as a boy and later counseled by both Nature (who urges a return to female identity) and Nurture (who argues for retaining a male identity). Medical writers and practitioners often pondered, as Green discusses, the gender of "hermaphrodites" and their meaning within God's plan.[24] And in the Byzantine east, as Ringrose shows, eunuchs adopted a gender distinctiveness that was built on much more than castration alone.

Nevertheless, throughout the Middle Ages, reproduction was understood as the key purpose of sexual activity. Thus, physicians and other medical practitioners tended to focus their care of women, as Green shows in her chapter, on reproductive health. Across centuries and across religious cultures, the care of women's bodies, whether by female or male practitioners, focused on preserving fertility and facilitating childbirth.

Engendering Christian Holiness

In the last thirty years, feminist scholars have transformed the study of medieval Christianity. Bynum's *Holy Feast and Holy Fast* redirected discussions away from theological and ecclesiastical hostility to women (and even nuns) to emphasize how women were able to shape their own Christian faith. The association of women with the flesh, Bynum argued, allowed women to identify with the body of Christ, and both female and male writers produced a dazzling array of positive associations linking the divine and the feminine. Bynum also demonstrated that although only priests could celebrate the Mass, holy women bypassed this male monopoly through their own experiences of Eucharistic miracles. In the wake of Bynum's work on the intersection between theology and practice, feminist scholars of medieval Christianity began to tell new and startling stories.

As a result, medievalists now see the medieval church as willing to play with gender binaries. God the Father, although a distinctly masculine figure, was not without tenderness. God the Son was also masculine, but sometimes given nurturing feminine attributes, as in Bynum's examination of "Jesus as mother." The Holy Spirit, often figured as a dove, was even less tied to one gender or the other. The medieval church itself—an institution in which only men were ordained and all women (even nuns) were laity— was often cast as a bride, with Christ as bridegroom. The cult of the saints, particularly veneration of the Virgin Mary, allowed ample room for feminine aspects to enter religious devotion (as Rubin shows). Mystics, among them many women, regularly played with a wide range of gendered and sexual metaphors in their discussions of the divine; so, too, did bishops and other church leaders.[25]

Feminist medievalists have also drawn attention to how medieval Christians deployed women, gender, and sexuality to guard the boundaries of their faith.[26] Women and gender were everywhere in the Christianization of Europe—as proselytizers, as converts, and as sites of anxiety as old faiths overlapped with new (see Bitel's chapter). And when the church came to deal with Christians whose faith diverged from orthodox teachings, especially from the twelfth century on, gender was again important. As John Arnold points out in his chapter, some heretics diverged from the Roman church in their gender rules (allowing, for example, preaching by women), and sometimes Rome's classification of acceptable divergence—whether a belief was merely idiosyncratic or heretical—hinged on gender conformity or nonconformity.

Whereas nuns were once *the* story of women in medieval Christianity, the ordinary pieties of Christian households now command more attention, as also do laywomen who pursued holiness outside formal communities. Nuns remain, however, an important part of our understandings of medieval society. Some scholars have proposed that nuns (and monks as well) became de-gendered by their vows, released from ordinary standards; others have argued that while monastics used gendered metaphors flexibly, they still clung to an overarching binary of gender. Regardless, most agree that the lives of nuns and monks were more similar than different (and thereby different from most laity). Diem argues that the forms of monasticism that dominated by the central Middle Ages may have been originally designed for women, and in the great monastic reforms of the twelfth century, as Griffiths shows, women worked as hard as men to create new types of religious practice, even if the eventual results were not entirely positive for them.

Finally and most dramatically, female piety today takes center stage in histories of medieval spirituality: the theology of Hildegard of Bingen, the heterodoxy of Marguerite Porete, the mysticism of Catherine of Siena, the eremiticism of Julian of Norwich, the striving holiness of Margery Kempe, and the quotidian devotion of countless ordinary women. By their own hand or through scribes, pious women wrote extensively about their devotions, visions, and theological insights. Men produced more texts, to be sure, but women's texts were often distinctively innovative (Kempe's book is, for example, the first autobiography in English), and female authors likely lie hidden behind a plethora of "anonymous" writings.[27] Forceful pious women, Mulder-Bakker demonstrates, also took leadership roles in many quasi-organized forms of lay piety. Some created or commissioned artworks of extraordinary power.[28] And everyday women—ordinary women, not writers, leaders, or artists— worshipped in homes and parishes where, like men, they drew on a range of Christian practices and artifacts that spoke not only to their humanity but also to their gender (see Deane and Ashley). There was, in short, far more flexibility and space for women within medieval Christianity than historians once imagined. In this research area, perhaps more than any other, feminist histories today speak more of opportunity and less of constraint.

TURNING POINTS AND PLACES

Joan Kelly long ago called on historians to gender our master narratives, but medievalists still usually identify epochal change with major events that have little to do with women or gender: the deposition of the last Western Roman emperor in 476; the plagues of 1347–1349; the Ottoman capture of Constantinople in 1453; the voyage of Columbus in 1492. Even in the 1990s, gender remained a glaringly overlooked category in a well-funded, international research project on the transformation of the Roman world into a medieval one.[29] More recently, feminist historians have suggested downplaying epochal change altogether—that is, focusing more on continuities. Working, as did Kelly, on the transition from medieval to modern, Judith Bennett has argued that while women's work changed, the status of that work did not: whenever a particular type of work became more prestigious, as with weaving or brewing, men took it over, and tasks identified as female remained just as low status, low-skilled, and poorly compensated as before.[30]

Today, feminist chronologies of the Middle Ages work within and around these debates. Historians are finally beginning to look at "late antiquity" with a focus less on geopolitical events and more on the way Christians, particularly Christian women, preserved and reconfigured aspects of Roman culture (see Cooper). We are also reassessing the all-important transitions that cluster around the year 1000. Some, like McNamara, find a wholesale reorientation of the gender system after 1000, as a newly celibate clergy excluded women from ecclesiastical and dynastic roles.[31] Others, like Berman in this volume, see this as a time of expanding opportunity for women and, indeed, even expanding female influence over the course of historical change. In both cases, stories of women and gender in the central Middle Ages play against a less glorious background than was once the case. The same western Europeans who built states, cathedrals, and universities between 1000 and 1300 also mounted crusades against Muslims, persecuted Jews, and grew increasingly anxious about sexual minorities.

The transitions of the fourteenth and fifteenth centuries are similarly now seen in ambivalent light. Some changes seem clearly negative: the retrenchment of some women's economic role as a result of the rise of mercantile capitalism (discussed by Howell) and the beginnings of witch-hunts (discussed by Stokes). Other changes—such as the first glimmerings of female advocacy in Europe (see Krueger)—are considerably more positive.

As reflected in the essays in this volume, feminist scholarship on the Middle Ages is at once scholarly and political. Feminist medievalists approach the artifacts of the past— the documents, texts, bones, and goods the dead have left for us—with academic rigor and honesty, striving to "get it right." But we also talk back to sources—asking questions and seeking answers that reflect current issues, both scholarly debates (did women's work status decline during the Middle Ages?) and broadly social concerns (should women be paid equally with men?). The extremes of Mary and Eve, of achievement and abasement, can no longer encompass this complex field. Yet the dichotomy speaks to a sort of truth. Medieval women worked hard, created much, and accomplished a great deal, but their achievements are all the more remarkable because they took place within a confined context—a medieval world in which men were human and women were different.

FURTHER READING

The contributors to the volume introduced by this essay have produced remarkable summations of specific areas of research. In addition, see these general resources:

Amt, Emilie, ed. *Women's Lives in Medieval Europe: A Sourcebook*. New York: Routledge, 1993.
Feminae: Medieval Women and Gender Index. The University of Iowa Libraries, <http://inpress.lib.uiowa.edu/feminae/Default.aspx>.

Larrington, Carolyne, ed. *Women and Writing in Medieval Europe: A Sourcebook.* London: New York: Routledge, 1995.

McCarthy, Conor, ed. *Love, Sex and Marriage in the Middle Ages: A Sourcebook.* London: Routledge, 2004.

Murray, Jacqueline, ed. *Love, Marriage, and Family in the Middle Ages: A Reader.* Peterborough, Ont.: Broadview Press, 2001.

Schaus, Margaret, ed. *Women and Gender in Medieval Europe: An Encyclopedia.* New York: Routledge, 2006.

Skinner, Patricia and Elisabeth Van Houts, *Medieval Writings on Secular Women.* London: Penguin, 2011.

Wilson, Katharina M., ed. *Medieval Women Writers.* Athens, Ga.: University of Georgia Press, 1984.

Wilson, Katharina M. and Nadia Margolis, eds. *Women in the Middle Ages: An Encyclopedia.* Westport, Conn.: Greenwood Press, 2004.

Notes

1. R. N. Swanson, "Angels Incarnate: Clergy and Masculinity from Gregorian Reform to Reformation," in D. M. Hadley, ed., *Masculinity in Medieval Europe* (London; New York: Longman, 1999), 160–77; Jacqueline Murray, "One Flesh, Two Sexes, Three Genders?" in Lisa M. Bitel and Felice Lifshitz, eds, *Gender and Christianity in Medieval Europe* (Philadelphia: University of Pennsylvania Press, 2008), 34–51.

2. Alain Boureau, *The Lord's First Night: The Myth of the Droit de Cuissage*, trans. Lydia G. Cochrane (Chicago: University of Chicago Press, 1998); idem, *The Myth of Pope Joan*, trans. Lydia G. Cochrane (Chicago: University of Chicago Press, 2001). Albrecht Classen, *The Medieval Chastity Belt: A Myth-Making Process* (New York: Palgrave Macmillan, 2007).

3. Barbara Newman, "Authority, Authenticity, and the Repression of Heloise," in *From Virile Woman to WomanChrist: Studies in Medieval Religion and Literature* (Philadelphia: University of Pennsylvania Press, 1995), 46–75.

4. Betty Bandel, "The English Chroniclers' Attitude Toward Women," *Journal of the History of Ideas*, 16 (1) (1955): 113–18. Eileen Power, *Medieval Women*, ed. M. M. Postan (Cambridge; New York: Cambridge University Press, 1975).

5. Susan Mosher Stuard, ed., *Women in Medieval Society* (Philadelphia: University of Pennsylvania Press, 1976); Shulamith Shahar, *The Fourth Estate: A History of Women in the Middle Ages* (London: Methuen, 1983).

6. David Herlihy and Christiane Klapisch-Zuber, *Tuscans and Their Families: A Study of the Florentine Catasto of 1427* (New Haven: Yale University Press, 1985); Herlihy, *Medieval Households* (Cambridge, Mass.: Harvard University Press, 1985); idem, "Land, Family and Women in Continental Europe, 701–1200," *Traditio*, 18 (1962): 89–120.

7. Caroline Walker Bynum, *Jesus as Mother: Studies in the Spirituality of the High Middle Ages* (Berkeley: University of California Press, 1982); idem, *Holy Feast and Holy Fast: The Religious Significance of Food to Medieval Women* (Berkeley: University of California Press, 1987).

8. Georges Duby, *The Knight, the Lady, and the Priest: The Making of Modern Marriage in Medieval France*, trans. Barbara Bray (New York: Pantheon Books, 1983); Marion F. Facinger, "A Study of Medieval Queenship: Capetian France, 987–1237," *Studies in*

Medieval and Renaissance History, 5 (1968): 3–48; Jo Ann McNamara and Suzanne Wemple, "The Power of Women Through the Family in Medieval Europe: 500–1100," *Feminist Studies*, 1 (3/4) (1973): 126–41; Joan Kelly-Gadol, "Did Women Have a Renaissance?" in Renate Bridenthal and Claudia Koontz, eds, *Becoming Visible: Women in European History* (Boston: Houghton Mifflin, 1977), reprinted in Joan Kelly, *Women, History, and Theory: The Essays of Joan Kelly* (Chicago: University of Chicago Press, 1984).

9. *Speculum*, 68 (2) (1993); Nancy F. Partner, ed., *Studying Medieval Women: Sex, Gender, Feminism* (Cambridge, Mass.: Medieval Academy of America, 1993).

10. Judith Butler, *Gender Trouble: Feminism and the Subversion of Identity* (New York: Routledge, 1990).

11. Joan W. Scott, "Gender: A Useful Category of Historical Analysis," *American Historical Review*, 91 (5) (1986): 1053–75; reprinted in *Gender and the Politics of History* (New York: Columbia University Press, 1988). Dyan Elliott, "The Three Ages of Joan Scott," *American Historical Review*, 113 (5) (December 2008): 1390–403.

12. Alcuin Blamires, ed., *Woman Defamed and Woman Defended: An Anthology of Medieval Texts* (Oxford: Clarendon Press, 1992), 12.

13. For exceptions, see Shennan Hutton, *Women and Economic Activities in Late Medieval Ghent* (New York: Palgrave Macmillan, 2011) and Ellen E. Kittell, "The Construction of Women's Social Identity in Medieval Douai: Evidence from Identifying Epithets," *Journal of Medieval History*, 25 (3) (1999): 215–27.

14. Maryanne Kowaleski and P. J. P. Goldberg, eds, *Medieval Domesticity: Home, Housing and Household in Medieval England* (Cambridge; New York: Cambridge University Press, 2008).

15. Felicity Riddy, "Mother Knows Best: Reading Social Change in a Courtesy Text," *Speculum*, 71 (1) (1996): 66–86.

16. Marilyn Oliva, "Nuns at Home: The Domesticity of Sacred Space," in Kowaleski and Goldberg, eds, *Medieval Domesticity*.

17. David Herlihy, *Opera Muliebria: Women and Work in Medieval Europe* (Philadelphia: Temple University Press, 1990); Constance H. Berman, "Women's Work in Family, Village, and Town after 1000 CE: Contributions to Economic Growth?" *Journal of Women's History*, 19 (2007): 10–32.

18. P. J. P. Goldberg, *Women, Work, and Life Cycle in a Medieval Economy: Women in York and Yorkshire, c. 1300–1520* (Oxford: Clarendon Press, 1992); Caroline M. Barron, "The 'Golden Age' of Women in Medieval London," *Reading Medieval Studies*, 15 (1989): 35–58; Marjorie Keniston McIntosh, *Working Women in English Society, 1300–1620* (Cambridge: Cambridge University Press, 2005); Judith M. Bennett, chapter 5 in *History Matters: Patriarchy and the Challenge of Feminism* (Philadelphia: University of Pennsylvania Press, 2006), 82–107.

19. Barbara Hanawalt, *The Wealth of Wives: Women, Law, and Economy in Late Medieval London* (New York: Oxford University Press, 2007).

20. Ruth Mazo Karras, *Common Women: Prostitution and Sexuality in Medieval England* (New York: Oxford University Press, 1996).

21. Vern L. Bullough, *Sex, Society, and History* (New York: Science History Publications, 1976); Michel Foucault, *Histoire de la sexualité* (Paris: Gallimard, 1976), translated as *The History of Sexuality: An Introduction*, vol. 1, trans. Robert Hurley (New York: Vintage Books, 1990).

22. John Boswell, *Christianity, Social Tolerance, and Homosexuality: Gay People in Western Europe from the Beginning of the Christian Era to the Fourteenth Century* (Chicago; London: University of Chicago Press, 1980); debate summarized in Ruth Mazo Karras,

Sexuality in Medieval Europe: Doing Unto Others, 2nd edn (Abingdon: Routledge, 2012), 5–10.

23. James A. Schultz, *Courtly Love, the Love of Courtliness, and the History of Sexuality* (Chicago: University of Chicago Press, 2006); Karma Lochrie, *Heterosyncrasies: Female Sexuality When Normal Wasn't* (Minneapolis: University of Minnesota Press, 2005); Karras, *Sexuality in Medieval Europe*; Helmut Puff, "Female Sodomy: The Trial of Katherina Hetzeldorfer (1477)," *Journal of Medieval and Early Modern Studies*, 30 (1) (2000): 41–61; Jacqueline Murray, "Twice Marginal and Twice Invisible: Lesbians in the Middle Ages," in Vern L. Bullough and James A. Brundage, eds, *Handbook of Medieval Sexuality* (New York: Garland, 1996), 191–223.

24. Joan Cadden, *Meanings of Sex Difference in the Middle Ages: Medicine, Science, and Culture* (Cambridge; New York: Cambridge University Press, 1993); Lorraine Daston and Katharine Park, "The Hermaphrodite and the Orders of Nature: Sexual Ambiguity in Early Modern France," in Louise Fradenburg and Carla Freccero, eds, *Premodern Sexualities* (New York: Routledge, 1996); Leah DeVun, "The Jesus Hermaphrodite: Science and Sex Difference in Premodern Europe," *Journal of the History of Ideas*, 69 (2) (2008): 193–218.

25. Barbara Newman, *God and the Goddesses: Vision, Poetry, and Belief in the Middle Ages* (Philadelphia: University of Pennsylvania Press, 2003).

26. David Nirenberg, "Conversion, Sex, and Segregation: Jews and Christians in Medieval Spain," *American Historical Review*, 107 (4) (2002): 1065–93.

27. Janet L. Nelson, "Gender and Genre in Women Historians of the Early Middle Ages," in *The Frankish World, 750–900* (London: Hambledon, 1996).

28. Jeffrey F. Hamburger, *Nuns as Artists: The Visual Culture of a Medieval Convent* (Berkeley: University of California Press, 1997).

29. Julia M. H. Smith, "Did Women Have a Transformation of the Roman World?" *Gender & History*, 12 (3) (2000): 552–71.

30. Bennett, *History Matters*.

31. Jo Ann McNamara, "The Herrenfrage: The Restructuring of the Gender System, 1050–1150," in Clare A. Lees, ed., *Medieval Masculinities: Regarding Men in the Middle Ages* (Minneapolis: University of Minnesota Press, 1994), 3–29.

PART I

GENDERED THINKING

CHAPTER 2

GENDER AND THE CHRISTIAN TRADITIONS

DYAN ELLIOTT

In modern parlance, gender is considered to be a cultural construction that can be detached from sexed bodies. Such a concept was alien to classical and medieval thinkers. Nevertheless, they had much to say about what we would consider to be gendered topics: the proper social roles for men and women; their relations to one another; their distinct physical and psychological make-up; and the behaviors and activities that could lead to either a commendable or despicable slippage between characteristics generally associated with a particular sex. These discussions often occurred in the course of addressing various crises and contemporary hot-button issues, providing a unique window into Christian society's shifting, and often competing, values. The church was fraught with a wide variety of gender troubles from its inception, giving rise to conflicts that are essential for understanding what was to come. While this might be regarded as a truism when seeking to understand any historical period, it takes on particular importance for religious traditions, like Christianity, in which theological arguments, polemics, and pastoral direction were steeped in precedent. There is no understanding medieval Christianity without some knowledge of the apostolic and patristic periods.

In classical culture, marriage was almost invariably the lot of every freeborn woman—an institution in which she was unilaterally deemed to be subordinate to her husband. Christianity challenged these social norms. According to Christian tradition, Jesus himself said: "The children of this world marry, and are given in marriage: But they which shall be accounted worthy to obtain that world, and the resurrection from the dead, neither marry, nor are given in marriage: Neither can they die any more: for they are equal unto the angels; and are the children of God, being the children of the resurrection" (Luke 20:34–36). When anticipating the end of the world, he also grimly remarked, "Woe to them that are with child and give suck in those days" (Luke 21:23). He further commended individuals who had made themselves "eunuchs for God" (Matt. 19:10–12). These remarks were enigmatic and fleeting, however. It fell to the apostle Paul, who had never met Christ and whose ministry only began after Christ's death, to address most directly subjects like marriage and appropriate gender roles. Since Paul believed that the end of the world was imminent and that any procreative imperative was therefore waived, he encouraged those capable of abstaining sexually to choose a life of celibacy, perceiving marriage and family life as distractions from God (I Cor. 7:29).

This tacit disparagement of sex by Paul (and perhaps Christ) resonated on many different levels. For some, Christianity seemed to promise a suspension of normative gender roles and social status alike. Scholars now believe that when Paul professed that there is "no male or female, but all one in Christ" (Gal. 3:28), he was quoting the contemporary baptismal formula—suggesting that baptism itself ushered in a new age. Some theologians, however, were inclined to go farther, asserting that the very division into male and female was not part of God's plan. According to this line of argument, humanity had originally been created as androgynous and only split into two sexes with the Fall, at which point death entered into the world and Adam and Eve were required to procreate.[1] The biblical claim that God cursed Eve by making her subject to Adam and condemned her to bring forth children in suffering helped to sustain this view (Gen. 3:16).

But Christianity's challenge to gender roles was not limited to learned discourse. Perpetua (d.203), a patrician matron of Carthage, was prepared to ignore the claims of her father, husband, and even her newborn child, instead choosing martyrdom on behalf of her faith. In the course of her imprisonment, moreover, she dreamed that she was transformed into a male gladiator to do battle with the devil, who took the form of a fierce Egyptian.[2] There were others who sought an alternative manner of martyrdom in the self-mortification (lit. making dead) of asceticism. Rejecting the institution of marriage, these Christian ascetics embraced lifelong chastity as a surer way to prepare themselves for the afterlife. The eastern desert fathers, the forerunners of monasticism, who separated themselves from society in favor of a harsh regime of asceticism, were of this persuasion.[3] There is early evidence that women were especially attracted to an ascetic life of dedicated virginity, perhaps looking to escape the dangers of childbirth, but also perhaps seeking a means of transcending the usual restrictions placed on their sex. For instance, in the various apocryphal gospels that circulated under the names of different apostles (works that were definitively rejected in the fourth century as part of the canon) there are innumerable stories of women on the brink of marriage accepting Christianity and embracing lifelong virginity. The *Acts of Paul and Thecla*, written sometime in the second century but popular throughout the Middle Ages, depicts the virgin Thecla as vehemently rejecting her upcoming marriage after hearing Paul preach on the blessedness of virginity. Her mother was especially provoked: thwarted in her matrimonial objectives for her daughter, the frustrated woman eventually sought to have Thecla executed. After triumphing over multiple spiritual and physical challenges, Thecla dressed herself like a man and proceeded to make multiple converts.

The attitude of Thecla's mother epitomizes a reaction against the more flexible gender roles fostered by aspects of early Christian culture. This was already apparent in some telling analogies present in Paul's own writings. He compared the husband's relationship with his wife to Christ's relationship to the church, conferring a divine stamp on marriage by affirming female subordination (Eph. 5:22–23). The husband was further enjoined to love his wife as he would his own body, tacitly aligning man with spirit and woman with flesh, and hence reinforcing the classical world's traditional prejudices.[4] The so-called pastoral epistles, the letters to Timothy and Titus, written by the next generation of Christians in Paul's voice, would, in turn, emphasize wifely submission even more sharply.

These tensions within the Christian tradition gave rise to some celebrated conflicts. The seven Vestal Virgins, who guarded the hearth of Rome, were an anomaly. This placed consecrated virgins in a position that implicitly challenged the gender hierarchy. Married women traditionally assumed a veil, which functioned as a symbol of both gender differentiation and submission. Tertullian (d. c.220), the Christian West's first great theological voice, believed that the consecrated virgins in his native city of Carthage should likewise be veiled in order to signify their subjection as women. The virgins resisted, however. We are not privy to the virgins' motives for refusing the veil; in fact, there are no female authored texts from the early church apart from Perpetua's prison diary. But according to Tertullian's representations, the virgins in question believed that their consecrated virginity not only allowed them to escape marriage, but gave them access to the liminal angelic life here on earth. As quasi-angels, they were naturally exempt from the subjection associated with the veil. Tertullian derisively represented their presumption as constituting "a third generic class, some monstrosity with a head of its own."[5]

Far from angels, the women in question were, in Tertullian's representation, "daughters of Eve," and he further suggested that the prelapsarian Eve's subjected womanhood took precedence over the alleged honor due to her as a virgin: "since she has the appellation *woman* before she was *wedded,* and never *virgin* while she *was* a *virgin.*" Not only does this emphasis confound arguments in favor of the special androgyny inherent in the virginal state, it further sets the stage for the remedial intervention of that exemplary virgin (and woman) par excellence, Mary. The Virgin Mary is an antidote to the evil instituted by the primordial virgin, Eve:

> it was while Eve was yet a virgin, that the ensnaring word had crept into her ear which was to build the edifice of death. Into a virgin's soul, in like manner, must be introduced that Word of God which was to raise the fabric of life; so that what had been reduced to ruin by this sex, might by the selfsame sex be recovered to salvation. As Eve believed the serpent, so Mary believed the angel.[6]

Tertullian ultimately resolves that consecrated virgins are, in fact, matrons since they are married to Christ. This juxtaposition of Eve and Mary as well as the image of the virgin as bride of Christ would remain classic tropes throughout the Middle Ages.

Not long after Tertullian's death, another crisis arose in Carthage that directly turned on gender roles—the problem of the *virgines subintroductae* (lit. "virgins led in surreptitiously"). It had come to the attention of Bishop Cyprian (d.258) that a certain deacon was cohabiting with several consecrated virgins, even sharing the same bed, allegedly in chastity. Cyprian vigorously forbade the practice, even requiring that the women receive a gynecological examination ensuring their intact virginity before being readmitted to the congregation.[7] Given how many theologians wrote against such households, it would seem that this way of life was a relatively widespread solution to the challenges of celibate life. Although their cohabitation was determined by practical considerations (housekeepers for the clerics; protectors for the women), their critics complained that clerics and their virginal roommates alike believed their chaste lifestyle could accommodate close relations between the sexes without undermining their virginal vocation. It is also probable that the individuals in question were in their own way reaping the benefits of the intimacy that a life of chastity seemed to afford them—experiencing the realized eschatology that dissipated both gender and the passions to which the fallen body was subject. This lifestyle could be placed on a continuum with the unveiled pride of Tertullian's virgins. John Chrysostom (d.407), who dedicated two treatises to denouncing the practice of clerics cohabiting with virgins, was deeply censorious, making it clear that relations with the opposite sex were invariably pleasurable and thus represented a breach of chastity. The kind of companionship such couples sought must needs be deferred to the afterlife "when bodily passions are henceforth undone and tyrannical desire has been quenched."[8]

The issues both of the veiling of and chaste cohabitation with virgins were but two skirmishes in the church's struggle to stabilize gender roles, thereby controlling independent virgins. The war was by and large won by the time of Ambrose (d.397), bishop of Milan and great promoter of consecrated virginity, who wrote four treatises on the subject. Ambrose introduced a ceremony for the consecration of a virgin that was modeled on secular marriage rites—literally marrying her to Christ and thus making her subordinate in the same way a woman was to her husband. He further advanced a regimen in which the virgin was urged to emulate the ultimate virgin, Mary, especially for her celebrated submission and reclusion. (The well-known *Protoevangelium of James*, an apocryphal gospel, depicted Mary as spending her youth in isolation in the temple, where she was fed by the hand of an angel.)[9] Beginning in the sixth century, Christ's brides would come to emulate Mary's seclusion, by and large living out their vocations in enclosed religious communities.

The rhetoric of the angelic life never disappeared, but by the fourth century, it retained practically none of its androgynous savor. Even so, there were a number of church fathers who perceived a vocation to chastity as mitigating women's traditional association with the flesh, referring to such women as honorary men. In the words of Jerome (d.420), "As long as a woman is for birth and children, she is as different from man as body is from soul. But when she wishes to serve Christ more than the world, then she will cease to be a woman, and will be called a man."[10] He often applied such imagery to the patrician women, both virgins and chaste widows, in the pious circle he cultivated. Because the women in question were immensely wealthy, their independent behavior provides frequently striking illustrations of this rhetoric. When the patrician Melania the Elder (d. *c*.409) was widowed at twenty-two, she moved to Rome, converted to Christianity, and, soon after, placed her ten-year-old son with a guardian in Rome and set off for Alexandria. It was there that Melania became the patroness of the theologian, Rufinus, with whom she would found a monastery in the Holy Land. She influenced her granddaughter Melania the Younger (d.439) to embrace a similar ascetic lifestyle. When the younger Melania subsequently convinced her husband to vow chastity, she proceeded to liquidate her property and travel the world. The patrician widow Paula (d.404) similarly abandoned friends and family to travel to the Holy Land with Jerome, where she founded a religious community for each of them.[11]

The concept of the "virile woman" could also be articulated in other concrete ways, as is demonstrated by the female ascetics who distinguished themselves in their struggles in the Egyptian desert.[12] In medieval hagiography, these legendary desert mothers were frequently depicted as so shriveled and wizened by their fasting that they were barely recognizable as women. For instance, St Pelagia had allegedly lived in voluptuous splendor until her run-in with a holy man, which sent her into a spiral of self-loathing. Her ensuing penance was so extreme, and her body so shrunken, that she called herself Pelagius, easily passing for a male. A related motif, associated with saints such as Marina and Margaret, depicts the predicament of a pious woman who was required to disguise herself as a monk, usually because her parents were dead and there were no female communities that she could enter. When the female-monk is maliciously accused of fathering a child, she accepts the blame out of humility. In either case, it was only on the deathbed that the truth of the woman's sex and sanctity were simultaneously revealed.[13]

Generally, however, gender border-crossings made the church fathers nervous. This is especially true when it came to men, who had nothing to gain from assuming a female persona, since the male sex was already considered superior in every way. This very sense of superiority could lead to male angst. For instance, ascetic efforts to discipline the male body rendered suspect certain inevitable, but unsolicited, bodily functions like nocturnal emissions: the very lack of control was likened to menstruation and, hence, perceived as effeminizing.[14] By the same token, Chrysostom was afraid that the cohabitation between the sexes had an effeminizing effect on men, whom he claimed began to gossip like women. The women, in turn, became lordly and domineering.[15]

In the fourth century, there was a short-lived effort to challenge the superiority of virginity. Jovinian had attempted to place marriage on a par with virginity by arguing that the Virgin Mary had herself endorsed the institution by virtue of her own marriage. In a similar vein, Helvidius had attacked the adulation of chastity by arguing that the biblical reference to "Christ's brethren" indicated that Mary and Joseph had children subsequent to Christ. Their contentions were handily defeated by Ambrose and Jerome. From this point on, an individual's reward in the afterlife was considered to be at least partially determined by his or her sexual past. On the basis of an exegesis from the Gospel of Matthew (13:8), it was advanced that virgins would receive a hundred-fold reward in heaven, chaste widows only sixtyfold reward, and the married a thirty-fold reward. In heaven, only unsullied virgins would have the privilege of following the Lamb (Christ)—a privilege described in the Revelation of St John (Rev. 3:4; 14:4).

Jerome defended virginal prerogatives in *Against Jovinian*, a treatise that consistently extolled virginity at the expense of marriage. Indeed, his denigration of the married state was so extreme that it raised something of an outcry in Rome. As a result, his contemporary Augustine (d.430), bishop of the North African city of Hippo, felt compelled to demonstrate that it was possible to praise virginity without vilifying marriage, leading to a series of treatises addressed to the triune hierarchy of virgins, widows, and the married. While never contesting the basic ranking, Augustine did his best to minimize the distance between these different states. This was especially true of the first treatise, *On Holy Virginity*, which, compared to the many panegyrics to virginity written over the course of the fourth century, provided a restrained and measured sense of the essence of virginity and the rewards it would accrue. Augustine repeatedly cautioned that mental integrity was to be valued over physical integrity and denounced the virgin's propensity for overweening pride in her condition. He also challenged the tacit assumption that the virgin was automatically ensured the first place in heaven, arguing that only God knew whose faith could stand the ultimate test of martyrdom. But the sexual hierarchy was never in danger of being displaced. Augustine conceded the superiority of virginity in *On the Good of Widowhood*, while still reassuring the widow that "she would have a better place than a married woman, among the members of Christ."[16]

Augustine's final and most ambitious treatise, *On the Good of Marriage*, had a less pastoral and more theological agenda, seeking to present marriage as not simply a lesser evil, but a good in its own right. This required revisiting the vexed question of whether marriage was part of God's original intention for Adam and Eve. Augustine's affirmative answer was central for upholding the basic dignity of the institution. But it also provided an opportunity for bolstering traditional gender roles. Augustine perceived marriage as "a certain true and friendly union of the one ruling, the other obeying," making it clear that Eve was created subordinate prior to the Fall, and that female subordination in marriage was part of God's plan. Following the contours of Roman law, moreover, Augustine saw consent as the essence of the marriage contract, initiating the "full vigor of the order of charity between husband and wife." This bond could not be undermined by a vow of chastity. In a later work he would insist that a marriage was complete without consummation, upholding the virginal marriage of Mary and Joseph as an exemplar.[17] So a husband's authority was in no way contingent upon consummation.

Good to his word, Augustine lambasted the patrician woman, Ecdicia, for assuming that the husband's rule was waived by a transition to chastity. After having convinced her husband to vow chastity, Ecdicia had not only begun to dress like a widow but also to give away her fortune to a couple of wandering monks without consulting her husband. The outraged husband retaliated by committing adultery, a sin that Augustine laid at Ecdicia's door. "He did not cease to be your husband because you were both refraining from carnal intercourse; on the contrary you continued to be husband and wife in a holier manner because you were carrying out a holier resolution, with mutual accord."[18] Not surprisingly, Augustine's writings did not favor the "virile woman" imagery.

The importance of the church fathers would remain paramount throughout the Middle Ages. Medieval clergy would continue to group women together according to their sexual status—regardless of their social roles. By the same token, Augustine was destined to become the foremost authority on marriage in Latin Christendom, ensuring that his impact on gender roles was immense. But the medieval debt to the church fathers was not just a question of later generations adhering to specific patristic doctrines; patristic authorities were ingrained into the way in which medieval think-ers thought and wrote. Not only did medieval authors cite patristic texts at length, but they often wove them silently and seamlessly into their own work, as they did also with scripture. These authorities could even be unwittingly invoked, as, for example, if a cleric made use of a sermon or reading in which the patristic source was not expressly acknowledged.

Patristic treatises also provided important models. For instance, the monk Aldhelm (d.709) wrote a treatise on virginity for Hildelith, abbess of Barking, consciously emu-lating Ambrose's writings on virginity for his sister, Marcellina. Aldhelm seems also to have taken a page from Augustine, however, in so far as the treatise tended to decenter the prerogatives of female virgins both by emphasizing virginity as a male virtue and blurring the boundaries between different forms of chastity.[19] Such an approach makes sense when one considers that Barking was a double monastery that would have con-tained not only monks and nuns, but also virgins and widows.

By and large, however, medieval authors would be more in line with Jerome, praising virginity at the expense of marriage. The poet Fortunatus (d.609) was a rather extreme exponent of this tradition. His various writings on virginity often featured graphic denunciations of the evils of the married state, including the dangers and discomforts of pregnancy:

[The pregnant woman] cannot hide a torpid womb with its enclosed fetus, / saddened, she lays down, burdened by the proof. / The heaving of body and soul between gasps, her health suspended in doubt, its stamina depleted / when, with its javelins, the wound of the uterus swells / and the woman, sick because of lust, gives birth to a monster. Unruly skin alone swelled out, beyond all human appearance / so that it shames the mother that she bore it with love. / Fleeing from her own relatives, ashamed, she carries it away / until she destroys the burden, deposited in a sack.[20]

The fact that this human tragedy was described primarily in terms of a "humiliation" seems to add insult to injury.

Although the papacy had urged clerical celibacy since the fourth century, it was only achieved in the course of the eleventh-century reform movement (see Berman in this volume). But the cost was high, and the institution of marriage paid the price. Not content with the Pauline position that the unmarried had more time for the Lord, the reforming rhetoric of the eleventh century and after stressed the polluting nature of marriage, leading to a disparagement of the married state parallel to the fourth-century chastity wars. The case against clerical marriage was in many ways indecipherable from an attack on women. Peter Damian (d.1072), one of the reform's ringleaders, argued that the priestly hands that held the virginal Christ (i.e., the consecrated host at Mass) must not be sullied by contact with the genitals of whores (i.e., the wives of priests). He further likened clerical wives to concubines of the devil.[21]

Much of this antimatrimonial rhetoric would be redressed during the twelfth century, a period fittingly referred to as a renaissance since it witnessed the revival of just about everything. The population soared, monumental buildings arose, cities and commerce reappeared, and there was a flourishing of letters—both in Latin (the language of the church) and the various vernacular languages. This reawakening included an incredible burgeoning of popular piety, exemplified in the rising cult of the Virgin Mary and devotion to the passion of Christ. It was also a period that considered the world with a new optimism. Rather than regarding nature through the lens of the corruption wrought by Adam's fall, ecclesiastical authorities were suddenly inclined to depict the contemplation of nature as a direct path to the creator. Humanity itself was now apprehended as a microcosmic figure of the divinely created macrocosmic order.

This spirit of optimism led to a reassessment of the institution of marriage through a selective deployment of Augustine. The Parisian monk Hugh of St Victor (d.1141), in particular, stressed the spiritual and consensual nature of the bond, which existed independently of the sex act, upholding Mary and Joseph as truly married (see McDougall in this volume). Hugh further maintained that marriage was not simply a sacrament created to repair the sin of Adam and Eve, but existed as an office prior to sin entering the world.[22] Adopting most of Hugh's arguments, Peter Lombard (d.1160), theologian and bishop of Paris, included marriage as a sacrament in his influential *Sentences*. The authority of this work ensured that marriage would be among the definitive list of seven sacraments.

The century's optimism accommodated the veneration of other female figures besides the Virgin Mary. There was also a burgeoning cult of Mary Magdalene. We also see a progressive fascination with the literary personification of philosophical and moral abstractions as female goddesses. Barbara Newman describes this work as an "imaginative theology," one which encourages thinking outside the box of a masculine monotheistic deity. One of the most famous examples occurs in Alan of Lille's poem *The Plaint of Nature*, articulated in the first person by the goddess Nature.[23] A reconsideration of the first mother, Eve, was also underway. For instance, Hugh of St Victor first made the point that Eve had not been created from Adam's head, as his lord, or foot, as his slave, but from his side, as his companion.[24] His contemporary Hildegard of Bingen (d.1179) had a vision in which Eve, emerging from Adam's side like a beautiful cloud decorated by a wash of stars, is overshadowed by a dark fetid cloud, signifying Satan. Such imagery is representative of the tendency to diminish Eve's culpability in the Fall, a feature apparent throughout Hildegard's writings. Hildegard also had a healthy vision of gender complementarity, beginning from the moment of conception: in adherence with the tradition associated with the second-century physician Galen, Hildegard saw men and women as both possessed of generative seed.[25]

Others, such as Peter Abelard (d.1141), struggled against the implicit antifeminism of the reform movement and its flight from women. Abelard experienced a very different trajectory than most career churchmen, a fact apparent from both his autobiography and his vivid correspondence with his estranged wife, Heloise. According to Abelard's account, while lecturing at the cathedral school of Paris he sought lodging with Fulbert, a canon of the cathedral, deliberately to seduce his brilliant niece, Heloise. Fulbert was delighted at the housing arrangement since Abelard had agreed to tutor Heloise. Teacher and pupil fell passionately in love, reveling in the sheer physicality of their relationship.

Not surprisingly, the two lovers were eventually discovered in a compromising situation and forced to separate. When Heloise learned she was pregnant, Abelard insisted on marrying her, against her better judgment. Abelard portrayed Heloise's opposition as recognition that such a marriage would necessarily destroy any career that Abelard might have in the church. Later, however, after a copy of Abelard's autobiography made its way into Heloise's hands, she supplemented this perspective with further testimony to her heartfelt aversion to the institution of marriage:

> But you kept silent about most of my arguments for preferring love to wedlock and freedom to chains. God is my witness that if Augustus, Emperor of the whole world, thought fit to honour me with marriage... it would be dearer and more honourable to be called not his Empress but your whore.[26]

Her conviction that such a marriage would only lead to disaster proved prophetic. Although the marriage was at least in part undertaken to placate Fulbert, the couple denied the marriage to outsiders, which aroused Fulbert's suspicions. The final straw was when Abelard foolishly attempted to conceal Heloise in the religious community of Argenteuil, where she had been raised, dressed like a nun (admittedly, without the veil). Fulbert thought, with some justification, that Abelard was forcing Heloise into religion—a traditional way of disposing of inconvenient wives. He hired some thugs to castrate Abelard, presumably out of retaliation for the shame Abelard had brought on Fulbert's family and his treatment of Heloise. Again at Abelard's insistence, the wretched couple separated and entered religious communities. Their son, Astrolabe, was raised by Abelard's sister.

Soon after, when Heloise (now abbess of Argenteuil) and her nuns were evicted from their property, Abelard stepped up and gave them the Paraclete, an oratory he had founded. Abelard went on to produce a number of works for the community of the Paraclete, including a history of female religious and a new rule, both of which were written explicitly at Heloise's request. It is clear from these and other writings that Abelard's relationship with Heloise had left a deep imprint on his perception of women and their role in the church. For instance, his history of nuns unpredictably downplays the central role of the consecrated virgin, instead tracing the female vocation to the widow Anna, who prophesied at Christ's circumcision.[27]

Anna is salient in another important way in so far as she was the prototype used in the rite for ordaining a deaconess, a title Abelard wished to secure for Heloise, and which he assimilated with her role as abbess throughout his ensuing rule. The office has an obscure past: there is a reference to a certain Phoebe as deaconess in the letters of Paul (Rom. 16:1–2). We also know that a number of clerical wives were ordained deaconesses in the early Middle Ages, though we do not know what their responsibilities were. Nevertheless, as the word ordination implies, the deaconess was not just consecrated, as was a nun, she was ordained to the ministry as a member of the clergy. The office had been under attack by church councils since the fifth century, at least in Gaul, while the eleventh-century reform put an end to all possibility of an official ministry for women. For this reason, Abelard's insistence on according Heloise the title of deaconess has been described by Gary Macy as "the last defense" of an ancient tradition that was fast succumbing to church reform.[28] Such efforts were capped by Abelard's argument for how woman was superior to man "in as much as she indeed was created in Paradise, but man without," contributing to the twelfth-century rehabilitation of Eve.[29]

Finally, both Abelard and Heloise were advocates of what they themselves referred to as the "ethic of pure intention," the belief that God assessed an individual on the basis of intentions as opposed to actions. This allowed Heloise to argue that, although her behavior leading up to their entrance in religion might seem wholly culpable in society's eyes, she was vindicated in God's eyes because her intentions were pure. For Abelard, the ethic of pure intention opened the way to hypothetical reasoning that would be especially advantageous to a nonvirgin undertaking a religious vocation. He contended that if a woman vowed chastity and never wavered in her resolve, nothing could remove her right to follow the Lamb—even if she were not a virgin. He reinforced this point by citing Augustine's comment on the rape of the Roman matron, Lucretia: "there were two in the bed, but only one committed adultery while the other remained whole."[30]

The twelfth century was also a period of institution building, in which the formulation of canon law made great strides (see McDougall in this volume). Such progress represented something of a mixed bag for women and gender roles, however. On the one hand, canon law corroborated theological efforts to dignify marriage by legally stabilizing the institution, upholding a vigorous policy of indissolubility. Since the vast majority of medieval women were married, this arguably worked in their favor. The reintroduction of Roman law also brought with it the nebulous concept of marital affection: basically, a conception of the correct attitude and feeling one should possess for one's spouse, without which no marriage could exist. This emphasis on the couple's feelings necessarily helped to elevate spousal affectivity. On the other hand, the reintroduction of Roman law reinforced a woman's subordinate position in marriage and society at large.[31] This subordination could also make inroads into a woman's spiritual autonomy. Although a husband could not order his wife to do anything sinful, she was nevertheless unable to distribute alms or even make a pious vow without her husband's permission.

The latter part of the twelfth century and the thirteenth century also witnessed the reintroduction of Latin translations of the major works of Aristotle, which had been lost to the West for centuries. One of the effects was confirmation of the twelfth century's new optimism toward the realm of the natural, with a direct impact on attitudes toward sex and gender. The early Middle Ages tended to regard sex with suspicion and the pleasure it elicited as an unmitigated evil. In contrast, the Dominican theologian Thomas Aquinas (d.1272) insisted that married sexuality was good because it was natural, implemented by a good creator to sustain his good creation. He even argued that a person could win merit through married sex. But the downside was Aristotle's view of woman as an imperfect or deformed male, handicapped by the lack of heat during conception and gestation, a pronouncement echoed by Aquinas and others. In contrast to the tradition associated with the Roman physician Galen, moreover, Aristotle also believed the form of the fetus was entirely imparted by the male seed (see Park in this volume). Women, having no seed of their own, merely provided the necessary material for the fetus.[32]

By the time Aquinas was writing, the cathedral school of Abelard's day had developed into the university, the ancestor of our own institutions of higher learning. Besides Aristotle and Galen, the medieval universities were newly exposed to various medical and scientific authorities such as the influential Persian physician and philosopher known to the west as Avicenna (d.1037). The works of the twelfth-century Trota of Salerno, a female physician and gynecologist, began to circulate. A number of theologians also began to write scientific treatises. Albert the Great (d.1280), teacher of Aquinas, was fascinated by the animal kingdom, including humans. He wrote extensively on sexual matters, not just focusing on reproduction, but providing explicit discussions of female puberty and masturbation.[33] Nevertheless, because traditional medical authorities tended to stress women's physical—and incumbent moral—inferiority, their influence often fostered an antifeminist streak that was especially widespread in clerical circles. A case in point is the late thirteenth-century *Secrets of Women*—a text wrongly attributed to Albert the Great that seems to have been generated in theological circles. It is an ugly compilation of misinformation that transformed clerical mistrust of women into projections of active female malice. Hence the traditional beliefs in the harmful effects of menstrual blood are enhanced by allegations that some women put iron in their vaginas in order to maliciously harm men. In all likelihood, this work influenced the inquisitor, Heinrich Kramer, author of the notorious *Malleus maleficarum* (*Hammer of Witches*, 1486). The *Malleus* probably contributed more than any other text to the perception that witchcraft was primarily a female crime.[34]

Yet if the inferiority of the female body was foundational in the view of women as agents of depravity, it was also central to the perception of women as agents of particular grace. Theologians tended to concur that it was precisely the inferiority of the female body, its greater fluidity and malleability, that made women more impressionable to spiritual influences, for good or for bad.[35] The thirteenth century witnessed the rise of female mystics, women who were believed to communicate with God in the course of revelations and trance-like states. The earliest mystics seem to have arisen in the Low Countries with the rise of the Beguine movement (see Mulder-Bakker in this volume). The beguines were women who lived a religious life in the world, often forming informal communities or "beguinages." The theologian James of Vitry (d.1240) wrote the life of Mary of Oignies (d.1213), one of the first Beguines, and this life was destined to become a template for the mystical experience. The work was couched in the language of the Song of Songs, and Mary was singled out as Christ's special bride. In addition to this voluptuous metaphoric overlay, Mary's spirituality was also depicted as deeply embodied: she wept uncontrollably for Christ's suffering, endured illness and pains inflicted by the devil, communed with God during raptures in which her body was insensible, experienced frantic hunger for the host.[36] Nor was Mary alone. As the work of Caroline Walker Bynum has suggested, women seemed much more inclined than men to experience mystical raptures, divinely inspired illness, or various physical markings, such as the stigmata. They were also more apt to engage in extreme ascetic acts and punishing fasts. The physicality of women's spirituality is, in part, related to the age-old association between woman and flesh. But while scholars formerly assumed that the women's extreme asceticism represented a rejection of the body, Bynum has argued that these women were, in fact, embracing the body, exploring its spiritual potential. Women's identification with the body acted as a bridge which enabled their association with the broken body of the suffering Christ. The holy women of this period were often perceived as representing the human side of Christ.[37]

Clearly the church's perception of women was wracked with many seeming contradictions and historical inversions. In the early church, Tertullian attempted to humble independent virgins by marrying them to Christ, a relationship that the beguines eventually came to celebrate through bridal mysticism. Jerome's *Against Jovinian* is one of the notorious misogynistic treatises of all time and yet, on a practical level, his core supporters were all women. Eve's liabilities in the early church were transformed into definite advantages at the hands of Abelard, who argued for the superiority of women's creation because Eve alone had been formed inside of Paradise. And yet Abelard would do considerable damage to women's dignity by arguing that only man was created in God's image, while woman was only created in God's "likeness."[38] The frailty of the female body prepared the way equally for intimacy with Christ and the devil. Such contradictions do but mirror the puzzle at the center of the faith: that Eve represented humanity's damnation; Mary its salvation. This pivotal anomaly, bequeathed by Tertullian to the medieval clergy, both sustained and normalized the clergy's fractured view of women.

FURTHER READING

Allen, Prudence. *The Concept of Woman: The Aristotelian Revolution, 750 BC–AD 1250*, vol. 1. Montreal: Eden Press, 1985.

Atkinson, Clarissa. "'Precious Balsam in a Fragile Glass': The Ideology of Virginity in the Later Middle Ages." *Journal of Family History*, 8 (1983): 131–43.

Blamires, Alcuin. *The Case for Women in Medieval Culture*. Oxford: Clarendon Press, 1997.

Bos, Elisabeth. "The Literature of Spiritual Formation for Women in France and England, 1080–1180," in Constant Mews, ed., *Listen Daughter: The* Speculum Virginum *and the Formation of Religious Women in the Middle Ages*. New York: Palgrave, 2001, 201–20.

Bynum, Caroline Walker. *Holy Feast and Holy Fast: The Religious Significance of Food to Medieval Women*. Berkeley; Los Angeles: University of California Press, 1987.

Bynum, Caroline Walker. *Jesus as Mother: Studies in the Spirituality of the High Middle Ages*. Berkeley; Los Angeles: University of California Press, 1982.

Farmer, Sharon. "Persuasive Voices: Clerical Images of Medieval Wives," *Speculum*, 61 (1986): 517–43.

Hollywood, Amy. *The Soul as Virgin Wife: Mechtild of Magdeburg, Marguerite Porete, and Meister Eckhart*. Notre Dame, Ind.: University of Notre Dame Press, 1995.

McCracken, Peggy. "The Curse of Eve: Female Bodies and Christian Bodies in Heloise's Third Letter," in Bonnie Wheeler, ed., *Listening to Heloise: The Voice of a Twelfth-Century Woman*. New York: St. Martin's Press, 2000, 217–32.

McNamara, Jo Ann. "The *Herrenfrage*: The Restructuring of the Gender System, 1050–1150," in Clare Lees, ed., *Medieval Masculinities: Regarding Men in the Middle Ages*. Minneapolis: University of Minnesota Press, 1994, 3–29.

Rubin, Miri. *Mother of God: A History of the Virgin Mary*. New Haven: Yale University Press, 2009.

Notes

1. John Bugge, *Virginitas: An Essay in the History of a Medieval Idea* (The Hague: Martinus Nijoff, 1975), 16–19.

2. W. H. Shewring, ed. and trans., *The Passion of SS. Perpetua and Felicity* (London: Sheed and Ward, 1931), ch. 10, p. 11; trans., 31. For an introduction to this text, see Maureen Tilly, "The Passion of Perpetua and Felicity," in Elisabeth Schüssler Fiorenza, ed., *Searching the Scriptures* (New York: Crossroad, 1994), 2: 829–58.

3. Peter Brown, *The Body and Society: Men, Women, and Sexual Renunciation in the Early Church* (New York: Columbia University Press, 1988), 213–40.

4. Dyan Elliott, "Flesh and Spirit: Women and the Body," in Alastair Minnis and Rosalynn Voaden, eds, *Medieval Holy Women in Christian Tradition* (Turnhout: Brepols, 2010), 13–46.

5. Wayne Meeks, "The Image of the Androgyne: Some Uses of a Symbol in Earliest Christianity," *History of Religions*, 13 (1974): 165–208; Dale Martin, *The Corinthian Body* (New Haven: Yale University Press, 1996), 233–37; Tertullian, *On the Veiling of Virgins*, ch. 7, *Ante-Nicene Fathers* (Edinburgh: T. & T. Clark, 1867–73) (=*ANF*), 4:31. See Brown, *Body and Society*, 80–82; Jo Ann McNamara, *A New Song: Celibate Women in the First Three Christian Centuries* (Binghamton, NY: Harrington Park Press, 1983), 109–12.

6. Tertullian, *On the Veiling of Virgins*, ch. 5, *ANF*, 4:30; idem, *On the Flesh of Christ*, ch. 17, *ANF*, 3:536; cf. his discussion of Mary's womanhood in *On the Veiling of Virgins*, ch. 6, *ANF*, 4:31.

7. Cyprian, Ep. 4: "To Pomponius," in *The Epistles of S. Cyprian, Bishop of Carthage and Martyr*, trans. Members of the English Church (Oxford: Henry Parker, 1844), 7–11.

8. John Chrysostom, see *Instruction and Refutation against Those Men Cohabiting with Virgins*, and *On the Necessity of Guarding Virginity*, in Elizabeth Clark, trans., *Jerome, Chrysostom, and Friends: Essays and Translations* (New York: Edwin Mellen Press, 1982), 164–208, 209–48, 204.

9. *The Protoevangelium of James*, ch. 8, *ANF*, 8:363.

10. See Jerome, *Commentarius in Epistolam ad Ephesios*, 3.5, as cited by Barbara Newman, *From Virile Woman to WomanChrist: Studies in Medieval Religion and Literature* (Philadelphia: University of Pennsylvania Press, 1995), 81. For the patristic background to this imagery, see Gillian Cloke, *"This Female Man of God": Women and Spiritual Power in the Patristic Age, AD 350–450* (London: Routledge, 1995). Also see Susanna Elm, *Virgins of God: The Making of Asceticism in Late Antiquity* (Oxford: Oxford University Press, 1994).

11. On Melania the Elder, see *The Lausiac History of Palladius*, trans. W. K. Lowther Clarke (London: Society for Promoting Christian Knowledge, 1918), chs 46 and 54 <http://www.ccel.org/ccel/pearse/morefathers/files/palladius_lausiac_02_text.htm>; for Melania the Younger, see ibid., ch. 61, and Gerontius' *Life of Melania, the Younger*, trans. Elizabeth Clark (New York: Edwin Mellen Press, 1984). See Jerome, Ep. 108: "To Eustochium on the death of her mother, Paula," *A Select Library of Nicene and Post-Nicene Fathers of the Church*

(New York: Christian Literature Co. [et al.], 1887–92; repr. Grand Rapids, Mich.: Eerdmans [et al.], 1952–), ser. 2, 6: 195–212 (=*LNPNFC*). Also see *The Lausiac History of Palladius*, ch. 41, which describes Paula as possessed of "manly qualities" in the pursuance of God's work, but hindered by Jerome.

12. David Brakke, *Demons and the Making of the Monk: Spiritual Combat in Early Christianity* (Cambridge, Mass.: Harvard University Press, 2006), 182–212.

13. James of Voragine, *The Golden Legend of Jacobus de Voragine*, trans. Granger Ryan and Helmut Ripperger (New York: Arno Press, 1969), 610–12, 317–18, 613–14.

14. Dyan Elliott, *Fallen Bodies: Pollution, Sexuality, and Demonology in the Middle Ages* (Philadelphia: University of Pennsylvania Press, 1999), ch. 2.

15. Chrysostom, *Instruction and Refutation*, chs 10–11, in Clark, trans., *Jerome, Chrysostom, and Friends*, 193–98.

16. Augustine, *On Holy Virginity, LNPNFC*, ser. 1, 3: 417–38; idem, *On the Good of Widowhood*, ch. 4, ibid., 442.

17. Augustine, *On the Good of Marriage*, chs 8, 1, 3, *LNPNFC*, ser. 1, 3: 402–403, 3: 399, 400; idem, *On Marriage and Concupiscence*, ch. 1, 12–13, *LNPNFC*, ser. 1, 5: 268–69.

18. Augustine, Ep. 262: "To Ecdicia," ch. 4, in Sister Wilfrid Parsons, trans., *Letters*, vol. 5: *(204–270)* (New York: Fathers of the Church, 1956), 263.

19. Aldhelm, *On Virginity (The Prose Version)*, in Michael Lapidge and Michael Herren, trans., *Aldhelm: The Prose Works* (Ipswich: D. S. Brewer, 1979). See Felice Lifshitz, "Priestly Women, Virginal Men: Litanies and their Discontents," in Lisa Bitel and Felice Lifshitz, eds., *Gender and Christianity in Medieval Europe* (Philadelphia: University of Pennsylvania Press, 2008), 97–101.

20. Fortunatus, *De virginitate*, lines 325–34, bk 8, carm. 3, *Monumenta Germaniae Historica, Auctores Antiquissimi*, 4 (Hannover: Impensis Bibliopolii Hahniani et al., 1826–), 1:189–90.

21. Elliott, *Fallen Bodies*, 100–106.

22. Hugh of St Victor, *On the Sacraments of the Christian Faith*, 2.11.5, 2.11.3, trans. Roy Deferrari (Cambridge, Mass.: Mediaeval Academy, 1951), 332, 325–27. See Penny Gold, "The Marriage of Mary and Joseph in the Twelfth-Century Ideology of Marriage," in Vern Bullough and James Brundage, eds, *Sexual Practices and the Medieval Church* (Buffalo: Pantheon Books, 1982), 102–17.

23. See Rachel Fulton, *From Judgment to Passion: Devotion to Christ and the Virgin Mary, 800–1200* (New York: Columbia University Press, 2002); Katherine Jansen, *The Making of Magdalen: Preaching and Popular Devotion in the Later Middle Ages* (Princeton, NJ: Princeton University Press, 2000); and Barbara Newman, *God and the Goddesses: Vision, Poetry, and Belief in the Middle Ages* (Philadelphia: University of Pennsylvania Press, 2003).

24. Hugh of St Victor, *On the Sacraments*, 1.6.35, 117.

25. Hildegard of Bingen, *Scivias* 1.2.9–10, trans. Columba Hart and Jane Bishop (New York: Paulist Press, 1990), 76–77. Barbara Newman, *Sister of Wisdom: St. Hildegard's Theology of the Feminine* (Berkeley: University of California, 1987), 107–20. On Hildegard and gender, see Prudence Allen, *The Concept of Woman: The Aristotelian Revolution 750 BC–AD 1250* (Grand Rapids, Mich.: W. B. Eerdmans, 1985), 292–314.

26. Heloise, Ep. 2, in Betty Radice, trans., *The Letters of Abelard and Heloise*, rev. M. T. Clanchy (Middlesex: Penguin Books, 2003), 51.

27. Ep. 7: "On the Origin of Nuns," in C. K. Scott-Moncrieff, trans., *The Letters of Abelard and Heloise* (New York: Alfred A. Knopf, 1942), 131–75. See Dyan Elliott, *The Bride of Christ Goes to Hell: Metaphor and Embodiment in the Lives of Pious Women, ca. 200–1500* (Philadelphia: University of Pennsylvania Press, 2012), 140–41.

28. Gary Macy, *The Hidden History of Female Ordination: Female Clergy in the Medieval West* (Oxford: Oxford University Press, 2008), 93–95. Cf. Mary McLaughlin, "Peter Abelard and the Dignity of Women: Twelfth Century 'Feminism' in Theory and Practice," in *Pierre Abélard; Pierre le Vénérable: Les courants philosophiques, littéraires et artistiques en Occident au milieu du XIIe siècle* (Paris: Editions du Centre national de la recherche scientifique, 1975), 298–301. Abelard's rule is in Ep. 8, *The Letters of Abelard and Heloise*, trans. Radice, 130–210.

29. Abelard, Ep. 7, *Letters of Abelard and Heloise*, trans. Scott-Moncrieff, 156. See McLaughlin, "Peter Abelard and the Dignity of Women," 301–303.

30. Heloise, Ep. 2, *Letters of Abelard and Heloise*, trans. Radice, 53. Abelard's views were expressed in the course of teaching and captured by a student. See Charles Burnett and David Luscombe, "A New Student for Peter Abelard: The Marginalia in British Library MS Cotton Faustina A.X," in José Francisco Meirinhos, ed., *Itinéraires de la raison: Etudes de philosophie médiévale offertes à Maria Cândida Pacheco* (Louvain-la-Neuve: Fédération Internationale des instituts d'études médiévales, 2005), 169–70.

31. James Brundage, *Law, Sex, and Christian Society in Medieval Europe* (Chicago: University of Chicago Press, 1987), 229–55, 41–42; John Noonan, "Marital Affection and the Canonists," *Studia Gratiana* 12 (1967): 481–509. For the canonist Gratian's emphasis on female subordination, see Dyan Elliott, *Spiritual Marriage: Sexual Abstinence in Medieval Wedlock* (Princeton, NJ: Princeton University Press, 1993), 155–57.

32. Thomas Aquinas, *Summa theologica*, pt 3 (supplement), q. 41, art. 3–4, <http://www.newadvent.org/summa/5041.htm>. Joan Cadden, *The Meanings of Sex Difference in the Middle Ages* (Cambridge: Cambridge University Press, 1993), 117–30, 133–34, 141–45, 247–48. Also see Ruth Mazo Karras, *Sexuality in Medieval Europe: Doing Unto Others* (New York: Routledge, 2005), 66–70.

33. See Elliott, *Fallen Bodies*, 45–46.

34. *Women's Secrets: A Translation of Pseudo-Albertus Magnus's* De Secretis Mulierum *with Commentaries*, trans. Helen Lemay Rodnite (Albany, NY: State University of New York, 1992), 88–90; Heinrich Kramer, *Malleus maleficarum*, 1.6, ed. and trans. Christopher Mackay (Cambridge; New York: Cambridge University Press, 2006), 2: 111–25. On the relationship between *Women's Secrets* and the *Malleus*, see Rodnite's introduction to *Women's Secrets*, 49–58.

35. Nancy Caciola, *Discerning Spirits: Divine and Demonic Possession in the Middle Ages* (Ithaca, NY: Cornell University Press, 2003); Dyan Elliott, *Proving Woman: Female Spirituality and Inquisitional Culture in the Later Middle Ages* (Princeton, NJ: Princeton University Press, 2004), 204–11.

36. James of Vitry, *Life of Mary of Oignies*, trans. Margot King, in Anneke Mulder-Bakker, ed., *Mary of Oignies: Mother of Salvation* (Turnhout: Brepols, 2006), 33–127.

37. Caroline Walker Bynum, "'And Woman His Humanity': Female Imagery in the Religious Writing of the Later Middle Ages," in *Fragmentation and Redemption: Essays on Gender and the Human Body in Medieval Religion* (New York: Zone Books, 1992), 171–89.

38. McLaughlin, "Peter Abelard and the Dignity of Women," 305–306.

CHAPTER 3

....

JEWISH TRADITIONS ABOUT WOMEN AND GENDER ROLES: FROM RABBINIC TEACHINGS TO MEDIEVAL PRACTICE

....

JUDITH R. BASKIN

MEDIEVAL Jewish attitudes about appropriate gender roles originated in the teachings of the rabbinic movement. Active in Palestine and Mesopotamia between the first and sixth centuries CE, these circles of sages, known as rabbis, created a voluminous litera-ture elucidating and expanding the legal and narrative traditions of the Hebrew Bible. The rabbinic movement understood its multivocal writings, completed over many cen-turies, to be a part of divine revelation (*Torah*), sharing biblical sanctity and authority. Over time rabbinic mandates and interpretations, which incorporated legal as well as nonlegal content, became normative for all Jewish communities and continued to grow and evolve throughout the Middle Ages. Not surprisingly, given the patriarchal envi-ronments in which they originated, rabbinic writings are wholly androcentric; women played no active part in the development and codification of these traditions, either in late ancient or medieval times.

Rabbinic legislation governed virtually all aspects of Jewish life in medieval times, including the appropriate roles and responsibilities for women and men. This hegem-ony of rabbinic law was possible because Jews, who were accorded autonomy in both Muslim and Christian societies, created highly organized systems of communal govern-ance and institutions according to rabbinic mandates. However, gendered behaviors, as well as language, dress, and cultural values, were also significantly shaped by the social customs and practices of the larger environments in which Jews lived at any given time.

Feminist scholars have only recently begun to investigate representations of women in rabbinic and medieval Jewish literatures, much less deploy gender as a category for analyzing Jewish societies in late ancient and medieval times. Such undertakings, which began in the 1980s, result from the growth and impact of women's studies as an academic endeavor and from the increasing numbers of women who have entered the field of Jewish studies, once almost entirely a male domain, in recent decades.

Constructions of Gender in Rabbinic Literature

The earliest written document of rabbinic Judaism is the *Mishnah* (cited hereafter as *M.*, followed by the title of the tractate), a compilation of legal rulings organized into six subject divisions and sixty-three distinct tractates; it was edited in early third-century Roman Palestine. The *Tosefta*, a roughly contemporaneous collection of additional legal rulings, follows the same order as the *Mishnah*. In the centuries following the completion of these two works, rabbinic authorities teaching in academies in Palestine and Mesopotamia, which Jews called Babylon, produced extensive commentaries on the *Mishnah*. Known as *gemara*, these widely ranging expansions of the *Mishnah* are primarily in Aramaic, the Semitic language that was dominant in Western Asia. The *gemara* produced in the rabbinic academies of Babylon was far more voluminous than the *gemara* produced in Palestine. At some point in the sixth century, the *Mishnah* and this more extensive *gemara* were combined and substantially redacted to form the *Babylonian Talmud* (cited here as *BT*, followed by the title of the tractate), which constituted the definitive compilation of Jewish law and practice for the next millennium and beyond. The less comprehensive *Jerusalem Talmud* (also known as the *Palestinian Talmud*), completed in the fourth to fifth century CE, also became part of rabbinic literature. Parallel to the *Mishnah*, *Tosefta* and *Talmud*s are *midrash* collections, exegetical compilations organized either as consecutive glosses on a biblical book or as thematically related homilies on a particular verse or group of verses.[1] In all these texts, rabbinic views about gender were built on the conviction of women's essential otherness from men. The talmudic statement that "women are a separate people" (*BT Shabbat* 62a) conveyed a basic belief that females were human entities created by God with physical characteristics, innate capacities, and social functions inherently dissimilar from those of males. Moreover, the ways in which women were perceived as essentially different were not only ineradicable but undesirable and inferior. The sages who produced rabbinic literature were highly conscious of human sexuality and its potential for disrupting an ordered society; women, in particular, were seen as both morally unreliable and constant sources of temptation to men. Thus, rabbinic social policy apportioned separate spheres and separate responsibilities to women and men and endeavored to confine women to the private realms of the family and its particular concerns. These private concerns could include economic undertakings that would benefit the household, and such activities were often an expected part of a woman's domestic role.

This template was already well established by late biblical times, as indicated by Proverbs 31:10–31, which described a gendered differentiation of roles. While the ideal wife (a likely understanding of the difficult term *eshet ḥayyil* [Proverbs 31:10], often translated "woman of valor") was involved in a range of domestic, entrepreneurial, and philanthropic activities, her husband sat with the elders in the gates (31:23); he was known by his words, she by "her works" (31:31).

In rabbinic and medieval times, women were active participants in the economic lives of their households, frequently venturing beyond the home in pursuit of business opportunities. But whatever women did in public, they did as private individuals. Rabbinic law and custom generally excluded women from the culturally valued and power-conferring activities of the Jewish community. Since these public endeavors had mostly to do with group worship at set times, study of religious texts, and the execution of judgments according to Jewish law, women were simultaneously ineligible for public leadership, as well as the spiritual and intellectual sustenance available to men.[2]

As long as women satisfied male expectations in their domestic roles, they were revered and honored for enhancing the lives of their families and particularly for enabling their male relatives to fulfill religious obligations. The Talmud related that women earned merit "by sending their sons to learn in the synagogue, and their husbands to study in the schools of the rabbis, and by waiting for their husbands until they returned from the rabbinic academies" (*BT Berakhot* 17a). In this religious system, a select group of men expounded the divine rulings that affected women's lives; women, the objects of these directives, had no standing to legislate for themselves or others. This is not to say that women lacked spiritual status. Women, like men, were responsible for obeying all of Judaism's prohibitions, as well as for observing the Sabbath and the holy days of the Jewish calendar (although male and female obligations on these days sometimes differed). Women were required to pray, although they were exempt from the requirement incumbent on men to participate in daily communal prayer at specific times according to a fixed Hebrew liturgy (*BT Berakhot* 20b). Rather, the timing and content of women's prayers could be spontaneous and in a vernacular language (*M. Sotah* 7:1).

An enduring result of this separate pattern of obligations was that medieval Jewish women were rarely taught Hebrew, the language of study and public worship. Women's central ritual observances were almost wholly domestic: these included preparation and serving of food according to rabbinic dietary laws (*kashrut*), and the observance of specified limitations on marital contact during and following the wife's menstrual period prior to her ritual immersion in a cleansing bath (*mikveh*). Women were also expected to kindle Sabbath and festival lights and to separate and burn a piece of the dough used in making Sabbath bread, a reminder of the offerings that had been part of sacrificial rituals in the Jerusalem Temple. Although these three "women's commandments" are explained more than once in rabbinic writings as punishments or atonements for Eve's responsibility in the death of Adam, and therefore in all human mortality, they doubtless provided satisfying and affirming spiritual avenues for sanctification of aspects of daily life.

The formulators of rabbinic Judaism were fully aware that their legal system privileged men, and they justified female subordination on the grounds of women's secondary place in human creation. The first female, after all, was fashioned from the body of the previously created male (Gen 2: 4–24); this removal by one step from the divine image was a frequent explanation for the moral and intellectual deficiencies attributed to women. Male primacy was explicit both in a daily morning prayer, in which men thanked God for not being created a woman (or a slave or a gentile), and in rabbinic enumerations detailing the drawbacks of being female (*Genesis Rabbah* 17:8; *BT Eruvin* 100b). Among the acknowledged liabilities were the pains of menstruation and childbirth, the demands of raising children, sexual passivity and restriction to one sexual partner, the requirement of veiling in public, a strong connection with death, and the subordination of self to a husband rather than realizing one's own spiritual and intellectual aspirations (*BT Eruvin* 100b). Yet as different from men as they were imagined to be, women were also acknowledged as the indispensable social mortar sustaining rabbinic society. They were praised as "bolsters to their husbands" (*BT Eruvin* 100b) whose ancillary services enabled and elevated men's study of the divine word to the highest rung of human endeavor.[3]

THE EVOLUTION OF LEGAL TRADITIONS

In medieval times, significant populations of Jews lived in the Muslim world of the Middle East, North Africa, and Spain; smaller enclaves resided in Christian Europe. Between the mid-sixth and eleventh centuries, Jewish legal authority rested with three rabbinic leaders, the Geonim (sing. Gaon). Two of the Geonim headed rabbinic academies near Baghdad; the third presided over a rabbinic academy in Palestine. Through legal enactments (*takkanot*; sing. *takkanah*) that responded to specific circumstances, the Geonim adjusted talmudic law (*halakhah*) to changing social realities; they also institutionalized local and regional customs. An important seventh-century enactment from Baghdad, for example, ruled that if a woman claimed in a rabbinic court that she could not bear to live with her husband, her husband could be forced to grant her an immediate divorce. One of the motivations behind this ruling was to provide Jewish women with an alternative to bringing their marital disputes to Muslim courts or even converting to Islam to escape an untenable marriage.[4] The Geonim also created something called "responsa literature" to answer the questions of distant constituencies; these rabbinic responses to questions sent from all over the Jewish world addressed virtually every aspect of life. The Geonim's responses, which circulated widely in small booklets and had the status of law, established precedents for similar quandaries; the particular circumstances of each reported situation provide vivid glimpses of everyday Jewish life.

By the eleventh century, the authority of the Geonim had declined as local centers of Jewish learning were established elsewhere, both in the Muslim world (North Africa, Egypt, and Spain) and in Italy, France, and Germany. This regionalization of

Jewish governance resulted in increasing geographical discrepancies in legal practice and local customs, and it led to the emergence of distinctive Jewish communities in Europe, including Sephardim (Jews in the Iberian Peninsula) and Ashkenazim (Jews in Germany and surrounding regions). The traditions of Jews in various parts of the Byzantine Empire and the Muslim Middle East and North Africa continued to develop in distinctive directions as well.[5]

Legal codes, a genre that also originated with the Geonim, were also important repositories of evolving Jewish law and practice. The most influential, comprehensive, and original medieval code is the *Mishneh Torah* of the Spanish-born Moses Maimonides (d.1204), which he completed in Egypt *c*.1178. The fourth division of this fourteen-section compilation, entitled "The Book of Women," deals with family law. Maimonides reflected an aspect of his Muslim environment when he wrote that "There is nothing more beautiful for a wife than sitting in the corner of her house" and suggested that women should not leave home to visit family and friends more than once or twice a month (*Mishneh Torah*, "Book of Women: Laws of Marriage" 13:11). In the *Mishneh Torah*, Maimonides also strongly discouraged girls' education in rabbinic writings on the grounds that women had no legal obligation to study. He argued that "most women's thought is oriented in a different direction, and not toward the study of *Torah* [divine revelation in its fullest sense, which included rabbinic writings], and as a result they will turn the words of *Torah* into frivolity" ("Book of Knowledge: Study of *Torah*" 1:13, based on *M. Sotah* 3:4). Regarding Bible study, Maimonides wrote that a father should not set out to teach biblical texts to his daughter, but if he did so, "it is not considered as if he taught her frivolity." In fact, some male relatives did instruct their daughters or sisters in the Bible in medieval Egypt, at least on an elementary level, since two letters in Maimonides' collected responsa concern a woman who ran a primary school for boys.[6]

Ordinances, responsa literature, and legal codes were also central in the evolving life of medieval Ashkenazic Jewry. Rabbinic leaders in France and Germany tended to share Maimonides' view that women should not be taught the complexities of Jewish law. In his *Sefer Mitzvot Gadol* (Large Book of Commandments), written in the early thirteenth century, Moses of Coucy explained that although "a woman is exempt from both the commandment to learn *Torah* and to teach her son, even so, if she aids her son and husband in their efforts to learn [through her economic support], she shares their reward for the fulfillment of that commandment." Interestingly, in the introduction to his *Sefer Mitzvot Katan* (Small Book of Commandments), Isaac ben Joseph of Corbeil (d.1280) encouraged women to master the commandments that applied to their lives, explaining that "The reading and studying of them will benefit them as the study of Talmud helps men."

Among important ordinances altering aspects of rabbinic law and practice for Jews in France and Germany was the eleventh-century ruling mandating monogamy. Attributed to Gershom ben Judah of Mainz (*c*.960–1028), known as "Light of the Exile," this prohibition of polygamy was never adopted by Jews living in Muslim regions. Gershom is also credited with the significant pronouncement that no woman could be divorced against her will. Both of these ordinances are likely responses to Christian mores and sensibilities, since Christianity forbade polygamy and made divorce virtually impossible. Both of these rulings improved women's legal position significantly[7] and indicate, together with the substantial dowries that were typical in this milieu, the high status and economic significance of women in northern European Jewish communities.[8]

At the end of the Middle Ages, the *Shulhan Arukh* (Set Table) of the Sephardic scholar Joseph Karo (d.1575 in Safed, Ottoman Palestine) became universally accepted as the authoritative code of Jewish law. One of its four sections, *Even ha-Ezer* (Stone of Help), is devoted to the laws of marriage, divorce, and related topics. Beginning in the 1570s the *Shulhan Arukh* was printed with a detailed commentary called the *Mappah* (Tablecloth), composed by the Ashkenazic legal authority Moses Isserles (d.1572). Isserles' commentary cited practices, including many details of family law, which had developed in Germany and Poland and often differed from Sephardic customs. As a result of his additions, the *Shulhan Arukh* became an essential legal resource for both Ashkenazim and Sephardim. Its rapid dissemination was facilitated by new printing technologies. The *Mappah* preserved the precept that women earn merit by supporting their husbands' and sons' scholarly endeavors (*BT Berakhot* 17a) and the view that a woman must be instructed in the laws that apply to her life. However, as with previous legal compilations, the *Shulhan Arukh* and the *Mappah* reflected male perspectives; the only female contributions to Jewish law in the medieval era were occasional female testimonies cited in responsa literature about the rulings on domestic matters of an esteemed male relative.

MEDIEVAL JEWISH FAMILY LAW

Legal issues affecting medieval Jewish women included marriage, divorce, inheritance, and care of children following a divorce or the death of a spouse. The marriage contract (*ketubbah*), a post-biblical innovation in Jewish practice, played a central role in all these circumstances. Written in Aramaic, the marriage contract was presented by a husband to his wife at the time of their betrothal. This document outlined the man's legal and financial obligations. Among other commitments, a husband promised to provide his wife with food, appropriate clothing, and conjugal rights, and he pledged that her dowry, as well as property she acquired during the marriage, would pass to her heirs. The *ketubbah* protected a woman financially by stipulating that should her husband divorce or predecease her, she would receive the dowry she had brought into the marriage as well as a deferred monetary pledge from her husband's resources. These payments enabled a widowed or divorced woman to negotiate a second marriage or establish an independent livelihood.

Divorce was always permitted in Judaism but the legal dissolution of a marriage could only be initiated by the husband (assuming, at least in Ashkenaz after 1000, that his wife did not object). A woman had no unilateral power to end her marriage in any circumstances. In some situations, such as infertility, spousal abuse,[9] desertion, or pronounced incompatibility, a wife could petition the rabbinic court to compel her unwilling husband to divorce her (*M. Ketubbot* 7:1–5, 10). Custody of children following a divorce, as demonstrated in numerous instances found in responsa literature, was often a contentious issue. Generally, boys of six years and older were placed in their father's care; younger boys would move to their father's household when they turned six. Daughters, however, stayed with their mothers until their marriages were arranged. However, if a divorcée chose to remarry or if she died, her daughters, too, would likely come under the care of her former husband or his family.[10]

Since a woman's dowry, as specified in her marriage contract, often comprised a significant portion of her parents' resources, a woman did not generally inherit wealth or property following her father's death, particularly if she had brothers. Similarly, a woman did not usually inherit anything from her husband following his death, beyond what was stated in her marriage contract. Some wealthy men in Christian Spain made wills in non-Jewish courts so that their wives could inherit all or parts of their estates, which would be worth considerably more than the promised *ketubbah* payment.[11] Most widows, however, had the choice of receiving the payment specified in the marriage contract in full, or of being supported from their husbands' estate. A woman with small children would likely take the latter option and join her deceased husband's extended family.

The medieval Jewish marriage contract enhanced women's status, prevented rash divorces, and limited the numbers of indigent widows and divorcées dependent on community support. It also could contain added protections, including the assurances found in marriage contracts from Muslim lands that a husband would not take a second wife without the first wife's consent, that he would not beat his wife, that he would not travel anywhere without her consent, and that he would not insist on a move to another locale that separated his wife from her parents against her will. A contract sometimes inventoried the objects that were part of the dowry, providing useful information for modern historians of medieval material culture. In addition to the unilateral marriage contract issued in the husband's name, which was generally the norm in Jewish practice, the Cairo Genizah, a repository of medieval Jewish documents from late antiquity through the later Middle Ages, preserved examples of *ketubbot* written according to the custom of "the land of Israel." These unusual contracts were based on a statement of mutual obligations by groom and bride, and they defined marriage as a partnership. Contrary to biblical and rabbinic precedent, they granted the wife the right to initiate divorce proceedings against her husband if she found herself unable to live with him.[12]

THE ROLE OF THE BODY

Rabbinic Judaism constructed an idealized social order in which only free unblemished Jewish males participated fully in Israel's covenant with God; entry into this covenant relationship was sacralized by circumcision. As many authorities saw it, women's bodies were irredeemably deficient since, according to rabbinic medical understanding, women lacked the ability to generate new life and simply served as the passive vessels in which a deposited potential life was nurtured. In *BT Berakhot* 51b, the Palestinian sage Ulla insisted that women's secondary obligations in the performance of commandments were justified by their secondary role in reproduction. In each instance, her husband was the active partner while she was the passive recipient who benefited from his performance. Similarly, dominant voices in rabbinic Judaism understood creation in God's image as applying only to men, since to be like God required the possession of fully functioning male sexual organs. They took for granted that the covenantal alliance marked on the flesh of the eight-day-old male infant through circumcision excluded women *de facto* from complete participation in Jewish worship and religious service.[13]

As early as the twelfth century, Christians claimed as part of their conversionary efforts that Judaism was deficient in its evaluation and treatment of women; they argued that both women and men entered Christianity through baptism, but only Jewish males could be circumcised. How then did women become Jews? The *Nizzahon Vetus* (Old Book of Polemic), a thirteenth-century anthology of Jewish rejoinders to Christian arguments, written in northern France or Germany, responded that married women's observance of the ritual purity regulations pertaining to menstruation and childbirth constituted their distinguishing performance of Jewishness. Moses Maimonides, on the other hand, argued that since Jewish women are undeniably Jews, and since many gentiles are also circumcised (as was the case among Muslims), it was obvious that circumcision was not equivalent to baptism as an essential initiation ritual. Rather, Maimonides stressed that membership in the community of Israel was based in proper belief, which was possible for both women and men.[14] However, while belief and practice might be the rational constituents of Jewish identity, Jews continued to understand the ritual circumcision of male infants as the entry into the covenant between God and Jewish men, a relationship that was not open to women.

Male anxiety about female biological functions was also a significant factor in rabbinic Judaism's elimination of women from direct participation in communal worship and study. Rabbinic Judaism was a religious system constructed on biblical foundations that likened ritual impurity to a state of spiritual death. Blood and other bodily emissions were primary sources of ritual pollution, as was contact with the dead. Women, due to their periodic flows of blood, which represented the loss of an opportunity for new life, were portrayed as sources of potential pollution and as portents of physical extinction. The Talmud expanded the biblical ordinances of Leviticus (12:4, 15:19–32, 18:19, and 20:18) into a complicated system of rules preventing any direct or indirect physical contact between husband and wife for specified periods of time, both postpartum and during and after menstruation. Although men could also be subject to various discharges and states of ritual impurity, rabbinic Judaism understood these as unusual and sporadic. Those particular to women, however, were normal and regular, and as a defining female characteristic, they were indicative of the risks women, in general, presented to male ritual purity. At some point after the early third-century codification of the *Mishnah*, the definition of a menstruating or postpartum woman (*niddah* in

Hebrew) was extended in rabbinic legislation from the actual duration of menstruation. Physical contact between husband and wife was thereafter prohibited for an additional seven "white" days. An atmosphere of asceticism, possibly related to mourning for the 70 CE destruction of the Jerusalem Temple and the continued state of exile, may have eased acceptance of this stricture.[15] At the end of the prescribed marital separation, the wife was required to immerse herself in a ritual bath (*mikveh*) before sexual relations could resume.

While rabbinic law was concerned with preserving men from the ritual pollution caused by contact with a menstruating woman, the procedures for calculating the interval of forbidden spousal contact relied heavily on a woman's knowledge of the stages of her menstrual cycle. Thus, a young woman had to be taught to be sensitive to hormonal changes indicating the onset of menstruation, and she had to be instructed to examine herself carefully so that she would know when her menses had ceased. Similarly, a wife was counseled to immerse herself in the ritual bath as soon as legally permitted so that she and her husband could return to sexual intimacy as quickly as possible.[16]

Male concerns about menstruation and female ritual immersion were prompted by fears that a woman in a state of *niddah* might transmit her ritual impurity to her husband. Thus, only married women were required to cleanse themselves in a ritual bath. Medieval rabbis were as convinced as their predecessors that women garnered merit through enabling male piety; in this instance, it was women's expeditious and conscientious observance of these commandments that enabled their husbands to remain ritually pure. There are no references to the possibility that being in a state of ritual impurity could have a spiritual or psychological impact on women themselves. When the thirteenth-century pietist Eleazar ben Judah of Worms enumerated the appropriate acts of penance for those who transgressed the prohibition against contact between a man and a *niddah*, he assumed that these acts of atonement, which included extensive fasting, lashing, and immersion in icy water, applied only to men. In such pietistic writings, women were generally imagined as objects that could occasion desire and sin in men, but not as self-conscious entities who might wish to expiate their own wrongdoing or advance their own sanctity.[17]

Although marital separation during the prohibited interval was often presented as a matter of concern only to husband and wife, some rabbinic and medieval writings linked contact with any menstruating woman to defilement and even to danger. Jewish customary law concerning the menstruating woman became increasingly stringent in the central Middle Ages, particularly in Jewish communities in Christian Europe. According to the *Baraita de-Niddah*, an influential text that was probably written in Palestine or Italy in the ninth or tenth century, a menstruating woman was forbidden to enter a synagogue, to come into contact with sacred books, to pray, or to recite God's name.[18] The thirteenth-century German pietistic compendium, *Sefer Ḥasidim* (Book of the Pious) warned that a man who looked at the face of a *niddah* at the moment her flow began would forget all of his accrued Talmud study (Bologna version, §1026). Eleazar ben Judah of Worms prohibited a menstruating woman from wearing eye make-up or jewelry; she was not to cook for her husband, prepare his bed, or pour water from one vessel to another; moreover, "...she was forbidden to enter a synagogue until she had immersed in water...a *niddah* who had sexual relations with her husband caused her sons to be stricken with leprosy, even for twenty generations." Some rabbinic authorities, including Maimonides, objected to the virtual demonization of the menstruating woman and to her exclusion from the synagogue, stating that ritual impurity does not bar any person from holding a *Torah* scroll or engaging in prayer and study. However, these customs continued in many Jewish communities in Christian Europe well into the early modern period with the endorsements of rabbinic authorities who praised compliant women for their piety. The larger environment probably also played a role in these customary exclusions, since the Christian setting in which Jews lived also had strong traditions about menstruation and the propriety of public religious roles for menstruating and postpartum women.[19] Moses Isserles reiterated this ambivalence in his sixteenth-century gloss on the *Shulḥan Arukh*, in which he affirmed that rabbinic law did not prohibit menstruating woman from participating in prayer. Nevertheless, he noted that the prevalent custom was to exclude the *niddah*. His commentary confirms that medieval and early modern women frequently attended synagogue and that being excluded was emotionally painful for them. This is evident in his ruling that "on the High Holidays and Yom Kippur [the most sacred days of the Jewish year] [*the niddah*] may enter the synagogue like other women, for otherwise it would cause her great sorrow to remain outside while everyone congregates in the synagogue" (*Oraḥ Ḥayyim* §88:1).

A medieval development related to the discussion of when women could and could not enter the synagogue was the institution of separate worship areas for men and women. According to rabbinic legal traditions, women were generally not obligated to fulfill commandments that had to be performed at specific times, such as communal prayer (*M. Kiddushin* 1:7; *BT Berakhot* 20a–20b). It was assumed that men represented their households during public worship and that female religious observance should take second place to family responsibilities. Moreover, rabbinic Judaism's construction of gender was predicated on a consciousness of the disruptive potentialities of human sexuality. Since women were not required to be present and since they might constitute distractions to men, it was felt that they should not occupy a central place in the synagogue sanctuary. One justification for the exemption of women from participation in communal worship was based on the talmudic statement, "The voice of woman is indecent" (*BT Berakhot* 24a). This derived from a ruling that a man could not recite certain prayers if he heard a woman singing because her voice might divert his concentration. Extrapolating from hearing to seeing, medieval practice came to insist that all pubescent girls and women who chose to attend synagogue must sit out of sound and sight to preserve men from distraction.

References to separate worship areas or rooms for women appear beginning in the tenth century. Separation of men and women during worship was prevalent in contemporaneous Christianity and Islam, although in most cases without a physical barrier between the sexes, and this likely had an influence on Jewish practice. What is clear is that over time it became customary for men to pray together in the main part of the synagogue sanctuary while women were relegated behind a visual barrier of some kind. Documents from the Cairo Genizah indicate that this practice was well established in Egypt by the tenth and eleventh centuries. Early medieval synagogues in Europe, built without specific areas for women, do not give evidence either of women's presence or absence. In the twelfth century, however, sections adjoining the main worship space began to be added to existing buildings, establishing women's annexes in attached rooms, as in the synagogue at Worms, or in upstairs rooms or basements. Often, learned women, generally daughters of scholars, led prayers for other women in these female spaces, an activity that was both approved and praised by rabbinic leaders.[20] By the seventeenth century, separate areas for women were regularly built into newly constructed synagogues in the form of upstairs galleries overlooking the main sanctuary. This architectural innovation became common throughout Europe, with opaque screens, grilles, or lattice work to prevent male congregants from seeing female worshipers.[21]

Ironically, some women used the laws pertaining to menstruation to their own advantage. In France and Germany refusing to immerse in the ritual bath at the appointed time became a strategy to end an unhappy marriage in cases where a husband refused to initiate a divorce. A wife who refused sexual relations could be designated a "rebellious wife" by a rabbinic court; she was subject to a daily fine, and when the value of her dowry had been exhausted, her husband was compelled to divorce her. Women who supported their families through entrepreneurial enterprises, especially moneylending, or who had achieved economic independence by other means could effect an exit from uncongenial marriages by refusing to visit the ritual bath.[22] Such acts of female agency became increasingly frequent in twelfth- and thirteenth-century Ashkenaz and prompted various rabbis to institute legal rulings to prevent women's expressions of independence, although with limited success. In this same era and locale, economic prosperity also led some women to assume religious practices from which they were exempt in rabbinic law and to assert authority in the communal realm. That women with significant resources would use their financial clout in these ways implies that some women, at least, had long resented their exclusion from the public performance of religious obligations and from community honors.[23]

GENDER AND JEWISH MYSTICISM

Women are absent from histories of medieval Jewish mysticism, often known as *kabbalah*, and there is virtually no evidence for female Jewish mystics prior to the seventeenth century; this is in striking contrast to the importance of female mystics in medieval Christianity and Islam. One reason was the highly intellectual nature of medieval Jewish mysticism. Given their limited educations in traditional Jewish learning, few if any women could have attained the requisite linguistic and textual expertise essential for initiation into mystical teachings. Other explanations for female exclusion from mystical circles include the association between women and the demonic that permeated medieval Jewish mystical speculation, as well as the prevalent conviction that physical impurity created an insurmountable obstacle to divine communion.[24]

Although women were absent from the ranks of medieval Jewish mystics, female imagery was a frequent characteristic of mystical traditions. In the Hebrew Bible and throughout later Jewish literature, marriage was often understood metaphorically as signifying the intimate bonds between God and human beings. Rabbinic interpretation of the Song of Songs, for example, assumed that the biblical book's love poetry was actually an allegory detailing the passion between God (understood to be the male lover) and the people of Israel (the female beloved).[25] In medieval mysticism, marital sexuality took on a specifically redemptive function. The late thirteenth-century *Zohar* (Book of Brightness), the central work of medieval Jewish mysticism, taught that each religiously inspired act of marital intercourse, particularly on the eve of Sabbath, ensured the presence of the *Shekhinah*, the nurturing and indwelling aspect of God that was most accessible to human experience. While the *Shekhinah* was understood to be feminine, the infinite and distant aspect of God, the *Ein Sof* ("eternal"), was constructed as masculine. Thus, conjugal union was believed to play a crucial role in restoring cosmic harmony in the divine realm by simultaneously presaging and enacting the ultimate reunification of the masculine and feminine aspects of the divine, believed to be in exile from each other.[26]

"The Holy Letter," a late thirteenth-century mystical text from Spain of unknown authorship, was among the earliest Jewish medieval works to present connubial sexuality as a salvific activity. This document provided guidance on enhancing the mutual pleasure of marital intercourse and also suggested sexual techniques and strategies that were said to result in the births of scholarly sons. According to "The Holy Letter," marital relations were to be infused with appropriate intention: both participants in sexual intercourse had to direct their thoughts towards God if they hoped to have worthy children and to produce the appropriate cosmic effect. In this mystical scenario, as opposed to the allegorical imagery connected with the Song of Songs, neither human partner represents the divine. Rather a man's performance of intercourse with the proper intention prompts the *Shekhinah* to establish her presence in the human realm, in effect as a second female partner in the marriage. Ironically, the male mystic was understood to achieve his spiritual goal through marital intercourse, even though his desire for his wife was deemed less important than his yearning for divine companionship.[27] The resulting dilemma for men of divided mystical and mundane loyalties remained unresolved in medieval Judaism, which had no option of a monastic and celibate life for either men or women.[28]

In the gender imagery that pervaded medieval Jewish mystical writings, the male, created in the divine image, was the dominant, primary sex, while females were passive and secondary. In sexual union female distinctiveness, and by analogy the feminine aspect of the divine, the *Shekhinah*, was effaced and absorbed by the preeminent male entity, the *Ein Sof*, from which she was originally derived. This notion of the reabsorption of the feminine by the masculine originated in the creation narrative of Genesis 2:18–24 and reiterated the conviction, so central to rabbinic constructions of gender, that woman, created out of man's body, was secondary in her relation to the divine. It also explains why the *Shekhinah* as bride of the *Ein Sof* was a positive symbol pointing to divine unity. The *Shekhinah* on her own, however, was sometimes represented as a menstruating woman (*niddah*); as such, she was a figure of danger, since the unconstrained female and her menstrual blood were linked to the demonic forces responsible for evil in the world.[29]

A similar development in thirteenth-century mystical writings was the appearance of the folklore figure of Lilith who was said to rule, with her male counterpart Samael, over an unholy realm of evil powers that paralleled the world of sanctity over which the *Shekhinah* and *Ein Sof* presided. Centuries of legends about the demon Lilith had already been synthesized in eleventh-century rabbinic speculation. Identified as the "first Eve" who was created simultaneously with Adam (Genesis 1), she refused to submit to Adam's assertion of mastery and established herself as an independent demonic being. In later Jewish folklore and popular mysticism, Lilith became the exemplar of rebellious wives and the fiendish enemy of married women and their children.[30]

CONCLUSION

Women's voices are almost completely missing from the documents that constitute our knowledge of medieval Jewish societies.[31] These texts, which provided legal guidance, spiritual sustenance, and intellectual stimulation, were written by men for male readers. However, they also reveal, sometimes inadvertently, that women were energetic and influential members of their communities, particularly in northern Europe. Endowed with large dowries and active in commerce, Ashkenazic Jewish women frequently provided the domestic support and financial resources that enabled men to concentrate on scholarship, teaching, and communal leadership. The dissonance between women's positive social and economic contributions and the negative ways in which they were frequently represented in medieval Jewish writings indicates the enduring impact of rabbinic traditions about women's reduced connection to the divine and their perceived potential for sexual disruption and ritual pollution.

FURTHER READING

Baskin, Judith R. "Jewish Women in Ashkenaz: Renegotiating Jewish Gender Roles in Northern Europe," in Carmen Caballero Navas and Esperanza Alfonso, eds, *Late Medieval Jewish Identities: Iberia and Beyond*. New York: Palgrave Macmillan, 2010, 79–90.
Baskin, Judith R. "Jewish Women in the Middle Ages," in idem, ed., *Jewish Women in Historical Perspective*, 2nd edn. Detroit: Wayne State University Press, 1998, 94–113.
Baskin, Judith R. "Male Piety, Female Bodies: Men, Women, and Ritual Immersion in Medieval Ashkenaz," *Journal of Jewish Law*, 17 (2007): 11–30.
Baskin, Judith R. "Medieval Jewish Models of Marriage," in Sherry Roush and Cristelle Baskins, eds, *The Medieval Marriage Scene: Prudence, Passion, Policy*. Tempe, AZ: Arizona Center for Medieval and Renaissance Studies, 2005, 1–22.

Baskin, Judith R. *Midrashic Women: Formations of the Feminine in Rabbinic Literature*. Hanover, NH: Brandeis/University Press of New England, 2002.

Baumgarten, Elisheva. *Mothers and Children: Jewish Family Life in Medieval Europe*. Princeton, NJ: Princeton University Press, 2007.

Biale, Rachel. *Women and Jewish Law: An Exploration of Women's Issues in Halakhic Sources*. New York: Schocken Books, 1984.

Dishon, Judith. "Images of Women in Medieval Hebrew Literature," in Judith R. Baskin, ed., *Women of the Word: Jewish Women and Jewish Writing*. Detroit: Wayne State University Press, 1994, 35–49.

Goitein, Shlomo Dov. *A Mediterranean Society: The Jewish Communities of the Arab World as Portrayed in the Documents of the Cairo Geniza*, 6 vols. Berkeley: University of California Press, 1967–93.

Grossman, Avraham. *Pious and Rebellious: Jewish Women in Medieval Europe*, trans. J. Chipman. Hanover, NH: Brandeis/University Press of New England, 2004.

Koren, Sharon Faye. *Forsaken: The Menstruant in Medieval Jewish Mysticism*. Hanover, NH: University Press of New England for Brandeis University Press, 2011.

Melammed, Renée Levine. "Sephardi Women in the Medieval and Early Modern Periods," in Baskin, ed., *Jewish Women in Historical Perspective*, 128–47.

Rosen, Tova. *Unveiling Eve: Reading Gender in Medieval Hebrew Literature*. Philadelphia: University of Pennsylvania Press, 2003.

NOTES

1. See Hayim Lapin, "The Rabbinic Movement," and Michael S. Berger, "The Centrality of Talmud," in Judith R. Baskin and Kenneth Seeskin, eds, *The Cambridge Guide to Jewish History, Religion, and Culture* (Cambridge; New York: Cambridge University Press, 2010), 58–84, 311–36.

2. On constructions of gender in rabbinic writings, see Judith R. Baskin, *Midrashic Women: Formations of the Feminine in Rabbinic Literature* (Hanover, NH: Brandeis/University Press of New England, 2002); Daniel Boyarin, *Carnal Israel: Reading Sex in Rabbinic Culture* (Berkeley: University of California Press, 1995); Miriam Peskowitz, *Spinning Fantasies: Rabbis, Gender, and History* (Berkeley: University of California Press, 1997); and the essays in Miriam Peskowitz and Laura Levitt, eds, *Judaism Since Gender* (New York: Routledge, 1997).

3. The rabbis generally discounted the egalitarian creation narrative of Genesis 1, see Baskin, *Midrashic Women*, 44–64; for perceived female disabilities, see ibid., 65–87. On rabbinic formations of preferred male gender roles and their long-term ramifications, see Daniel Boyarin, *Unheroic Conduct: The Rise of Heterosexuality and the Invention of the Jewish Man* (Berkeley: University of California Press, 1997).

4. Gideon Libson, "Halakhah and Law in the Period of the Geonim," in N. S. Hecht, B. S. Jackson, et al., eds, *An Introduction to the History and Sources of Jewish Law* (Oxford; New York: Clarendon Press, 1996), 235–38.

5. See Norman A. Stillman, "The Jewish Experience in the Muslim World," and Robert Chazan, "Jewish Life in Western Christendom," in Baskin and Seeskin, eds, *Cambridge Guide*, 85–112 and 113–39, for the general contours of these distinctive medieval communities.

6. On Jewish gender roles in the Muslim world, see S. D. Goitein, *A Mediterranean Society: The Jewish Communities of the Arab World as Portrayed in the Documents of the Cairo Genizah*, 6 vols (Berkeley: University of California Press, 1967–1993), particularly, vol. 3, *The Family*; for Muslim and Christian Spain, see Renée Levine Melammed, "Sephardi Women in the

Medieval and Early Modern Periods," in Judith R. Baskin, *Jewish Women in Historical Perspective*, 2nd edn (Detroit: Wayne State University Press, 1998), 128–47.

7. See Elisheva Baumgarten, "Gender and Daily Life in Jewish Communities," Chapter 14 in this volume.

8. On these legal rulings and on Jewish gender roles and relations in Ashkenaz in general, see Baumgarten, "Gender and Daily Life in Jewish Communities," and Judith R. Baskin, "Jewish Women in the Middle Ages," in idem, ed., *Jewish Women in Historical Perspective*, 94–113; Elisheva Baumgarten, *Mothers and Children: Jewish Family Life in Medieval Europe* (Princeton: Princeton University Press, 2007); and Avraham Grossman, *Pious and Rebellious: Jewish Women in Medieval Europe*, trans. J. Chipman (Hanover, NH: University Press of New England, 2004).

9. For varying attitudes about violence towards wives, see Grossman, *Pious and Rebellious*, 47–48, 212–30.

10. On divorce in Jewish law, see Rachel Biale, *Women and Jewish Law: An Exploration of Women's Issues in Halakhic Sources* (New York: Schocken Books, 1984; repr. 1995), 70–101; on the surprising frequency of divorce in medieval Jewish societies, see Goitein, *A Mediterranean Society*, 3: 263, 274; Grossman, *Pious and Rebellious*, 131–33, 230–40, 250–52.

11. On wealthy Jewish men in Christian Spain who filed wills in Christian courts to benefit their wives or otherwise left significant parts of their estates to their wives, contrary to halakhic norms, see Grossman, *Pious and Rebellious*, 113–14, 127 and Melammed, "Sephardi Women," 135–36.

12. On the development of the marriage contract and its importance, see Biale, *Women and Jewish Law*, 44–69; Goitein, *A Mediterranean Society*, 3: 114–25; Baskin, "Jewish Women," 104–105; Grossman, *Pious and Rebellious*, 68–70 and *passim*.

13. On the dilemmas inherent in ancient and rabbinic Judaism's perception of God as masculine and the corollary that human masculinity was expressed through procreation, see Howard Eilberg-Schwartz, *God's Phallus and Other Problems for Men and Monotheism* (Boston: Beacon Press, 1994). For discussion of the links among circumcision, male fertility, and Jewish identity, see Shaye J. D. Cohen, *Why Aren't Jewish Women Circumcised? Gender and Covenant in Judaism* (Berkeley: University of California Press, 2005).

14. David Berger, *The Jewish-Christian Debate in the High Middle Ages: A Critical Edition of the Nizzahon Vetus with an Introduction, Translation, and Commentary* (Philadelphia: Jewish Publication Society of America, 1979); Cohen, *Why Aren't Jewish Women Circumcised?* 185.

15. *Niddah* literally means "one who is excluded" or "expelled." On this topic, see Shaye J. D. Cohen, "Menstruants and the Sacred in Judaism and Christianity," in Sarah B. Pomeroy, ed., *Women's History and Ancient History* (Chapel Hill: University of North Carolina Press, 1991), 273–99; Biale, *Women and Jewish Law*, 147–74; Tirzah Meacham, "An Abbreviated History of the Development of the Jewish Menstrual Laws," in Rahel S. Wasserfall, ed., *Women and Water: Menstruation in Jewish Life and Law* (Hanover, NH: Brandeis University Press, 1999), 23–39; Charlotte Elisheva Fonrobert, *Menstrual Purity: Rabbinic and Christian Reconstructions of Biblical Gender* (Stanford University Press: Stanford, 2000); Baskin, *Midrashic Women*, 22–29, and for the medieval era, Sharon Faye Koren, *Forsaken: The Menstruant in Medieval Jewish Mysticism* (Hanover, NH: University Press of New England for Brandeis University Press, 2011).

16. Judith R. Baskin, "Women and Ritual Immersion in Medieval Ashkenaz: The Sexual Politics of Piety," in Lawrence Fine, ed., *Judaism in Practice: From the Middle Ages Through the Early Modern Period* (Princeton: Princeton University Press, 2000), 131–42.

17. See Judith R. Baskin, "From Separation to Displacement: The Problem of Women in *Sefer Hasidim*," *Association for Jewish Studies Review*, 19 (1) (1994): 1–18; on Eleazar ben Judah of Worms and his family, see Baumgarten, "Gender and Daily Life in Jewish Communities."

18. On the *Baraïta de-Niddah*, see the translation and commentary by Evyatar Marienberg, *La Baraita de-Niddah: Un texte juif pseudo-talmudique sur les lois religieuses relatives à la menstruation* (Brepols: Turnhout, 2012); and Koren, *Forsaken*, 28–42.

19. See Cohen, "Menstruants and the Sacred," and Judith R. Baskin, "Male Piety, Female Bodies: Men, Women, and Ritual Immersion in Medieval Ashkenaz," *Journal of Jewish Law*, 17 (2007): 11–30. For an extensive discussion of similar practices in Islam and Christianity, see Koren, *Forsaken*, 127–71.

20. Baskin, *Midrashic Women*, 29–36; Lee Levine, *The Ancient Synagogue: The First Thousand Years*, 2nd edn (New Haven: Yale University Press, 2005); Goitein, *A Mediterranean Society*, 2: 144; and see also Baumgarten, "Gender and Daily Life in Jewish Communities."

21. Carol Herselle Krinsky, *Synagogues of Europe: Architecture, History, Meaning* (New York: Dover Publications, 1996).

22. Baskin, "Male Piety, Female Bodies," and Grossman, *Pious and Rebellious*, 240–44.

23. Grossman, *Pious and Rebellious*, 174–97; Martha Keil, "Public Roles of Jewish Women in Fourteenth and Fifteenth-Century Ashkenaz: Business, Community, and Ritual," in Christoph Cluse, ed., *The Jews of Europe in the Middle Ages (Tenth to Fifteenth Centuries)* (Turnhout: Brepols, 2004), 317–30.

24. Koren, *Forsaken*, 43–60.

25. See Gershon Cohen, "The Song of Songs and the Jewish Religious Mentality," in *Studies in the Variety of Rabbinic Cultures* (Philadelphia: Jewish Publication Society, 1991), 3–17.

26. David Biale, *Eros and the Jews: From Biblical Israel to Contemporary America* (Berkeley: University of California Press, 1992), 89, 101–11; Peter Schäfer, *Mirror of His Beauty: Feminine Images of God from the Bible to the Early Kabbalah* (Princeton: Princeton University Press, 2002).

27. On this work, see Biale, *Eros and the* Jews, 101–11; and Seymour J. Cohen, trans. and introduction, *The Holy Letter: A Study in Jewish Morality* (Northvale, NJ: Jason Aronson, 1993).

28. Biale, *Eros and the Jews*, 113–18; Moshe Idel, "Sexual Metaphors and Praxis in the Kabbalah," in David Kraemer, ed., *The Jewish Family: Metaphor and Memory* (New York: Oxford University Press, 1989), 205; Judith R. Baskin, "From Separation to Displacement: The Problem of Women in *Sefer Hasidim*," *Association for Jewish Studies Review*, 19 (1994): 1–18.

29. Koren, *Forsaken*, 63–123.

30. Joseph Dan, "Samael, Lilith, and the Concept of Evil," *Association for Jewish Studies Review*, 5 (1980): 17–40; and Koren, *Forsaken*, 91, 118. A major source on Lilith is the eighth- or ninth-century *Alphabet of Ben Sira*. An annotated English translation by Norman Bronznick appears in David Stern and Mark Jay Mirsky, eds, *Rabbinic Fantasies: Imaginative Narratives from Classical Hebrew Literature* (Philadelphia: Jewish Publication Society, 1990), 167–202; for Lilith, see 183–84. On the Lilith legend in the Middle Ages, and on amulets and other defenses against her, see Joshua Trachtenberg, *Jewish Magic and Superstition* (New York: Jewish Publication Society, 1970), 36–37, 101, 169.

31. The major exceptions are some letters in the Cairo Genizah documents and a few Arabic and Hebrew poems from Muslim Spain.

....

CHAPTER 4

WOMEN AND GENDER IN
ISLAMIC TRADITIONS

....

JONATHAN P. BERKEY

ISLAM began in the Near East in the early seventh century, in lands that in late antiquity had been important but contested centers of Roman and Persian civilization: Arabia, then the Fertile Crescent, Egypt, Iran. By the mid-eighth century, Muslims ruled over an enormous swath of territory, from Spain in the west to the borders of China in the east. Generalizations about the historical experiences of people living in such a large area are intrinsically dangerous. Identifying those experiences as "Islamic" is also problematic since it may have been as late as the tenth or eleventh century that Muslims formed a numerical majority in the territories ruled by Muslim states, at least outside of Arabia. Moreover, at some hard-to-define point in Islam's first centuries, the community splintered permanently into majority (Sunni) and minority (Shi`i) factions. By the Middle Ages, a pietistic movement (Sufism) transformed the religious experiences of both Sunnis and Shi`is.

Nonetheless, Muslims did fairly rapidly construct a discursive tradition, based on the revelations which came to Muhammad (the Qur'an) and reports about his words and deeds (*hadith*). That discourse achieved its fullest expression in a sophisticated jurisprudence (*fiqh*) which Muslims recognized as normative. (Sunni *fiqh* and Shi`i *fiqh* differ more in their theoretical underpinnings than in substantive law.) And since it was normative, this jurisprudence came to have a homogenizing effect on the diverse Muslim societies.

The gendering of the world was one of the assumptions of that discourse. Gender was part of the fabric of the universe. "O people," the Qur'an proclaims, "be pious toward your Lord, who has created you from a single soul, and created from it its mate, and from those two has spread abroad a multitude of men and women" (4.1). Not surprisingly, the role and status of women formed an important theme of the discursive tradition that shaped normative Islam. The Qur'an contains little positive law, but it does make numerous pronouncements about Muhammad's wives, and about relations between male and female members of the community. The texts in which the later medieval lawyers shaped the contours of Islamic law are obsessed with women: their rights and responsibilities; their status relative to men concerning property, inheritance, ritual, and other matters; marriage and the family and the differing obligations of men and women to it.

The lawyers' pronouncements must, however, be read with caution. In the first place, the intimate sphere of family life and gender relations was arguably influenced as much by inherited practices as by normative injunction. Moreover, the student of women and gender in Islamic history must negotiate the treacherous terrain of prejudice today. That prejudice is shaped by diverse, even contradictory assumptions, ranging from the eroticized fantasies of Orientalist painters about the Muslim harem to the widespread feeling that "Islam" oppresses its women. It is impossible, and also unwise, to investigate women and gender in medieval Islam without acknowledging the complex and politically charged question of women in the contemporary Islamic world, and how debates over women and gender now may shape our understanding of the past. Many in the West today perceive in the Islamic world a resurgence of "traditional" Islam. Phenomena such as the increase in the popularity of the veil are taken to mark what has been called "the revenge of God," and the triumph of a patriarchy which is deeply embedded in, if not intrinsic to Islam. There certainly were patriarchal elements woven into the fabric of the historical experience of Islam. Yet the return of the veil has coincided with the erosion of the economic and social foundations on which past Islamic patriarchies have rested. So, for example, many of those in the forefront of the movement to reclaim the veil have been highly educated professional women, often working in the public sphere— autonomous agents, in other words, who have chosen to wear the veil for political or ideological reasons, rather than as passive victims of male command. The complexity surrounding the issue of the veil should remind us that Islam is not a static category, but one that Muslims have continually constructed and reconstructed in the face of the contingencies they have faced. Consequently, looking at medieval Islam through the lens of women and gender can help to illuminate much larger questions about the historical development of the Muslim tradition.

In the Early Islamic Crucible

On all matters, not just on questions concerning women, the situation in pre- and early Islamic Arabia figured prominently in later expressions of normative Islam. Like Judaism and Christianity, Islam is an intensely historical religion. It is true that many scholars question the historical reliability of the earliest Islamic sources. Because most took their present form long after the events they describe, they arguably reflect later realities more than conditions at the time. But Muslims have long taken the practices of Muhammad and his companions as described in those sources as binding precedent. In a nutshell, they have asked the question, "What would Muhammad do?" His example, and that of his companions, called *sunna*, "normative practice," is known through stories (*hadith*) that were recounted orally and later written down.

Both historians and polemicists debate whether the arrival of Islam improved or worsened the status of women in Arabia. One line of thought, influenced by early twentieth-century anthropological theories of human social evolution, perceived in the rise of Islam a marker of an ongoing advance in the human social condition. The impact on women of this pattern of social evolution was complex. Structures and practices rooted in urban, literate, bourgeois society eclipsed older matrilineal and even matriarchal social conventions. These new social structures may have been patriarchal, squeezing out older social patterns (for example, polyandry) in which women were less constrained. On the other hand, they also reflected a concern for the value of individual humans, both male and female.[1]

This confident, optimistic teleology is now out of fashion, but some scholars now perceive in the Qur'an's message a more unambiguous revolution in gender relations in favor of women. Without a doubt, the rise of an ethical monotheism put an end to certain pre-Islamic practices that discriminated against women—for example, female infanticide (see 81:8–9). At the heart of the Qur'an, Muslim feminists have argued, lies a bedrock egalitarian spirit. A key verse is 33:35:

> Lo! men who surrender unto God, and women who surrender, and men who believe and women who believe, and men who obey and women who obey, and men who speak the truth and women who speak the truth, and men who persevere [in righteousness] and women who persevere, and men who are humble and women who are humble, and men who give alms and women who give alms, and men who fast and women who fast, and men who guard their modesty and women who guard [their modesty], and men who remember God frequently and women who remember—God has prepared for them forgiveness and a vast reward.

Here people are distinguished by their degree of piety, not their gender. The setting for the revelation of 33:35 is critical. Muhammad's wife Umm Salama had asked him why men were frequently mentioned in the revelations, but not women. This verse was God's answer. Feminist commentators construe this as affirming that God "spoke of the two sexes in terms of total equality as believers."[2]

The situation in Arabia before and during Muhammad's day was complex, and probably reflects a society in transition, one that was already coming to resemble more closely the patriarchal societies of the Fertile Crescent. There are signs that practice varied between Mecca, a city that served as the hub of an international trading network and where Muhammad was born and began his career, and Medina, the oasis settlement to which Muhammad and his companions fled in 622 to escape persecution in Mecca. In Mecca, whose leading men maintained close contacts with trading partners in Damascus and other cities of the Fertile Crescent and who would have been aware of the patriarchal mores and practices of their urban residents, some women may have lived restricted lives. The people of Medina, by contrast, retained closer ties to the Bedouin, whose nomadic life made strict seclusion of women impracticable. One of the Meccans who accompanied Muhammad to Medina is recorded as having ruefully remarked: "We men of Quraysh [the leading tribe in Mecca] used to dominate our women. When we came to the Ansar [the

Medinese 'helpers' of the prophet, i.e., 'when we arrived in Medina'], we found that they let themselves be dominated by their women. Then our women began to copy their habits."[3]

The record suggests that women in pre-Islamic Arabia were simultaneously freer and more vulnerable than their later Muslim sisters. Female infanticide was not the only pre-Islamic practice in which men served as arbiters of women's fate. In some cases women were treated as a form of chattel: a widow, for example, might be inherited by a dead man's heir (provided she was not his mother), to be disposed of as he saw fit. On the other hand, the institution of marriage in the pre-Islamic period was more fluid, and descriptions of its forms must have startled later Muslims accustomed to the rigidly patriarchal institution embraced by the Islamic lawyers. Muhammad's wife Aisha once described the various forms of marriage that were practiced among the Arabs before Islam, including several that were distinctly polyandrous. Other sources suggest that at least some women among the pre-Islamic Arabs retained the right to divorce their husbands.[4]

Women in pre- and early Islamic Arabia also played public, even political, roles that would be closed to them in later centuries. Recited during large public gatherings of the tribes, poetry was the principal art form of the pre-Islamic Arabs, and while most poets were men, some were women. There is no indication that women fought alongside men in the intertribal warfare that was characteristic of pre-Islamic Bedouin life, but women did accompany men into battle in supporting roles. In one famous incident, a woman belonging to the leading family of Muhammad's opponents publicly taunted the Muslims after their defeat in battle, dramatically ripping open the body and biting into the liver of one fallen Muslim in revenge for his killing of her kinsman. Muslim sources portray the prophet's first wife, Khadija, living an autonomous life before her marriage to Muhammad. A wealthy widow active in the international trade, she hired the young Muhammad as her agent and then, impressed by his character, proposed marriage to him.

Evidence from the Qur'an itself is mixed. On the one hand, while the gender equality which Muslim feminists perceive in 33:35 may reflect one strand of the Qur'anic worldview, it is offset by the stark imbalance expressed in 4:34:

> Men are in charge of women because God has made some of them to excel others and because they spend out of their property [i.e., to maintain the family]. The good women are therefore obedient, guarding the unseen as God has guarded. As for those women from whom you fear discord, admonish them, and leave them alone in the beds, and beat them; then if they obey you, do not seek a way against them, for surely God is High, Great.

This verse, far more than 33:35, informed the views of the later jurists concerning relations between the sexes. Having accepted the fundamental social superiority of men, the jurists were able to stretch the scope of other Qur'anic injunctions and make the gender imbalance a fundamental principle of Islamic law. So, for example, the Qur'anic passage referring to women's attire is ambiguous as to what degree of covering is required.

> And say to the believing women that they should lower their gaze and guard their modesty; that they should display of their adornment only what would [normally]

appear; that they should draw their veils over their bosoms and not display their adornment except to their husbands, their fathers, their husband's fathers, their sons, their husbands' sons, their brothers or their brothers' sons, or their sisters' sons, or their women, or those whom their right hands possess [i.e., slaves], or male servants free of physical needs [i.e., eunuchs], or children who are not acquainted with the private parts of women; and that they should not strike their feet in order to draw attention to their hidden ornaments. And turn together towards God, O believers, that you may prosper. (24:31)

Nonetheless, under the lawyers' guidance, veiling and seclusion became a common phenomenon in medieval Islamic cities, at least for those Muslims who could afford to practice it.

On the other hand, the Qur'an's overriding goal seems to be to encourage the formation and preservation of stable families, while recognizing the dignity of the individuals who compose them. Marriage is strongly encouraged. "Marry those women who please you—two, three, or four," the scripture enjoins (4:3). The jurists understood the verse to permit Muslim men to be married simultaneously to four women (although it was probably originally meant simply to ensure that the surfeit of women in the nascent Muslim community would find husbands). Women, by contrast, were restricted to one husband at any one time, another clear manifestation of the patriarchal principles current at the time and embedded in Islamic law. Men, however, are repeatedly required to treat their wives kindly, and equally so. "But if you fear that you will not treat them justly," 4:3 continues, "then [marry] one only." Divorce is allowed, and as a general rule the opportunity to initiate it is restricted to men—another marker of the gender imbalance affirmed by Qur'anic legislation. At the same time, divorce is discouraged—of all things permitted by God, divorce is the one he hates the most, as Muhammad is famously alleged to have said—and the restrictions the Qur'an places on men's ability to divorce their wives probably aimed at tightening up much looser pre-Islamic practice. The Qur'an presumes that men will provide for their wives and children, and it requires that they adequately compensate those wives whom they divorce.

Not surprisingly, the prophet's wives have served as exemplars for later Muslim women. Their experience was not binding on posterity. In the later years of his life Muhammad was married to considerably more than four women, but his case was understood to be exceptional. So was that of his wives. Muhammad's wives submitted to special restrictions that did not apply to others: for example, they were required to live in seclusion and were forbidden from remarriage after Muhammad's death. Nonetheless, as "mothers of the believers," the prophet's wives played important roles in shaping the later tradition.

This was especially true of Aisha. Aisha was a controversial figure, playing a divisive part in the political struggles that followed the prophet's death, as we will see. But Muslims revere her as the prophet's favorite wife, albeit also his youngest (betrothed at age six, joined with Muhammad at age nine). It was to Aisha's residence that Muhammad was taken during his final illness. Her status made her the ultimate source for a significant proportion of the *hadith*, especially those concerning Muslim ritual. And so it is somewhat startling to hear her complain after Muhammad's death that Muslims "equate [women] with dogs and donkeys," i.e., unclean creatures who, if they came between a praying Muslim and the *qibla* (the direction facing the Ka`ba in Mecca), would invalidate a Muslim man's prayers. Yet while he was alive, she said, "the prophet would come in and pray while I lay before him on the bed."⁵ In her words we hear an echo of the tensions and competing imperatives concerning women, their social status, and their relations with men that were already manifest in the earliest Muslim society.

Sex and Sensibility

However important the example of Muhammad and his companions, Islam is far more than a simple product of the Arabian environment in which it first appeared. Many of the principles and practices adopted by the Islamic tradition were the product of the interaction of the new religion with the values and customs it encountered among the Jewish, Christian, and Zoroastrian peoples of the Near East. This is especially true regarding gender issues and matters involving women. There is little doubt that the subordination of women, along with their seclusion and restrictions on their public activities, was deeply rooted in the cities of the Roman and Sasanian empires. There, at least among the middle and upper classes, practices such as veiling were fairly common. And it was in the cities of newly conquered Syria, Iraq, Iran, and Egypt, far more than in Arabia, that Islamic law took shape.

Social patterns in the societies conquered by the early Muslims help to explain the patriarchal and discriminatory elements that are unmistakably woven into the fabric of Islamic law. The Islamic jurists relied on the Qur'an and *hadith*, but the law emerged from other sources as well, chief among them the consensus (*ijma`*) of the jurists themselves. *Ijma`* in practice eclipsed even the Qur'an and *hadith* as a source of Islamic law, most famously in the matter of adultery. The Qur'an clearly stipulates one punishment: "The adulterer and the adulteress, scourge each one of them with a hundred lashes" (24:2). But the consensus of the jurists in favor of a stricter ruling was so strong that it eventually prevailed over the Qur'anic text, so that the *shari'a* (Islamic law) required that adult, married offenders be punished by death by stoning. *Ijma`* proved to be the channel through which Muslims absorbed and adopted as their own the patriarchal values and practices of Roman and Sasanian societies.

The medieval Islamic past is extraordinarily well documented, at least from the eighth century on. Muslim authors produced a torrent of texts: works of history, law, theology, and philosophy, as well as the literature of entertainment in a myriad of forms. Virtually none of that literature, however, was produced by women. Women were not entirely excluded from public intellectual life, but their voices have left little discernible trace in the surviving texts. The recollections of Aisha may have interjected a woman's perspective into the community's memory of the prophet, but the later compilers and commentators on the *hadith* were exclusively men. Women and women's thoughts may lie behind certain texts, particularly in the field of popular literature—some of the tales in the *Thousand and One Nights* come to mind—but that is neither certain nor provable. In a tradition as scripturally based as Islam, defined by an evolving series of interconnected commentaries on the scriptural foundations of the faith, the absence of women's voices is critical.

The problem is not simply that women themselves are silent as historical sources. It is also that male writers were silent about the women they knew. The jurists had a great deal to say about women in the abstract, but their discourse was prescriptive rather than descriptive. Discussions of particular women were restricted by the code of honor and shame that was common throughout the Mediterranean world, which located a man's honor in the chastity of his women, his sisters, wives, and daughters. Medieval authors frequently refer to women with circumlocutions, especially various words built on the Arabic root *h/r/m* (as in the anglicized "harem"), which indicates something forbidden, unlawful, sacred, or taboo. (Significantly, *h/r/m* is also the root for the word *haram*, used to identify the holy sites of Mecca and Medina that are closed to non-Muslims, that is, to outsiders.) Muslim men, had they been aware of Pericles's funeral oration to the Athenians, would have heartily agreed with his conclusion that the best thing to be said about women is that nothing be said about them. The resulting reticence *about* Muslim women amplified their own historical silence.

Discussions of women in the juristic literature tended to focus on matters arising from sexual relations. There is no parallel in Islam to the Christian ideal of virginity. Sex, and sexual desire, is in and of itself a good thing. The Qur'an instructs its (male) listeners in almost earthy terms: "Your women are a tillage for you" (2:233). It was not only men who might legitimately enjoy sex. During one domestic crisis, Muhammad had withdrawn in anger from his wives, and refused temporarily to cohabit with any of them. A revelation came to the prophet chastising him for having foresworn normal sexual relations with his wives: "O Prophet! Why have you forbidden that which God has permitted—that you should seek to please your wives?" (66:1). The jurists had no doubt that sexual desire and its satisfaction were good, both for men and women. They recognized a wife's right to the sexual attentions of her husband, and some identified a husband's impotence as legitimate grounds on which his wife might seek a divorce. Others went further and determined that a husband could not practice coitus interruptus without his wife's consent, because it might lessen her sexual pleasure as well as deny her progeny. Islamic societies were not unusual in producing a lively tradition of erotic literature and manuals for lovemaking, but it is striking that many of these works were written by scholars trained in the religious and juristic sciences.[6]

Nonetheless, the Muslim tradition shared with other cultures, particularly those of the larger Mediterranean world, a fear of unrestrained female sexuality. The female sexual predators who populate tales such as those in *A Thousand and One Nights* are comical figures, but also give expression to widely held assumptions about the voracious sexual appetite of women. Women were frequently referred to as a *fitna*, a "temptation" or "distraction," an Arabic word which has rich and disturbing connotations, suggestive of social disruption and the breakdown of order. Such assumptions were linked to broader misogynist attitudes—for example, that women were less intelligent and less rational, therefore irresponsible in matters of religion, and so in a very real sense inferior. According to a widely cited (although probably apocryphal) *hadith*, Muhammad reported that "a majority of the inhabitants of hell are women."[7] Such assumptions had practical implications. So, for example, the jurists, basing themselves on a Qur'anic text (2:282), insisted that the testimony of a woman was worth only half that of a man.[8]

The jurists' preeminent concern was preserving the gender boundary. The difference between men and women was a part of the fabric of God's creation; it was to be expected that proper social relations should reflect the natural order of things. In the second half of the eighth century, the caliph al-Mansur (r. 754–775) went so far as to have a separate bridge for women constructed over the Tigris River in Baghdad. Hence, also, the close attention which the jurists paid to clothing. Drawing on *hadith* that condemned men wearing women's and women wearing men's clothing, the jurists articulated detailed normative guidelines delineating what was proper dress for the different sexes: that men, for example, should never wear gold or silk.

The most visible manifestation of the jurists' concern to keep women separate was the seclusion to which some Muslim women were subject. The use of the veil in public and the sequestering of women in the private quarters of a house were old practices in the Middle East. Among the Byzantine and Sasanian urban middle and upper classes, they served to mark a woman as married or in some other way as sexually unavailable. After the wars of conquest, most Muslim Arabs, despite their desert origins, settled in the cities of the conquered territories, where they absorbed the attitudes and copied the practices of their non-Muslim neighbors. By the fourteenth century, veiling and seclusion were common enough that a Moroccan scholar named Ibn Battuta, who spent most of his life traveling through the Muslim world, expressed disgust when, on the fringes of that world, he encountered what he considered deviant behavior: the wives of Muslim scholars among the Tuareg, who routinely mixed with unrelated men, or the Muslim women of the Maldives who, following local custom, wore loose clothing which left their breasts exposed.[9]

The prevalence of veiling and seclusion should not, however, lead us to believe that Muslim women led completely sequestered lives. Veiling was largely an urban phenomenon, but the vast majority of medieval Muslim women (and men) lived outside cities. In peasant and pastoral societies, where women played essential economic roles, veiling and strict seclusion were often impractical. Even in the cities, the practice was probably less widespread than Ibn Battuta's injured sensibilities might suggest. Among the large majority of families who could not afford slaves to shop for them in public markets and perform other household chores, women must frequently have crossed the private threshold to deal with the outside world. Among the laboring classes, some professional occupations were largely the preserve of women: coiffeuses, midwives, attendants in bathhouses (when they were open to women), and others.[10] Seclusion was the ideal, one that looms large in the historical sources because their educated and affluent authors held it dear, but social reality was considerably more complex.

All of this—the positive attitude toward sex and sexual desire; assumptions about the disruptive force of female sexuality and the related misogyny; the obsession with preserving the boundary between male and female—had practical consequences for women's lives, most profoundly in the Islamic law of marriage and divorce. The jurists were adamant that sexual energies be directed into proper, licit activities. The principal channel for sexual activity was *nikah*, "marriage," the root meaning of which is "sexual relations."[11] For women, indeed, wedlock to one man at any given moment was the *only* licit channel. Women could have more than one husband, but only on a serial basis, if they remarried after divorce or widowhood, and we know from historical and biographical literature that such remarriage was common. Men, by contrast, had the options of multiple nonserial marriages, as well as taking as many concubines (female slaves purchased for the purpose of sex) as they could afford.

Sex outside the licit channels was roundly condemned, but here again the jurists' prescriptions were not fully descriptive of social reality. Erotic treatises and the literature of entertainment make it clear that, not surprisingly, transgressive sexuality was not unknown. The wild sexual escapades of tales in the *Thousand and One Nights* are comical, but could not have been completely untethered from social reality. *Zina*, illicit sexual behavior, included homoerotic activity as well as adultery. Nonetheless, it has been argued that the cult of male honor which placed such limits on heterosexual activity may have made homoeroticism less dangerous and disruptive of social values, and consequently more tolerated (or at least ignored) than adultery. This may have been especially true of sexual encounters between women, precisely because of their restricted public presence.[12]

Within marriage itself, a woman's position was equivocal, reflecting the competing attitudes and assumptions of the jurists. On the one hand, the lawyers confirmed that women possessed certain rights and privileges. One of the reasons why "men are in charge of women," according to the Qur'an, is that "they [men] spend out of their property [i.e., to maintain the family]," and the *shari'a* affirmed that financial responsibility for the family rested with the husband. Marriage is a legal contract in Islamic law, and among its stipulations is that the husband pay a suitable sum (*mahr*) to the woman, not to her father or family. Even concubines, while technically slaves, had rights. If, for example, a concubine gave birth to her master's child, she could no longer be sold, and was guaranteed her freedom on her master's death; her child, moreover, was free and fully legitimate. Divorce, on the other hand, was an arena of stark inequality. The rules on divorce were complex, but the bottom line is that men, and men alone, were granted a unilateral right to divorce their spouses.

These imbalances reflect a gendered hierarchy of rights which was endemic in classical Islamic law, if not in the Qur'an. The legal superiority of men over women that we have already seen in the areas of sexual rights, access to divorce, and testimony in the courts affected other areas of life as well. According to the complex rules of inheritance, a male heir claimed twice the share of a female. Women were encouraged to pray at home, rather than in mosques, but if they did pray in a public space, they were required to do so behind the men, affirming in spatial terms the hierarchy which placed the male over the female.

The critical function which the gender hierarchy played for the Islamic jurists is on vivid and surprising display in the intricate care that they took over what at first glance seems a rather arcane matter: how to deal with hermaphrodites.[13] Hermaphrodites posed a problem because they challenged the gendered nature of God's creation. Islamic law was built on the distinction between male and female: what, then, should be done with an individual who appeared to be both? The jurists assumed that a hermaphrodite was in fact either male or female—God after all had gendered humankind—and so they established precise and detailed guidelines for how to determine the gender of an individual with ambiguous genitalia. Where, however, a definitive judgment was impossible, the rules worked out by the jurists demonstrated their concern to preserve both the boundary between men and women and the hierarchy that put males on top. So, for example, in a mixed congregation, a hermaphrodite should pray behind the men, but in front of the women. In that way, should the hermaphrodite turn out to be female, the validity of no male's prayers would be threatened by having a woman stand in front of him. In inheritance, an ambiguous hermaphrodite was to receive the portion allotted to a female, presumably because the more serious danger lay in the possibility that a woman might inherit the larger portion stipulated for a man.

The *shari'a* was a normative discourse, which had a powerful impact on the lives of women and men, but which nonetheless was prescriptive rather than descriptive. Local custom might undermine even those protections extended to women by the law. The patriarchal values and sexual taboos that contributed to the subordination of women were broader than the *shari'a* and Islam—they were shared by many non-Muslims in the Mediterranean world—and sometimes came into conflict with it. So, for example, while Islamic law requires that brides receive a *mahr* and guarantees female property rights, local practice might vary: the bride's father might appropriate some or all of the *mahr*, and a woman's right to inherit family property, especially land, might give way to the pressures in a peasant economy to keep landholding intact.[14] An even more debilitating practice, common in a few parts of the Muslim world, was that sometimes referred to as "female circumcision," the excision of some or all of a girl's external genitalia. The practice was not enjoined by Islamic law; some jurists approved, but many others rejected or simply ignored it. But the practice was deeply rooted in some places, and where, as in Egypt, it addressed and reinforced the patriarchal urge to control and limit female sexuality, popular custom trumped the reservations of the jurists.[15]

AGENCY AND AUTHORITY

In the private sphere, women wielded a degree of power, making decisions that affected their own lives as well as those of others. There were also certain areas of public life in which women held positions of responsibility. But it is difficult to identify precise ways in which women significantly shaped the contours of public life, or the Islamic tradition itself. The situation might be described this way: women possessed agency, but generally lacked authority.

Within the family, women exercised considerable power over daily affairs, the administration of the household, even questions as significant as who would be chosen as wives for their sons. Older women were particularly empowered, as they assumed responsibility over the females of their extended families, including their daughters-in-law.[16] The reluctance of medieval authors to discuss intimate matters of family life makes it difficult to penetrate the world of the premodern Muslim family. Modern parallels, however, suggest that under certain circumstances women could exercise considerable responsibility over family life.[17]

Politics was probably the area in which women's authority was most thoroughly circumscribed. Almost from the beginning, the Islamic tradition looked askance at female participation in politics, as the legacy of the Prophet's wife Aisha makes clear. Aisha emerged as a wielder of political power (although never a formal candidate for leadership of the community) in the tumultuous years following Muhammad's death. Indeed, she was a central figure in a rebellion against the fourth caliph, `Ali ibn Abi Talib, Muhammad's cousin and son-in-law. The political crisis surrounding that rebellion was a complex one. Among other things, it helped to precipitate the split between Sunni and Shi`i branches of Islam, the Shi`is emerging as the defenders of `Ali and his descendants and of their right to lead the community. Shi`is, therefore, were naturally hostile to Aisha's political activities. But it was not only Shi`is who cast this rebellion as a *fitna*, the same term that was sometimes applied to women generally. Most later Sunni commentators also disapproved of Aisha's actions, and read her example as a lesson confirming the received wisdom that women should not participate in political life.[18]

That received wisdom had multiple roots. Qur'anic passages could be read as supporting the exclusion of women from political life—for example 33:33, in which the Prophet's wives were commanded to "stay in your houses." Many *hadith*, too, left room for the later jurists to find in Prophetic admonition a rejection of female participation in politics—for example, one in which Muhammad remarked that "those who entrust their affairs to women will never know prosperity."[19] Nizam al-Mulk, chief minister to the Saljuq sultan of Baghdad in the late eleventh century and the author of an important treatise on rulership, was contemptuous of meddling by the women of the royal family in political affairs. His views grew out of his experience with one particular woman in the royal family he served, but also reflected a broader hostility to women's participation in politics in the Persian political traditions which increasingly shaped medieval Islamic thought.[20] Over time, the opposition to women in politics became more firmly fixed. The trajectory is apparent from the fate of *sura* (chapter) 27 of the Qur'an at the hands of later exegetes. *Sura* 27, which tells the story of Solomon and the Queen of Sheba, remarks that the people of Sheba were ruled by a queen, but simply reports the fact, without comment and without betraying any sense of unease. Medieval Muslim commentators, however, found the fact remarkable and disturbing, and so explained the story (away) by recasting it as a tale illustrating male superiority and the dangers attendant when women held political power.[21]

The picture is complicated, however, by the fact that in Islamic history, the exercise of political power routinely blurred the lines between the public and the private. Although Islamic law was never comfortable with the idea of dynasties, political power came to be invested in particular families or kin groups. Within the ruling family, as in any family, women wielded a certain degree of influence. It was the meddling of the women of the sultan's harem which annoyed Nizam al-Mulk, but despite his admonition, there is a long, almost continuous tradition of the wives, concubines, and mothers of the ruler influencing affairs of state.[22]

The influence of women on politics probably reached its height in the later Middle Ages, with the rise of regimes reflecting the power and interests of the new Turco-Mongol masters of the Middle East. These former nomads considered the "state" an extension of the ruling household, so that the authority of the regime was a divisible piece of property shared among the members of the ruling family and their retainers. In Central Asian political traditions, too, women often played substantial roles. Indeed, Ibn Battuta was surprised during his travels in the region by the outsized and very public influence women exerted among the Turkish and Mongol tribes.[23]

Despite the power that women might wield within the private sphere of the royal family, women only rarely held the formal trappings of political authority. There was no question of a woman serving as caliph; with few exceptions, the jurists agreed that the caliph must be a man. But by the later Middle Ages, the caliphate was an attenuated institution. Real power was held by local rulers, usually referred to as *sultans*. There are very few instances of women claiming to be sultans themselves—one from Yemen in the eleventh and twelfth centuries, another from a Turkish regime in north India in the thirteenth century—so few that they really are exceptions that prove the rule. The most famous involved Shajar al-Durr, the consort of a ruler of Egypt who died in 1247, who briefly held the title of sultan, and had her name stamped on coins and mentioned during the Friday congregational prayers, until opposition to a woman holding power forced her to marry another important figure within the regime and to rule jointly with him. Her case, in other words, can be read as an extreme version of the general rule of Islamic history that women exercised political power only through the blurring of the distinction between public and private in the political sphere—that they had agency, that is, but lacked authority.

In another area of public life, women had a surprisingly important role. The religious sphere created plentiful space for meaningful female participation, starting with their role as benefactors of religious institutions. Mosques, schools, Sufi convents—all such establishments were generally the product of individual acts of charity, rather than official undertakings of the government. Since Islamic law afforded women full rights to hold and dispose of property, women as well as men—at least the wealthy among them—might be moved to create and endow religious institutions, and even to manage their endowments.[24]

In public religious activity, too, women played an important role. The nature of Islamic education and its transmission created space for participation by women. The transmission of religious knowledge—for example, the recitation of important religious texts, such as the compendia of *hadith*—was perceived as a spiritual as well as an academic activity, from which female Muslims as well as males might benefit. Moreover, the system of transmitting religious knowledge from one generation to the next never relied upon institutional degrees, but was measured instead by the personal relationships established between teacher and pupil and by the reputations of the individual scholars involved. Consequently, if a woman acquired for herself a reputation as a repository of learning—if, for example, she became known for the depth of her memory, or the number and quality of her teachers, or if she became the last person in a given city to transmit important religious texts on the authority of a renowned scholar—she herself might become a much sought-after authority for younger students. As a result, women were frequently mentioned in biographical dictionaries (one of the major primary sources for medieval social history) for their scholarly accomplishments, especially as transmitters of *hadith*. Indeed, many of the most prominent male academics of the day counted numerous women among those on whose authority they transmitted the textual foundations of Muslim learning.[25]

However, it is striking that women made their mark in the transmission of *hadith*, which privileged memory and accuracy, rather than in those academic fields which put *hadith* to use. As one scholar has put it, "women might absorb normative knowledge through hadith, but because they were denied access to the exclusively male medieval study of law and theology, they could not determine its practical application to their own lives."[26] Authorship and authority here become almost coterminous, and the absence of female authors of religious and jurisprudential texts reflects and helps to explain their lack of authority. According to some jurists, women might (at least in theory) serve as *mufti*s, jurists entitled to issue nonbinding opinions on questions of law, and others (a minority) even recognized their right to be *qadi*s, "judges" of the Islamic courts. But in fact women rarely if ever served as such. An influential eleventh-century treatise on Islamic governance expressed the more common view that the first qualification of one who wished to serve as *qadi* is that he be a man.[27]

At more popular levels, however, the scope for female participation was much broader. In the streets, in informal sessions in mosques or homes, sometimes in special institutions set up to provide shelter for poor or widowed women, female scholars or preachers delivered pious homilies to gatherings of women and provided them with religious instruction.[28] Especially in Sufi circles, women played an important role. One of the earliest and most revered Islamic mystics was a woman, Rabi`a of Basra, who acquired fame as an ascetic and as a poet of divine love. One reason that Sufi mysticism proved popular with women may have been its tendency to undermine or overcome the social barriers that cut through both premodern societies and Islamic law: barriers of wealth, personal status, and especially gender. Indeed, accounts of female mystics such as Rabi`a often explicitly suggest that they overcame the gender barrier by achieving the status of men.[29] The feminine and the female are not of course exactly coterminous, but it may nonetheless be significant that some Sufi mystics, in particular Ibn `Arabi (d.1240), ascribed the "creative imagination" of the divinity to a feminine principle.[30] More practically, the Sufi orders which became enormously popular in the later Middle

Ages often included women as members, and several Middle Eastern cities included hospices established specifically to house female mystics.

In Sufi mysticism as in other areas of medieval Islamic life, women were in no meaningful sense the equals of men. Neither, however, were they completely powerless creatures. Defining the tradition was largely beyond their reach, but within that tradition, women played important roles in shaping the contours of the lives lived in medieval Islamic society.

FURTHER READING

Ahmed, Leila. *Women and Gender in Islam: Historical Roots of a Modern Debate*. New Haven: Yale University Press, 1992.

Babayan, Kathryn and Afsaneh Najmabadi, eds. *Islamicate Sexualities: Translations Across Temporal Geographies of Desire*. Cambridge, Mass.: Harvard University Press, 2008.

Hambly, Gavin R. G., ed. *Women in the Medieval Islamic World: Power, Patronage, and Piety*. New York: St. Martin's Press, 1998.

Keddie, Nikki and Beth Baron, eds. *Women in Middle Eastern History: Shifting Boundaries in Sex and Gender*. New Haven: Yale University Press, 1991.

Malti-Douglas, Fedwa. *Woman's Body, Woman's Word: Gender and Discourse in Arabo-Islamic Writing*. Princeton: Princeton University Press, 1991.

Meisami, Julie Scott. "Writing Medieval Women: Representations and Misrepresentations," in Julia Bray, ed., *Writing and Representation in Medieval Islam: Muslim Horizons*. London: Routledge, 2006, 47–87.

Mernissi, Fatima. *The Veil and the Male Elite: A Feminist Interpretation of Women's Rights in Islam*. Reading, Mass.: Addison Wesley, 1991.

Nashat, Guity and Judith Tucker. *Women in the Middle East and North Africa: Restoring Women to History*. Bloomington: Indiana University Press, 1999.

Roded, Ruth. *Women in Islamic Biographical Collections: From Ibn Sa`d to Who's Who*. Boulder: Lynne Reiner, 1994.

Sonbol, Amira El-Azhary, ed. *Beyond the Exotic: Women's Histories in Islamic Societies*. Syracuse: Syracuse University Press, 2005.

NOTES

1. See, for example, W. Montgomery Watt, *Muhammad at Medina* (Oxford: Clarendon Press, 1956), 373–85.
2. Fatima Mernissi, *The Veil and the Male Elite* (Reading, Mass: Addison Wesley, 1991), 118.
3. Watt, *Muhammad at Medina*, 381–82.
4. Watt, *Muhammad at Medina*, 378–79, 381.
5. Leila Ahmed, *Women and Gender in Islam: Historical Roots of a Modern Debate* (New Haven: Yale University Press, 1992), 47.
6. On sex and the law, see Ze'v Maghen, *Virtues of the Flesh: Passion and Purity in Early Islamic Jurisprudence* (Leiden: Brill, 2005), esp. 14–31, and Basim Musallam, *Sex and Society in Islam* (Cambridge: Cambridge University Press, 1983), esp. 31–33. On erotic manuals, see Abdelwahab Bouhdiba, *Sexuality in Islam* (London: Routledge and Kegan Paul, 1985), 140–58.

7. Denise Spellberg, *Politics, Gender, and the Islamic Past: The Legacy of 'A'isha bint Abi Bakr* (New York: Columbia University Press, 1994), 139, and Marion Katz, *Body of Text: The Emergence of the Sunni Law of Ritual Purity* (Albany: SUNY Press, 2002), 196–97.

8. Mohammad Fadel, "Two Women, One Man: Knowledge, Power, and Gender in Medieval Sunni Legal Thought," *International Journal of Middle East Studies*, 29 (1997): 187–204.

9. Ross Dunn, *The Adventures of Ibn Battuta* (Berkeley: California University Press, 1986), 234–35, 299–300.

10. Hoda Lutfi, "Manners and Customs of Fourteenth-Century Cairene Women: Female Anarchy versus Males Shar'i Order in Muslim Prescriptive Treatises," in Nikki Keddie and Beth Baron, eds, *Women in Middle Eastern History: Shifting Boundaries in Sex and Gender* (New Haven: Yale University Press, 1991), 103–106; Maya Shatzmiller, *Labour in the Medieval Islamic World* (Leiden: E. J. Brill, 1994), 347–68.

11. See Susan Spectorsky, *Chapters on Marriage and Divorce: Reponses of Ibn Hanbal and Ibn Rahwayh* (Austin: University of Texas Press, 1993).

12. Sahar Amer, "Medieval Arab Lesbians and Lesbian-Like Women," *Journal of the History of Sexuality*, 18 (2009), 221–23. On illicit sex generally, see Everett Rowson, "The Categorization of Gender and Sexual Irregularity in Medieval Arabic Vice Lists," in Julia Epstein and Kristina Straub, eds, *Body Guards: The Cultural Politics of Gender Ambiguity* (New York: Routledge, 1991), 50–79.

13. Paula Sanders, "Gendering the Ungendered Body: Hermaphrodites in Medieval Islamic Law," in Keddie and Baron, eds, *Women in Middle Eastern History*, 74–95.

14. Deniz Kandiyoti, "Islam and Patriarchy: A Comparative Perspective," in Keddie and Baron, eds, *Women in Middle Eastern History*, 32. On the impact of patriarchy on Mediterranean social and economic patterns more broadly, see Germaine Tillion, *The Republic of Cousins: Women's Oppression in Mediterranean Society*, trans. Quinton Hoare (London: Al Saqi Books, 1983).

15. Jonathan Berkey, "Circumcision Circumscribed: Female Excision and Cultural Accommodation in the Medieval Near East," *International Journal of Middle East Studies*, 28 (1996): 19–38.

16. Kandiyoti, "Islam and Patriarchy," 32–33.

17. See, for example, Elizabeth Fernea, *Guests of the Sheik* (New York: Doubleday, 1965).

18. See Spellberg, *Politics, Gender and the Islamic Past*, 101–49; Nabia Abbott, *Aishah, the Beloved of Mohammed* (Chicago: University of Chicago Press, 1942), 82–176.

19. Spellberg, *Politics, Gender, and the Islamic Past*, 139.

20. Omid Safi, *The Politics of Knowledge in Premodern Islam: Negotiating Ideology and Religious Inquiry* (Chapel Hill: University of North Carolina Press, 2006), 71–74.

21. Jacob Lassner, *Demonizing the Queen of Sheba: Boundaries of Gender and Culture in Postbiblical Judaism and Medieval Islam* (Chicago: University of Chicago Press, 1993), 36–87.

22. For an early modern example, see Leslie Peirce, *The Imperial Harem: Women and Sovereignty in the Ottoman Empire* (Oxford: Oxford University Press, 1993).

23. Dunn, *Adventures of Ibn Battuta*, 168.

24. Carl Petry, "Class Solidarity versus Gender Gain: Women as Custodians of Property in Late Medieval Egypt," in Keddie and Baron, eds, *Women in Middle Eastern History*, 122–42.

25. Jonathan P. Berkey, *The Transmission of Knowledge in Medieval Cairo: A Social History of Islamic Education* (Princeton: Princeton University Press, 1992), 161–81.

26. Denise Spellberg, "History Then, History Now: The Role of Medieval Islamic Religio-Political Sources in Shaping the Modern Debate on Gender," in Amira El-Azhary Sonbol, ed., *Beyond the Exotic: Women's Histories in Islamic Societies* (Syracuse: Syracuse University Press, 2005), 8.

27. Al-Mawardi, *The Ordinances of Government*, trans. Wafaa Wahba (Reading: Garnet, 1996), 72. See also Fadel, "Two Women, One Man," 190.

28. Berkey, *The Transmission of Knowledge*, 173–75; Jonathan P. Berkey, *Popular Preaching and Religious Authority in the Medieval Islamic Near East* (Seattle: University of Washington Press, 2001), 31–32.

29. A. J. Arberry, *Muslim Saints and Mystics* (London: Routledge, 1966), 40; Margaret Smith, *Rabi`a the Mystic and Her Fellow-Saints in Islam* (Cambridge: Cambridge University Press, 2010); Jamal Elias, "Female and Feminine in Islamic Mysticism," *The Muslim World*, 78 (1988): 211.

30. Henry Corbin, *Creative Imagination in the Sufism of Ibn `Arabi* (Princeton: Princeton University Press, 1969); Ralph Austin, "The Feminine Dimension in Ibn 'Arabi's Thought," *Journal of the Muhyiddin Ibn `Arabi Society*, 2 (1984): 5–14.

CHAPTER 5

THE POLITICAL TRADITIONS OF FEMALE RULERSHIP IN MEDIEVAL EUROPE

AMALIE FÖßEL

SCHOLARS have long associated the political power of women in the Middle Ages with the empresses, queens, and influential noblewomen who are the subjects of narrative histories. In research women like these have been labeled as "exceptional women." This term refers to noblewomen who were in charge in difficult political circumstances, who exercised influence, who managed important social networks and kinship ties or a large fortune for political goals, or who acted as regents and exercised rulership in their own right. This model contrasts the few "exceptional women," such as the empresses Adelheid and Theophanu in the tenth century, with the majority of women of the high nobility, who had no real significance in the political organization of their realms.

The new approaches of gender history and recent studies on the mechanisms of power in premodern societies have opened new perspectives on the complexity of political and social relationships. One important realization has been that lordly dominions of the early and central Middle Ages should be understood primarily as realms of political communication, which functioned by means of ritual practices. Thus, a wide range of ritualized forms of communication were used to organize, reinforce, and modify the rudimentary existing political institutions. In this model, social networks and kinship ties formed the pillars supporting early medieval domains, which functioned through interaction among various groups and through specific family strategies and mechanisms aimed at increasing their power.

These modern approaches, which place the agents and their concerns at the forefront, can be fruitful for studying the scope of political action for noblewomen and their gender-specific strategies. In recent years, these approaches have been increasingly tested, critically reflected, revised, enhanced, and modified in an ongoing vivid discourse.[1] Research discourse in the field of gender and politics has become very complex and distinctive. A prominent place in it is occupied by the arguments of Jo Ann McNamara and Suzanne Wemple, who both postulate a structural change beginning around the year 1000 that, in the long run, brought a loss of power for women in many contexts. This thesis is based on the idea that noblewomen in the ninth, tenth, and early eleventh centuries were rich and powerful because their membership in influential families privileged them. They had extensive titles of property, which were transferred from their families of blood or marriage, and they were able to increase their wealth without restrictions due to the absence of public order.[2]

McNamara argues that this changed strikingly during the eleventh century and sees women at a disadvantage, which reached its theoretical culmination in the work of Thomas Aquinas and his recourse to Aristotelian teachings on the inferiority of women. Many explanations have been offered for a decrease in women's power over the course of the Middle Ages. In addition to the increasingly hierarchical elements in church, state, and society, some scholars have indicated the process of state formation and the attendant expansion of the administrative apparatus. The exclusion of women from the universities and the associated educational and career opportunities made the inequality of the sexes glaringly complete and became an enduring phenomenon. In the end, the conceptual division of the sexes and the idea of masculinity and femininity were powerful products of the early second millennium, implying positive effects for men and negative consequences for women.[3]

These wide-ranging and multifaceted observations and theories, only briefly described here, can be understood as a new idea of a modern, gender-based master narrative of European history. In this context, further critical analysis is necessary that considers not only German and English kingdoms, but also further continental European developments in the central and late Middle Ages. Yet despite a multitude of contributions, the current state of the field of gender and politics lacks comparative studies with synchronic as well as diachronic orientations. Most of the numerous studies of the political competence of aristocratic women take a biographical approach, while there are still too few comparative studies with chronologically and geographically broader ambitions.

In what follows, I will survey the traditions of political activity of the female elite in medieval Europe, illustrated with examples from my own research concerning the political lordship and legitimation strategies of medieval empresses and queens.[4] The perceptions of power structures and arenas for action among the high nobility function as a case study and form a frame of reference for female holders of territorial political responsibility and their participation in rulership. The focus is on the monarchies of the central and western European heartland with their various constitutional structures. At its center stand four thematic categories: patterns of perception concerning gender and power, models for female lordship practices, queenly titles as a political tradition, and the implementation of gender and power.

PATTERNS OF PERCEPTION: GENDER AND POWER

Any discussion of the traditions for women's political activity in medieval Europe must begin from the principle that contemporary political conceptions reflected the patriarchal social order and legitimated male hierarchy. In other words, they included the conviction that men were born to rule and women to be ruled. The handbooks known as "Mirrors for Princes," with their practical instructions for a just reign, were written by men, for men, and were full of characteristically male attributes such as strength and virtue. The concept of political responsibility for women had no place in them. This gender difference found a momentous theoretical restatement in Thomas Aquinas's retrieval of the Aristotelian concept of the woman as incomplete man. The chroniclers of the early and central Middle Ages, by contrast, had provided quite a different view of women. They viewed them as female rulers who were perceived by their contemporaries as political actors and were praised or criticized for their actions. This was especially true for the female upper nobility, who reigned not only as proxies for their husbands and sons, but also as heiresses of their fathers in their own right. It was also true for abbesses, who acted by virtue of their office on behalf of their orders and cloisters.

It is significant how female practices of lordship were perceived and evaluated by contemporaries, possibly culminating in assigned traditional gender-specific characteristics. Politically successful women were described as possessing masculine reason and vigor, by which they were able to overcome their own feminine frailty and to exercise leadership like a man. This concept drew upon traditional models that, especially in the early Middle Ages, described influential and assertive women who were socially gendered as masculine using the term *virago*, which came from the Latin for "acting like a man."[5]

THE CONSTRUCTION OF THE QUEEN AS INSTITUTION AND MODEL IN CORONATION *ORDINES*

In the tenth century, the Ottonians developed a tradition of crowning and anointing empresses as a form of legitimation. In the Carolingian era these acts of consecration had only been sporadically used. The first documentary evidence mentions the consecration of Bertrada, wife of Pippin I, in 754. The first demonstrable coronation with a golden circlet and the bestowal of the title *augusta* is that of Irmingard, first wife of Charlemagne's son Louis the Pious, in 816. The crown of the Lombard queen

Theudelinde from the late sixth century, preserved in the treasury of Monza cathedral, is older than these documentary sources, but it does not necessarily indicate a coronation, especially since there is no associated textual evidence. We have similarly scant knowledge about the coronations of queens in the other early medieval kingdoms of the Goths, Vandals, Burgundians, Thuringians, and Merovingians.[6]

Under Carolingian rule, it was not common to crown and anoint royal wives, and in particular the three spiritual acts of consecration, anointing, and coronation were not combined, as they would be from the tenth century onward. However, two events in the West Frankish kingdom of Charles the Bald can serve as a model in this respect. In the first, the king had his daughter Judith crowned and anointed upon her marriage to the Anglo-Saxon king Aethelwulf on October 1, 856.[7] Ten years later, in 866, her mother Irmentrud was crowned and anointed in Soissons after twenty-four years of marriage to Charles. Scholars emphasize that the anointing in particular was a central component in this context, as it bestowed upon the queen a sacral aura.[8]

The coronation of Adelheid as empress in Rome in 962 under the Ottonians marked a sharp change from practice in the East Frankish Carolingian realm, where there was no tradition of the coronation of the king's wife, and provided a pattern for later generations. As had been the case for Judith and Irmentrud among the West Franks, a written order of liturgy, an *Ordo*, was developed. The coronation of the empress was to take place in Rome, that of the queen in a German cathedral. The latter first took place in Paderborn in 1002 when Kunigunde, wife of Henry II, was crowned queen of the Romans and the Germans. Both coronation ceremonies founded a tradition, and their central passages continued to be used until the end of the Middle Ages. When a new king took power, it was common for his wife to be crowned queen in a separate ceremony, and for her to travel with the king to Rome later in order to be elevated to empress and *augusta* along with him, in the same ceremony.

As a theoretical foundation for the scope of political action for empresses and queens, the coronation *Ordines* depict an image of an ideal type of queen and provide a model for her as ruler, wife, and mother. A twofold model is apparent that depicts biblical examples of femininity on the one hand and describes concrete ways of exerting influence as a royal wife on the other.[9]

This ideal queen displayed specific characteristics. The first was the overcoming of inconstancy, the struggle against feminine fragility which a queen had to undertake. The Old Testament widow Judith functioned as the type of a clever and brave woman because, with personal initiative, feminine subtlety, and great determination, she seduced and beheaded Holofernes, who was threatening her city, thus demonstrating greater courage than the men of her city.

The second characteristic was motherhood, especially the bearing of an heir to the throne to preserve the dynasty. All the biblical matriarchs—Sarah (wife of Abraham), Rebecca (wife of Isaac), Leah and Rachel (wives of Jacob)—were invoked as examples for queens. They were the mothers of mankind because they produced the long-desired heirs (the fathers of the tribe of Israel), and their descendants populated the world.

The third aspect dealt directly with political power and cited the example of the Old Testament queen Esther for her piety, wisdom, and courage. She rescued the Israelites from the predations of the power-greedy Haman and, as a result, was elevated by the Persian king Ahasuerus to be his wife and co-ruler. She became the archetypal model for medieval queenship. The foundation of her power was her marriage to the king. The participation of the queen in earthly lordship as a divinely established authority by virtue of marriage was one of the integral components of each coronation ceremony as a publicly staged act of legitimation.

In the *Ordines*, anointing functioned as an act of purification and was closely associated with humility and moral integrity as necessary virtues for a queen. In the subsequent crowning, the crown itself was interpreted as a dazzling symbol of a character shining with the gold of wisdom and the jewels of virtue.

The coronation *Ordo* can be read as a "Mirror for Queens." At its center stood selected female Old Testament archetypes, who enjoyed a close relationship to God because of their belief in his power, which they had personally experienced. Judith and Esther in particular were associated with displays of masculine strength. They became examples for queens because they used power in a typically masculine way for the good of their people and were rewarded for it. The biblical examples legitimated the queen's participation in government as a God-given element of earthly lordship. The model of the *consortium regni* (association in royal lordship) was bolstered by the inclusion of these passages in the ceremony immediately before the anointing, the central act of purification. The reference to Esther also expanded the political content compared to the *Ordines* of the Carolingian era, which did not include the formula of *consortium regni* and its reinforcement of shared lordship. The Carolingian *Ordines* had focused more on general virtuousness and especially the blessing of noble progeny.

Thus, rulers of the Carolingian period had known the co-reign of the queen in a different form. The queen managed the royal household and supported the king in the ruling of the kingdom in that she, along with him and their progeny, presided over the court and bore responsibility for their staff. Together with her chamberlains, she was responsible "for the proper furnishing of the court and especially for the trappings of the king, but also for the annual gifts of the vassals, except for the provision of food and drink and the upkeep of the horses," according to Hincmar of Reims. This meant that she needed to anticipate what would be required well enough in advance that these items were not lacking when they were needed. Though diplomatic gifts were usually managed by the chamberlain, the king could also delegate this duty to the queen, since she was also responsible for the smooth functioning of the court. To her also fell the supervision of the *camerarius*, the highest administrator of income and provisions.[10] In the Ottonian period, however, the queen's role grew to include many official duties like intervention on behalf of lay and ecclesiastical figures or the ruling in the name of child kings.

TITLES OF THE QUEEN

The official titles for queens formed a long-standing foundation for political authority. The predominant standardized formulas contain only a small amount of gender-specific language regarding lordship. Through coronation in Rome by the pope, a queen of Rome was promoted to *imperatrix augusta* (elevated empress). This titulature paralleled the combination of masculine functional titles and honorific titles used in the Roman Empire. Only the title *augusta* is documented as an honorific term for the wives of the ancient Roman emperors. Many, but not all, of the emperors' wives were given this title in order to express their prominence in Roman society and their value to the emperor.[11]

The description *consors regni* (associate in royal lordship) is part of the imperial tradition of the central Middle Ages. After 962, the Ottonian chancellery and chroniclers began to use this formula, though it had been articulated in late antiquity and was used sporadically in Carolingian and tenth-century Italian sources. This development seems to be connected with Empress Adelheid, wife of Otto I. Charters of the Italian King Lothar I, Adelheid's first husband, describe her already as a partner in royal government, as *consors regni*. The clear emphasis on the *consortium* concept in the imperial coronation of 962 probably came from Adelheid herself, who may also have personally arranged for the addition of the new Esther passage in the *Ordo*.[12] The *consors* formula was first used as a component of the empress's title in a charter of Otto I dated March 13, 962, six weeks after the Roman coronation. In this charter, the emperor confirmed the privileges of the bishop's church in Lucca "at the request and admonition of Adelheid, our beloved wife and associate in our royal lordship."[13]

In the mid-eleventh century, the chancellery of the Salian rulers developed a new titulature. It highlighted the interrelation of marriage and lordship by combining both in one formula: "associate in our bed and empire." The conceptual foundation of co-rulership cannot be more clearly expressed: the *consortium* of the queen was based on her marriage to the king.[14] With a few exceptions, this formula remained exclusively reserved for empresses. Among the exceptions is the West Frankish queen Adelheid (*c*.945/60–*c*.1004), widow of Hugh Capet, who is described as "the associate and partaker of our realm" in a letter by Gerbert of Aurillac; according to this title she would have had comparable rank to the Ottonian empresses Theophanu and Adelheid.[15]

The titulature was enhanced through devotional formulas indicating that earthly lordship was due to the grace of God (*gratia dei*) and that temporal authority should be understood as divinely established. This rationale first appeared during the eighth century. While the Merovingians had based their monarchy on the kinship-based concept of the royal sanctity of their clan, the Carolingians legitimized their lordship through anointing. This new basis for lordship was trenchantly encapsulated in the formula *gratia dei*. At first it was used for male rulers, but as it spread throughout medieval Europe it was included in the titulature of empresses as well as queens, and eventually became an indispensable component of it.

GENDER AND POWER: THE PRACTICE OF RULERSHIP

A discussion of political traditions and rulership must describe not only ideals and perceptions, but also the circumstances and possibilities of agency. Reigning queens, who ruled on the basis of their own heirship rights, possessed broad powers. Regent queens, who ruled in the name of their own underage sons and grandsons, exercised temporary rulership rights. Queen consorts exercised partial rulership as the wives of kings, whether they performed political duties alongside them or acted as their temporary representatives.

Medieval kingdoms developed different legal traditions. Almost all European kingdoms practiced hereditary monarchy in which women could inherit. After the end of the Frankish Empire with its principle of divided dynastic succession, the Ottonian East Frankish successor kingdom instituted the indivisibility of the Empire and the succession of the firstborn son. From the beginning, this arrangement of succession was overlaid and shaped through the principle of election by ecclesiastical and lay magnates. Nevertheless, the dynastic conception, which made possible the regency of mothers, dominated at first. After the acceptance of the idea of succession by election and the implementation of electoral rights of the prince-electors in the thirteenth century, only adult rulers came to power, and only the Habsburgs in the fifteenth century were able to establish themselves as the first long-term dynasty.

The monarchy developed differently in France; here, the dynastic principle persisted after the end of the West Frankish Carolingians, when the politically adept Hugh Capet took the throne. His descendants reigned in unbroken succession until 1328. The end of his dynasty was marked by the succession of the brothers Louis X, Philip V, and Charles IV, who died without leaving male heirs. From among the many cadet branches of the family, it was Philip VI who asserted the throne and founded the Valois dynasty, which reigned until 1589.

Changes in rulership were accompanied by discussions of female succession. This possibility was raised in France in 1316 and 1328, when the daughters of Louis X and Charles IV made claims to the throne. In both situations, the royal council and an assembly of magnates decided against female succession by referring to the so-called Salic Law, which prohibited female inheritance. When Louis X died in 1316, he left a five-year-old daughter Jeanne, who was passed over in favor of her uncle. Her heirship rights were recognized only for the kingdom of Navarre, so that she could be crowned as Joan II of Navarre in Pamplona in 1329, together with her husband Philip of Évreux. After the death of Charles IV in 1328, the dictum that a woman should have no share in a kingdom (*mulier vero in regno nullam habeat portione*), discussed in French legal and political tracts of the time, was newly applied in order to preempt the claims of two different parties. First, Charles IV left a pregnant widow; if she had had a son, he would have been Charles's natural successor. Therefore an interim committee of regency was installed that was spearheaded by Philip of Valois. Two months later, when Charles's widow brought not a son but a daughter into the world, the incumbent regent Philip of Valois was elevated to king.

The accession of Philip also negated the claim of the English King Edward III, who had made a bid for the French crown as the son of Isabella of France, grandson of Philip the Fair, and nephew of the last three Capetians. The Salic Law was referred to and a declaration was issued by the peers, barons, and jurists, who rejected the transmission of claims to the throne through royal daughters and therefore also rejected the obvious aspirations of Edward, as a foreign king. Edward and his mother Isabella did not accept this decision, which famously provided a major cause for the so-called Hundred Years' War, which began in 1337 with the crossing of English troops to the continent. The political disputes of 1316 and 1328 made France into the only European monarchy whose dynastic principles allowed no cognatic-based succession to the throne.[16]

REIGNING QUEENS

A study of royal successions in other European hereditary monarchies shows that dynastic contingency led to female succession, especially in the fourteenth century and the first half of the fifteenth century.[17] Queens were legitimated through inheritance, especially in the southwestern European kingdoms of Castile-Léon, Navarre, Sicily, and Naples, but also in Poland, Hungary, and Bohemia, as well as in Scandinavia. Dynastic accidents apparently made such situations rarer in earlier times. Exceptions were Urraca, queen of Castile-Léon (1109–1126), Petronilla of Aragón (1137–1162), Joan I of Navarre (1273–1303), and Empress Constance of Sicily (1194–1198). Empress Matilda, daughter of Henry I of England and widow of Emperor Henry V, struggled for many years against her cousin and rival, Stephen of Blois, to establish her claim to the throne as the heir of her father (1125–1154), and in the long term, the claim of her son, later Henry II of England.[18] In all, only Castile-Léon and Navarre experienced the rule of three or more queens, which gives a certain plausibility to the thesis of Theresa Earenfight that queens took a far more active role in government in Aragón and Castile than elsewhere in Europe and operated there as "partners in politics."[19]

Two princesses inherited the royal office in Sicily, Naples, and Hungary. In all other monarchies, a female claimant to the throne occurred only once. In the interest of completeness, the full list of female claimants includes the kingdoms already mentioned plus Margaret of Norway (1286–1290) in Scotland, Isabella in Mallorca in 1375, and Beatrice (1383–1385) in Portugal, though Beatrice, married to Juan I of Castile, could not enforce the claim to the throne she inherited from her father and had to yield it to her uncle João of Avis.

Thus the monarchies of medieval Europe, with the exception of France and the Holy Roman Empire, recognized female succession, and hereditary rights could be passed through cognatic lines. Out of one hundred changes in rulers between 1350 and 1450, female claims were relevant in twelve cases.[20] It remains to be asked how these claims were handled, under which circumstances women achieved the throne, and which political traditions played a role in this.

Cognatic successions were more or less a last resort. Women could only establish themselves if a male claimant to the throne was not available or was a foreign prince whom the kingdom was reluctant to accept. Reluctance to accept a foreign ruler could be to the advantage of the female heir, but it could also be turned to her disadvantage. This is what occurred in Portugal in 1385. The high nobility decided against the succession of the hereditary princess Beatrice and her Castilian husband and in favor of her father's illegitimate brother, who secured his succession as João I through his victory over a Castilian host at Aljubarrota.

Most female rulers were daughters who succeeded their fathers. The first case in medieval Europe was Urraca of Castile-Léon, who was the only surviving legitimate child of her father after the death of her half-brother. Before his death in 1109, Alfonso I the Great had his magnates confirm her succession and arranged a new marriage for her—a widow with two children—with the Aragonese king Alfonso VI.[21]

Twice in the period under discussion, mothers succeeded their sons, for whom they had been acting as regents. The situation of Margaret of Denmark is particularly noteworthy. She ruled her father's kingdom as his only living child after his death in 1375. Denmark was an electoral monarchy, and Margaret was named regent for her five-year-old son in return for recognizing broad privileges for nobles and clerics. The Danish nobles' decision in her favor also constituted a refusal of the claim of Albert of Mecklenburg, the ten-year-old son of her deceased sister. Margaret of Denmark, who outlived her husband and her son, did not remarry, and ruled the three Scandinavian kingdoms in a personal union for two decades, eventually adopting her great-nephew Eric of Pomerania and naming him as her successor.[22]

In two cases, sisters succeeded their brothers, and only once did a granddaughter succeed her grandfather. This took place in 1343 in Naples when Joan I fulfilled the will of her grandfather, King Robert the Wise, as the heir to his throne. Her succession was fiercely contested by several parties, including her own husband Andrew of Anjou, the younger brother of King Louis the Great of Hungary. Nonetheless, she successfully established herself and ruled in her own name for almost three decades, while only the first two of her four husbands were crowned. Her second husband Louis of Taranto in particular was involved in her government and acted as an important political advisor.

The circumstances under which women took the throne varied significantly and seldom proceeded without problems. Direct relationship with the dead king and individual hereditary right were of fundamental importance. Both played a crucial role if there were no male successors or the political decision-makers did not accept male claimants because they were foreign princes or minors. The dominance of male-line-based (agnatic) claims over female-line-based (cognatic) claims is unmistakable. This is proved by situations in which the claims of a daughter were superseded by those of a grandchild. Thus, Constance of Sicily as well as Margaret of Denmark—the latter only temporarily—ruled in their own names and at the same time functioned as regents for their sons, whom they had crowned as kings early in order to secure the succession to the throne.

Besides lone rule or rule together with a son, a queen who succeeded to the throne could also share communal rule with her husband. Blanche of Navarre is an example of this. As the wife of Martin I the Younger, Blanche first became queen of Sicily, which she ruled for several years after his death, until she was expelled as a childless widow in 1415 and returned to the kingdom of her father, Charles III of Navarre. She married John of Aragon, ten years her junior, and after 1425 ruled the kingdom in common with him. When she died in 1441, Navarre should have fallen to her son Charles, the prince of Viana. Her father Charles III had already decreed it and she had confirmed it. Yet after Blanche's death, Charles was prevented from succeeding by his father, who had entered a new marriage with all the assets of Charles's inheritance. The young Charles struggled against him for many years, but in vain.

In addition to the rulership of a queen ruling in her own right who included her husband in the business of governing, heiresses could also be represented by *gubernatores* (governors). Joan I of Navarre, the sole claimant to the throne as the daughter of King Henry I, grew up at the French court and married Philip IV the Fair of France at a young age. After the death of her father in 1274, Navarre and its politically affiliated county of Champagne became subject to France and were ruled by *gubernatores*. Nonetheless, in later years, Joan personally administered both realms. When Count Henry III of Bar invaded Champagne, the queen commanded a host that opposed him, won a victory at the battle of Commines in 1297, and took the count prisoner. In Navarre, she established a lasting peace. After her death in 1305, her oldest son Louis X inherited the kingdom; after his death in 1316, her granddaughter and namesake, who had been excluded from succession to the French throne (as discussed above), inherited it from her grandmother and her father and ruled as Joan II in Navarre.

These few examples stand for many others. In summing up, it can be observed that female rights to the throne were anchored in the hereditary monarchies of medieval Europe. But, although part of the political tradition, female ascension to the throne was rather an infrequent dynastic accident, and was primarily realized in southwestern European kingdoms. These exemplary cases show that circumstances of succession, the operating conditions, and modalities of rulership varied greatly and depended on the current political situations and the life circumstances of the protagonists. Because female claims to the throne were a last resort, it is scarcely surprising that even when they ruled in their own right, queens with minor sons simultaneously acted as regents and tutors for the crown prince, and thus played a role that was also the only one open to queens in the German Empire and France in the central Middle Ages.

REGENT QUEENS

Except for the Merovingian era, when queens could exert substantial influence on behalf of their sons and grandsons, female regency first became a major phenomenon in the late tenth century. In the East Frankish kingdom, the empresses Adelheid and Theophanu were the first to serve as regents, for Otto III, their grandson and son respectively. This was not a matter of course, but rather had to be decided through a power struggle. Duke Henry II of Bavaria, the uncle of Otto III, claimed kingship for himself. He took custody of the already-crowned child king and attempted to win the approval of the bishops and princes by any means. The empresses also did so, declaring early on their intention to take over the regency. They found committed allies in Gerbert of Aurillac, the prominent intellectual who later became Pope Sylvester II, as well as the powerful Adalbero, archbishop of Reims. In the end, the episcopate and the nobility backed the rulership of the empresses as they must have had worries that the duke sought not simply the post of regent for Otto III, but the kingship itself. Therefore, a Saxon assembly of princes led by the Archbishop of Mainz and Chancellor Willigis did a political about-face and settled the dispute in favor of the female regency of the imperial ladies. This founded a political tradition in favor of mothers as regents.

The well-informed Annals of Quedlinburg made Adelheid, the mother of Otto II and hence Theophanu's mother-in-law, the focus of subsequent events. Reliable messengers were sent to her, informing her about the state of affairs and urgently requesting her, with the "power of her presence and her counsel," to restore order to the fraying empire. Thereupon, Adelheid asserted divine support for her plans and set out the steps that needed to be taken. Magnates from all parts of the realm were summoned to a court audience, and a representative assembly was established. Here, the empresses took over "the care of the empire and the childhood of the king," as the Annals put it.[23] The Bavarian duke had to accept and submit to this broad "support." The consensus became permanent and with it the recognition of the authority of women and their political allies, the bishops Willigis of Mainz and Hildebold of Worms.

The reputation achieved during this regency may have substantially contributed to the central role that the queens of the Holy Roman Empire played thereafter in imperial politics, and to the fact that when a regent was next needed, for Henry IV, it was beyond dispute that it should be his mother. The formal decision was already made before the death of Henry III in 1056. The assumption of real rulership by Agnes of Poitou took place without problems and she enjoyed great support at first, but as she made political mistakes and it became increasingly apparent that she relied too much on the advice of individual persons, opposition grew. This led to the kidnapping of Henry IV in Kaiserswerth by a group of bishops led by Archbishop Anno of Cologne, and the empress was expelled.

Contemporary chroniclers described the event with gender-specific language. The regency of the empress was equated with that of a male regent as long as she fulfilled the expectations of the elite and followed the praxis of building political consensus. When this was no longer the case, the usual female stereotypes asserted themselves. In addition to the allegation that Henry IV had received a bad upbringing, there were loud complaints about the empress's manipulation by wicked counselors and the inadequate involvement of the imperial princes in political decisions. Then came allegations of corruption and injustice and finally fundamental doubts about the rulership of a woman. According to the anonymous author of Henry's biography, the *Vita Henrici*, at the beginning of her regency the empress acted as a woman endowed with manly understanding (*virilis ingenii femina*). Later, he reported, people said that it was not fitting that a woman should rule the empire, although there was also talk of many queens who had ruled the empire with manly wisdom.[24]

Except for the regency of Empress Constance for Frederick II in Sicily, which took place under entirely different circumstances, Empress Agnes's regency for Henry IV was the last in the German Empire during the Middle Ages, since the Empire developed into an electoral monarchy and had no more child kings. Things developed quite differently in France, where the first regency of a queen occurred after the death of Henry I in 1060. Anne of Kiev ruled on behalf of the minor Philip I, though in tandem with Count Baldwin V of Flanders. When she entered a highly controversial marriage one year later, she lost her position of power and had to leave court.[25] French queens in the eleventh century simply did not have enough authority to secure a position comparable to that of female regents in the Empire. Unlike Anne, Agnes of Poitou did not lose her status as empress after the political fiasco described above. She gave up direct governing authority, but she did not entirely withdraw from imperial politics and still exercised political influence. Especially in later years, she was extremely busy as an emissary between Henry IV, the pope, and the nobles who opposed Henry.

Female regencies became a long-term part of the political traditions of European monarchies. From the late twelfth century, it was increasingly standard practice for the mother of a minor successor to the throne to be installed as regent. The official competencies associated with this function, which brought queens into a more central political position than they held during the lifetimes of their husbands, fundamentally strengthened their place in the political structure. This thesis can be confirmed for the Ottonian Empire. It may also apply in large part to France, where the regency of Blanche of Castile for Louis IX the Pious particularly tended in this direction.

Queen Consorts

In the central Middle Ages, the queen's influence on political decisions in the French court as the wife of the ruler was much less pronounced than in the German Empire, where queens had the reputation of being influential figures to whom one could turn with requests for intercession.

In the Ottonian Empire, as in no other European monarchy, the queen's power of intervention developed into a major duty and took on an institutional character. Queenly advocacy provides an especially appropriate example for distinguishing among different political traditions. As a king's wife, a queen enjoyed a personal closeness to the ruler, and by shrewd action she had a prime opportunity to act as a counselor and thus exercise influence over political decisions. In addition to these highly individualized opportunities for influence, the German Empire of the central Middle Ages established an institutionalized form of the queen's power of intervention, which became the "job" for each queen in the tenth century. Empress Adelheid no longer merely exerted patronage on behalf of a small group of cloisters, churches, and their superintendents, but rather received petitioners for her advocacy from the entire extent of the Empire. It is obvious that she sought to augment her influence in daily political life by means of intervention. Charters reveal that after her Roman coronation in 962, she intervened in almost half of all grants made by the emperor.

This focused effort by Adelheid, who brought the petitions of many people to the attention of the emperor and the court, strengthened her personal authority and made her appear a virtual co-ruler. In this process the queen's agency consolidated, turned from being a personal competence into something more institutionalized, and stamped the image of the queen on the court and the Empire. Until well into the twelfth century, queens intervened in one fourth to one third of royal charters. In times of regency, intervention functioned as a specific political instrument that indicated official political responsibility.

The institutionalization of the power of intervention indicated a high degree of acceptance by contemporaries. The queen became the most important advocate and partner in securing the emperor's approval for a request. No bishop or duke had greater influence in this respect. This changed in the twelfth century, when a marked decline is visible under Empress Beatrice, the wife of Frederick I Barbarossa, which resulted from a new practice in document production. The intervention formula was discontinued in favor of a witness formula. The queen, however, was listed as a witness only in rare exceptional cases. This institutionalized form of intervention no longer occurred in the late medieval German Empire; is also not detectable in this form for the queens of other monarchies.

Other forms of power can be identified for England in the eleventh and twelfth centuries. According to the *Domesday Book*, queens were lavishly endowed with lordly domains after the conquest of 1066. In contrast, in the German Empire (and to my knowledge also in France), the ownership rights with which individual queens were endowed varied considerably. While the empresses Adelheid and Theophanu were unfathomably wealthy, the empress Kunigunde occasionally had no material resources, and indeed had to relinquish the holding of Bamberg, which was part of her endowment, and struggle to obtain a settlement. A shift to limiting a queen's holdings began in England in the mid-twelfth century during the reign of Henry II. Eleanor of Aquitaine commanded notably less income in England than her predecessors. She is the first one mentioned in the sources as the recipient of the so-called "queen's gold," a surtax on money paid to the king. In the fourteenth century, this developed into a major source of income, in addition to the allocation of landed estates and variable supplementary grants by the king. Unlike in the German Empire with its highly varied endowments, in England it was the practice to fix the endowment of the queen at a specified sum, around four thousand marks or four thousand pounds. Unlike in the German Empire, a specific set of holdings was reserved for English queens of the thirteenth and the first half of the fourteenth century.[26] The stipulation of a fairly stable monetary sum and the development of a core group of queens' estates are two important indicators of the institutionalized status of English queens.

CONCLUSIONS

The practice of female rulership and political influence in medieval Europe took place in different legal contexts and assumed different political forms. The idea of a political partnership as a *consortium* and the association with Esther were part of the political theory of the early and central Middle Ages and continued into the later Middle Ages. Disparate images and evaluations of female rulership were constructed by means of gender-specific *topoi*. A capacity for political participation that went beyond the typical feminine domains of wife and mother was created by the association of women with masculine categories, and the merging of feminine virtues like friendliness and godliness with masculine virtues like discipline, strength, and cleverness. Female rulership was legitimized and evaluated positively by merging masculine and feminine ideals; reducing female rulers to negative feminine stereotypes like weakness and suggestibility was a means to justify their inability to rule.

In the thirteenth century, the argument shifted. Until then, female power was understood in a more or less institutional form through the concept of the *consortium*, but in the late Middle Ages—with its aristocratic women who ruled in their own right and its increasingly important female regencies—the political participation of women took on a new dimension that was more and more unambiguously based on legal criteria. This concrete, effective juristic-political argument in favor of female rulership was opposed by scientific-biological discourse, which took up the Aristotelian theorem of the incomplete woman and solidified into a negative view of women. With the formation of hierarchical administrations at the monarchical and territorial level, women lost public functions as well as political competences. The model of the *consortium*, which in earlier centuries was based in a theologically grounded political tradition, was narrowed down to a model of political participation defined by legal arguments. Below the institutional legal level, direct influence on the ruler and the court, so difficult to detect in the sources and so subject to individual variations, formed for centuries a basis for power which should not be underestimated, and found expression in the image of the female representatives of ruling houses.

Translation Philip Grace

FURTHER READING

Duby, Georges and Michelle Perrot, eds. A History of Women in the West, vol. 2, Silences of the Middle Ages, ed. Christiane Klapische-Zuber, trans. Arthur Goldhammer. Cambridge, MA: Harvard University Press, 1998.

Duggan, Anne J., ed. *Queens and Queenship in Medieval Europe: Proceedings of a Conference held at King's College, London, April 1995*. Woodbridge: Boydell Press, 1997.

Fößel, Amalie, ed. *Die Kaiserinnen des Mittelalters*. Regensburg: Verlag Friedrich Pustet, 2011.

Gilsdorf, Sean, ed. *Queenship and Sanctity: The Lives of Mathilda and the Epitaph of Adelheid*. Washington, DC: The Catholic University of America Press, 2004.

Lebecq, Stéphane et al., eds. *Femmes et pouvoirs des femmes à Byzance et en Occident (VIe–XIe siècles): Colloque international organisé les 28, 29 et 30 mars 1996 à Bruxelles et Villeneuve d'Ascq.* Villeneuve-d'Ascq: Centre de recherche sur l'histoire de l'Europe du Nord-Ouest, 1999.

Schaus, Margaret, ed. *Women and Gender in Medieval Europe: An Encyclopedia.* New York: Routledge, 2006.

Stafford, Pauline. *Queens, Concubines, and Dowagers: The King's Wife in the Early Middle Ages.* London: Leicester University Press, 1998.

Stafford, Pauline and Anneke B. Mulder-Bakker, eds. *Gendering the Middle Ages.* Oxford: Blackwell Publishers, 2001.

Turner, Ralph V. *Eleanor of Aquitaine: Queen of France, Queen of England.* New Haven; London: Yale University Press, 2009.

NOTES

1. See for example two foundational collected volumes by the editorial duo Mary C. Erler and Maryanne Kowaleski on the theme of gender and politics, which explore closely related problems: *Women and Power in the Middle Ages* (Athens; London: University of Georgia Press, 1988), and *Gendering the Master Narrative: Women and Power in the Middle Ages* (Ithaca; London: Cornell University Press, 2003).

2. Jo Ann McNamara and Suzanne Wemple, "The Power of Women through the Family in Medieval Europe, 500–1100," *Feminist Studies*, 1 (1973): 126–41.

3. Jo Ann McNamara, "Women and Power through the Family Revisited," in Erler and Kowaleski, eds, *Gendering the Master Narrative*, 17–30.

4. Amalie Fößel, *Die Königin im mittelalterlichen Reich: Herrschaftsausübung, Herrschaftsrechte, Handlungsspielräume* (Stuttgart: Thorbecke, 2000), 319–32. For a summary of its central conclusions, see Amalie Fößel, "Gender and Rulership in the Medieval German Empire," *History Compass*, 7 (1) (2009): 55–65.

5. Kimberly A. LoPrete, "Gendering Viragos: Medieval Perceptions of Powerful Women," in Christine Meek and Catherine Lawless, eds, *Victims or Viragos?* Studies on Medieval and Early Modern Women, 4 (Portland: Four Courts Press, 2005), 17–38.

6. Martina Hartmann, *Die Königin im frühen Mittelalter* (Stuttgart: Kohlhammer, 2009).

7. Coronatio Iudithae Karoli II. filiae, in Richard A. Jackson, ed., *Ordines Coronationis Franciae: Text and Ordines for the Coronation of Frankish and French Kings and Queens in the Middle Ages*, vol. 1 (Philadelphia: University of Pennsylvania Press, 1995), Ordo V, 73–79.

8. Coronatio Hermintrudis reginae, in Jackson, ed., *Ordines*, Ordo VI, 80–86. Cf. Janet L. Nelson, "Early Medieval Rites of Queen-Making and the Shaping of Medieval Queenship," in Anne J. Duggan, ed., *Queens and Queenship in Medieval Europe* (Woodbridge: The Boydell Press, 1997), 301–15.

9. *Die Ordines für die Weihe und Krönung des Kaisers und der Kaiserin*, ed. Reinhard Elze, Monumenta Germaniae Historica: Fontes iuris Germanici antiqui, 9 (Hannover: Hahnsche Buchhandlung, 1960), no. III, 6–9; cf. Fößel, *Königin*, 17–49.

10. Hincmar of Reims, *De ordine palatii*, ed. and trans. Thomas Gross and Rudolf Schieffer, Monumenta Germaniae Historica: Fontes iuris Germanici antiqui, 3 (Hannover: Hahnsche Buchhandlung, 1980).

11. Anne Kolb, ed., *Augustae: Machtbewusste Frauen am römischen Kaiserhof?* (Berlin: Akademie Verlag, 2010).

12. On the biography of Adelheid, see most recently Amalie Fößel, "Adelheid," in idem, ed., *Die Kaiserinnen des Mittelalters* (Regensburg: Verlag Friedrich Pustet, 2011), 37–61.

13. "...prece et admonitione dilecte nostre coniugis Adelehide regnique nostri consortis," in *Die Urkunden Konrads I., Heinrichs I. und Ottos I.*, ed. Theodor Sickel, MGH Diplomata regum et imperatorum Germaniae, 1 (Hannover: Hahnsche Buchhandlung, 1879–84), no. 238. On the historical development of the formula, cf. Fößel, *Königin*, 56–66.

14. First used in a charter from November 19, 1048, published in Speyer, in *Die Urkunden Heinrichs III.*, ed. Harry Bresslau and Paul Kehr, MGH Diplomata regum et imperatorum Germaniae, 5 (Berlin: Hahnsche Buchhandlung, 1926–1931), no. 225: "...nostra thori nostrique regni consors...imperatrix augusta..."

15. *Die Briefsammlung Gerberts von Reims*, ed. F. Weigle, MGH Briefe der deutschen Kaiserzeit, 2 (Weimar: Hahnsche Buchhandlung, 1966), esp. 120. On the effects of titles on negotiations between the kingdoms, see Amalie Fößel, "Frauen an der Spitze Europas: Lebensstrategien und Lebensentwürfe von Königinnen des 10. Jahrhunderts," in Franz Staab and Thorsten Unger, eds, *Kaiserin Adelheid und ihre Klostergründung in Selz* (Speyer: Pfälzische Gesellschaft zur Förderung der Wissenschaften, 2005), 69–89.

16. Philippe Contamine, "'Le royaume de France ne peut tomber en fille': Une théorie politique à la fin du Moyen Age," in Gert Melville, ed., *Institutionen und Geschichte: Theoretische Aspekte und mittelalterliche Befunde* (Cologne; Weimar; Vienna: Böhlau, 1992), 187–207.

17. See the list by Arnim Wolf, "Reigning Queens in Medieval Europe: When, Where, and Why," in John Carmi Parsons, ed., *Medieval Queenship* (New York: Palgrave, 1993), 169–88.

18. Marjorie Chibnall, *The Empress Matilda: Queen Consort, Queen Mother and Lady of the English* (Oxford: John Wiley & Sons, 1991).

19. Theresa Earenfight, "Partners in Politics," in idem, ed., *Queenship and Political Power in Medieval and Early Modern Spain* (Aldershot: Ashgate Publishing, 2005), xiii–xxviii.

20. These numbers are taken from Wolf, "Reigning Queens."

21. Bernard F. Reilly, *The Kingdom of Léon-Castilla under Queen Urraca (1109–1126)* (Princeton, NJ: Princeton University Press, 1982); Ursula Vones-Liebenstein, "Une femme gardienne du royaume? Régentes en temps de guerre," in Philippe Contamine and Oliver Guyuotjeannin, eds, *La guerre, la violence et les gens au Moyen Age*, vol. 2: *Guerre et Gens* (Paris: Comité des travaux historiques et scientifiques, 1996), 9–22.

22. Inge Skovgaard-Petersen, "Queenship in Medieval Denmark," in Parsons, ed., *Medieval Queenship*, 25–42.

23. *Die Annales Quedlinburgenses*, ed. Martina Giese, MGH: Scriptores Rerum Germanicarum, 72 (Hannover: Hahnsche Buchhandlung, 2004).

24. *Vita Heinrici IV. imperatoris*, ed. Wilhelm Eberhard, MGH: Scriptores Rerum Germanicarum, 58 (Hannover: Hahnsche Buchhandlung, 1899), cap. 2, 13ff.

25. Robert-Henri Bautier, "Anne de Kiev, reine de France, et la politique royale au XIe siècle: Étude critique de la documentation," in idem, *Recherches sur l'histoire de la France médiévale: Des Mérovingiens aux premiers Capétiens* (Aldershot: Variorum, 1991), no. VIII, 539–64.

26. Amalie Fößel, "The Queen's Wealth in the Middle Ages," *Majestas*, 13 (2005): 23–45.

CHAPTER 6

....

MEDICINE AND NATURAL PHILOSOPHY: NATURALISTIC TRADITIONS

....

KATHARINE PARK

INSTEAD of distinguishing between sex difference, understood primarily as a physical category, and gender, understood primarily as a social category, the authors and compilers discussed here tended to collapse the two concepts into a single form of difference that they referred to indifferently as "sex" (Latin *sexus*). In this matter as in others, they believed that the divinely created natural order, which included the form and functioning of the human body, served as a kind of scripture, displaying the Creator's intentions for the social as well as the physical world; for example, if God made women physically weaker than men, according to the Christian encyclopedist Isidore of Seville (c.560–636), it was because "he intended for them to be subjected to men, lest lust drive men, when rejected by women, to desire a different form of satisfaction or seek out the male sex."[1] Here, Isidore superposed three forms of inequality, all of which he understood as divinely ordained: women are physically weaker than men; women are subject to male control, to the point of physical coercion; and coitus between men is morally inferior to coitus between a woman and a man. Where a modern commentator might interpret these three propositions as referring to separable realities, physical, political or social, and sexual or moral, Isidore understood them as a seamless whole.

This essay surveys accounts of the sexed body in the works of medieval writers on medicine and natural philosophy in Jewish, Islamic, and Latin Christian culture. (Natural philosophy aimed to give a general theoretical account of the workings of the natural world, including the bodies of animals such as humans, making it approximately—but only approximately—the medieval analogue of "science" in the modern sense.) While both fields in all three religious communities were wholly dominated by male scholars and were as a result highly androcentric, medical writers, who interacted regularly with female patients and were concerned with the health of women as well as men, tended to adopt a more positive and nuanced view of women's bodies and women's nature. On the surface, writing on these matters shows a good deal of continuity over the millennium between 500 and 1500, focused as it was on transmitting and interpreting ancient texts. Especially influential were works attributed to a small number of Greek scholars, of whom the most influential were Hippocrates (mostly fifth to fourth century BCE); Aristotle (fourth century BCE); Soranus (early second century CE); and Galen (mid- to late second century CE).[2]

While this rich but intellectually circumscribed classical heritage lent coherence to their discussions, medieval scholars, like their ancient models, differed on many points, depending on the texts they had to hand and the faiths, social orders, and institutions that shaped their viewpoints. For example, the treatment of sexuality by Christian authors, for whom sexual disobedience lay at the center of human rebellion against divine authority, differed from that of many Muslim medical writers, who believed that sexual pleasure was one of God's gifts to humanity. Throughout the Middle Ages, in other words, scholars picked and chose among the ancient works useful and available to them—a function of context and circumstances—and adapted, cannibalized, and commented on them in the ways that made the most sense to them and their imagined audiences. At the same time, virtually all medieval writers on medicine and natural philosophy, Christians, Muslims, or Jews, were committed to the naturalistic explanation of bodily functions and phenomena—to the idea that creation was the work of one God, who, with rare exceptions, worked through rationally discernible chains of cause and effect rooted in his created, physical order. Thus medieval scholars, like many modern ones, for that matter, considered what we might call ideological constructions concerning sex and gender to be facts of nature discerned by human reason.

This essay focuses on three topics that dominated medieval writing on the gendered body: sex difference, generation, and sexual pleasure or desire. I have organized my exposition chronologically and, within that framework, by linguistic and religious tradition. These traditions map fairly neatly onto broad geographical subdivisions of the medieval world, understood as embracing both the Islamicate lands, from the Middle East to Spain, where Islam was the dominant religion and Arabic the shared language of scientific discourse; and western Europe, where Christians wrote in Latin and Jews, on the whole, in Hebrew. Arabic scholarship effectively disappeared from Europe after the Christian reconquest of Muslim Spain, and Byzantine medicine and natural philosophy are, regrettably, not treated here.

Sex Difference in the Early Medieval West, 500–1050

While scholars in Byzantium and the Middle East had access to a wide range of Greek works relating to sex difference, their Western European counterparts worked in a textually impoverished environment. Few scientific works had been translated into Latin, and the gradual transformation of the western Roman Empire into a fragmented and increasingly rural society over the course of the fourth through sixth centuries had led to a precipitous decline in the knowledge of Greek and the availability of Greek texts. This was particularly true of the large and demanding oeuvres of Galen and Aristotle, which were to form the backbone of learned writing on sex difference in the Islamicate world throughout the Middle Ages and in western Europe beginning in the late eleventh century. Before then, the scientific culture of the Latin west centered on the few Greek works that had been translated into Latin during the last centuries of the Empire, together with Latin synopses and compendia, which were further adapted and extracted in monastic scriptoria.

It is impossible to elicit a consistent theory-based model of sex difference from these fragmentary and internally inconsistent texts. Their discussions were dominated by ideas derived from the gynecological works of Soranus, whose anti-theoretical stance (that of the Greek medical sect known as "Methodism") agreed with monastic tastes for practicality, on the one hand, and opinions compatible with Christian doctrine, on the other. De-emphasizing sex difference, Soranus described male and female bodies as structurally and functionally alike, with the exception of a handful of non-essential organs devoted to reproduction. In both types of bodies, he argued, the process of digesting food produces a residue that is consumed in physical activity or evacuated through excretion, emission of semen and/or menses, or periodic bloodletting. These ideas informed his *Gynaikeia* ("women's things"), a treatise for midwives that was translated into Latin several times over the course of the fourth through sixth centuries and was broadly influential in the European west.

The anatomical and physiological sections of Isidore of Seville's *Etymologies*, an influential early medieval Latin Christian encyclopedia, show the impact of Soranic ideas. While Isidore presented the existence of two sexes as a natural fact, he described male and female bodies as similar, with a few notable exceptions, of which the most substantial concerned their genitals; while both men and women have testicles, external and internal respectively, only men have penises and only women have wombs (11.1.73–147). Beyond that, Isidore was vague. Men eject seed, and women menstruate, and both are involved in the shaping of the fetus, but the relationship between the menses and female seed (as for Soranus) is unclear. Isidore nowhere mentioned the material basis of sex difference that grounded the theories of Hippocrates, Aristotle, and Galen: the polarities of hot and dry, cold and wet that were thought to distinguish male and female bodies respectively. Lacking this theoretical foundation, his account of the relatively few differences between men and women dissolves into a welter of unrelated morphological details, most of them superficial, like the size of the chest, the shape of the cheeks, and the presence or absence of facial hair.

Isidore's lack of interest in an overarching theory of sexed anatomy and physiology was balanced by his attention to the moral and spiritual meanings with which sex difference was freighted in Christian culture. He noted that "man, *vir*, is so named because he has greater strength [*vis*] than woman," while "woman, *mulier*, is named from softness [*mollities*]"; the last term had connotations of sexual license as well as spiritual weakness, which Isidore compounded by reminding his reader that, as in the case of Eve, "the female is more lustful than the male" (11.2.17–24). Women's spiritual and moral imperfection is reflected in the noxious qualities of menstrual blood. "On contact with this gore," Isidore wrote, "crops do not germinate, wine sours, plants die, trees lose their fruit, iron rusts, copper blackens. If dogs eat it, they contract rabies" (11.1.141).

Isidore compiled his *Etymologies* in the city of Seville, where he had at least indirect access to the learned traditions of antiquity through classical handbooks and school texts. A century later, Seville had fallen to the Arabs, the threadbare urban fabric of Christian Europe had largely disintegrated, and what little remained of ancient medical traditions survived mostly in monastic libraries. Nonetheless, the influence of Soranus continued to dominate writing on sex and gender. Of the various Latin abbreviations of the *Gynaikeia* that circulated in early medieval Europe, the most common was a brief, practical summary in question-and-answer format attributed to the otherwise unknown "Muscio" (probably sixth century), who, following Soranus, rejected the core Hippocratic idea that sexual activity and menstruation, which evacuated the noxious residues of digestion in the form of seed and blood, were essential to prevent serious illness in women. Muscio noted that although certain females do not menstruate "according to nature"—notably girls, old women, singers, and athletes—their condition does not require medical intervention as long as they "experience no bodily distress." On the contrary, he described perpetual virginity as "very healthy," especially for women, given the illnesses associated with coitus, pregnancy, and childbirth.[3] The general effect of these passages was to emphasize the benefits of chastity and consequently to portray women's health, like men's, as separable from their sexual and reproductive functions, rather than defined by them.

Monica Green has identified the puzzle presented by the influence of Soranus's *Gynaikeia* on early medieval monastic writing on women's bodies: why was a manual written for the instruction of Greek midwives preserved, adapted, and circulated by male Christian monks? (No Soranic manuscripts have been associated with women's monasteries.) In addition to satisfying the curiosity of supposedly celibate men about an important but unfamiliar realm of human experience, and conveying information that might be useful in a pastoral capacity, Muscio's text confirmed the universality of the Christian ideal of sexual continence, since it presented perpetual virginity as a plausible goal for women as well as men—a doctrine that ran counter to Galenic and Hippocratic views.[4] Indeed, Muscio's inclusion of female singers and women engaged in strenuous activity among those able to embrace a healthy non-reproductive life was particularly relevant to monastic women, since the Benedictine Rule made no provision for sexual differences in fasting and physical exertion. On a deeper level, the Soranic body resonated with the goal of early Christian asceticism to eradicate the cycle of human procreation that perpetuated original sin. In this way, virgin and childless women became exemplars for the repression of the procreative body, both male and female, in early Christian theology, while the identification of women with sexual intemperance, as in Isidore's *Etymologies*, made their acts of sexual and reproductive renunciation doubly resonant.[5]

SEX, GENERATION, AND SEXUALITY IN THE ISLAMICATE WORLD: ARABIC TRADITIONS, 800–1300

While Latin writing on sex difference in early medieval Europe was dominated by the influence of Soranus, the situation was very different in the eastern Mediterranean, where Galenic and, to a lesser degree, Hippocratic teachings were authoritative in the medical tradition, and Aristotelian teachings in the natural philosophical one. Unimpeded by linguistic barriers, the works of all three authors circulated widely in the Byzantine world and, unlike Soranus's *Gynaikeia*, were quickly translated into Arabic in the seventh and eighth centuries. The accounts of gendered bodies in the works of Aristotle and Galen were comprehensive, detailed, and highly theorized, situated in a general account of human anatomy and physiology, in contrast to the practically oriented Soranic compilations of the Christian west. They were also focused on procreative sexuality, rather than the ideal of virginity or sexual restraint, which led them, unlike Isidore, to emphasize differences between male and female bodies rather than dismissing the genitals as non-essential. As elaborated by Arabic translators, compilers, and theorists beginning the ninth century, these accounts came to form the core of learned writing on sex difference in Arabic and, eventually, Hebrew and Latin.[6]

The Arabic model of sex difference found its most complete expression in a series of medical encyclopedias, of which the most influential were two tenth-century works—*al-Kitāb al-Kāmil fī aṣ-ṣināʿa aṭ-ṭibbiya* ("Complete Representation of the Medical Art," *Pantegni* in Latin) by the Persian physician Alī ibn al-ʿAbbās al-Majūsī (Haly Abbas in Latin) and the *Zād al-musāfir* ("Provision of the Voyager," *Viaticum* in Latin) by al-Majūsī's North African contemporary, Abū Jaʿfar Aḥmad ibn Ibrāhīm ibn al-Jazzār—and an early eleventh-century one, *al-Qānūn fī aṭ-ṭibb* ("Canon of medicine," *Liber canonis* in Latin) by Abū Alī al-Ḥusayn ibn Sīnā (Avicenna in Latin), also Persian. Their authors took views Galen had developed in several individual works—views that were not always consistent with one another—and transformed these into a coherent system of theory and practice for the use of scholars, physicians, and medical students. All three encyclopedias circulated widely in the Islamicate world and were translated into Latin in the eleventh and twelfth centuries and into Hebrew in the twelfth and thirteenth.

Following Galen, al-Majūsī, Ibn al-Jazzār, and Ibn Sīnā located the fundamental difference between male and female bodies in their complexions: males were hot and dry and females cold and wet. Despite this difference, however, men's and women's sexual physiologies were analogous, in that both sexes secreted seed, the release of which was accompanied by pleasure. Both male and female seed were required for generation. In the words of al-Majūsī, citing both Galen and Hippocrates, "the fetus is completely formed only by the mixing of the man's seed with that of the woman and subsequently nourished, during gestation, by the mother's menstrual blood."[7] In addition to its role in generation, the regular emission of seed by men and women was thought to have important health benefits by evacuating the harmful by-products of digestion—an idea Galen shared with Hippocrates and Soranus. This function was particularly important for women, whose digestion was impeded by their cool, moist complexions and who therefore required an additional outlet in the form of regular menstruation, while most men, owing to their hotter temperament, required no more than the usual daily excretions supplemented by the slow growth of hair and nails. In contrast, women who did not emit seed or menstruate risked the potentially fatal illness of uterine suffocation, where noxious vapors from digestive wastes and, even more dangerous, putrefying seed spread inside the body, attacking the brain and other organs, or even forcing the uterus out of its natural place. (This last was a point on which al-Majūsī and Ibn Sīnā differed from Galen, who had rejected the Hippocratic notion of the wandering womb on anatomical grounds.) Remedies prescribed for suffocation included remedies to bring on the menses (in the case of women of childbearing age), coitus, and masturbation by a midwife. Lovesickness, an analogous condition primarily associated with men and caused by what Ibn al-Jazzār described as "an intense natural need to expel a great excess of humors," could likewise be remedied by coitus.

These views had important corollaries for learned understandings of gender and sexuality. For one thing, the emission of female seed was essential for fertility. As a result, physicians were legitimately concerned to enhance female pleasure in coitus and might recommend remedies such as extended foreplay and masturbation by a midwife, intended to help the woman ejaculate. These recommendations reflect a generally positive view of human sexuality in medieval Islamic culture, which understood sexual intercourse as part of divine creation, good in itself, not merely for reproduction and health. In the words of Abū Muḥammad ibn Qutayba, a ninth-century philologist and master of the *hadith* (authoritative reports of the words of Muhammad), one legitimate function of sex is "attaining pleasure and enjoying God's bounty." This principle applied to both sexes, and women could petition for divorce on the basis of sexual incompatibility. Indeed, Ibn Qutayba noted, sexual pleasure "is the benefit that is experienced in paradise where there is no procreation and no congestion to be drained." In medicine, these values found expression in medical treatises on sexual hygiene, which emphasized the importance of sexual pleasure for health and happiness and gave specific recommendations for positions, practices, and medications that would enhance both partners' sexual enjoyment.[8]

Muslim views concerning the importance of sexual pleasure and the role of male and female seed in procreation were reflected in a relatively accepting attitude toward birth control. Abortion was controversial among physicians, because it violated the Hippocratic oath. It was not prohibited by Islamic law, however, and abortifacients were easily procured from pharmacists. The use of contraceptives was widely accepted, not least because, since conception required the uniting of male and female seed, neither of these two substances counted for much on its own; thus preventing them from mingling could do little harm. This attitude, which contrasted with the biblical prohibitions on the spilling of male seed that influenced medieval Christian and, especially, Jewish views, meant that masturbation might be viewed as permissible under certain circumstances, such as while the woman was menstruating. (All three religions prohibited sex during menstruation, albeit to greatly differing degrees.)

The Muslim theologian and philosopher, Abū Ḥāmid al-Ghazālī (d.1111, Algazel in Latin) made a strong case for the lawfulness of coitus interruptus as a form of birth control.[9] Many medical treatises also included lists of contraceptive prescriptions in the form of penile ointments, vaginal pessaries, and occasionally oral medicines or amulets. Similar preparations might be used to bring on menstruation, in the case of women suffering from menstrual retention, or to abort fetuses in the uncontroversial case of women who could not bear children without endangering their own health. Muslim authors differed in the enthusiasm with which they recommended such measures but not, apparently, on religious grounds; for example, while Ibn Sīnā had few qualms about women's use of contraceptives and emmenagogues, al-Majūsī feared that they might be used to hide the results of extra-marital affairs.[10]

Finally, some learned physicians discussed same-sex sexual practices in naturalistic terms. The conceptual framework that shaped these discussions differed from the modern western category of homosexuality. Arabic medical writers focused not on same-sex desire but on gendered roles in intercourse: men were by nature penetrators and women, penetrated. While Islamic law prohibited anal sex, particularly with adult men, boys' cooler, more female complexions and presumably receptive role made the practice more "natural," meaning that men's desire for boys was more likely to be seen as a moral and religious transgression rather than a physical flaw. In contrast, some (thought not all) physicians used the language of illness to refer to men who wished to be anally penetrated. In his treatise on the "hidden illness," for example, the ninth-century Persian physician Muḥammad ibn Zakariyā al-Rāzī (Razes or Rhazes in Latin) described this as a chronic condition, *ubnah*, which he ascribed to men on the feminine end of the complexional spectrum; because their penis and testicles are not fully extruded, he argued, the secretion of seed creates a tickling effect in the rectum, which is pleasurable when scratched. He recommended treating the resulting disposition to passive anal sex by drugs, diet, massage, and baths to heat and draw down the genitals, or by suppositories and enemas to cool the hind parts.[11] At least one physician gave a complexional explanation to the corresponding inclination in women—a desire to rub their genitals against those of other women—attributing it to an excess of heat and attendant itching in the labia, which could be alleviated by the emission of cool female seed.[12] This kind of sexual activity between women, unlike that between men, drew little medical or moral attention, given the focus on penetration as the essence of the sexual act, and was in fact seen as a potentially beneficial way to evacuate harmful excess seed.

It is important not to minimize the differences among Arabic writers on sex, gender, and sexuality. As Sherry Gadelrab has shown, the field was characterized by pluralism and complexity, reflecting the availability in Arabic of sometimes contradictory Greek works, as well as the coexistence of competing learned discourses, theological, legal, and medical or natural philosophical. And medical and natural philosophical theory did not always agree, not least on the key issue of women's contribution to generation, which underpinned efforts to naturalize a wide range of ideas and practices relating to gender roles. Invoking the existence of "female testicles" (which we would call ovaries), Galen had presented male and female seed as analogous in nature and function, contradicting Aristotle, the principal authority for natural philosophers, who had identified female seed with the menses and insisted on its purely passive and material role in generation: "the female always provides the material," he wrote in *Generation of Animals*, while "the male provides that which fashions the material into shape [i.e., the form, life principle, or soul]; this, in our view, is the specific characteristic of each of the sexes: that is what it means to be male or female...." Unlike Galen, Aristotle described men's and women's bodies as contraries, where the latter were defined by passivity and privation as failed versions of the former. Respectful of both Greek authorities, many Arabic medical writers attempted to reconcile these contrasting views. Ibn Sīnā's position was particularly influential. In his *Canon*, written for medical practitioners, who, he pointed out, had no need to understand the finer points of human physiology, he endorsed female seed and female sexual pleasure as essential to conception; in contrast, in his compendium of natural philosophy, *al-Shifā* (*Healing*), he followed Aristotle, describing female seed as a more digested form of menstrual blood, "fit to be matter and not the principle of movement."[13]

This tension between Aristotelian and Galenic positions on female seed persisted over the course of the later Middle Ages, with authors on the whole inclined to find a middle way between them, not least because, pace Aristotle, several much-quoted *hadiths* described male and female seed as equally necessary for generation, and necessary in the same ways.[14] The main outlier in this respect was the Andalusian scholar Al-Walīd Muḥammad ibn Rushd (1126–1198, Averroes in Latin), who adopted a strict Aristotelian position on sex difference and generation in his *al-Kulliyāt fī al-ṭibb* ("Generalities of Medicine," *Colliget* in Latin). Unlike Ibn Sīnā and most other Muslim writers, Ibn Rushd insisted that since women did not secrete seed except in the form of menstrual blood, they could conceive without orgasm, citing as proof the testimony of several women, including a neighbor who claimed to have become pregnant while bathing in water in which men had previously ejaculated.[15] While Ibn Rushd's stance on female passivity in generation had little impact on Muslim medical and natural philosophical writers, his work had much greater influence on Jewish and Christian scholars in the later Middle Ages, as it resonated with some of the more misogynist elements in both religious traditions.

Throughout the medieval period, Jewish scholars living in Muslim territories subscribed to many of the views concerning sex difference that informed Islamic medical and natural philosophical writing, while occasionally introducing variations characteristic of their faith. For example, the tension between Galenic and Aristotelian positions on women's role in generation found in the work of Ibn Sina also marked that of Maimonides (1135–1204, Mūsā ibn Maymun in Arabic, Moshe ben Maimon or Rambam in Hebrew), one of the greatest Jewish scholars of the Islamicate world; Maimonides trained and practiced as a physician but, like his Muslim compatriot Ibn Rushd, was also influenced by the strong tradition of Aristotelian studies in Cordoba. The view that women, like men, produced seed that actively contributed to generation was strongly endorsed by biblical and Midrashic testimonies, as well as by Islamic *hadiths*,[16] which made it natural for Maimonides to follow the general strategy laid out by Ibn Sina, adopting the Galenic position in his medical encyclopedia *Kitāb al-Fuṣūl* (*Book of Aphorisms*), while arguing along Aristotelian lines in his philosophical and theological treatise *Dalalat al-ha'irin* (*Guide for the Perplexed*). However, his caustic remarks in the latter go far beyond Ibn Sīnā's naturalistic *al-Shifa* in emphasizing women's moral inferiority, passivity, and "essential otherness from men."[17] In the *Guide*, Maimonides also used the Aristotelian association of men with form and women with matter to reinforce that idea that women, like matter, were inherently promiscuous and that God had therefore conferred on men, who represented the "very noble" formal principle in generation, "power, rule, and dominion" over them.[18]

On the matter of menstruation, however, Maimonides's Galenism seems to have pushed him toward a relatively moderate interpretation of Jewish law, which, as Baskin describes,[19] treated the menses as a potent source of ritual pollution rather than a natural process essential to women's health. At the same time, one of his medical aphorisms explained how to differentiate the menses from other forms of vaginal discharge; this would have helped Jewish physicians and their patients determine when to apply the laws that interdicted all physical contact between men and menstruating women (*niddah*, meaning "separated"), whose pollution encompassed not only their entire bodies but also everything with which they came in physical contact. Other Jewish writers adduced Aristotelian arguments to naturalize more stringent versions of the taboo, explaining that menstrual pollution, like a contagious illness, might extend beyond the *niddah*'s body, requiring men to avoid not only any form of touch, as Maimonides required, but also eye contact and physical proximity. In his Hebrew polemic *Magen avot* (*Shield of the Fathers*), for example, the Majorcan physician Simon ben Zemah Duran (1361–1444), later chief rabbi of Algiers, explained that the eyes of the *niddah* emit a haze of bloody vapor into the surrounding air, so that "when a woman looks at herself in a mirror at the beginning of her period, you can see on it drops of blood, as is mentioned in [Aristotle's] *On Sleep and Waking*."[20]

A starker set of tensions between Jewish religious law and Islamic medical tradition is reflected in Jewish writing relating to contraception. While Muslim physicians embraced birth control and tolerated abortion under certain circumstances, Jewish medical writers faced scriptural obstacles to both in the biblical commandment to be fruitful and multiply, and the harsh condemnation in Genesis 38:10 of Onan's use of coitus interruptus, the primary form of birth control practiced in the Islamicate world. Where Jewish law did permit birth control, as in the case of women with medical conditions that contraindicated pregnancy and childbirth, other methods were advised, such as ointments and pessaries, while abortion was not endorsed under any circumstances. Paradoxically, the lack of a parallel prohibition regarding female seed, together with the restriction of the duty of procreation to men, meant that female masturbation and same-sex relations among women did not in fact violate religious law, although such behavior was discouraged as a moral vice.[21]

SEX, GENDER, AND GENERATION IN WESTERN EUROPE: HEBREW AND LATIN TRADITIONS, 1150–1450

The intellectual situation was more complicated in western Europe than in the Islamicate world, where Jews and Muslims shared a common language for medical and scientific discourse and a common set of authoritative texts, both ancient and contemporary. In Christian Europe, however, Christian scholars continued to write in Latin, while Jewish scholars in Spain, Italy, and Provence increasingly adopted Hebrew, previously used almost exclusively in religious contexts, as a language for scientific discourse. The Hebrew corpus of writing on women and gender is particularly complex, as its compilers worked to absorb materials from both Latin and Arabic; this required the creation of a technical vocabulary that had not previously existed in Hebrew and adjustment of the contents of both traditions to Jewish religious doctrine and sensibilities.

Both processes are evident in the *Sefer ha-Toledet* (*Book of Generation*), the most widely copied Hebrew work on gynecology, which was one of twenty-four medical texts—Hippocratic, Galenic, and Soranic—translated from Latin to Hebrew in the late twelfth century by an unknown scholar, probably in Provence. The Hebrew author based the *Book of Generation* on Muscio's sixth-century adaptation of Soranus's *Gynaikeia*—discussed in the first part of this essay—recasting it as a dialogue between the biblical Dinah and her father Jacob (cf. Genesis 34); this begins with a long lament in which Dinah rues her illness and infertility in words that echo the Talmudic tractate on *niddah* and combine Galenic medical doctrine ("cold and moisture rule me and every breeze bothers my functions") with biblical imagery ("the field of my body is ravaged, the earth wasted, without grain or sprout or grass for the work of man"). Dinah's father then instructs her on women's health, fertility, and childbirth, following the Soranic text with a few key alterations: the Hebrew translator omitted passages explaining that women who do not menstruate can be healthy and that pregnancy is unhealthy, and moderated a sentence praising perpetual virginity. In this way, a treatise that in early medieval Christian hands could be used to detach women's health from the cycle of procreative sexuality was recast to reinsert women into a familial and generative framework.[22]

Among Latin scholars, in contrast, the Soranic tradition was swamped over the course of the late eleventh and twelfth centuries by Arabic Galenism as represented in al-Majūsī's *Pantegni* and Ibn al-Jazzār's *Viaticum*, which were translated into Latin at the Italian monastery of Monte Cassino together with other Arabic medical treatises imported from his native North Africa by Constantinus Africanus (1017–1087) and circulated under his name. These works gave Latin scholars access to the core Galenic teachings concerning the gendered body: (1) women and men differ by virtue of their complexions (cold and wet, hot and dry respectively), which results in physiological differences; (2) both women and men produce seed necessary for generation and cannot conceive without pleasure; (3) in order to avoid serious illness, most notably suffocation of the uterus, women of childbearing age require regular menstruation and emission of seed; (4) the physician's duties include dispensing advice about how to bring a woman to orgasm when pregnancy is desired, how to prevent conception when it is not, and how to treat a wide range of women's illnesses, including amenorrhea and suffocation of the uterus as a result of celibacy or virginity.

Some of these ideas sat uneasily with Christian sensibilities. Although the learned Christian culture of twelfth-century Europe, increasingly located in courts and urban schools, was less monastic and less dominated by the ideal of virginity than in the early Middle Ages, sexual continence was still central to medieval Christian doctrine, in which the Fall was understood in sexual terms. The human propensity to lust was particularly associated with the daughters of Eve and reflected in menstruation, "a specifically womanly mark of the Fall."[23] Because the only justification for sexual activity was procreation (in contrast to Islamic and Jewish teachings, which stressed its social and affective functions), the Church condemned all non-procreative behaviors, resulting in a long tradition of ecclesiastical provisions against abortion and contraception; the latter went well beyond Jewish concerns regarding the spilling of male seed. These prohibitions found remarkably little purchase in eleventh- and twelfth-century Latin medical works based on Arabic originals, which hewed closely to the naturalizing approach of Arabic Galenism. While Constantinus Africanus, working in a monastic setting, tacitly suppressed Ibn al-Jazzār's chapter on abortifacients (though not his discussion of contraceptives) when he translated the *Viaticum*, most Latin Christian writers, as Monica Green has shown, adopted the Galenic view that fertility control was an integral part of women's health care.[24]

Menstruation, too, was largely detached from discourses of sin and pollution in Latin medical works based on the Constantinian translations, such as the much-copied *De sinthomatibus mulierum* (*On the Conditions of Women*) produced in Salerno, an important center of medical instruction. Although the author framed his discussion of sex difference with a clear reference to the creation of Adam and Eve, he made no reference to the Fall; rather, he attributed the complexional difference between men and women to God's concern for symmetry and treated generation as part of the divine plan for creation rather than the result of human sin. Menstruation, too, reflected God's providence rather than his wrath: established to "temper [women's] poverty of heat," the menses are necessary for fertility—hence their vernacular characterization as "flowers," forerunners of fruit—and, like men's nocturnal emissions, form part of the self-regulatory system of the human body.[25] Nonetheless, women's cold, wet nature means that they are "by nature weaker than men" and more subject to illness, particularly "around the organs devoted to the work of Nature," i.e., generation.

The same naturalizing impulse shaped the works of twelfth-century natural philosophers, who found in the Constantinian texts a powerful conceptual system for explaining natural phenomena of all sorts, including sex difference. Particularly influential was the *Dragmaticon philosophie* (*Philosophical Dialogue*, *c*.1148) of William of Conches, cast as a discussion between a "philosopher" and William's patron, the "Duke of Normandy and Count of Anjou." William prefaced the section on humankind with four chapters on sex and generation, which bear the unmistakable imprint of al-Majūsī's *Pantegni*. He strongly endorsed the importance of female seed and female pleasure in generation, using this principle to explain why prostitutes rarely conceive (they experience little enjoyment during intercourse with their clients) and, conversely, why women who take pleasure in sex with their husbands are sometimes infertile (they suffer from defects in the constitution of the womb or the complexion of the male or female seed). Even within this Galenic framework, however, there are traces of the Christian suspicion of female sexuality. To the Duke's objection that women who have been raped have been known to conceive "despite their protest and weeping," the Philosopher replies that "although...a raped woman does not assent with her rational will, she does have carnal pleasure."[26] This jarring claim, which harkens back to a passage in Soranus rather than al-Majūsī, reflects the persistent Christian association of women with sexual intemperance and danger, as does the Duke's claim, endorsed by the Philosopher, that a woman not herself infected by sex with a "leprous man" can nevertheless infect subsequent male partners (6.8). Not all twelfth-century writers took these new ideas in the same direction, however: the German abbess Hildegard of Bingen (1098–1179) used them to elaborate an idiosyncratic discussion of sex difference that avoided many of the tropes of Christian misogyny.[27]

At the same time, however, Hildegard rejected the existence of female seed, denying women an active role in generation. While unusual in the twelfth century, this notion gained currency over the course of the thirteenth and fourteenth centuries with the ongoing assimilation of the works of Aristotle and Arabic writers influenced by him, above all Ibn Rushd. Latin medical writers followed Ibn Sīnā's attempts in the *Canon* to reconcile Galen's endorsement of female seed with Aristotle's rejection of it, while stressing women's passivity in generation. Natural philosophers inclined to the one-seed position with very little demur.[28] This increasing emphasis on the asymmetry of male and female contributions to generation fostered an emphasis on female moral and physiological inferiority, in line with Aristotle's description of females as defective males.[29] Among the implications of this position, as Ibn Rushd had argued in the *Colliget*, was that women may conceive without pleasure; on this view, the question of how raped women may become pregnant, which puzzled the Duke in William of Conches's *Dragmaticon*, completely disappears. In fact, if female pleasure is unnecessary for conception, women's notorious appetite for sexual enjoyment, previously naturalized as essential for fertility and health, becomes a manifestation of willfulness and perversity.

The growing prominence of misogynistic themes in Latin writing on women's bodies among physicians and, especially, natural philosophers reflects a change in the character of learned discourse, increasingly centered in universities and in schools associated with the Dominican Order and, except in Italy, dominated by male clerical elites. Latin discussions of the inferiority of women's bodies focused not only on their passivity but also on the nature of the menses themselves. Harking back to Pliny and Aristotle, learned writers began to describe these as literally toxic: intercourse with a menstruating woman may harm her male partner and resulting offspring, and post-menopausal women, who lose the ability to purge this poison, may emit toxic vapors capable of killing young children. In the influential and notoriously misogynistic *De secretis mulierum* (*On the Secrets of Women*, late thirteenth century), for example, the author invoked Aristotle's passage on the spotted mirror, explaining that the retained menses "first infect the eyes, then the eyes infect the air, which infects the child."[30]

Late medieval Christian scholars' increasing reluctance to attribute generative agency to female seed, together with their concern to give a naturalistic explanation for the polluting nature of the menses, echo the views of their Jewish counterparts, such as Simon Duran in his *Magen avot*, discussed above. This raises the interesting question of interactions between the two communities and in which direction the predominant influence flowed—a topic that deserves more exploration.[31] Alternatively, the two traditions might have arrived at similar conclusions through their shared biblical heritage, compounded by the growing influence of Aristotle's *Generation of Animals* and of his interpreter Ibn Rushd's *Colliget*, which had been translated into both Hebrew and Latin in the thirteenth century.

While Christian medical writers were less inclined than natural philosophical ones to expressions of outright misogyny, one finds in their works as well an increasing tendency to intersperse moralistic judgments with naturalistic explanations, particularly on sexual topics. In contrast, Latin medical writers, like their Arabic predecessors, continued to view non-procreative sexual practices such as masturbation and contraception as sometimes permissible and necessary in the context of women's health care, but they were increasingly uneasy about same-sex sexual acts, especially among men. They never invoked the theological and legal category of sodomy;[32] this was not part of the medical tradition or of medical discourse. Rather, they either passed over the question of same-sex sexual desire in silence or identified it, following Ibn Sīnā, as a moral rather than a medical issue, better treated by punishment than by therapy. Exceptionally, Pietro d'Abano, an early fourteenth-century Italian master of medicine, also embraced a natural explanation of the inclination to passive anal sex, attributing it, like al-Rāzī, to a genital anomaly that rendered the anus rather than the penis sensitive to stimulation, but even he qualified the resulting behaviors as "filthy," "perverse," and "wicked."[33]

A "ONE-SEX BODY"?

In describing medieval scientific accounts of sex, generation, and sexuality, I have avoided alluding to the "one-sex body," the phrase Thomas Laqueur invented to characterize what he described as the dominant model of sex difference in the period covered by this essay (and well beyond). By this he meant the idea, laid out in Galen's *On the Use of Parts*, that "women were essentially men in whom a lack of vital heat—of perfection— had resulted in the retention, inside, of structures that in the male are visible without…. In this world the vagina is imagined as an interior penis, the labia as foreskin, the uterus as scrotum, and the ovaries as testicles." Furthermore, according to Laqueur (though not to Galen in this work or elsewhere), because sex difference depends ultimately on complexional heat, women can in fact turn into men if something causes their bodies to become hotter, turning their genitals inside out.[34]

In fact, as this essay demonstrates, the story was much more complicated. As Laqueur's invocation of *On the Use of Parts* implies, his "one-sex" model was at its core Galenic; thus its presence or absence depends largely on the currency of Galenic ideas and the availability of key Galenic texts, notably *On the Use of Parts*, which was by no means ubiquitous. Unsurprisingly, the model does not figure at all in early medieval Latin writing on sex difference, which was dominated by the influence of Soranus and lacked both anatomical specificity and a theoretical substructure based on the complexions and the humors. In contrast, it found clear expression where the Galenic tradition was most highly developed, in the works of Greek and Arabic writers of the Eastern Mediterranean and Islamicate world. Al-Rāzī sketched its major tenets in his treatise *On the Hidden Illness*. Indeed, his prescriptions for heating and drawing down the genitals of men afflicted with *ubnah*, the disposition to passive anal sex, imply the possibility of a dilute form of sex transformation, where a feminized male may be made more masculine with the assistance of his physician. This idea appears more fully in the *Canon* of Ibn Sīnā, who laid out the Galenic homologies between the male and female genitals in detail and described a condition in which an increase in complexional heat caused a part of the female genitals (likely the clitoris) to grow spontaneously into something like a penis—a condition for which he recommended surgical excision.[35] Significantly, however, this theory was never hegemonic even in Arabic Galenism: following Galen's *Anatomy of the Uterus* rather than *On the Use of Parts*, al-Majūsī compared the uterus to the bladder, not the scrotum, while the thirteenth-century Syrian physician Ibn al-Nafis rejected the genital homologies altogether. The uterus does not resemble the scrotum, he wrote, and Galen's inside-out model of the female genitals would place women's testes (our ovaries) *inside* their wombs; in fact, he argued, the uterus, which accommodates the fetus, has no male analogue.[36]

More to the point, since Laqueur's book focuses on the western tradition, the reception of these Galenic ideas by Latin and Hebrew writers was very patchy. More striking was the imperviousness of most European medical authors to the homologies between the male and female genitals, despite the centrality of Ibn Sīnā's *Canon* to the contemporary medical curriculum. The homologies appear in passing in a handful of texts, mostly surgical, where they were probably intended to help students of surgery visualize the anatomy involved. In works of internal medicine, however, accounts of sexed anatomy never mentioned the homologies, let alone spontaneous or medically assisted sex transformation. Rather, Latin writing on women's bodies emphasized aspects of female reproductive physiology and anatomy with no male equivalents: pregnancy, menstruation, and the characteristically female illness of uterine suffocation. The first full and clear Latin expressions of the elements that make up Laqueur's "one-sex" body appeared only at the very end of the fifteenth century, when Galen's *On the Use of Parts*, virtually unknown in medieval Europe, began to be widely read, cited, and eventually printed for the first time.[37] This development, however, is part of a later, simpler story, related to the revival of classical studies associated with the intellectual movement of Renaissance humanism. In contrast, the history of medical and natural philosophical thought in the Middle Ages, Latin, Arabic, and Hebrew, is far longer, more complex, and episodic. And while Laqueur's conviction concerning the ideological constructedness of scientific writing on sex difference, modern as well as medieval, is undoubtedly correct, his model of the "one-sex" body collapses chronologies, confuses textual traditions, and ignores problems of transmission in ways that obscure the richness and diversity of medieval writing on sex and gender.

FURTHER READING

Barkaï, Ron. *Les infortunes de Dinah; ou, la gynécologie juive au Moyen Age*. Paris: Editions du Cerf, 1991.

Barkaï, Ron. *A History of Jewish Gynecological Texts in the Middle Ages*. Leiden: Brill, 1998.

Caballero-Navas, Carmen. "Medicine and Pharmacy for Women: The Encounter of Jewish Thinking and Practices with the Arabic and Christian Medical Traditions." *European Review*, 16 (2) (May 2008): 249–59.

Cadden, Joan. *Meanings of Sex Difference in the Middle Ages: Medicine, Science and Culture*. Cambridge: Cambridge University Press, 1993.

Gadelrab, Sherry Sayed. "Discourses on Sex Differences in Medieval Scholarly Islamic Thought." *Journal of the History of Medicine and Allied Sciences*, 66 (1) (January 2011): 40–81.

Green, Monica H., ed. and trans. *The Trotula: A Medieval Compendium of Women's Medicine*. Philadelphia: University of Pennsylvania Press, 2001.

Green, Monica H. *Making Women's Medicine Masculine: The Rise of Male Authority in Pre-Modern Gynecology*. Oxford: Oxford University Press, 2008.

Jacquart, Danielle, and Claude Thomasset. *Sexuality and Medicine in the Middle Ages*. Trans. Matthew Adamson. Princeton: Princeton University Press, 1988.

Musallam, Basim. *Sex and Society in Islam: Birth Control Before the Nineteenth Century*. Cambridge: Cambridge University Press, 1983.

Park, Katharine. "Cadden, Laqueur, and the 'One-Sex Body.'" *Medieval Feminist Forum (MFF)*, 46 (1) (2010): 96–100; available online at <http://ir.uiowa.edu/mff/vol46/iss1/>, accessed 30 November 2012.

NOTES

1. Isidore of Seville, *Etymologiarum sive originum libri XX*, 11.2.19, ed. W. M. Lindsay, 2 vols (Oxford: Clarendon Press, 1911), vol. 2.
2. See Joan Cadden, *Meanings of Sex Difference in the Middle Ages: Medicine, Science and Culture* (Cambridge: Cambridge University Press, 1993), 13–39.
3. Muscio, 1.26–30; 2.8–9, in Valentin Rose, ed., *Sorani Gynaeciorum vetus translatio latina . . .* (Leipzig: B. G. Teubner, 1882), 12–13 and 49–50.
4. Monica H. Green, *Making Women's Medicine Masculine: The Rise of Male Authority in Pre-Modern Gynecology* (Oxford: Oxford University Press, 2008), 35.
5. Linda L. Coon, *Dark Age Bodies: Gender and Monastic Practice in the Early Medieval West* (Philadelphia: University of Pennsylvania Press, 2011), 235; Peter Brown, *Body and*

Society: Men, Women, and Sexual Renunciation in Early Christianity (New York: Columbia University Press, 1988), epilogue.

6. Overview in Sherry Sayed Gadelrab, "Discourses on Sex Differences in Medieval Scholarly Islamic Thought," *Journal of the History of Medicine and Allied Sciences*, 66 (1) (January 2010), 40–81; Danielle Jacquart and Claude Thomasset, *Sexuality and Medicine in the Middle Ages*, trans. Matthew Adamson (Princeton: Princeton University Press, 1988) discusses both Arabic and Latin traditions. I am grateful to Ahmed Ragab for his help with Arabic materials.

7. Al-Majūsī, *Kitāb al-Kāmil*, 1.3.34, in Pieter de Koning, trans., *Trois traités d'anatomie arabes*, ed. Fuat Sezgin (Frankfurt am Main: Institut für Geschichte der arabisch-islamischen Wissenschaften an der Johann Wolfgang Goethe Universität, 1986), 393–94.

8. Ibn Sīnā, *Liber canonis* (Venice, 1507; rpt. Hildesheim: G. Olms, 1964), 3.20.2.44, fol. 358r; 3.21.1.9, fol. 363v–64r; Ahmed Dallal, "Sexualities: Scientific Discourses, Premodern," in Fuad Joseph et al., eds, *Encyclopedia of Women and Islamic Cultures*, 6 vols (Leiden: Brill, 2003–2007), vol. 3: *Family, Body, Sexuality, and Health*, 405 (quotations from Ibn Qutayba). See in general Jacquart and Thomasset, *Sexuality and Medicine*, 122–28; and Basim Musallam, *Sex and Society in Islam: Birth Control Before the Nineteenth Century* (Cambridge: Cambridge University Press, 1983).

9. Abū Ḥāmid al-Ghazālī, *Marriage and Sexuality in Islam: A Translation of al-Ghazali's Book on the Etiquette of Marriage from the Iḥya*, trans. Madelain Farah (Salt Lake City, Ut.: University of Utah Press, 1984), 108–10.

10. Al-Majūsī, *Kitāb al-Kāmil*, 2.8.28; see in general Musallam, *Sex and Society*, ch. 4 (quotation on 70).

11. Franz Rosenthal, "Ar-Razi on the Hidden Illness," *Bulletin of the History of Medicine*, 52 (1978): 45–60 (quotation on 56). See in general Khaled El-Rouayheb, *Before Homosexuality in the Arab-Islamic World, 1500–1800* (Chicago: University of Chicago Press, 2005), esp. introduction and ch. 1.

12. Saher Amer, "Medieval Arab Lesbians and Lesbian-Like Women," *Journal of the History of Sexuality*, 18 (2) (May 2009), 215–17.

13. Aristotle, *Generation of Animals*, 738b20–24, trans. A. L. Peck (Cambridge, Mass.: Harvard University Press, 1979), 185. On this debate, see Gadelrab, "Sex Differences," 66–67; and Musallam, *Sex and Society*, ch. 3 (quotation from Ibn Sina on p. 48).

14. Musallam, *Sex and Society*, 50–53.

15. Ibn Rushd, *Colliget*, 2.10, in *Abhomeron Abynzohar. Colliget Auerroys* (Venice: Gregorius de Gregoriis, 1514). See Gerrit Bos and Resianne Fontaine, "Medico-Philosophical Controversies in Nathan b. Yo'el Falaquera's 'Sefer Sori ha-Guf,'" *The Jewish Quarterly Review*, n.s., 90 (1/2) (July–October 1999), 54–56.

16. Pieter Willem van der Horst, "Sarah's Seminal Emission: Hebrews 11:11 in the Light of Ancient Embryology," in David L. Balch, Everett Ferguson, and Wayne A. Meeks, eds, *Greeks, Romans, and Christians* (Minneapolis: Fortress Press, 1990), 287–302.

17. As Judith Baskin notes in "Jewish Traditions about Women and Gender Roles: From Rabbinic Teachings to Medieval Practice," Chapter 3 in this volume.

18. Moses Maimonides, *The Medical Aphorisms of Moses Maimonides*, 16.10 and 17, trans. Fred Rosner and Suessman Muntner, 2 vols (New York: Yeshiva University Press, 1970–1971), vol. 2, 34–36; Moses Maimonides, *Guide for the Perplexed*, 3.8, trans. M. Friedländer (New York: Dover, 1956), 261–64. See in general Carmen Caballero-Navas, "Maimonides' Contribution to Women's Healthcare and his Influence on the Hebrew Gynaecological

Corpus," in Carlos Fraenkel, ed., *Traditions of Maimonideanism* (Leiden: Brill, 2009), 37–41; and Ron Barkaï, *Les infortunes de Dinah; ou, la gynécologie juive au Moyen Age* (Paris: Les Editions du Cerf, 1991).

19. See note 17.

20. Simon ben Zemah Duran, *Magen avot*, trans. Henri Jahier and A. Fingerhuth, "Extrait du *Maguen Aboth*, le 'Bouclier des Pères,'" *Revue d'histoire de la medicine hébraique*, 28 (October 1955), 193. The passage appears in Aristotle's *On Dreams* (459b24–460a23).

21. Barkaï, *Infortunes de Dinah*, 68 and 92–94; Carmen Caballero-Navas, "Medicine and Pharmacy for Women: The Encounter of Jewish Thinking and Practice with the Arabic and Christian Medical Traditions," *European Review*, 16 (2) (2008), 256–57.

22. *Sefer ha-Toledet*, trans. Michel Garel, in Barkaï, *Infortunes de Dinah*, 129–223 (quotations on 130 and 137). See in general Ron Barkaï, *A History of Jewish Gynecological Texts in the Middle Ages* (Leiden; New York: Brill, 1998), ch. 1.

23. Cadden, *Meanings of Sex Difference*, 174.

24. Monica H. Green, "Constantinus Africanus and the Conflict Between Science and Religion," in G. R. Dunstan, ed., *The Human Embryo: Aristotle and the Arabic and European Traditions* (Exeter: Exeter University Press, 1990), 47–69.

25. *De sinthomatibus mulierum*, trans. Monica H. Green, in Monica H. Green, ed. and trans., *The Trotula: A Medieval Compendium of Women's Medicine* (Philadelphia: University of Pennsylvania Press, 2001), introduction and 72–73 (quotation).

26. William of Conches, *Dragmaticon philosophiae*, 6.7, in *William of Conches: A Dialogue on Natural Philosophy (Dragmaticon philosophiae)*, trans. Italo Ronca and Matthew Curr (Notre Dame, Ind.: University of Notre Dame Press, 1997), 137–38 (quotation). See Cadden, *Meanings of Sex Difference*, ch. 2, esp. 95–96. Cf. Caelius Aurelianus, *Gynaecia*, 1.48.

27. Cadden, *Meanings of Sex Difference*, 70–88, esp. 78.

28. Nancy G. Siraisi, *Taddeo Alderotti and His Pupils: Two Generations of Italian Medical Learning* (Princeton: Princeton University Press, 1981), 195–201.

29. Cadden, *Meanings of Sex Difference*, ch. 3; Jacquart and Thomasset, *Sexuality and Medicine*, 65–70.

30. Fernando Salmon and Montserrat Cabré, "Fascinating Women: The Evil Eye in Medical Scholasticism," in Roger French et al., eds, *Medicine from the Black Death to the French Disease* (Aldershot: Ashgate Press, 1998), 53–84. On the *Secrets of Women* tradition, see Green, *Making Women's Medicine*, ch. 5.

31. *Sefer ha-Toledet*, trans. Michel Garel, in Barkaï, *Infortunes de Dinah*, 51n.–52n.

32. Discussed by Helmut Puff in "Same-Sex Possibilities," Chapter 24 in this volume.

33. Joan Cadden, "'Nothing Natural Is Shameful': Vestiges of a Debate about Sex and Science in a Group of Late-Medieval Manuscripts," *Speculum*, 76 (1) (January 2001): 66–89. See also Jacquart and Thomasset, *Sexuality and Medicine*, ch. 5.

34. Thomas Laqueur, *Making Sex: Body and Gender from the Greeks to Freud* (Cambridge, Mass.: Harvard University Press, 1990), 5 (quotation) and 124–30.

35. Ibn Sīnā, *al-Qānūn*, 3.21.1.1, in de Koning, *Trois traités*, 746.

36. Al-Majūsī, *Kitāb al-Kāmil*, 1.3.33, in de Koning, *Trois traités*, 387–89; Gadelrab, "Discourses," 72–75.

37. Katharine Park, "Cadden, Laqueur, and the 'One-Sex Body,'" *Medieval Feminist Forum (MFF)*, 46 (1) (2010): 96–100; available online at <http://ir.uiowa.edu/mff/vol46/iss1/>; Katharine Park, "Itineraries of the 'One-Sex Body': A History of an Idea" (in preparation).

PART II

LOOKING THROUGH THE LAW

CHAPTER 7

··

WOMEN AND LAWS IN EARLY MEDIEVAL EUROPE

··

JANET L. NELSON AND ALICE RIO

In "The Power of Women Through the Family, 500–1100," Jo Ann McNamara and Suzanne Wemple claimed they would "rely heavily on the Germanic codes to chart the changes that occurred in the early Middle Ages."[1] This (selective) reliance led them to conclude that "by the mid-eighth century...the private rights of women to the control of property had been established, giving them, as daughters, sisters, mothers, and wives, a position of economic equality within the family." Generalizing across 500–1100, McNamara and Wemple pointed to allegedly women-friendly legal trends visible in women's increasing capacity to inherit, to receive dower from husbands, and to manage their own property in "an age when private power was almost synonymous with public power." McNamara and Wemple's upbeat thesis and their briefly sketched antithesis of women's worsening position after c.1100 typify larger narratives of golden age followed by decline, of agency won and lost, and private succumbing to public power, which have loomed large in the historiography of medieval women.

Complementing the rise and fall of "women's power through the family" was another big story, inspired by the work of the French historian Georges Duby, and largely based on French material. Duby argued that between the tenth century and the twelfth, changes in family structure and legal custom reinforced male lineages, making patrimonial land the basis of family power and consciousness, and, shifting the weight of marital endowment from dower to dowry, closed off daughters' inheritance rights and left women fundamentally disadvantaged vis-à-vis their earlier medieval predecessors. This narrative dominated the historiography until the 1990s, when Pauline Stafford brought into the discussion the crucial concept of life cycle, questioned the model of change in the central Middle Ages, stressed the variety of particular women's circumstances, noted the ambivalence of the church's role (at once protecting and threatening women's property rights, especially dower), and called for debate.[2]

Warily mindful of the propensity of women—and of law codes—to become the stuff of myth, we revisit notions of the family as women's refuge, and of women as possessing agency and power.[3] We focus on early medieval law codes, and ask why their prescriptions concerning women could be so diverse yet show recurrent similarities, and why they were responsive to everyday practical situations yet so ideologically loaded. Since laws about women were made and applied by men, our approach necessarily takes into account gender and power.

We see these texts, not as mirrors of reality, but still as much more than a form of discourse to be *de*coded. For early medieval western Europeans, the legal context had changed dramatically with the transfer of political control from the Roman Empire to kingdoms dominated by rulers of particular peoples able to draw on two earlier models of written laws: Roman, still in use in much of the former western Roman Empire, and Jewish, embodied in the Old Testament of the Christian Bible. Just as those laws helped define the identities of Romans and Jews, early medieval law codes helped define the identity of peoples and, increasingly during the sixth and seventh centuries, territories with settled populations. The codes of the Burgundians (517) and the Visigoths (its earliest form appearing *c*.500, with revisions down to *c*.700) incorporated much that was Roman and Christian. The western Franks were at the other extreme: settled in areas to the west of the river Meuse, they had a code, *Lex Salica* (*c*.500) whose content showed little sign of Christianity, or of Romanity, though it was in Latin and systematically organized. Between *c*.600 and *c*.800, Rhineland Franks, Lombards, Bavarians, Alemans, Thuringians, Anglo-Saxons, and other groups each acquired codes of their own. These can seem bizarrely, pointlessly, detailed: "The issues selected for legislative record sometimes seem to have been dictated by arbitrary obsession rather than rational choice."[4] Yet once Burgundian and Lombard kings had issued codes, their successors added revisions explicitly informed by real cases—what could be more practical? The clearest sign of laws' relationship to reality is the way lawmakers responded to pressures to change them according to the priorities of elite men. All law codes from this period show similar basic concerns to safeguard men's honor by both protecting and restraining women, alongside significant differences in women's valuation, or regulations over marriage, or women's access to property. What logic did they follow? How did gender play out in them?

PRICE AND VALUE

One of the primary concerns of law codes was to set compensation tariffs for injuries, in lists ranging from a severed ear to homicide. Besides the nature of the injury, the status of the victim was another important variable, and historians have long used these price lists as maps for legal and social hierarchies. It would not be unreasonable to expect them to yield insights into gender hierarchies as well. But here the evidence becomes problematic: whereas injury clauses discuss men of every kind of status, they rarely refer to women, and only in a very restricted range of situations, above all sexual assault and injury during pregnancy.

The most plausible explanation could be that laws only mentioned women specifically when their being women rather than men made a difference to the nature of the crime. The standard use of the masculine as a grammatical default, as in the standard beginning *si quis* ("if anyone…"), can be misleading: *quis* should be read as *homo* (a person), not *vir* (a man). When law codes did not mention women in their price lists, this may have been simply because there was no difference in penalty.[5] This becomes clear when one considers that women were also not identified separately as perpetrators of crime, except, once again, for specialist female crimes such as abortion or infanticide. The distinction was only made in cases in which gender happened to pose a practical problem in the application of punishment, as when the penalty for a man was castration (*PLS*, XL.11). This suggests it was absent from other clauses because all other punishments were applicable to both sexes; women, whether victims or perpetrators, were not singled out unless they constituted special cases. *Si quis* remains difficult to interpret in that it could be used in clauses which applied only to men, most obviously those relating to public office or the army, as well as in some that applied to both sexes (it was never, so far as one can tell, used to refer only to women). In order to avoid deriving an exaggerated image of gender differentiation in matters of injury or crime from this source material, it is important to understand from the start that areas of differentiation according to gender are relatively few. These areas of difference do, however, remain significant, and play a crucial part in any gendered analysis. Despite the likely general applicability of injury clauses, many lawmakers were keen to place violence done to women and violence done to men in separate spheres: this is clear from their unsympathetic treatment of women who had sustained injuries in inappropriately unfeminine contexts, such as taking part in a brawl. Some refused even to consider the possibility that women could be involved in larger-scale violence: Lombard kings ruled that women could not engage in—nor, in what later became a problematic loophole, be found legally responsible for—activities such as feuding, housebreaking, or attacking villages.[6]

Lawmakers were less ambivalent in thinking about women as victims of sexual violence, which was treated extensively across the law codes. *Raptus*, a complicated category that could include abduction as well as rape, was punished mostly as a disruption to marriage strategies, giving this offense a distinctive character (see below). Other forms of assault were usually similar across the codes, with incremental fines according to the seriousness of the offense: lifting a woman's dress above her knees; touching a finger or a hand; more expensively, an elbow; more expensively still, a breast. Some law codes show concern over assaults on women's hair: removing their headdresses or letting their hair fall to their shoulders.[7] This was sometimes punished as sexual assault, but the emphasis could also be on humiliation: Burgundian law deals in the same clause with uncovering a woman's hair before witnesses and insulting her. Uncovering a woman's hair or body could constitute a deliberate strategy of public humiliation extending to her family, as in the real case treated in Lombard law of a man who stole a woman's clothes from the riverbank while she was bathing, forcing her to return home naked. The culprit had to pay his *wergeld* (the compensation value attached to his own life) to her family, in the expectation that he would otherwise be killed in retaliation (Liutprand 135). This blurring of the lines between sexual violence and humiliation—mimicking sexual assault by act-ing out some of its motions, but with different aims—is telling in itself. Women, as we shall see in relation to marriage, were the weak link in a family's protection of its honor; attacks against them hit a family at its most vulnerable point. This is reflected in the punishment of insults aimed at women: in Salic law, calling a woman a whore was more heavily fined than any insult aimed at men (*PLS*, XXX.3).

Apart from sexual attacks, beatings during pregnancy are the other main category of physical harm to women considered in the codes ("if someone hits a pregnant woman in the belly or the back with fists or shoes," *PLS*, *Capit.* III.104.4). Contraception, abortion, and infanticide, as opposed to cases in which miscarriage was the accidental by-product of an attack, constituted a separate group of offenses, treated sometimes more harshly than unintentional termination of pregnancy, sometimes less.[8]

Compensations for homicide (*wergeld*) have received more attention from gender historians, because they discriminated more—not only between men and women, but also between different kinds of woman: in this they differed from injury, where com-pensation, as argued earlier, could be more gender-blind. This may be because homi-cides—unlike most injuries, which presumably mattered most to the victim—entailed a definitive loss for the family, so that the worth of the victim needed to be assessed more precisely.

This could make *wergelds* a promising starting point from which to explore gender hierarchy. The picture, however, is far from coherent. Women were worth sometimes less than men, sometimes more, sometimes the same. This diversity in treatment also applied in discriminating between different women. Fertility has been highlighted as the most important variable, following Salic law, long privileged as archetypical:[9]

> If someone kills a free girl before she is able to have children … 200 *solidi*. If someone kills a free woman after she has started having children … 600 *solidi*. After middle age and after she can no longer have children … 200 *solidi*. (XLI.15–17)

The importance attached to fertility in other law codes, however, is less clear. The only other codes to take age into account are Ribuarian law (12–13) and Thuringian law (48–49), both influenced by Salic law; in the Visigothic laws, age was a less gendered cat-egory, since it also made a difference to men (VIII.4.16). Others distinguished among women on the same basis as among men: according to status. Even in the Thuringian code, status trumped life cycle: although a merely free woman's value varied according to age, a noblewoman was worth 600 *solidi* regardless.

All this makes it difficult to identify any simple principle governing the impact of gen-der on *wergeld* payments. Many codes offer completely opposite answers to such basic questions as whether a virgin was more valuable than a nonvirgin, a fertile woman more valuable than a prepubescent or postmenopausal one, or even whether a man was more valuable than a woman.

It is worth considering possible reasons for this apparently random distribution. Could the societies of the different barbarian kingdoms have had so little in common in their evaluation of women's value? Possible explanations could include varying degrees of influence of Roman law, or significant demographic imbalance at the times these codes were compiled, leading to fluctuations in women's value on the marriage market. Neither of these, however, stands up to scrutiny, because there seems to be no correlation between geographical location and high or low valuations of women: the more Romanized Southern European codes are no more consistent, and Saxony and Frisia are so close geographically that it is unlikely they could have experienced very different demographic conditions, but whereas Frisian law places compensation for women on the same level as for men, Saxon law, probably compiled around the same time, doubles it.

Since these differences do not fall into any pattern, perhaps one should not insist on reading these price lists as corresponding to real, experienced hierarchies. Early medieval lawmakers, in the process of drawing up such lists, had to submit the working social and gender order of their own societies to a degree of interpretation; this was the difficult task of turning the logic of practice into the more totalizing and unforgiving logic of law.[10] In some cases, this process was relatively straightforward: lawmakers came up with similar answers when it came to determining the hierarchy governing status (free, unfree, and in-between). When it came to gender, however, their answers diverged to a surprising extent, suggesting that the practical logic of gender relations was less easily reducible to a single set of rules. It seems likely that these wildly contradictory assessments of women's value point not to huge differences in reality, but to different interpretative results caused by ambiguities in practice. And it does seem that women's place in early medieval society and family *was* a fundamentally ambiguous and conflicted one, likely to lead to very different answers (as it has among modern historians): a highly prized asset and a crucial form of symbolic capital on the one hand, but also a heavy financial burden, a liability, and a weakness in men's safeguarding of their honor. These conflicting characteristics—as both asset and burden—are evident in the two main topic categories where written law concerned itself with women: marriage and property.

Marriage

The protective streak in the laws was essentially concerned with what outsiders might do to women: most injuries are envisaged as happening "on the road." It seems clear, however, that women, then as now, were most vulnerable in the home, at the hands of their own kin. Legislators gave great leeway to the men of a household to discipline their women, and, as laws sometimes acknowledged (Rothari 182, 195; Liutprand 120), a woman's family could constitute the greatest threat to her welfare—*pace* McNamara and Wemple's notion of "power through the family."

Laws, unsurprisingly, discuss marriage only in so far as things could go wrong. This creates a distorted picture, but also one that vividly illustrates the core tensions involved in marriage strategies. The ideal which all law codes sought to promote was one of predictability: a marriage between social equals, negotiated in advance between families, with neither party reneging on the agreement, no third party interfering, and leading to a definitive alliance. Several interest groups had to agree to follow this script through to the end. The woman, as symbolic capital, had to retain her initial exchange value throughout, including after the marriage itself, in order to avoid a catastrophic breakdown in the process or the nullification of its benefits. The means by which a woman might depreciate, whether by her unsanctioned sexual activity, unwarranted repudiation by her husband, or the actions of her family or possible abductors, constituted a crucial concern for lawmakers, who tried to guard against all possible threats.

Before marriage, the specter of the *raptor*, the abductor capable of throwing all the best-laid plans into disarray, loomed large. The link between *raptus* and coercion is not constant: some laws, like the Visigothic code (III.3), used the word only when the woman had not consented, but others used it as a blanket category for all unarranged marriages, including elopement. Families, of course, could use coercion themselves in arranging daughters' marriages, and few laws tried to deny them this right. All codes, on the other hand, tried to guard against *raptores*, and even the most succinct set the compensation to be paid to men with prior claims: the woman's family, and the prospective husband if a betrothal had already been made. Most lawmakers took it as their priority to allow the woman's family to salvage what they could of a bad situation by forcing the abductor to compensate them for the lowering of her exchange value. Marriage could usually follow if the abductor and the woman's family wished it; some laws assumed it would. More rarely, lawmakers forbade the progression from *raptus* to marriage, instead specifying more severe penalties, such as death or enslavement for the abductor. This created a greater disincentive for abduction, but at the same time, by forbidding private settlement, did less to mitigate the loss to families, avenged but left with a less marriageable daughter. Such laws prioritized the aim of diminishing the frequency of this crime over the interests of families who fell victim to it, and are found in kingdoms (Visigothic Spain, Carolingian Francia) where lawmakers appeared most committed to a notion of the public good.[11]

Raptus counted as one of a limited number of changes in a woman's circumstances recognized as drastic enough to make the initial arrangement no longer fair or honorable to a betrothed man. Laws could express the hope that he would still marry the woman, but could not make it obligatory; even Carolingian capitularies, normally so insistent that betrothal should be as final a commitment as marriage, allowed him to marry another woman without having to do penance. Lawmakers recognized very few legitimate grounds for dissolving a betrothal: in Lombard law, if the woman had become leprous, possessed, or blind in both eyes, or if a feud had erupted between the families (Rothari 180; Liutprand 119). Beyond such cases, all parties had to offer substantial compensation for going back on a betrothal—the highest-risk moment, when some investment had already been made but the relationship not finalized. Most laws assumed that the betrothed man would be the one to change his mind, but the woman's family was also discouraged from looking elsewhere, and could be harshly punished for arranging a subsequent abduction.[12]

Law codes allowed divorce in even fewer circumstances, some of which seem rather outlandish: in the Burgundian code, a wife could be discarded for grave-robbing and performing magic. Most lawmakers were remarkably reluctant to allow divorce, even in cases of extreme change in circumstances, as when one of the spouses became or was discovered to be unfree. As with betrothal, most laws on divorce seem designed to stop husbands leaving their wives rather than the other way around, with two exceptions, so far apart in outcome it is difficult to generalize from them: the Burgundian code, which says a woman who left her husband should be drowned in mud; and Æthelberht's code, which says a woman who left her husband should be entitled to half his property. Legislation on divorce was meant to protect women and their families from the dishonor evidently attached to being discarded. This was also a concern when a man went back on a betrothal; Bavarian (VIII.15) and Alemannian (LII) laws clearly had the need for public vindication of the jilted bride in mind when they ruled that a betrothed man who wanted to marry another woman had to swear with twelve oath-helpers that this was "not because he found any fault or vice in her, but because of his love for the other woman."[13]

The one factor generally agreed to constitute a legitimate cause for dissolving a marriage was adultery by the woman; in nearly all such laws, the operational words were "if she has committed no wrong." If abductors and wavering bridegrooms constituted the main threats before marriage, the behavior of the woman herself was the greatest concern after it.[14]

A woman's sexual behavior, of course, mattered at any stage of life: since she always belonged to someone else (her husband if she was married; her family if she was not; her master if she was unfree), any sexual relationship she undertook outside marriage infringed on at least one other person's rights, and diminished someone else's honor. This is evident from the use of the word *adulterium* in laws to refer not just to adultery, but to any unsanctioned sexual activity by women, including virgins, widows, and slaves. Indeed, laws seem to expect the reactions of fathers and husbands to be similar, some of them giving fathers the right to kill a daughter's lover caught in the act in their own house.[15] Transgressing in the context of the household was a great affront to the honor of whatever man stood at its head, since his authority partly depended on his ability to control the sexual behavior of his women. The Visigothic code extended suspicion to doctors, threatening them with a fine if they treated a woman at home without the presence of a family member (XI.1.1). Heads of households who proved unwilling or unable to discipline their own women were taken to task, and laws sometimes envisaged royal authority stepping in to inflict punishment when families failed to.[16]

Outside the realm of the family home, the difference between married and unmarried women becomes more apparent. Even Visigothic laws, which allowed a father to kill his daughter if she had sex "in their own home," contemplated an unmarried woman's "going to a man's house for sex" with more equanimity, merely stating that he was not obliged to marry her afterwards. Many law codes made some allowance for a woman arranging her own marriage, as long as she had not been betrothed to someone else. The main thrust of laws on this matter was to protect the woman's family and her husband against any claims she might later make: typically she forfeited any right to her inheritance, and her husband was not obliged to give her a dower.[17] Having had sex in her father's home, by contrast, was evidently too egregious a challenge to paternal authority to be cancelled out by such a disconnection.

Punishment of married women's adultery was often left to the discretion of husbands, and laws typically devote more attention to the punishment of their lovers: the clause in the laws of Cnut, according to which an unfaithful wife was punished by the loss of her ears and her nose, as well as her property, is exceptional (II Cnut 53). It is nevertheless clear that unfaithful wives could be punished extravagantly harshly. Visigothic laws handed over the adulterous couple to the husband to punish as he liked (III.4.1); Lombard law stipulated death for both wife and lover in cases of adultery, and left the husband free to choose any punishment, short of death or mutilation, if someone groped his wife with her consent (Rothari 211; Liutprand 121). Later Italian Carolingian capitularies enslaved the couple to the husband; if he sold them, their new owners were to prevent them from continuing their relationship (I, nos 157, c. 3; 158, c. 2). Outside this southern context, consequences are rarely stated, but it is clear that repudiation might be the least of the worries of an unfaithful wife. One capitulary prescribing the efforts a bishop should make to protect an adulterous woman from her husband's fury had the bishop rely on persuasion rather than any more concrete means of preventing her husband from killing her: all he could do, apart from trying to find her a place to hide, was quote to her husband Augustine's arguments against the double standard (II, no. 252, c. 46).

Unlike other forms of gift exchange, where an alliance could be maintained over time by continual reiteration, a marriage could only be done once. The subsequent work of preserving the relationship between families was concentrated on the wife herself and depended on her behavior, in which all of the parties retained a controlling interest: her husband most obviously, but also her husband's family and her own.[18] The Visigothic code gives a chilling example of the role of relatives; it encouraged the husband's family to intervene "if wives who hate their husbands and pollute themselves by adultery, through potions or other magic, weaken the mind of their husbands so that they will not accuse them publicly." If the adultery was proven, these relatives stood to gain from the woman's confiscated property, offering them a clear incentive to accuse her (III.4.13). The dangerous ease with which a woman could lower her husband's honor and unbalance the original exchange was an essential cause for concern, making her sexual policing even more crucial than before marriage—and more people than ever had a say in it.

WOMEN AND PROPERTY

Gender made a difference in access to property, and women's life cycle affected the timing of access. Lawmakers aimed not to set out general principles or normal practice in matters of property, but to intervene in social relations. It was clear women should be provided for, less clear who should be responsible for that provision. Landed property was very often held by family groups, with individuals having only qualified and temporary rights—women's generally more qualified and more often temporary than men's. Any property earmarked for the support of a woman was necessarily, if only temporarily, immobilized and withdrawn from the control of the rest of the family group—whether her own relatives, if the property came to her through inheritance, or her husband's, if it came to her from him. Women's rights to such material support were regularly contested by their in-laws and relatives. Lawmakers came up with different answers as to which side should bear the principal burden of responsibility, and successive laws preserve the trace of constant negotiations on this topic, with elite families bringing their cases before royal justice as problems came up.

Only Visigothic law explicitly provided for sons and daughters to inherit equally if parents died intestate (IV.2.1). Most other law codes protected the cohesion of family property by placing severe limits on women's access to property, by restricting it either to particular circumstances (if there were no sons[19]), or to particular, distinctively female categories or sources of property: the law of the Frankish Chamavians distinguished between the inheritance "in forest, land, slaves and movables" of a father, which was to pass to a son, and the mother's inheritance (unspecified) which was to go to a daughter (XLII); Burgundian law stated that if a girl died before being married, her share of the inheritance should go to her sisters, not her brothers (LI.4–5), and that only daughters could inherit their mother's jewelry (LI.3; LXXXVI.2); Thuringian law laid down that a sole surviving daughter could inherit slaves, movables, and jewelry from her parents, but not land, weapons, or armor, which must go to the nearest male relative (26–32).

Lombard law seems most categorical in denying women control over property; it also offers the best examples of legislators changing tack because of unforeseen and increasingly complicated problems, clearly brought before them in a steady stream. Rothari (636–52) decreed, "No free woman living by the law of the Lombards can live under her own legal control, but she must always be under the guardianship (*mundium*) of some man or the king. She may not give away any property, movable or immovable, without the consent of whoever has her *mundium*" (Rothari 204). Further laws then had to be issued to guard women against these guardians (Liutprand 22, 29). Lombard lawmakers also initially excluded daughters from any inheritance unless there was no legitimate son (Rothari 158), but later earmarked property for women. Liutprand (712–44) forbade a father to will away more than two-thirds of his property; he must leave his daughter a third of it (Liutprand 65). Liutprand had ruled that "a Lombard may reward his sons for good service out of his property"; Aistulf (749–756), noting that "nothing was said about daughters," ordered that they too could be rewarded for service (Liutprand 113; Aistulf 13). A contentious case triggered Liutprand's amended legislation on unmarried women, all of whom—whether brotherless daughters living in their father's house or sisters living in their brother's house—were to inherit equally on the death of the paterfamilias: "But now there is a dispute between brothers and sisters over the inheritance of their niece who died unmarried." Her uncles, it was resolved, should get her share, and aunts' inheritance would remain the same (Liutprand 145). Aistulf then had to plug a further gap in Liutprand's ruling, now citing the plight of aunts, "who cannot inherit from their nephew because nothing is said about them in the previous edict, and while they remain unmarried in their house without inheritance, suffering need, marry slaves" (Aistulf 10). Aistulf ordered nephews to ensure their aunts "should not suffer from poverty, nor lack food, clothing nor service," and to arrange their entry into a convent should they desire it; he also ruled aunts could now inherit from their nephews if they died childless or intestate.[20] Such laws provide rare glimpses of the practical difficulties of supporting women in large, tension-ridden, households. Other law codes show much the same negotiations at play, though rarely with such explicit reference to gaps in earlier legislation. Frankish lawmakers similarly responded to actual cases by issuing new rulings.[21]

Dower, given to wives by their husbands' families on the betrothal and/or wedding day (Frankish *dos*, Burgundian *wittimon*, Lombard *morgingap* or *meta*), was important both to the women it supported and to the other family members who might stand to lose by its assignment and retained an interest in it.[22] Visigothic and Lombard laws' concern to place caps on dower amounts presumably reflects the lobbying of husbands' families for safeguards against marriage arrangements which they felt placed unbalanced demands on them (*LVisig.* III.1.5; Liutprand 7, 89, and 103). Frankish lawmakers said nothing on "normal" dower payment at marriage, but presupposed its existence when requiring the division of the wife's dower on either spouse's death if the marriage had been childless.[23] Dower mattered most when a woman's position within her own family had become more precarious; the arrangements for *wittimon* set out in Burgundian law for the case of a girl "who marries and has no father or brothers" identified the plural interests potentially harbored within the wife's natal family: the girl's paternal uncle, her sisters, her mother, and her mother's relatives (LXVI). Thuringian law, by assigning daughters a share of the father's or mother's inheritance in movables only, clearly assumed the woman would move after her parents' deaths (or had already moved), to live in dependence on husband or kinsfolk, or a religious community.

Friction often arose in cases involving widows' property. A widow, especially if she had children, was depicted in the Bible as the archetypical person in need of protection (Deut. 10:18, 14:29, 11:11; Is. 1:17, 23). Widowhood was a life-cycle stage experienced (probably) by most women and foreseen by those who endowed them.[24] Whatever property a woman inherited from her own family, inheritance from a dead husband in the form of dower was of special importance to her. The laws obliquely represent divergent responses to widows' neediness. Whereas Roman law sometimes depicted women as frail and irrational, Visigothic law made the widow the guardian of her children.[25] Anglo-Saxon lawmakers provided support for the widow with offspring in the deceased's family home and from his property.[26] In Lombard Italy, Rothari ruled that the widow could return to the home of her father or brother if they retrieved guardianship over her (Rothari 199). *Lex Ribuaria* assigned the widow 50 *solidi* and "one third of everything [the couple had] worked together" (41.2). A capitulary of 821 further specified this as "one third of whatever [the couple had] acquired together and worked together as property held from and owing dues to a lord (*in beneficio*)" (I, no. 148, c. 9), showing that, even as conditional tenures of land proliferated under the Carolingian kings, royal intervention protected small-scale landholders, women as well as men, against claims of lords or kin.[27]

Limiting the widow's rights in her late husband's property to usufruct (a life-interest in the land) helped secure the children's rights in the long term; but if there were stepchildren from a previous marriage, her and her own children's interests might be at odds with theirs. Aistulf, concerned to protect those interested others, set a limit of "half the property, under usufruct" on what a dying Lombard could leave his wife (Aistulf 14). The widow's dower was explicitly stated in some laws to be hers for life only.[28] Laws aimed at making the widow's dower more secure indicate points where her interests and those of her husband and his family pulled against each other.

Despite some ecclesiastical hostility, many widows chose to remarry. Frankish lawmakers had laid down different rules about what would happen to rights over the widow's dower in such a case. In 819, a panel of men learned in law made a judgment, confirmed by the king, that overrode earlier written rules, instead specifying the arrangement should be reached "by the will and consent of the relatives, as their ancestors have done until now." Visigothic law required the widow, if she wanted to keep all her property, to wait for at least a year before remarriage. Lombard law allowed the widow, on remarriage, to keep her dower provided her new husband handed over half of its value to the first husband's relatives. In England, the Second Code of Cnut (1020/1) punished a widow who remarried within a year of her husband's death by loss of dower as well as of other property.[29]

Charters show that dower-land was often bequeathed by a widow, or her heirs, to churches, whose new rights would then compete with residual rights held by her late husband's kin. Frankish formularies show that the wife (and sometimes the husband too) was sometimes forbidden to alienate any of her dower, which would revert to the *husband's* family, with potentially disruptive effects on her natal family's calculations. The interest of children in their mother's dower could lead to other kinds of tension, especially if she was widowed and remarried, or if she predeceased them and the father remarried.[30] Widows' wills highlighting the importance of dower as a legally safeguarded life-interest also show its fragility in face of the rival claims of a deceased husband's well-entrenched kin or a powerful lord. A widow's "free power" (*libera potestas*) could be anything but.

Conclusion

The optimistic line of thought developed by McNamara and Wemple presents laws as the guarantee of domestic stability, allowing the family to remain a haven of relative peace and security for women. Law codes seem unlikely to support such optimism, because by their very nature they deal with situations that arise when things have gone wrong. Yet, though they distort by obscuring normal situations in which no dispute arose, they do expose tensions and conflicts which tended to crop up over such questions as how to control the behavior of women, while at the same time ensuring material support for them, and how that burden should be shared out within and between families. These concerns, which would have presented themselves in all family contexts, though they seldom blew up into scandal, are very like those evidenced in social practice as presented in charters. Because particular cases created a demand for rulings in matters of family law, it is, paradoxically, in this most private of contexts that the greatest demand can be detected for the input of legislators and for judgment in royal courts. Precisely here are to be found reference to actualities, most spectacularly in scandals brought before assemblies, where the private erupted onto the public scene.[31] The resulting legislation represented a consensus view hammered out between kings and aristocrats. What united both the private and public scenes and all of the participants was a fundamental ambivalence. The relationship between women and the law would remain chronically and gender-distinctively unresolved.

FURTHER READING

Bougard, François, Laurent Feller, and Régine Le Jan, eds. *Dots et douaires dans le haut moyen âge*. Rome: Ecole française de Rome, 2002.

McKitterick, Rosamond. *The Carolingians and the Written Word*. Cambridge: Cambridge University Press, 1989.

McNamara, Jo Ann and Suzanne Wemple. "The Power of Women Through the Family in Medieval Europe, 500–1100," in Mary Erler and Maryanne Kowaleski, eds, *Women and Power in the Middle Ages*. Athens: University of Georgia Press, 1988, 83–101.

Nelson, Janet L. "The Wary Widow," in Wendy Davies and Paul Fouracre, eds, *Property and Power in the Early Middle Ages*. Cambridge: Cambridge University Press, 1995, 82–113.

Parisse, Michel, ed. *Veuves et veuvage dans le haut moyen âge*. Paris: Picard, 1993.

Stafford, Pauline. "*La mutation familiale*: A Suitable Case for Caution," in Joyce Hill and Mary Swan, eds, *The Community, the Family and the Saint: Patterns of Power in Early Medieval Europe*. Turnhout: Brepols, 1998, 103–25.

Stafford, Pauline. *Gender, Family and the Legitimation of Power: England from the Ninth to Early Twelfth Century*. Aldershot: Ashgate, 2006.

Wormald, Patrick. *Legal Culture in the Early Medieval West: Law as Text, Image and Experience*. London: Hambledon Press, 1999.

Wormald, Patrick. *The Making of English Law: King Alfred to the Twelfth Century*, vol. I: *Legislation and its Limits*. Oxford: Blackwell, 1999.

NOTES

We use the following abbreviations to refer to primary sources:

Capitularia: Capitularia regum Francorum, ed. Alfred Boretius (Hanover: MGH, 1883, 1897).

CJ, Nov.J.: Code and *Novellae* of Justinian: trans. Samuel P. Scott, *The Civil Law* (Cincinnati: Central Trust Co., 1932).

CTh.: *Codex Theodosianus: The Theodosian Code*, trans. Colin Pharr et al. (Princeton: Princeton University Press, 1951).

LAlam.: *Leges Alamannorum*, ed. Karl Lehmann and Karl A. Eckhardt (Hanover: MGH, 1966).

LVisig.: *Leges Visigothorum*, ed. Karl Zeumer (Hanover: MGH, 1902).

LBai.: *Lex Baiwariorum*, ed. Ernest von Schwind (Hanover: MGH, 1926).

LFCham.: *Lex Francorum Chamavorum*, ed. Karl A. Eckhardt, *Die Gesetze des Karolingerreiches, 714–911* (Weimar: H. Böhlaus Nachfolger, 1934).

LFris.: *Lex Frisionum*, ed. Karl A. Eckhardt and Albrecht Eckhardt (Berlin: MGH, 1982).

LRib.: *Lex Ribuaria*, ed. Franz Beyerle and Rudolf Buchner (Hanover: MGH, 1954).

LSax.: *Lex Saxonum*, ed. Karl F. de Richthofen (Hanover: MGH, 1866).

LThur.: *Lex Thuringorum*, ed. Karl F. de Richthofen (Hanover: MGH, 1875–89).

LibConst.: *Liber Constitutionum*, ed. Ludwig M. de Salis, *Leges Burgundionum* (Hanover: MGH, 1892).

PLS: *Pactus Legis Salicae*, ed. Karl A. Eckhardt (Hanover: MGH, 1962).

Lombard laws: Aistulf, Liutprand, Rothari: *Leges Langobardorum*, ed. Friedrich Bluhme (Hanover: MGH, 1869).

Anglo-Saxon laws and related material (we thank Julie Mumby for access to her spreadsheet): Æthelberht, Hlothere and Eadric, Ine, Alfred: *The Laws of the Earliest English Kings*, ed. and trans. Frederick L. Attenborough (Cambridge: Cambridge University Press, 1922); Cnut: *The Laws of the Kings of England from Edmund to Henry I*, ed. and trans. Agnes J. Robertson (Cambridge: Cambridge University Press, 1925); *Wifmannes Beweddung, Northumbrian Priests' Law: Die Gesetze der Angelsachsen*, I, ed. Felix Liebermann (Halle: Niemayer, 1903).

1. *Feminist Studies*, 1 (1973): 126–41, repr. in Mary C. Erler and Maryanne Kowaleski, eds, *Women and Power in the Middle Ages* (Athens: University of Georgia Press, 1988), 83–101, cited here (quotations at 90, 93, and 97).
2. Georges Duby, "Structures familiales dans le Moyen Age occidental," in *Mâle Moyen Age: De l'amour et autres essais* (Paris: Flammarion, 1988), 129–38; Diane Owen Hughes, "From Brideprice to Dowry in Mediterranean Europe," *Journal of Family History*, 3 (1978): 262–96. Pauline Stafford, "*La mutation familiale*: A Suitable Case for Caution," in Joyce Hill and Mary Swan, eds, *The Community, the Family, and the Saint* (Turnhout: Brepols, 1998), 103–25.
3. See Ruth Mazo Karras, "The History of Marriage and the Myth of *Friedelehe*," *Early Medieval Europe*, 14 (2006): 119–51; Janet L. Nelson, "The Problematic in the Private," *Social History*, 15 (1990): 355–64; Pauline Stafford, *Gender, Family and the Legitimation of Power: England from the Ninth to Early Twelfth Century* (Aldershot: Ashgate, 2006).
4. Patrick Wormald, "*Lex scripta* and *verbum regis*," in P. H. Sawyer and I. N. Wood, eds, *Early Medieval Kingship* (Leeds: The Editors, 1977), 105–38, repr. in Patrick Wormald, *Legal Culture in the Early Medieval West: Law as Text, Image, and Experience* (London: Hambledon Press, 1999), 1–43, at 12.
5. In the three codes where sex made a systematic difference in all cases, women were included in injury lists: *LBai.* IV.30; *LAlam.* LIX.2; *LSax.* 15. The gender neutrality of *si quis* is noted in Guy Halsall, *Settlement and Social Organization: The Merovingian Region of Metz* (Cambridge: Cambridge University Press, 1995), 63. For a table of injury lists, see Patrick Wormald, "The *leges barbarorum*: Law and Ethnicity in the Post-Roman West," in Hans-Werner Goetz, Jorg Jarnut, and Walter Pohl, eds, *Regna and Gentes: The Relationship*

between Late Antique and Early Medieval Peoples and Kingdoms in the Transformation of the Roman World (Leiden: Brill, 2003), 21–53, at 47–53.

6. Brawls: *LBai.* IV.30; *LibConst.* XCII.2; Rothari 378; Liutprand 123. Feud: Liutprand 13. Housebreaking and larger-scale violence: Rothari 278; Liutprand 141. Ross Balzaretti, "'These are things that men do, not women': The Social Regulation of Female Violence in Langobard Italy," in Guy Halsall, ed., *Violence and Society in the Early Medieval West* (Woodbridge: Boydell, 1998), 175–92, at 186–88.

7. Sexual assault: *PLS* XX; *LRib.* 43; *LBai.* VIII.3–4; *LAlam.* LVI; *LFris.* XXII.88–89; Alfred 11, 18. Only the Visigothic code considers the rape of one man by another (III.5.4). Hair: *PLS, Capit.* III.104; *LBai.* VIII.5; *LibConst.* XXXIII, XCII.

8. Beatings during pregnancy: *LVisig.* VI.3.2; Rothari 75, 334; *LBai.* VIII.19; *LAlam.* LXX; Alfred 9. Abortion: *PLS* XIX.4; *LVisig.* VI.3.1, VI.3.7; *LBai.* VIII.18, VIII.20–21; *LAlam.* LXXXVIII; *LFris.* V.1–2.

9. Wemple, *Women in Frankish Society*, 29; Lisa Bitel, *Women in Early Medieval Europe, 400–1100* (Cambridge: Cambridge University Press, 2002), 70 ("Most legal codes followed this system of valuation"). Compare Rothari 201; *LAlam.* LIX.2, LX.2; *LBai.* IV.30; *LFris.* Add. Sap. V.

10. Pierre Bourdieu, *The Logic of Practice*, trans. Richard Nice (Stanford: Stanford University Press, 1990), 101–103.

11. *LibConst.* XII; *PLS* XIII, XV.2; *LRib.* 38–39; *LBai.* VIII.6, VIII.16; *LAlam.* XCVII.4; *LFris.* IX.8, IX.11; *LFCham.* XLVII; *LThur.* 46–47. Women punished for colluding with *raptores*: *PLS Capit.* VI.2.2; *LSax.* 40. Laws forbidding marriage without the woman's consent: Rothari 195; Liutprand 120; *Capitularia* I, nos 8, c. 7 and 15, c. 6; II Cnut 74. Marriage after a *raptus*: Rothari 187, 191; *LAlam.* LI; *LSax.* 49; Æthelberht 82–84; laws forbidding such marriages: *LVisig.* III.3; *PLS Capit.* VI.2.2; *Capitularia* I, nos 138, c. 23; 139, c. 9; 156, c. 1; II, nos 228, c. 10; 293, c. 65–66. In practice, even capitularies recognized that families made deals with abductors (no. 293, c. 68). Einhard himself interceded in favor of one: "it seems better to me that she be joined to that man again…than that she should be scorned by everyone" (Einhard, letter 60, trans. Paul Dutton, *Charlemagne's Courtier* (Peterborough, Ontario: Broadview, 1998), no. 55, at 158).

12. Going back on a betrothal: *PLS* LXVa; *LVisig.* III.1.3; Rothari 178, Liutprand 119; *LBai.* VIII.15; *LAlam.* LII. Cf. Count Stephen's efforts to break his betrothal in the late 850s: Janet L. Nelson, *Charles the Bald* (London, 1992), 174, 185, 196. Initiated by the woman's family: *LVisig.* III.3.3–4; Rothari 192; Ine 31.

13. Grave-robbing and magic: *LibConst.* XXXIV.3; cf. *CTh.* III.16.1. Unfree status: *LVisig.* IX.1.16, III.2.7; *LFris.* VI.1; *Capitularia* I, nos 15, c. 8, and 16, c. 6 and 13; II, nos 201, c. 15 (added in Paris BnF lat. 4613) and 252, *canon. extrav.* 2. For a woman leaving her husband: *LibConst.* XXXIV.1; Æthelberht 79–80. In Carolingian capitularies a woman could cite nonconsummation of the marriage as a reason for divorce: *Capitularia* I, nos 15, c. 20; 16, c. 17; 112, c. 46.

14. On the requirement of innocence: *Capitularia* II, no. 193, c. 3; *LibConst.* XXXIV.2; Grimoald 6; *LBai.* VIII.14; *Northumbrian Priests' Law* 64–65. Adultery: *LibConst.* XXXIV.3; *Capitularia* I, nos 12, c. 9; 180, c. 36. Only the Visigothic code treated fornication as a legitimate cause for divorce on both sides (III.6.2–3).

15. *LVisig.* III.4.5; *LibConst.* LXVIII; Rothari 212; Alfred 42.7; "William I" 35; *LBai.* VIII.1; *LFris.* V.1.

16. Royal authority stepping in: Rothari 189, 221; Liutprand 24; *LVisig.* III.2.3; parents prostituting their daughter: *LVisig.* III.4.17; cf. *Capitularia* II, no. 228, c. 9, on fathers allowing their daughters to become corrupted "in their own house."

17. *LVisig.* III.2.8, III.4.7–8. See also *LibConst.* XII.4–5, XLIV.2, LXI, C; Rothari 188–89, 214; Liutprand 114; *LBai.* VIII.8, VIII.17; *LAlam.* LIII; *LFris.* IX.11. The husband sometimes had to pay a fine, but a lower one than for abduction.

18. Bishops might also express an interest, though they could also be quick to pass on a difficult conjugal case to the wisdom of "married men," as was the fate of Northild, discussed in Janet L. Nelson, "England and the Continent in the Ninth Century: IV, Bodies and Minds," *Transactions of the Royal Historical Society*, 15 (2005): 1–27, at 20.

19. *LSax.* 41, 44; *LAlam.* LV; *LThur.* 26; Rothari 158; *PLS* LIX.6, on which see Thomas Anderson, "Roman Military Colonies in Gaul...and the Forgotten Meaning of *Pactus Legis Salicae* 59.5," *Early Medieval Europe*, 4 (1995): 129–44; *LRib.* 57.4.

20. For the convent option, see Susan Wood, *The Proprietary Church in the Medieval West* (Oxford: Oxford University Press, 2006), 124–25, 130–37, 178–80.

21. *PLS Capit.* IV. 108; *PLS Capit.* I. 67.

22. Régine Le Jan, "Aux origines du douaire médiéval (Ve-Xe siècles)," in Michel Parisse, ed., *Veuves et veuvage dans le haut moyen âge* (Paris, 1993), 53–67; Cristina La Rocca, "*Multas amaritudines filius meus mihi fecit*: Conflitti intra-familiari nell'Italia longobarda (secolo VIII)," in *Les transferts patrimoniaux en Europe occidentale, VIIIe–Xe siècle* (Rome: Ecole française de Rome, 1999), 933–50; and contributions to François Bougard, Laurent Feller, and Régine Le Jan, eds, *Dots et douaires dans le haut moyen âge* (Rome: Ecole française de Rome, 2002), esp. Laurent Feller, "'Morgengabe', dot, *tertia*," 1–25.

23. *PLS Capit.* IV.110; *LRib.* 41, 50. See Karras, "The History of Marriage," 142.

24. On frictions, see *Les transferts*, though La Rocca, "*Multas amaritudines*" has a distinctive view. Brigitte Pohl-Resl, "Vorsorge, Memoria und soziales Ereignis: Frauen als Schenkerinnen in der bayerischen und alamennischen Urkunden des 8. und 9. Jahrhunderts," *Mitteilungen des Instituts für Österreichische Geschichtsforschung*, 103 (1995): 265–87, confronts laws with charter evidence. On widows: Robert Hajdu, "The Position of Noblewomen in the *pays des coutumes*, 1100–1300," *Journal of Family History*, 5 (1980): 122–44, at 130, estimated nearly two-thirds of his twelfth-century sample were widowed; Janet L. Nelson, "The Wary Widow," in Wendy Davies and Paul Fouracre, eds, *Property and Power in the Early Middle Ages* (Cambridge: Cambridge University Press, 1995), 82–113.

25. Diocletian, *CJ* II.12.18, V.35.2–3; *Nov.J.* 118.5 and 94 (see Gillian Clark, *Women in Late Antiquity* (Oxford, 1993), 56–62); *LVisig.* III.1.7, IV.3.1; cf. *LibConst.* LXXXV.

26. Ine 38; cf. Æthelberht 78, Hlothere and Eadric 6.

27. Paul Fouracre, "The Use of the Term *beneficium* in Frankish sources: A Society Based on Favours?" in Wendy Davies and Paul Fouracre, eds, *The Languages of Gift in the Early Middle Ages* (Cambridge: Cambridge University Press, 2010), 62–88, at 71.

28. *LVisig.* III.1.5; *LSax.* 47; *LBai.* XV.7.

29. *PLS* XLIV and *Capit.* III.100; *Capitularia* I, no. 142, c. 8. *LVisig.* III.2.1. Rothari 182; Liutprand 127; II Cnut 73; *LAlam.* LIV.

30. Formularies of Angers 40, 41, 54, and Marculf I.12; II.7–9: *Formulae Merowingici et Karolini Aevi*, ed. Karl Zeumer (Hanover: MGH, 1886); *The Formularies of Angers and Marculf: Two Merovingian Legal Handbooks*, trans. Alice Rio (Liverpool: Liverpool University Press, 2008). Cf. *LibConst.* XXIV.1, and *LVisig.* IV.5.2–4. For similar tensions in Angevin England, see Janet S. Loengard, "'Of the Gift of Her Husband': English Dower and its Consequences in the Year 1200," in Julius Kirshner and Suzanne F. Wemple, eds, *Women of the Medieval World* (Oxford: Blackwell, 1985), 215–55; cf. Stafford, "*La mutation familiale*," 115–19.

31. As in the cases of Northild and Stephen, above nn. 12, 18.

CHAPTER 8

··

CONFLICTS OVER GENDER IN CIVIC COURTS

··

CAROL LANSING

ONE of the places where medieval people actively used gender categories to construct or debate identity was civic courts. Surviving records of court process can reveal conflicts over gender expectations, moments when people disagreed. This essay examines some of those conflicts. The goal is not a general survey of civic courts or legal categories but rather a close look at practice: how individuals sought to use the judicial system and played on ideas about male and female nature to do so. The essay touches on issues of female legal capacity and gender norms and asks how people manipulated those norms and discourses in practice. It is an extended look at a rape case from the criminal court of the Italian town of Bologna in 1295. The case is a particularly vivid example of a power struggle waged in and out of the court over class and gender expectations, revealing the twists and turns a case could take, and also how expectations for men and women at different social levels influenced that process.

Evidence from civic courts can be revealing for several reasons. Records of cases often include reported speech: people told the court stories about their lives and the lives and character of their neighbors. These stories, often told in response to an interrogation and usually translated into the formulaic Latin of the law, are hardly a direct glimpse of social experience, but they had at least to be plausible.[1] At a distance of seven or eight centuries, they are often as close as historians can get. In addition, participants in court cases included low-status people, who do not show up in most records because they had little property and thus had little need for the notarial contracts that are the basis of most studies of medieval townsfolk in southern Europe. The kinds of evidence that appear in court records were very much shaped by the twelfth-century revival of Roman law.[2] A thirteenth-century court adjudicated cases on the basis of local statutes and also what was termed *ius comune*, law common to all, which meant canon law, custom, and also Roman law. These legal norms were based on long-standing assumptions about men and women, including limited female capacity and the sexual double standard. However, the complex requirements for proof in Roman law also opened up the possibility of debate over gender norms. Partial proof could be based on *fama*, that is, reputation and status. Witnesses testifying to *fama* discussed what aspects of behavior determined a person's status, which could become an implicit debate over gender expectations. What behaviors indicated an honest woman? When did a husband's discipline of his wife cross the line and become *saevitia*, savage cruelty? Discussions of *fama* even gave witnesses the opportunity to disagree with legal norms.

The courts of the thirteenth and fourteenth centuries were a crucial part of the growing apparatus of government, exercising the power to coerce and to punish. Towns expanded the reach of their courts to serve as sites for not only dispute resolution, but also active investigation of crime. Recent studies have explored aspects of judicial coercion, including the growing use of civic prisons, as well as mechanisms for debt collection and the enforcement of taxation.[3] In many ways, the judicial system operated as an extension of the interests of elite patriarchal families: in Florence, at least, a wealthy family could get rid of a troublesome son by dumping him in the town's prison and could even cut his hamstrings to keep him there.[4] And yet, savvy townsfolk at much lower social levels were quick to use and even manipulate the courts for their own ends. This was particularly true in Bologna, a town that hosted the most sophisticated university legal faculty in Europe. The town was crawling with lawyers and notaries. Accusations to the courts were usually pressure tactics, intended to force an opponent to an outside settlement.[5] Men and women tried to use the court to exact vengeance, to get rid of a pesky neighbor or kinsman, even to protect themselves. This means that sentences from civic courts cannot simply be taken at face value: often, they were not the real goal. Careful reading of a case requires an understanding not only of the court's procedure, but also of the broader social and political context, as the tale of Tomasina and Nicolao will show.

AN ANONYMOUS CHARGE OF RAPE

In August 1295, the judge in charge of Bologna's criminal court received a notification that a man named Nicolao of the Bentivoglio family had entered the house of a woman named Tomasina Lanfredi.[6] He "grabbed her by force and violently knew her, holding a knife to her throat and saying to her 'Unless you do my will, I will kill you.'" The unnamed notifier asked the court "to inquire, find the truth, and when the truth has been found punish the malefactor." Tomasina, "because of Nicolao's power and her fear," had not dared to accuse him. A notification to the court could be anonymous: a person could simply leave a note in a box outside the civic palace. This meant there were no repercussions for the person who lodged it, and they could throw in whatever charges they chose. The choice to lodge an accusation was riskier: it could not be anonymous, and every charge had to be proved or the accuser was liable for a fine. People used accusations most often as pressure tactics, to force a settlement outside the court. The court was obligated to pursue a notification if possible, by holding an ex officio inquest. The point of this system was to build the court's ability to investigate crime, but in practice, people used notifications for all sorts of reasons. Effective notification usually included a list of witnesses. In this case, the notifier listed sixteen, eleven of them from Tomasina's parish, San Egidio.

The court held an initial inquest on Saturday, August 13. The first witness was Tomasina herself, the alleged victim. She was read the text of the notification, in Italian, and responded on oath that it was not true. In fact, on a Saturday evening in June, Nicolao de Bentivoglio did come to her house, along with Benvenuta, her godmother. Godparenthood or spiritual kinship was a close and trusted relationship. Benvenuta knocked on her door and when Tomasina asked who was knocking, replied, "I am Benvenuta, your godmother." Tomasina, believing Benvenuta to be alone, opened the door and Nicolao as well as Benvenuta quickly entered. When Tomasina saw him, she pushed with her hands on his chest, saying, "Why did you come here, since my husband Bonamico is in bed?" Nicolao answered that he was not using force. She said: "Remove yourself from the house because I do not want you to stay here." He replied that he did not want to leave. She told him she would cry out for help, and he got up, took her by the sleeve and said to her, "You are already making a big fuss about me." She immediately cried out for help and he took her by the throat with his hand but did no harm to her, and then he left the house and she closed the door. The only person present was Benvenuta.

The court questioned further witnesses on August 17. A *domina* Bona knew nothing because she had been out in the country at the harvest, gleaning. The title *domina*, *Madonna* in the original Italian, indicated a respectable woman. Benvenuta the godmother was questioned, and gave a more elaborate version of Tomasina's story. Nicolao had told her he wanted to stable his horse at Tomasina's house, and asked Benvenuta to come with him. When he entered the house and Tomasina asked him "Who are you who enter my house?" he responded that he was not there for anything evil: he just wanted to stable his horse, since he had been waiting for a friend to ride with him out to his villa, and the friend had not arrived. When they entered, Tomasina said, "Alas for me, who are you who have entered my house?" Ultimately, Tomasina placed her hands on his chest and told him to get out, because her husband Bonamico had told her not to stable anyone's horse when he was absent. Asked whether Nicolao touched Tomasina or harmed her, she answered that he touched her on the chest with his hand, saying, "I don't want a big noise because I did not come here for any evil purpose." And he did no evil. This, she stated, is all she knew. Afterwards, he went with his horse to Boninconte's house and, she believed, stayed there all night.

Two further witnesses, a man and a woman, testified only that they had heard Tomasina cry out for help. A third witness, the rector of a hospital, had heard that Nicolao was at her house, but not that he had done any harm. Bonamico Bonjohanis, nicknamed Micolo, who as we will see kept Tomasina as his concubine, testified that he had been out in the country for eight days, and on his return had heard only that she had cried out for help. Four more witnesses said roughly the same thing: they had heard that Nicolao entered her house against her will. In effect, eleven witnesses supported Tomasina's story, testifying to some sort of trouble, but not to rape.

Then the story began to unravel. Jacobo Guasparelli said he had not been there, but he had heard from neighbors that Nicolao had entered her house because he wanted to know her carnally. Beatrisia said it was public knowledge (*pubblica fama*) in the parish of San Egidio that Nicolao had forced Tomasina, and that he had placed a knife at her throat. Beatrisia had heard that Tomasina accepted money from Nicolao not to speak the truth; some said fifty gold pennies, others said fifty pounds.

Beatrisia's husband Johane Bonacolsi agreed. He had not been there, but it was common knowledge in the street of San Donato (where Nicolao lived) that he had entered her house against her will and raped her, and that many people were drawn to the fracas. Further, Tomasina was paid fifty Bolognese pounds to not incriminate Nicolao. It was the priest of her parish church, San Egidio, who made an oral agreement between them, making Nicolao give her fifty pounds to keep silent. He had also heard that the friends of Nicolao had made big efforts to keep him from being incriminated. Thus far, all the witnesses except the victim and her godmother had testified to *pubblica fama*, neighborhood gossip.

RAPE AND EXPECTATIONS FOR ELITE MEN

Let us pause and consider the social dynamic. Why would Tomasina not dare to accuse Nicolao, as the notifier asserted? It was rare for women to accuse men of rape. The charge was hard to prove and could easily damage a woman's reputation. As Trevor Dean has argued, "Of all the crimes perpetrated against women, rape stands out for the ineffectiveness of the law."[7] One English study found that twenty eyre records dated from 1202–1276 included 142 rape cases, compared to 3,492 homicides, with an overall conviction rate for rape of 6 percent.[8] Rape laws were often vague, penalties often varied by status and also tended in practice to be light. Medieval laws on rape were heavily influenced by Roman law. The legal terms commonly used in Italian civic statutes were *stuprum*, which literally meant to debauch or defile, and *raptus*, a term that in late Roman law had meant abduction and rape, but by the thirteenth century could simply mean abduction.[9] Even the famed jurist Alberto Gandino found the term confusing. After he served a term as a judge in Bologna the legality of one of his judicial actions was questioned because he had had a man suspected of *raptus* tortured, which was legal in a case of carnal knowledge, but not in a case of abduction.[10] Gandino was exonerated. The thirteenth-century Bolognese statute addressed *stuprum*, holding that a person guilty of *stuprum* by force of a widow or virgin was to be punished at the discretion of the *podestà*, or chief magistrate, according to the quality of the persons and actions.[11] Despite the statutes, in practice when people lodged accusations of rape, they usually used precise language: carnal knowledge with force against the victim's will. *Stuprum* after all could mean sexual defilement without coitus. Presumably, accusers wanted the judge to know the exact charge and that evidence of a lack of consent existed. A woman and her family might use a rape accusation in an effort to force a marriage between the alleged rapist and victim, as in a case from fifteenth-century Paris analyzed by Edna Ruth Yahil.[12] Otherwise, they would hesitate, since the law was ineffective and the damage to a woman's reputation could outweigh the satisfactions of justice. A case, after all, would be very public; in Bologna, as in many Italian towns, women had to testify on the steps of the town hall, rather than within the judge's chamber.

However, in this case the notifier said that Tomasina did not accuse Nicolao, because of "her fear and his power." Who was Nicolao? An understanding of his status requires a brief look at contemporary politics. This was the period of the rise of guild-based republics in Italy, a change ultimately driven by the commercial revolution. An older knightly elite was gradually replaced or absorbed into newer commercial and professional classes: guildsmen, notaries, lawyers, merchants, bankers. Bologna led the way, as a group of guilds led by the notaries were able to take control of civic government and rewrote the constitution to base eligibility for civic office and other privileges on guild membership. The regime in 1287 crafted a set of ordinances that placed severe restrictions on a long list of noble families, termed magnates, barring them from civic office and imposing stiff penalties for crime, on the grounds that they were "rapacious wolves," violent threats to civic order. Requirements for proof were eased. The Bolognese ordinances were copied by most guild republics over the next few decades.

This means that if Nicolao had been a magnate, it would have been relatively easy to charge him in court. Nobles were associated with rape, in contemporary discourse and also in practice. Dramatic evidence survives from mid-fourteenth-century Florence, in the form of anonymous denunciations of magnate violence to a special tribunal dedicated to enforcing the anti-magnate laws, the Executor of the Ordinances of Justice. The proportion of denunciations for rape to the Executor was four times higher than to the ordinary criminal court.[13] Why? It may well be that nobles were more apt to commit rape. They were accustomed to high status and the exercise of power, and denunciations to the Florentine Executor certainly depict a noble culture of impunity. Some rapes surely were opportunistic, but many were demonstrably premeditated. One noble was denounced for going to a village house with a group of his men, carrying a ladder which he used to climb in through a window. He punched a married woman, threatened her with a knife at her throat to keep silent, "and in this way forced this good woman." And even in these cases with eased requirements for proof, rape charges tended to be ineffective. The Executor's court held an inquest and questioned eleven witnesses, including the woman's brother-in-law. All of them denied any knowledge and the case was dropped.[14]

Denunciations to the Executor also suggest that nobles at times used abduction and rape as a calculated weapon of lordship. Three cases from the tribunal over a five-year period, 1343–1348, depict rural nobles attempting to abduct and rape respectable women. In two cases, the nobles succeeded and kept the abducted women as concubines, which was effectively sexual enslavement.[15] Then, when the women's husbands or kinsmen protested, the nobles retaliated with violence. In both cases, the noble was charged with having the man killed. In the third case, the woman and her husband successfully resisted an attempted rape and then an attempted abduction by their landlord.

Significantly, the denunciations to the Executor addressed not the alleged rapes and abductions, but rather the violent retaliation against the women's kinsmen. In fact, there is no evidence that the families sought the return of the dishonored women. These cases depict nobles using rape as a weapon of lordship, a way not only to get women but to dominate and humiliate male subjects. To use Susan Brownmiller's phrase, these rapes were "messages between men." Kathryn Gravdal has shown a similar pattern in medieval French literature and law: accounts of rape came to be about the men and not the female victims.[16]

Nicolao, however, was not a magnate and was not supposed to be a rapacious wolf. Ironically, he was powerful because he belonged to the exact class responsible for efforts to restrain magnate violence. He was a member of the Bentivoglio, a rising family at the heart of Bologna's popular regime. In the 1290s, family members were well placed in two powerful guilds at the forefront of the regime, the butchers and the notaries. In 1294, fourteen Bentivoglio belonged to the butchers' guild, which gave them access to civic office and political power. Family members were rapidly gaining wealth and held extensive rural lands, as Nicolao's reference to riding out to his villa suggests. The lands were probably used for raising cattle. Nicolao may have been one of nine sons of Bentivoglio, the family founder. If so, he would have been inscribed in the butchers' guild, which held a series of important popular offices in the 1280s. Ironically, this Nicolao surely took part in crafting the ordinances that restricted the magnates because of their violence.[17] However, the Nicolao imputed in the notification could just possibly have been a grandson of the founder. Whatever the case, he was a man from a family with resources, great political clout, and legal privilege because of its offices.

WEAPONS OF THE WEAK

However, sheer intimidation of Tomasina simply does not make sense of this case. Why, if Tomasina did not accuse Nicolao "because of her fear and his power," did he and his friends arrange to pay her a hefty fifty pound bribe? They must have had some reason to think that she was willing to accuse him in court. This speaks to the long-discussed question of "weapons of the weak": the strategies low-status people used to resist the powerful.[18] It is possible that she and her friends, or her lover Micolo, put pressure on Nicolao and his friends. In fact, the Bentivoglio family's standing in the popular regime evidently made him particularly vulnerable. A respectable guildsman and officeholder should not give way to sexual appetite and commit rape. As Johane Bonacolsi had heard, Nicolao's friends made big efforts to avoid having him inculpated for this. This strengthens the case that the Nicolao implicated in the case was the man who played a prominent role in the popular government. In 1295, the regime was on shaky ground, engaged in a desperate war with Azzo VIII d'Este of Ferrara. The last thing the regime needed was the public disgrace of an important popular leader.

Pressure tactics that revolved around the threat of an accusation in court were common, especially among Bologna's savvy population. Again, the goal of an accusation was usually to get a person to settle. In one vivid case from 1298, a woman named Blonda notified the court that her neighbor Meglior was a sorceress, prostitute, and pimp who snatched young girls from their families so that she could sell their virginity. An inquest was held, and Meglior's defense against this dramatic charge included a series of witnesses who pointed out that Blonda's son had recently been banned from Bologna for an assault on Meglior. It was notorious in the neighborhood that Blonda, in response, had threatened Meglior with the courts. If she did not relax the young man's ban, Blonda had said, then she would lodge notifications and accusations that would get Meglior burned.[19] She chose charges based on gender expectations, ideas about women of bad character.

When people settled their disputes, they effectively ended the court process. Often, they also recorded the settlement in a legal contract drawn up by a notary. Settlements in the form of peace pacts were extremely common. Shona Kelly Wray analyzed 177 dispute settlements in Bolognese notarial records from the year 1337 and found that in 122 of them the parties explicitly made peace pacts.[20] A peace could be used to end court proceedings, reduce penalties, or—more commonly—to end a sentence of banishment imposed after a particular crime, which was apparently Blonda's goal in her lurid charge against Meglior. Nicolao and Tomasina surely settled without a notarial contract.

The court thus could serve as a weapon of the weak, in this case indirectly. It is striking that the bribe to Tomasina was thought necessary to preempt any court process. Nicolao had a reputation to protect, and chose an expensive private settlement. The point is important. Despite the ineffectiveness of the law, it is too simple to assume that medieval elites could rape with impunity. Clearly his reputation and that of his family as upstanding members of the *popolo*—and perhaps even the reputation of the regime itself—were at risk. In other words, gender expectations for men of his political class were at play in the case. It is also fascinating that the parish priest was the go-between, suggesting that he was trusted on both sides and also maybe a bit flexible in his ethics. The settlement that he brokered in fact aided both sides, since neither had a strong motive to go to court.

Torture and Status

How did the case play out? On August 19, Nicolao made an appearance to defend himself, in response to the court's summons. He told a story close to Benvenuta's: he had entered the house, wanting a place to rest and to stable his horse. When Tomasina told him to leave, he did touch her chest, she cried out, and he left. On August 20, however, he confessed to premeditated rape. He said had gone to the house that evening "with the spirit and intention of penetrating her." She said her husband Bonamico was there, but he was not. He grabbed her by the throat so she could not cry out, threw her to the ground near the door and "forcibly against her will knew her carnally." Benvenuta, the godmother, had not known that he wanted to penetrate Tomasina, and quickly left.

Why did he change his story and confess? It is probable that he was tortured. The requirements for proof were stringent: two eyewitnesses or a confession. Roman law courts could torture if they had strong indications that a charge was true, but needed proof. However, as Sarah Blanshei has shown, all Bolognese were not equal before the law. Nicolao, as a Bentivoglio, was a privileged person and could be tortured only with permission of an official termed the Capitano del Popolo, in the presence of senior advisors to the regime.[21] This would have been unlikely in a simple rape case, especially if the victim was a low-status concubine. However, the criminal court had broad powers to use torture if it suspected false testimony, something considered far more serious than rape. Torture could not cause permanent harm or death, and a confession given under torture had to be repeated away from the place of torture. One piece of evidence that suggests torture is the fact that Nicolao was called to the judge's bench in the town hall on August 21 to reaffirm that his confession was true. Given six days to prepare a defense, he hired a lawyer. On August 23, someone, surely a friend of Tomasina, lodged another notification: two months earlier, Petruciolo, a winecarrier and a notorious thief, persuaded Tomasina to open the door. Nicolao rushed in and attempted to rape her, but was prevented by the crowd of people drawn by her cries.[22] The charge was against Petruciolo, but the notification depicting an earlier attempt at rape was surely intended to influence Nicolao's case.

FAMA AND FEMALE CHARACTER

Once Nicolao confessed to premeditated forcible carnal knowledge, the case hinged not on his actions but on gender norms, putting the focus on Tomasina's character. The rationale for this defense was simple. Thirteenth-century jurists, probably influenced by church law, held that the victim of a rape had to be an honest woman, a woman of good legal standing.[23] The case thus became a debate over the definition of what it meant to be an honest woman. *Fama* could refer to reputation in the streets, or to a specific legal condition. Bad *fama* might mean reputation or the local gossip, or it could refer to a legal disability due to a court action. For example, a person convicted of heresy suffered legal disabilities that included being barred from summoning witnesses.[24] Witness testimony might be about public *fama* (reputation), but it also could be eyewitness reports of behavior that indicated status.[25] Witnesses were now brought in by both sides not to report neighborhood gossip, but to describe Tomasina's status. Was she an honest woman? Significantly, there was disagreement over what defined a woman as *inhonesta*. Was it marital status? Sexual behavior? How her man treated her? How she earned her living?

The court heard six witnesses, who testified not to events but to Tomasina's good character: was she an honest married woman? A widow from the neighborhood said she did not know whether Tomasina was married to Bonamico. She did know that she had stayed at his request over eight years, and that the couple had a daughter. Sometimes, she had seen Tomasina wear a ring. She lived in the house at his instance, and whenever Bonamico wished, he went there, ate, drank, and lay with her, and had conversation with her. Sometimes Bonamico lived with his father. Tomasina, the widow testified, was considered a good woman, and to her knowledge did not have bad *fama*. Two more women, both married, similarly testified that Tomasina was not Bonamico's wife, but that he stayed with her as a husband does with a wife. She was considered a good, honest woman, and anything else was calumny. Two men testified that Bonamico often stayed with her like a wife, and treated her as an honest woman.

Bonamico's testimony clarified her status. He had never espoused her, but he had certainly promised to take her as a wife. For over eight years, he had treated her as a wife in bed and at table and in other necessities. He considered her an honest woman. This meant that Tomasina was an *amasia*, a common but murky social category best translated as concubine or lover. *Amasie* are hard to study because they show up in few records other than those of the criminal courts in Bologna, Florence, and surely elsewhere.[26] They did not obviously fit the court's dichotomous categories, either as honest unmarried woman or *inhonesta*. Significantly, there was disagreement over whether an *amasia* could be *honesta*. Again, was female reputation defined by marital status, by how her man treated her, by her sexual behavior, or by how she earned her living?

Some women, probably including Tomasina, presumably lived in apparently monogamous relationships with men of higher status. These were women who lacked dowries, which with rare exceptions barred them from marriage. The man might, like Bonamico, treat an *amasia* as if she were his wife, but she had no legal rights, and the children were not legitimate. There was a structural tension between *amasie* and wives. A number of cases mention men who kept an *amasia* for a time, then threw her and their children out when they married. In one case, a husband was said to have thrown out his young wife in favor of a prior concubine and children when the wife's dowry was left unpaid.[27] In another case from 1295, another Tomasina, in this case the injured wife, notified the court that her husband had thrown her out two years before and denied her marital affection and material support, giving them instead to his concubine, Fina. Further, Fina had insulted her in the main piazza, charging her with being a whore and having five lovers. This Tomasina was able to produce a dowry instrument: the modest sum of 25 pounds, paid ten years before by her widowed mother. Her witnesses agreed that Fina had been the husband's concubine for two years and received food, drink, and housing from him. Tomasina, who was living with her mother, characterized herself as a poor little woman, a phrase used in legal proceedings to signal defenselessness.[28] The husband and Fina did not show up in court and were therefore convicted in absentia, banned from Bologna until they paid 100 pound fines.

In another inquest, a wife blamed a concubine in what was probably an attempt to restrain an abusive and irresponsible husband. The charge was that a prostitute named Caterina used love magic and other blandishments to seduce the husband, so that he beat up and attempted to kill his wife Matilda. Matilda ultimately fled his house "utterly ill and badly beaten, naked, impoverished, and tearful, and returned to her father's house."[29] Further, the husband had kept Caterina for two years and had a daughter by her. However, neighborhood witnesses in the initial inquest painted a different picture: the husband had beaten Matilda fifteen days before but she was now perfectly fine, and he had fled the neighborhood out of fear of her kinsmen's retribution. No witness mentioned Caterina or magic. The husband finally did show up in court and denied having any relationship with Caterina, but admitted to pulling his wife's hair. He was absolved. Surely the tale of magic and seduction was a way to save face and also bring him to heel. The alternative for an abused wife was to charge her husband in a church court; if she could literally prove he treated her with savage cruelty, she might obtain a separation from him, though of course she could not remarry while he lived. Blaming a concubine for his behavior preserved the marriage. In a number of marital homicide cases, *amasie* were accused of persuading their men to murder their wives.

Other *amasie* lived independently and had relations with several men. In Bologna, some offered not only sex but food and perhaps shampoos to a few students they termed their *dominos*, lords, who in turn paid their expenses. The status also could be demonstrably involuntary: the women abducted by nobles, who are discussed above, were termed *amasie*.

Could *amasie* be honest women? Some witnesses answered yes, and spoke of behavioral norms that had little to do with sex. The defense of a woman named Guicciardina, who was accused of prostitution, is revealing. She earned her living selling candles, oils, and herbs. A witness stated that she was considered a woman of good reputation and good condition, and the people of her neighborhood treated her as a good woman and freely associated with her; he had never heard that she did any evil. "She was the *amasia* of a student but in all other things she was held to be a good woman."[30] Clearly, the witness did not accept the dichotomous view of female identity based on sexual behavior.

Tomasina, like Guicciardina, was a concubine who was able to provide witnesses who characterized her as a respectable woman. Then, on August 22, she confessed that Nicolao had forcibly raped her. Again, she may have been tortured, since she also was potentially guilty of false testimony. Like Nicolao, she was required to affirm her confession in the chamber where the *podestà*'s court heard legal cases. The following day, Nicolao's defense was read, and his witnesses summoned. The legal argument was simple: Tomasina is a woman of vile condition and dishonest life, and has been vile and *inhonesta* in the neighborhood for many years. Nicolao produced four guarantors, all of them Bentivoglio relatives, and promised to pay a 600 pound fine if condemned. He then was released from prison. On August 23, eight witnesses testified on his behalf. All but one were from the parish, and two were women. The witnesses disparaged Tomasina's reputation by playing on contemporary attitudes about female honor: she had a sharp tongue, and was promiscuous and guilty of ill treatment of children. One married woman stated that Tomasina was the *amasia* of Micolo. She was a woman who used her tongue to say evil things of her neighbors; asked how she knew this, the witness replied that she herself had heard Tomasina. She had a bad reputation. How did she know? A woman named Divicia from a nearby village gave birth to a dead baby boy in

Tomasina's house, and died of the birth. Divicia was said to have been pregnant by the son of a widow. The next three witnesses, all male, stated that Tomasina was not a good woman because she was an *amasia*. Further witnesses said roughly the same thing; one mentioned her sharp tongue, testifying that she said shameful things of good married woman. The final witness said that she lived as Bonamico's *amasia*, but also lay with other men. Questioned further, he stated that four years before, he knew her carnally at her instigation, and she bore a son. Many times she asked him to take his boy. He gave her money so that she could raise the child. He sent her away "because she did not regulate her life well."

These were common ideas about disreputable women, and they often showed up in contemporary exchanges of insults. When people insulted a man, they usually disparaged the sexual reputation of his female relatives: you are the son of a whore. Insulting a woman meant attacking her sexual behavior and perhaps her treatment of children: you whore, you drowned your babies in the well. Sexual insults could be imaginative. Rosa, a fisherman's daughter, charged Johana with shouting insults at her in the main piazza, including prostitution, bigamy, and necrophilia. Rosa produced five women as witnesses, who gave various versions. One reported that Johana had threatened to prove "with good witnesses" that Rosa was a whore and a female pimp. Another quoted: "You are a whore and a pimp, you have two husbands, you dug up the dead Jacomino Chavalatium from his tomb and put him on top of you, and your husband Michele is not your husband."[31] Johana was convicted and assessed a 25 pound fine. Two days later, she retaliated, charging Rosa with insulting her by calling her a whore and pimp who has many lovers, but without success.

How did the rape case end? Nicolao was convicted and fined 300 pounds. The record does not state the crime for which he was convicted, but 300 pounds was the penalty for false testimony.[32] In effect, Nicolao was imprisoned, probably tortured, convicted, and fined, far more serious consequences than a simple conviction for the rape of a concubine. Why did the case turn out in this way? The real question is why the notification to the court was made after Tomasina evidently was paid off to keep silent. The answer, unfortunately, is hard to know. It was probably not Tomasina or Micolo who lodged the notification, since the result was that they had to lie to the court, risking a 300 pound fine for false testimony. Someone else wanted to injure Nicolao, perhaps a political or commercial rival. Or perhaps people in the neighborhood knew of the rape, were angry, and wanted justice. It is tempting to conclude that Tomasina's friends and neighbors trapped Nicolao by getting him to bribe her to keep silent and then lodging the notification that set him up to proffer false testimony. There is no way to know.

It is worth noting that a 2011 case in New York involving Dominique Strauss-Kahn, a prominent French politician, evolved in a way that was strikingly similar to the case of Tomasina v. Nicolao. Strauss-Kahn was charged with the rape of a low-status woman, a hotel maid named Nafissatou Diallo. The forensic evidence for rape was evidently strong, and, unlike Tomasina, Diallo did accuse her alleged attacker. Nevertheless, the prosecutors dropped the case because of questions about Diallo's reliability as a witness. As in the thirteenth-century Tomasina v. Nicolao case, the rape case hinged not on evidence of the man's actions but the character of the alleged victim. The continuity is striking. On the one hand, a well-publicized rape charge then as now could damage an elite man's reputation: Strauss-Kahn, much like Nicolao Bentivoglio, suffered imprisonment, humiliation, and the apparent end of his political career. On the other hand, the attitudes about rape victims that existed in the thirteenth century persist into the twenty-first: a rape case can still fail because of perceived doubts about the victim's morality that have nothing to do with the evidence in the case.

Coda: Comic Parody of a Sex Charge

Boccaccio in the *Decameron* included a story about an adultery case that is a mocking reflection on gender in an Italian civic court. It can draw together many of the themes of this essay. In the tale, a nobleman in Prato caught his wife committing adultery, charged her in court, and had her summoned. The statute in Prato, the narrator reports, did not distinguish between a woman guilty of adultery and a prostitute, and prescribed death by burning in either case. The wife, Madonna Filippa, scorned advice to flee into exile, and instead appeared before the *podestà*. She confessed to the adultery and then challenged the law, on two grounds. First, Filippa argued that laws should not be enacted without the consent of all those whom they affect. Her argument was based on a maxim of Roman law that was central to fourteenth-century political thought, *Quod omnes tangit*: "what touches all must be approved by all." Prato's adultery law bound only women, she pointed out, and no woman was ever even asked to consent to the law. It thus deserved to be called a bad law. Then, she turned to sexuality. She asked her husband whether she had ever denied him his enjoyment of her body, and when he admitted that she had always gratified him, she responded, "If he has ever had of me as much as he wants and as pleases him, what am I to do with the surplus? Must I cast it to the dogs?" Her argument played on the obligations of the marriage debt, and also the idea from Galen—the ancient medical authority—that women whose libidos were not satisfied could be poisoned by excess female semen. Her defense also echoed the contemporary tendency to view female sexuality as a commodity, with a surplus depicted as if wasted food. The people of Prato, who had flocked to watch the adultery trial, laughed loud and long at her wit, insisted that she was in the right, and had the *podestà* change the statute to penalize only prostitutes.[33] The husband left humiliated, the wife triumphant.

Filippa's arguments played on exactly the gender expectations that influenced judicial process. The first parodied a legal argument, a challenge that underscored the limited legal capacity of women. And yet, as we have seen, women could and did use the court to further their interests. The second argument accepted the notion of rapacious female libido, the notion that influenced the sexual double standard imbedded in the law. It was, after all, the sexual behavior of Tomasina, not Nicolao, that ultimately was at issue in the rape case. Finally, Filippa's argument played on the commodification of female sexuality at the center of the marriage and the dowry system, which consigned

Tomasina to life as a concubine: what is a woman to do with her surplus sexuality? The tale was of course a joke, not a serious critique. And yet, at the heart of the joke was the recognition that these gender expectations were cultural constructions that could be questioned and even mocked.

FURTHER READING

Blanshei, Sarah Rubin. *Politics and Justice in Late Medieval Bologna*. Leiden: Brill, 2010.

Brundage, James. "Rape and Seduction in the Medieval Canon Law," in Vern L. Bullough and James Brundage, eds, *Sexual Practices and the Medieval Church*. Buffalo, NY: Prometheus Books, 1982, 141–48.

Cohn, Samuel. *Women in the Streets: Essays on Sex and Power in Renaissance Italy*. Baltimore: Johns Hopkins University Press, 1996.

Dean, Trevor. *Crime and Justice in Late Medieval Italy*. Cambridge: Cambridge University Press, 2007.

Dean, Trevor. *Crime in Medieval Europe, 1200–1550*. Harlow, England; New York: Longman, 2001.

Gravdal, Kathryn. *Ravishing Maidens: Writing Rape in Medieval French Literature and Law*. Philadelphia: University of Pennsylvania Press, 1991.

Karras, Ruth Mazo. *Sexuality in Medieval Europe: Doing Unto Others*, 2nd edn. New York: Routledge, 2012.

Kuehn, Thomas. "*Fama* as a Legal Status in Renaissance Florence," in Thelma Fenster and Daniel Lord Smail, eds, *Fama: The Politics of Talk and Reputation in Medieval Europe*. Ithaca, NY: Cornell University Press, 2003, 27–46.

Lansing, Carol. "Concubines, Lovers, Prostitutes: Infamy and Female Identity in Medieval Bologna," in Paula Findlen, Michelle Fontaine, and Duane Osheim, eds, *Beyond Florence: The Contours of Medieval and Early Modern Italy*. Stanford: Stanford University Press, 2003, 85–100.

Vallerani, Massimo. *Medieval Public Justice*. Washington, DC: Catholic University of America Press, 2012.

NOTES

1. For a close analysis of these issues in a medieval English rape case, see Barbara Hanawalt, "Whose Story Was This? Rape Narratives in Medieval English Courts," in *"Of Good and Ill Repute": Gender and Social Control in Medieval England* (New York: Oxford University Press, 1998), 124–41.
2. As Marie Kelleher explains in "Later Medieval Law in Community Context," in this volume, Chapter 9.
3. Guy Geltner, *The Medieval Prison: A Social History* (Princeton: Princeton University Press, 2008); Daniel Lord Smail, "Violence and Predation in Late Medieval Mediterranean Europe," *Comparative Studies in Society and History*, 54 (1) (2012): 7–34.
4. Christiane Klapisch-Zuber, "The Devil in Prison," in Michael Rocke and Peter Arnade, eds, *Power, Gender and Ritual in Europe and the Americas* (Toronto: Centre for Reformation and Renaissance Studies, 2008), 95–112.
5. Massimo Vallerani, *Medieval Public Justice* (Washington, DC: Catholic University of America Press, 2012).

6. Archivio di Stato di Bologna (hereafter ASBo), Curia del Podestà, *Libri inquisitionum et testium*, busta 35, filza 6, 32r–42r.

7. Trevor Dean, *Crime in Medieval Europe, 1200–1550* (Harlow, England; New York: Longman, 2001), 82. See Ruth Mazo Karras, *Sexuality in Medieval Europe: Doing Unto Others*, 2nd edn (New York: Routledge, 2012), 145–51, 161–66.

8. Ruth Kittel, "Rape in Thirteenth-Century England: A Study of the Common-Law Courts," in D. Kelly Weisberg, ed., *Women and the Law: The Social Historical Perspective*, vol. 2 (Cambridge, Mass.: Schenkman, 1982), 101–15. See Hanawalt, "*Of Good and Ill Repute,*" 131–32.

9. See James Brundage, "Rape and Seduction in the Medieval Canon Law," in Vern L. Bullough and James Brundage, eds, *Sexual Practices and the Medieval Church* (Buffalo, NY: Prometheus Books, 1982), 141–48. On the evolution of understandings of *raptus* in late medieval English law, see Henry Ansgar Kelly, "Statutes of Rapes and Alleged Ravishers of Wives: A Context for the Charges Against Thomas Malory, Knight," *Viator*, 28 (1997): 361–419.

10. Hermann U. Kantorowicz, *Albertus Gandinus und das Strafrecht der Scholastik*, vol. 2: *Die Theorie* (Berlin; Leipzig: Walter de Gruyter, 1926), 398–99. See Sarah Rubin Blanshei, *Politics and Justice in Late Medieval Bologna* (Leiden: Brill, 2010), 322–23.

11. Gina Fasoli and Pietro Sella, eds, *Statuti di Bologna dell'anno 1288* (Città del Vaticano: Biblioteca Apostolica Vaticana, 1937), book IV, rubric 30.

12. Edna Ruth Yahil, "A Rape Trial in Saint Eloi: Sex, Seduction, and Justice in the Seigneurial Courts of Medieval Paris," in Michael Goodich, ed., *Voices from the Bench: The Narratives of Lesser Folk in Medieval Trials* (New York; Basingstoke: Palgrave Macmillan, 2006), 251–71.

13. See Claudia Caduff, "Magnati e popolani nel contado fiorentino: Dinamiche sociali e rapporti di potere nel Trecento," *Rivista di storia dell'agricoltura*, 33 (2) (December 1993): 15–63; Christiane Klapisch-Zuber, *Retour à la cité: Les magnates de Florence, 1340–1440* (Paris: Editions de l'Ecole des Hautes Etudes en Sciences Sociales, 2006), ch. 4.

14. Archivio di Stato di Firenze (hereafter ASF), Atti del Esecutore degli Ordinamenti di Giustizia, 96, 97r–8v. The denunciation was recorded at ASF, Capitano 69, 13v–14r.

15. Carol Lansing, "Magnate Violence Revisited," in John Easton Law and Bernadette Paton, eds, *Communes and Despots in Medieval and Renaissance Italy* (Farnham, Surrey: Ashgate, 2010), 35–48. The cases are Atti del Esecutore degli Ordinamenti di Giustizia, 51, 51r–52r; 54, 84r–86r; 33, 41r–42r; Capitano del Popolo 35, 3r; Capitano del Popolo 35, 4v–5r. Atti del Esecutore degli Ordinamenti di Giustizia, 50, 25r–30r; 48r–50r; 54, 81r–83r; 69, 5r–12v. See also Carol Lansing, "Humiliation and the Exercise of Power in the Florentine Contado in the Mid-Fourteenth Century," in *Emotions, Passions and Power in Renaissance Italy*, ed. Fabrizio Ricciardelli and Andre Zorzi (Amsterdam, Amsterdam University Press 2015), 77–90.

16. Kathryn Gravdal, *Ravishing Maidens: Writing Rape in Medieval French Literature and Law* (Philadelphia: University of Pennsylvania Press, 1991).

17. These included *anziano*, consul, and advisor to the guild in 1285 and 1287. See Armando Antonelli and Marco Poli, *Il Palazzo dei Bentivoglio nelle fonti del tempo* (Venice: Marsilio, 2006), 15, and the many studies they cite. Sarah Blanshei ranked the Bentivoglio tenth among families holding twenty or more terms of office in the main town council; Blanshei, *Politics and Justice*, 544.

18. James C. Scott, *Weapons of the Weak: Everyday Forms of Peasant Resistance* (New Haven: Yale University Press, 1985).

19. ASBo, Curia del Podestà, *Libri Inquistitionum et testium*, 46, 2, 41r–47v.

20. Shona Kelly Wray, "Instruments of Concord: Making Peace and Settling Disputes Through a Notary in the City and Contado of Late Medieval Bologna," *Journal of Social History*, 42 (3) (spring 2009): 733–60. See also Katherine Jansen, "Peacemaking in the Oltrarno, 1287–1297," in Francis Andrews, Christoph Egger, and Constance M. Rousseau, eds, *Pope, Church, and Society: Essays in Honor of Brenda M. Bolton* (Leiden: Brill, 2004), 327–44.

21. Blanshei, *Politics and Justice*, 321, 331.

22. ASBo, Curia del Podestà, *Libri inquisitionum et testium*, busta 35, filza 4, 24r–26v.

23. Brundage, "Rape and Seduction," 144–45.

24. See Thomas Kuehn, "*Fama* as a Legal Status in Renaissance Florence," in Thelma Fenster and Daniel Lord Smail, eds, *Fama: The Politics of Talk and Reputation in Medieval Europe* (Ithaca, NY: Cornell University Press, 2003), 27–46. Francesco Migliorino, *Fama e infamia: Problemi della società medievale nel pensiero giuridico nei secoli XII e XIII* (Catania: Editrice Giannota, 1985).

25. Blanshei, *Politics and Justice*, 184–85.

26. See Carol Lansing, "Concubines, Lovers, Prostitutes: Infamy and Female Identity in Medieval Bologna," in Paula Findlen, Michelle Fontaine, and Duane Osheim, eds, *Beyond Florence: The Contours of Medieval and Early Modern Italy* (Stanford: Stanford University Press, 2003), 85–100.

27. ASBo, *Inquisitionum et testium*, 3, 23v–4v.

28. ASBo, *Inquisitionum et testium*, 35, filza 2, 20r–2r. For another case of an *amasia* stealing a husband and description of a shamed wife, see *Inquisitionum et testium*, 35, filza 3, 73r.

29. "totaliter infirma et tribulata agravata nuda miseria et lacrimosa ad domum patris rentravit." ASBo, *Inquisitionum et testium*, 35, filza 3, 73r.

30. ASBo, *Libri Inquisitionum et testium*, 19, 6, 18r–v.

31. ASBo, *Accusationes*, 8b, filza 10, 56v–58r.

32. *Statuti di Bologna*, book IV, rubric 51, 213.

33. Boccaccio, *Decameron*, day 6, story 7. See Kenneth Pennington, "A Note to *Decameron* 6.7: The Wit of Madonna Filippa," *Speculum*, 52 (4) (1977): 902–905.

CHAPTER 9

··

LATER MEDIEVAL LAW IN
COMMUNITY CONTEXT

··

MARIE A. KELLEHER

DURING the central and late Middle Ages, the legal landscape of Western Europe underwent a major transformation as the *ius commune*—the combination of revived Roman
law and rationalized canon law taught in medieval universities—made its way into
Western European law codes and legal thinking. The layering of this new law over the
various legal traditions that existed at that time forced legislators, jurists, and litigators
to incorporate the ideas that lay behind that law into their thinking about broad socio-
legal concepts, including ideas about gender. Historians have tended to represent the
relationship between women and law in the central and late Middle Ages as necessarily
oppositional: when a woman was confronted by a legal system that restricted her public
role, enforced a sexual double standard, and accepted male domination of women as a
given, her primary role would be victim, her only avenue for agency, resistance. Studies
that focus primarily or solely on the substantive law (that is, the actual ordinances and
edicts) that arose out of this new legal culture, however, often fail to take into account
the *ius commune*'s influence on procedural law and the profound impact that changes
in this area made on the formation of women's legal and social identities. Women were
expected to behave in a manner consonant with the multiple and overlapping gender assumptions of the substantive law and took pains to represent themselves along
these lines. The actual impact of these carefully crafted self-representations, however,
depended on the existence of procedures that integrated community knowledge with
the learned law. The law of the central and late Middle Ages thus provided both the general parameters for women's roles and the courtroom procedure for translating those
general ideas into legal reality—a process that depended on the active participation of
both women and their communities.

THE *IUS COMMUNE* AND GENDER

Although medieval women's legal subordination did not originate with the *ius commune*, the new body of law provided an ideological framework for the existing gender system. While it is difficult to generalize about any prior "Germanic" socio-legal concepts, including ideas about gender, secular law codes of the early Middle Ages tended to assume that most women would be on unequal footing with most men.[1] Even the law of the early medieval Church, which in its early years promoted a radical spiritual equality between men and women, increasingly restricted women's access to public authority in the temporal realm.[2] But whether secular or ecclesiastical, most early medieval law treated women's inferior status on an ad hoc basis, declining to elucidate any consistent general theory behind that status. This situation changed over the course of the twelfth and thirteenth centuries, as scholars of both Roman and canon law worked to compile and systematize the many disparate legal collections that then existed throughout Western Europe. While the regulation of women's behavior was not these scholars' primary objective, their compilations provided a rationalized conception of women's fundamentally weaker nature that would shape women's legal and social identities for centuries to come.

In the field of canon law, the most important early product of this process of legal systematization was the work of a twelfth-century canonist known to history as Gratian, whose "Concord of Discordant Canons," better known as the *Decretum*, aimed to arrange and resolve the apparent contradictions of the many diverse canon law texts being used by church courts at that time. Around the same time, a similar process was taking place in secular law: in the towns of northern Italy, and especially in the city of Bologna, jurists had begun to work through the long-neglected corpus of Roman law that had been compiled during the reign of the Emperor Justinian (r. 527–65), a corpus that was itself based on law dating back several centuries earlier. Jurists of the central Middle Ages, first in Italy, then throughout Europe, commented extensively on both of these bodies of law, and students in the emerging "schools" of law that sprang up around these jurists studied a combined curriculum of Roman and canon law that came to be known as the *ius commune*, which formed the basis of continental law for the rest of the Middle Ages. Even in England, where the legal system was based on the precedent-centered common law, the *ius commune* exercised an important influence: it formed a part of the basic curriculum of the university law faculties at Oxford and Cambridge (as opposed to the common-law-focused education that took place at England's Inns of Court beginning in the fourteenth century); it provided the governing principles for several jurisdictions outside the common-law courts; and it was an important resource for resolving weighty constitutional or diplomatic matters.[3]

The Roman-law portion of the *ius commune* differed from early medieval law in more than merely content and organization. Individual pieces of Roman legislation (and, to a lesser degree, of canon law) proceeded from a set of underlying principles and legal assumptions rather than merely from precedent. This package of principles was instru-mental in the development of a legal theory of gender in the central and late Middle Ages. The Roman jurists who wrote the law that the medieval West would inherit assumed that women constituted a distinct legal class whose inherent sex-specific inca-pacities demanded both special legal protections and special limitations on their legal agency. Roman women could be witnesses in legal proceedings, but not witnesses to documents (an exclusion that also applied to minors, slaves, and lunatics). In addition, most women needed the consent of a tutor to make their own wills or undertake other legal acts. And while the few women who were *sui iuris* (that is, full legal persons not under the power of a tutor, guardian, or male head of household) could sign contracts and undertake legal action on their own behalf, even they could not do so on behalf of others, for to do so would be "beyond the female sex."[4]

By the period of the early Roman Empire, however, the existence of a growing class of *sui iuris* women (as well as other women who used the court system to exercise a degree of control over their property) had begun to undermine the legal assump-tion of inherent female incapacity. Even some of the greatest legal minds of the age were beginning to have their doubts: the prominent second-century jurist Gaius, for example, called the notion of inherent female incapacity "specious, rather than true."[5] Nevertheless, even as the legal guardianship of women declined, the notion of female helplessness remained a commonplace in late Roman culture, and women who litigated publicly or frequently were depicted by contemporaries as monstrous or unnatural.[6] Thus, a legal assumption of women as naturally incapacitated by reason of their sex combined with larger cultural notions of natural female modesty to create a legal philosophy that considered protection to be the first duty that the law and its agents owed women. By the time these gender ideas were revived in the central and late Middle Ages, they had been stripped of their late Roman context—in which many women exercised *sui iuris* rights that belied the principle of female incapacity—and were received as a system of self-evident beliefs about women's basic nature, with cor-responding legal implications.

Canon law of the central and late Middle Ages also contributed to the development of a legal theory of gender, sometimes softening the Romanist position, sometimes rein-forcing it. One area where canonists differed from Romanists was in arguing for spir-itual equality between men and women, a position that would seem to be at odds with the Roman-law assumption of inherent female inferiority to men. But for canonists, equality in the spiritual realm was perfectly compatible with inequality in the tempo-ral one. Canon law of the central and late Middle Ages generally regarded man as the "head" of woman and woman as the "body" of man—in other words, canon law pro-vided a model of male–female relations that assumed both gender complementarity and inherent female inferiority. Gratian's etymology (borrowed from late classical sources) of the words "man" and "woman" is perhaps the most straightforward indication of his gender ideas: "man (*vir*) is so-called not because of his sex, but because of his virtue (*vir-tute*) of soul; woman (*mulier*) so-called not because of the sex of her body, but because of her softness (*mollitie*) of mind."[7] Even if canonists did not fully articulate the more relentlessly negative view of women that appeared in the writings of some medieval theologians, they did take women's natural inferiority for granted.

Although canon law and Roman law were designed with two different purposes in mind, the two bodies of law shared an underlying assumption that women, while legal persons, were not the equals of men. Together, the two laws provided medieval jurists with a powerful conceptual vocabulary of gendered incapacity. This vocabulary reinforced the notion that women were a distinct legal class whose own inherent weaknesses and disabilities required that the law and its agents protect them, both from others and from themselves.

GENDER IN (LEGAL) THEORY AND PRACTICE

These legal assumptions about women were borne along with the *ius commune* as its influence spread throughout Western Europe. The statutes of the urban Italian communes generally treated women as physically and morally weak and in need of protection.[8] In Castile, the thirteenth-century *Siete partidas* ("seven-part [code]") of Alfonso X anticipated that women would be in court on occasion, but also assumed that their litigation would be limited to matters regarding those women's family members or family property. More generally, the *Partidas* reflect a vision of women as permanent minors whose legal actions would be mediated by a male relative or procurator whose job it was to look out for their best interests.[9] In the neighboring Crown of Aragon, *ius commune* assumptions about female vulnerability at times appeared baldly in the statutes: the Code of Tortosa (1272–79) echoed Roman ideas of female modesty in its provision that women should not be compelled to appear personally in court for any contract that they cosigned with their husbands, and another thirteenth-century law from Valencia asserted that a husband could not encumber the property his wife brought to a marriage without her consent because "the fragility of the female sex should not be turned against her or result in the diminution of her goods."[10] And in the counties and quasi-independent towns of southern France, where jurists did not hesitate to adduce women's weak, frivolous, and lighthearted nature, a survey of property litigation suggests that courts assumed most women would be under male jurisdiction, though exceptions might be made for widows or women whose status as independent tradeswomen meant they had to be able to defend their sole property interests in court.[11]

It is important to note that these legal ideas about women's inferiority or dependency may mask a more nuanced picture of women's legal status. In some cases, courts made exceptions for clearly exceptional situations. The courts of Byzantine southern Italy, for example, were known to grant extensive independent legal authority to married women who lived in port areas where their husbands were regularly absent for long periods of time, suggesting that Roman-law ideas about women were flexible enough to accommodate situations in which individual women had to act in ways that did not accord well with more general legal assumptions about a woman's inherent incapacity or vulnerability.[12] But divergences between legal theory and courtroom practice were not limited to exceptional cases; they also resulted from the intermingling during the late medieval centuries of *ius commune* ideas and older customary law. Even in the towns of northern Italy, the crucible of the *ius commune* revolution, local legal traditions continued to exercise a strong influence over women's position in society and in the family. For example, the Lombard concept of *mundium*, or complete patrimonial power over a woman, provided elite male jurists with grounds to ignore *ius commune* provisions for women's inheritance and thereby ensure that most property descended to men. The degree of patriarchal control varied from one Italian city (and one indigenous legal tradition) to the next: some cities, like Milan and Venice, declined to invent particular statutes regarding women's legal incapacity; others, like Bergamo, placed women under the *de facto* (if not *de jure*) guardianship of their husbands; still others, like Florence, required the consent of a husband or guardian for almost any legal action a woman wished to undertake.[13] In all cases, however, Italian women's status as legal agents was the result of a blending of two traditions—both patriarchal, but with different underlying frameworks that could, in time, have different consequences for the women caught up in them.

This competition between legal traditions becomes more apparent the further away one gets from the Mediterranean littoral, and its effects on the relationship between women and law become correspondingly more pronounced. In France, for example, historians of law have long recognized two separate territories, in terms of legal culture: the "land of customary law" in the north and the "land of written law" in the south. The laws of the southern French counties and territories were more strongly influenced by the *ius commune*, in part because their proximity to Mediterranean networks of exchange meant more frequent contact with other *ius commune*-influenced polities, but possibly also due to a greater residual influence of Roman legal ideas on their own customary law traditions.[14] In the north, customary law remained the more important force in women's lives, in some areas well into the early modern era: while jurists echoed Roman-law rhetoric in citing women's weak and frivolous nature, individual women continued to exercise important control over property and rights of guardianship. A similar bifurcation of medieval women's legal status can be found in some regions of the Low Countries, where couples might choose between one marital property regime based in customary law that emphasized the household as a (male-headed) unit, and another based in Roman contract law that assumed a separation of marital goods.[15]

Probably the most important example of this legal competition (or syncretism, as the case may be) comes from England. English lawyers and judges—especially those who studied at the legal faculties of Oxford and Cambridge—would have received basic training in the *ius commune* as a part of their formal studies. Yet England's common law was, like the customary law of the continent, built on a foundation of precedent and exigency, as opposed to Roman law's set of general principles from which individual laws were derived.[16] The one important area where general principle (rather than precedent) was the major driving force in women's status was the legal fiction of coverture, according to which the law treated husband and wife as one person, thereby effectively barring a married woman from contracting, suing, or being sued independently of her husband in the common-law courts. Some urban working wives did have themselves declared independent legal persons—*femmes soles*—and were therefore able, like widows and single women, to make and sign contracts in their own right. But only a very limited group of women were ever eligible to claim this status, and even fewer actually took advantage of it. In general, and with the exception of criminal cases, a husband in later medieval England was legally responsible for his wife's actions because the two were one person in the eyes of the law. In other words, the common-law courts of England went much further than treating women as permanent minors; married women in England might find themselves effectively effaced as legal subjects. On the other hand, jurisdictions outside the common-law courts—for example, the manorial courts, the ecclesiastical courts, and equity jurisdictions like the Courts of Requests or Chancery—provide evidence of large gaps in the seemingly solid armor of coverture: in practice, nonaristocratic women maintained substantial property of their own, usually through marriage settlements, and English widows routinely enjoyed greater control over property than the common law allowed them.[17] In other words, even in the one legal system that is paradigmatic of women's degraded legal status, a plurality of traditions rendered women's independent legal action possible.

MULTIPLE LEGAL IDENTITIES FOR WOMEN

Women in the central and late Middle Ages had to deal not only with multiple legal traditions but also with multiple identities within those traditions. Embracing the gendered conceptual vocabulary of the *ius commune* was an indispensible feature of the legal strategies of female litigants in this period, as they and their legal counsel worked both to present the facts of the case and (perhaps more importantly) to tell a story about who a woman was, couched in terms of assumptions about women's essential nature. A particular case from early fourteenth-century Spain is illustrative of this legal strategizing. In September 1303, Ermessenda de Cabrenys, a member of the minor nobility in the region around the northern Catalan city of Girona, was called to appear before the local arm of the royal courts to answer charges against her (unspecified, but likely involving one or more of the debts that she owed, as attested to in documents bound together with the court summons and the plaintiff's response). It was not Ermessenda herself who appeared in court, however, but her procurator Berenguer de Devesia. Reaching back to the law of the fifth-century Theodosian Code and the sixth-century Code of Justinian, Ermessenda's procurator argued that because his client was a *materfamilias*—a term of ancient Roman origin that comprehended both sex and status, but not motherhood per se—it was inappropriate for the magistrates to compel her to mix with the "crowds of men" at the law courts. She was prepared to pay the fine demanded by the king's legal representative, but would not consent to appear in person before the royal court in Girona, as to do so would be an affront to her status. The procurator's stated concern was thus not the payment itself but rather the impropriety of his client being forced to leave her own home to answer a charge in public.[18]

An analysis of this case could very easily—and not inaccurately—turn on the disjuncture between law and practice. Ermessenda's procurator was using a provision of Roman law with a specific gender meaning—that the nature of women made it inappropriate for them to be compelled to associate with the unfamiliar men who populated the male world of the law courts—in order to assert his client's immunity; this, despite the fact that Ermessenda's previous business dealings had already proven her quite capable of undertaking public action on her own behalf. But Ermessenda's case before the royal court of Girona also illustrates how women's own litigation played a part in reinforcing gendered legal assumptions. Ermessenda's construction of her legal identity played upon ideas about gender inherited from the Roman law of the *ius commune*: her procurator referred to her "matronly modesty" and argued that the court's order that she present herself personally was "contrary to the modesty and shame of females."[19] In this case, Ermessenda's procurator was asserting that his client, who seems to have been a wealthy (if improvident) woman and a force to be reckoned with in the Girona region, was, because of disabilities inherent in her sex, too emotionally fragile to appear personally in the male world of the courtroom. Since Ermessenda had offered to pay the fine in either case, the advantage she was seeking was probably not financial in nature; rather, she may have been attempting to prevent erosion of her legal sovereignty as a minor territorial landlord living in her own domains outside the direct jurisdiction of the Girona officials. Whatever her motivations, the nature of her response serves as an example of how women might use ostensibly negative legal stereotypes to their own advantage.

In addition to representing herself in terms of the overall legal-cultural category of "woman," a female litigant or her representative had to consider her relational status (e.g. daughter, wife, widow) when constructing her courtroom identity. Relational identities such as these predated the *ius commune*, and may already have been central to women's legal standing under early medieval law. But the *ius commune* naturalized these categories, making it essential for women to take them into account in their litigation. One example of the importance of women's relational identity can be found in cases concerning property. Legal ideas about women's inherent incapacity meant that most adult women had recourse to a provision of Roman law (the Velleian *senatus consultum*, *c*.46 CE) that stated that a woman could not be compelled to take part in public business transactions, thereby freeing a wife from economic liability for any contracts her husband made without her direct participation.[20] Yet the way medieval women interacted with this law differed substantially, depending on their relational status: a married woman whose husband was squandering her dowry could plead her privileges under the Velleian *senatus consultum* in order to have her properties sequestered from her husband's creditors, while a widow claiming guardianship of her minor children would formally renounce this same privilege in order to take on the rights and responsibilities of an independent head of household.[21]

Relational status also affected the way that violence against women was measured; rape litigation provides a good illustration of this point. According to the Catalan Code of Tortosa, a man found guilty of raping a virgin should either marry her or give her a marriage portion as he would a wife. The rapist of a married woman, however, faced hanging, while a rapist whose victim was neither a virgin nor married was required to provide enough money for her to find a husband appropriate to her station.[22] These varied levels of punishment for the same crime provide a clue as to what was at stake in different types of rape prosecutions, and women represented themselves accordingly. Women who were young, virginal, or unmarried tended to emphasize those facts about themselves in order to underline their innocence and the harm done, both to their persons and their marriage prospects. Married women, who stood to gain little (financial compensation for rape of a married woman was rare) and lose much (in terms of reputation, both theirs and their husbands'), rarely brought charges of rape before the courts. And unmarried women who were not minors or virgins seldom prosecuted for rape unless they were willing and able to prove their reputations along with the charges they were bringing against their assailants.

This final point about the reputation of unmarried women illustrates yet another aspect of legal identity that women had to negotiate: the binary of respectable versus disreputable. Many rape cases from areas all over late medieval Europe emphasize either the victim's youth or her virginity, often employing terms like "deflowered" or "corrupted" to underline the fundamentally transformative nature of the damage done in the act.[23] Convincing use of a virginity narrative could increase the penalty on the convicted assailant, but it was also a way of asserting the victim's unblemished reputation prior to the attack. Reputation was important in other types of women's litigation as well: in cases of marital violence or neglect, for example, married women went out of their way to prove that they had been good wives and good women, opposing their behavior to that of their ne'er-do-well husbands or the "depraved" women with whom their husbands may have been consorting. But the necessary obverse of this legal strategy was that a woman whose reputation was questionable could be subject to physical violence with little or no legal remedy.

LAW AND COMMUNITY

In all of these cases, we see female litigants actively engaging with legal concepts of gender, drawn either directly or indirectly from the *ius commune*, as part of a process of translating their circumstances and their own identities into legally actionable terms. This meant that women had to speak the language of the learned law and its many overlapping categories, each with its own set of demands on any individual woman's behavior and self-representation. But women and their legal counsel were not the only ones to play a role in this process of definition. Public opinion about a woman, together with her own self-representation, determined an individual woman's place within these overlapping sets of legal identities, and the procedural innovations of the *ius commune* were what gave legal weight to both.

When considering the interaction of litigation and ideas about gender, one of the most important developments in procedural law during the central and late Middle Ages was the admissibility of reputation as evidence in preliminary proceedings (which integrated the common knowledge of all members of a community, both male and female) with the specialized knowledge of legal professionals (who were exclusively male). This general, often unsubstantiated knowledge about events came under the rubric of *fama*, a concept present in both Roman and canon law, loosely translatable here as "common knowledge" or "rumor."[24] *Fama* could mean talk about the facts of a case, but it also might encompass a community's beliefs about a particular person. An 1199 decretal by Pope Innocent III had established that an individual's bad reputation could serve in an inquest as part of the grounds for bringing a case to trial, and later commentators clarified that publicly flaunted misconduct (as opposed to the open secrets that produced *fama*) could likewise serve as grounds for launching an inquest into the crime itself. Most significantly, reputation within a community could be the "reasonable cause" that sparked a full-fledged inquest into a particular case. That is, reputation and rumor could decide matters of law (i.e., whether there was a case to be made), but not matters of guilt or innocence.[25]

By the late Middle Ages, inquiries into a person's *fama* within a community had become routine in criminal inquests, and while ordinary people might not have understood all the nuances of legal procedure, they seem to have had a good grasp of *fama*. In a 1203 case from Tuscany, witnesses asked to specify what they meant when they used that term replied that it was "what all say publicly;" in Pisa in 1192 a witness defined *fama* as "what the majority of men say."[26] And when questioned as to what they meant when they said something was *fama*, the answers of witnesses questioned in one case from fourteenth-century Catalonia varied slightly from person to person, but were generally similar: *fama* was "what people say," "what the people say all over the place," or "that which the majority of people in any place affirm to be true."[27]

In a legal culture where a woman's reputation within a community could become part of the discourse surrounding the relative propriety of her activities, *fama* could be critical in creating or undermining a woman's attempts to represent herself before a court in terms of the many legal categories to which she belonged. Even if a "witness" had not personally seen or heard the crime in question, procedural rules of the central and late Middle Ages allowed testimony that amounted to reports of common gossip, not only as to the offense committed but also with regards to the reputations of both the offenders and victims. Female reputation could extend to any number of ways that an individual woman failed to conform to an entire complex of gender ideals. In northwestern Europe, especially, reputation increasingly came to encompass prosecutions for actionable language or "scolding," both of which fell disproportionately on women.[28]

Sexual reputation was, however, by far the most common grounds for calling a woman's *fama* into question. In one case from the courts of fifteenth-century Florence, Giovanni della Casa, member of a prosperous Florentine family with merchant and banking interests, did not deny that he had carried on a sexual relationship with Lusanna, an artisan's daughter who claimed to be his wife. His strategy, rather, was to argue in court that his lover had been sexually involved with several neighborhood men before their own affair took place, and to that end he produced witnesses who reported that Lusanna's low sexual reputation was public knowledge. She was, according to several of her neighbors, a "bad woman" whose sexual affairs both before and after her (first) husband Andrea's death brought shame on herself, her husband, and her family.[29] In another case, this one from the Catalan town of Vilafranca, when Valentí Golet stood accused of having murdered his wife Blanquina, royal prosecutors questioned several of his neighbors as to how well they had known the victim, and whether they "knew or had heard tell" anything about her reputation (*fama*). According to witnesses, it was common knowledge in town that she had been four or five months pregnant when Valentí had married her, and that she had carried on an affair with Romeu Comes, a royal official in the same town, as well as with other men, both before and during her marriage.[30]

Neighbors' reports on *fama* thus went beyond the local talk about events to delve into the reputations of the people involved, illustrating how community knowledge about a woman's behavior played a critical role in the formation and enforcement of the legal discourse that surrounded her. A woman who successfully presented herself in the law's terms was laying claim to the various legal protections available to women of distinct relational statuses, to respectable people of both sexes, and to women in general. Conversely, a woman who could not successfully represent herself as adhering to these many overlapping sets of behavioral expectations could find herself excluded from the protection of the law. In the worst-case scenario, a woman's bad reputation among her neighbors and associates could transform into *infamia*, a legal condition that translated into a diminution or loss of legal personality.[31] The manifest existence of individual nonconforming women did not, however, trouble overall legal assumptions about women more generally; rather, these women were simply removed from the protected legal class of "woman" and had to muddle through as best they could, with neither the protections reserved for women nor the full legal authority enjoyed by men.

The precise legal status of these women of "evil fame" varied widely from one place to another in the late medieval West. For example, medieval ordinances from the French town of Eyrieu required a man who raped a prostitute to pay a fine of 100 sous, and prostitutes in later medieval Languedoc may have been able to sue for rape. In Castile, on the other hand, men who raped prostitutes faced lighter penalties than men whose victims were more respectable women, and the Customs of the Catalan city of Tortosa explicitly excluded "public whores" from the list of rape victims to whom compensation had to be paid.[32]

A more common result of damaged reputation was loss of community, as offended neighbors worked to expel women whose actions or reputation placed them outside the bounds of acceptable female behavior. In late fifteenth-century England, the town of Great Yarmouth banished the married woman Alice Dymmok for "harboring suspicious persons," "promoting immorality," cursing her neighbors, and being a general nuisance. Around the same time, Margaret Morgan's unsavory reputation prompted neighbors in one London ward after another to expel her from their midst: according to witnesses, the first expulsion (from Langbourne ward) had taken place because Margaret was "of ill fame and in the parish commonly said, held, and reputed an adulteress and a whore."[33] Further south, in the year 1330, King Alfonso IV of the Crown of Aragon ordered the councilors of the city of Barcelona to respond to the complaints of "good men and women" to eject the prostitutes from the neighborhood in which they were living, "lest they [the prostitutes] cast a shadow upon the chastity and pure reputation of others." The king noted that the councilors should not be deterred even if the "base and public women" in question protested that they owned the houses they were being ejected from, because those women were not actually being deprived of their property, which they could always rent out to others.[34] The women who fell afoul of community opinion in these cases did not lose their status as legal persons. They were, however, subject to a degree of legal discrimination and even outright violence that other women were not. The determination of the level of legal disability to which an individual woman would be subject rested on her *fama*—born in community interactions, then given legal weight through the procedural law of the *ius commune*.

We should note that not all exclusions from the protected class of "woman" were imposed upon women from without. As noted earlier, some women, especially widows, deliberately opted out of the Velleian *senatus consultum*'s special protections for women, as part of the process of shaping a new legal identity as independent heads of household and administrators of the family estate. By claiming this status, together with all its privileges and responsibilities, a widow was in a sense agreeing to govern herself, since there was no man there to do so. The increased level of surveillance that went along with this independent status could severely constrain a widow's behavior. But, as shown above, the dynamics of the law–gender–community relationship were even more severe for women who were removed against their will from the protected category of "women."

CONCLUSIONS

The *ius commune* revolution of the central and late Middle Ages has often been regarded as a turning point for the relationship between women and law. Most notably, historians point to the reintroduction of Roman law and the injection of its patriarchal ideas about women into the thinking of legislators and jurists. The lopsided gender assumptions inherent in Roman law were partly ameliorated by canon law, but canonists were more interested in women's spiritual equality than in the more mundane issues that brought women before the secular courts.

Yet it may be that historians have been right about the *ius commune* and women, but for the wrong reasons, lending too much agency to an impersonal body of law and not enough to women themselves. Substantive law provided a theoretical foundation for many aspects of women's subordinate status, but it could not have functioned well without women's active participation. As the broader gender assumptions that lay behind the laws of the *ius commune* made their way into both law codes and the legal imaginations of the men who adjudicated cases according to those laws, women and their legal representatives had to adopt the gendered conceptual vocabulary of the new law to structure their legal narratives and to represent who they were within both their families and their communities. Thus, the procedural law of the *ius commune* played as great a role as substantive law in determining women's status during this period. By making community dynamics a part of litigation, canonists and civilians fused the language of the learned law—including its centuries-old ideas about gender—to community knowledge and to women's own strategic use of the law's gendered conceptual vocabulary. This process rendered women and their communities essential participants in the process of turning abstract legal ideas about women into reality through the process of litigation, specifically in accordance with the procedural rules of the *ius commune* itself.

FURTHER READING

Bellomo, Manlio. *The Common Legal Past of Europe, 1000–1800.* Trans. Lydia G. Cochrane. Washington, DC: Catholic University of America Press, 1995.

Fenster, Thelma and Daniel Lord Smail, eds. *Fama: The Politics of Talk and Reputation in Medieval Europe.* Ithaca, NY: Cornell University Press, 2003.

Gardner, Jane F. *Women in Roman Law and Society.* Bloomington, IN: Indiana University Press, 1986.

Hanawalt, Barbara. "'Of Good and Ill Repute': The Limits of Community Tolerance," in *"Of Good and Ill Repute": Gender and Social Control in Medieval England.* Oxford: Oxford University Press, 1998, 1–17.

Karras, Ruth Mazo. *Common Women: Prostitution and Sexuality in Medieval England.* New York: Oxford University Press, 1996.

Kelleher, Marie A. *The Measure of Woman: Law and Female Identity in the Crown of Aragon.* Philadelphia: University of Pennsylvania Press, 2010.

Kuehn, Thomas. "Person and Gender in the Laws," in Judith Brown and Robert Davis, eds, *Gender and Society in Renaissance Italy.* London: Longman, 1998, 87–106.

Lansing, Carol. "Girls in Trouble in Late Medieval Bologna," in Konrad Eisenbichler, ed., *The Premodern Teenager: Youth in Society 1150–1650.* Toronto: Centre for Reformation and Renaissance Studies, 2002, 293–309.

Reyerson, Kathryn and Thomas Kuehn. "Women and Law in France and Italy," in Linda E. Mitchell, ed., *Women in Medieval Western European Culture.* New York: Garland, 1999, 131–41.

Skinner, Patricia. "Disputes and Disparity: Women in Court in Medieval Southern Italy." *Reading Medieval Studies,* 22 (1996): 85–105.

Synek, Eva M. "'Ex utroque sexu et fidelium tres ordines'—The Status of Women in Early Medieval Canon Law." *Gender and History,* 12 (2000): 595–621.

NOTES

1. Lisa M. Bitel, *Women in Early Medieval Europe* (Cambridge: Cambridge University Press, 2002), 67–71.
2. Eva M. Synek, "'Ex utroque sexu et fidelium tres ordines'—The Status of Women in Early Medieval Canon Law," *Gender and History,* 12 (2000): 595–621.

3. Manlio Bellomo, *The Common Legal Past of Europe, 1000–1800*, trans. Lydia G. Cochrane (Washington, DC: Catholic University of America Press, 1995), 55–77 and 112–17; James A. Brundage, *The Medieval Origins of the Legal Profession: Canonists, Civilians, and Courts* (Chicago: University of Chicago Press, 2008), 75–125; for England, see R. H. Helmholz, *The Ius Commune in England* (Oxford: Oxford University Press, 2001), esp. 3–15; and Brundage, *The Medieval Origins of the Legal Profession*, 248 and 368–69.

4. Jane F. Gardner, *Women in Roman Law and Society* (Bloomington, IN: Indiana University Press, 1986), 18–22.

5. Gaius, *Inst.* 1.190, as reproduced in Judith Evans Grubbs, ed., *Women and the Law in the Roman Empire: A Sourcebook on Marriage, Divorce, and Widowhood* (London: Routledge, 2002), 29.

6. Gardner, *Women in Roman Law and Society*, 262–63.

7. René Metz, "Le statut de la femme en droit canonique medieval," *Recueils de la société Jean Bodin*, 12 (1962): 86–89. See also Gratian, C. 33 q. 5 d.p.c. 20 for head/body metaphor, and C. 33 q. 7 d.p.c. 17 for his etymology of "man" and "woman."

8. Maria Teresa Guerra Medici. *Orientamenti civilistici e canonistici sulla condizione della donna* (Naples: Edizioni scientifiche italiane, 1996), 45.

9. Diana Arauz Mercado, *La protección jurídica de la mujer en Castilla y León (siglos XII–XIV)* (Valladolid: Junta de Castilla y León, Consejería de Cultura y Turismo, 2007), 291–95; see also María Francisca Gámez Montalvo, *Régimen jurídico de la mujer en la familia castellana medieval* (Granada: Comares, 1998), 13–14.

10. *Código de las Costumbres de Tortosa* [hereafter *C. Tort.*], ed. D. Bienvenido Oliver (Madrid: Ginesta, 1876), IV.7.1; *Furs de València*, ed. Germà Colón and Arcadi Garcia (Barcelona: Barcino, 1970–2007), IV.XIX.1 and 28.

11. Kathryn Reyerson and Thomas Kuehn, "Women and Law in France and Italy," in Linda E. Mitchell, ed., *Women in Medieval Western European Culture* (New York and London: Garland, 1999), 133–34; Rebecca Winer, *Women, Wealth, and Community in Perpignan, c.1250–1300: Christians, Jews, and Enslaved Muslims in a Medieval Mediterranean Town* (Burlington, Vt.: Ashgate, 2006), esp. chapter 2, "The Christian Woman as Daughter, Wife, Mother, and Widow."

12. Patricia Skinner, "Disputes and Disparity: Women in Court in Medieval Southern Italy," *Reading Medieval Studies*, 22 (1996): 88–91.

13. Reyerson and Kuehn, "Women and Law in France and Italy," esp. 136–38; and Thomas Kuehn, "Person and Gender in the Laws," in Judith Brown and Robert Davis, eds, *Gender and Society in Renaissance Italy* (London and New York: Longman, 1998), 97–101.

14. Bellomo, *The Common Legal Past of Europe*, 101–106.

15. For France, see Barbara B. Diefendorf, "Women and Property in *Ancien Régime* France: Theory and Practice in Dauphiné and Paris," in John Brewer and Susan Staves, eds, *Early Modern Conceptions of Property* (London and New York: Routledge, 1996), 175–77; for the Low Countries, see Martha C. Howell, *The Marriage Exchange: Property, Social Place, and Gender in Cities of the Low Countries, 1300–1550* (Chicago: University of Chicago Press, 1998).

16. R. C. Van Caenegem, *The Birth of the English Common Law* (Cambridge: Cambridge University Press, 1973), 88–91.

17. Amy Louise Erickson, *Women and Property in Early Modern England* (London and New York: Routledge, 1993); Barbara A. Hanawalt, *Wealth of Wives: Women, Law, and Economy in Late Medieval London* (Oxford: Oxford University Press, 2007), 9–13 and

98–104; Janet S. Loengard, "Common Law for Margery: Separate but Not Equal," in Mitchell, ed., *Women in Medieval Western European Culture*, 117–29. For *femmes soles*, see Marjorie K. McIntosh, "The Benefits and Drawbacks of Femme Sole Status in England, 1300–1630," *Journal of British Studies*, 44 (2005): 410–38.

18. Arxiu de la Corona d'Aragó [hereafter ACA], Cancelleria, Processos en quart, 1303-F, first part, 1v–3r. Marie A. Kelleher, *The Measure of Woman: Law and Female Identity in the Crown of Aragon* (Philadelphia: University of Pennsylvania Press, 2010), 15–16.

19. ACA, Cancelleria, Processos en quart, 1303-F, first part, 5v–6r.

20. *Digest* (of Justinian), 16.1.1–2.

21. Kelleher, *The Measure of Woman*, 59–61 and 66–68; Julius Kirshner, "Wives' Claims Against Insolvent Husbands in Late Medieval Italy," in Julius Kirshner and Suzanne Fonay Wemple, eds, *Women of the Medieval World: Essays in Honor of John H. Mundy* (Oxford: Basil Blackwell, 1985), 256–303.

22. *C. Tort.* 9.2.1–3.

23. Kathryn Gravdal, *Ravishing Maidens: Writing Rape in Medieval French Literature and Law* (Philadelphia: University of Pennsylvania Press, 1991), 128–30; Kelleher, *The Measure of Woman*, 136–38; Guido Ruggiero, *The Boundaries of Eros: Sex Crimes and Sexuality in Renaissance Venice* (Oxford: Oxford University Press, 1985), 98–102.

24. For a brief overview of the medieval use of this concept, see Thelma Fenster and Daniel Lord Smail, eds, *Fama: The Politics of Talk and Reputation in Medieval Europe* (Ithaca, NY: Cornell University Press, 2003), especially the editors' introduction to the volume, pp. 1–11.

25. Lotte Kéry, "Inquisitio—denunciatio—exceptio: Möglichkeiten der Verfahrenseinleitung im Dekretalenrecht," *Zeitschrift der Savigny-Stiftung für Rechtsgeschichte—Kanonistische Abteilung*, 118 (2001): 239–43; Henry Ansgar Kelly, "Inquisition and the Prosecution of Heresy: Misconceptions and Abuses," *Church History*, 58 (1989), 446; Thomas Kuehn, "Fama as Legal Status in Renaissance Florence," in Fenster and Smail, eds., *Fama*, 29. For specific canon law citations, see *Liber extra* 5.3.31 and 5.1.24.

26. Chris Wickham, "Fama and the Law in Twelfth-Century Tuscany," in Fenster and Smail, eds, *Fama*, 203.

27. ACA, Cancelleria, Processos en foli 3/2 (1296), 4r–7v.

28. Sandy Bardsley, *Venomous Tongues: Speech and Gender in Late Medieval England* (Philadelphia: University of Pennsylvania Press, 2006); see also Ellen E. Kittell, "Reconciliation or Punishment: Women, Community, and Malefaction in the Medieval County of Flanders," in Ellen E. Kittell and Mary A. Suydam, eds, *The Texture of Society: Medieval Women in the Southern Low Countries* (New York: Palgrave Macmillan, 2004), 16.

29. Gene Brucker, *Giovanni and Lusanna: Love and Marriage in Renaissance Florence* (Berkeley: University of California Press, 1986), 26–27 and 89.

30. ACA, Cancelleria, Processos en foli 126/19 (1378).

31. Peter Landau, *Die Entstehung des kanonischen Infamiebegriffs von Gratian bis zur Glossa ordinaria* (Cologne and Graz: Böhlau, 1966), 3–4. See also Edward Peters, "Wounded Names: The Medieval Doctrine of Infamy," in Edward B. King and Susan J. Ridyard, eds, *Law in Mediaeval Life and Thought*, Sewanee Mediaeval Studies, 5 (Sewanee, Tenn.: The University of the South, 1990), 69, and Winfried Trusen, "Der Inquisitionsprozeß: Seine

historischen Grundlagen und frühen Formen," *Zeitschrift der Savigny-Stiftung für Rechtsgeschichte—Kanonistische Abteilung*, 74 (1988): 180.

32. For France, see Annik Porteau-Bitker, "Criminalité et délinquance féminines dans le droit pénal des XIIIe et XIVe siècles," *Revue historique de droit français et étranger*, 58 (1980): 13–56, and Leah Lydia Otis, *Prostitution in Medieval Society: The History of an Urban Institution in Languedoc* (Chicago: University of Chicago Press, 1985), 64–68; for Castile, see Ricardo Córdoba de la Llave, *El instinto diabólico: agresiones sexuales en la Castilla medieval* (Córdoba: Universidad de Córdoba, 1994), 25–26; for Tortosa, see *C. Tort.* 9.2.3.

33. Ruth Mazo Karras, *Common Women: Prostitution and Sexuality in Medieval England* (Oxford: Oxford University Press, 1996), 68–69.

34. *Constitucions i altres drets de Catalunya* (Barcelona: n.p., 1704; repr. Barcelona: Base, 1973), *Pragmáticas* IX.3.2.

CHAPTER 10

···

BRIDEPRICE, DOWRY, AND OTHER MARITAL ASSIGNS

···

SUSAN MOSHER STUARD

Marriage gifts provided a significant transfer of family wealth in medieval times. Today our chief transfer of family-held wealth occurs with the death of the senior generation; medieval families differed somewhat by transferring large sums at the marriages of their offspring—traditionally to their sons but by the central Middle Ages often to their daughters instead. Medieval people recognized that lack of resources would restrict opportunities for young couples to establish new households, open land to cultivation, or follow a trade, or for a husband to pursue a promising career or business with some assurance that his widow and orphaned children would have a living in the event of his death. Generational sharing of the expense of establishing newlyweds in households abetted economic growth.

Dowry practice in ancient Rome had involved a gift given by the bride's family that was considered, in terms of Roman law, her *legitim*, or share of her natal family inheritance, sometimes referred to as her "falcidian quarter," although it was unlikely to represent a quarter of her family's wealth. Late medieval cities like Florence adopted this Roman dowry system; it was part of a Mediterranean-wide revival of ancient precedent. The story of marriage gifts in the intervening sixth through the eleventh centuries is complicated, allowing some insights into how marriage gifts to women came to shape the economy, the demographic regime, and attitudes toward gender in medieval Europe.

In Florence as late as the fifteenth century, most men married when they "still lived as sons, younger brothers, or more distant relatives ... under someone else's roof."[1] This was the large household pattern that characterized southern Europe, and it was a contrast to the smaller household units found farther north. In Florence, generous wedding gifts from the bride's family could remedy a bridegroom's dependence upon his natal household, so that he, sometimes twice his bride's age at marriage, could set about creating his own *casa* (household). In this way, the town's lineages, both great and small, spread to all corners of the community, capturing youthful energy and ambition backed by timely infusions of wedding wealth.

Much of the scholarship on marriage gifts is concerned with where these gifts of dowry went wrong or grew out of all proportion, leading to litigation, contested marriages, marital troubles, even outright crime. This study will look at that literature, as well as the dramatic reversal of the direction in which marital wealth flowed at marriage, a momentous alteration that occurred sometime between the eleventh and the thirteenth centuries and reintroduced Roman *dos* (dowry) to Mediterranean cities. By 1500 this transformation had made inroads into European marriage practices north of the Alps.

From the sixth to the tenth century, the so-called "male" dowry may be found in the laws of the Lombards. A quarter of family wealth was given to a son when he married so that he could sustain his new household. In other regions, custom or law specified a different portion for the marrying son, even as much as one third. This has generally been considered a feature of Germanic customary practice because evidence of these gifts may be found in Frankish, Saxon, Burgundian, Visigothic, Alamannic, and Lombardic laws, and the payment served as evidence for valid marriage.[2] Men whose families could afford to provide this wherewithal could marry and establish households. By the early eleventh century, at the latest, a modification took place: a *morgengabe* (morning gift) marking the formal act of consummation of a marriage became the chief assign from husband to wife, placing the marrying couple on a more independent footing from their parents since it rendered irrelevant an exchange of guardianship by payment. Earlier Lombardic ideas that guardianship was transferred through a gift of wealth at marriage vanished.

A family's distribution of wealth to their son, the bridegroom, in all likelihood promoted intermarriage from the sixth to the eleventh centuries. Anecdotal evidence about powerful dynastic families indicates that marriages were made in which one spouse was an Arian while the other followed Christian dogma as proclaimed by Rome, or in which Germans married Romans or their Latinized subjects. Gifts, often lavish ones, marked these occasions; indeed some gifts were impressive enough to be recorded in great detail. This generous gift-giving for unions that crossed cultural, religious, and language barriers may have encouraged assimilation.

After the eleventh century, in a more adequately documented age, Italian townspeople, and those in towns in southern France and in Spain, replaced the Germanic *morgengabe* awarded to the bride by her husband with Roman dowry as the chief marital assign. In the Adriatic region, no change occurred at all because the area had always been loyal to the late Roman practice of a dowry from the bride's family as the major gift at marriage. In northwest Italy the transition to dowry occurred first in towns. In 1975, Eleanor Riemer also pointed out how the study of inherited Roman law texts convinced civic officials to mandate dowry from a bride's family so that a community like Siena might live "in all things according to Roman law."[3] In 1978, Diane Owen Hughes wrote a pathbreaking analysis of how this change affected the lives of urban families in Italy.[4]

In Italian towns that mandated dowries at marriage, gifts were soon hedged with complex statute law restraints: how the gift was to be given, when, to whom, and in what form (generally money), and how it was to be managed once given. Laws mandated restitution of dowry if the wedding did not occur. Laws were also clear that a dowry belonged to the wife, but the husband managed the sum with the legal requirement that he preserve and increase the gift but never squander it. This requirement raised the issue of risk in the burgeoning commercial economy in the Mediterranean world. If husbands invested dowries as required by statute law, there were unavoidable risks; returning an intact dowry to a wife upon her husband's death was a tall order, as many families found out to their dismay.

The contrast between *morgengabe* and dowry, once given, lay not necessarily with which spouse owned the gift—both assigns were actually possessions of the wife—but with who controlled the gift.[5] The wife had control over the *morgengabe*, which was likely to be given in kind (land, slaves, animals, equipment, houses, ornaments, clothes, and arms). This gift symbolized a marriage based neither on the consent of the parties (as was true in late Roman law and in medieval canon law) nor on rights through purchase (as in the earlier Lombardic practice of *mundium* or guardianship), but on a contract marking their union. Women held the right to control their marriage gifts and when brides' families began to award dowry, this right disappeared.

Pierre Bonnassie, in studying the records of the Vivas family that lived just outside Barcelona's walls in the years after 1000, noted that dowry in cash was awarded to daughters when they married, while sons received land, which might not be formally divided until the death of the father. Bonnassie noted that families' desire to hold lands intact for the patriline drove this change to cash awards for brides.[6] Wedding gifts in cash for daughters' marriages protected family landholdings while providing support for daughters and cementing good relations with sons-in-law. Clearly wedding gifts in cash also promoted the monetization of the economy wherever they spread from the eleventh century and beyond, although more analysis of the process is needed. The award of "good" coin, which was often specified in charters that accompanied dowries, became a point of honor in Italian towns. Special coins *"in sugello"* (under special seal) or secured in purses distinguished this money from workaday cash as the best coin available, and it was to be protected and guarded with care.

One impediment to the study of the reversal of the direction in which wealth flowed at marriage, that is, from *morgengabe* to Roman dowry, has been the long-standing controversy among Italian historians over the consequence of Germanic or Roman law and custom in the emergence of medieval Italy. Ample evidence exists to support both Romanists and Germanists, particularly in regard to the development of Italian civil law.[7] As noted above, the *morgengabe* that was replaced by Roman dowry was not the brideprice of early Germanic law but an outright gift to the bride with no transfer of guardianship implied. According to Thomas Kuehn, Florentines seem to have self-consciously revived a form of Germanic guardianship *(mundualdus)* by the fourteenth century, but it was quite distinct from awarding gifts at marriage.[8] Nor did Italian husbands cease the practice of awarding their own gifts to their brides, even while Roman dowry represented the principal transfer of wealth. The husband's marital gift was given to his bride, but was policed by statute law so that it remained a small gift in relation to dowry.

The statute laws that came to surround the awarding of Roman dowry in towns are as consequential for women's history as the awards themselves. Juristic sources—the twelfth-century *Concordance of Discordant Canons*, known as Gratian's *Decretum*, later explications of canon laws of marriage like those of Giovanni d'Andrea (*c*.1275–1348), and *consilia* (legal opinions) of Baldus Ubaldi (*c*.1327–1400) and Bartolus of Sassoferrato (1313–1357)—help scholars to understand the theory underlying numerous lawsuits.

Civil law and canon law did not necessarily agree when marriage disputes arose, so many *consilia* offered by the legal scholars who commented on marriage were attempts to reconcile the two. Canon law allowed girls who were twelve and boys who were fourteen to give legal consent to their marriages. Children's emancipation from parental control in civil law clashed with this doctrine of consent; marriage did not emancipate daughters at all in Florence.[9] Bartolus of Sassoferrato noted that one of the differences between canon and civil law was that "in civil law the *patria potestas* lasts in every age of a child, but in canon law *patria potestas* comes to an end at adulthood, at marriage, whether carnal or spiritual, and at the taking of orders."[10] It is an understatement to note that disputes resulted.

In contrast to *morgengabe*, the new Roman dowry was controlled by the husband, and sometimes his family, despite the fact it was the wife's property. This too led to disputes. Acting independently of her husband's family, widowed Bianca Spini (1380–1446/50) returned to her family's palace next to the church of Santa Trinità at age 47. Her father gave her the handsome sum of 800 florins, allowing her to snub her husband's family, with whom she contested the huge sum of 1,115 florins, of which 850 were her dowry. Apparently, she never resolved this dispute, but since she wrote her own will, scholars know that she left adequate money to decorate the family chapel at Santa Trinità at her death.[11] Canon law allowed married or widowed women to write wills and claimed jurisdiction over them. A wife might write a will to the benefit of her brothers and sisters, or even her parents, which might well oppose the interests of her husband's patriline or even her own children, who were part of their father's lineage and whose rights were protected by civil statute law.

In legal terms, dowries placed married women in a distinctive position. Families attempted rather startling legal maneuvers to take advantage of the fact that a dowried woman could not be held responsible for her male relatives' debts under civil law. A Florentine woman did not share her husband's political exile and, exempt from paying his debts, sometimes undertook ventures in trade unencumbered by his obligations. Brothers might repudiate an inheritance in favor of their sister because the inheritance was laden with debt and she was not held responsible for paying it. This ploy was invoked in the interest of the bride's natal family, rather than in the interest of the woman herself, which is one reason why historians sometimes couch the issue in terms of whether married women were mere pawns or players under the dotal regime. Many dowry disputes ended disastrously for widows who needed dowry returned to them for bread and board. Their lives were caught up in a complex set of conflicting demands from husband's kin and natal family. A woman's dowry and legal disabilities played out in elaborate schemes to preserve familial wealth among agnatic kin (natal relatives) and cognates (the family into which a bride married), with both sides trying to prosper and avoid burdensome debts at the same time. The needs of a widow and her children could be lost in the face of the strategies undertaken by either or both sides. Ideally, at her death a woman's dowry would be divided among her offspring, but even this ideal was transgressed. The stakes rose higher as dowries rose in value; elaborate legal ploys seem to have become more complex in response to civil statute laws that had become more specific over the decades. In Ragusa/Dubrovnik, the sums awarded as dowries more than doubled from 1235 to 1440, when they leveled out at about 1,600 *hyperpera*.[12] In the decades following the Black Plague (1347–1350), dowries served as an important conduit for the wealth of orphaned heiresses who enriched other families that survived. In Venice, the curve of dowry increase was even steeper, and the 800 to 1000 ducat dowries awarded by members of the patriciate and the wealthiest *cittadini originarii* (nonpatrician citizens) of the fourteenth and fifteenth centuries represented fortunes. Other cities attempted to keep up with the munificence displayed by the wealthiest and most powerful city states. As a consequence, dowries came to represent not just security for the future but great wealth, with the potential for increased honor and prestige for new husbands.

Take, for example, the handsome dowry received by Giannino della Piazza from Nicolo Sturion, a very wealthy *cittadino originario* of Venice, when he married Nicolo's eldest daughter Maria in 1390. The devout Maria was very unhappy in her marriage and returned home almost immediately. Giannino left town to become a knight in the war between Francesco Gonzaga, ruler of Mantua, and Giangaleazzo Visconti, duke of Milan. This required an entire equipage, including expensive war horses, and it is almost certain that Giannino used Maria's dowry for that purpose. He was not heard of again in Venice. The Sturion family was simply left without recourse, although they responded compassionately and welcomed their daughter back to their home, where she devoted her young life to pursuing sainthood.[13] They gained no advantages from prestigious new connections, but their great wealth allowed them to absorb this serious financial loss. Other families hoping to obtain a well-connected bridegroom with a large gift of dowry suffered serious setbacks from a fiasco like the marriage of Gianinno and Maria.

Much recent scholarship has labeled the dotal regime a marriage market, sometimes using terms like "marriage bargain" or "barter" or other phrases referring to hard-edged negotiations for dowry sums. It is important to remember, however, that brides were not for purchase where Roman dowry was given. Rather, the bride's family obtained an enterprising son-in-law for their investment of dotal funds. They hoped the groom would prove to be a good husband and ally who would enrich the bride's family, even as that family fulfilled its legal obligations for the daughter's future welfare. In the cities of Italy, promising young bachelors set high demands for dotal funds when they married, and the most successful made upwardly mobile marriages. They took full advantage of in-laws' manifest need for a future return of favors and contacts.

A great deal rested on how, and how well, one married, and this was particularly the case among wealthy families. The honor of both families was involved when contracting a marriage. Although laws restricted the groom's gift to his bride, he and his family could indulge their pursuit of greater honor and prestige by awarding nondotal gifts of clothes, jewels, and house furnishings at the wedding. Both families could increase the solemn pomp of the occasion when the bride was conducted to her husband's home with a lavish display of gifts and rich costumes. The successful marriage strategist and fiercely independent widow Alessandra Strozzi (1406–1471) wrote to her son Filippo about his newfound bride and dowry, "Get the jewels ready, and beautiful ones, for a wife is found! Being beautiful and Filippo Strozzi's wife, she needs to have fine jewels – since, just as you are honored in everything else, you should not be lacking in this."[14] When it came to the marriage of her daughter Caterina, Alessandra Strozzi could rely upon the generosity of the upwardly mobile silk merchant and bridegroom Marco Parenti to provide more in gifts like fine silk than she had offered for her daughter's dowry.

But other brides' families worried just as much as grooms' families about honoring weddings and providing finery for the bride. In 1353 in Florence, the guardians, not the parents, of Tommasa Niccolini provided an impressive trousseau including fine new green cloth for a cloak and elegant new crimson for a dress, although her second dress was to be sewn from green cloth that was on hand.[15] The laws of Venice permitted four elaborate wedding dresses, but trains were limited in length and certain decorative effects, such as a border embroidered with pearls, were forbidden by sumptuary laws in 1299 and 1334. In Venice, rich ornaments with pearls woven into the hair raised the concern of the lawmakers as well. Most of the laws' restrictions were directed at women, youth, and children, while men were exempted. This did not mean that men, including bridegrooms, dressed soberly or cheaply. Men wore even heavier ornaments than women, and these were largely fashioned out of gilded silver and often studded with jewels. In addition, men continued to purchase new luxury goods over a lifetime while it was understood that a bride's trousseau would provide her formal wardrobe for the entire span of her married life.[16]

Rich gifts kept marriages, particularly the marriages of the wealthy, in the spotlight. Yet the practice of dowry also trickled down in cities until in late medieval Italy, southern France, and Spain, women without dowries were unlikely to marry at all, helping to create a new cadre of singlewomen in cities and towns. Some were domestic slaves who could not marry; others worked at contract labor, which meant they worked for a span of years (ten or twelve years was not unusual) earning room and board with the promise of a sum of money for dowry paid at the end of the term. This sum made some of them desirable prospects for marriage in town even if they were originally from the countryside; where this failed, women did not wed. Those who did marry, using as a dowry their lump sum wage paid at the end of service, usually wed later than wealthy young women, who were likely to marry in their teens, even their early teens. Yet even among the well-to-do, finding sums for dowry for four, five, or six daughters became a very heavy burden. This problem led families to send at least one daughter to a convent, which also required a dowry, but a considerably smaller one than that demanded by an aspiring husband.

The pressures that spread this dotal regime throughout Italy are not difficult to identify. Men enjoyed increasing privileges in civil life in medieval Italy, so it was no wonder that they wished to hold out for dowry awards and other marital gifts that could
further their ambitions. They managed the awards, invested them, or used them to
gain tools and materials for a trade, relied on them for necessary household fixtures,
furniture, and linens, and generally became better off simply by the fact that they had
married. Furthermore, they drew great honor from receiving dowry. Men might reasonably expect more than one dowry gift in a lifetime, as in the example of Gregorio Dati
(1362–1435), who collected four dowries before his death.[17] In his *Zibaldone* (daybook),
Giovanni Rucellai (1475–1525) proudly viewed his grandfather's four dowries collected
at successive marriages as a foundation of the family's great achievements and prosperity.[18] Sanctioned by law and custom, the transfer of wealth to men at marriage became
the norm at every level of society.

It was a different story for women. The issue centers on whether owning and managing wedding wealth, as women had earlier with *morgengabe*, equipped women to own
and manage inherited wealth or the money earned by their own labor over the years
of a marriage. There are very few archival holdings in cities for the twelfth century, but
Genoa, where *morgengabe* still existed in the early twelfth century, provides a number
of notarial records or what are frequently labeled "documents of practice," including
records of women's contributions to the economic life of the prospering city. At the highest level of Genoese society, noblewomen ran gold thread manufactures in their homes.
They also hired skilled servants to wind foil on silk thread, a difficult and highly specialized task.[19] Artisan women worked in home industries with their husbands or pursued manufactures on their own.[20] Mark Angelos has found that some Genoese women
invested heavily in *commenda* (maritime trade) contracts between 1155 and 1216. These
women were members of established merchant families as well as prosperous artisans.
Some invested money in their husbands' names while their husbands traveled for trade;
other invested with sons or brothers.[21] At the least, women learned the management of
capital and, given the swift rise of Genoa as a maritime power, it appears that drawing
on the skills of both women and men played a role in the community's initial twelfth-
century success.

Unfortunately, the thirteenth and fourteenth centuries are not well documented
due to the loss of records, so it is difficult to trace what happened to women from those
groups who had enjoyed high profiles in the bustling economic life of twelfth-century
Genoa. Still, it is apparent that Genoese women lost opportunities over the following
centuries. Often historians equate property rights with work identity in urban life; in
twelfth-century Genoa, the enlargement of women's roles in production and trade
appears to have correlated with women's management of such wealth as wedding gifts.
Unfortunately for women, this proficiency was subsequently transformed here as elsewhere in Italy. When notarial records become available again for Genoa, that is, near
the end of the medieval era, there is almost no trace of these earlier productive jobs for
women, and the city had entered a different phase wherein investment did not call upon
women's participation. The Genoese were content to "retire" women to the sidelines

where they lived under a dotal regime just as in neighboring cities. Women owned their dowries and might in some instances inherit other wealth, but they did not manage their own investment properties.

Did the loss of managerial rights over wedding gifts lead to the loss of control of the fruits of one's labor for women elsewhere? Although few cities have records as ample as those of Genoa, Eleanor Riemer found that Sienese women lost investment opportunities over the course of the thirteenth century.[22] David Herlihy, who was interested in women's work identity, stated that in Florence, at least, women workers' productivity and actual contribution to the economy had diminished by the later Middle Ages. Of course he may have been a victim of the records, or lack thereof, because notarial collections only become ample for study in Florence late in the fourteenth century. A number of scholars have challenged Herlihy's findings: in the vertically organized silk industry that used the putting-out system, it is difficult to identify the women who "threw" silk, the essential first step in producing silk thread. It may be that women continued to be productive but their work was subsumed into the household and credited to their male relatives.[23]

For whatever reason, over the course of the later medieval centuries women became increasingly invisible in notarial records. This has added to interpretive differences among scholars. Christiane Klapisch-Zuber, Manlio Bellomo, and Isabelle Chabot present the more negative view of women's plight under the dotal regime. For Klapisch-Zuber, not only were women's economic roles curtailed but their social lives were increasingly restricted and even wedding gifts of jewels from their husbands and their families became more like loans to be returned once another bride entered the lineage.[24] Klapisch-Zuber traced the growth of cultural artifacts like marriage chests painted with scenes from the story of poor Griselda, who was utterly subjugated to the whim of her wealthy husband. Griselda's story ran diametrically counter to the actual direction in which significant wealth moved at marriage, creating its own irony. Still, by the middle of the fourteenth century, wealthy husbands were expected to supply fine clothes and jewels for their brides, and warnings about husbands' gifts belonging to the patriline and its *casa* were incorporated into the legend. Griselda came to her marriage with nothing except her shift, so later she might be stripped of all possessions—even clothing—by her husband's command and she had to bear this meekly: "the husband's dressing of his bride still possessed the quality of compelling ritual action."[25] It would be a difficult admonition for a bride to ignore.

For legal historians like Julius Kirshner, Anthony Molho, and Thomas Kuehn, the situation of women in dotal regimes seems less severe. They note the many legal ploys available to women, who did gain certain benefits from awards of dowry. A dowried woman could demand a detailed inventory of her deceased husband's household assets to gain restitution. Because her children might prefer to inherit her assets and to repudiate those of a debt-ridden father, she was placed in a position of power. But cautions abounded: the Italian jurist Odofredus (d.1265) had observed that the law favored masculine control, so "ladies [might well] guard their documents with great care."[26] Perhaps the question came down to the relative social positions of the bride and groom. When highly ambitious and unscrupulous bachelors contracted lucrative marriages, the bride's financial welfare was at risk. Among marriages more equal in wealth and social standing, great pride in brides' illustrious connections prompted husbands to treat dowry awards circumspectly.[27] In Giovanni Rucellai's *Zibaldone*, Molho found "an image of the city of Florence,…intermarrying among themselves generation upon generation…, [that] created a community of interests and a thick web of solidarities."[28] At this level of society, dowries were understood to be mutually beneficial, and were often exchanged among families encouraging fair play.

In time, dowries became a matter of state policy. In the 1970s Julius Kirshner and Anthony Molho showed how the dowry fund or *Monte delle Doti* (established 1425) in late medieval Florence revealed the high consequence of dowries; it had become a matter of honor to set aside sums to provide awards for daughters. Once great sums were invested in this government-run fund, dowry shares became in turn a new underpinning for urban finance.[29] Florence was in need of funds since it was at war with Milan at the time the fund was established. The dowry fund paid off handsomely in the next few years: over 12 percent for a seven-and-a-half-year investment and over 11 percent for a fifteen-year term. The fund also answered concerns that dowry be paid on time and in cash, common problems when fathers of brides sometimes delayed payments well beyond the wedding date. Historians' concentration on Florentine initiatives when considering questions relating to dowry has been driven in part by this decision to incorporate the quintessential private familial obligation to provide dowry with a communally organized and managed fund. Parents began investing in the fund upon the birth of a daughter and added further money as time passed. Enthusiastic participation in the fund created a pool of capital for investment that in turn strengthened the commune.

In Venice, where marriages were more likely to be restricted to persons of one's own social standing, especially after the *Serrata* (closing of the patriciate) in the late fourteenth century, women attained enhanced opportunities to bequeath their wealth.[30] Patrician women would not expect to work at manufacturing or crafts in any case, and dowries held long-standing and traditional roles in family life. Still, Venice was no less concerned with honor than other cities, and courts saw lawsuits involving dowry at all levels of society, noble and non-noble alike. Immensely wealthy noble families were even willing to produce a dowry that would attract a king. With a magnificent dowry, Caterina Cornaro (1454–1510) was married to Louis, king of Cyprus, and enthroned, a first step toward making the island a Venetian possession. In major cities, the giving of dowry had become a matter of state by the end of the Middle Ages.

In Venice as well, bequests for dowries for "poor but deserving" girls or specific bequests for the dowries of poorer relatives, even rather distant ones, stressed the increasing consequence of dowry. While there may have been exceptions, Venetians assumed that a girl lacking a dowry would not marry. The earliest orphanages made provision in their constitutions for dowries for inmates, although it would have been prohibitively expensive to provide funds for all the orphans for whom endowed foundations and convents were responsible; the frequent dedication of orphanages to St Nicholas, patron saint of girls without dowries, reflected this concern.

The study of Roman law in university centers like Paris may have encouraged the adoption of dowry into marriage practices in northern cities. So, too, did northern imitation of Italian cities, which were known far and wide for the importance of their dowries, as well as their impressive mercantile and manufacturing economies. Colonies of wealthy Italian merchants established themselves in northern cities where their behaviors were closely observed. Any marriage contracted with an Italian family would include consideration of the sum to be given in dowry, so deeply was the practice entrenched in the understanding of family position and honor. Italians celebrated weddings with pomp and lavish entertaining; the sums given in dowry were no more secret abroad than they had been at home in Italy. Weddings were very public celebrations of a family's status and connections, beginning with the bride and her possessions carried to her husband's home.

Yet historians, often focused on national experience, have seldom acknowledged the influence of Italian models on the spread of a dotal regime through much of northwestern Europe. Georges Duby has noted that competing views of marriage, one aristocratic and the other ecclesiastical, created serious tensions, if not actual impasse, in the lives and marriage strategies of nobles in twelfth-century France, but he found no role for any outside precedents.[31] Nonetheless, in northern France "brideprice and *morgengabe* both gradually gave way to the practice of dowry coming from the bride's family," according to Kathryn Reyerson, while in London, dowry from the bride's family as well as dower from the groom were well established by the second half of the fourteenth century.[32] London brides brought wealth, often in real estate, to husbands; as rich widows with both a dowry and dower returned to them, they became economic powers to be reckoned with and were sought in second marriages, although the dotal system was as subject to misuse here as elsewhere. Procedures that established dowry in England, northern France, or the neighboring Low Countries reflected new statute laws, but recent scholarship credits local initiatives in reforming northern marriage law rather than any Roman law promptings, examples provided by Italian merchants, or hires of university-trained lawyers.

Nevertheless, the distinction between owning and managing dowries traveled with dowry wherever it went, suggesting direct influence from the Mediterranean south rather than reinvention that reflected only indigenous decision-making. In Italian *consilia* and statute law, and in canon case law, separation of women's ownership and men's management of marriage gifts was a distinctive *medieval*, rather than ancient, feature of Roman dowry. This same feature was found in southern France and Spain. Trained lawyers would comprehend that separation of the two was not an inherited feature of ancient Roman law codes. It is worth investigating whether legislators in northern towns had some level of knowledge of how dowry was given and managed where it first began its reign in medieval Europe in southern towns and cities.

In the case of late medieval law reforms enacted in towns like Douai, a middle way between dowry and community property evolved that, according to Martha Howell, created a clumsy compromise employing a dowry but safeguarding a wife's interests.[33] Women's productive roles in the economic life of cities were supported longer in northern Europe than in the south, but in prosperous towns in Flanders, Roman law had begun to influence marriage property laws by 1500.[34] It is, as yet, unclear how much women's authority over their wealth might have lessened once new urban laws that separated ownership and management of dowry in marriage were passed.

Dowry may have carried social cachet wherever it traveled in the medieval world, and this snob appeal may have obscured the real restraints Roman dowry placed on women. As dowry competition pushed marriage age lower and lower for women, marriages were often contracted when the bride was just a little past the age of puberty. Under the dotal regime the greatest consequences for women lay in the arguments rolled out to justify depriving women of management rights over their wealth during the years of their marriages. No such justifications were necessary under English common law, which simply chose one spouse (the husband) as sole legal and financial authority for the married couple. In the south, however, married women had once managed their *morgengabe* wealth, and inherited late Roman law provisos were decidedly lacking in justifications for depriving women of control of property. In late antiquity, daughters possessed legal capacities and inherited along with their brothers. Men did not exert guardianship over women, and there was significantly less masculine bias in the inheritance of family property than would be true in the medieval era. Women did not possess public rights under this law, but they were remarkably equal in private law. This returns the question to the origins of statute laws devised in Mediterranean cities that affirmed married women's ownership but restrained women from managing dowry over the duration of the marriage. Some justification outside the provisions of inherited late Roman law was needed to deprive women of their former control of property, and to this end medieval legal experts and scholars turned to ancient philosophy.

The slow recovery of Aristotle by medieval scholars, first in Latin allusions, quotations, and commentary, and later of entire texts of his politics and philosophy, inspired such wonder that Aristotle was widely known as The Philosopher to medieval scholars. On the assumption that the ancient world possessed a coherent worldview sustaining law and social practice, medieval scholars found no trouble in applying Aristotle's maxims to justify depriving women of positive legal rights, specifically removing women's authority to manage their dotal wealth. With Gratian may be found the opening salvo: "Woman should be subject to her husband's rule and she possesses no authority, either to teach, to bear witness, to give surety, or to judge."[35] Linking statute laws about a wife's subordination to incapacity arguments introduced a significant gender distinction into the issue of managing wealth—that is, wedding gifts. Indeed, it helped make gender a more salient category of distinction in medieval society.

In the thirteenth century, Thomas Aquinas firmly advanced Aristotle's mode of analysis. He found polar schemes in Aristotle that he affirmed as essential to God's natural order. In Question 92 of the *Summa theologica*, Aquinas addressed the question of "woman" secondarily and in juxtaposition to "man," to whom he gave a place halfway between the beasts and the angels in God's earthly creation. He employed Aristotle's aligned polarities of maleness and femaleness. Man signified limit, odd, one, right, square, at rest, straight, light, and good. The traits defining femaleness were opposed: unlimited, even, plurality, left, oblong, moving, curved, darkness, and evil. Man was made in the image of God and was therefore active, formative, and tending toward perfection, unlike woman, who was passive, material, and deprived of the tendency toward perfection. The scheme was simple, which recommended it to those seeking justification or a rationale for laws.[36]

When it came to the law, Gratian and lawyers who followed him employed the polarity of capacity and incapacity, that is, authority and lacking authority. This was critical to the exercise of legal and financial rights. The argument, following ancient models, was generally cast in the singular, that is, it concerned "man" and "woman," which functioned as categorical imperatives brooking no exceptions. Woman's incapacity, in contrast to man's capacity, was simple, axiomatic, and easily applied. These qualities promoted the use of the incapacity argument, which may be found not only in laws but in sermons, homilies, and writings by university scholars on law, medicine, and theology. These polarities may well be notional thought in contrast to carefully reasoned logical arguments (also inherited from ancient writings) but that may have added to their appeal rather than detracted. Woman's incapacity, which first appeared in Western thought as an axiomatic phrase, slipped into the intellectual baggage of later generations where it remains to this day.

Not all medieval women married, although most of them did. Nor were all brides provided by their natal families with Roman dowry, but an increasing number of them were provided with this gift as the medieval era progressed. Respectability attached itself to the awarding of this assign, which in turn promoted its adoption by others. From the twelfth century onward, arguments about female incapacity were firmly attached to dowry and may have traveled with it to new communities. There remain too many recorded instances in which women sued for their own rights in marriage or as widows to conclude that women, or their families, actually believed in women's incapacity. It was instead a useful legal neologism. Still, any stricture placed on women that was justified by an incapacity argument encouraged its broad application. Generally speaking, this influence could not help but detract from women's legal standing wherever it was invoked. A woman was justifiably proud to have a handsome sum made contingent upon her marriage, but in the long run, women lost more from the awarding of dowry than they gained.

FURTHER READING

Bellomo, Manlio. *La condizione giuridica della donna in Italia. Vicende antiche e moderne.* Turin: Eri, 1970.

Bellomo, Manlio. *Ricerche sui rapporti patrimoniali tra coniugi.* Milan: Giuffre, 1961.

Botticini, Maristella. "A Loveless Economy? Intergenerational Altruism and the Marriage Market in a Tuscan Town, 1415–1436," *Journal of Economic History,* 59 (1) (March 1999), 104–21.

Dean, Trevor and Kate Lowe, eds. *Marriage in Italy.* Cambridge: Cambridge University Press, 1998.

Karras, Ruth Mazo. "The History of Marriage and the Myth of Friedelehe," *Early Medieval Europe*, 14 (2) (2006): 119–51.

Kirshner, Julius and Jacques Pluss. "Two Fourteenth-Century Opinions on Dowries, Paraphernalia and Non-Dotal Goods," *Bulletin of Medieval Canon Law*, n.s., 9 (1979): 65–77.

Meek, Christine and Catherine Lawless, eds. *Studies on Medieval and Early Modern Women: Pawns or Players?* Dublin: Four Courts Press, 2003.

Murray, Jacqueline, ed. *Conflicted Identities and Multiple Masculinities: Men in the Medieval West*. New York: Garland, 1999.

Sperling, Jutta Gisela and Shona Kelly Wray, eds. *Across the Religious Divide, Women, Property and Law in the Wider Mediterranean (ca. 1300–1800)* New York: Routledge, 2010.

Stuard, Susan Mosher. *Considering Medieval Women and Gender*. Aldershot: Ashgate Press, 2010.

Zordan, Giorgio. "I vari aspetti del comunione familiare di beni nell Venezia dei secoli XI–XII," *Studi veneziani*, 8 (1966): 127–94.

Notes

1. David Herlihy and Christiane Klapisch-Zuber, *Tuscans and Their Families* (New Haven: Yale University Press, 1985), 228. The authors characterize this pattern as viri-local.
2. For a list of legists who commented on marriage, see Julius Kirshner, "Wives' Claims Against Insolvent Husbands," in Julius Kirshner and Suzanne F. Wemple, eds, *Women of the Medieval World* (Oxford: Blackwell, 1985), 266–67.
3. Eleanor Riemer, *Women in the Medieval City: Sources and Uses of Wealth of Sienese Women in the Thirteenth Century* (dissertation, New York University, 1975), 60–66.
4. Diane Owen Hughes, "From Brideprice to Dowry in Mediterranean Europe," *Journal of Family History*, 3 (1978): 266–76.
5. Hughes, "From Brideprice to Dowry," 275.
6. Pierre Bonnassie, "A Family of the Barcelona Countryside and its Economic Activities Around the Year 1000," in Sylvia Thrupp, ed., *Early Medieval Society* (New York: Appleton Century Crofts, 1967), 103–23.
7. Manlio Bellomo, *The Common Legal Past of Europe*, trans. Lydia Cochrane (Washington, DC: Catholic University of America Press, 1995).
8. Thomas Kuehn, *Law, Family, and Women: Toward a Legal Anthropology of Medieval Italy* (Chicago: University of Chicago Press, 1991), chapter 9, "'Cum Consensu Mundualdi': Legal Guardianship of Women in Quattrocento Florence," 212–37.
9. Thomas Kuehn, "Women, Marriage, and the *Patria Potestas* in Late Medieval Florence," *Tijdschrift voor Rechtsgeschedenis*, 49 (1981): 127–47, see esp. 131–32.
10. Bartolus de Saxoferrato, *Tractatus de differentia inter ius canonicum et civile*, in *Opera omnia* (Venice, 1570), vol. 9, fol. 153r, cited by Thomas Kuehn in full, "Women, Marriage, and the *Patria Potestas*," 132.
11. Kevin J. F. Murphy, "'Lilium inter spinas': Bianca Spini and the Decoration of the Spini Chapel in Santa Trinità," *Italian History and Culture*, 8 (2002): 51–65.
12. Susan Mosher Stuard, "Dowry Increase and Increments in Wealth in Medieval Ragusa (Dubrovnik)," *Journal of Economic History*, 41 (1981): 795–811.
13. Susan Mosher Stuard, "The *Legenda* of Maria of Venice," in Ruth Mazo Karras, Joel Kaye, and E. Ann Matter, eds, *Law and the Illicit in Medieval Europe* (Philadelphia: University of Pennsylvania Press, 2008), 197–210.

14. Mark Phillips, ed., *The Memoir of Marco Parenti* (Princeton: Princeton University Press, 1987), 133, taken from the correspondence of Alessandra Strozzi.

15. Ginevra Nicccolini da Camugliano, *Chronicles of a Florentine Family, 1200–1470* (London: J. Cape, 1933), 66.

16. Susan Mosher Stuard, *Gilding the Market: Luxury and Fashion in Fourteenth-Century Italy* (Philadelphia: University of Pennsylvania Press, 2006). On pawns of gifts by husbands see Jane Bestor, "Marriage Transactions in Renaissance Italy," *Past & Present*, 164 (1999): 4–46.

17. Gene Brucker, ed., *Two Memoirs of Renaissance Florence: The Diaries of Buonacorso Piti and Gregorio Dati*, trans. Julia Martines (Prospect Heights: Waveland Press, 1967), 107–41.

18. Giovanni Rucellai, *Giovanni Rucellai ed il suo zibaldone*, I, ed. Alessandro Perosa (London: Warburg Institute, 1960).

19. William Bonds, "Genoese Noblewomen and Gold Thread Manufacturing," *Medievalia et Humanistica*, old ser., 17 (1966): 79–81.

20. Diane Owen Hughes, "Urban Growth and Family Structure in Medieval Genoa," *Past & Present*, 66 (1975): 3–28.

21. Mark Angelos, "Urban Women, Investment, and the Commercial Revolution," in Linda Mitchell, ed., *Women in Medieval Western European Culture* (New York: Garland 1999), 257–72.

22. Eleanor Riemer, "Women, Dowries, and Capital Investment in Thirteenth-Century Siena," in Marion A. Kaplan, ed., *The Marriage Bargain: Women and Dowries in European History* (New York: Haworth Press, 1985), 59–80.

23. David Herlihy, *Opera Muliebria* (New York: McGraw Hill, 1990). See also Luca Mola, "L'industria della seta a Lucca nel tardo Medioevo: Emigrazione della manodopera e creazione di una rete produttive a Bologna e Venezia," in Simonetta Davaciocchi, ed., *La seta in Europa, sec. XIII–XX* (Florence: Le Monnier, 1993), 435–45. Judith Brown has also contested Herlihy's findings: see Judith Brown and Jordan Goodman, "Women and Industry in Florence," *Journal of Economic History*, 40 (1980): 73–80.

24. Manlio Bellomo, *La condizione giuridica della donna in Italia: Vicende antiche e moderne* (Turin: Eri, 1970); Isabelle Chabot, "'La Sposa in Nero': La ritualizzazione del lutto della vedove Fiorentine (secoli XIV–XV)" *Quaderni Storici*, 86 (1994): 421–62; Christiane Klapisch-Zuber, "The Griselda Complex," in *Women, Family and Ritual in Renaissance Italy*, trans. Lydia G. Cochrane (Chicago: University of Chicago Press, 1985), 213–46.

25. Klapisch-Zuber, "Griselda," 229.

26. Maria Teresa Guerra Medici, "'City Air': Women in the Medieval City," in Giovanna Casagrande, ed., *Donne tra Medioevo ed Età Moderna in Italia* (Perugia: Morlacchi Editore, 2004), 28. The author cites Odofredo, *Lectura sup. Codicem*, ed. Lyon 1552, *de edendo*, f. 57r.

27. Anthony Mohlo, *Marriage Alliance in Late Medieval Florence* (Cambridge, Mass.: Harvard University Press, 1995).

28. Anthony Molho, Roberto Barducci, Gabriella Battista, and Francesco Donnini, "Genealogy and Marriage Alliance: Memories of Power in Late Medieval Florence," in Samuel K. Cohn Jr. and Steven A. Epstein, eds, *Portraits of Medieval and Renaissance Living* (Ann Arbor: University of Michigan Press, 1996), 41.

29. Julius Kirshner and Anthony Molho, "The Dowry Fund and the Marriage Market in Early Quattrocento Florence," *Journal of Modern History*, 50 (1978): 403–38.

30. Stanley Chojnacki, *Women and Men in Renaissance Venice* (Baltimore: Johns Hopkins University Press, 2000).

31. Georges Duby, *Medieval Marriage: Two Models from Twelfth-Century France*, trans. Elborg Forster (Baltimore: Johns Hopkins University Press, 1978).

32. Kathryn Reyerson and Thomas Kuehn, "Women and Law in France and Italy," in Linda Mitchell, ed., *Women in Medieval Western European Culture* (New York: Garland 1999), 133; and Jean Hilaire, *Le régime des biens entre époux dans la region de Montpellier du début du XIII siècle à la fin du XVI siècle* (Montpellier: Causse, Gaille & Casatelnau, 1957), 56–88; for England, see Barbara Hanawalt, *The Wealth of Wives, Women, Law, and Economy in Medieval London* (New York: Oxford University Press, 2007), 50–117.

33. See Martha C. Howell, *The Marriage Exchange, Property, Social Place, and Gender in Cities of the Low Countries, 1300–1550* (Chicago: University of Chicago Press, 1998), 212–17; Robert Jacob, *Les époux, le seigneur et la cité: Coutume et pratiques matrimoniales des bourgeois et paysans de France du Nord au moyen âge* (Brussels: Facultés Universitaires Saint-Louis, 1990), 207–15. For regions under written law, see Jean Hilaire, *Le régime des biens entreépoux*, 136–91.

34. Philippe Godding, *Le droit privé dans les Pay-Bas méridionnaux du 12 siècle au 18 siècle* (Brussels: Palais des Académies, 1987), 142–43, item 192.

35. There is no satisfactory critical edition of Gratian's *Decretum*. Emil Freidberg, ed., *Corpus Juris Canonici*, vol. I (Graz: Bernard Tauchnitz, 1911) is the text most frequently cited.

36. Thomas Aquinas, *Summa theologiae*, ed. Edmund Hill, vol. 13 (1 a. 90–102) (London: Blackfriars, 1964), 34–47, I q. 92, 1.

CHAPTER 11

···

WOMEN AND GENDER IN CANON LAW

···

SARA MCDOUGALL

THE law of the Catholic church, or canon law, understood men and women as distinct and different. Following Roman law, even hermaphrodites had to be categorized as one or the other.[1] Canon law thus required the division of all Christians into two categories of male or female with even more consistency than the divide they sought to maintain between clergy and laity in their efforts to separate sacred persons and powers from temporal persons and powers. This division of Christians into male and female had consequences, since in this system, gender difference also meant gender inequality. Many, even most, positions within the ecclesiastical hierarchy excluded women. No woman, for example, could become a priest or serve as an ecclesiastical judge or advocate. In these matters, at least, canon law did not allow room for space between male and female. What is far less clear is the place of gender in canon law and legal practice in other matters.

Modern scholars currently lack a firm understanding of how medieval canonists thought about gender in organizing Christian society. Gender scholars have only just begun to tackle medieval canon law. This law does seem to require the division of all Christians into two categories of male or female, but what is harder to understand are the practical implications of this distinction. Recent studies examining the canon law on fornication, slander, and clerical concubinage have revealed a great deal of complexity, in prescriptive law and especially in the legal practice regarding gender. What all this meant for the status of women and the role of gender more broadly, however, remains rather obscure.

Scholars generally assume that canon law diminished the status of women.[2] Nevertheless, while canon law defined men and women as different, with different and unequal rights and responsibilities, it was not without important equalities that applied to all Christians irrespective of gender. In particular, women as wives were considered the equals of their husbands in many respects, as René Metz observed in an important article on the status of women in canon law.[3] Focusing on marriage as a rare moment of equality—if a limited and complex equality—for women, this chapter seeks the balance of gender equalities and inequalities as found in both legal theory (canon law) and in legal practice (church courts). As this chapter will show, Christian marriage provided women as wives (and only as wives) a distinct opportunity for a complicated equality with their husbands, a radical departure in a hierarchically organized society.

Canon law defined marriage as the exclusive and indissoluble bond of one man to one woman (only), as husband and wife, respectively. To say that marriage provided an opportunity for gender equality seems strange, since men as husbands and women as wives had different legal standings, with husbands holding authority over their wives. According to canonists and theologians, Christian marriages had to include this hierarchical relationship, because all Christian marriages ultimately had to resemble the hierarchical unions of Adam to Eve or Christ to the church. Late antique and medieval legal systems perceived this male supremacy as both natural and necessary. At the same time, however, the hierarchical structure of marriage did not exclude some measure of equality for spouses. Marriage also was understood as a partnership. Taken from Adam's side, Eve shared one flesh with Adam, and they were understood to live as companions with largely reciprocal duties and obligations. Regardless of gender, as Saint Paul wrote [I Corinthians 7:1–3], in marrying, both husbands and wives lost power over their own bodies to the other spouse.

In addition to scripture, as just shown, canon law derived from the writings of the church fathers, church councils, and also Roman law, which from the twelfth century played an especially important role in the organization of a vast corpus of long-accepted ideas and issues that canonists cited, interpreted, and sometimes Christianized. By the early Middle Ages, a diverse corpus of texts laid out the rules of the church, designating sacred offices, rituals, and spaces, and describing also how all Christians should live. In what is known as the "classical" period of canon law in the west, beginning at around 1100, canonists began to assemble more systematic compilations, and in the twelfth century at Bologna the compilation now known as Gratian's *Decretum* was produced. Made in two recensions by two men both referred to as Gratian, this text was intended to resolve and synthesize "discordant canons," the existing mass of various and often contradictory church teachings. Each canon included a main question or two, an offering of at least tangentially related excerpts from various legal and ecclesiastical authorities, and the pronouncement of a reconciled conclusion. Subsequent collections of papal decretals and commentary culminated in the thirteenth century with the work of Raymond of Peñafort, known as the *Liber Extra* (meaning the book added to the *Decretum*), and continuing thereafter. In addition to these fundamentally important collections of law and commentary, canon law is also found in synodal statutes produced by local ecclesiastics, which offer nuanced examples of the local functioning of canon law.

The first reference tool for any scholar interested in the medieval canon law of marriage and its relationship to women is James Brundage's mighty tome surveying the development of canon law ideas of marriage and sex.[4] As to gendered analysis of this material, Susan Mosher Stuard's essay on the limitation of husbands' power in Gratian's *Decretum* provides an excellent example. As Stuard explains, the *Decretum* teaches that wives had to submit to their husband's authority. But the context and conclusion of this discussion of husbandly authority was a rule stating that a husband could not become a monk without his wife's permission.[5] Clearly a husband's authority had limits, and wives had certain rights. Charles Reid argues that medieval husbands and wives shared four important rights in common, regardless of sex: the right to consent to marriage, the right to ask for marital debt or conjugal (sexual) duty, the right to leave a marriage when they either suspected it was invalid or had grounds to sue for separation, and finally the right to choose one's own place of burial, death being the point at which a spouse's ownership of the other spouse's body ceased.[6] Canon law, in theory, offered this complex mix of mutual rights and obligations alongside the hierarchical structure that placed husbands above wives.

Law is one thing, practice quite another. The study of the place of women and wives in the courtroom has developed considerably in recent years, with gender studies lagging behind. One promising site of study on questions of gender, marriage, and canon law is the papal penitentiary.[7] It was to this institution in Rome that thousands of supplicants or their advocates flocked in search of dispensations, absolutions, and licenses. We still await a full analysis of how men and women petitioned the court and on what grounds, and how the court responded to male or female suits. We know more about local courts, thanks especially to Charles Donahue's pioneering comparative study of five courts in England and northwestern Europe.[8] While quite diverse, court practice was largely, as Donahue stresses, in keeping with what the canon law demanded for marriage. Practices in Italian, Spanish, and southern German courts more closely resemble English courts than those of northern France or Belgium; there, marriage law applied in quite different ways, with courts adopting a far more proactive and regulatory character in their efforts to prevent and punish illicit sex and illegal marriages.

If courts for the most part adhered to the canon law as studied in medieval universities and as articulated by Pope Alexander III, we can also find a variety of deviations from what canon law, in theory, required. We find gender differences where we are not supposed to and near-equalities when there should be—as far as the canon law was concerned—differences. At least three divergences between the learned law and court practice had important implications for women in particular. Church courts almost always allowed women and other persons technically excluded from bringing suits or giving testimony to participate on a seemingly equal basis with the "honest and upright" men to whom the learned law granted the greatest legal privileges. Also, as discussed in more detail below, several courts gave spouses permission to separate—to remain married but live apart—on grounds that exceed the bounds of canonically permitted separations. Finally, a court in southern Germany granted spouses married to absent partners the right to remarry with seeming total disregard for the canonical requirement of proof of death before remarriage.[9]

These deviations between law and legal practice are relatively small when compared to those found in the ecclesiastical courts of Byzantium. Byzantine courts operated at considerable distance from the written law. We find a legal culture and courtrooms riddled with idiosyncrasies and far from free of political or social influence. As total enforcement of many of the rules governing remarriage, separation, or divorce as laid out in either the western or the Byzantine legal systems would have been rather draconian, these "divergences" cannot be taken as negative, above all where women were concerned.[10]

There is a great deal more we would like to know about the place of women in marriage litigation. Some cases seem to have been more readily brought to court by men than women, but which kinds of cases and why? In choosing either male or female witnesses to offer evidence, did litigants draw upon gender norms in society as well as canonical limitations on a woman's testimony? Were female litigants more likely to be supported by female deponents and vice versa?[11] In England, at least, women initiated marriage litigation more often than men and were generally more successful.[12] But in assessing the role of gender in this litigation, how should scholars correct for how well or poorly men, women, or their advocates made their cases, or the court's sympathy for some types of cases regardless of the gender of the litigant? Courts in England seemed especially keen to enforce marriage by making decisions that created or recognized marriages, and reluctant to grant a dissolution or to rule that no marriage had taken place. The success of these suits, then, had more to do with the nature of the claim than the gender of the plaintiff. But that said, can we know for certain if plaintiffs got what they wanted in winning their cases? What if a plaintiff had some goal in litigation other than "success," that is, what if they wanted something other than winning their suit? We will keep these questions in mind while looking at five areas of canon law norms and practices concerning marriage. The first two categories will be marriage formation and remarriage; next, married life and then, adultery; as a fifth category, legal separation and the dissolution of marriage. Each section will begin with an overview of the laws and then turn to legal practice. The focus will be on western canon law, with some reference to Byzantine law.

MARRIAGE FORMATION

The laws of marriage developed in quite different ways in the west and in Byzantium. Beginning in the tenth century Byzantine marriages required parental consent and a public ceremony, while by the mid-twelfth century western canon law came to prioritize the spouses' free consent over both parental consent and publicity. One similarity shared in the east and the west also points to the one clear gender difference. In keeping with Roman legal traditions, both places maintained the legal age for marriage as twelve for women and fourteen for men. Strikingly, outside of the age of consent, the many rules for marriage formation offer no differences in the treatment of male and female betrothed. The very different requirements canon law and medieval society generally had for men versus women suggests that there should have been many more differences, but all the canon law explicitly required is this age difference of two years.

From the twelfth century on, the western canon law of marriage required, above all, the freely given consent of the principals. Both partners had to have reached the respective ages of reason or maturity, and both had to consent. The agreement of both parties, regardless of gender, was equally necessary. Once they had consented to the marriage, they were both equally bound, regardless of whether the marriage had been approved by their parents, publicized with banns, or blessed by a priest. Canon law urged a couple to seek publicity and a priest's blessing, but it did not require it. Thus couples could validly marry quite informally, a "clandestine marriage." Once married, either by an exchange of promises in the present tense "I marry you," or by vows in the future tense, "I will marry you," followed by consummation, this couple had indissolubly wed. Neither could desert the other.

Such were the rules. However, if a couple had married without witnesses or without banns or other publicity, what if one spouse or the other subsequently decided not to honor the marriage? What if a woman or a man claimed a marriage had taken place when no such words had in reality been exchanged? Disputes over clandestine marriage often took the form of an allegedly deceived and possibly pregnant young woman seeking to enforce promises of marriage made by a man she considered her husband. In most circumstances in which no witnesses could be found, canon law generally recommended that a court take a man's word over that of a woman. With questions of marriage formation, however, rather than a clear inclination to believe men over women, scholars have often found instead that some courts, especially in England, seem more inclined to decide in favor of whichever party claimed the existence of a marriage. Other courts held to a policy that the party who claimed that an exchange of promises had taken place bore the burden of proof. If both parties agreed that promises had in fact been exchanged, it also mattered whether the consent had been freely given. Even if made by a present-tense exchange of vows or future-tense vows followed by consummation, marriage made out of "force and fear" was no marriage, the canonists determined, as long as the force and fear seemed sufficient to shake "a steady man" or, we might add, a steady woman.[13]

Marriage practice varied enormously in western Europe and violated canon law rules on marriage formation in a variety of ways. For example, in Verona, many couples, especially non-noble and poorer couples, married in private homes with few witnesses and without publicity or a church blessing. Sometimes, husbands in particular later denied that a marriage had taken place.[14] In Sweden, marriages often took place at the church door, but these marriages also adhered to older, secular traditions that required the consent of the bride's "marriage guardian," usually her father or closest living male relative, in addition to the consent of the spouses themselves. A priest who blessed the marriage of a couple without the marriage guardian's consent could face a considerable fine levied by his local church court.[15]

Differences in local practice also contributed to differences in the nature of litigation over marriage formation in ecclesiastical courts. In fifteenth-century Venice, men and women sought the enforcement of a marriage at about the same rate, but Cecilia Cristellon has shown how the gender of the complainant shaped judicial responses to such suits.[16] Women, and only women, faced intense, extensive interrogation. Judges often ordered their confinement in a convent for some days, to allow them time and space to reflect (separated from the potentially overbearing influence of relatives) before giving testimony in court. Men in similar circumstances were never sent to a monastery. The courts considered the temporary enclosure of a young boy inappropriate treatment for a male. Unsurprisingly, the response of Venetian ecclesiastical judges to marriage suits also had a good deal to do with the social status of both parties, as well as their sex. Judges often seemed sympathetic towards the plight of a socially weak and potentially deceived woman, but these judges were reluctant to bind a high-status man in marriage to a lowborn woman.

Judges in fifteenth-century Saragossa shared this reluctance with their Venetian colleagues. Court action, however, differed from Venice in that women brought suits seeking enforcement of marriage more often than men. As Martine Charageat argues, these contested marriage claims broke down along gender lines. Women were plaintiffs in sixty-six out of ninety-one enforcement suits in Saragossa. These cases largely fit the pattern of a man and a woman who had a sexual relationship, perhaps founded on a promise of marriage, but a promise that the man no longer wished to honor. When faced with the accusation that he had promised to marry a woman and had slept with her, the man freely admitted to sexual relations but fiercely denied having made any promise to marry. Women, on the other hand, often admitted promises to marry, but regularly denied any sexual relations prior to marriage, except when they made use of such allegations to compel men to admit to a promise of marriage. Women felt less compromised by words they had exchanged than what they had done with their bodies.[17]

Promises to marry made in public also proved a source of litigation. Across Europe, both men and women claimed that they had married out of fear, and so had not truly consented.[18] In these cases of "force and fear," women often claimed intimidation by their parents, while men claimed that they had promised to marry because the girls' families had threatened them. Scholars working on Italian records have found a number of cases in which efforts to have a marriage dissolved on the grounds of lack of consent were strengthened by the legal incapacity of the wife, who had married before reaching the age of consent.[19] The age of these sometime-brides stands apart from other places in Europe, where women generally married much later, or at least over the age of twelve. Married so young, these Italian women, if they survived childbirth, often outlived their older husbands and sometimes remarried.

Remarriage

The rules governing remarriage in canon law were explicitly gender-neutral. Widows and widowers both could remarry, or not, with the same constraints. Byzantine law placed restrictions on the number of marriages a Christian of either sex could enter into in succession, with penances and temporary abstention from the sacraments following even the permissible remarriages. In the west, widows and widowers could remarry freely. Even the traditional Roman rule that a widow had to wait a certain number of months before remarriage (usually twelve) was explicitly rejected in western canon law. Widows and widowers both could choose the better path of celibacy. Or they could remarry as quickly as they liked, especially if they were young and had reason to fear that they might otherwise commit sexual sin.

The manner in which a widow or widower might remarry did face some circumscription, however. Canon law deprived both widows and widowers of the nuptial blessing offered at first marriages. While the withholding of this blessing applied to both genders in the canon law, major theological treatises and some local synodal statutes suggest that the marital history of the woman alone was what mattered in such circumstances. Widows and widowers who wished to remarry also faced, in principle, another rule that applied to men and women alike. Beginning in the late twelfth century, canon law required that one married to a long-absent or missing spouse (and wishing to remarry) prove the distant spouse had died. As found in the synodal statutes of northern France, a wife might have to seek witnesses to her husband's death. A widower newly arrived in a diocese, meanwhile, might have to produce a letter from his parish priest back home, attesting that his wife had died. If the synodal statutes expressed these rules in gendered terms, assuming a wife would be left behind while a husband might rove, the law also required traveling wives and stay-at-home husbands to provide proof before remarriage.

Ecclesiastical courts present a very mixed record of enforcement of the rules for remarriage. Priests seem to have given the nuptial blessing to widows and widowers with some regularity, and they paid fines as recompense with less regularity. Those seeking to marry were at least sometimes asked for documentation in some dioceses, but more often and in most places people who wanted to marry could do so without needing to document their freedom and fitness to do so. Notably, if gender-neutral in principle, the rules prohibiting remarriage without proof of an absent spouse's death were applied by the courts with a clear gender bias. Rather surprisingly, across Europe, wherever courts prosecuted fraudulent or hasty remarriages, men were punished far more often and much more harshly than women. Women did commit bigamy, but prosecution of female bigamy did not result in the harsh punishments inflicted upon male bigamists.[20] This seems to have been because female bigamy, while sinful, did not transgress gender norms as much as did male bigamy. A man's abandonment of a first marriage and fraudulent creation of a second was a serious abrogation of his duty as head of household. The husband was responsible for the marriage's success. Even when it was the wife who ran away and married someone else, the fault ultimately lay with the husband. As for an abandoned wife, if she sought male headship in the form of another husband, such an act at least placed her back under male control.

MARRIED LIFE

If the only legally established gendered difference in marriage formation was different ages of consent for men and for women, we might nevertheless expect many more differences to emerge in the rights and obligations of a husband and wife in their married life together. In fact, the western canon law of marriage offers few explicit differences in governing the behavior of husbands and wives. These few differences, however, may well have held real practical importance, with broad implications for practice even in situations in which the law called for gender-neutral treatment of spouses. Most of all, a wife had to obey her husband, and this obedience might well have had a role in shaping all else a wife could legally do.

On the whole, the similarities seem to outweigh the differences. Both husband and wife could not remarry while the other spouse lived. Neither spouse could refuse to have sexual relations with the other, nor should either abandon the conjugal domicile. Neither spouse could take a vow of celibacy or enter religious life without the other's permission. Each spouse could demand an annulment if they suspected their marriage was invalid, and each could seek a legal separation on certain grounds. As for differences, we have only four. A man became capable of marrying at fourteen, whereas his wife could marry at twelve. Second, a wife owed her husband obedience over and above the obedience she owed her parents. Meanwhile, a husband did not have to obey his wife, but he could not neglect her or his many obligations to her and to their children. Third, if a wife had a child, she could not return to church until she underwent a rite of purification, but her husband had no ritual of purification.[21] Fourth, a husband could seek a legal separation from his wife on suspicion of adultery alone while a wife needed some grounds on which to base her accusation. Every other thing required of a wife was equally required of a husband.

Many of these reciprocal rules for spouses stem from canonists' interpretation of the marital debt, the requirement that spouses make themselves sexually available to each other. Canonists presented the marital debt in starkly equal terms for husbands and wives. In marrying, husbands lost ownership of their bodies, which belonged to their wives, as well as vice versa. Regardless of gender, whoever rendered the debt to the demanding spouse was almost always doing a good and virtuous thing, as it prevented the other spouse from indulging in some other sinful behavior. Gender does not seem to have affected the determination of what one spouse could do or not do, even in the more improbable situations for sexual intercourse that canonists considered, such as, for example, when one spouse asks the other for sex in a church. Seemingly regardless of gender, there is only the request and the rendering of the debt, and while the asking is more or less appropriate or sinful, the rendering is almost always meritorious.

Many scholars have taken the marital debt as an important example of equality between spouses.[22] Other scholars, however, in studying the efforts of female would-be saints to escape the carnal urgings of their husbands, have maintained that the marital debt in effect functioned to allow men to have sex with their wives on demand, but not the reverse.[23] For a better understanding of relations of spouses in canon law, we must understand how canonists and judges resolved the tension between the competing principles of inequality and parity. What was the balance between the rule that wives had to be obedient to their husbands, on the one hand, and on the other hand, the rule requiring equality of spouses in asking for and rendering the marital debt, with its implications for so many other aspects of married life?

On this and other matters, further analysis of the laws as well as litigation may yield some answers. Of particular interest is the issue of one spouse leaving the conjugal domicile—for work, for pilgrimage, for warfare, to visit ill parents, or any of the other myriad reasons—and thereby depriving the other spouse of the marital debt. When did spouses actually have to seek permission? There may have been a perceived difference in husbands' versus wives' abandonment, intended as temporary or not, of the conjugal domicile. Husbands more often had to travel for work or war. Nevertheless, there may have been at least some limitations on a husband's freedom of movement. The fact that when a husband wished to join the crusades, and his wife refused to allow him to go, the matter required papal attention, indicates that a rule that required spouses ask each other's permission to part, and a rule that included husbands, must have in principle existed. Innocent III decided that the spiritual importance of crusading overrode the obligation to stay home, but this rule may have had extremely limited application.[24]

Scholarship on desertion of the conjugal domicile, including that of Sara Butler, Martine Charageat, and Corinne Wieben, has focused more on husbands' use of the court to seek the return of an errant wife than on the reverse.[25] If their focus on husbands in these studies has obscured from our view wives' efforts to retrieve absent husbands, so far we have little evidence to suggest otherwise. In fifteenth-century Venice, for example, out of sixty-one requests for resumption of cohabitation, wives initiated only 18 percent of the requests, while husbands initiated 82 percent of the requests. In an additional gender difference, these women were rarely successful in these few claims. This might suggest that the courts acted more often to assist husbands with their errant wives.[26] In addition to this example, we would like to know much more about what an abandoned wife could or did do in a law court. Did wives, like husbands, also ask the court to menace their spouses with excommunication and fines if they did not return home? At least some wives did make use of the court to seek improvement of their married lives. As Anne Lefebvre-Teillard has shown, a northern French official might intervene in a number of instances. A husband might be enjoined to treat his wife well, not to beat her excessively or without cause, or even not to beat her at all, on penalty of excommunication and imprisonment and a fine. Another husband might be simply ordered to return home.[27] According to Lefebvre-Teillard, both husbands and wives abandoned the conjugal domicile, and relatively often, but the church did not fight very strongly against this tendency. It remains to be seen if husbands more often sought the return of errant wives, and if wives were ordered home more often than husbands.

ADULTERY

Adultery is another area in which western canon law demanded equality for spouses in theory, at least. In Byzantium, however, only the extramarital activity of a wife—and this extramarital activity most loosely defined and on the slightest suspicion—counted as adultery. In so defining adultery, and especially in defining (female) adultery as grounds for divorce, the Byzantine law showed more fidelity to Roman law traditions, and far less principled equality for husbands and wives than found in the western canon law. According to Angeliki Laiou, for a wife's behavior to qualify as adultery in Byzantium, a wife had only to leave her home without permission overnight, travel in the company of a man other than her husband, or attend frequent baths or banquets. For a man's extra-marital sexual behavior to qualify as grounds for divorce, the man had to bring his mistress to live in their home, or live with this other woman in another house in the same city. Male extramarital behavior, as Laiou explains, was only a serious problem when it so denigrated the wife's (and her family's) honor, otherwise it was tolerated. Female adultery, meanwhile, was seen as a pollution so powerful that a husband sinned in staying with an adulterous wife. Laiou describes canonists as "somewhat embarrassed and ambivalent" about this gender bias in defining and handling adultery. Saint Basil wrote "disapprovingly, but accepting the fact" that while divine law condemned husband and wife equally for extramarital sex, "custom" required that wives face divorce and punishment but not husbands. "The reason" according to Basil "is not easy to understand, but this is the prevailing custom."[28]

Meanwhile, western canon law complied with the insistence of the church fathers who argued that adulterous husbands and wives ought to be treated the same. Quoting Saint Ambrose, Gratian's *Decretum* called all extramarital sex, that of husbands and that of wives, adultery: "What is not permitted to wives is not permitted to husbands. Chastity is expected of husbands as well as wives."[29] Husbands and wives could have sex with each other, but no one else. But canon law seemingly competed with a reality in which husbands could get away with adultery while their wives could not. Canonists observed that husbands readily brought adultery accusations against their wives, while wives largely suffered in silence, or if they did attempt to accuse their husbands, the courts ignored or rejected the accusations. They also expressed concerns about extrajudicial or secular court treatment of wives suspected of adultery. Throughout the Middle Ages, canonists shared the evidently quite unimaginative fear that husbands might kill their wives if they caught them at adultery. Indeed, some secular legal traditions even permitted such extrajudicial violence or forgave it.

If no canonist endorsed the murder of an adulterous wife, canonists and especially theologians did not always maintain a strictly gender-neutral treatment of adultery. For many theologians and some canonists, a husband's adultery seemed less problematic, criminal, or dangerous than a wife's adultery. Thomas Aquinas argued that a wife's adultery was far worse than that of a husband, as the wife's adultery might disrupt a patri-line. Pope Innocent IV went so far as to excuse husbands' adultery as a lesser evil than wives' adultery on the grounds that women resembled the church while men resembled Christ. As Innocent explained, the female church could only have one spouse, Christ, and so her adultery was unforgivable. Christ, meanwhile had married both the Old and New Testaments, and so a husband's adultery seemed a lesser violation. On the other hand, canonists sometimes pressed toward the other extreme. Adulterous husbands are occasionally described as worse offenders than wives in that they, as the stronger sex, should be more able to resist temptation. Husbands are sometimes even blamed for the adultery committed by their wives. As heads of household and responsible for their wives' behavior, they should prevent any adultery. Additionally, Leah Otis-Cour and Shannon McSheffrey have argued that tolerance of male adultery greatly diminished by the fifteenth century.[30] As I am finding in my own research, some late medieval church courts—and even more remarkably, secular courts—exhibit a surprising tendency to prosecute husbands for adultery with unmarried women, even including prostitutes.

Legal Separation and Dissolution of Marriages

In the early Middle Ages, marriage operated on flexible terms. Couples could, and did, divorce and remarry on a wide variety of grounds. Annulments were granted on account of a vast range of impediments, which could have emerged both before and after a marriage had taken place. Beginning at around 1100 the canon law shifted quite dramatically to allow for fewer grounds of annulment. Increasingly, only marriages that could be proven invalid based on the impediments of lack of consent, incest, affinity, or impotence might be annulled. For other matters, western canon law developed a sort of middle ground called a "legal separation." Spouses granted such a separation remained married, but were released from many of the normal requirements of married life, such as the rendering of the conjugal debt.

From a legal standpoint these separations in no way meant an end to a marriage. Above all, neither spouse could legally remarry while the other lived. The principle of indissolubility had such importance to canonists that while they might allow spouses to separate their goods or their persons in some limited circumstances, these spouses remained married. Even if they lived apart and were no longer required to render the conjugal debt, the marriage remained. Turning to legal practice, we find, of course, numerous variations in the law as employed by the court and by litigants, and also in the extrajudicial behaviors of married people. In practice, spouses probably ignored the rules and remarried after a separation. Even more, it seems most probable that spouses in many parts of western Europe separated and remarried without any recourse to ecclesiastical judgment.

Western canon law provided for legal separation in two main instances: entrance into religious life and adultery. Canonists maintained that the wish to take religious vows could not supersede marital obligations, neither for a husband nor for a wife. Whichever spouse wished to enter religious life could not do so without the consent of the other. That other spouse ideally also entered religious life or at least promised to live chastely, and could not remarry unless his or her spouse died. These rules had no clear gender difference in the law, and no gender differences in legal practice have been identified thus far. Separations for adultery, and separations granted on other grounds such as cruelty, operated with more clear differences.

For medieval canonists, Matthew 5:32 and 19:9 implied that a separation was possible because of adultery. If either spouse suspected adultery, the aggrieved party could seek a legal separation from an ecclesiastical court. As mentioned above, the husband had legal and social advantages over the wife in bringing such a claim, including the principle that he could act on suspicion alone but his wife needed proof. While entrance into religious life and adultery offered the only grounds for a separation recognized by the Catholic church, canonists found ways to define adultery quite expansively. Latin renderings of Matthew 5:32 and 19:9, used as the basis for the legal right to separate, used the word *fornicatio* rather than *adulterium*. Doctrinal texts on marriage maintained this tendency to describe adulterous relationships (extramarital sexual relationships involving at least one married person) as fornication (illicit sex), and this terminology provided canonists with an opportunity to expand the grounds on which separation might be allowed. Canonists made use of the word *fornicatio* to grant separations for a number of different kinds of "fornications" including "spiritual fornication," by which they meant heresy, or conversion. Christine Meek found a remarkable case in which an Italian woman sought a separation from her husband on the grounds that he, while a slave in Tunis, had converted to Islam and married a Muslim woman.[31]

Stretching the bounds of *fornicatio* still further, canonists eventually also allowed separations on the grounds of cruelty. Initially, canonists did not allow for separation on the grounds of cruelty unless a spouse's life was in danger. It appears that only in the fifteenth century did any canonist, namely Panormitanus (d. 1445), allow less extreme cases of cruelty as grounds for a separation of bed and board. Meanwhile, in practice, well before the time of Panormitanus, some ecclesiastical courts granted separations on a wide range of grounds, including cruelty and violence.[32] Courts also granted a separation of goods to wives whose husbands had squandered their dowries, which may or may not have accompanied a separation of bodies as well. Scholars have found large numbers of separation cases in Italy, northern France, and Belgium. Among the cases of separation brought in Italy, we find that husbands initiated suits more often than wives. When Italian wives did seek separations, they came to court most often after already having left their husbands, either on their own initiative or in response to a complaint lodged by the husband. These wives sought the return of their dowries or the right to live apart.[33]

Unlike legal separation, the dissolution of a marriage usually rendered that marriage fully null and void, thus granting spouses the freedom to remarry. In Byzantium and in the west, both husbands and wives sought nullification of their marriages on the grounds that the union lacked validity from its outset. Spouses could claim a number of impediments to their marriages and often offered courts a wide range among which to choose. Church courts could dissolve marriages made within forbidden degrees of relationship by blood or by marriage. Marriage to a godparent or the godparent's immediate family was also prohibited and therefore potentially grounds for annulment, as was marriage with someone closely related to a former sexual partner or former betrothed. Also, marriages might be dissolved because a prior marriage, a prior bond, rendered the subsequent marriage invalid. Gendered analysis of whether husbands or wives might be more likely to claim consanguinity, sexual affinity, or prior bond as invalidating a marriage, and how courts handled these suits, would be of considerable interest.

Western church courts could also dissolve marriages on one final, salacious ground. Dissolution of a marriage on the grounds of frigidity or impotence has been the subject of considerable study.[34] The subject is a particularly rich one for discussions of gender, as the bias favored wives seeking a dissolution rather than husbands. Canon law accorded the right to seek the dissolution of a marriage on the grounds that a spouse—male or female—was permanently frigid or otherwise unable to have sex. The impotent or frigid partner was forbidden remarriage, but their spouse could remarry, as long as the incapable partner did not somehow develop the capacity for sexual relations. In that case, the prior marriage had to be resumed. The law itself usually discussed this rule in terms of impotent husbands whose wives wished to remarry, but frigid women also came under discussion in western canon law. Legal practice appears to have followed the tendency found in the law, handling male impotence far more often than female frigidity or physical incapacity. Scholars working with court records from across Europe have located dozens of such cases, mostly of male impotence, but with a few examples of female frigidity. Whatever the gender of the impotent or frigid spouse, scholars have found as well many examples of fraudulent practices on the part of spouses who made use of the dissolution to remarry. If the impotence or frigidity was cured in a new (illegal) union, both original spouses were invariably ordered to resume their prior marriages.

While in the Middle Ages the western tradition came to severely restrict the grounds for annulment, Byzantine canon law retained many of the older grounds for dissolution which in the west had shifted to legal separations. In Byzantium the husband of a convicted adulteress could remarry, as could a husband whose wife had become a nun. Meanwhile, wives had far fewer legal options for divorce. One exception is found with impotence, one of the few grounds that also remained open to western Christian spouses. However little Byzantine canon law permitted wives, ecclesiastical courts proved willing to grant them far more than the law allowed. Courts granted at least some wives married to absent and missing husbands the right to remarry. Courts also allowed divorces on the grounds of "implacable hatred," usually an implacable hatred that the wife was said to feel towards her husband, and it seems both could then remarry. While we can argue that in these cases, Byzantine courts did a great deal seemingly to equalize the options for wives in giving them access to these grounds for divorce, it is important to recognize the context in which these court actions took place. If courts sometimes allowed wives more than the law permitted, in other cases wives were punished more harshly than required by law.[35]

CONCLUSIONS

To write about gender equalities and inequalities in medieval canon law calls for important choices in presentation. It would be easy to complain that while canonists called for equality for spouses of both sexes in the marital debt and many related matters, they nevertheless fell far short of producing a law that maintained these egalitarian stand-ards. But how many law codes achieve their ideals in practice? It is better to appreciate that canon law, with its roots in the earliest centuries of Christianity, was the product of a Judeo-Roman world. In this world, husbands and wives were supposed to be unequal in their respective rights and obligations as spouses, and only female extramarital sexual activity was criminalized. Christians had to start, for example, by pleading with men not to kill wives suspected of adultery. Perhaps we can best proceed, as attempted in this essay, by writing with awareness of the ways in which canonists fell short of their own claims, but also with awareness of the prior legal and cultural differences, and the real differences present in both Byzantine and western medieval perceptions of the duties and moral obligations of husbands and wives.

The canon law of marriage was a complex structure of give and take, moving in and out of the binaries that placed men and women, as husbands and as wives, into separate categories. Canonists pushed harder than theologians in insisting that wives and hus-bands be treated the same, a difference in approach that merits further study. As a group, however, canonists were divided on what they thought should be forbidden to wives or allowed to husbands. Canonists were divided as well on what equalities there could be in marriage, and on the reception members of each sex ought to find in an ecclesiastical court, depending upon their gender and the nature of their crime. In ecclesiastical court practice, men and women engaged in a variety of court actions to establish, improve, or put an end to a marriage. Judges engaged in a variety of proceedings instigated to regu-late marriage practice in the diocese, with varying impact on husbands and wives and upon men and women. If gender loomed large in these proceedings, it was also open to extensive manipulation and interpretation on the part of the men and women who fre-quented medieval courtrooms.

FURTHER READING

Charageat, Martine. "La confrontation des genres au tribunal au Moyen Age (XIVe–XVIe siècles): Une relecture des relations de couples en conflit." *Genre & Histoire*, 5 (Fall 2009): 1–23.

Laiou, Angeliki. "Evolution of Status of Women in Marriage and in Family Law," in Society for the Law of the Oriental Churches, L.E. Mitchell, ed., *Mütter, Nonne, Diakonin: Frauenbilder im Recht der Ostkirchen*, Kanon. Egling an der Paar: Kovar, 2000, 71–86.

McDougall, Sara. "Bigamy: A Male Crime in Medieval Europe?" *Gender & History*, 22 (2) (August 2010): 430–46.

Metz, René. "Le statut de la femme en droit canonique medieval." *Recueils de la société Jean Bodin*, 12 (1962): 86–89.

Reid, Jr, Charles. *Power Over the Body, Equality in the Family: Rights and Domestic Relations in Medieval Canon Law*. Grand Rapids, Mich.: William B. Eerdmans, 2004.

Schmugge, Ludwig. "Female Petitioners in the Papal Penitentiary." *Gender & History*, 12 (3) (November, 2000): 685–703.

Stuard, Susan Mosher. "Burdens of Matrimony: Husbanding and Gender in Medieval Italy," in Barbara Rosenwein and Lester Little, eds, *Debating the Middle Ages: Issues and Readings*. Oxford: Blackwell, 1998, 290–98.

Notes

1. Yan Thomas, "The Division of the Sexes in Roman Law," in Georges Duby and Michelle Perrot, gen. eds, Pauline Schmitt Pantel, ed., *A History of Women in the West*, vol. 2: *From Ancient Goddesses to Christian Saints* (Cambridge, Mass.: Harvard University Press, 1992), 83–138.

2. Daniela Müller, "Vir caput mulieris," in Norbert Brieskorn, Paul Mikat, Daniela Müller, and Dietmar Willoweit, eds, *Vom mittelalterlichen Recht zur neuzeitlichen Rechtswissenschaft* (Munich: Ferdinand Schöningh, 1994), 223–45, esp. 232–33.

3. See discussion by Marie Kelleher, "Later Medieval Law in Community Context," Chapter 9 in this volume.

4. James Brundage, *Law, Sex and Christian Society in Medieval Europe* (Chicago: University of Chicago Press, 1987).

5. Susan Mosher Stuard, "Burdens of Matrimony: Husbanding and Gender in Medieval Italy," in Barbara Rosenwein and Lester Little, eds, *Debating the Middle Ages: Issues and Readings* (Oxford: Blackwell, 1998), 290–98, esp. 293.

6. Charles Reid, Jr, *Power Over the Body, Equality in the Family: Rights and Domestic Relations in Medieval Canon Law* (Grand Rapids, Mich.: William B. Eerdmans, 2004).

7. Ludwig Schmugge, "Female Petitioners in the Papal Penitentiary," *Gender & History*, 12 (3) (November 2000): 685–703.

8. Charles Donahue, *Law, Marriage, and Society in the Later Middle Ages: Arguments about Marriage in Five Courts* (Cambridge: Cambridge University Press, 2007).

9. Christina Deutsch, "Zwischen Leben und Tod: Die Verschollenen und ihre Hinterbliebenen im Spätmittelalter," *Trajekte: Zeitschrift des Zentrums für Literatur- und Kulturforschung Berlin*, 14 (2007): 12–16.

10. Angeliki Laiou, "Evolution of Status of Women in Marriage and in Family Law," in Society for the Law of the Oriental Churches, ed., *Mütter, Nonne, Diakonin: Frauenbilder im Recht der Ostkirchen*, Kanon (Egling an der Paar: Kovar, 2000), 71–86, esp. 79–82; and Angeliki Laiou, *Mariage, amour et parenté à Byzance aux Xie–XIIIe siècles* (Paris: De Boccard, 1992).

11. P. J. P. Goldberg, "Gender and Matrimonial Litigation in the Church Courts in the Later Middle Ages: The Evidence of the Court of York," *Gender & History*, 19 (1) (April 2007): 43–59, esp. 45.

12. Donahue, *Law*, see esp. chapter 3.

13. X 4.1.15 [*Corpus Iuris Canonici*, Book 4, Title 1, chapter 15]. Reid, *Power*, 45–47.

14. Emlyn Eisenach, *Husbands, Wives, and Concubines: Marriage, Family, and Social Order in Sixteenth-Century Verona* (Kirksville, Mo.: Truman State University Press, 2004), 95.

15. Mia Korpiola, *Between Betrothal and Bedding: Marriage Formation in Sweden 1200–1600* (Leiden: Brill, 2009), 179–81.

16. Cecilia Cristellon, *Charitas versus eros: Il matrimonio, la Chiesa e i suoi giudici nella Venezia del Rinascimento (1420–1545)* (PhD thesis, European University Institute, 2005), 132–45.

17. Martine Charageat, "La confrontation des genres au tribunal au Moyen Age (XIVe–XVIe siècles): Une relecture des relations de couples en conflit," *Genre & Histoire*, 5 (Fall 2009): 1–23, esp. 10–18.

18. Sara Butler, "'I Will Never Consent to be Wedded With You': Coerced Marriage in the Courts of Medieval England," *Canadian Journal of History*, 39 (2) (August 2004): 247–70; several examples from Italy can be found in Silvana Seidel Menchi and Diego Quaglioni,

eds, *Matrimoni in dubbio: Unioni controverse e nozze clandestine in Italia dal XIV al XVIII secolo* (Bologna: Societa editrice il Mulino, 2001).

19. Christine Meek, "Un'unione incerta: La vicenda di Neria, figlia dell'organista, e di Baldassino, merciaio pistoiese (Lucca 1396–1397)," in Menchi and Quaglioni, eds, *Matrimoni in dubbio*, 107–22.

20. Sara McDougall, "Bigamy: A Male Crime in Medieval Europe?" *Gender & History*, 22 (2) (August 2010): 430–46.

21. Scholars have traditionally understood purification, or churching, as a source of shame for women, but it also has been read as a ritual exclusive to wives, rather than unmarried women, and a sign of prestige. See Paula Reider, *On the Purification of Women: Churching in Northern France*, 1100–1500 (New York: Palgrave MacMillan, 2006).

22. Elizabeth Makowski, "The Conjugal Debt and Medieval Canon Law," in Julia Bolton Holloway, Constance S. Wright, and John Bechtold, eds, *Equally in God's Image: Women in the Middle Ages* (New York: Peter Lang, 1990), 129–43; James Brundage, *Sex*, 241; Reid, *Power*, 120–26; see also Dyan Elliott, "Sex in Holy Places: An Exploration of a Medieval Anxiety," *Journal of Women's History*, 6 (3) (Fall 1994): 6–34.

23. Dyan Elliott, *Spiritual Marriage: Sexual Abstinence in Medieval Wedlock* (Princeton: Princeton University Press, 1993): 148–55.

24. James Brundage, "The Crusader's Wife: A Canonistic Quandary," *Studia Gratiana*, 12 (1967): 425–42; idem, "The Crusader's Wife Revisited," *Studia Gratiana*, 14 (1969): 241–52.

25. Sara Butler, "Runaway Wives: Husband Desertion in Medieval England," *Journal of Social History*, 40 (2) (Winter 2006): 337–59; Corinne Wieben, "'As Men Do with Their Wives': Domestic Violence in Fourteenth-Century Lucca," *California Italian Studies Journal*, 1 (2) (2010): 1–13; Charageat, "Confrontation"; see also Brundage, *Law*, 453, n. 188.

26. Cristellon, *I Tribunali*, 402: in 118 cases between 1420 and 1500, 39 percent were initiated by women and 61 percent by men. There were thirty-seven requests for separations, with 72 percent initiated by women and 27 percent by men. There were sixty-one requests for resumption of cohabitation, with 18 percent initiated by women, while 82 percent were initiated by men; Stanley Chojnacki, "Il divorzio di Cateruzza: Rappresentazione femminile ed esito processuale (Venezia 1465)," in Silvana Seidel Menchi and Diego Quaglioni, eds, *Coniugi nemici: La separazione in Italia dal XII al XVIII secolo* (Bologna: Il mulino, 2000), 371–416.

27. Anne Lefebvre-Teillard, *Les Officialités à la veille du concile de Trente* (Paris: Sirey, 1973), 112.

28. Laiou, "Evolution," 77.

29. *Corpus Iuris Canonici* v. 1: C. 32 q. 4 c. 4.

30. Shannon McSheffrey, "Men and Masculinity in Late Medieval London Civic Culture: Governance, Patriarchy, and Reputation," in Jacqueline Murray ed., *Conflicted Identities and Multiple Masculinities: Men in the Medieval West* (New York: Garland Press, 1999), 243–78, esp. 260–66; Leah Otis-Cour, "'De juro novo': Dealing with Adultery in the Fifteenth-Century Toulousain," *Speculum*, 84 (2) (2009): 347–92.

31. Christine Meek, "'Simone ha aderito alla fede de Maometto': La 'fornicazione spirituale' come causa di separazione (Lucca 1424)," in Menchi and Quaglioni, eds, *Coniugi nemici*, 121–39.

32. Donahue, *Law*, 522–24.

33. Eisenach, *Husbands*, 179.

34. Jacqueline Murray, "On the Origins and Role of 'Wise Women' in Cases for Annulment on the Grounds of Male Impotence," *Journal of Medieval History*, 16 (3) (1990): 235–49; Catherine Rider, *Magic and Impotence in the Middle Ages* (Oxford: Oxford University Press, 2006).

35. Laiou, "Evolution," 80–83.

PART III

DOMESTIC LIVES

CHAPTER 12

....

GENDERING DEMOGRAPHIC CHANGE IN THE MIDDLE AGES

....

MARYANNE KOWALESKI

HISTORICAL demography lays out essential parameters for the history of medieval women: how long they lived (mortality), how many children they had (fertility), and how often and far they moved about (migration). This essay explores what we know about these parameters by drawing on not only the documentary analyses of historical demographers, but also the pioneering archaeological work of paleodemographers. Whether analyzing texts or skeletons, both sorts of demographers rely heavily on indirect or proxy measures because their direct sources are so poor: few censuses, no systematic records of births or deaths, and difficulties dating and sexing human skeletons. Historians, for example, infer population growth from rising grain prices and rents (since these suggest demand outstripped supply), and archaeologists infer nutritional deprivation in childhood from a decline in adult average height or other skeletal conditions. Demographers' reliance on indirect or proxy measures has thus made intense methodological debate a hallmark of their scholarship.

Because of women's central role in human fertility, historical demographers have always treated sex and gender as major categories of analysis. Yet they have tended to concentrate more on how sex ratios and marriage rates affected overall population trends than on how, for example, gender relations might be responsible for different sex ratios in town and country, or how often and when women married. This problem is especially acute for medievalists, who have until recently focused on estimating, primarily from tax records, the total size of populations. Scholars now broadly agree on the main trends, while acknowledging significant local and regional variations. Western Europe's population was falling by the third century as the political stability of the Roman Empire faltered; decline continued with the first wave of barbarian settlement in the fourth century, the outbreak of severe plague in the mid- and late sixth century, and the collapse of cities and long-distance trade in the fifth through seventh centuries.

Population stabilized and probably even increased slightly during the eighth and early ninth centuries, but Viking, Magyar, and Muslim invasions in the late ninth and early tenth centuries undercut recovery in many regions. From c.1050, however, population increased rapidly until c.1300 when, according to many scholars, Europe's population had extended beyond its resources, precipitating a Malthusian crisis in which a weakened population was especially susceptible to disease and famine. The Great Famine of 1315–1322 increased mortality rates by 10 to 15 percent in some areas, but the largest population decline came with the Black Death of 1347–1350, when one third to one half of Europe's population died. For reasons that are not yet clearly understood, the population was slow to recover from the Black Death. Survivors should have married earlier and produced larger families because of the reduced pressure on food resources, but the population failed to grow. Most scholars currently explain this population stagnation—which lasted until the end of the fifteenth century and into the early sixteenth century in many regions—by the influence of high mortality from subsequent outbreaks of plague and other epidemics. But others attribute this stagnation to fertility, pointing to economic and cultural factors that encouraged women to marry late or not at all.

This master narrative is the product of much labor and the subject of much debate. It reflects the achievement of a discipline that has in the last forty years developed innovative methodologies to calculate not only rates of mortality, fertility, and migration, but also such crucial measures for women's history as sex ratio (the number of men for every 100 women), household size, and proportions married. These measures have tremendous possibilities for helping us understand how the decisions and choices of ordinary women and men—the poorly documented majority—shaped changes in the size and structure of medieval populations.

MORTALITY

Most medieval demographers identify the death rate as the prime factor in population change; it is also easier to measure than fertility or migration. They usually focus on specific groups for whom the date of death is known, particularly elite men such as monks or aristocrats, but calculations are complicated because dates of birth or entrance into religious community are hard to find. The best data, for English monks during the difficult years of the fifteenth century, show a mortality rate of 25–30 per thousand per year, rising to 40 and even 60 per thousand in bad years, compared to about 8 per thousand in the world today. The dangers affecting medieval populations are even evident among well-off English landowners whose life expectancy at birth (another way to assess mortality) was only 25–30 years in the fourteenth century (compared to 67 years today). Members of Florentine merchant families in 1250–1500 had a life expectancy of about 35 years, though this is a probably a high estimate since it is based on births and deaths recorded in family memoirs, which tend to under-record deaths of babies. Estimates further down the social ladder are even more contentious; one assessment puts the death rate of male peasants in England before the Black Death at 40–50 per thousand, with a life expectancy at birth of 25–28 years, and a grimmer forecast of 20–25 years for less substantial peasants, while another for the post-plague period puts it closer to 32 years, albeit using a completely different set of sources. None of these measures offers any firm data on female mortality.[1]

Despite the scarcity of hard evidence, most scholars believe that female life expectancy was lower than men's in the early Middle Ages.[2] The documentary evidence rests to a great extent on skewed sex ratios found in the Carolingian estate surveys or polyptychs. The normal sex ratio at birth is about 105 (105 boys born for every 100 girls), but declines to 100 by adulthood. Most of the estate surveys of the late eighth to early ninth century show high sex ratios (that is, an excess of males), ranging from the strikingly imbalanced average adult ratios of 120 to 140 on several northern French estates to the lower averages of 112 on lands in central Italy, to 102 among Provençal serfs. Emily Coleman has interpreted the skewed sex ratios on the estates of St Germain-des-Prés as evidence of female infanticide, but others have convincingly argued that recording bias was responsible for undercounting adult women. The only polyptych to give the ages of all children, a Provençal survey of St Victor's estates, also does not suggest any differential neglect of female infants or girls.

Evidence assembled from literary texts, law codes, gravestones, and cemeteries has also been interpreted as indicating a persistently low number of adult women in the early Middle Ages. In the Anglo-Saxon cemetery of Raunds Furnells, for example, only 46 percent of the men died before age 35, but 71 percent of women were dead by that age; similar if not so stark differentials have been found in other Anglo-Saxon cemeteries. Robin Fleming speculates that the dearth of adult women may explain why peasants marshaled their resources by increasingly settling in nucleated villages and why they were attracted to sites with labor-saving mills. Carol Clover hypothesizes that a similar shortage of women in early Scandinavia may have spurred not only polygamy and concubinage (possession of scarce women being a male status symbol), but also early female marriage, easier female divorce, frequent female remarriage, heightened male competition for women (in the form of duels or abductions), and even the male migration behind Viking raids. These intriguing speculations, however, assume that people were reacting to a new increase in female mortality when in fact we have no evidence that such a change occurred.[3]

Another argument for changing female mortality rates comes from Vern Bullough, who speculates that death rates declined around the turn of the millennium because agricultural advances improved diets. He blamed iron deficiency for the lower life expectancies of early medieval women and argued that nutritional improvements increased female longevity and equalized sex ratios by the later Middle Ages. Late medieval records for northern Europe do show more women than men in towns, but fewer women in the population at large, although the tax and manorial records that provide these data are notorious for their under-enumeration of women and girls.[4] The skeletal evidence at first glance is less equivocal. Analyses of cemetery evidence from across

Europe from the eleventh through fifteenth centuries show sex ratios that generally average about 112 to 122, with many considerably higher.[5]

What could have produced this seeming shortage of women in medieval populations? Female infanticide, though more through differential neglect than deliberate exposure, has been identified as one possibility. There is certainly modern evidence of food discrimination against female children in parts of modern Asia and Africa where female mortality is high, and an ominous correlation in nineteenth-century Britain between large families and high female infant mortality.[6] Medieval society clearly undervalued females, which could have resulted in differential treatment and access to food, particularly during hard times. Studies of medieval child abandonment, for example, have found that girls were more likely to be abandoned than were boys, and some medieval treatises recommended breastfeeding boys several months longer than girls, although in some places—such as early medieval Provence—weaning did not vary by sex.[7] Unfortunately, close analyses of medieval cemetery data provide no corroborating evidence. First, the surviving infant skeletons are notoriously difficult to sex. Second, although there is some slight archaeological and documentary evidence that gender might have influenced access to food, there is no concrete proof that medieval females suffered more nutritional deficiencies or inferior care than males. Indeed, most skeletal studies find more evidence of poor health in males than females, although disparities of age, wealth, and habitat environment influence health more than sex. Third, methods for sexing skeletons, particularly when they are not well preserved, have also been shown to be biased in favor of males.[8]

Others have argued that the dangers of pregnancy and childbirth must have caused earlier female mortality and thus the imbalanced sex ratios we see in the documentary and cemetery record. The demands of pregnancy and lactation can negatively affect women's health when their diets are scarce in calcium, but skeletons of medieval women over age 50 show the same incidence of osteoporosis as modern women.[9] Many demographers who point to the dangers of pregnancy and childbirth as the chief factors in early female mortality cite anecdotal evidence, much of it gathered from the elite, whose women were more at risk because of their very young age at marriage and their continual pregnancies; others rely on considerable adjustment of figures (Herlihy and Klapisch-Zuber) or unquestioning acceptance of cemetery data (Benedictow). Women certainly died in childbirth, but studies of maternal mortality in the early modern period indicate lower rates than anticipated, not high enough to account for the strikingly imbalanced sex ratios gathered from many medieval records and cemeteries.[10] Nor is the skeletal evidence conclusive on this point. Although some cemeteries have yielded evidence that medieval women tended to die during their peak years of fertility while male mortality was on average later and thus life expectancy greater, these studies do not account for mortality under the age of 20 since it is so difficult to sex young skeletons. Others have found no significant difference between male and female mortality; indeed, paleopathologists now tend to downplay the link between pregnancy and high female mortality.[11]

There have also been efforts to determine if the plague affected men and women dif-ferently, but interpretations of the often conflicting data vary. For example, medieval burial records from Florence, Arezzo, and Siena show that more men died during plague years, although women were often the first victims of attacks; these measures of plague mortality do not, however, take account of the (as yet unknown) sex ratio of the at-risk population. In contrast, one of the foremost historians of the Black Death, Ole Benedictow, is convinced that medieval women must have been more affected by plague because the early modern and modern documentary evidence for female super-mortality during plagues is so firm, although some of the best early modern plague data actually show greater male plague mortality.[12] The medieval skeletal evidence does not support his view since the majority of plague cemeteries show greater male than female mortality, with sex ratios reaching 177 at the Black Death cemetery at East Smithfield, London. But the skeletal evidence itself is questionable. On the one hand, the evidence needs to be seen in light of the large number of unsexed skeletons and choices about who would be buried in specially-made cemeteries like East Smithfield. High sex ratios were also common to all medieval cemetery populations, regardless of whether they were affected by plague or not; a recent comparison of medieval Danish skeletons from plague and non-plague cemeteries concludes that sex did not strongly affect risk of death during plague years. On the other hand, studies of osteological stress mark-ers suggest that men were more vulnerable to medieval plague. It is also curious that when female plague mortality was higher than men's, as in a parish in Switzerland in 1349, a small town in France in the late fourteenth century, and mid-fifteenth century Cremona, demographers usually explain this pattern as an anomaly.[13] The evidence is thus inconclusive and still open to debate.

The relationship between mortality and gender has also been front and center in the ongoing debate about whether women's paid labor increased after the Black Death, when extremely high mortality made labor scarce and wages high. Some argue that these economic conditions could have provided women with an opportunity to earn more income and take on occupations previously held by men. Women's greater entry into the commercial work force, particularly if they migrated to towns where work was abundant, might have also delayed the age when women married, thus helping to explain the stagnating population of the later Middle Ages.[14] Others, however, empha-size the long-term continuity in the low-level jobs and remuneration of women workers, thus downplaying the impact of mortality crises working through the economy to alter gender roles.[15] A similar debate centers on whether the high mortality of the Black Death produced more female heirs and landowners who thus enjoyed more economic agency; recent reviews of the English evidence, however, indicate that women in general did not benefit from the greater availability of land after the plague.[16]

All told, we currently have more debate than consensus in understanding the rela-tionship between mortality and gender. Many sources suggest that female mortality was more acute than male mortality, especially before c.1000. But given the notorious underreporting of females in medieval records, the difficulties sexing pre-adolescent and post-50 skeletons, and the gender bias that has even crept into the scientific labs of archaeologists,[17] it is difficult to endorse the interpretation that the high sex ratios found in medieval documents and cemeteries meant that medieval women regularly died at younger ages than their brothers, fathers, and sons. If women were in such short supply, why did they marry so late in much of northwestern Europe during the fifteenth century, and why were Italian parents at that time placing so many of their daughters in convents?

FERTILITY

Fertility rates (the average number of births by women of childbearing age within a particular population) are rarely available for the Middle Ages, except for a few wealthy bourgeois women whose husbands kept diaries recording the births of offspring. Scholars must, therefore, rely on more uncertain proxy measures, such as bulges in age pyramids constructed from taxed populations (interpreted as periods of plentiful births) or falls in the number of registered baptisms (said to reflect a declining birth rate) or estimates based on sources like the churching fees assessed on women who had recently given birth. Demographers also rely on modeling; that is, they ask what fertility rate would be necessary to maintain or grow a population, given known or postulated mortality rates and patterns; the aim is to match an appropriate "model life table" in order to calculate fertility rates. Based on the mortality data for fifteenth-century England (which, it should be remembered, relate mainly to monks and noblemen), women would have had to bear more than five children on average to maintain the population. This high fertility rate is difficult to achieve even in better-fed societies. It also requires early (under 20 years of age) and almost universal marriage; neither were characteristic of fifteenth-century England.[18]

Female nuptiality, also called the marriage rate and measured as the number of women who married per thousand, is a key element of fertility since the vast majority of medieval births occurred within marriage. Because specific data on marriage rates are hard to come by for the Middle Ages, demographers tend to measure nuptiality indirectly, either via the female age at marriage or the proportions of women who married. These numbers reflect crucial trends in society because women who marry before the age of 20 bear more children than women who marry late, after age 25. Paleodemographers postulate early marital ages when they find high mortality among female adolescents aged 15–20, and a later marital age when female mortality peaks at ages 25–30, but this view too readily assumes, as we have seen, that female mortality was closely related to the rigors of childbirth.[19] Historians do not fare much better since the scarce data available for female age at marriage is largely for wealthier women; efforts to mine Carolingian polyptychs, manorial court rolls, or village genealogies have yielded conflicting evidence and no consensus.[20] For ordinary women, the best evidence comes from Italian tax assessments that record the gender and age of household members, which show a trend toward later marriages and a wider age gap between spouses. In 1427, for example, women's average age at marriage in Tuscany was around 18 years in both town and countryside, but had risen to 21 by the end of the century. Men married in their mid-twenties in 1427; by the end of the century, they were marrying in their late twenties or even early thirties. This changing pattern explains many distinctive features of late medieval Italy. Young women's difficulties finding husbands from among a smaller cohort of older men (smaller because more men had died by age 30) may have prompted the intense dowry inflation of the era, as well as a substantial increase in numbers of Italian nuns.[21] The large number of widows in Tuscany and elsewhere in the Mediterranean must have been influenced in part by the widening age gap between spouses, although their remarriage was further discouraged by the region's inheritance systems and notions of honor.

This so-called "Mediterranean" model of marriage in southern Europe was very different from the "northwestern European" pattern of marriage, which was typified by a relatively late age at marriage for women (at least 23 for women and 26 for men), as well as a high proportion (around 10–20 percent) of people who never married.[22] Reliable data from early modern parish registers show that this pattern of late marriage dominated in the British Isles, Scandinavia, the Low Countries, Germany, and northern France by the sixteenth century, and medievalists have assiduously sought its traces in the fourteenth and fifteenth centuries. One key component was increasingly in place by c.1400: "life-cycle service," whereby adolescents left home for work and delayed marriage until they accumulated the resources to set up independent households. In medieval towns especially, it is clear that servants constituted more than the 6–10 percent of the population accepted as evidence of the northwestern European marriage pattern.

We know more about the second major factor in determining female nuptiality: the proportions of women who married. Tax records showing large proportions of single-women (over the age of 12–15 and never-married) reflect a late age at marriage and thus a lower fertility rate. Once again we see a contrast between northern and southern Europe. Almost 30 percent of all women recorded in the 1377 English poll tax were single, with higher proportions in towns, but in Tuscany singlewomen accounted for only around 18 percent of the population, and 21 percent in Florence itself, a pattern seen throughout most of southern Europe. This contrast is particularly strong in the percentage of singlewomen who never married, a measure that more than any other factor influences the size of premodern populations. In 1427 Florence, for instance, about 4 percent of women reached the age of 50 without marrying and a miniscule 2 percent of their rural counterparts. We have no directly comparative data for northern Europe, but the high proportions of unmarried adult women (including widows) in the English poll tax, as well as the larger percentage of women who were servants, suggest that lifelong singlewomen were considerably more numerous there than in Tuscany. It is important to keep in mind, however, that these larger trends could mask marked differences even within regions in the age at first marriage, prevalence of live-in servants, or household size.[23]

In the absence of firm data on age at marriage or proportions who married, demographers also infer fertility rates from the changing size of households, particularly the average number of children in a household or family, a somewhat tenuous practice.

Wills, censuses, and taxes provide these data, but often for households rather than fami-lies, and they often exclude the young or the unmarried (particularly daughters) who had left home. The peasant households recorded in the ninth-century polyptychs had an average household size of about 5 (3 children) per household, though we do not know how many survived to adulthood; those in the Rhineland had 5–6 per household (3–4 children).[24] These households seem to have been small nuclear families given the limited vocabulary of kinship employed, the absence of married brothers living together (a dis-tinctive household form called *frérèches*), and archaeological evidence of peasant dwell-ings. The excess number of bachelors in these communities, which led to the skewed sex ratios noted in the discussion of mortality above, has been explained in the case of Provence by the earlier age at which girls married compared to boys and by the migra-tion of young wives out of the community. Yet there is no consensus about what these patterns tell us about the exact age at marriage for women; some interpret the evidence as an early age at marriage (14–15 and, according to one scholar, as young as 10–12), but others see a later age at marriage. Analysis of the fuller data in the Provençal survey, which gives the ages and sex of all household members, allowed Monique Zerner-Chardavoine to calculate a (very) rough fertility rate by assessing the number of chil-dren aged 0–4 years old born to married women of childbearing age in the population. On two demesnes, this ratio was almost as high as that calculated for Tuscan women in 1427, which can be interpreted as typical of a population in which women marry young and can respond quickly to mortality crises by having more children. Such data are wel-come given the paucity of information about the fertility of early medieval women, but they are by no means conclusive, not least because the ratio was considerably lower on another demesne, suggesting a later age at marriage, and because the numbers do not include nonmarried women of childbearing age, a group that was probably larger in Carolingian Provence than late medieval Tuscany.[25]

For later centuries, household size is known from a plentiful group of hearth taxes, but these sources usually record only the head of the household, so that efforts have been oriented primarily towards finding the best multiplier in order to calculate the total size of the household and thus changes in the community's population from one tax period to another. Deciding which multiplier to use also dominates discussions on the English poll tax of 1377, considered one of the best demographic sources for all of medieval Europe. It lists all household members over 14, but requires a multiplier to account for the percentage of the population that was under 14 or evaded the tax, a fig-ure that ranges from 1.5 to 1.9. These and other late medieval household taxes, however, can yield useful data, especially when several survive for the same place and include information about wealth and/or occupation. In the Burgundian town of Chalons, for example, almost 19 percent of all households in 1360 were headed by women, and the proportion rose to 44 percent among households headed by a servant. In the next gen-eration, female householders declined a bit, but the proportion of singlewomen and widows among servant-headed householders rose to 54 percent. Although the author of this study explains this change as a function of high mortality, it also suggests declining fertility rates, with more women either never-married or not-remarried.[26] Almost all tax registers show that female heads of households (widows, but particularly singlewomen) were much poorer than their male counterparts; again, this poverty might go some way toward explaining the low fertility rates of Europe after the Black Death.

Female age at marriage and proportions married were important determinants of fertility, but other factors could also influence how many children a woman bore. Medieval people tended to react to mortality crises like the Black Death by practicing earlier and more universal marriage, an effect visible in bulges in age pyramids or the rare marriage register, such as that for Givry in Burgundy, where marriages increased almost fivefold in the year after the plague. This short-term strategy was less effective in southern Europe where the age at marriage was already low and most everyone married. Economic conditions could also affect nuptiality and remarriage. When land was scarce, as in England during the first half of the fourteenth century, remarriage among land-owning widows of reproductive age became more common than in later decades, when land was relatively abundant and cheap. When labor was short, as in the late Middle Ages, some argue that women could take advantage of rising wages and the chance to move into more lucrative positions previously held by men, developments that tended to promote a later age at marriage. Social status and class could also exert a powerful effect since less well-off women from an artisanal or laboring background married at an older age than richer women, even in strongholds of the Mediterranean regime of marriage. Customary inheritance practices also influenced whether and when young men and women married.[27]

The ability of women to become pregnant could also be stymied by subsistence crises and nutritional deficiencies. The age of menarche is strongly influenced by nutrition; in the modern world, girls start menstruating around age 12–13 but in the medieval world it was probably at least 14 or later. Peak fertility lags behind menstruation by several years, so that medieval women became most fertile in their late teens. Menopause is and was around 50, but births after the early thirties seem to have been rare, probably because of the greater difficulties that women over 30 have in becoming pregnant, but birth control may have also been a factor. Breastfeeding was one way to limit fertility, especially when combined with culturally prescribed periods of abstinence from sex after childbirth. A technique developed to analyze the amounts and proportions of stable isotopes of nitrogen in the tooth enamel of skeletons indicates that English peasant women breast-fed their infants for about eighteen months; it would have taken these women another eight months to ovulate, providing a 24- to 29-month interval between births.[28] This period could be shortened if mothers sent their infants out to be wet-nursed, a practice restricted to the wealthy in most of northern Europe, although in Florence, we know that it spread from the landed and civic elites into the middling classes by the late fourteenth century. This practice raised fertility amongst the wealthy, whose higher standard of living also ensured that more of their children reached adulthood. Yet these mothers may have been more susceptible to anemia because of the stress of repeated pregnancies and more frequent menstruation.

A more fraught question revolves around the extent to which medieval couples practiced contraception. There is now considerable evidence that birth control, especially *coitus interruptus*, was fairly widespread by the early fourteenth century. Herbal potions with contraceptive properties were known in the classical and early medieval periods, though it is unclear how much or how effectively these techniques could be practiced by medieval women.[29] Religious teaching was firmly against birth control, although it took some centuries before the current Catholic doctrine on abortion was fully articulated. Deliberate birth control could be behind the well-known tendency for poorer women to have fewer children, but prolonged breastfeeding, acting as a wet nurse, or just poor nutrition might have rendered such direct intervention unnecessary.

Migration

Studies of migration have focused almost exclusively on men, although new methodologies are now challenging previous assumptions that most medieval migrants were male. DNA analyses have been particularly revealing. One recent study, for instance, demonstrates that some modern Icelanders descend from a native North American woman who was most likely captured by Vikings around the year 1000. Isotope analysis (which reveals where an individual grew up, based on dietary evidence left in bones, especially in tooth enamel) shows that a woman buried in a Norse colony on the Isle of Lewis *c.*900 was raised in southern England, even though she was laid alongside others who came from Norway and children born in the Hebrides, leading to speculation that the woman may have been captured in a raid and then enslaved. Similar evidence from Bavaria also reveals the movement of women in the great migrations of the fifth and sixth centuries, when documentary sources are scarce and focus more on the military activities of men; about one third of the cemetery population did not grow up locally, and most of these were women. "Foreign" grave goods found with pre-Christian burials provide further evidence of the long distances that women could travel, as does the discovery of women in Normandy and Bavaria whose skulls had been bound so tightly during childhood that they became cone-shaped with a distinctive, elongated forehead, a practice associated with Hunnic culture. Such patterns are attributed primarily to virilocality—that is, women moving to their husbands' communities when they married—as well as to war, capture, and slavery.[30]

Documentary sources are less revealing about female migration, but historians have not, in any case, paid much attention to the information they offer on women. The Castilian resettlement of conquered regions in southern Spain, for instance, generated some very detailed sources including data on wives, widows, and even singlewomen, but few scholars have bothered to analyze the gendered component of this great movement. A shortage of settlers, particularly women, was recognized in laws (*fueros*) that gave special privileges and tax exemptions to married men who resided with their wives in frontier towns.[31] Further work on the gendered dimension of the forced and voluntary removal of the Muslim population (when more female than male Muslims may have stayed as servants or slaves) is also needed.

Most medieval migrants moved over short distances, usually less than twenty miles. Male migration to towns, tracked via admissions to citizenship, apprenticeship, and surname studies, has received the most attention. Women shared many of the characteristics of male migrants in terms of moving primarily when they were young, in their late teens to late twenties, usually searching for economic opportunities. But women's migratory patterns could also differ from men's. Some studies show that women migrated in greater numbers than men and may have been influenced to move more by personal reasons, rather than landlessness or the lack of economic opportunity at home. Women were especially attracted to towns, where by the later Middle Ages there were clearly more female than male residents. It is unclear, however, whether young women were more often "pulled" into towns by hopes of better work or a freer lifestyle or "pushed" from the countryside by inheritance customs that favored sons, the prejudices of lords against female tenants, or simply a general lack of economic opportunities for women. A very large number of female migrants also moved to be with new husbands or to accompany their families when they migrated to a new settlement. Although female migration to towns has been used to explain imbalanced sex ratios in a wide range of rural communities, including those documented by the Carolingian polyptychs and medieval English cemeteries, urban "receiving" populations were too small, even in the more urbanized later Middle Ages, to account for the shortfall of women in the countryside.[32]

The gendered impact of medieval migration deserves far more attention. Studies of early modern singlewomen who moved to cities show, for example, that they were generally poorer and delayed marriage longer than women born in the city.[33] Because migrant women earned their own living and were more distant from their parents, they may have had more say in choosing a husband, which was reflected by a smaller spousal age gap. But the downside was that migrant women also needed to work for many years to accumulate a dowry, and their marriage partners were from lower social-status groups. They also tended to remain poor and single more often than their city-born sisters. Unlike mortality and fertility, moreover, there is virtually no comparative work on the gendered dimension of medieval migration, nothing that would tell us, for instance, why there is no northern parallel for the secondary migration of older widows from the Tuscan countryside to cities such as Florence.

CONCLUSION

Medieval demography is a still a new frontier for feminist scholars, but it is the field most likely to show the powerful role of the undocumented, non-elite majority in shaping the medieval world. Demographers and paleodemographers are increasingly aware that women's life stories—where they came from, what they ate, how they supported themselves, when they married, and how many babies they had—were critical variables in the rise and fall of medieval populations. For those who are interested less in population and more in women, demography can address crucial questions. Did women die earlier than men and if so, why? How big a problem was maternal mortality in childbirth? How many women had children? How did the size of families differ by wealth or region? When and over what distances did women and men leave their natal homes? Even more promising are new explorations of the relationship between gender and demographic change fueled by isotopic and DNA analyses. Recent analyses of bone material, for example, now allow us to identify gendered patterns of behavior, including work-related markers found on female skeletons from the village of Wharram Percy that indicate medieval peasant women spent many hours on their haunches, presumably tending a fire or grinding grain.[34] Gendered behavior is also behind such skeletal indicators of aggression as the facial fractures and cranial trauma more often seen in male than female skeletons, particularly when found on medieval battlefields or in cemeteries used for hanged felons.[35] Feminist scholars have much to learn from these recent advances.

FURTHER READING

Benedictow, Ole Jørgen. *The Medieval Demographic System of the Nordic Countries.* Oslo: Middelalderforlaget, 1993.

Burguière, André et al., eds. *A History of the Family,* volume I: *Distant Worlds, Ancient Worlds,* trans. Sarah Hanbury Tenison, Rosemary Morris, and Andrew Wilson. Cambridge, Mass.: Belknap Press of Harvard University Press, 1996.

Chamberlain, Andrew. *Demography in Archaeology.* Cambridge: Cambridge University Press, 2006.

Dupâquier, Jacques, ed. *Histoire de la population française,* volume I: *Des origines à la Renaissance.* Paris: Presses universitaires de France, 1988.

Goldberg, P. J. P. *Women, Work, and Life Cycle in a Medieval Economy: Women in York and Yorkshire, c.1300–1520.* Oxford: Clarendon Press, 1992.

Herlihy, David and Christiane Klapisch-Zuber. *Tuscans and Their Families: A Study of the Florentine Catasto of 1427.* New Haven: Yale University Press, 1985, abridged version of *Les Toscanes et leur familles: Une étude du Catasto florentin de 1427.* Paris: Editions de L'Ecole des Hautes Etudes en Sciences Sociales. Presses de la Fondation Nationale des Sciences Politiques, 1978.

Klapisch-Zuber, Christiane. "Plague and Family Life," in Michael Jones, ed., *The New Cambridge Medieval History,* volume VI: *c. 1300–c. 1415.* Cambridge: Cambridge University Press, 2000, 124–54.

Kowaleski, Maryanne. "Singlewomen in Medieval and Early Modern Europe: The Demographic Perspective," in Judith M. Bennett and Amy M. Froide, eds, *Singlewomen in the European Past, 1250–1800.* Philadelphia: University of Pennsylvania Press, 38–81, 325–44.

Mays, S., C. Harding, and C. Heighway. *The Churchyard: Wharram, A Study of Settlement on the Yorkshire Wolds, XI.* York: York University Archaeological Publications, 2007.

Smith, R. M. "Hypothèses sur la nuptialité en Angleterre aux XIIIe-XIVe siècles," *Annales: économies, sociétiès, civilisations,* 38 (1983): 107–36.

Notes

1. David Loschky and Ben D. Childers, "Early English Mortality," *Journal of Interdisciplinary History*, 24 (1993): 85–97; Richard M. Smith, "Measuring Adult Mortality in an Age of Plague: England, 1349–1540," in Mark Bailey and Stephen Rigby, eds, *Town and Countryside in the Age of the Black Death: Essays in Honour of John Hatcher* (Turnhout: Brepols, 2012), 47–73; John Hatcher, A. J. Piper, and David Stone, "Monastic Mortality: Durham Priory, 1395–1529," *Economic History Review*, 2nd ser., 59 (2006): 667–87; David Herlihy and Christiane Klapisch-Zuber, *Tuscans and Their Families: A Study of the Florentine Catasto of 1427* (New Haven: Yale University Press, 1985), 83–84; L. R. Poos, *A Rural Society after the Black Death: Essex 1350–1525* (Cambridge: Cambridge University Press, 1991), 118. For attempts to estimate female mortality and replacement rates, see Robert S. Gottfried, *Epidemic Disease in Fifteenth-Century England: The Medical Response and the Demographic Consequences* (New Brunswick: Rutgers University Press, 1978), 187–222; Zvi Razi, *Life, Marriage, and Death in a Medieval Parish: Economy, Society, and Demography in Halesowen, 1270–1400* (Cambridge: Cambridge University Press, 1980).

2. Vern Bullough and Cameron Campbell, "Female Longevity and Diet in the Middle Ages," *Speculum*, 55 (2) (1980): 417–25; Emily Coleman, "Infanticide in the Early Middle Ages," in Susan Mosher Stuard, ed., *Women in Medieval Society* (Philadelphia: University of Pennsylvania Press, 1976), 47–70; Robert-Henri Bautier, "Haut Moyen Age," in Jacques Dupâquier, ed., *Histoire de la population française*, volume 1: *Des origines à la Renaissance* (Paris: Presses universitaires de France, 1988), 185–87; Monique Zerner-Chardavoine, "Enfants et jeunes au IXe siècle: La démographie du polyptyque de Marseille, 813–14," *Provence historique*, 30 (1981): 335–80.

3. Carol J. Clover, "The Politics of Scarcity: Notes on the Sex Ratio in Early Scandinavia," in Helen Damico and Alexandra Hennessey Olsen, eds, *New Readings on Women in Old English Literature* (Bloomington: Indiana University Press, 1990), 100–34; Josiah Cox Russell, *Late Ancient and Medieval Population Control* (Philadelphia: American Philosophical Society, 1985), 64–65, 75–76, 153–60; Tony Waldron, *Counting the Dead: The Epidemiology of Skeletal Populations* (Chichester: John Wiley, 1994), 23; Robin Fleming, *Britain after Rome: The Fall and Rise, 400–1070* (New York: Penguin, 2010), 352–53.

4. Vern Bullough, "Nutrition, Women, and Sex Ratios," *Perspectives in Biology and Medicine*, 30 (1987): 450–60. Josiah Cox Russell, *British Medieval Population* (Albuquerque: University of New Mexico Press, 1948), 150–55, 166–69; Roger Mols, *Introduction à la démographie historique des villes d'Europe du 14e au 18e siècle*, 3 vols (Louvain: Editions J. Duculot, 1954–56), 2: 186–87; 3: 129; Herlihy and Klapisch-Zuber, *Tuscans and Their Families*, 131–58.

5. Ole Jørgen Benedictow, *The Medieval Demographic System of the Nordic Countries* (Oslo: Middelalderforlaget, 1993), 58–60; S. Mays, "The Human Remains," in S. Mays, C. Harding, and C. Heighway, eds, *The Churchyard: Wharram, A Study of Settlement on the Yorkshire Wolds, XI* (York: York University Archaeological Publications, 2007), 91–92; Anne L. Grauer, "Where Were the Women?" in Alan C. Swedlund and D. Ann Herring, eds, *Human Biologists in the Archives: Demography, Health, Nutrition, and Genetics in Historical Populations* (West Nyack, NY: Cambridge University Press, 2002), 274–77.

6. John Caldwell and Pat Caldwell, "Women's Position and Child Mortality and Morbidity in Less Developed Countries," in Nora Federic, Karen Oppenheim Mason, and Sølvi Sogner, eds, *Women's Position and Demographic Change* (Oxford: Clarendon Press, 1993), 122–39; Richard Wall, "Inferring Differential Neglect of Females from Mortality Data," *Annales de démographie historique*, 18 (1981): 119–40.

7. Herlihy and Klapisch-Zuber, *Tuscans and Their Families*, 145–46; Valerie A. Fildes, *Breasts, Bottles, and Babies: A History of Infant Feeding* (Edinburgh: Edinburgh University Press, 1986), 48; Zerner-Chardavoine, "Enfants et jeunes."

8. Andrew T. Chamberlain, *Demography in Archaeology* (Cambridge: Cambridge University Press, 2006), 90–95, 98–105; A. Alduc-Le Bagousse, "Maturation osseuse—majorité légale: la place des adolescents en paléoanthropolgie," in Luc Buchet, ed., *La femme pendant le Moyen Age et l'époque moderne* (Paris: CNRS, 1994), 31–40; Charlotte A. Roberts and Margaret Cox, *Health and Disease in Britain: From Pre-history to the Present Day* (Stroud, UK: Sutton Publishing, 2003), 278–79; Mays, "Human Remains," 91–92, 139; Anne L. Grauer and Patricia Stuart-Macadam, eds, *Sex and Gender in Paleopathological Perspective* (Cambridge: Cambridge University Press, 1998); Charlotte A. Roberts, Mary E. Lewis, and Philip Boocock, "Infectious Disease, Sex, and Gender: The Complexity of It All," in Grauer and Stuart-Macadam, eds, *Sex and Gender*, 93–113; Simon Mays, *The Archaeology of Human Bones* (London and New York: Routledge, 2nd ed., 2010), 47–50. See also Donald J. Ortner, "Male-Female Immune Reactivity and its Implications for Interpreting Evidence in Human Skeletal Paleopathology," in Grauer and Stuart-Macadam, eds, *Sex and Gender*, 79–92, for a discussion of the implications of women's better immune systems.

9. Mays, "Human Remains," 177–81.

10. Elisabeth Carpentier and Michel Le Mené, *La France du XIe au XVe siècle: Population, société, économie* (Paris: Presses Universitaires de France, 1996), 57. Herlihy and Klapisch-Zuber, *Tuscans and Their Families*, 277; Benedictow, *Nordic Countries*, 62–75; Roger Schofield, "Did the Mothers Really Die? Three Centuries of Maternal Mortality in 'The World We Have Lost,'" in Lloyd Bonfield, Richard M. Smith, and Keith Wrightson, eds, *The World We Have Gained: Histories of Population and Social Structure: Essays Presented to Peter Laslett on his Seventieth Birthday* (Oxford: Basil Blackwell, 1986), 231–60.

11. Grauer, "Where Were the Women?" 277–78; Svenja Weise and Jesper L. Boldsen, "'Dangerous Fertile Ages' for Women: A Universal Medieval Pattern?" AAPA Abstracts, *American Journal of Physical Anthropology*, 132 (2007): 246; Roberts and Cox, *Health and Disease*, 278.

12. Ann G. Carmichael, *Plague and the Poor in Renaissance Florence* (Cambridge: Cambridge University Press, 1986), 91, 93; Samuel K. Cohn, Jr, *The Black Death Transformed: Disease and Culture in Early Renaissance Europe* (New York: Oxford University Press, 2003), 210–12; Ole J. Benedictow, *The Black Death 1346–1353: The Complete History* (Woodbridge: Boydell Press, 2004), 266–67; Mary F. Hollingsworth and T. H. Hollingsworth, "Plague Mortality Rates by Age and Sex in the Parish of St. Botolph's without Bishopsgate, London, 1603," *Population Studies*, 25 (1971): 131–46.

13. Ian Grainger et al., *The Black Death Cemetery, East Smithfield, London* (London: Museum of London Archaeology Service, 2008), 43, 48–49, 55; Sharon N. DeWitte, "The Effect of Sex on Risk of Mortality during the Black Death in London, A.D. 1349–1350," *American Journal of Physical Anthropology*, 138 (2) (2009): 222–34; Sharon N. DeWitte, "Sex Differentials in Frailty in Medieval England," *American Journal of Physical Anthropology*, 143 (2) (2010): 285–97; Pierre Dubuis, *Le jeu de la vie et de la mort: La population du Valais (XIVe-XVIe s.)* (Lausanne: Faculté des lettres, Université de Lausanne, 1994), 101, 122–25; Christian Gullere, "La mortalité de 1372 à 1407," in Olivier Guyotjeannin, ed., *Population et démographie au Moyen Age* (Paris: Editions du CTHS, 1995), 138–40.

14. P. J. P. Goldberg, *Women, Work, and Life Cycle in a Medieval Economy: Women in York and Yorkshire, c.1300–1520* (Oxford: Clarendon Press, 1992); Tine de Moor and Jan Luiten van Zanden, "Girl Power: The European Marriage Pattern (EMP) and Labour Markets in

the North Sea Region in the Late Medieval and Early Modern Period," *Economic History Review*, 2nd ser., 63 (2010): 1–33.

15. Judith M. Bennett, *History Matters: Patriarchy and the Challenge of Feminism* (Philadelphia: University of Pennsylvania Press, 2006), 54–107.

16. Sandy Bardsley, "Peasant Women and Inheritance of Land in Fourteenth-Century England," unpublished paper given at the 10th Anglo-American Seminar on Medieval Economy and Society, Durham, UK, July 2010; Jane Whittle, "Rural Economies," Chapter 20 in this volume.

17. For the bias towards males in sexing skeletons, see Chamberlain, *Demography in Archaeology*, 90–91.

18. Christiane Klapisch-Zuber, "Plague and Family Life," in Michael Jones, ed., *The New Cambridge Medieval History*, volume VI: *c. 1300–c. 1415* (Cambridge: Cambridge University Press, 2000), 140; Poos, *A Rural Society after the Black Death*, 120–127; A. Hinde, *England's Population: A History Since the Domesday Survey* (New York: Oxford University Press, 2003), 12–13, 58–62.

19. Grauer, "Where Were the Women?" 278; Benedictow, *Nordic Countries*, 52, 55–56.

20. M. Kowaleski, "Singlewomen in Medieval and Early Modern Europe: The Demographic Perspective," in Judith M. Bennett and Amy M. Froide, eds, *Singlewomen in the European Past, 1250–1800* (Philadelphia: University of Pennsylvania Press, 1999), 38–81, 325–44.

21. Herlihy and Klapisch-Zuber, *Tuscans and Their Families*, 87–88, 203–11, 222–26.

22. For this and the following paragraph, see Kowaleski, "Singlewomen."

23. Bas van Bavel, *Manors and Markets: Economy and Society in the Low Countries, 500–1600* (Oxford: Oxford University Press, 2010), 284–91.

24. Pierre Toubert, "The Carolingian Moment (Eighth–Tenth Century)," in André Burguière et al., eds, *A History of the Family*, volume I, trans. Sarah Hanbury Tenison, Rosemary Morris, and Andrew Wilson (Cambridge, MA: Belknap Press of Harvard University Press, 1996), 381–84.

25. Zerner-Chardavoine, "Enfants et jeunes," 368–71.

26. Henri Dubois, "L'histoire démographique de Chalon-sur-Saône à la fin due XIVe siècle et au début du XVe d'après les 'Cherches de Feux,'" in *La démographie médiévale: Sources et méthodes* (Nice, 1972), 96–97.

27. Benedictow, *Nordic Countries*, 271; Peter Franklin, "Peasant Widows' 'Liberation' and Remarriage before the Black Death," *Economic History Review*, 2nd ser., 39 (1986): 186–204; Goldberg, *Women, Work, and Life Cycle*; Tovah Bender, "The Case of the Missing Girls: Sex Ratios in Fifteenth-Century Tuscany," *Journal of Women's History*, 23 (4) (2011): 155–75; van Bavel, *Manors and Markets*, 282–91.

28. Chamberlain, *Demography in Archaeology*, 54–55; Benedictow, *Nordic Countries*, 49–52; Mays, "Human Remains," 102–103, 189–90.

29. Peter Biller, "Birth Control in the West in the Thirteenth and Early Fourteenth Centuries," *Past & Present*, 94 (1982): 3–26; John M. Riddle, *Eve's Herbs: A History of Contraception and Abortion in the West* (Cambridge, MA: Harvard University Press, 1997).

30. Chamberlain, *Demography in Archaeology*, 9–10, 146–48; Sigríður Sunna Ebenesersdóttir et al., "A New Subclade of mtDNA Haplogroup C1 Found in Icelanders: Evidence of Pre-Columbian Contact?" *American Journal of Physical Anthropology*, 144 (1) (2011): 92–99; Fleming, *Britain after Rome*, 359; Susanne Hakenbeck et al., "Diet and Mobility in Early Medieval Bavaria: A Study of Carbon and Nitrogen Stable Isotopes," *American Journal of Physical Anthropology*, 143 (2010): 235–49; L. Buchet and C. Pilet, "Des femmes orientales en basse Normandie au Ve siècle," in Buchet, ed., *La femme pendant le Moyen Age*, 111–27.

31. Heath Dillard, *Daughters of the Reconquest: Women in Castilian Town Society, 1100–1300* (Cambridge: Cambridge University Press, 1984), 13–34.

32. E. D. Jones, "Some Spalding Priory Vagabonds of the Twelve-Sixties," *Historical Research*, 73 (2009): 93–104; Jane Whittle, "Population Mobility in Rural Norfolk Among Landholders and Others c. 1440–c. 1600," in Christopher Dyer, ed., *The Self-Contained Village? The Social History of Rural Communities, 1250–1900* (Hatfield: University of Hertfordshire Press, 2007), 28–45; David Postles, "Migration and Mobility in a Less Mature Economy: English Internal Migration, c. 1200–1350," *Social History*, 25 (2000): 285–99; René Germain, "Les migrations comme facteur d'équilibre démographique (Bourbonnais, XIVe-XVe siècles)," in Guyotjeannin, ed., *Population et démographie*, 251–66; Goldberg, *Women, Work, and Life Cycle*, 280–394; Poos, *A Rural Society after the Black Death*, 159–230; Jean-Pierre Devroey, "Men and Women in Early Medieval Serfdom: The Ninth-Century North Frankish Evidence," *Past & Present*, 166 (2000): 20–21; Grauer, "Where Were the Women?" 278.

33. Kowaleski, "Singlewomen," 57–58.

34. Mays, "Human Remains," 125–27.

35. Piers D. Mitchell, "The Integration of the Palaeopathology and Medical History of the Crusades," *International Journal of Osteoarchaeology*, 9 (5) (1999): 333–43; V. Fiorato, A. Boylston, and C. Knüssel, *Blood Red Roses: The Archaeology of a Mass Grave from the Battle of Towton AD 1461* (Oxford: Oxbow Books, 2001); Ann Stirland, "Patterns of Trauma in a Unique Medieval Parish Cemetery," *International Journal of Osteoarchaeology*, 6 (1) (1995): 92–100.

CHAPTER 13

....

GENDERS AND MATERIAL CULTURE

....

KATHERINE L. FRENCH

INTRODUCTION

....

THE quickening economy of the twelfth and thirteenth centuries offered medieval people new goods, new markets, and new ways of expressing identity and respectability. Expanding material culture also challenged existing values and changed behavior in ways we are only beginning to discern. What did new cuts of clothing mean for existing notions of modesty? Did new eating habits undermine household order? What did more expansive and furnished interiors mean for the gendering of space?

Art historian and theorist of material culture Jules David Prown argues that "human-made objects reflect, consciously or unconsciously, directly or indirectly the beliefs of the individuals who commissioned, fabricated, purchased, or used them, and by extension the beliefs of the larger society to which these individuals belonged."[1] Because we have relatively few writings by medieval women, the objects they owned and used, or representations of those objects in use, offer us an alternative view of their everyday life unfettered by the rhetorical devices and clerical biases of so many literary works. These very material possessions especially help us see women's agency, as well as the ways in which women and men negotiated space, personal interaction, and gender.

CLOTHING

....

When God expelled Adam and Eve from the Garden of Eden, they invented clothing to hide their newfound nakedness. Embedded in this creation story is the idea that clothing not only protects from the elements, but also projects, reinforces, and upsets prevailing cultural values. Clothing was a particularly fraught site of cultural contention;

medieval moralists worried with some reason that consumers would be tempted to imitate their betters, would fall into sinful pride, or would deceptively use luxurious clothing to sexual ends, a charge especially levied against women.

Clothing is ancient, but fashion is recent. How recent, however, is the subject of much scholarly debate. In the early twentieth century, Paul Post argued that fashion developed in fourteenth-century Burgundy, when young men, inspired by the shapes of armor, began to wear short coats that emphasized their legs instead of the more typical long robes. Stella Mary Newton also believed that fashion emerged in the fourteenth century, but in Sicily when Walter of Brienne introduced French court styles to Florentine and Catalan mercenaries stationed there. Rosita Levi Pisetzky counters that Italians, not the French, originated medieval fashion in the fourteenth century; in her view, Italy's proximity to and trade with eastern markets offered its merchants choices in cloth and cuts of clothing that were unavailable in the rest of Europe. Those with available capital began to imitate and complement what they saw worn by Muslims, Slavs, and others. Recently, Sarah-Grace Heller has reframed the debate by arguing that "fashion seems to stage its own birth again and again, because a fundamental characteristic of fashion is declaring the past invalid in favor of a new, improved present."[2] For Heller, fashion is conceptual rather than visual, and it is defined by a desire for uniqueness and admiration; because medieval visual evidence fails to record adequately the desire for "novel consumption" before the fourteenth century, scholars relying on images necessarily dated fashion's advent to that time.[3]

Medieval fashions tended to change on two different levels: details, such as edging, sleeve shape, or necklines changed frequently, while silhouette—the shape of the body created by clothing—changed more slowly. Layering and edging created color contrasts and individual styles. In the fourteenth century, men's fashions—influenced by military dress—changed much more rapidly than women's. Fashion started as an elite concern. Tight-fitted tailoring was more expensive; it required more work and created oddly shaped and largely unusable scraps that wasted cloth. The taste for change, however, quickly percolated down the social scale. The ever-newer styles encouraged disposing of out-of-date clothing before it was worn out, creating an extensive used clothing market, in which styles were passed down, clothes reconfigured, with colors slightly faded, for the second- and third-hand consumer. Laborers wore practical cuts and preferred sturdy, soil-resistant materials such as leather and hemp, but they too sought bright colors for their shirts and tunics. Popular tales such as fabliaux show them coveting new details and trimmings, such as fur to line their hats.

Color was central to fashion. Manufacturers usually dyed yarn rather than cloth, so that weavers could produce medleys, cloth with a warp of one color and a weft of another. In the thirteenth century, blues, greens, and reds were prestige colors, and dyestuffs were an important trade commodity. The most prized was cloth dyed in a variety of red to purple hues with kermes, a dye produced from an insect; its high cost expressed both wealth and power. After knighting, for example, some young men received scarlet cloaks as a sure sign of their new status. By the mid-fifteenth century, dark hues, especially black, became more fashionable. They set off gold braiding and other edgings for sleeves and hems.

Combining colors—in the form of stripes, checks, or parti-colored cloths coupled with dagged or slashed sleeves—also carried meanings that changed over time. Some retinues reserved such styles for fools and minstrels, as shown in twelfth- and thirteenth-century illustrations. In the John the Baptist Roll, a late twelfth-century Alsatian manuscript, Herod's servants wear parti-colored attire. Because of their frivolous or loose associations, parti-colored clothes were sometimes publicly regulated. A 1269 Icelandic rule outlawed parti-colored clothing for priests, and thirty years later, a Norwegian rule prohibited all wearing of "divided, slashed clothing and all kinds of German style of clothing...checked, parted, or slashed cut of clothes..."[4] These negative connotations were gradually replaced by positive ones, and in the fourteenth century, multicolored clothes were an acceptable part of courtly fashion, worn by even the highest nobles.

By the fourteenth century, men's and women's clothing was increasingly differentiated. Men typically wore three layers of clothing. Underclothes consisted of linen breeches, a shirt, and hose for the legs. A belt held up the hose and breeches. Over the underclothes went a doublet, a buttoned hip-length jacket. Covering both layers was a final coat or gown, often called a *houppelande*. Young men began to leave off the houppelande in the fourteenth century, in order to show off tight-fitting doublets that displayed their legs and emphasized their torsos. The change was not welcomed by all. A fourteenth-century French chronicler complained that "noblemen and their squires took to wearing tunics so short and tight that they revealed what modesty bids us hide. This was a most astonishing thing for the people."[5] By the fifteenth century the houppelande had disappeared altogether.

Women, like men, also typically wore three layers of clothes. Women's underclothing consisted of a smock or chemise and hose. Next came a kirtle, a long garment originally with short or no sleeves, worn over the smock, chemise, and hose. Over time, kirtles became increasingly fitted, with ever-lengthening sleeves. Over kirtles, women wore a variety of outer tunics, such as the houppelande, or a sleeveless tabard or *pelisse*. At the same time men gave up the houppelande, women changed to gowns, a more form-fitted garment that emphasized the waist and the wearer's height. Thus by the fourteenth century, both genders wore close-fitting but differentiating garments.

Special occasions demanded special clothing. Although there were no prescribed colors for wedding dresses, many brides dressed specially for the event and remembered what they had worn. Elizabeth Tymprly of East Hamsted (Buckinghamshire) left to a church "my wedding gown to make a vestment thereof."[6] New mothers of the Florentine bourgeoisie had elaborate outfits for the ritual visiting and gift-giving that followed a successful birth. In the fourteenth and fifteenth centuries, the birth outfit consisted of a cloak that covered an elaborately embroidered nightshirt, and by the late fifteenth century, a vest joined the ensemble. There were also special clothes and blankets for the infant's procession to baptism.[7] While the birth remained a female affair, clothing the new mother and bringing the child to church was a masculine business, and special clothing signaled the father's success at procreating heirs and providing for his family.

Women's head coverings further marked their relationships to men. Women typically covered their heads and did not cut their hair, a sign of their sexuality. Covered hair signaled controlled sexuality and deference. In the thirteenth century, French and English women covered their heads with linen caps or kerchiefs, square or triangular pieces of cloth, held in place by two linen bands: a *barbet* passed under the chin and a *filet* went around the forehead. Over the barbet and kerchief could go veils and an assortment of other coverings. This style declined in the early fourteenth century, but inspired the wimple, a linen veil that covered the head and neck, worn by widows and nuns. Stories about St Veronica's veil or the Virgin's head covering promoted the associations of kerchiefs with virtue, modesty, and chastity. When St Veronica wiped Jesus's sweat from his brow with her veil, on his way to Calvary, it miraculously left an image of his face. According to Nicolas Love's vernacular devotional text, *Myrrour of the Blessid Lif of Ihesu Crist*, Mary wrapped Jesus "in the kerchief of her head" when he was born and again at his death, covering him with it after the crucifixion.[8]

Women's hair became more visible in the late Middle Ages, and they braided it in elaborate styles, or caught it up in hair nets. For elite women, head coverings were also a means of accentuating the long profile created by their gowns. The *hennin*, a tall conical headdress, first appeared around 1430. Women often hung veils from their hennin. By the late fifteenth century, women's headdresses could be quite elaborate, with two points and a variety of scarves, veils, and drapes supported by wire frames. Preachers frequently denounced these headdresses, because the "horns" invoked the devil. Such headgear must have hindered women's mobility, perhaps creating new standards of restricted movement for elite women. Unmarried Italian elite women, for their part, adorned their hair with braids, circlets, or crowns. Men also wore a variety of head coverings, but they were less restricting and did not hold the same sexualized meanings.

Shoe shape and height also contributed to the construction of status. In the central Middle Ages, women's status shoes were often laced, with cut-out patterns, while fashionable men wore tight boots. In Italy, urban elites wore platform shoes called *pianelle*, which gave them added height and visibility and elevated them above the muddy streets. Women's pianelle were especially tall and elaborately decorated with designs on the edge of the platform and bows and ruffles on the body of the shoe. Throughout much of late medieval Europe, pointed shoes were fashionable, with points becoming so extreme in some instances that wearers tied them to their knees. Even the feet of plated armor included pointed toes. According to legend, Swiss peasants were able to beat the Habsburg army by unseating the knights, whose pointed armored shoes were so long and inflexible they could not walk.[9] At the very end of the Middle Ages, pointed shoes gave way to more practical square-toed shoes.

Accessories were another important element of sartorial statements. One of the most important accessories for nobles and peasants alike was a belt or girdle. The abundance of white-metal, or tin alloy, accessories found by London archaeologists suggests a large market for cheap belts and buckles. Belts could be thick and short, or long and slender, with the end hanging nearly to the feet; they could sit at the waist or on the hips, accentuating the curve of the hips, stomach, and legs. Some, like the fourteenth-century murder victim excavated by archaeologists in Bocksten, Sweden, wore plain leather belts. Others favored quite elaborate styles, as demonstrated by the silver belt that one Duccio Puccii purchased for the huge sum of thirty ducats in Ragusa.[10] Both men and women wore belted girdles, but they had a particular resonance among women, who sometimes turned to holy girdles for assistance in childbirth.

From these belts hung purses, pouches, daggers, prayer beads, amulets, and house keys. These objects were decorative, useful, and often gender-specific. Both sexes carried purses and pouches. Keys on a belt symbolized housewifery, while daggers were more masculine. The English chronicler Henry Knighton denounced women at tournaments for imitating men by hanging little daggers from their low-slung belts. Knighton's concerns tap into an association of women's girdles with their fertility and sexuality. The daggers were too suggestive of male sexuality, and in his eyes made women appear mannish.[11] Beads used as rosaries were also gendered: women tended to have long sets of beads while men's were shorter. Beads were made out of a variety of materials, from precious and semi-precious stones to glass, bone, and even metal. The 1486 shop inventory of John Skyrwyth, a London leather seller, contained thousands of pounds of glass, bone, stone, and metal beads of various colors and designs.[12] Beads were a popular manifestation of piety, but medieval lapidaries also promoted the apotropaic qualities of the gemstones that made up rosaries: coral would stop excessive menstruation and promote fertility; jet provoked menstruation; and amber eased women with childbirth. Rings and beads of coral, jet, and amber make up a significant portion of the jewelry found in excavations of medieval sites in London.

The importance of such goods to women was expressed on their deathbeds, when they more frequently than men bequeathed clothing and accessories. In so doing, a woman often drew upon the symbolic importance of her clothing and accessories, trying to imprint the virtues she associated with the object on its recipient, as when a mother left her daughter her a coral bead rosary. Frequently, women bequeathed their clothing and jewelry to images of the saints in their church. For example, in 1523, Agnes Awmbler of Barroby (Lincolnshire) gave a kerchief to "the image of Our Lady within the choir." Women also requested that their clothing be turned into liturgical items. Janet Yngyll, also from Lincolnshire, left her kerchief to be a *corporas*, a cloth holder for the host. With their fertility connotations, girdles, such as the red silk one harnessed with silver and gilt that Alice Montague left to her parish of Queen Camel (Somerset), were appropriate remembrances for successful mothers. The gift of a girdle also symbolized faith. According to legend, Mary threw down her girdle to Thomas as proof of her assumption, and a woman's gift of a girdle reversed this exchange, symbolizing her faith in life after death.[13]

Fashion was more than a means of differentiating genders, demonstrating power, and expressing piety. Because clothing was so critical in indicating status, it was dangerous—an indulgent form of pride, a deceptive means of hiding identity, or even worse, a means of creating a new one. Moralists believed that the pursuit of status-driven fashion reflected vanity and pride. In his chronicle, John of Reading, a late fourteenth-century monk at Westminster Abbey, described new styles of clothing in terms of the dangerous morality he believed they promoted:

> Ever since the arrival of the Hainaulters [servants and attendants of Edward III's queen, Philippa of Hainault] about eighteen years ago [1326], the English have been madly following outlandish ways, changing their grotesque fashions of clothing yearly. They have abandoned the old decent style of long, full garments for clothes which are short, tight, impractical, slashed, every part laced, strapped or buttoned up, with the sleeves of the gowns and the tippets of the hoods hanging down to absurd lengths, so that if the truth be told, their clothes and footwear make them look more like torturers, or even demons, than men... Women flowed with the tides of fashion in this and other things even more eagerly, wearing clothes that were so tight that they wore a fox tail hanging down inside their skirts at the back, to hide their arses. The sin of pride manifested in this way must surely bring down misfortune in the future.[14]

The social and moral significance of clothing becomes apparent in the sumptuary legislation that spread across Europe between the thirteenth and sixteenth centuries. Sumptuary legislation regulated all forms of luxury, from behavior at funerals to food at weddings. But it was the regulation of clothing, particularly women's clothing, where sumptuary legislation found its fullest expression. Governments frequently connected the excessive cost of women's clothing to a host of ills, from a weak economy to declining birthrates. Men were implicated only insofar as they had to enforce the laws in their homes and pay fines if their wives and daughters were caught violating this legislation. If they failed to pay, they could not hold public office. Governments continually had to revise their sumptuary laws because women easily avoided prosecution by modifying their clothing. When Florence began to address men's fashions in 1377, it tried to limit the length of their pointed shoes, the shortness of their tunics, and the amount of silver in their belts. German cities' sumptuary legislation accused men and women who wore pointed-toed shoes or luxurious furs of lacking proper fear of God.[15]

Because clothing spoke to status and respectability, sumptuary legislation also tried to distinguish prostitutes from respectable women. In Pisa, prostitutes had to wear a yellow filet around their foreheads, while in Florence, prostitutes affixed bells to their hoods or shawls. As with lepers, the prostitutes' bells identified them as impure. Sometimes legislators tried to limit fashions by restricting them to the reviled prostitutes; both Florence and Siena tried to outlaw high-heeled shoes, gloves, and belts by permitting only prostitutes to wear them. London's regulations for prostitutes' clothing were less specific, but driven by the same concerns. They could not dress like "good or noble dames and damsels"; they were later told not to wear furred hoods; and by 1351, they were required to wear unlined "rayed" or striped hoods (an example of the lingering negative connotations of parti-colored clothing).[16] By forcing prostitutes to dress identifiably, governments sought to define such women as publicly dissolute.

Jews and Muslims living in Christian areas also had to wear identifying marks. In 1215, ostensibly to prevent interfaith marriage and concubinage, the Fourth Lateran Council mandated that Jews and Muslims wear distinguishing clothes, although the specific sign and its enforcement were left up to local authorities. Ultimately, different regions created their own identifying systems. In fourteenth-century Portugal, Muslims wore a crescent moon of colored cloth on their outer garments, while Jews wore a six-pointed red star. In England, shortly before their expulsion in 1290, Jews were required to wear a symbol shaped like the two stone tablets of the Ten Commandments, while in thirteenth-century Austria and in fourteenth- and fifteenth-century Holy Roman Empire, Jews wore a pointed-red hat (called a *Judenhut*) with a brim twisted into a pair of horns. In 1432, Jewish women in Perugia had to wear earrings and long mantles over their heads, fashions once common but by then long out-of-date. In this way, Perugians tried to set Jewish women outside respectable women's fashion system. (The legislation also stipulated that mantles could not be made of "monkish black," lest Jewish women be mistaken for nuns.) Jewish communities issued their own sumptuary codes designed to conceal ostentation and limit their visibility. The regulations from the Jewish community in Forlì stated that "No man shall be permitted a silk or velvet cloak except if it is completely hidden. Neither shall women wear any silk or velvet dress except in a way that it is completely hidden."[17] The range of legislation that sought to regulate dress by religious faith is striking, but these laws suggest that Jews, Christians, and Muslims did not, in fact, dress differently. If the differences had been obvious, no laws would have been required.

Men and women did, however, dress differently, and anyone who adopted the clothing of the other gender was seen as presenting a false or inappropriate identity. By wearing male clothing, women assumed male privileges of power, authority, and freedom of movement; when men wore women's clothes, they were assumed to be trying to gain sexual access to women. Joan of Arc (d.1431) is perhaps the most famous and best-documented cross-dresser. In her efforts to rid France of the English, she cut her hair short, carried weapons, and wore spurs and a breastplate to lead her troops into battle. She claimed God instructed her to dress this way. While officially she was condemned and executed for heresy, wearing men's clothing figured prominently in her indictment. At her trial she insisted on remaining in men's clothes, but also insisted on her virginity and her skill at sewing and spinning. After her conviction for heresy in May of 1431, she abjured, then briefly wore women's clothing, and then reverted to men's clothing; the court interpreted her renewed cross-dressing as a sign of relapse into heresy. The fraught political context of her trial made the outcome a foregone conclusion, but the ambivalence of her identity and behavior were problematic even for the French, who supported her.

Medieval examples of cross-dressing men are rarer and are usually confined to carnival, theater, or other moments of explicit inversion. The possibly apocryphal tale of Ulrich von Lichtenstein, a thirteenth-century knight from Styria in modern-day Austria, is one such instance. As the narrator of the poem *Frauendienst* (*Service of the Lady*), he recounts traveling across Europe dressed as a woman and fighting in tournaments. Most observers never fell for his disguise, but participated in his game as a form of carnival. While there have been efforts to validate Ulrich's existence and experiences, scholars remain divided over the issue of the authenticity of his tale.[18]

More illuminating perhaps is the case of Eleanor Rykener, arrested in London for prostitution in 1394. Upon examination by the authorities, Eleanor was identified as

John. The outcome of the case does not survive, but Rykener's testimony tells of male transvestism, male same-sex intercourse, and considerable fluidity of sexuality and sexual behavior. Rykener moved back and forth between male and female dress, as well as between "sex as a man" and "sex as a woman." For the court, prostitution appeared less of a problem than how to conceptualize Rykener's gender identity. John/Eleanor Rykener's repeated movement back and forth between genders suggests that, for medieval Londoners at least, gender was as much performative as it was physical. Whenever John/Eleanor Rykener dressed and acted as a woman, she was a woman: genitalia did not define gender identity.[19]

Household Furnishings

Ideally, medieval European dwellings were divided into two sections: a hall and an enclosed room. In many places, there was also a third section, the service room. The hall was a place to receive people; through scale, decor, and furnishings, it expressed the householder's social standing and ambitions. The smaller enclosed room, variously called a parlor, chamber, or solar, was a more intimate space for the household's personal use. A service room, if there was one, might include housing for animals, storage, food preparation, and a kitchen and or bakehouse, which was usually in a separate building because of the danger of fire. When there was no kitchen, cooking was done on an open hearth in the middle of the hall or, as was common in towns, eschewed altogether in favor of purchasing prepared food. Small houses combined the three areas into one space, while the dwellings of the wealthy expanded on these three sections with additional, specialized rooms.

The hall provided a communal space where the household ate and conducted business. The hall of a manor house or castle was large enough to accommodate a retinue and to display seigniorial authority. Visibility was an important aspect of household hierarchy and seigniorial status. In his thirteenth-century instructions to the Countess of Lincoln, bishop Grosseteste wrote

> Make your own household to sit in the hall as much as you may...and sit you ever in the middle of the high board (table), that your visage and cheer be showed to all men...so much as you may without peril of sickness and weariness eat you in the hall afore your many, for that shall be to your profit and worship.[20]

Even in peasant and artisan houses, halls still were places to display hierarchy and household order.

Grosseteste might have admonished the Countess of Lincoln to be so prominent in her hall because she had to overcome the masculinity of castles, which were built more for military concerns than familial ones. As keeps gave way in the thirteenth century to less fortified buildings within a defensive curtain wall, rooms and buildings with domestic purposes appear, but even thereafter, castles contained more men than women. At Warwick castle in the fifteenth century, the household included ten women and forty men. These few women might have spent much of their time in separate facilities, as suggested by excavations of spindle whorls, a thimble, and other evidence of women's handwork in a side room off the main hall of Saxholmen castle (Sweden). Queens built their own separate spaces within castles. Queen Eleanor of Castile (d.1290) had her own cloister, chambers, and garden at King's Langley (Hertfordshire).[21] In this world, the hall was a masculine space where even a woman as powerful as the Countess of Lincoln had a household comprised mostly of men.

Lacking the vast resources of the nobility, most people lived more modestly, without separate spaces for men and women. Limited and movable furnishings facilitated flexibility. While moralists urged husbands and fathers to keep their women at home occupied with household chores, this advice often fell on deaf ears. Elite Mediterranean women were generally kept at home, but they were a small (if well-documented) group. The families of ordinary women—south as well as north—could not afford to confine their women, and northern elites, who might have afforded it, did not care to do so. We might reasonably wonder how closely medieval people associated the home with women.[22] Within the hall of a peasant's longhouse, the housewife cooked, cleaned, spun, and cared for infants. But men also cared for children, and they probably mended tools or broken household items in the house as well. The same might be said for manor houses and urban homes. While lords heard petitions from underlings and merchants conducted business, women tended children or spun nearby. Their presence affirmed the lord's position and made the hall a site of gender negotiation as well.

Halls were physically and visually imposing. The hall was usually the first room visitors entered. In fifteenth-century England, elaborate timber framing opened the hall to the roof. Limited but solid furniture conveyed durability and strength. In fifteenth-century Italian halls, neoclassical décor and an emphasis on symmetry conveyed gravitas and rationality. The hall's large scale further emphasized hierarchy and order; in halls, lesser folk observed the powerful, and vice versa.

As Grosseteste's instructions show, eating before the household was fundamental to maintaining the seigniorial position. Lords and peasants alike ate from long trestle tables that were put away at the end of the meal. Elites ate, drank, and served off pewter, silver, or even gold dishes, while everyone else used locally produced ceramics. For most of the period, people ate off shared plates or trenchers. Often trenchers were made of hard bread. At the end of the meal the diner ate the juice-soaked trencher, tossed it to the household dogs, or gave it to the poor. Over the course of the fifteenth century, diners in the Rhineland and Low Countries began eating off individual dishes. Continental images of the "Last Supper" or the "Marriage at Cana" in this period often show individual place settings.[23] By the mid-fourteenth century, affordable stoneware imported into England and France from Rhenish and Spanish potteries allowed humble consumers across Europe to imitate the dining habits of the elite, suggesting that their eating habits probably began to change as well. People freely mixed stoneware and pewter. The new diversity of dishes presented users, often female domestic servants and housewives, with many choices; some dishes were created for particular functions, such as bowls for liquids and plates for solids, but others served multiple functions. In Northamptonshire, archaeologists have found that housewives used shallow bowls as both milk skimmers and grain measurers.[24] Whether women were servants or housewives, the increase in dishware changed their work within the house. As with clothing, choice about how to use the growing variety of dishes allowed women new agency in performing their household tasks.

Within households, food and food preparation was a housewife's responsibility; even if servants prepared and served the food, the housewife still oversaw provisioning, meal preparations, and serving. A husband and wife were to eat together; the legal language for divorce—"*a mensa et thoro*" (from table and bed)—emphasized the importance of conjugal commensality. As part of her religious observances, Margery Kempe stopped eating with her husband on Fridays, much to his distress. When she sought to negotiate a chaste marriage, one of his stipulations was that she resume eating with him. With Eucharistic resonances, a wife serving and then eating with her husband reinforced the sacramental nature of the marriage that created a household and its head, the husband. Late fifteenth-century English advice on choosing a wife sums up the essence of a properly ordered marriage by turning to mealtime dynamics. The prospective groom is advised to value meekness over wealth, warning that a courteous and good wife who "serves you well and pleasantly...with rest and peace, a fulsome meal of honest fare [is better] than to have an hundred dishes with grumblings & with much care."[25]

Manners further maintained status boundaries during meals. Over the course of the Middle Ages, elaborate seating arrangements evolved for feasts, and proper behavior at the table became important. In the image of a feast in the fourteenth-century *Luttrell Psalter*, the lord was at the center of the table, flanked by members of his family. Continental depictions sometimes show women segregated from the men at their own table or together at the lower end. At castle feasts, women left the hall before the heavy drinking began. While honored guests and lords had comfortable seats with backs and armrests (near the fire), others sat on stools or benches. A peasant householder might have sat in a chair in his own home, but at the manor-house harvest feast, he shared a bench with others at the far end of the hall.[26] Diners used knives and spoons, but no forks. They washed their hands before and during the meal and used napkins. Even in peasant and artisan households, where meals were less elaborate and social distinctions narrower, seating arrangements, napkins, and manners contributed to household order.

Food itself was also an important marker of identity and occasion. Nobles ate an abundance of game, roasted on a spit; peasants boiled their meat when there was any, with the majority of their diet comprising grains and legumes. So closely were status and identity associated with diet that in his poem *Mirour de l'omme* (*Mirror of Man*) written sometime before 1378, John Gower wrote, "The labourers of olden times were not accustomed to eat wheat bread; their bread was made of beans and of other corn, and their drink was water. Then cheese and milk were as a feast to them; rarely had they any other feast than this."[27] French, Spanish, and English sumptuary legislation tried to regulate diets as well as clothing. English servants (of lords), grooms, and artisans were only to eat meat once a day "and at other times other food appropriate to their estate, such as milk, butter and cheese."[28] Menus also marked occasions. During childbirth, Italian women ate poultry and sweetmeats to keep up their strength, because they were believed to be easy to digest. In northern Europe, women in labor restored their strength with caudle, a spiced and sweetened wine. Visitors to the birthing room shared in this food, giving it a ceremonial and social function as well as a medicinal one.[29]

While the hall emphasized and promoted visibility, privacy was the goal of the chamber or solar, a smaller room off the hall. Privacy became increasingly important at the end of the Middle Ages. In Florence, a groom furnished his chamber, and his bride contributed an elaborately carved and painted marriage chest (*forziere*), filled with dowry goods. Servants displayed the forziere when the bride processed from her parents' house to her new husband's house. The forziere's images and contents promoted a vision of marriage and wifely behavior centered on duty, beauty, fertility, and piety. The contents might include combs, mirrors, girdles, sewing equipment, and rosaries, all of which would help the new bride conform to the social expectations placed on her.[30] Marriage chests were also common in Germany.

The chamber was a place to sleep, read, hold private conversations, and do handwork. Accommodating these various functions required numerous furnishings. The dominant piece of furniture was a bed, often an imposing and expensive item. There was a tremendous variety of beds. Wealthy Italian elites had beds with chests attached on three sides. The chests provided storage and a place to sit. Beds had canopies and headboards, draped with curtains. John Williams of Westminster had a tester (curtain over a headboard) with an image of the Assumption.[31] Beds used by servants and children often lacked frames, consisting of a mattress on the floor. English and French children and servants also slept in truckle (or trundle) beds, which slid underneath the larger bedstead when not in use. The householder and spouse, nursing infants, and perhaps young children slept in the chamber, while others in the household slept in the hall, in service rooms, or in attics. The ability to eat and work in one space and sleep in another distinguished the householder from the rest of his or her household. Chambers might also have tables for intimate dining, benches or chairs for handwork or reading, and small desks and chests for storage and additional seating. Among elites, wives sometimes had their own chambers.

Bedding and linen were also elaborate and decorative. Mattresses of straw or feathers were covered with sheets, blankets, quilts, and bedspreads. Accompanying the linens were a variety of pillows, bolsters, and other cushions. Elite Italian and Spanish bedding was often of silk, with Middle Eastern designs. The luxury of these fittings can be seen in Italian illustrations of the "Birth of the Virgin" or the "Birth of John the Baptist," which show finely appointed bedding, with plaid blankets and embroidered curtains.

Beds were both masculine and feminine spaces. On the one hand, as the place where male heirs were conceived, beds were symbols of patrimony and patriarchy. On the other hand, beds were also female spaces that spoke to the labors of childbirth. Even though most women used stools to give birth, they returned to beds to recover, nurse, and receive guests. Among those with means, special furnishings such as new bed linens transformed the chamber into a birthing room. Margaret of Burgundy (1399–1441) advised her sister-in-law Isabel of Portugal (1397–1471), wife of Duke Philip the Good of Burgundy to hang her bed with green silk canopies. She also advised that the room be shut for eight days after the birth and only lit by two candles. The child's room should have the same colors as the mother's room and tapestries with the mother's coats of arms. Florentine mothers received elaborately painted childbirth trays (*desco da parto*), upon which female attendants carried food to the new mother. They were decorated to highlight the father's lineage and the arrival of a male heir as a civic duty.[32]

Other life events compounded the bed's symbolism. Women, both mothers and wet nurses, nursed babies at night in their beds, and people died in bed. Women frequently cared for the ill and dying, and then prepared the body for burial, again transforming the bed and the bedroom into another sort of female-controlled space. Even in everyday life, the space was the responsibility of women. The *Ménagier* of Paris put great stock in his bed, giving his young wife detailed instructions for keeping it free of fleas.[33] With lives beginning and ending in beds, they even became the default place for many religious ceremonies. Marriages were completed by consummation—in a bed. Childbirth might require an emergency baptism by the midwife—in a bed. Priests performed last rites for the dying—in a bed. The bed and by extension, the bedroom, became by these actions a sacramental place. In this context, it is perhaps not surprising that religious imagery adorned John Williams's Westminster bed.

Single-room dwellings had no division between hall and chamber. Often inhabited by poor widows, singlewomen, or young bachelors, these small, mean dwellings underscored the low status of the not-married, the young and old, and the newly arrived. Inhabitants sent out for food, or used a common kitchen in the back of the property. Lacking a separate hall, they ate, worked, and slept in the same space. While households of one created new kinds of domesticities, they were seldom defined as respectable or socially established. The lack of a hall also marked them as poor.

The arrangements of houses reveal strong messages about status, but they contain no readily articulated assumptions about gender. By attending to the ways medieval people lived in houses, however, we can understand how they lived out or compromised on their values and assumptions about gender. While moralists were clear that women belonged at home and away from the gaze of strangers, in practice, houses were not so explicitly gendered.

CONCLUSION

Material culture carries values and expectations that are not readily expressed verbally, giving scholars access to unspoken assumptions about medieval men's and women's everyday experiences. Medieval men and women used material culture to establish identity, maintain reputation, and manage their relationships. By the later Middle Ages, they could do this with relative ease, whether by adopting new styles, imitating the customs of their social superiors, or adapting foreign aesthetics to local uses. Middle Eastern designs on bedding might indicate the foreign status of the wife who brought the bedding with her when she married, but might just as easily indicate the husband's position as a well-traveled and well-connected merchant. Material culture was an important site of identity negotiations, whether about status, gender, ethnicity, or reputation.

The mutability of material culture posed several problems. Identity formation was not a one-way process, as the repeated attempts to update sumptuary legislation show. Authorities, whether civic or familial, tried to fix identities and the use of clothing, housing, and ritual to express identity, but they never succeeded. "Respectable" women wanted to wear the shoes and gloves prescribed as suitable only for prostitutes. New types of dishes or cheaper chairs introduced new opportunities, along with new values and behaviors. Objects have no fixed meaning or use; bowls intended as milk strainers could also be used to sift grain. While these changes and instabilities offered women opportunities for agency and creativity, men and women were not adversaries in their use of material culture. As spouses, offspring, and employers and employees, men and women both lived and worked together, and as such, they shared in striving for more than individual survival. Most were invested in social stability and their family's respectability and prosperity. The expanding consumer culture of late medieval Europe brought social anxieties, institutional expectations, and everyday tensions, but the objects themselves—and their uses—were also important. Although moralists might write that women belonged in the home, when confronted with the realities of everyday life, men and women typically shared spaces while performing gendered tasks. Even though late medieval people often deployed new clothes or furnishings to promote stability, they brought change.

FURTHER READING

Ajmar-Wollheim, Marta and Flora Dennis, eds. *At Home in Renaissance Italy*. London: Victoria and Albert Museum, 2006.

Carlin, Martha. "Fast Food and Urban Living Standards in Medieval England," in Martha Carlin and Joel T. Rosenthal, eds, *Food and Eating in Medieval Europe*. London: The Hambledon Press, 1998, 27–52.

Eames, Penelope. *Furniture in England, France, and the Netherlands from the Twelfth to the Fifteenth Century*. London: Furniture History Society, 1977.

Gaimster, David and Paul Stamper, eds. *The Age of Transition: The Archaeology of Culture, 1400–1600*. Oxford: Oxbow, 1997.

Girouard, Mark. *Life in the English Country House: A Social and Architectural History*. New Haven: Yale University Press, 1978.

Heller, Sarah-Grace. *Fashion in Medieval France*. Cambridge: D. S. Brewer, 2007.

Hughes, Diane Owen. "Distinguishing Signs: Ear-rings, Jews and Franciscan Rhetoric in the Italian Renaissance City," *Past & Present*, 112 (1986): 3–59.

Killerby, Catherine Kovesi. *Sumptuary Law in Italy, 1200–1500*. Oxford: Oxford University Press, 2002.

Musacchio, Jacqueline M. *The Art and Ritual of Childbirth in Renaissance Italy*. New Haven: Yale University Press, 1999.

Piponnier, Françoise and Perrine Mane. *Dress in the Middle Ages*, trans. Caroline Beamish. New Haven: Yale University Press, 1997.

Sonnenfeld, Albert, ed. *Food: A Culinary History*. New York: Penguin Books, 2000.

Wolfthal, Diane. *In and Out of the Marital Bed: Seeing Sex in Renaissance Europe*. New Haven: Yale University Press, 2010.

NOTES

1. Jules David Prown, "The Truth of Material Culture: History or Fiction," in Steven Lubar and W. David Kingery, eds, *History From Things: Essays on Material Culture* (Washington, DC: Smithsonian Institution Press, 1993), 1.
2. Susan Mosher Stuard, *Gilding the Market: Luxury and Fashion in Fourteenth-Century Italy* (Philadelphia: University of Pennsylvania Press, 2006); Stella Mary Newton, *Fashion in the Age of the Black Prince: A Study of the Years 1340–1365* (Woodbridge: Boydell Press, 1980); Françoise Piponnier and Perrine Mane, *Dress in the Middle Ages*, trans. Caroline Beamish (New Haven: Yale University Press, 1997); Sarah-Grace Heller, *Fashion in Medieval France* (Cambridge: D. S. Brewer, 2007), 59.
3. Heller, *Fashion in Medieval France*, 59.
4. Quoted in Ruth Mellinkoff, *Outcasts: Signs of Otherness in Northern European Art of the Late Middle Ages*, vol. 1 (Berkeley: University of California Press, 1993), 7, 9.
5. Quoted in Fernand Braudel, *Civilization and Capitalism, 15th–18th Centuries*, trans. Siân Reynolds, vol. 1: *The Structures of Everyday Life* (New York: Harper and Row, 1981), 317.
6. Katherine L. French, *The Good Women of the Parish: Gender and Religion after the Black Death* (Philadelphia: University of Pennsylvania Press, 2008), 44.
7. Jacqueline M. Musacchio, *The Art and Ritual of Childbirth in Renaissance Italy* (New Haven: Yale University Press, 1999), 38–48; French, *Good Women*, 60.
8. Nicholas Love, *The Mirror of the Blessed Life of Jesus Christ: A Reading Text*, ed. Michael G. Sargent, rev. edn (Exeter: University of Exeter Press, 2004), 38.
9. Maria Guiseppina Muzzarelli, "Sumptuous Shoes: Making and Wearing in Medieval Italy," in Giorgio Riello and Peter McNeil, eds, *Shoes: A History from Sandals to Sneakers* (Oxford: Berg, 2006), 50–75.
10. Geoff Egan and Frances Pritchard, *Dress Accessories, 1150–1450* (Woodbridge: Boydell Press, 2002), 18, 35; Stuard, *Gilding the Market*, 56.
11. "Chronicle of Henry Knighton," in Rosemary Horrox, ed., *The Black Death* (Manchester; New York: Manchester University Press, 1994).
12. The National Archive (London), PROB2/15.
13. French, *Good Women*, 43–44; F. W. Weaver, ed., *Somerset Medieval Wills*, vol. 1 (London: Somerset Record Society, 1901), 385; Christian Peters, *Patterns of Piety: Women, Gender, and Religion in Late Medieval and Reformation England* (Cambridge: Cambridge University Press, 2003), 51–52.
14. "Chronicle of John of Reading," in Rosemary Horrox, ed., *The Black Death* (Manchester; New York: Manchester University Press, 1994), 131.
15. Catherine Kovesi Killerby, *Sumptuary Law in Italy, 1200–1500* (Oxford: Oxford University Press, 2002), 113; Stuard, *Gilding the Market*, 68–69; Gerhard Jaritz, "*Ira Dei*, Material

Culture, and Behavior in the Late Middle Ages: Evidence from German-Speaking Europe," *Essays in Medieval Studies*, 18 (2001): 56.

16. Diane Owen Hughes, "Distinguishing Signs: Ear-rings, Jews and Franciscan Rhetoric in the Italian Renaissance City," *Past & Present*, 112 (1986): 25; Ruth Mazo Karras, *Common Women: Prostitution and Sexuality in Medieval England* (New York: Oxford University Press, 1996), 21.

17. Piponnier and Mane, *Dress in the Middle Ages*, 137; Israel Abrahams, *Jewish Life in the Middle Ages* (repr. New York: Athaneum, 1969), 298; Hughes, "Distinguishing Signs," 27.

18. Vern L. Bullough and Bonnie Bullough, *Cross Dressing, Sex, and Gender* (Philadelphia: University of Pennsylvania Press, 1993), 62–64.

19. David Lorenzo Boyd and Ruth Mazo Karras, "*Ut cum muliere*: A Male Transvestite Prostitute in Fourteenth-Century London," in Louise Fradenburg and Carla Freccero, eds, *Premodern Sexualities* (New York; London: Routledge, 1996), 99–116.

20. Quoted in Mark Girouard, *Life in the English Country House: A Social and Architectural History* (New Haven: Yale University Press, 1978), 30.

21. Girouard, *Life in the English Country House*, 27; Eval Svensson, *The Medieval Household: Daily Life in Castles and Farmsteads: Scandinavian Examples in their European Context* (Turnhout: Brepols, 2008), 168–70; Roberta Gilchrist, "Medieval Bodies in the Material World: Gender, Stigma, and the Body," in Sarah Kay and Miri Rubin, eds, *Framing Medieval Bodies* (Manchester: Manchester University Press, 1994), 51.

22. Barbara Hanawalt, *The Ties that Bound: Peasant Families in Medieval England* (New York: Oxford University Press, 1986); P. J. P. Goldberg, "The Public and the Private: Women in the Pre-Plague Economy," in Peter R. Coss and S. D. Lloyd, eds, *Thirteenth-Century England III: Proceedings of the Newcastle-upon-Tyne Conference, 1989* (Woodbridge, Suffolk: Boydell Press, 1991), 75–81.

23. Hipólito Rafael Oliva Herrer, "Peasant *Domus* and Material Culture in Northern Castile in the Later Middle Ages," in Cordelia Beattie, Anna Maslakovic, and Sarah Rees Jones, eds, *The Medieval Household in Christian Europe, c. 850–1550* (Turnhout: Brepols, 2003), 482; Alejandra Gutierrez, "Cheapish and Spanish: Meaning and Design on Imported Pottery," *Medieval Ceramics*, 21 (1997): 74; David Gaimster and Beverley Nenk, "English Households in Transition, c. 1400–1550: The Ceramic Evidence," in David Gaimster and Paul Stamper, eds, *The Age of Transition: The Archaeology of Culture, 1400–1600* (Oxford: Oxbow, 1997): 174.

24. Paul Blinkhorn, "The Trials of Being a Utensil: Pottery Function at the Medieval Hamlet of West Cotton, Northamptonshire," *Medieval Ceramics*, 22–23 (1998–99): 37–46.

25. "How the Wise Man Taught his Son," in Frederick J. Furnivall, ed., *The Babees Book*, Early English Text Society, original ser. 32 (London: Kegan Paul, Trench, Trübner, 1868): 50–51.

26. Françoise Piponnier, "From Hearth to Table: Late Medieval Cooking Equipment," in Albert Sonnenfeld, ed., *Food: A Culinary History* (New York: Penguin Books, 2000), 344; Penelope Eames, *Furniture in England, France, and the Netherlands from the Twelfth to the Fifteenth Century* (London: Furniture History Society, 1977), xix, 181.

27. Quoted in John Hatcher, "England in the Aftermath of the Black Death," *Past & Present*, 144 (1994): 16.

28. Frances Elizabeth Baldwin, *Sumptuary Legislation and Personal Regulation in England* (Baltimore: The Johns Hopkins University Press, 1926), 47; quoted in Rosemary Horrox, ed., *The Black Death* (Manchester; New York: Manchester University Press, 1994), 340.

29. Musacchio, *Art and Ritual of Childbirth*, 40–41; Adrian Wilson, "The Ceremony of Childbirth and its Reception," in Valerie Fildes, ed., *Women as Mothers in Pre-Industrial England* (London: Routledge, 1990), 73–74.

30. Jacqueline Musacchio, *Art, Marriage, and Family in the Florentine Renaissance Palace* (New Haven: Yale University Press, 2009), 159–89.

31. Westminster City Archives, Bracy, 26–27v.

32. Musacchio, *Art and Ritual of Childbirth*, 38; Elizabeth L'Estrange, *Holy Motherhood: Gender, Dynasty and Visual Culture in the Later Middle* Ages (Manchester: Manchester University Press, 2008), 16, 76.

33. Diane Wolfthal, *In and Out of the Marital Bed: Seeing Sex in Renaissance Europe* (New Haven: Yale University Press, 2010), 13–18; *The Good Wife's Guide: Le Ménagier de Paris: A Household Book*, trans. Gina L. Greco and Christine M. Rose (Ithaca: Cornell University Press, 2009), 139.

CHAPTER 14

....

GENDER AND DAILY LIFE IN JEWISH COMMUNITIES

....

ELISHEVA BAUMGARTEN

In a poem written in memory of his wife, Dulcia (d.1196), murdered together with their two daughters during an attack on their house, Eleazar ben Judah of Worms (d.1232), a well-known author and leader of the German-Jewish community, described the many deeds that made Dulcia a pious, God-fearing woman, as well as an ideal wife and mother. Eleazar ben Judah modeled his eulogy on the last chapter of Proverbs (Prov. 31:10–31), starting each line with a quote from Proverbs and then elaborating on Dulcia's own life. He begins:

> *Who can find a woman of valor* (Ps. 31:10) like my pious wife, Mistress Dulcia?
> A woman of valor, her husband's crown, a daughter of benefactors
> *A God-fearing woman* (Ps. 31:30), renowned for her good deeds,
> *Her husband trusted her implicitly* (Ps. 31:11), she fed and clothed him in dignity,
> So he could sit among the elders of the land, and provide Torah study and good
> deeds.[1]

The account of Dulcia's deeds, only a few dozen lines long, constitutes the fullest description of a medieval Jewish woman's life that has survived in any known source to date and is one of the only texts that describes a specific woman. It is representative of the Hebrew sources that have reached us from the Middle Ages in many ways. It was written by a man, and indeed we have no text written by a Jewish woman from the medieval period. It was most concerned with different aspects of religious observance, the topic that is paramount in many of the Hebrew texts that have been preserved from this period. It connected medieval life to the Bible—a common practice among medieval Jews who saw themselves living in direct connection to biblical events. And, of course, it was written according to the literary conventions of its time.

This essay builds from the details of Dulcia's life as described posthumously by her husband. Dulcia was an atypical, elite Jewish woman, but she was typically active in her community and local culture. Like other medieval Jewish women, Dulcia was presented first and foremost as a daughter, mother, and wife. These were the expected roles of every Jewish woman, and while there were certainly women who did not marry, these seem to have been few and there are almost no records of them. Dulcia was an active businesswoman and moneylender. Like many of her Jewish neighbors she was also an involved member of her community. Finally, Dulcia died as the result of a Christian attack, although in this case the attack did not stem from anti-Jewish motivations per se; rather, her killers were two criminals in search of money. In fact, the city officials in Worms caught and executed one of the criminals shortly after the event. However, the relationship between medieval Jews and Christians that is reflected in her murder illustrates the complexities of Jewish life in Christian Europe.[2]

The living conditions and cultural circumstances in which Dulcia lived are representative of a way of life that characterized Ashkenazic Jews (that is, Jews in medieval Germany and northern France) during the twelfth and thirteenth centuries when these communities were at their zenith. The circumstances of Jews in Ashkenaz changed drastically at the end of the thirteenth and the early fourteenth centuries when many Jewish communities experienced severe attacks (in Germany, the Rindfleisch events of 1298) or expulsion (England 1290; France 1306; Germany during the Black Death). Thereafter, Jews began to move to Poland in large numbers, taking eastward their customs and way of life.

In following Dulcia and her Jewish counterparts in twelfth- and thirteenth-century Ashkenaz, this essay sees Jewish communities as embedded in their Christian surroundings. Some aspects of Jewish life—activities within the synagogue, religious education, and marriage arrangements—were by definition only between Jews, but medieval Jewish women lived in more complex and integrated surroundings. Jews lived in close quarters with Christians and had many business dealings with them. Not only was space shared by Jews and Christians, time was as well. The Jews lived within the rhythms of medieval cities, knowing the pattern of Christian festivities and often unwillingly adapting themselves to Christian time.[3] As part of the need to accommodate Christian circumstances, Jewish authorities even amended traditional restrictions regarding trade with non-Jews during non-Jewish holidays. Furthermore, Jews and Christians shared basic markets of materials and produce. They lived in the same climate, had access to the same foods, built their houses and made their clothes and their books out of the same materials.

Despite these shared aspects of time, space, and material culture, facets which historians have often overlooked or played down until recently, Jewish daily life was still distinct. Jews entered Christian space; Jews dealt and even dwelt with Christians; Jews and Christians shared ovens and wells. But these myriad interactions were accompanied by other practices that emphasized the distinction between the two religious groups.

Family and Households

She is like the merchant ships (Ps. 31:14), She feeds her husband (so he can) study Torah,
Daughters saw her (Ps. 31:29) and declared her happy, *her wares were so fine* (Ps. 31:18),
She gives food to her household (Ps. 31:15) and bread to the boys…
She extends a hand to the poor (Ps. 31:20),
Feeding her boys,[4] daughters, and husband.

Dulcia's life as a mother and wife was fairly typical. She was a mother of three children, aged fifteen, twelve, and six at the time of her death; scholars suggest that most medieval Jewish families had between two and four living children.[5] Dulcia most probably was in her mid-thirties when she was killed, which would indicate that she, like most Jewish women, had her first child in her late teens, shortly after her marriage. As was common, the names in her family fit a known pattern by which Jewish women had names in local vernaculars (in Dulcia's case, the name is Italian, perhaps indicating her family's origin), whereas men had names that were more ethnic.[6] The house in which Dulcia lived was that of her nuclear family, shared by some of her husband's students. Based on responsa literature, one of the few sources for details of living patterns, it seems that most couples, like Dulcia and Eleazar, lived independent of their parents, certainly after a few years of support. At times a Jewish couple settled next door to parents, but each nuclear unit maintained an independent household.[7]

Medieval Jews lived in communities that were made up of individual families, often related to each other. In most cases these communities obtained from local or regional authorities permission to dwell and work within cities. These families were granted privileges by the local or regional authorities allowing them to dwell within the cities and conduct their business. The privileges also permitted Jewish communal self-government as well as some form of economic autonomy. For the most part, in northern Europe, Jews lived within cities, although single families often lived in rural areas. Most larger urban centers had Jewish communities, and these communities grew throughout the twelfth and thirteenth centuries.[8]

Jews, like other ethnic, social, and occupational groups in medieval towns, tended to live in clusters. Since there were no ghettos before the sixteenth century, however, their neighborhoods were not exclusively Jewish. Jews lived in close proximity to their Christian neighbors, often within a single courtyard. Moreover, as different maps of medieval urban centers have demonstrated, the Jewish quarter was usually situated in the center of the city, close to the cathedral and other important civic structures.[9] Few recent studies have investigated the interior of Jewish homes, but physical conditions were likely similar to those of their Christian neighbors.

Gender divisions of labor within the Jewish homes were also similar to those among Christians. Like Christian women, Jewish women were, in theory, responsible for the care of their young children, and mothers were first separated from their sons when they began their formal schooling, either at home with a tutor or in a local school, often situated in the synagogue. Men were considered responsible for their sons' education and for making sure their sons had professions. Girls received their education from tutors within the home or from their mothers and female relatives.[10] It was not considered fitting for fathers to be involved in childcare, and this belief was so strong that new widowers with young children could remarry immediately—during the seven-day mourning period after the death of their wives—so that the new wife could immediately begin to care for their young ones.

Yet despite medieval texts that upheld ancient traditions about the division of labor, daily life did not conform in many cases to these theoretical ideals. Women were often said to encourage their children to study, and in fact, moral treatises praised women for ensuring that their sons and husbands studied the Torah. Fathers are reported not only as caring for their young children but as responsible for their behavior, despite the clear instructions that these children should be their mother's tasks. Cooking tasks and food preparation seem to have been considered as both men's and women's responsibilities, although women were especially conversant in laws pertaining to the preparation of food.[11] This more diversified division of domestic duties remained constant for many centuries, even as other aspects of Jewish families and communities changed.

MEDIEVAL JEWISH MARRIAGE:
PRACTICES AND REFORMS

Marriage created and solidified connections between families and between communities. The first lines of the poem about Dulcia state that she was the "daughter of benefactors," and she might have been born into an Ashkenazic family of Italian origin; such families were often considered the most respectable in Jewish communities. Her marriage to a prominent rabbi reinforced, as did other marriages, ties between scholarship and ancestry. Dulcia and her husband Eleazar probably were also typical of most couples in that they married in their mid-teens. This age of marriage remained fairly constant until the early modern period.[12]

In both law and practice, Jewish marriage and divorce underwent a substantial revolution during the central Middle Ages, much as in Christian society where marriage became universally recognized as a Christian sacrament. While Jewish alterations were not quite as dramatic as Christian ones, which redefined the sacramental nature of marriage and the church's control over it, they too were significant.

To begin with, the process of getting married changed, with the ceremony no longer split between engagement (*kiddushin* or *erusin*) and marriage (*nissuin*). Solomon, son of Isaac, known by the acronym Rashi (d.1105), discussed the financial wisdom of holding the two events together; one celebration saved parents a significant amount of money.

However, there was an additional, even more substantial benefit to the new practice. Once a woman was engaged, even if she was a minor, she then needed a formal divorce if the union was not completed with full-fledged marriage. Although some Jews continued to keep two separate rituals separated by months and even years up to the late thirteenth century, this system was slowly replaced by an independent engagement ritual that was socially binding but did not require divorce if breached. This new ritual brought with it a new profession as well, that of the matchmaker.[13]

Moreover, the combined betrothal and marriage ritual itself changed. Elliott Horowitz and Esther Cohen have suggested that much like the sanctification of Christian marriage, Jewish marriage underwent a sanctification of sorts in the central Middle Ages. One of the seven traditional wedding blessings changed and the version accepted in northern Europe stated: "Blessed art thou ... Who sanctifies Israel by means of marriage and betrothal (*huppah* and *kiddushin*)." Also, instead of the biblical stipulation that two witnesses could declare the marriage, it became increasingly common for a marriage to be completed in the presence of a rabbi and a quorum (*minyan*) from the community.[14]

Process and ritual mattered a great deal, but the most important changes in marriage related to the contract itself. Most famous were the statutes attributed to Gershom ben Judah of Mainz (*c*.960–1028) known as "Light of the Exile," which determined that women could not be divorced against their will and that a man could not have two wives at once. Although scholars have devoted much of their attention to the latter statute relating to bigamy, the former had consequences that were formidable as the requirement of women to consent to divorce was a significant change from accepted Jewish law until this time which allowed men to divorce their wives regardless of the women's desires.[15]

According to traditional Jewish law, a man could divorce his wife without her consent, whereas Jewish women could demand divorce under a small number of instances such as their husbands' impotence or conversion to another religion. Women required their husbands' consent to the divorce. Gershom ben Judah's statute was revolutionary in that it limited men's ability to divorce their wives, requiring a formal writ of divorce given with the approval of a court and witnesses, a process that became more and more formalized throughout the Middle Ages. By the thirteenth century, divorce writs were often granted only if rabbinic courts of three different jurisdictions agreed. As one fifteenth-century rabbi commented, these strict demands prevented the swiftness with which some men initiated divorce, increased the cost of divorce, and reduced its appeal. Legal authorities also made it harder for women to initiate divorces, especially women who were defined as "rebellious wives" because they refused to have conjugal relations with their husbands. In these cases, medieval rabbis changed a practice that had been accepted since the early Middle Ages. Earlier tradition was to grant these "rebellious" women divorces and provide them with the money from the marriage contract (*ketubbah*). Thirteenth-century rabbis in northern Europe demanded that such women give up their *ketubbah* money, leaving these women in financial positions that were more difficult.[16]

These restrictions in divorce moved at different paces from the tenth to the fifteenth centuries, first limiting men's abilities to divorce their wives, and only shifting in the thirteenth and fourteenth centuries toward diminishing women's ability to instigate divorce. Some rabbis suggested that wives had become more eager to divorce than before. Whether wives were in fact more rebellious, they were certainly less able to divorce their husbands after c.1250 than before. Viewed in the context of Christian prohibition of divorce and growing emphasis on the sanctity of marriage, these changes suggest an ongoing conversation between Jews and Christians over the merits of marriage and the undesirability of its dissolution.

The practice of levirate marriage also changed during the central Middle Ages. According to biblical law, if a man died without offspring, his widow was either to marry his brother or reject him through the rite of *halizah* (whereby the widow removed her shoe, threw it at the brother-in-law, spat at him, and thereby freed them both from the obligation) (Deut. 25:5–10). Levirate marriage was practiced in medieval Ashkenaz, although many community leaders openly stated that *halizah* was to be preferred and suggested, even in the eleventh century, that a widow should not be forced to marry her brother-in-law. One twelfth-century authority, Rabbenu Tam (Jacob ben Meir, 1100–1171), even suggested that the practice of levirate marriage should be forbidden. Nevertheless, some brothers-in-law still refused to release widows from levirate marriage or demanded money in return for release, sometimes dragging out the cases for years.[17]

Economics of Marriage, Divorce, and Inheritance

The economics of family life also changed during the Middle Ages. Financial arrangements played a major role in marriage negotiations and the creation of new households. In the tenth and eleventh centuries, the bride's family usually provided a dowry at the time of marriage; the groom's family's contribution to the household would come later when he inherited a share of family wealth from his father. In this way the business of marriage was seen as a mutual arrangement to which each side of the family contributed at different points in the couple's life. A woman without a dowry was unlikely to find a partner and the higher the dowry, the better the match she could make. This practice was not unique to medieval Jews, and at least the initial dowry payment mirrored similar practices among Christians. By the later Middle Ages, men's families no longer provided funds later in the marriage, but instead at its outset. With both parents contributing to a new household, Jews were better able to set up their children in what had become, due to anti-Jewish restrictions, a more difficult economic climate.

In addition, the ownership of a woman's dowry, if she died soon after her wedding without any heirs, became a contested matter during the twelfth century. Did the groom's family inherit the money despite the failure to create a child—that is, a biological bond between the families? During the twelfth century, Rabbenu Tam instituted a practice according to which families whose daughters died shortly after marriage without offspring were entitled to the return of the dowry. Increasingly during the twelfth and thirteenth centuries, both families had the right to demand their money back if one of the partners died without offspring.

The financial situation of divorced women was perilous, especially those who divorced with young children. They were entitled to the sum stated in their wedding contract (*ketubbah*), a sum that was often set quite high but not fully redeemed in practice. They were also entitled to their dowries, but they often did not receive these monies since they had been the husband's responsibility throughout the marriage and he often claimed the money had been lost. Divorced mothers did receive alimony but they also had to support their children, until the age of six for sons and until marriage for daughters. As a result, many divorced women were left with little money and in most cases they were also homeless as one of the immediate effects of divorce was their departure from the shared home. If they were young, they often became burdens on their parents. Remarriage was an option, especially because families were anxious that divorced daughters might seek sexual satisfaction outside of marriage. At the same time, there was some concern that remarried mothers might neglect their children from earlier marriages. As a result, divorced mothers could not, in theory, remarry until their youngest child was more than two years old.[18]

In contrast to divorced women, widows fared better economically. Unlike biblical and late antique practices that offered a widow a home and subsistence but left the bulk of her husband's estate to his children, medieval widows were first in line of inheritance and became the executors of their husbands' estates, whether large or small. In fact, many husbands explicitly designated their widows as their chief heirs in their wills, and the favored treatment of widows sometimes caused discontent, especially among stepchildren.[19]

Everyday Economic Activities

> Her labor provides him with books, her very name means "pleasant"…
> *See how her hands held the distaff* (Ps. 31:19) to spin cords for (binding) books,
> Zealous in everything, she spun (cords) for (sewing) tefillin (phylacteries) and megillot (scrolls), gut for (stitching together) Torah scrolls.

Before she was murdered by intruders in her home, Dulcia was a prominent businesswoman, lending money and manufacturing some forty Torah scrolls. Eleazar ben Judah also stated that Dulcia supported him from money she lent, something that seems to have been quite unusual. Yet it was not rare for Jewish women to be involved in trade, moneylending, and other businesses. Jewish women might even have specialized in working with Christian women. William Chester Jordan has demonstrated that Jewish women in Picardy often did separate business with Christian women, sometimes even forming partnerships with them.[20] According to Jordan's study, women's business was more modest, their transactions usually amounting to only one-third the value of those of men.

Women from wealthy families were often given property, money, or jewelry as part of their dowries, and in some cases their wedding contracts stipulated that they possessed these goods absolutely, with no oversight from their husbands. Some women ran businesses independent from their husbands, often with their brothers or other kin. However, most couples ran their family enterprises, however small or large, together. There is evidence that Jewish women, like men, often travelled for business, met with non-Jews, and actively pursued retribution in court for business deals gone awry.

Scholars have suggested three central explanations for the expanded role of women in the medieval Jewish economy. First, because northern European Jewish communities were relatively new (founded during the ninth century) and small, women took an active role, certainly more active than that which has been attributed to them in other regions in late antiquity. Second, perhaps Jewish women expanded their economic activities in emulation of their Christian neighbors; it was common in medieval towns to find women, Christian or Jewish, in workshops and markets. Third, Jewish women have been noted as especially active in families whose husbands traveled and left family businesses under the care of wives. This was, once again, not so different from Christian women.[21] While travel to distant Muslim lands all but ceased after attacks on Jewish communities that accompanied the First Crusade in 1096, intra-European travel was still a constant in medieval life, and both women and men traveled regularly. Although there are fewer texts that discuss women who traveled than those that discuss men's travels, the number of women who are referred to as traveling is surprising. As was true among Christians, the economic activities of women generated some negative comment. In the streets and shops of medieval towns and cities, Jewish women actively took part in local businesses, whether as widows, individuals, or partners with their husbands. But some rabbis worried about women's abilities to dispense large amounts of money and assume financial responsibilities. Such practices deviated from Talmudic law and in fact blatantly contradicted it. While some rabbis and legal authorities attempted to limit women's involvement in economic matters, it seems that in practice women remained active partners in business, especially joint family ventures, well into the early modern period.[22]

Religious Practice

> She looked for white wool (Ps. 31:13) with which to make tzitzit, *she spun with enthusiasm* (Ps. 31:13)
> She foresees how to do many commandments, all who see her praise her...

> She freely did the will of her Creator, day and night.
> *Her lamp will not go out at night* (Ps. 31:18)—she makes wicks
> For the synagogue and schools she says Psalms
> She sings hymns and prayers, she recites petitions…
> In all the towns, she taught women (so they can chant) songs
> She knows the order of the morning and evening prayers,
> And she comes early to synagogue, stays late
> She stands throughout Yom Kippur, sings and prepares the candles
> She honors the Sabbaths and Holidays as well as Torah scholars.

At least a third of the poem about Dulcia is devoted to her religious activities. Her husband emphasized her communal work such as feeding the poor, clothing brides, and preparing the dead for burial, as well as her personal devotion and worship. He also noted her status within the community as Dulcia was a leader—she taught women in her community and in other cities how to pray and led the women in prayer. As the wife of a community leader and a member of the Rhineland or Ashkenazic "Pietists" (*Hasidei Ashkenaz*) who constantly searched for ways to sanctify their lives, Dulcia's religious activities were unusually extensive.[23] Yet most of the deeds attributed to her were also recorded in connection to other women and in fact were characteristic of pious men who were not very learned.

Like Dulcia, who is said to have gone to the synagogue early and remained there until late, most medieval women attended synagogue regularly, not only on Sabbath but also on weekdays. Indeed, some sources suggest that women, like men, attended synagogue twice a day, and there are reports of servants and Christian business acquaintances coming to the synagogue to call them out for business matters. Archeological evidence indicates that central medieval synagogues, some of which were destroyed during the First Crusade, did not have a separate women's section, rather women seem to have prayed within the main sanctuary in a part allocated for them. After the First Crusade, some synagogues were rebuilt with a separate room attached to the main sanctuary by small windows. A number of tombstones throughout the medieval period note women who, like Dulcia, were leaders of women's prayers. These female prayer-leaders, like those who instructed other women on ritual activities, were often the daughters or relatives of male cantors.[24]

In the thirteenth century, however, women's synagogue attendance began to change, because it became more common for menstruating women to avoid synagogues. While eleventh- and twelfth-century sources note that only especially pious women might choose not to attend the synagogue during menstruation, this custom slowly became expected of all women. In some cases, some women prayed outside the synagogue, while others simply did not go to the synagogue at all.[25]

The synagogue and its vicinity hosted many other community and personal events, such as circumcision rituals, marriage ceremonies, and court proceedings. Marriage rituals took place in the synagogue courtyard, circumcisions inside the sanctuary, and legal proceedings often in the synagogue's foyer. Moreover, in many Ashkenazic communities during the Middle Ages the sanctuary of the synagogue became a court of sorts, especially for the resolution of difficult or long-standing grievances. A community member, male or female, could interrupt prayers to demand that a grievance be addressed. Such interruptions suggest that women were formidable and confident actors in the public sphere.[26] Many medieval women also publicly manifested their personal piety. While Torah study was first and foremost the reserve of men, medieval Jewish women are noted in the sources as praying, giving charity, and fasting, much like many of the men did. Fasting was a common practice among medieval Jews, for communal events as well as for personal penance or petitions. Many of these pious acts were also displayed in the synagogue.

Dulcia and others also instructed other women on matters of religious practice. These female leaders were usually mentioned as leading by example in areas that were part of female expertise, such as candle-lighting on the Sabbath or ritual purity practices related to menstruation. Women were also referred to as authorities on the rules of keeping kosher and as expert makers of ritual garments. Those mentioned by name are in almost all cases the sisters, wives, and daughters of rabbinic authorities. Some of them are said to have received their instructions from their male relatives. For example, Bellette the sister of Isaac b. Menahem of LeMans (eleventh century) was said to have instructed the women in her community on how to prepare for immersing in the ritual bath. In Bellette's case, the author emphasized that she instructed the women of the community in her brother's name.[27] One can only wonder what other behaviors were recommended by these women who clearly had a position of authority, with or without their male relatives' consent.

In relation to holidays and daily activities, medieval Jewish women sometimes followed commandments that had been defined in ancient sources as the obligation of men alone. These commandments, known as "positive time-bound commandments," included hearing the *shofar* (horn) blown on Rosh Hashanah and participating in some of the rituals of Succoth and Passover. They also included wearing *tefillin* (phylacteries) and *tzitzit* (fringes attached to clothing).[28] The women who took these obligations upon themselves usually belonged to elite families, in which the men were also performing these commandments; this was, in other words, a religious practice that was governed not only by gender but also by class. In the eleventh and twelfth centuries, women notably insisted on their right to shoulder these religious obligations, but the practice was slowly eroded by the end of the thirteenth century and the early fourteenth century. By then, rabbinic leaders had extended many religious observances and practices beyond the rabbinic elite and turned commandments such as phylacteries into an obligation practiced by all adult men and not just by a select few. Alongside these changes in male ritual observances grew a steady resistance to female participation. This growing restriction on female ritual practice was yet another area in which the gender relations within the Jewish communities seem to have mirrored Christian communities.[29]

Finally, despite the many religious activities of medieval women, it is necessary to note that women, no matter how central, pious, or important, were not represented formally in any community institutions. They were not members of the community courts, synagogue committees, charity collectors, or the leaders (*parnasim*) of the community.

These were all men, as were the legal authorities (often, in fact, the same men), and they saw women as subservient, in religious practices as in all matters.

JEWS AND CHRISTIANS: SHARED SPACES AND SEPARATE REALMS

As noted at the outset of this essay, Jews conducted their lives separately, within their own community institutions and frameworks, as well as in conjunction with their neighbors. Not only did Jews and Christians live in close quarters and within the same material and physical culture, they also shared ideas and values. Gender-based divisions and understandings of daily labor and of religiosity were often shared, despite the obvious differences between Jewish and Christian theology and practice.

Time and space were simultaneously shared and distinct. Jews lived within the medieval Christian city and according to its rhythm. Jewish and Christian women, to some extent even more than the men, were in daily contact. Some Christians went into Jewish homes for business as this was the locus in which most Jewish business was conducted; others, especially women, resided within Jewish houses, as house servants, wet nurses, or nannies. The church and the rabbis were very aware of this coresidence and attempted often to outlaw it or to control and contain it. Medieval sources regularly describe the presence of non-Jews in the house, whether lighting the fire on the Sabbath, cooking, or observing Christian holidays and rituals. Jews also entered Christian space, whether Christian houses of worship or neighbors' homes. Jewish children were left at Christian wet nurses' homes, pledges were returned, and trade took place. Jews and Christians knew where to find each other—seeking each other out at home, at the synagogue, and in church. Some sources contain evidence of Jews and Christians sharing meals and exchanging gifts as well.[30]

Despite these shared aspects of time, space, and material culture, Jewish daily life also manifested differences between Jews and their neighbors. For example, despite shared urban space and similar daily rhythms, Jewish and Christian calendars rarely intersected: the two communities observed different weekly days of rest as well as distinct holidays. Daily rituals, like praying and fasting for both men and women, whether Jewish or Christian, indicated an immediate belonging to one community or the other. Food preparation is a good example, especially because many food issues involved women who dealt with servants, neighbors, and the actual tasks of cooking. Jewish laws of keeping kosher forbade the eating of certain kinds of meat. Even when the meat came from an animal that was considered kosher, the animal had to be slaughtered correctly by a Jew, and certain restrictions applied to the way it was cooked. Animals were often raised by non-Jews in partnership with Jews, then slaughtered by Jews, who would subsequently sell to their Christian neighbors animals that did not meet the Jewish ritual standards. This practice generated some interfaith tensions, as it could appear that Christians were consuming substandard meat rejected by Jews.[31] Feasts and fasts in both communities also emphasized Jewish and Christian difference. Medieval Jews and Christians fasted frequently during the year, as part of the annual cycle and as expressions of personal piety and devotion. These fast days were rarely shared; Christians often fasted on Wednesdays and Fridays, whereas Friday was never a Jewish fast day and Mondays and Thursdays were. Jews fasted during the weeks after Passover; Christians fasted before and during Lent. The practical details of how members of both religions, male and female, observed these fasts marked difference. Fasting and festivity also dictated other mundane behaviors such as when one could or should wash oneself. Jews bathed on Fridays as a rule, Christians did not.

Material objects and culture also created distinctions. Jews and Christians kept separate cooking utensils as part of the food differentiation addressed above. Also, although Jews had their own distinctive ceremonial objects, like Torah scrolls, phylacteries, prayer shawls, and *shofar*, many of which were part of male ritual use, they did not possess or revere holy objects in the manner of their Christian neighbors. Relics were present and regularly used by Christians not only in public church ceremonies but also at home; Christian processions honored saints' bones or other remains, and a cure for a sick Christian might be hastened with a rock from Jesus's tomb. When the number of sacred relics increased in Christian Europe during the crusades, it further extended this material distinction between Jewish and Christian communities.

Medicinal materials were much the same and to a certain extent they were more the realm of women than of men as women grew herbs and applied cures to their households. Jews and Christians shared markets and diseases, but religion made a difference. Jewish and Christian doctors and midwives are known to have cooperated over the years, often consulting with each other or taking over for one another. The medicinal substances used by practitioners of both religions were fairly similar, as most came from local environments or markets. Yet religious belief deeply informed how these substances were used—the formulae, the verses recited at application, even the theories that explained their effectiveness. And, of course, because medical practice so often involved matters of life and death, practitioners of a different faith were sometimes avoided or distrusted.

Conclusions

Jewish women were often excluded from traditional centers of learning and seem to have not participated in learned theological and theoretical conversations during the medieval period.[32] This was largely true of Christian women as well. Yet this exclusion does not seem to have affected Jewish women's sense of belonging, religious belief, or involvement in daily devotional activities. Examining the place of gender conceptions and women's activities within medieval settings, one is struck by both the distinctions and the similarities between the lives of Jews and Christians, and more specifically Jewish and Christian women. Nineteenth-century scholars imagined medieval Jewish homes as havens in a hostile Christian world. Today, we see those homes as distinctly Jewish yet also comfortably embedded in Christian surroundings.

Jewish life in medieval Europe certainly entailed difference from the surrounding Christian culture. After all, Jews, unlike Christians, did not promote celibacy as a religious practice. At the same time, however, Jews maintained a gendered hierarchy very similar to that which existed in medieval Christian society. Women were expected to be subservient to their husbands and fathers (unless they were divorced or widowed), and in all cases, they were expected to obey their community's male leadership. They had a specific gendered status both before Jewish courts and as part of Jewish ritual. And they shared with Christian women the experiences of growing restrictions—in divorce and business—from the twelfth and thirteenth centuries. Two communities: two similar gender orders. We will understand both communities better if our future research into the shared worlds of medieval Jews and Christians weighs shared gendered frameworks alongside religious differences.

FURTHER READING

Abrahams, Israel. *Jewish Life in the Middle Ages*. London: Goldston Publishing, 1932.

Agus, Irving. *Urban Civilization in Pre-Crusade Europe*. New York: Yeshiva University Press, 1965.

Baumgarten, Elisheva. *Mothers and Children: Jewish Family Life in Medieval Europe*. Princeton: Princeton University Press, 2004.

Baskin, Judith R. "Dolce of Worms: The Lives and Deaths of an Exemplary Medieval Jewish Woman and her Daughters," in Lawrence Fine, ed., *Judaism in Practice: From the Middle Ages Through the Early Modern Period*. Princeton: Princeton University Press, 2001.

Chazan, Robert. *Reassessing Jewish Life in Medieval Europe*. New York: Cambridge University Press, 2010.

Cluse, Christoph, ed. *The Jews of Europe in the Middle Ages (Tenth to Fifteenth Centuries)*. Turnhout: Brepols, 2004.

Grayzel, Solomon. *The Church and the Jews in the Thirteenth Century*. New York: Hermon Press, 1966.

Grossman, Avraham. *Pious and Rebellious: Jewish Women in Medieval Europe*. Waltham: University of New England Press, 2004.

Katz, Jacob. "Marriage and Sexual Life among the Jews at the Close of the Middle Ages." [Hebrew] *Zion, 10* (1945): 21–54.

Marcus, Ivan. *Rituals of Childhood: Jewish Acculturation in Medieval Europe*. New Haven: Yale University Press, 1996.

Rosman, Moshe. *How Jewish is Jewish History?* Oxford; Portland, OR: Littman Library, 2007.

Stow, Kenneth. *Alienated Minority: The Jews of Medieval Latin Europe*. Cambridge, Mass.: Harvard University Press, 1992.

NOTES

1. Two translations are available: Ivan G. Marcus, "Mothers, Martyrs and Moneymakers: Some Jewish Women in Medieval Europe," *Conservative Judaism, 38* (1986), 34–45, and Judith R. Baskin, "Dolce of Worms: The Lives and Deaths of an Exemplary Medieval Jewish Woman and her Daughters," in Lawrence Fine, ed., *Judaism in Practice: From the Middle Ages through the Early Modern Period* (Princeton: Princeton University Press, 2001), 436–37. I have combined both these translations with slight adjustments throughout the essay, relying primarily on Marcus's translation.

2. This has been the topic of much recent research. For some conceptualizations of this relationship, see Kenneth Stow, *Alienated Minority: The Jews of Medieval Latin Europe* (Cambridge, Mass.: Harvard University Press, 1992); Ivan Marcus, *Rituals of Childhood: Jewish Acculturation in Medieval Europe* (New Haven: Yale University Press, 1996); Israel J. Yuval, *Two Nations in Your Womb: Perceptions of Jews and Christians in Late Antiquity and the Middle Ages* (Berkeley: University of California Press, 2006); Jonathan Elukin, *Living Together, Living Apart: Rethinking Jewish–Christian Relations in the Middle Ages* (Princeton: Princeton University Press, 2007); Robert Chazan, *Reassessing Jewish Life in Medieval Europe* (New York: Cambridge University Press, 2010).

3. Joanne M. Pierce, "Holy Week and Easter in the Middle Ages," in Paul Bradshaw and Lawrence Hoffman, eds, *Passover and Easter: Origin and History to Modern Times* (Notre Dame: University of Notre Dame Press, 1999), 161–85.

4. The plural of boys indicates her husband's students. Dulcia herself had only one son.

5. Kenneth R. Stow, "The Jewish Family in the Rhineland: Form and Function," *American Historical Review, 92* (1987), 1085–110; Abraham Grossman, *The Early Sages of Ashkenaz: Their Lives, Leadership, and Works* [Hebrew] (Jerusalem: Magnes Press, 2001), 8 n. 32, 10.

6. Dulcia's daughters' names were Bellette and Hannah; see Baskin, "Dolce of Worms." Goitein shows the same pattern in Muslim lands; see Shlomo Dov Goitein, *A Mediterranean Society* (Berkeley: University of California Press, 1983), 3: 2–14.

7. Irving Agus, *Urban Civilization in Pre-Crusade Europe*, volumes 1 and 2 (New York: Yeshiva University Press, 1965) collected a large number of the tenth- and eleventh-century responses and translated them into English. Within the section on the family there are many examples of living patterns; see volume 2: 554–729.

8. For the privileges and their recipients, see Jonathan Ray, "The Jew in the Text: What Christian Charters Tell Us about Medieval Jewish Society," *Medieval Encounters, 16* (2010), 246–48. For rural communities, see Michael Toch, "Jewish Peasants in the Middle Ages? Agriculture and Jewish Land Ownership in the Eighth–Twelfth Centuries," [Hebrew] *Zion, 75* (2010), 291–312.

9. For example: Matthias Schmandt, "Cologne, Jewish Centre on the Lower Rhine," in Christoph Cluse, ed., *The Jews of Europe in the Middle Ages (Tenth to Fifteenth Centuries)* (Turnhout: Brepols, 2004), 367–77; Pam Manix, "Oxford: Mapping the Medieval Jewry," in ibid, 405–20; Werner Transier, "Speyer: The Jewish Community in the Middle Ages," in ibid, 435–47; Gerald Bönnen, "Worms: The Jews between the City, the Bishop and the Crown," in ibid, 449–57. For Provence, see Danièle Iancu-Agou, *Provincia Judaica: Dictionnaire des géographie historique des juifs en Provence médiévale* (Paris-Louvain: Peeters, 2010). Many of the descriptions of the cities are accompanied by maps that show the centrality of the *rue de juiverie* (Street of the Jews) or *Judenviertel* (Jewish quarter) and its proximity to central urban sites.

10. Ephraim Kanarfogel, *Jewish Education and Society in the High Middle Ages* (Detroit: Wayne State University Press, 1992) describes the education process. See also Marcus, *Rituals*; Elisheva Baumgarten, *Mothers and Children: Jewish Family Life in Medieval Europe* (Princeton: Princeton University Press, 2004), 200 n. 45.

11. Judith Baskin, "Jewish Traditions about Women and Gender Roles: From Rabbinic Teachings to Medieval Practice," Chapter 3 in this volume; Baumgarten, *Mothers and Children*, 154–65. For food, see R. Jacob Mulin, in Yitzchok Satz, ed., *Shut Maharil (Responsa of Rabbi Yaacov Molin-Maharil)* [Hebrew] (Jerusalem: Machon Yerushlayim, 1979), 314–15, #199.

12. Jacob Katz, "Marriage and Sexual Life Among the Jews at the Close of the Middle Ages," [Hebrew] *Zion, 10* (1945), 21–54.

13. Avraham Grossman, *Pious and Rebellious: Jewish Women in Medieval Europe* (Waltham: University of New England Press, 2004), 49–67 outlines the process of marriage.

14. Esther Cohen and Elliott Horowitz, "In Search of the Sacred: Jews, Christians and Rituals of Marriage in the Later Middle Ages," *Journal of Medieval and Renaissance Studies, 20* (1990), 225–50. The biblical stipulation continued to hold, although some communities repeated the nuptial blessing; see Zeev W. Falk, *Jewish Matrimonial Law in the Middle Ages* (Oxford: Oxford University Press, 1966), 58–64.

15. Susan Mosher Stuard, "Brideprice, Dowry, and Other Marital Assigns," Chapter 10 in this volume; Baskin, "Jewish Traditions"; Grossman, *Pious and Rebellious*, 68–101.

16. Grossman, *Pious and Rebellious*, 240–44; Falk, *Jewish Matrimonial Law*, 13–34; R. Jacob Molin, in Shlomo Spitzer, ed., *Sefer Maharil: Minhagim* (Jerusalem: Machon Yerushalayim, 1989), Laws of Divorce, 493.

17. Grossman, *Pious and Rebellious*, 90–101, summarizes the conclusions of Jacob Katz, "Yibbum veHalizah baTekufah haBetar Talmudit," *Tarbiz, 51* (1981), 59–106.

18. Israel J. Yuval, "Monetary Arrangements and Marriage in Medieval Ashkenaz," in Menahem Ben-Sasson, ed., *Religion and Economy: Connections and Interactions* [Hebrew] (Jerusalem: Merkaz Shazar, 1995), 191–208; Baumgarten, *Mothers and Children*, 144–53.

19. Grossman, *Pious and Rebellious*. It should be noted that although Grossman has outlined many of these topics, research on them is still very rudimentary and I expect these conclusions to be modified and nuanced in future studies.

20. William C. Jordan, *Women and Credit in Pre-Industrial and Developing Society* (Philadelphia: University of Pennsylvania Press, 1993); Martha Keil, "Public Roles of Jewish Women in Fourteenth and Fifteenth-Century Ashkenaz: Business, Community and Ritual," in Cluse, ed., *Jews of Europe*, 317–30; Grossman, *Pious and Rebellious*, 117–21.

21. As discussed by Kathryn Reyerson, in "Urban Economies," Chapter 19 in this volume.

22. Alyssa Gray, "Married Women and 'Tsedaqah' in Medieval Jewish Law: Gender and the Discourse of Legal Obligation," *Jewish Law Association Studies, 17* (2007), 168–212; Debra Kaplan, "'Because Our Wives Trade and Do Business With Our Goods': Gender, Work, and Jewish–Christian Relations," in Elisheva Carlebach and Jacob J. Schachter, eds., *New Perspectives on Jewish-Christian Relations* (Leiden: Brill, 2011), 241–64.

23. For the history of the Ashkenazic Pietists, see Ivan G. Marcus, *Piety and Society: The Jewish Pietists of Medieval Germany* (Leiden: Brill, 1981).

24. For women's synagogues, an issue that needs yet to be explored, see Richard Krautheimer, *Mittelalterliche Synagogen* (Berlin: Frankfurter Verlags-Anstalt, 1927), 110–12; Monika

Porsche, "Speyer: The Medieval Synagogue," in Cluse, ed., *Jews of Europe*, 428–29. Dulcia herself was such a prayer leader. Others appeared on tombstones; see Grossman, *Pious and Rebellious*, 181.

25. Elisheva Baumgarten, "'And They Do Nicely': A Reappraisal of Menstruating Women's Refusal to Enter the Sanctuary in Medieval Ashkenaz," in Rami Reiner et al., eds, *Ta Shma: Essays in Memory of Israel M. Ta Shma* [Hebrew] (Alon Shvut: Tevunot, 2011), 85–104; Moshe Rosman, *How Jewish is Jewish History?* (Oxford; Portland, OR: Littman Library, 2007), 131–54.

26. Avraham Grossman, "The Origins and Essence of the Custom of 'Stopping the Service,'" [Hebrew] *Mil'et*, 1 (1983): 199–221.

27. Many of these women were already noted by Abraham Berliner in the Hebrew version of his *Aus dem inneren Leben der deutschen Juden im Mittelalter* (Berlin: Julius Benzian, 1871), published in Hebrew in Warsaw 1900, 8–9.

28. Bitkha Har-Shefi, *Women and Halakha in the Years 1050–1350 CE: Between Custom and Law* (Jerusalem: Hebrew University of Jerusalem, 2002).

29. Baumgarten, *Mothers and Children*, 85–91.

30. Solomon Grayzel, *The Church and the Jews in the Thirteenth Century* (New York: Hermon Press, 1966) outlined Christian legislation; Jacob Katz, *The "Shabbes Goy": A Study in Halakhic Flexibility*, trans. Yoel Lerner (Philadelphia: Jewish Publication Society, 1989) discussed some aspects of Jewish legislation.

31. Grayzel, *Church and the Jews*, 42.

32. As noted by Judith Baskin in "Jewish Traditions."

CHAPTER 15

....

CAROLINGIAN
DOMESTICITIES

....

RACHEL STONE

In 836, Einhard, the biographer of Charlemagne, wrote a letter lamenting the death of his wife Imma. His grief had still not abated, partly, said Einhard, because of the extent of his domestic loss: "I am keenly aware of these losses every day, in every act, in every deed, in the whole management of the *domus* and *familia*, and in every appointment and assignment which pertains to the service of God and man."[1]

Any discussion of Carolingian "domesticity" must first escape from the word's modern connotations of a private, apolitical sphere. The Latin term *domus* had multiple meanings: it could be used for a physical house, for the household that resided within it, or for the extended kindred, including both cognates and agnates. The same multiple meanings are visible in the term *familia*. Its original meaning encompassed all those under the legal control of the Roman *paterfamilias*, a group which comprised slaves and legitimate children, but not normally a man's wife. The meaning of the word, however, had become extended by the early Middle Ages, so that it might refer to either narrow or broad groups of blood relatives, not necessarily coresident. *Familia* could also refer solely to the domestic workers within a household, or to all free and unfree dependents of an individual or an organization, such as a monastery.[2] Carolingian domesticity, at least for aristocratic women like Imma, was therefore more akin to managing a substantial family business than being solely a wife and mother.

Einhard and Imma had jointly managed two estates east of the Rhine, granted to them by Louis the Pious. At both they erected large basilicas, and at one (Seligenstadt), Einhard installed the precious relics of the martyrs Marcellinus and Peter; the site became a place of pilgrimage and miracle stories. Einhard and Imma had probably been married for around twenty years when she died. We do not know of any children from the marriage, but it is possible that Imma had children from a previous union, as one of her two surviving letters advises someone who may be her grandson (the other pleads for an unfree man who had taken refuge at Seligenstadt after marrying a free woman).

Imma was a friend of several bishops: we know the exact date of her death (December 13, 835) from records kept by Bishop Gozbald of Würzburg.

The early Middle Ages are conventionally seen as a "dark age," a static and shadowy period, lacking civilization and with a poor source base. In fact, there were many social, economic, and political changes between 500–1000 CE, with the breakdown of the Roman Empire in Western Europe leading to new, relatively small-scale Christian militarized societies. These changes are often poorly documented, but the relative bulk of material from Carolingian Francia (the empire of Charlemagne and his successors, stretching from Catalonia to western Hungary) offers a rare chance to see how an early medieval society, based socially, economically, and ideologically on domestic patriarchies, developed as a coherent system. The estates and households of nobles such as Einhard and Imma were the basic building blocks of Carolingian civil society, dominating the expanding economy of the eighth and ninth centuries. Politically, it was through court-connected men such as Einhard that Carolingian rulers were able to influence often distant local societies. Well-born couples also came to play key ideological roles in Carolingian religious and moral reforms.

Eighth- and ninth-century Francia also provides some of the earliest medieval sources for the lives of women who, like Imma, were neither queens nor saints. Women's precise roles in noble households are often hard to ascertain, though we can presume parallels with the experiences of better-documented royal women. Yet by combining normative sources (such as legislation and moral tracts), narratives (such as histories and hagiographies), documents (such as charters and letters), and archaeological evidence (such as building layouts), we can discern some patterns of aristocratic domestic life. Occasionally, we also get glimpses into the lives of nonaristocratic women.

MARRIAGE

In the mid-twentieth century, Karl Schmid and Georges Duby argued for a change in aristocratic ideas of kinship. The early Middle Ages were marked by the key sociopolitical role of the clan or *Sippe*, a large group linked by bilateral and undifferentiated kinship. In contrast, a "feudal mutation" around the year 1000 also involved a "family mutation," in which a much narrower sense of kin developed, with the emphasis on patrilineage and the transmission of property in the male line. Primogeniture became increasingly common. More recent research has weakened the contrast between the two periods. Early medieval bilateral kinship already included biases toward the male line, and kin could be treated differently for different purposes. Men keen to acknowledge distant kin on some occasions, such as in prayers for the dead, often had far more restricted ideas of family when it came to passing on their inheritance. Social advancement meant using any available kinship ties to the powerful; after wealth and office had been achieved, however, those regarded as "official" relatives might come to be restricted. The Carolingian royal house, in particular, developed a strong patrilineal consciousness once they had attained power, a pattern later copied by comital families.[3]

There is little evidence for the political importance of the *Sippe*, in the sense of groups capable of coordinated action, in the Merovingian or Carolingian period; indeed, there could be bitter rivalries between closely related men. Such broad kinship ties were, however, significant for patronage relationships, particularly with the emergence in the eighth and ninth century of an imperial aristocracy, where members of the same elite family could hold power in widely dispersed regions of the expanding Carolingian empire. Nobles who moved between Carolingian kingdoms could thus relatively easily use existing kinship networks to forge new local connections.

Marriage was one of the key ways of making and renewing these social connections, and it was thus vitally important not only for the couple involved, but also their families. The hagiographer Hucbald commented that St Rictrudis and her husband Adalbald both had the qualities normally sought in marriage partners: Rictrudis had "beauty, birth, riches, and character [*mores*]," Adalbald "virtue [*virtus*], birth, beauty, and wisdom." Female wealth and character here balanced out male wisdom and (manly) virtue. Jonas of Orléans also showed the importance of female wealth, condemning men who wanted to divorce and remarry when their wives became ill or their inheritance squandered. Some early medieval hagiography describes fathers forcing or attempting to force their sons and daughters into marriage. Archbishop Hincmar of Rheims, however, claimed—perhaps in exaggeration—that fathers had less say, starting one anecdote about a troubled marriage:

> A certain young man of noble birth fell passionately in love with a woman of not ignoble ancestry. And seeking her legally from her parents, he won assent from her father, but the girl's mother totally refused his request. But, what rarely happens, the father prevailed in agreeing to the young man's entreaties.[4]

The main focus of early medieval secular and religious edicts on marriage was on alliance-building and its potential problems.[5] Positive definitions of what made a lawful marriage were rarely given; one of the few exceptions is Hincmar's statement that a full marriage was made when a woman was "legitimately betrothed, endowed, and honored with public nuptials," and sexual consummation followed.

As Hincmar's comments suggest, marriage was a process of stages, with an initial engagement followed by an actual marriage. Occasionally, such an engagement might be prolonged; Count Stephen of the Auvergne, whose complicated marital problems became a *cause célèbre* in the late 850s, attempted to delay marriage for several years, before being forced by his intended father-in-law, Count Raymond of Toulouse, to go through with the ceremony.[6]

At the time of the marriage itself, the bride was "handed over" by her relatives (*traditio*) or "led home" by her husband (*deductio*). Several Carolingian capitularies demanded that weddings must be "public," one adding that this should be done by both nobles and the "ignoble."[7] Although clerical authors encouraged the couple to have a marriage blessing, and we possess the orders of service for several such marriages, these services were not essential. Indeed, Jonas of Orléans argued that nuptial blessings should only be given when the bride was a virgin.[8]

Marriage was an important social structure throughout the early Middle Ages and beyond; during the Carolingian period it also became a key moral structure, with prohibitions more sharply defined and regulated. The earliest Carolingian church councils in the 740s already laid considerable emphasis on the need to avoid "adulterous and incestuous marriages." By the end of Charlemagne's reign, a substantial body of both secular and religious legislation regulated marital and sexual life. These laws focused on the concept of a single, legitimate form of marriage; they cracked down on *raptus* (the abduction of or elopement with a woman for the purpose of marriage); they greatly extended the reach of "incestuous" marriage (all consanguineous kin as well as affines and the "spiritual kin" created by godparenthood); and they prohibited divorce and remarriage.

Historians have traditionally seen these reforms to marital practice as imposed by kings and clerics on a reluctant laity. Georges Duby, for example, argued for the existence of two "models" of marriage: clerical and lay.[9] Yet in fact, the laity of both sexes had contradictory interests in rules on marriage and divorce, depending on their particular familial roles. A nobleman might want the ability to repudiate his own wife and remarry, but would object if his daughter's husband tried to do the same; marriage via (consensual) abduction might appeal to a young man and woman, but be resisted by the woman's parents.

Carolingian attempts to regulate marriage are better seen as a complex negotiation between religious principles and social interests, creating an ideal of marriage shared by both clerics and the laity, which nevertheless allowed a certain flexibility in practice. This is seen, for example, in Hincmar's intervention in the marriage dispute of Count Stephen in 860. Stephen had reluctantly completed his marriage to Count Raymond's daughter, but not consummated it, claiming that it would be incestuous, since he had previously slept with a relative of his bride. Hincmar argued, contrary to patristic tradition, that consummation was necessary to make a valid marriage, allowing a face-saving end to an unwanted alliance.

Repeated Carolingian enactments against both *raptus* and consanguineous marriage reflect an alliance between clerical reformers and parents at the expense of younger men. Well-born daughters, especially princesses, were a particular target for abductions and elopements; bans on *raptus* theoretically prevented an enterprising young man marrying a young woman to whom he could otherwise not aspire.[10] Similarly, in a world without written genealogies, older generations gained power from new rules that required complex tracing of kinship before a couple married. Even prohibitions on divorce can be seen partly as an attempt to enhance further the stability of alliances made by parents for strategic reasons; such divorces had probably been relatively infrequent among the upper classes even in the Merovingian period.

At a practical level, these reforms clearly encouraged exogamous marriage; known marriages to close kin are fewer among the Carolingian aristocracy than in earlier Frankish elites, although late Carolingian Catalonia was marked by unusual endogamy.

A scattering of marriage disputes recorded from the ninth century suggest that the principle of indissoluble marriage was also generally accepted, even while occasional strenuous attempts were made to end particular marriages. King Lothar II of Lotharingia spent more than ten years attempting to rid himself legally of his wife, Theutberga; the contrast with Charlemagne's straightforward repudiation of a Lombard bride almost a century earlier is revealing.[11]

While some women suffered from the changing rules on marriages, others took advantage of them, for example by exploiting the rule that a man could not marry (or stay married to) his child's godmother. Some women were more forceful: the Council of Metz in 893 recorded how a woman called Ava separated from her husband, with the support of her brother Folcrius and other relatives, and how Folcrius then castrated Ava's priest Folcardus when he protested at this.

The key role of powerful male kin is visible here; without such men, a wife or a sister was far more vulnerable. Lothar's marriage to Theutberga, for example, was clearly linked to his need for the support of her brother Hubert. Once Lothar and Hubert became estranged, Theutberga was accused of incest with her brother, and put on trial for her life. During the rebellion against Louis the Pious by his sons in 833–834, Gerberga, the sister of Louis's favorite, Bernard of Septimania, was executed by the rebels.[12]

Carolingian rulers and churchmen also made attempts to protect women from violence, or at least the domestic violence of a husband's private anger. There were repeated denunciations of wife-killing, and churchmen were prepared to offer sanctuary to wives claiming to be in fear of their lives. Although some authors have claimed that indissoluble marriage led to an increase in uxoricide, the evidence of queens suggests that Carolingian society was less dangerous for wives than before. The wives of Carolingian rulers faced legal accusations of adultery and threats of divorce, but, unlike Merovingian royal women, they were never murdered.[13]

HOUSEHOLD ECONOMIES:
PEASANTS AND NOBLES

The Carolingian economy was predominantly agricultural, and the main basis for wealth was landowning; the greatest Frankish aristocrats were already conspicuously wealthy by the seventh century, owning land in several different regions of the kingdom. Agricultural exploitation took several forms. Large landowners collected rent and dues from free or unfree tenants, but a new model, the bipartite estate, developed in the central regions between the Seine, Meuse, and Rhine in the late Merovingian period and gradually spread outwards. Lords of such estates directly exploited some land (the demesne) themselves, working it by imposing labor services on the dependent peasant tenures around this central demesne, in addition to their tenants' traditional payments in money or kind. In other areas, however, such as Catalonia and

Italy, the aristocracy was generally less wealthy, and a more substantial class of free peasant proprietors remained.

Polyptychs (estate inventories) provide important evidence on the lives of free and unfree tenants on estates owned by rulers and churches. They show us, for example, that both free and unfree peasants usually lived in nuclear families. These families were virilocal, with new wives moving to their husband's estates on marriage, and had on average four to six people in a household. Bilateral kinship ties are suggested by children named after kin on both sides of the family; unlike in the classical world, the unfree did not have distinctive "slave" names. The polyptychs also show those outside such nuclear families: women living on their own on small and marginal tenures, and both male and female domestic laborers (normally young, unmarried, and unfree or semi-free) employed in aristocratic households.

In contrast to these marginal groups, nuclear families enjoyed an enhanced status. Capitularies (royal ordinances) demanded that unfree families should not be split up and sold separately; the marriages of the unfree were seen as valid, not simply as *de facto* partnerships, as in the ancient world. Unfree households—a nuclear family living on their own patch of land—had been common since at least the late Roman period, but now they took on a new legal and ideological significance. The *servus* (unfree man) was granted some of the attributes of a domestic patriarch; masculine authority within a household was no longer a preserve of elite men. Marriage also offered the possibility of social mobility for unfree men, who were more likely than unfree women to marry a spouse of higher legal status.[14]

Within peasant households, some—though by no means all—labor was gendered, reinforcing the economic codependence of a peasant couple. A capitulary of Charlemagne prohibiting Sunday work refers to bans on men plowing, reaping, and hedging, among other duties, and to women sewing, laundering in public, or shearing sheep on the Sabbath. The dues demanded by landlords from female dependents might include specific quantities of spun wool or flax.[15]

The complexity of managing large estates is revealed by the capitulary *De villis*, a document probably attributable to Charlemagne, which gives orders for royal estates and shows the specific role played by the queen in their management, able to instruct and control estate officials in the same way her husband does. There is a parallel in the life of St Liutberga, who, as a girl, was visited in her convent by a widowed Saxon noblewoman, Gisla, who was traveling around her estates in order to manage them. Gisla persuaded Liutbirga to leave the convent and trained her to help in administering this property. Liutbirga in turn assisted Gisla's son Bernard in managing his lands after Gisla's death, and as a recluse, also instructed young girls sent to her in psalmody and textile work. One particular supervisory role for noblewomen was probably the management of *gynaecea* (workshops for female textile workers, most of them probably unfree[16]), which were common in monasteries and royal estates, but also existed on lay estates. Valerie Garver has suggested other forms of estate work that noblewomen may have supervised, from gardening and poultry-keeping to the production of candles and brewing.[17]

The influential view of Henri Pirenne in the 1930s that the Carolingian economy was based on agricultural self-sufficiency, and marked by an absence of towns, markets, or trade, has been overturned by more recent research.[18] Archaeological excavations in the northern part of the empire reveal agglomerations of peasant farmsteads, with individual household units consisting of a central longhouse (typically around 12 x 5 meters), along with smaller buildings such as storage pits and ovens, all surrounded by a ditch. There is often evidence of craft activities connected with both genders in such settlements (textile production, bone- and antler-working, iron-working) and of access to imported goods, such as pottery. In contrast, some Mediterranean areas, such as parts of Tuscany, have only very simple and scattered houses, with little sign of villages.

Elite homes, meanwhile, looked like simpler versions of Carolingian palaces, with stone churches and large stone halls. The hall built in the ninth century at Thier d'Olne in Englis (eastern Belgium), for example, measured 27 x 18 meters and was decorated with painted plaster. Noble households ate game, and pigs and cows slaughtered in their prime, in contrast to the mature cattle eaten by those in humbler settlements.[19] Such aristocratic consumption may have played a key role in generating Carolingian economic growth, by stimulating demand and encouraging more intensive agriculture.

Other forms of noble consumption are visible in model dowry documents specifying the value of the "gold and silver and jewels" to be given to the bride. The will of Eberhard of Friuli and his wife Gisela (the daughter of Louis the Pious) from c.863 also demonstrates the rich material culture available to the highest nobility. Their sons received gold-decorated belts, swords, and tunics, as well as armor; both sons and daughters were given silver drinking-cups, manuscripts, and liturgical equipment. Forms of conspicuous consumption were thus often gendered, but male display was equal to female display or even greater. The rejection of fine clothing was a virtue of both male and female saints in Carolingian hagiography, and moralists warned both religious men and women of the dangers of luxurious dress. In contrast, many Carolingian texts celebrated the rich costumes and feasting of both elite men and women.[20]

Elite women themselves were often responsible for the production and management of this rich material culture. Gift exchange played an important role in maintaining social bonds; a treatise on the organization of the palace, written by Hincmar in 882 and probably drawing on older material, describes the queen as particularly responsible for the management of the palace and the annual gifts to officials. Several Carolingian queens gave gifts of their own embroidery: the most famous example is the belt given to Bishop Witgar of Augsburg in the late ninth century by Emma, the wife of Louis the German, which still survives.[21] Hospitality, too, was an important form of gift exchange, and we have occasional references to queens organizing or presiding over feasting. It is likely that noblewomen, too, were involved in organizing such exchanges within their own households.

WOMEN'S ECONOMIC RESOURCES

Women at all social levels thus played important economic roles, whether contributing labor to a peasant holding or helping to manage extensive estates. To what extent did they benefit themselves as well as their families in doing so? One of the key determinants of women's domestic position has always been their independent access to wealth. Unfortunately, we rarely know about the full extent of individuals' wealth; instead we normally see only their donations to churches and monasteries. Legal texts on transfers of property not only show considerable regional variation, but do not necessarily correspond either to the model documents known as formularies or to actual practice. Many transactions, especially involving moveable goods, probably were never written down.

Despite these limitations, broad patterns and norms of resource-holding reveal something about women's economic situation. Two basic facts are clear. One was that in most regions women, including married women, could not only own their own property, but also control it; some monastic charters, for example, show donations made by married women without any reference to their husbands. The second key aspect was that women owned substantially less land than men. Statistics using charter evidence show women acting as principal donors in around 5–15 percent of cases. Women's landholding was probably also more vulnerable to challenge from other parties: they seem to have been involved in proportionally more property disputes than men.[22]

While a land market existed in some regions of the Carolingian empire, the main economic resources of laywomen came from noncommercial transactions, particularly inheritance, dowry, and gifts. Eberhard and Gisela's will, for example, grants lands held jointly by them to both sons and daughters. The statements of barbarian law codes about inheritance varied, but they tended to combine the basic principle of partibility (children sharing equally) with restrictions on daughters' inheritance. The exact interpretation of such laws is difficult, as is their relationship to practice; early medieval law was more a starting point for negotiations than a fixed framework.[23]

Assessing dowry practices is similarly difficult, with the further complication of unstable terminology; over the course of the early Middle Ages, *dos* changed from its classical Roman meaning of wealth given by the bride's parents (the "direct dowry") to the "indirect dowry" given by a husband to his wife either at her betrothal or after the marriage. There were also regional vernacular terms, which again were not necessarily consistent: the term *morgengabe*, for example, originally referred to the gift given by the husband to his wife on the day after the wedding ceremony, but in central Italy came to be used for all a husband's gifts to her.[24] References to a "third share" (*tertia*) for a widow did not necessarily apply to all of a husband's property, but could refer only to property acquired subsequent to the marriage. The continued existence of multiple dowry formulae shows the element of choice that was possible.

As with inheritance, "laws" on dowries should not be taken as definitive. Nor should we simply accept at face value the frequent statements by Carolingian churchmen that a dowry was a necessary condition for a valid marriage, although it is likely that it was an expected element of a marriage among the elite. A dowry did also form one way of distinguishing a wife from a concubine; the settling of disputes over *raptus* might involve endowing the woman concerned to confirm her status as a new wife.[25]

Legal stipulations and practices on dowry were complex partly because dowry was at the center of contradictory expectations about property and families. The main purpose of the dowry was to provide for the wife if she were widowed, but it could also be used as a resource for the immediate needs of the couple during their marriage. The lands given by a husband in indirect dowry were often deliberately chosen from outside his family patrimony (the long-established familial properties); instead the preference was for land that he had purchased or that his mother had inherited. The dowry, intended for the long-term support of the wife, was paradoxically therefore often the portion of the couple's land that was most easily sold or donated.

There was also the possibility of "giving without giving." Some land transfers were not immediate and firm; they might, for example, simply assign future claims to property after the husband's death. Some dowries provided for a fixed share of the husband's property (such as the *tertia* or *quarta*), and these might have conferred claims rather than actual transfers, especially since a man might inherit or buy additional property during a marriage. Yet the Abruzzo region of Italy had a market in "quarter portions," suggesting that such future claims had here been translated into immediate control of lands.

Moreover, wives and widows did not always control dowries and might have to bend to the conflicting interests of their families. Some formulae give a wife full control during her husband's lifetime, while others create a community of property; widows might be granted only the usufruct of their *dos* or alternatively full rights over it. On her husband's death, a widow's claims on property might meet counterclaims from her children and her deceased husband's other heirs.

Women's resources were further affected by new rules that allowed spousal cooperation in the land market. Roman law had prohibited gift-giving between spouses; but early medieval spouses, even though they had no automatic right to inherit from each other, could ensure provision for the survivor by grants made during their lifetime. For example, in 900, the nobleman Guy and his wife Imma donated land to St Martin's at Tours, receiving it back as a lifetime grant. Some of this land had been given jointly to Imma and her first husband, Ebolus, and she had obviously retained full rights to it on his death, rather than it passing to children or in-laws.

There were thus no clear "rules" for early medieval inheritances and dowries; the closer we look, the more exceptions and complications appear, even within regions. Specific decisions reflected the wealth and power of the particular families allying, the number and sex of children from a given marriage, and the age and sex of the surviving spouse. Yet relationships within the nuclear family, too, played an important role: one formula, possibly reflecting an actual case, shows a widowed father disputing with his children over the lands he had given their mother as dowry.[26] Despite the key social role of the conjugal family, harmony within it could not be taken for granted.

THE MORAL HOUSEHOLD

Although households have always played crucial social and economic roles, especially in the preindustrial world, they also came to play a particularly important ideological role in the Carolingian empire. As compared both to late antique attitudes, and those during the tenth- and eleventh-century Gregorian reforms, Carolingian ideology is notable for its more positive view of lay life, marriage, and women.

This ideology grew both from new relationships between monasteries and lay society and from the specific political programs of Carolingian rulers. Late antique ascetics, such as Jerome, emphasized marriage as a trap from which the pious, especially girls of marriageable age, should flee: married people were denigrated as inferior in order to encourage conversion to asceticism. Female virginity in particular was exalted. From the sixth century, however, western monasticism was marked by the increasing recruitment of oblates (child monks) rather than adult converts, and close ties to the outside world via the exchange of spiritual and material gifts. Religious writers thus developed a more positive view of those laypeople who supported monasteries via their donations and the oblation of their children, while remaining themselves in secular life. The oblation of boys also offered a ready supply of virginal male recruits, reducing the uniquely numinous quality of female virgins. With less of a pressing need to steer young women away from marriage and into the religious life, an older ideology hostile to married life now disappeared.[27]

Carolingian religious reformers also saw an important moral role for both laymen and laywoman, especially among the nobility. Rulers wanted all elite men, religious and secular, to cooperate politically. This encouraged an ideology celebrating the moral worth of both the professed religious and also the lay nobleman, whose distinctive characteristics were marriage and participation in warfare. The households of such noblemen ideologically paralleled the kingdom, places both of ordered hierarchy and a careful combination of love and obedience. A model sermon, probably from around 802, shows these expectations:

> Let wives be subject to husbands in all goodness and chastity, keeping themselves from fornication, sorcery and avarice...Let them nurture their sons in the fear of God...Let husbands love their wives and not say dishonorable [*inhonesta*] words to them, ruling their houses [*domus*] in goodness...Let sons love and honor their parents; let them not be disobedient to them.[28]

During the late eighth and early ninth centuries, several Carolingian moral manuals sought to instruct lay aristocrats in correct conduct. Although addressed only to men, they show the important joint moral role of aristocratic husbands and wives. Jonas of Orléans entitled one chapter of his treatise: "That married people should know they ought to exercise a pastoral ministry in their homes," while the books of Eberhard and Gisela show their household "as a place of stringent self-improvement, the moral and corrective drives of Charlemagne's *renovatio* [renewal] shrunk to the scale of a single family."[29]

The life of Liutbirga discussed above shows the particular role of mothers and other women as educators within such ordered households. Another example is given by the manual written in around 841 by the noblewoman Dhuoda for her teenage son William. Dhuoda did not see instructing her son in practical, moral, and spiritual matters as in any way unusual; all that was atypical was her need to do this in writing, since William was at Charles the Bald's court, effectively held as a hostage. Dhuoda's work also shows the wide intellectual resources (biblical, patristic, and even classical) to which a well-educated Carolingian laywoman could gain access.[30] A more institutional but still domestic role for women can be seen in the children, male as well as female, raised by nuns, such as Liutbirga herself or the author Paschasius Radbertus.

Within the moral noble household, wives were subordinate to their husbands: Dhuoda calls Bernard her *senior* (lord). Yet in turn they had authority over others: Carolingian patriarchy did not imply the universal subjugation of women to men, but a more complex set of hierarchies. This is clear in a passage in which Hincmar of Rheims comments on the tenth commandment:

> The law of the Almighty God divides all things into three kinds, which men are seen to have subject to them in earthly matters or to possess, since in the Ten Commandments, He defines it and says, "*Neither shalt thou desire his wife, nor his slave nor his slave girl, nor his ox, nor his sheep, nor his ass, nor any thing that is his.*" In these words, without doubt, the dignity of the wife should be considered in one way, the condition of slaves and slave girls in another, and in another the vileness of brute animals or unfeeling things.[31]

Here, a statement from an earlier patriarchal society is interpreted within the Carolingian world's own somewhat softened view of male superiority and the significance of unfreedom. Elite men still remained on top, but the exact valuation given to subordinate groups could be modified to reflect social realities and needs.

CONCLUSION: THE POLITICAL HOUSEHOLD

Einhard's letters reveal a network of patronage in which local dignitaries acted as brokers of royal favors and rulers in return could be assured continuing forms of military and other service. Local and transregional groups of practical kin and friends were held together far more by such transactions than abstract concepts of the *Sippe*. Women were disadvantaged in the maintenance and development of such networks by their relative lack of resources. Not only did they hold less land than men; apart from queens and abbesses, they were not allowed to hold office. A Romanized concept of secular office as held at royal command, rather than inherited, meant that there are few parallels to the "lordly women" visible in eleventh-century France.

Yet women were still sometimes able to influence events, as a number of letters to and from royal and noble women indicate. As discussed above, they shared in the important political task of arranging marriages. Women with court connections were keen to exploit these. Dhuoda saw herself as a courtier, mentioning how she had been married at the royal palace at Aachen; she hoped to use her manual to influence the young courtiers surrounding William, and possibly even Charles the Bald. A charter from 816 from the church of Freising refers to a benefice it gave to a woman called Mezcunde, because she had helped the church "when in the lord's court, she was an attendant of the king's daughter."[32] Women also played a prominent role in another important form of networking, that of the connection of the living and the dead. The task of preserving and transmitting family memories, and especially arranging intercessory prayer for those who had died, often seems to have been a particular responsibility of aristocratic women, both religious and lay.[33]

It is within this specific political and social context that Carolingian ideas of domesticity need to be considered. Christianity has repeatedly reinvented its ideology of families and households as social circumstances changed. As the late antique aristocracy adopted Christianity, they blended the Pauline idea of the holy household with an existing classical model of the senatorial couple. This glorified a cultured civilian husband, in harmonious concord with the Roman matron, who sat within a well-ordered household, symbolically busy with her wool-working. Such a lay civilian elite, however, largely disappeared in the post-Roman world, and new images of both men and women reflected this. Analysis of Merovingian grave goods suggests an emphasis on women's childbearing role rather than their domestic work; sources of the period normally mention only women who are queens or saints.[34]

Carolingian social ideology once again became centered on the household, but not necessarily the housewife. Frankish sources say relatively little about married women's domestic tasks: these had more economic importance than ideological significance. Several lives of Carolingian religious women, such as that of Liutbirga, stress the saint's devotion to textile work. In contrast, St Rictrudis, a rare married female saint, is not shown with such skills, and if Dhuoda did knit, sew, or weave for her family, she says nothing of this in her manual.

Instead, the ideological focus of Carolingian domesticity was on the role of women as moral exemplars and instructors, both in their own household and beyond. In a world where power was largely mediated through personal connections, Carolingian women's formal exclusion from most of the "public" sphere of office and law courts carried less significance than it later would. The married woman had an honored, if subordinate, place within wider social networks; it may have been the loss of these networks, as much as his own domestic comfort, that led Einhard to his bitter laments on the death of Imma.

Further Reading

Bougard, François, Laurent Feller, and Régine Le Jan, eds. *Dots et douaires dans le haut moyen âge*. Rome: Ecole français de Rome, 2002.

Garver, Valerie L. *Women and Aristocratic Culture in the Carolingian World*. Ithaca: Cornell University Press, 2009.

Goetz, Hans-Werner. *Frauen im frühen Mittelalter: Frauenbild und Frauenleben im Frankenreich*. Weimar: Böhlau, 1995.

Goetz, Hans-Werner, ed. *Weibliche Lebensgestaltung im frühen Mittelalter*. Cologne: Böhlau, 1991.

Heene, Katrien. *The Legacy of Paradise: Marriage, Motherhood, and Woman in Carolingian Edifying Literature*. Frankfurt am Main: Peter Lang, 1997.

Le Jan, Régine. *Famille et pouvoir dans le monde franc (VIIe–Xe siècle): Essai d'anthropologie sociale*. Paris: Publications de la Sorbonne, 1995.

Reynolds, Philip Lyndon. *Marriage in the Western Church: The Christianization of Marriage During the Patristic and Early Medieval Periods*. Leiden: Brill, 1994.

Stafford, Pauline. *Queens, Concubines, and Dowagers: The King's Wife in the Early Middle Ages*. Athens: University of Georgia Press, 1983.

Stone, Rachel. *Morality and Masculinity in the Carolingian Empire*. Cambridge: Cambridge University Press, 2011.

Toubert, Pierre. "The Carolingian Moment (Eighth–Tenth Century)," in André Burguière et al, eds, *A History of the Family, vol. 1: Distant Worlds, Ancient Worlds*. Cambridge: Polity Press, 1996, 379–406.

Wormald, Patrick and Janet L. Nelson, eds. *Lay Intellectuals in the Carolingian World*. Cambridge: Cambridge University Press, 2007.

Notes

1. Lupus, *Epistola* 3, ed. Ernst Dümmler, MGH Epp. 6 (Berlin: Weidmann, 1925), 10. On Imma and Einhard see Julia M. H. Smith, "Einhard: The Sinner and the Saints," *Transactions of the Royal Historical Society*, 6th ser., 13 (2003): 55–77; Matthew J. Innes, "Practices of Property in the Carolingian Empire," in Jennifer R. Davis and Michael McCormick, eds, *The Long Morning of Medieval Europe: New Directions in Early Medieval Studies* (Aldershot: Ashgate, 2008), 247–66 at 259–62. Imma's two letters are edited as Einhard, *Epistolae* 37–38, ed. K. Hampe, MGH Epp. 5 (Berlin: Weidmann, 1899), 128–29, and included in the translations of Einhard's letters by Paul Edward Dutton, *Carolingian Civilization: A Reader* (Peterborough, Ontario: Broadview, 1993), 283–310.

2. I have used the term unfree for the early medieval period rather than slave or serf: see Alice Rio, "Freedom and Unfreedom in Early Medieval Francia: The Evidence of the Legal Formulae," *Past & Present*, 193 (2006): 7–40.

3. Régine Le Jan, *Famille et pouvoir dans le monde franc (VIIe–Xe siècle): Essai d'anthropologie sociale* (Paris: Publications de la Sorbonne, 1995); Pauline Stafford, "*La mutation familiale*: A Suitable Case for Caution," in Joyce Hill and Mary Swan, eds, *The Community, the Family, and the Saint: Patterns of Power in Early Medieval Europe* (Turnhout: Brepols, 1998), 103–25; Constance Brittain Bouchard, *Those of My Blood: Constructing Noble Families in Medieval Francia* (Philadelphia: University of Pennsylvania Press, 2001).

4. Hucbald, *Vita sanctae Rictrudis*, c. 5 (PL 132, col. 834); Jonas of Orléans, *De institutione laicali* 2-12 (PL 106, col. 189); Hincmar, *De divortio Lotharii regis et Theutbergae reginae*, ed. Letha Böhringer, MGH Concilia 4, Supplementum 1 (Hanover: Hahn, 1992), *Responsio* 15, 205. I am currently preparing a translation of this text with Charles West for Manchester University Press; a draft is available at the *Collaborative Hincmar Project Blog*, <http://hincmar.blogspot.com>.
5. As Janet Nelson and Alice Rio discuss in "Women and Laws in Early Medieval Europe," in this volume, Chapter 8.
6. Stephen's marriage is discussed later in this section. Hincmar's letter on the marriage is edited as Hincmar, *Epistola* 136, ed. Ernst Perels, MGH Epp. 8 (Berlin: Weidmann, 1939), 88–107; a draft translation is available at the *Collaborative Hincmar Project Blog*, <http://hincmar.blogspot.com>. For Hincmar's views on marriage, see Jean Devisse, *Hincmar, Archevêque de Reims 845–882* (Geneva: Droz, 1975–76), vol. 1, 367–466; Rachel Stone, "'Bound From Either Side': The Limits of Power in Carolingian Marriage Disputes, 840–870," *Gender and History*, 19 (2007): 467–82.
7. Council of Ver 755, c. 15, ed. Alfred Boretius, MGH *Capitularia regum Francorum*, 1 (Hanover: Hahn, 1883), no. 14, 36. On Carolingian marriage and divorce see Philip Lyndon Reynolds, *Marriage in the Western Church: The Christianization of Marriage during the Patristic and Early Medieval Periods* (Leiden: Brill, 1994); Emmanuelle Santinelli, ed., *Répudiation, séparation, divorce dans l'Occident médiéval* (Valenciennes: Presses Universitaires de Valenciennes, 2007); Rachel Stone, *Morality and Masculinity in the Carolingian Empire* (Cambridge: Cambridge University Press, 2011), 247–78.
8. *De institutione laicali* 2–2 (col. 170–71). This is one of several hints within the sources that lack of virginity did not necessarily make a girl unmarriageable: see Stone, *Morality*, 283.
9. Georges Duby, *Medieval Marriage: Two Models from Twelfth-Century France*, trans. Elborg Forster (Baltimore: Johns Hopkins University Press, 1978).
10. Rachel Stone, "The Invention of a Theology of Abduction: Hincmar of Rheims on *Raptus*," *Journal of Ecclesiastical History*, 60 (2009): 433–48; Sylvie Joye, *La femme ravie: Le mariage par rapt dans les sociétés occidentales du haut Moyen Age* (Turnhout: Brepols, 2012).
11. Martin Aurell, *Les noces du comte: Mariage et pouvoir en Catalogne (785–1213)* (Paris: Publications de la Sorbonne, 1995); Stuart Airlie, "Private Bodies and the Body Politic in the Divorce Case of Lothar II," *Past & Present*, 161 (1998): 3–38; Karl Heidecker, *The Divorce of Lothar II: Christian Marriage and Political Power in the Carolingian World*, trans. Tanis M. Guest (Ithaca: Cornell University Press, 2010).
12. Council of Metz 893, c. 10, in Giovanni Domenico Mansi and Philippe Labbe, eds, *Sacrorum conciliorum: nova et amplissima collectio* (Graz: Akademische Druck- und Verlagsanstalt, 1960–1), vol. 18A, col. 80; *Annales Bertiniani*, ed. Georg Waitz, MGH SRG 5 (Hanover: Hahn, 1883), s.a. 834, 9.
13. Suzanne Fonay Wemple, *Women in Frankish Society: Marriage and the Cloister, 500–900* (Philadelphia: University of Pennsylvania Press, 1981), 104; Geneviève Bührer-Thierry, "La reine adultère," *Cahiers de civilisation medieval*, 35 (1992): 299–312; Nira Pancer, *Sans peur et sans vergogne: De l'honneur et des femmes aux premiers temps mérovingiens (VIe—VIIe siècles)* (Paris: Albin Michel, 2001), 286.
14. *Carolingian Polyptyques*, <http://www.le.ac.uk/hi/polyptyques/index.html>; Carl I. Hammer, "The Handmaid's Tale: Morganatic Relationships in Early-Mediaeval Bavaria," *Continuity and Change*, 10 (1995): 345–68; Jean-Pierre Devroey, "Men and Women in Early Medieval Serfdom: The Ninth-Century North Frankish Evidence," *Past & Present*,

166 (2000): 3–30; Isabelle Réal, *Vies de saints, vie de famille: Représentation et système de la parenté dans le Royaume mérovingien, 481–751, d'après les sources hagiographiques* (Turnhout: Brepols, 2001), 284–98.

15. *Admonitio generalis*, ed. Boretius, MGH Cap 1, no. 22, c. 81, 61, translated in P. D. King, *Charlemagne: Translated Sources* (Lambrigg, Kendal: P. D. King, 1987), 218–19; David Herlihy, *Opera Muliebria: Women and Work in Medieval Europe* (New York: McGraw-Hill, 1990), 25–48; Ludolf Kuchenbuch, "*Opus feminile*: Das Geschlechterverhältnis im Spiegel von Frauenarbeiten im früheren Mittelalter," in Hans-Werner Goetz, ed., *Weibliche Lebensgestaltung im frühen Mittelalter* (Cologne: Böhlau, 1991), 139–75.

16. As Sally McKee discusses in "Slavery," in this volume, Chapter 18.

17. *Capitulare de villis*, ed. Boretius, MGH Cap 1, no. 32, 83–91, translated in H. R. Loyn and John Percival, eds, *The Reign of Charlemagne: Documents on Carolingian Government and Administration* (London: Arnold, 1975), 64–73; *Das Leben der Liutbirg: Eine Quelle zur Geschichte der Sachsen in karolingischer Zeit*, ed. Ottokar Menzel (Leipzig: K.W. Hiersemann, 1937), trans. in Frederick S. Paxton, ed., *Anchoress and Abbess in Ninth-Century Saxony: The Lives of Liutbirga of Wendhausen and Hathumoda of Gandersheim* (Washington, DC: Catholic University of America Press, 2009); Valerie Garver, "Learned Women? Liutberga and the Instruction of Carolingian Women," in Patrick Wormald and Janet L. Nelson, eds, *Lay Intellectuals in the Carolingian World* (Cambridge: Cambridge University Press, 2007), 121–38; Valerie L. Garver, *Women and Aristocratic Culture in the Carolingian World* (Ithaca: Cornell University Press, 2009), 204–15.

18. Adriaan Verhulst, *The Carolingian Economy* (Cambridge: Cambridge University Press, 2002); Chris Wickham, *Framing the Early Middle Ages: Europe and the Mediterranean, 400–800* (Oxford: Oxford University Press, 2005); Chris Wickham, "Rethinking the Structure of the Early Medieval Economy," in Davis and McCormick, eds, *Long Morning*, 19–32.

19. *Un village au temps de Charlemagne: Moines et paysans de l'abbaye de Saint-Denis du VIIe siècle à l'An Mil* (Paris: Editions de la Réunion des musées nationaux, 1988); Christopher Loveluck, "Rural Settlement Hierarchy in the Age of Charlemagne," in Joanna Story, ed., *Charlemagne: Empire and Society* (Manchester: Manchester University Press, 2005), 230–58.

20. Marculfi Formulae 2–15, *Formulae Merowingici et Karolini aevi*, ed. Karl Zeumer, MGH Legum Sectio V (Hanover: Hahn, 1886), 85, translated by Alice Rio, *The Formularies of Angers and Marculf: Two Merovingian Legal Handbooks* (Liverpool: Liverpool University Press, 2008), 198–99. On Eberhard and Gisela, see Christina La Rocca and Luigi Provero, "The Dead and their Gifts: The Will of Eberhard, Count of Friuli, and his Wife Gisela, Daughter of Louis the Pious (863–864)," in Frans Theuws and Janet L. Nelson, eds, *Rituals of Power: From Late Antiquity to the Early Middle Ages* (Leiden: Brill, 2000), 225–80, Paul J. E. Kershaw, "Eberhard of Friuli, a Carolingian Lay Intellectual," in Wormald and Nelson, eds, *Lay Intellectuals*, 77–105. On the moral aspects of elite consumption, see Katrien Heene, *The Legacy of Paradise: Marriage, Motherhood and Woman in Carolingian Edifying Literature* (Frankfurt am Main: Peter Lang, 1997), 232–33; Garver, *Women and Aristocratic Culture*, 35–36, 40–51; Stone, *Morality*, 236–39.

21. Hincmar, *De ordine palatii*, ed. and trans. Thomas Gross and Rudolf Schieffer, MGH *Fontes iuris Germanici antiqui in usum scholarum separatim editi*, 3 (Hanover: Hahn, 1980), c. 22, 72–74. Text translated in Dutton, *Carolingian Civilization*, 485–99. On the Witgar belt, see Eric J. Goldberg, "*Regina nitens sanctissima Hemma*: Queen Emma (827–876),

Bishop Witgar of Augsburg, and the Witgar-Belt," in Björn Weiler and Simon MacLean, eds, *Representations of Power in Medieval Germany 800–1500* (Turnhout: Brepols, 2006), 57–95; Garver, *Women and Aristocratic Culture*, 223–27, 253–58.

22. David Herlihy, "Land, Family and Women in Continental Europe, 701–1200," *Traditio*, 18 (1962), 89–120; Wemple, *Women in Frankish Society*, 106–20; Lluis To Figueras, "Les femmes dans la société catalane des IXe–XIe siècles," in *La femme dans l'histoire et la société méridionales (IXe–XIXe s.)* (Montpellier: Fédération historique du Languedoc méditerranéen et du Roussillon, 1995), 51–65 at 55–58. For a specific example of how a woman might take precautions to ensure the carrying out of her decisions, see Janet L. Nelson, "The Wary Widow," in Wendy Davies and Paul Fouracre, eds, *Property and Power in the Early Middle Ages* (Cambridge: Cambridge University Press, 1995), 82–113.

23. See Nelson and Rio, "Women and Laws."

24. Laurent Feller, "'Morgengabe', dot, *tertia*: rapport introductif," in François Bougard, Laurent Feller, and Régine Le Jan, eds, *Dots et douaires dans le haut moyenâge* (Rome: Ecole française de Rome, 2002), 1–25 at 20–1.

25. Régine Le Jan-Hennebicque, "Aux origines du douaire médiéval (VIe–Xe siècles)," in Michel Parisse, ed., *Veuves et veuvage dans le Haut Moyen Age: Table ronde organisée à Göttingen par la Mission historique française en Allemagne* (Paris: Picard, 1993), 107–21; Bougard, Feller, and Le Jan, *Dots et douaires*; Philip L. Reynolds and John Witte, eds, *To Have and to Hold: Marrying and its Documentation in Western Christendom, 400–1600* (Cambridge: Cambridge University Press, 2007).

26. Pierre Gasnault, "Les actes privés de l'abbaye de Saint-Martin de Tours du VIIIe au XIIe siècle," *Bibliothèque de l'Ecole des chartes*, 112 (1954): 24–66, at pp. 55–60; Marculfi Formulae 2–9, 80–81. Translation: Rio, *Formularies of Angers and Marculf*, 192–93.

27. Rachel Stone, "Masculinity Without Conflict: Noblemen in Eighth- and Ninth-Century Francia," in John H. Arnold and Sean Brady, eds, *What Is Masculinity? Historical Dynamics from Antiquity to the Contemporary World* (Basingstoke: Palgrave, 2011), 76–93; Rachel Stone, "'In What Way Can Those Who Have Left The World Be Distinguished?' Masculinity and the Difference Between Carolingian Men," in Cordelia Beattie and Kirsten A. Fenton, eds, *Intersections of Gender, Religion and Ethnicity in the Middle Ages* (Basingstoke: Palgrave, 2011), 12–33; Albrecht Diem, "The Gender of the Religious: Wo/men and the Invention of Monasticism," in this volume, Chapter 27.

28. Missi cuiusdam admonito, ed. Boretius, MGH Cap. 1, no. 121, 240.

29. *De institutione laicali* 2–16 (col. 197); Kershaw, "Eberhard," 102.

30. Steven A. Stofferahn, "The Many Faces in Dhuoda's Mirror: The *Liber Manualis* and a Century of Scholarship," *Magistra*, 4 (1998): 89–134; Janet L. Nelson, "Dhuoda," in Wormald and Nelson, eds, *Lay Intellectuals*, 106–20.

31. *De divortio*, Responsio 5, 145.

32. Hans-Werner Goetz, *Frauen im frühen Mittelalter: Frauenbild und Frauenleben im Frankenreich* (Weimar: Böhlau, 1995), 361–92; Dhuoda, *Handbook for her Warrior Son: Liber Manualis*, ed. and trans. Marcelle Thiébaux, Cambridge Medieval Classics 8 (Cambridge: Cambridge University Press, 1998), Preface, 48; Theodor Bitterauf, ed., *Die Traditionen des Hochstifts Freising* (Munich: M. Rieger, 1905), no. 358, 306–307.

33. Elisabeth van Houts, *Memory and Gender in Medieval Europe, 900–1200* (Basingstoke: Macmillan, 1999); Matthew Innes, "Keeping it in the Family: Women and

Aristocratic Memory, 700–1200," in Elisabeth van Houts, ed., *Medieval Memories: Men, Women and the Past, 700–1300* (Harlow: Longman, 2001), 17–35; Garver, *Women and Aristocratic Culture*, 68–121.

34. Guy Halsall, "Female Status and Power in Early Merovingian Central Austrasia: The Burial Evidence," *Early Medieval Europe*, 5 (1996): 1–24; Julia M. H. Smith, "Did Women Have a Transformation of the Roman World?" *Gender and History*, 12 (2000): 552–71; Guy Halsall, "Gender and the End of Empire," *Journal of Medieval and Early Modern Studies*, 34 (2004): 17–39; Kate Cooper, *The Fall of the Roman Household* (Cambridge: Cambridge University Press, 2007).

CHAPTER 16

....

PUBLIC AND PRIVATE SPACE AND GENDER IN MEDIEVAL EUROPE

....

SARAH REES JONES

IN his popular work *On the Rule of Princes* (*c.*1280), Giles of Rome provided a clear account of the dependence of public on private space and of the role of both in the sustenance of families and cities.[1] According to Giles, a city started with a house in which children were born and raised; as households proliferated, a street was formed; this street (which he described as a "collection of children") eventually merged with other streets to create a neighborhood; and from many neighborhoods, a city grew. In this typical "Aristotelian" view, the home life of families and children was a constituent part of the city, but house, street, and city had different, mutually interdependent roles to play in both the reproduction of children and the reproduction of wealth. The house provided daily necessities, and the street enabled the buying and selling of more luxurious items. Indeed, he continued, if any house needed to buy and sell goods necessary to its daily survival then it was a corrupt house that survived not as "men that are at home, nor as citizens [should], but as pilgrims and wayfaring men."

This concept of space, with its cyclical movement of human bodies between household, street, and city, does not map on to a simple binary of private and public. However it does suggest that the reproduction of society, through the reproduction of children, was considered an essential function of the spaces of the city. This was an idea that was loaded with symbolic meaning (associating earthly regeneration with the incarnation of God as man), and even within Giles of Rome's text we can see that it implicitly supported the development of normative gender roles which were defined by the different kinds of labor considered appropriate to such reproduction. Women as the childbearers became associated with the production of "daily necessities" anchored in the home. Men, by contrast, were those who traveled abroad to organize and produce more sophisticated types of wealth. This essay will explore the degree to which the development of this binary of female and male contributed to the emergence of a binary of private and public space in social practice and in architecture by around 1500.

The built environment of medieval towns (and many villages as well) was designed and regulated throughout Europe and throughout the Middle Ages. The space of the street was never just market space (as Henri Pirenne once argued), nor was it solely for the display of political power (as suggested by Marc Boone). Spaces were also organized to reflect contemporary beliefs in the indivisible union between personal virtue and the common good; an idea that was the foundation of larger economic and political systems. By the later Middle Ages, the corporate common good was celebrated annually in processions, ritualized punishments, and street theater. Many ideals of hierarchy, social status, and religious orthodoxy informed these occasions, but so, too, did ideals about the proper behavior of women and men. In some times and places, moral anxieties about women's independent activity in the street restricted the movement of women of high status and stigmatized the necessary work of poorer women. But male identities, too, were shaped by concern for the common good. Men were, for example, pressured to join guilds and could be dishonored by trading independently in public market places. Space in medieval cities, towns and larger villages was economic, political, *and* highly gendered.

To date, relatively little work has brought together medieval space and gender: the two fields have been prolific but discrete. Over the past sixty years, we have made great advances in analyzing the developing physical forms of medieval towns and villages across Europe.[2] Historians and cartographers have cooperated in projects such as the European Historic Towns Atlas to map the essential public spaces and buildings of towns both large and small. In many places, painstakingly detailed research has reconstructed the history of individual streets, houses, and building plots, while archaeology has revolutionized our understanding of the development of both urban and rural settlement in the Middle Ages. This scholarship has greatly increased our empirical knowledge of medieval spaces, yet these studies have rarely considered gender, perhaps because archaeology and historical cartography have yielded little data that are explicitly gendered.[3]

New approaches, following the "postmodern turn," have generated a large body of scholarship focused on the social construction, symbolic value, and representation of space. Two excellent collections of essays edited by Sarah Kay and Miri Rubin in 1994, and by Virginia Cheiffo Raguin and Sarah Stanbury in 2005, have set out the exciting possibilities for applying these new approaches to the study of gender through a focus on the relationship between the body and lived space, particularly within the context of religious practice. Yet all too often gender still does not receive the attention it deserves in studies of secular space. A seminal article on archaeological approaches to the performance of space emphasized the diversity of personal perspectives, yet ignored gender.[4] In *Medieval Practices of Space* (2000), gender was highlighted as a particular concern, but was barely addressed in the essays, while in 2002 the journal issue, *The Productivity of Urban Space in Northern Europe*, addressed issues of gender more fully but still concluded that "a history of women's work and gender relations awaits location in a larger framework of spatial reorganization."

Work that has incorporated gender into studies of space has often focused overenthu-siastically on a seemingly normative divide between male public and female private. It has become commonplace to associate women, especially married women, with domes-tic space. Yet "public" and "private" have meant different things to different historians. Martha Howell has argued that a medieval concept of ungendered "common space" was replaced by a different idea of male "public space," which was separate from a private domestic sphere and oriented towards politics and commerce. Around 1100, she argues, there was no such thing as public space in medieval towns, either conceptually or actu-ally: streets were narrow and unregulated. By the sixteenth century, however, something like a public sphere was coming into being, and public spaces associated with politi-cal discourses and commercial institutions were controlled by men to the detriment of women. It was only with the emergence of this conception of a male public sphere that actual public spaces and buildings were created in towns. While I would suggest that the association between the street and public discourse was much older than Howell allows (that towns and villages were planned for political purposes before as well as after 1100), nevertheless her argument makes the important point that neither perception nor use of space was constant.

Most scholars use the term "public" much less precisely than Howell to describe spaces (such as the street) accessible to all, in contrast to private spaces such as homes or religious buildings to which access was restricted by personal or institutional owner-ship. Yet many medieval spaces did not easily fit into this neat division. The precincts of castles and palaces, urban walls and towers, courtrooms, and churches and synagogues were restricted to certain people on some occasions but made more widely available on others. The ritualized use and elaborate design of such spaces played a key role in the reproduction of public authority.[5] Only exceptionally did women appear in official per-formances in such public places, and often their role was either allegorical or reflected an extension of male authority (as in the coronation of queens).[6]

The assumption of public and private, male and female, as rigid binaries do not, there-fore, aid our understanding. Individual women and men moved not between two dis-crete categories of public and private space, but between different continuous modes of spatial experience (the intimate or personal, the private or domestic, and the public or political). In York in 1405, a local rebellion against the king fractured the political classes and divided families, and in its wake, intimate matters (such as declarations of chastity) were deployed to resolve conflicts that were both highly political and highly personal.[7] While the ideal of chastity was conventionally represented as a matter of inti-mate domestic virtue (particularly for young girls), it was here also used publicly as a common creed to facilitate public reconciliation with the king. If public and private were not discrete categories, neither were masculine and feminine. Caroline Walker Bynum in particular has emphasized the flexibility of medieval gendering.[8] A growing cultural interest in the passion of Christ's body, particularly after the development of the cult of Corpus Christi from 1246, was associated with exploration of the feminine char-acteristics of his bodily suffering: of how he nurtured, taught, and even mothered the world through his passion. This, she argues, created a productive ambiguity about the overlapping identities of men and women in which some women could, through control of their bodies, achieve positions of public spiritual authority.

The idea of private woman and public man was thus always somewhat attenuated and varied in practice. Debate surrounds three key issues: the degree to which women were restricted to a domestic sphere in practice; the extent to which cultural practices changed over time; and variations in practice geographically. All recognize that, as Thomas Kuehn and Anne Jacobson Schutte have put it, we need to resist the neat "equation of public space gendered as male space and private space gendered as female."[9]

PRIVATE PROPERTY

To what degree were women restricted in practice to a private sphere? The answer to this question varies by social status, time, and region, and suggests that the regulation and use of space was at least as important as the design of the space itself. Social status was extremely important. Propertied women were everywhere more likely to be chaperoned or restricted in their movements than were poorer women whose families relied on their labor in the fields and streets. Some of the most successful studies of the gendered use of space have focused on spaces clearly assigned to one sex, often in elite contexts such as palaces or religious houses. The pioneering work of Roberta Gilchrist in particular has argued that "increasing status seems to be accompanied by greater segregation of women's quarters."[10] At least from the thirteenth century, aristocratic and royal women were commonly provided with separate apartments in which they could hold court (and also deer parks in which they might hunt). Eleanor of Provence was given a separate suite of rooms in Windsor Castle after her marriage to the English king Henry III in 1236, while the "Plesaunce" in Greenwich was constructed after 1447 as a residence for Queen Margaret of Anjou. The spaces designed for nuns were also different from those of monks. Gilchrist suggests that nunneries were located in marginal sites and were provided with relatively modest material resources and facilities (such as latrines and kitchens). Whereas in male houses the most private and least accessible space was allocated to the chapter house (the site of monastic government), in nunneries it was the dormitory.

By the fifteenth century, discrete female establishments figured prominently in didactic and fictional literature for elite women.[11] Such works as *The Doctrine of the Heart* and the *Assembly of Ladies* established a genre of writing in which women were imagined as powerful political and spiritual figures through their control of their own bodies and by extension, their management of well-governed households, convents, anchorholds, or courts. This conflation of the well-governed body with the well-governed home was not uniquely feminine. The genre first emerged in the context of works for princes, such as the household ordinances promulgated by the King of Aragon in 1276.[12] Yet, as it developed, this genre did more than any other to associate virtuous women with domestic chores, and by the fifteenth century it had percolated down to works for bourgeois readers through such poems as "How the Goodwife Taught her Daughter" and the so-called "Ballad of the Tyrannical Husband."

These texts prescribed how women should behave; women's actual practices can be discerned through studies of the personal ownership and occupation of real estate. Local property law and custom varied greatly across Europe and across the Middle Ages. Yet, in general, women's control of space through the ownership of houses and land was much inferior to that of men, particularly with regard to long-term planning and large-scale activity. This inferiority became part of feminine gendered identity. As Latin Europe slowly moved from broad kinship systems to narrower ones that privileged patrilineal descent from fathers to sons, female property ownership weakened. Although we might imagine this as a cumulative process across the Middle Ages, some scholars have identified particular periods (during the fourth, eleventh, and fifteenth centuries) when the legal opportunities for women to own real estate were reduced particularly sharply.[13] These changes coincided with the growing importance of marriage as a mechanism for controlling wealth, and they affirmed the primacy of women's roles as wives and mothers. It was primarily through the provision of dowry (a marital gift from parents) and dower (the conjugal portion due to a widow) that women exercised some economic and political influence as owners of property. Noble, bourgeois, and peasant women played critical roles in augmenting the estates of their husbands (through their dowries), and in enabling the safe passage of property from one generation to the next (through legitimate procreation and careful stewardship of estates), but they were usually denied the right to control their assets independently. It was particularly hard for women to lease property, buy property, or even devise it to heirs. Nor could women as easily as men raise or advance large sums of credit secured on land. Without doubt, women worked alongside their families, and some were left in temporary charge of businesses. But both the laws of property and the use of property combined to reinforce female inferiority to men. Landownership, then, was one crucial aspect of the gendering of space in which binary divisions of male and female were extremely influential. Female control of wealth was often restricted primarily to the home in which they lived, and it was more likely, as a result, to be contained in furnishings and personal items than in titles to land or large sums of money. Howell goes so far as to suggest that the reduction of female property rights in the cities of the Low Countries in the later fifteenth century was replaced by an increasing emphasis on women's role in choosing and displaying such moveable goods: femininity became associated with shopping and the lavish decoration of interior domestic spaces.

DOMESTIC SPACES

Similar gendered distinctions can also be observed in poorer households. The much smaller homes of laborers and petty craft workers, typically containing between one and four rooms, certainly meant that most spaces were multifunctional, and women could not be segregated spatially from men. Nevertheless, Barbara Hanawalt and Jane Whittle have suggested that a gendered division of space existed in peasant communities, with the core of women's work centered in the home and men's work in the fields and forests. Jeremy Goldberg has disagreed. He argues that women worked outside in the fields (weeding and harvesting, for example) as much as in the home, and that they shared leisure spaces, such as the pub and the church, with the men of the village. In urban contexts, where artisan workshops were located inside the home, different types of labor (including childcare) were, he argues, shared by both sexes. This marital companionship meant that "gender was not an especially significant factor in the organization and use of space."[14]

However, even Goldberg concedes that domestic chores, such as cooking and laundering (and one might add childbearing and weaning), were regarded as women's work and that their spaces were gendered. Also, certain occupations maintained clear gendered divisions of labor: fishwives, spinsters, embroiderers, and candlemakers were typical occupations for women working alongside men in the victualing and clothing trades. Thus, even in small homes, labor and space were, to some degree, gendered.

The gendering of domestic space within the home was particularly significant in such areas as the hall and the bedchamber as Jennifer Deane discusses (ch. 17).[15] Both were multifunctional spaces, shared by men and women. In elite houses, the hall was a large central space, relatively easily accessed by visitors, and used to display status through feasting and lavish hospitality. The host typically sat on an elevated platform at the far end. The bedroom, by contrast, was an intimate and less accessible space. Strangers might gain access to it only by passing through other rooms where they were overseen by others. Nevertheless it was the bedchamber which developed great importance as the center of public and private power.[16] By the later fourteenth century King Charles V of France received his most favored political guests in the royal bedchamber in his royal palace at the Louvre in Paris. Queens maintained their own chambers, but although the public authority of both king and queen was enacted through their manipulation of intimate space, their political power was not equal. Among more ordinary people, the bedchamber also acquired a particular public significance in relation to marriage. In fifteenth-century London, the bedchamber was a common choice for the location of public betrothals, while in Florence, it was the place where a new husband's most luxurious possessions were shown to his wife prior to the consummation of their marriage. This rise of the symbolic use of the bedchamber, among all who could afford such chambers, conflated private and public life, while reinforcing the fundamentally different identities of men and women through their publicly sanctioned sexual roles. In one sense, the bedchamber was a special place shared by both sexes, but in another it was the key space in which the different functions assigned to men and women were most affirmed and reinforced.

Ordinary people were better able to emulate the living standards of their social superiors from the later thirteenth century, as Katherine French discusses (ch. 13). New building technologies and increased standards of living enabled both rural and urban dwellers to construct more complicated domestic structures with a larger number of rooms. By the fourteenth century, even small town houses supplemented the main room with an upper room, permitting the separation of sleeping from living quarters to some degree, while single-storey peasant longhouses used partitions to create separate rooms. Across Europe a diversification of domestic housing types is well attested among all social classes. However, some general patterns may be drawn. In both later medieval England and northern Castile, more houses included halls as central communal spaces and also more chambers such as parlors and bedchambers, while more specialist work spaces were arranged around internal courtyards, away from the street.[17] Urban homes tended to contain more elaborate and sophisticated possessions than did those of their "country cousins," but increasing commercialization promoted more imitation. All this meant that it became possible by the fifteenth century for more people to live in multi-roomed homes, where they were able to reproduce some aspects of the gendered division of space found in wealthier houses. These included not only bedchambers but other private rooms, in particular the countinghouse or office, in which men's identities were displayed in artifacts that spoke to their prowess as soldiers and businessmen. Richard Toky, a London grocer, kept in his countinghouse in 1391 a suit of armor along with the books and instruments of his trade.[18] The new masculine identities which these new spaces supported took some time to be accommodated to the prevalent gender ideals. Chaucer played with the moral dilemma of the home office in the *Shipman's Tale*: the wife cuckolds her husband, a merchant, in part because he prefers to spend long evenings alone upstairs in his countinghouse rather than in their bedchamber with her.

GENDERED CONDUCT OUTSIDE THE HOME

Perhaps the most pernicious consequence of the gendering of spatial conduct for all women was apparent in the treatment of the street and other public spaces. Working women, precisely because of their high visibility outside the home, were particularly at risk of being treated as vulgar, morally inferior, and incapable of virtue. Commercial activity by women was discouraged, especially work which had them walking the streets, such as the hawking of goods. Explicit laws were passed to this effect: in twelfth-century Seville market rules forbade women from sitting by the riverbank if men appeared, or from walking on the same path with them on festival days. The same laws discouraged barbers, who provided medical services, from treating women in private places where they could not be overseen, and they also instructed all traders to be cautious in dealing with women. In other places such norms were implicit in social practice, and over time they produced a distinctive male-orientated world of official public commerce. Judith Bennett has argued that in England men gradually took over responsibility for, and changed the commercial nature of, the production of ale, which had traditionally been an industry associated with women's work in the home.[19] Men everywhere dominated the trade guilds and companies that developed to protect the interests of manufacturers and traders.

The major concern expressed about women's activities, whether in formal or informal situations, was that they might enable unsanctioned or undesired sexual contact. Even priests were cautioned against the dangers of hearing women's confessions, and they were often suspected of breaching their oaths of celibacy as a result of this special access to women. In 1421 the priest of St Leonard's Church in Fasterlane (London) was even accused of using the confessional to procure women for prostitution.[20] Where space did not segregate the sexes, the promotion of marriage as a virtuous state, especially after the Fourth Lateran Council in 1215, encouraged self-policing in conduct whenever men and women mingled, whether in public or private spaces.

Women who could or would not accommodate to these rules, such as singlewomen or women working outside the home, were marginalized accordingly.[21] In late medieval England, singlewomen were discriminated against in the workforce and likely to find themselves compelled into service. Fraternities of maidens and wives that had once actively raised funds for their parish churches during Hocktide and other festivities gradually disappeared. Preferred activities for women outside the home were restricted to extensions of domestic duties, such as shopping, collecting water, washing clothes in rivers, or mourning in funeral processions. Even these activities were seen as opportunities for inappropriate contact with the opposite sex. In Perugia in 1342, double punishments were set for men who molested women at the public fountain, and in London it was expected that all such activities would be overseen by either the head of the household or his wife. While punishments for infringing these rules were imposed on men, women at large in public spaces risked loss of reputation. Negative comment was particularly directed at women who hawked goods in the open or went out to enjoy themselves, like "the noble and common women" of Padua who were described in 1318 as attending festivals "more to sin with men than for the remission of sins." These restrictions damaged the moral as well as economic status of women. The term "common," for example, was generally used in a positive register to describe public space (the common hall, the common market) or members of a public community (common citizens, the common clerk). But the term took on a decidedly negative meaning when applied to "common women" who were implicated in selling sexual services outside marriage and outside the home.[22] Such women might also find themselves constrained spatially to marginal locations or small, cheap rooms crowded into narrow courtyards or along busy streets, such as the "Baudesrents" in London in 1425, whose inhabitants threw their urine into the street for lack of private toilets.[23]

This tension between morally questionable public women and morally upright private women was played out for all to see in liturgical processions, political parades, and street theater.[24] The performers in these public ceremonials were usually men, although women might play a noted role as spectators, as in fifteenth-century Florence, where "women and girls" lined the processional route on the city's patronal feast day. In the York Corpus Christi play of the Flood, Noah's wife, an invented character, was portrayed as so overly attached to the attractions of the street (her gossips, friends, and family) that she is reluctant to join her husband in the ark (she eventually does). Reenactments of St George slaying the dragon (sometimes portrayed as a female dragon, as in Aarhus,

Denmark) and rescuing the princess were understood as a victory over the vices that threatened virtuous femininity and settled domestic life. And in 1392, Richard Maidstone's poetic description of Richard II's entry into London emphasized the king's marital virtue and steadfast loyalty to both wife and city.

It was certainly the case that such normative discourses and aspirational behaviors contrasted with other popular uses of space, though they are less well documented. We can uncover these in part by reading against prescriptive records: women were told not to wear extravagant clothing and not to dance singing and shouting down the streets late at night; men were told not to allow their horses to wander free in the streets where they might trample playing children; adolescent boys were told not to hang around on street corners or carry knives; farmers were told not to remove the cobbles from the king's highway; and housewives were told not to throw their household waste onto the streets. Some festivities and spaces came to seem suspicious. Bologna in 1288 banned its May Day festivities in which young women were crowned as May queens and paraded through the streets. Taverns in towns were particularly suspected as places of immoral conduct by men and women; in the countryside, the "greenwood" was a similar cause for concern. Clearly such behaviors were common and flourished into the post-medieval era, providing a source of entertainment for both rich and poor.[25]

Yet even private spaces were susceptible to public oversight. Householders reported neighbors who behaved badly; they accused them of creating a nuisance and reported on their sexual and marital relations.[26] And so it seems that normative conventions were winning the day, as indicated both by increasing evidence for their enforcement and by the increasingly negative rhetoric directed at transgressors. This ever-closer association between morality and the gendering of space had far-reaching implications. The association between poverty and immorality, for example, affected opportunities for employment, housing, and treatment in courts of law, and even opportunities for marriage and a settled domestic life.

The gendering of space, then, varied according to status and changed over time. It is less clear how consistently these practices spread across Europe or even within particular regions. Local practice could vary from one neighborhood to another in such matters as the design of houses, their furnishing, or the enforcement of rules of conduct. Katherine French has shown, for example, how the seating of women in English churches varied from one parish to another, even if women always occupied less central positions than the men.[27] Locality (and its particular regulation by individuals and institutions) provided an important context for personal experiences of gender and space.

Even within a common framework of normative discourse across Latin Christian Europe, it is often argued that northern or "continental" European women enjoyed greater personal freedom in their use of space than did women in "Mediterranean" regions. The larger age gap between young brides and older husbands in some Mediterranean cities may explain the tendency to establish official brothels whose "common women" were seen as protecting the honor of private daughters, wives, and widows by providing unmarried men with a necessary sexual outlet. These differences have been somewhat exaggerated. In Italy, for example, the major restrictions on female conduct applied predominantly to wealthy noble and mercantile families, and women in working families were often, as in the north, outside their homes. The precocious wealth and literacy of Italian elites may have brought their practices to our attention a bit too emphatically. However, in some Mediterranean communities, practices not commonly found in the north (such as slavery or bonded labor) and the greater presence of Jews and Muslims (as in a city like Seville) resulted in anxieties about marriage that crossed social, ethnic, and religious boundaries. This, in turn, resulted in a heightened attention to female conduct with men in public and private. Interfaith marriages between Christians, Jews, and Muslims were universally discouraged, and all three religions punished women in such relationships particularly severely.[28] These harsh attitudes to women as the carriers of religious identity were literally beaten onto women's bodies and mapped onto social space resulting in major changes to the built environment after the expulsion of Jews and Muslims in the fifteenth century.

THE DESIGN AND GOVERNMENT OF PUBLIC AND PRIVATE SPACE

The argument that normative rules did influence practice is akin to Giles of Rome's belief that architecture and town-planning could shape ethical conduct. Indeed, this classical principle had long been reflected in the design of public and private space. From at least the eighth century, the planning of lived space was associated with good government;[29] public or common spaces were not to be dark, cluttered, disorganized, and organic, but instead spacious and planned to fulfill a rational function. Towns were designed to support markets, encourage traffic, and draw the immigration through which towns actually grew (in contrast to the natural reproduction imagined by Giles of Rome). Two urban forms predominated. In the "street" form, a central broad main street, often widening into a large marketing area at one end, provided the spine of the settlement, with parallel back lanes running behind long narrow house plots on either side. Major streets could be up to 40 m wide and 2 km long, providing ample space for public associations of all kinds. Side and back streets were much narrower. In the "market" form, settlements were built on a rough grid of parallel and cross streets, often centered on a market square. In the modern city of Zagreb, both forms can be seen in the city's two original medieval nuclei built on neighboring hill tops: Kaptol, the cathedral city founded in 1094, follows the street form, while Gradec, the market town founded in the thirteenth century, is laid out as a regular grid around a central market. Modern observers have often failed to see this regularity in medieval plans because settlements were often continuously re-planned, and side streets were encroached upon and enclosed. Larger towns thus developed complex aggregate forms, and as a result, they now look less organized and more chaotic than the original planners often intended.

In all these settlements, public and private spaces were established in a strictly governed relationship to each other. Houseplots fronting onto streets were laid out with arithmetic regularity, measured in multiples of two human arm lengths (roughly 2 m) and extending backwards across an entire block. These private plots were also commonly divided into two or three informal zones. The zone nearest the street was used for retail and workshop spaces and also for smaller or low-status housing such as cottages and rented rooms. Larger houses of wealthier residents, such as successful artisans and merchants, were typically set back from the street in a middle zone of the plot. Behind the main house stretched gardens, yards, industrial premises or warehousing (if the length of the plot allowed). The very largest private mansions might extend over the full area of their original plot and incorporate neighboring plots as well, such as the extraordinary example of the Palazzo Strozzi in Florence begun in 1489. This zoning of private space produced and supported the social and gendered organization of domestic space. The middle zone of a plot offered wealthier urbanites some privacy from the life of the street and also allowed them the space to support gendered divisions within their accommodation. Those who lived in the zone nearest the street, however, lacked many essential amenities (such as privies, kitchens, or yards) and either depended on shared facilities (at first with the larger house behind, later through public charitable provision) or spent most of their time outside the home. For these people, space was too limited for it to be explicitly gendered. The very structure of planned towns created a clear social hierarchy, and these different urban spaces could be associated with different practices of domesticity and gendered behaviour.

Such regular planning of settlements as a deliberate political act, designed to promote "the peace of God," is well evidenced throughout Europe between the tenth and fourteenth centuries from the planning of new towns in countries bordering the Baltic and the North Sea around 1000, to the redevelopment of large cities such as Paris by Philip II or of Prague by Charles IV or even the planning of the small Scottish borough of Whithorn under David II in the mid-1300s. Such planning spread across Latin Christian Europe with the development of monasticism and the kingship. In Mediterranean Europe, Arabic, Turkish, and Islamic influences created different relationships between public and private space which privileged enclosed over open spaces, and resulted in narrower streets separating developments around internal courtyards. In cities such as Cordoba, Seville, and Toledo, centuries of progressive redevelopment and adaptation under rulers of different faiths created highly complex plans, with many contrasting features. In Toledo, the eventual expulsion of Jews and Muslims was followed, after 1492, by a deliberate refashioning of both streets and houses into forms associated with Latin Christianity: wide streets lined by narrow tenements with shops to the front and houses to the rear replaced narrow lanes and courtyards in the fifteenth and sixteenth centuries.[30] Just as opposition to interfaith relationships had been played out on women's bodies in medieval Spain, so the removal of those possibilities resulted in the creation of new public and private spaces, changing the physical contexts in which men and women interacted.

Throughout the Middle Ages the masculine nature of public space was most expressed in the development of hierarchical, male-dominated local public government institutions—such as town councils or manorial courts—which took responsibility for the maintenance of streets and the protection of towns. They paved streets, built and repaired bridges and hospitals, provided clean supplies of public water, and created rules for social conduct in public places. By the twelfth century, urban corporations also began to construct public buildings such as tollbooths, town halls, guild halls, and market halls. In Tallinn, a new town hall and large market square were established around 1248 when the town was chartered by King Eric IV of Denmark. In the later fourteenth and fifteenth centuries, these public buildings (rather like houses) became much more elaborate, adding private rooms for different court and council meetings. At the same time, many larger villages and small towns acquired similar purpose-built meeting rooms for the first time. Buildings and law reinforced each other, and the decoration of public buildings was another medium through which messages about gender could be conveyed. Ambrogio Lorenzetti's frescoes in the *palazzo publico* in Siena (1338) dwelt on matters of gender in the well-governed city. Peace and prosperity were championed by the feminized allegorical figure of security and symbolically represented by the chaste and beautiful women of the well-governed town; both were contrasted with women's exposure to rape under tyrannical and fractious regimes. Background scenes show men at work in a variety of trades and crafts, but women do not work—they are allegorical or sexual. Public buildings provided a new kind of public space, but as places of government, they were more explicitly and institutionally male than were the public streets, markets, and fields.

These male governors eventually shaped not only their proud town halls, but also the very nature of public and private and the interrelationship between them. By the fourteenth century in London, the height and size of windows overlooking neighboring properties was regulated. As a result windows overlooking neighboring properties were restricted, while upper windows overlooking the street became larger and more decorative. As the liminal space where public street intersected with private interior, such windows also became sites for the promotion of the family's honor and public status through the display of coats of arms and other devices displaying patrilineal descents and matrimonial alliances, and they were popularly understood as a safe vantage point from which "pretty young girls" could enjoy the spectacles of street life.[31] Windows and doors became fantasy sites for the interaction of public and private, and they were incorporated into gendered rituals of courtship and marriage. Chaucer's Criseyde first caught sight of Troilus (and recognized her love for him) as he processed along the main street beneath her window, while in stories of betrothals from the London and York church courts, couples tell of exchanging love tokens by windows and doors, and even undertaking betrothals.[32] In Jan Van Eyck's portrait of the Arnolfini marriage (1434), the betrothed couple stand close to the window, the man near to the window (and the overshoes he will wear to walk the streets); the woman stands near the bed where the marriage will be consummated.

CONCLUSION

For Giles of Rome, the well-managed home and the well-managed street were essential for society, and his view illustrates well the ways in which medieval Europeans grew to understand the relationship between private and public space to be intimately associated with gendered and social conduct. The use of space was as important as space itself. Outside of elite institutions, it was hard to distinguish male and female space through architecture alone, and as a result, the regulation of personal conduct in otherwise ungendered spaces was crucial in the very construction of gender. The gendering of space was subtle. It varied over time and place, and depended on the acceptance of normative codes of conduct.

Medieval ideas of gender did not imagine only a simple binary of masculine males and feminine females, and in the spatial organization of society, the elevation of the ideal of marriage as a normative discourse affected men as much as it did women. However, over the course of the Middle Ages, a heightened focus on the procreative functions of civilized society (evident for example in the importance placed on bedchambers) reinforced ideas of a "natural" binary difference. This was evident in the increasing discrimination against women as landowners, and in the evolving designs of houses which increasingly emphasized the importance of private space as a means of developing and publicly asserting moral and social capital. New ideas and practices of gender were layered over older spatial environments, which had once worked to differentiate social status more than gender. For those who could not afford grand homes, their less gendered use of space came to be increasingly impugned as unchaste and immoral. By 1375, "*commune as the strete*" was a euphemism for "promiscuous" for men as well as women.[33]

FURTHER READING

Arnade, Peter J., Martha C. Howell, and Walter Simons, eds. Special issue of *Journal of Interdisciplinary History* 32/4 (*The Productivity of Urban Space in Northern Europe*). Spring 2002.

Beattie, Cordelia, Anna Maslakovic, and Sarah Rees Jones, eds. *The Medieval Household in Christian Europe, c. 850–1550: Managing Power, Wealth, and the Body*. Turnhout: Brepols, 2003.

Boone, Marc and Peter Stabel, eds. *Shaping Urban Identity in Medieval Europe*. Louvain-Apeldoorn: Garant, 2000.

Erler, Mary C. and Maryanne Kowaleski, eds. *Gendering the Master Narrative: Women and Power*. Ithaca: Cornell University Press, 2003.

Gilchrist, Roberta. *Gender and Material Culture: The Archaeology of Religious Women*. London; New York: Routledge, 1994.

Hanawalt, Barbara A. *The Wealth of Wives: Women, Law, and Economy in Late Medieval London*. Oxford; New York: Oxford University Press, 2007.

Hanawalt, Barbara A. and Michael Kobialka, eds. *Medieval Practices of Space*. Minneapolis: University of Minnesota Press, 2000.

Howell, Martha C. *The Marriage Exchange: Property, Social Place, and Gender in Cities of the Low Countries, 1300–1550*. Chicago: University of Chicago Press, 1998.

Karras, Ruth Mazo. *Common Women: Prostitution and Sexuality in Medieval England*. New York: Oxford University Press, 1996.

Kay, Sarah and Miri Rubin, eds. *Framing Medieval Bodies*. Manchester; New York: Manchester University Press, 1994.

Kowaleski, Maryanne and P. J. P. Goldberg, eds. *Medieval Domesticity: Home, Housing and Household in Medieval England*. Cambridge; New York: Cambridge University Press, 2008, 14–36.

McSheffrey, Shannon. *Marriage, Sex, and Civic Culture in Late Medieval London*. Philadelphia: University of Pennsylvania Press, 2006.

Raguin, Virginia Chieffo and Sarah Stanbury, eds. *Women's Space: Patronage, Place, and Gender in the Medieval Church*. Albany, NY: State University of New York Press, 2005.

Riddy, Felicity. "Mother Knows Best: Reading Social Change in a Courtesy Text," *Speculum*, 71(1) (1996): 66–86.

NOTES

1. Giles of Rome, *The Governance of Kings and Princes: John Trevisa's Middle English Translation of the* De regimine principum *of Aegidius Romanus*, ed. David C. Fowler, Charles F. Briggs, and Paul G. Remley (New York: Garland, 1997), 164–68.
2. European Historic Towns Atlas, <http://www.ucd.ie/twnatlas/catalog.html>, accessed March 29, 2011.
3. Nigel Baker and Richard Holt, *Urban Growth and the Medieval Church: Gloucester and Worcester* (Aldershot: Ashgate, 2004); Derek Keene, *Survey of Medieval Winchester*, 2 vols (Oxford: Clarendon Press; New York: Oxford University Press, 1985); Derek Keene and Vanessa Harding, *Historical Gazetteer of London Before the Great Fire, Part 1, Cheapside* (Cambridge; Alexandria, Va.: Chadwyck-Healey, 1987). At the International Congress of Medieval Archaeology (Paris, 2007) almost every paper discussed space but few mentioned gender. One exception was a paper about women artisans by Gitte Hansen, "Women's Oldest Profession? Evidence from Twelfth-Century Bergen, Norway," <http://medieval-europe-paris-2007.univ-paris1.fr/G.Hansen.pdf>, accessed March 29, 2011.
4. David Austin, "Private and Public: An Archaeological Consideration of Things," in Harry Kühnel et al., eds, *Die Vielfalt der Dinge: Neue Wege zur Analyse mittelalterlicher Sachkultur* (Wien: Verlag der Österreichischen Akademie der Wissenschaften), 163–205.
5. John M. Steane, *The Archaeology of Power: England and Northern Europe, AD 800–1600* (London: Tempus, 2001).
6. Joanna Laynesmith, *The Last Medieval Queens: English Queenship 1445–1503* (Oxford; New York: Oxford University Press, 2004).
7. Sarah Rees Jones and Felicity Riddy, "The Bolton Hours of York: Female Domestic Piety and the Public Sphere," in Anneke Mulder-Bakke and Jocelyn Wogan-Browne, eds, *Household, Women, and Christianities in Late Antiquity and the Middle Ages* (Turnhout: Brepols, 2006), 215–54.
8. Caroline Walker Bynum, *Fragmentation and Redemption: Essays on Gender and the Human Body in Medieval Religion* (New York: Zone Books; Cambridge, Mass.: Distributed by MIT Press, 1991).

9. Thomas Kuehn and Anne Jacobson Schutte, "Introduction," in Anne Jacobson Schutte, Thomas Kuehn, and Silvana Seidel Menchi, eds, *Time, Space, and Women's Lives in Early Modern Europe* (Kirksville, Mo.: Truman State University Press, 2001), xv.

10. Roberta Gilchrist, "Medieval Bodies in the Material World: Gender, Stigma, and the Body," in Sarah Kay and Miri Rubin, eds, *Framing Medieval Bodies* (Manchester; New York: Manchester University Press, 1994), 50–51, 53.

11. See essays in Cordelia Beattie, Anna Maslakovic, and Sarah Rees Jones, eds, *The Medieval Household in Christian Europe, c. 850–1550: Managing Power, Wealth, and the Body* (Turnhout: Brepols, 2003).

12. Marta Van Landingham, *Transforming the State: King, Court and Political Culture in the Realms of Aragon (1213–1387)* (Leiden: Brill, 2002).

13. Kate Cooper, *The Fall of the Roman Household* (Cambridge: Cambridge University Press, 2007); Jo Ann McNamara and Suzanne Wemple, "The Power of Women Through the Family in Medieval Europe, 500–1100," in Mary C. Erler and Maryanne Kowaleski, eds, *Women and Power in the Middle Ages* (Athens: University of Georgia Press, 1988), 83–101; Thomas Kuehn, *Law, Family, and Women: Towards a Legal Anthropology of Renaissance Italy* (Chicago: University of Chicago Press, 1994); Martha C. Howell, *The Marriage Exchange: Property, Social Place, and Gender in Cities of the Low Countries, 1300–1550* (Chicago: University of Chicago Press, 1998); essays by Jo Ann McNamara and Sarah Rees Jones in Mary C. Erler and Maryanne Kowaleski (eds), *Gendering the Master Narrative: Women and Power* (Ithaca: Cornell University Press, 2003); Barbara A. Hanawalt, *The Wealth of Wives: Women, Law, and Economy in Late Medieval London* (Oxford; New York: Oxford University Press, 2007).

14. Barbara A. Hanawalt, *The Ties that Bound: Peasant Families in Medieval England* (New York: Oxford University Press, 1986), chapter 9; Jane Whittle, "Housewives and Servants in Rural England, 1440–1650: Evidence of Women's Work from Probate Documents," *Transactions of the Royal Historical Society*, 6th ser., 15 (2005): 63–64, 51–75; P. J. P. Goldberg, "Space and Gender in the Later Medieval English House," *Viator*, 42 (2) (2011): 205–32 at 229.

15. Maryanne Kowaleski and P. J. P. Goldberg, eds, *Medieval Domesticity: Home, Housing and Household in Medieval England* (Cambridge; New York: Cambridge University Press, 2008); Jane Grenville, *Medieval Housing* (London; Washington: Leicester University Press, 1997); John Schofield, *Medieval London Houses* (New Haven, Conn: Yale University Press, 1994).

16. Mary Whiteley, "Public and Private Space in Royal and Princely Chateaux in Late Medieval France," in Annie Renoux, ed., *Palais royaux et princiers au Moyen Age* (Le Mans: Publications de l'Université du Maine, 1996), 71–75; A. Richardson, "Gender and Space in English Royal Palaces c. 1160–c. 1547: A Study in Access Analysis and Imagery," *Medieval Archaeology*, 47 (2003): 131–65; Laynesmith, *Last Medieval Queens*, 112–18, 138; Shannon McSheffrey, "Place, Space, and Situation: Public and Private in the Making of Marriage in Late-Medieval London," *Speculum*, 79 (2004): 960–90; Richard A. Goldthwaite, *Wealth and the Demand for Art in Italy, 1300–1600* (Baltimore: Johns Hopkins University Press), 228–29.

17. Beattie et al., eds, *Medieval Household*; Matthew Johnson, *Housing Culture: Traditional Architecture in an English Landscape* (London: UCL Press, 1993); and see references in note 15 above.

18. A. H. Thomas, ed., *Calendar of Select Pleas and Memoranda of the City of London, 1381–1412* (Cambridge: Cambridge University Press, 1932), 212–13.

19. Maryanne Kowaleski, ed., *Medieval Towns: A Reader* (Toronto: Broad View Press, 2006), 118–20; Judith M. Bennett, *Ale, Beer, and Brewsters: Women's Work in a Changing World, 1300–1600* (New York: Oxford University Press, 1996).

20. A. H. Thomas, ed., *Calendar of Plea and Memoranda Rolls Preserved Among the Archives of the Corporation of the City of London at the Guildhall, A.D. 1413–1437* (Cambridge: Cambridge University Press, 1943), 127.
21. Judith M. Bennett, "Compulsory Service in Later Medieval England," *Past & Present, 209* (1) (2010): 7–51; Katherine French, "'To Free Them from Binding': Women in the Late Medieval English Parish," *The Journal of Interdisciplinary History, 27* (3) (1997): 387–412; Trevor Dean, *The Towns of Italy in the Later Middle Ages* (Manchester; New York: Manchester University Press), 55; Shannon McSheffrey, *Love and Marriage in Late Medieval London* (Kalamazoo: Western Michigan University, 1995), 19.
22. Lyndal Roper, "'The Common Man', 'The Common Good', 'Common Women': Gender and Meaning in the German Reformation Commune," *Social History, 12* (1) (1987): 1–21; Kowaleski, *Medieval Towns*, 120.
23. Thomas, ed., *Calendar of Pleas, 1413–1437*, 127.
24. Dean, *Towns of Italy*, 74; Richard Beadle and Pam King, *The York Mystery Plays: A Selection in Modern Spelling* (Oxford: Clarendon Press, 1984), 21–32; Alexander Barclay, *The Life of St. George*, ed. William Nelson (London: Oxford University Press for the Early English Text Society, 1960); Richard Maidstone, *Concordia (The Reconciliation of Richard II with London)*, trans. A. G. Rigg, ed. David R. Carlson (Kalamazoo: Medieval Institute Publications for the Consortium for the Teaching of the Middle Ages, 2003).
25. Dean, *Towns of Italy*, 201; Frank Rexroth, *Deviance and Power in Late Medieval London* (Cambridge; New York: Cambridge University Press, 2007).
26. Thomas, ed., *Calendar of Pleas, 1413–1437*, 1115–159; Shannon McSheffrey, *Marriage, Sex, and Civic Culture in Late Medieval London* (Philadelphia: University of Pennsylvania Press, 2006).
27. Katherine L. French, "The Seat Under Our Lady: Gender and Seating in Late Medieval English Parish Churches," in Virginia Chieffo Raguin and Sarah Stanbury, eds, *Women's Space: Patronage, Place, and Gender in the Medieval Church* (Albany, NY: State University of New York Press, 2005).
28. P. J. P. Goldberg, "Pigs and Prostitutes: Streetwalking in Comparative Perspective," in Katherine J. Lewis, Noël James Menuge, and Kim M. Phillips, eds, *Young Medieval Women* (New York: St. Martin's Press, 1999); David Nirenburg, "Love Between Muslim and Jew in Medieval Spain: A Triangular Affair," in Harvey J. Hames, ed., *Jews, Muslims, and Christians In and Around the Crown of Aragon: Essays in Honour of Professor Elena Lourie* (Leiden; Boston: Brill, 2004).
29. Robert Bartlett, *The Making of Europe: Conquest, Colonization and Cultural Change, 950–1350* (London: Penguin, 1993); Keith D. Lilley, *City and Cosmos: The Medieval World in Urban Form* (London: Reaktion Books, 2009); Sarah Rees Jones, "Building Domesticity in the City: English Urban Housing before the Black Death," in Kowaleski and Goldberg, eds, *Medieval Domesticity*.
30. Jean Passini, "Algunos apectos del espacio domestic medieval en la ciudad de Toledo," in Beatriz Arízaga Bolumburo and Jesús Á. Solórzano Telechea, eds, *El espacio urbano en la Europa medieval* (Logrono: Gobierno de La Rioja, 2006), 245–72.
31. Maidstone, *Concordia*, lines 255–60.
32. Geoffrey Chaucer, *Troilus and Criseyde*, Book 2, lines 1114–239.
33. Gower, *Confessio Amantis*, 5: 2497.

CHAPTER 17

....

PIOUS DOMESTICITIES

....

JENNIFER KOLPACOFF DEANE

OF all the ideas shaping medieval imaginations, none was more potent than that of the home and its associations with heart and hearth, bread and bedchamber, warmth and welcome. Culturally speaking, home was safe haven. Scripture itself was laced with the language of kinship, from fatherhood, motherhood, and the yearning for children to miraculous births, eating and feeding, sexual pleasures, sibling rivalries, marital struggles, and so on.[1] If the church, and by extension medieval churches, were Christ's house, the inverse was also true, for domestic space was a vivid manifestation of God's church. By 1500, home was no longer simply a place in which to recite prayers and to live well, for home was host to the spirit and hospitality within it was highly gendered. The intersections of home and holiness created cultural patterns integral to medieval history, colored by broad economic, social, and political shifts, but also uniquely stitched by local communities and individual lives.

Scholarship in medieval religion and gender studies exploded during the 1980s and 1990s, as have more recent histories of the household, spatial studies, and explorations of lay sanctity. This chapter integrates the two, focusing both on medieval peoples' pious practices at home, and the ways in which gender inflected their beliefs and behaviors. The essay thus unfolds along three axes: the social (who is engaging in the practice, and are they individuals, small groups, or large communities?), the temporal (how long does a particular fusion of the sacred and domestic endure in time?), and the material (how tangible or visible are these practices, and with what consequences?).

In the following, I use the term "household" in a socio-spatial sense, as the place in which personal social bonds are forged daily by coresidents. I employ "home" in an affective sense, referring to the emotional meanings medieval people assigned to the household. These are imperfect distinctions, since households were certainly economic and political institutions as well, but it will nonetheless help us trace the particular ways in which medieval people infused piety into their routine domestic lives. As noted by scholars across disciplines in recent years, the very distinctions between "secular" and "sacral," or "public" and "private" so fundamental to modern historiography are insufficient for mapping the premodern European past. Medieval households were never entirely secular, nor were they private in the modern sense of the word.[2] As such, they were particularly interesting sites of contact among lay believers, Christian authority, and religious ritual.

HOME AND THE HOLY

Home served as an essential unit in societies across the ancient world. Babies were conceived and born at home, food was gathered and shared, mothers and fathers variously labored, and men and women died at home. Jesus's prescription "Peace be to this house" (Matt. 10:12) suggested that hospitable dwellings were placed under God's protection, and the early Christian writer Tertullian (160–220 CE) referred to the routine practice of making the sign of the cross as a blessing upon entering a fellow believer's home. By the early Middle Ages, a new range of pious at-home behaviors had become possible. Women were to teach their children the basic prayers and creeds of the faith, a practice that continued to the end of the Middle Ages and beyond. Joan of Arc reported in 1431, for example, that she had learned the Our Father, Hail Mary, and Nicene Creed from, and only from, her mother. Children learned from their parents to revere local holy people, and families celebrated feast days with their neighbors. Laypeople could perform blessings, petition saints in childbirth or crisis, and sometimes even briefly wield sacramental authority: parents could baptize a dying infant, for example, and if no priest were available, any Christian could hear a dying person's confession.

Domestic spirituality, however, bore particular significance for women. Scripture and patristic writings admonished women to withdraw from the public eye, passages whose gender assumptions would reverberate across the Middle Ages. As the house churches of the late antique era were replaced by purpose-built churches managed by clerics, female religious influence become more limited. Yet home remained a potent staging point for devotion across the Middle Ages. After all, Jesus had also directed his followers to meld piety and domesticity: "when you pray, go into your room, close the door and pray to your Father, who is unseen. Then your Father, who sees what is done in secret, will reward you" (Matt. 6:5–6). His message spoke to women as well as men.[3]

Inspired by the apostolic model of humility combined with activity, medieval people re-envisioned the convergence of gendered household service and wholesome spirituality. The New Testament figure of Martha serves as a litmus test for gendered notions of pious domesticity, resonating quietly but with surprising consistency across the medieval centuries. As described in the books of Luke and John, Martha was sister to Lazarus (whom Jesus raised from the dead) and to Mary of Bethany. Luke relates Jesus's visit as follows:

> Now as they went on their way, he entered a certain village, where a woman named Martha welcomed him into her home. She had a sister named Mary, who sat at the Lord's feet and listened to what he was saying. But Martha was distracted by her

many tasks; so she came to him and asked, 'Lord, do you not care that my sister has left me to do all the work by myself? Tell her then to help me.' But the Lord answered her, 'Martha, Martha, you are worried and distracted by many things; there is need of only one thing. Mary has chosen the better part, which will not be taken away from her.' (Luke 10:38–42).

Not all medieval Christians agreed that Mary had the better part, however. Many, such as St Ambrose (c.340–397), defended Martha's active hospitality ("Martha should not be rebuked in her good service"), arguing that such devout busy-ness was ultimately rooted in contemplation. Over a century later, the Merovingian saint Radegund (c.520–586) was described by her biographer as "a new Martha," tired from her labors in the kitchen but tireless in her efforts at Christian service. The theologian Peter Abelard (1079–1142) similarly emphasized the spiritual features of Martha's activity, referring to her food preparation as internally restoring Jesus while Mary's oils only soothed him externally.

In the later Middle Ages, the relationship among Martha, Mary, and Jesus continued to hold powerful symbolic value. An early fifteenth-century translation of Augustine's *City of God*, for example, illustrates the active and contemplative lives with an image of the two sisters encountering the resurrected Christ at their home (Figure 17.1). On the left, a haloed Mary kneels on the grass before the wounded Jesus. To the right is Martha, also haloed but larger in scale than Mary; contained within the walls of the house and yet also standing on the same grass, she kneads circles of dough reminiscent

FIGURE 17.1 Jesus with Mary and Martha (c.1410–1412). Koninklijke Bibliotheek, Den Haag, Museum Meermanno Westreenianum, 10 A 12, fol. 191r.

of Eucharist wafers and enacts the practical life. The "holy hostess," as Martha was described by Jacob de Voragine in the popular thirteenth-century *Golden Legend*, represented a positive symbol of domestic piety that was being quietly enacted in medieval homes across Europe.

INDIVIDUAL PIETIES

Drawing from cultural, scriptural, and local traditions, medieval people infused domestic spaces with an array of spiritual meanings. Some brought the sacred into the household, placing a saint's bone, sacred objects, or other relic in the house. Since such holy things both represented and enacted the miraculous, their presence transformed the house into a site of joining between heaven and earth. Medieval people also developed other ways of exploring the spiritual facets of home, and it is these intensely personal, impermanent expressions of pious domesticity that concern us here.

Despite, or perhaps because of, the intimacy associated with sleeping and sexuality, bedrooms were an especially meaningful place for personal prayer. All Christians were exhorted to recite the Lord's Prayer, and the practice of seeking the divine while kneeling in the bedroom was a common means of conflating the mundane and divine. Domestic blessings from across medieval Europe suggest that by the later Middle Ages, such rituals had moved from emphasizing physical protection of the household to understanding home as a place to seek salvation. A fifteenth-century blessing of a wedding bed, for example, recasts the piece of furniture as a site of union, both human and divine.[4] The reverse could also be true: for women and men attempting to live chastely within marriage, such as the thirteenth-century Mary of Oignies and her husband, the bedroom became a meaningful site because of carnal behavior *not* enacted.

Medieval laypeople also recognized spiritual opportunities within the prosaic realm of the kitchen, and the spiritual interpretation of feminine food practices and Eucharistic devotion has been particularly well explored.[5] Beyond the ascetic rigors of an extraordinary few, however, simpler opportunities abounded in the visceral daily routines of gathering, chopping, heating, and supervising necessary to nourish those in residence. Women's labor facilitated meatless Fridays, for example, and Lenten observances. Cooking for celebrations or charity, setting the table in hospitality, and serving in humility were also daily tasks that, as discussed below, melded with gendered Christian aspirations.

In the early fourteenth century, the lay visionary Douceline and her father fed and served the poor whom their brother and son, the Franciscan Hugh of Digne, "for the love of God…was accustomed to looking after in his home."[6] In another pious play on food, an early fifteenth-century devotional guide directed an English layman to "make a cross on the table out of five bread-crumbs; but do not let anyone see this, except your wife."[7] Manliness precluded that others witness his humble practice, suitable only for the eyes of a devoted housewife.

Sanctified crumbs might have appeared differently, however, to the wife who ground the grain, kneaded the dough, patiently waited for it to rise before tending the fire that transformed it into wholesome bread, and then cleaned the table (crumbs and all) after the meal. Sources are of course scarce, as women's daily routines and tasks were not typically documented until clergy or other literate people inserted them into a hagiographical or inquisitorial record. Future studies of domestic devotion might fruitfully draw insight from anthropological and sociological models or from comparative analysis with premodern Jewish or Muslim households.

Pious domestic settings were not limited to those of laity, for clergy of all levels and appointments also inhabited households. The routines of the all-male clerical households of cathedral canons and others are beyond the scope of this chapter, but the domestic arrangements of parish priests were also locations where gender, piety, and the home intersected.[8] As one consequence of the eleventh-century Gregorian reform (c.1050–1080), which sought to enforce clerical celibacy and to eliminate lay interference in the church, priests' homes represented potential sites of sexual sin, where wives, mistresses, and even female housekeepers were thought to pose a spiritual threat. Despite reformers' warnings, sexual relationships certainly occurred between clergy and local women after the Gregorian reforms. However, clerical testaments and other sources suggest that long-standing platonic bonds also developed between priests and the women who tended to them at home. Thus women who baked communion bread or prepared meals for priests variously combined spiritual meaning with domestic labor. Such women were often beguines whose domestic service to clergy was a conscious blend of spiritual service and physical work, and whose efforts were frequently acknowledged in bequests.

Domestic piety was also encouraged in literature such as the household guide known as the *Ménagier de Paris* (c.1393), written by an experienced elderly man for his new fifteen-year-old wife. Before setting out recipes, management directives, and reminders to wifely obedience, the author first addressed spiritual concerns. In fact, the very first section of the book directs the young wife's attention to prayer in the bedroom: "at the hour you hear the Matins ringing, you praise and hail our Lord with some greeting or prayer before you fall back to sleep." Additional prayers in both Latin and French are included for beginning and ending the day, fusing spiritual humility with domestic authority. The wife's work for home and family in turn inspires her husband, who will then "desire to see [her] again as the poor hermits, penitents, and abstinent monks desire to see the face of Jesus Christ."[9] The good wife was first and foremost a pious working wife, and her orderly, prayerful household a testament to the Christian family.

The mid-thirteenth century devotional text *The Doctrine of the Heart* similarly depicts the relevance of household labor to piety. Originally written in Latin by the Dominican Hugh of St Cher (d.1263), it exhorts readers through insistently domestic imagery. Written in the wake of the Fourth Lateran Council's requirement of annual confession in 1215, for example, the text points to the internal cleansing necessary for the devoted soul's hospitable reception of Christ in the Eucharist: "the interior must be cleaned with a broom of confession, which sweeps sin through the door of the mouth."[10]

The necessity of cleaning as a prerequisite to hospitality was certainly familiar to lay, particularly female, audiences. Despite the text's decidedly clerical cast, the fact that late medieval vernacular translations appeared in English, Dutch, French, German, Italian, and Spanish illustrates a popular appreciation of these domestic devotional themes.

Late medieval clerics also wrote texts known as the Christian day group (*les journées chrétiennes*), ostensibly to help married women weave spiritual significance into daily work. In one fifteenth-century guide for young women, for example, the Carthusian author instructs the female reader to rise early and pray, and immediately thereafter to "turn your attention to the housework: wake up the servants, light the fire, sweep, start breakfast, dress the children, make the beds, do the laundry, take care of the chickens, etc., while meditating on the celestial hierarchies, the reasons for the damnation of Lucifer, the creation of the world in six days, etc."[11] Although such texts again clearly represent clerical attitudes, one may not presume an easy dichotomy of idealized clerical theories imposed on a passive female audience. Like so many other popular devotional writings, Christian day texts were likely in part a response to the existing practices and spiritual desires of the women who read them.

Penitents and devoted laypeople of various sorts who lived in family dwellings also infused domestic spaces with spiritual meaning. Frequently associated with the Dominicans or Franciscans, such women and men lived at home either alone, with birth family, or with a spouse and children. Enacting their own regimen of daily devotions, penitents often engaged in daily cycles of prayers modeled after monastic hours.[12] Similarly, Douceline of Digne is reported to have "divided the night into three parts: she would spend the greatest part in reading and in prayer; next she would rest; then she would get up and say her matins."[13] Attested to in a variety of disparate source material, such practices suggest a fundamental symmetry between the rhythms of lay household piety and those of monasteries in the later Middle Ages.

Just as monks were expected obediently to labor within their own communities, housework as a manifestation of humility and service was also a staple in the lives of penitent women. The biographer of the young Italian Dominican penitent Osanna of Mantua, for example, noted her undertaking such household drudgery as cleaning, removing garbage, and making beds.[14] Since Osanna came from an elite family, the uncomplaining assumption of such labors was especially to her spiritual credit. Holy women from more humble backgrounds also worked in domestic service as a means of self-support. Examples include the penitent Sybillina of Pavia, who worked as a servant before going blind, or "Dame Agnes the Beguine," specifically tasked in the *Menagier* with serving, instructing, and teaching the wife "wise and mature conduct."[15] We can guess, but cannot know, the extent to which penitents invested economically necessary work with pious meaning. Yet the remarkable late medieval popularity of saintly laywomen suggests that holy domesticity resonated even more broadly than has been recognized.

Not all individual recastings of domestic activity remained internalized, however. In some cases, household residents insistently assigned new meaning to a particular room, as did the young Florentine widow Umiliana de'Cerchi who, pressured by family to enter the social world of marriage and reproduction, conceptually transformed her bedroom into a site for ascetic devotion. "What did she lack of the monastic life, who lived in such continuous silence and observance? What less did she possess than the holy hermits, who found herself a solitude in the midst of the city and converted her bedchamber into a prison cell?" queried a clerical admirer.[16] The imaginative consecration of a bedroom as a cell was more than mere semantics, for it allowed her to negotiate for herself a life of dedicated virginity in the world.

The Italian Dominican penitent and mystic Catherine of Siena (1347–1380) also urged others to construct imaginative pious spaces, to "build a cell inside your mind, from which you can never flee." According to her biographer Raymond of Capua, Catherine achieved perfection "not in a monastery or in the desert, but in the house of her own father, without anyone's help, and even while being hindered by all her family members."[17] Although her family fought Catherine's reinterpretation of domestic space, they ultimately yielded to her conviction. Her physical cell retained its specifically holy meaning within the household, a material manifestation of her interior cell of the mind.

Catherine's perception of spiritual value in the domestic prompted her to appreciate St Martha's role as well: in a 1374 letter, she referred to the saint as "the loving hostess who welcomed Christ the God-Man, and now she is living in the Father's house, that is, in the very being of God."[18] For Catherine, as for so many others, the active and contemplative were complementary rather than opposed. The evident appeal of such a model to ordinary pious laywomen, whether within or beyond penitent circles, merits further consideration.

Communal Recastings

Another striking manifestation of vibrant lay piety in the years following the eleventh century was the repurposing of existing domestic space for new communities. In contrast to the fleeting individual reimaginings discussed earlier, these households were characterized by self-conscious membership and some degree of recognition by neighbors, supporters, local authorities, or opponents. And although such communal recastings were only semi-permanent (depending as they did upon residents' commitment to a particular pious lifestyle), they served profound socio-spiritual needs within local circles for decades and even centuries.

Physical structures themselves were not usually altered during the transformation of a domestic structure to a space of consciously enacted piety, but the change was nonetheless significant and often distinctly visible. And because contemporaries interacted with such communities, whether in supportive or critical ways, the textual record is much richer than for the individual practices explored above. Yet the development of devotional practices among beguines, tertiaries, Sisters and Brothers of the Common Life, and various "houses of poverty" have to date been studied in isolation from one another, separated by doctrine, region, or historiography, and with particular attention to whether a movement was orthodox or heretical. A horizontal view across such diverse gatherings reveals, however, that all emerged from a shared cultural wellspring of religious behaviors, household practices, and gendered notions of authority and community. As a member of a mid-fifteenth-century sisterhood in Deventer put it, the ideal was a woman "glued" to a house out of love for God and her chosen way of life.[19]

From the early thirteenth century on, for example, significant numbers of single-women drew together in a phenomenal array of communities across medieval Europe. Labels are tricky to apply to these communities, since such women were variously known across different regions and languages as *beguines, bizzoche, pinzochere,* and *beatas,* or simply as sisters, virgins, or poor women. Some housed women from established and often well-educated families, while others were particularly designated for poor or indigent women. More often membership was mixed, the beguine house's social strata mirroring local society. Such diversity precludes easy generalization, as does the tremendous variation in size, organization, and patronage of these houses. What lay religious women's houses did share across time and space, however, was a surprisingly consistent blend of social and spiritual expectations—a broadly agreed-upon blend of Martha and Mary.

Subject like all Christians to the spiritual authority of a local parish priest, these women's daily lives were shaped by specific regulations written by donors, clergy, secular officials, and sometimes the mistress or a resident-donor of the house. Within these groupings, residents developed locally observed patterns and behaviors, following in their donated homes a regimen of daily devotions akin to those of sisters in orders. Beguine house rules from the fourteenth and early fifteenth centuries, for example, often call for the women to say twenty-eight Our Fathers at matins, fourteen at vespers, and seven at all the other hours; literate women were to recite more, illiterate women according to their abilities.

Just as central medieval abbots responsible for running monastic households were assigned "the part of Martha," beguines also found the sister of Bethany a particularly useful and evocative model.[20] The mistresses of many communities in Germany and the Low Countries were called the "Martha," for example; and in a direct parallel to monastic roles, women in such homes frequently took on specific roles with titles such as "kitchen Martha," "cellar Martha," and "door Martha." Like their penitential sisters living at home, those in lay religious communities integrated prayer with daily tasks, locating spiritual opportunities in such activities as cleaning, cooking, and care for sick and suffering bodies.

Rooted in traditional concepts of household and faith, these communities provided secure environments for singlewomen and widows at all stages of life to express devotion to God through a standard set of gendered skills. The twelfth-century beguine leader Yvette of Huy, for example, "learned from the book of experience" and applied her earlier knowledge of household management to shaping her community and serving that "heavenly housewife," the Virgin Mary.[21] More than a social safety valve for singlewomen, these households were broadly understood as occupying a specifically Christian niche: that of the chaste, devout, humble, yet skilled female servant.

By the later thirteenth century, however, clerical elites increasingly worried that behind positive models of Christian apostolic ideals evoked by these communities lurked the specter of wickedness. They worried particularly about mobile women whose uncloistered lives breached boundaries (it was thought) between unregulated and regulated, domestic and sacral. Largely hostile decrees from the Council of Vienne were circulated in 1317 in an attempt to clarify proper attitudes toward lay religious communities and to distinguish the pious from the heretical. Over the course of the following century, popes repeatedly urged bishops and local authorities on the one hand to uproot heretical beguines (thought to be preaching "Free Spirit" mysticism or otherwise challenging clerical authority), but on the other to ensure that they left devout ones in peace. The resulting confusion underscores the extent to which women's pious domesticities were in fact very difficult to distinguish in terms of actual practice. All drew upon traditionally gendered scriptural models in their fusion of spiritual and household roles, and it was the evident similarities to monastic life that prompted the most concern. Thus were charges of hypocrisy among the most common criticisms leveled at lay religious women.

Picking up on the affinity of pious laywomen for Martha, some opponents cynically depicted them as alternating between spiritual and sexual indulgence. In the scathing words of the thirteenth-century poet Rutebeuf, "Last year she wept, now she prays, next year she'll take a husband. Now she is Martha, then she is Mary; now she is chaste, then she gets a husband."[22] Suggesting palpable discomfort with the overlap between bedroom, kitchen, gender, and piety, the scornful phrase reflects mounting concern that lay Christians—especially women—should not be blending the spheres of sacred and secular, or blurring the all-important distinctions in women's status and mobility.

Men also formed and participated in new pious communities, in both approved and persecuted traditions. These have been comparatively neglected in the literature, perhaps in part because they were substantially fewer. Medieval men had many more spiritual options available to them, and concerns about female mobility did not, of course, apply. Although "beghards" are often referred to as the masculine equivalent of beguines, they far more frequently moved in itinerant groups, and there is little evidence that they regarded themselves as participating in a shared spiritual life with the women. However, more work remains to be done on beghards in settled communities (such as those in the Low Countries or Germany), the extent to which various groups modeled themselves more specifically on monastic models, and how they understood their relationship to piety and domesticity.

Other types of brotherhoods and sisterhoods are nevertheless well documented, although primarily from inquisitorial sources. Forged by bonds of spiritual kinship as well as family ties, same-sex pious communities associated with heretical movements dotted the late medieval landscape. Occitanian Good Women (known in later inquisitorial and historiographical circles as Cathars), for example, provided vital spiritual guidance in communal households; so too did members of the Poor of Lyon and Lombardy (known by their critics as Waldensians) and beguins (lay southern adherents of the Spiritual Franciscans). Many of these communities were acknowledged by local contemporaries as dedicated to a pious lifestyle. Women in particular took in female relatives or girls from other families, instructing, nurturing, supervising, catechizing, serving as socio-spiritual role models, and running the household as a vital link within broader communal networks. Inquisitors and supporters alike frequently referred to such communities as "houses of poverty," underscoring (albeit for quite different purposes) the members' claims to spiritual aspiration.

Mixed-sex family households within heretical networks also came under increased suspicion in the later Middle Ages. Parents, children, and other relations among Wycliffites or Lollards, beguins, Good Men and Women, and various groups of Poor across Europe established meeting places, traded books and other texts, preached, discussed God over meals and beer, and invited like-minded people into their homes. In particular, these pious domesticities allowed men critical of clerical hierarchies to assume an authoritative preacher's voice. Masters and other charismatic leaders traveled extensively between far-flung pockets of support to preach secretly and minister; along the way, they could expect warm welcome, food, and shelter in the homes of the faithful, where women would (like Martha and Mary) both serve and worship.

Sometimes a single home took on communal spiritual meaning, as in the house churches of the Poor or domestic meeting places of beguins. Women cleaned and prepared these spaces, provided refreshments to guests, and likely prayed quietly before or after meetings. Moreover, as members struggled to protect themselves and their friends against mounting inquisitorial pressure, family homes harbored those in flight and even contained the relics—flesh and bone—of their executed comrades.[23] As John Arnold notes (Chapter 31), feminine roles among such households thus echoed rather than escaped the traditional: women provided hospitality and household care, they read and listened, prayed, instructed children and girls, and formed networks of relationship. Whether considered righteous or suspect by onlookers, these homes were broadly recognizable by a substantial overlap of domestic and spiritual, no part of which was in itself explicitly unusual. In another example, and despite Lollard rejection of much late medieval devotion associated with women, the faith of the accused fifteenth-century Englishwoman Margery Baxter was "not automatically but elaborately and consciously, a *domestic* faith, with the house, family, and the maintenance of both at the center of her religious values, a yardstick to take the measure of doctrine."[24] Although anticlerical sentiment among dissenting communities was certainly responsible for locating an even greater devotional emphasis in the household than in other Christian homes, that difference is arguably more a matter of degree than of kind.

MATERIAL TRANSFORMATIONS

The expanding commercial economy of the central and later Middle Ages also prompted Christians to channel wealth into material expressions of piety and civic pride. Ranging from anchorholds and court beguinages to private chapels in wealthy homes, these later medieval buildings testify to changing conceptions of space, spirituality, and gendered authority. In recent decades, scholars have generated an extensive body of work on anchorholds, cells or rooms attached to churches in which sanctified individuals led enclosed lives. Although there were male anchorites, the practice was especially popular among women whose voluntary embrace of immobility paradoxically earned them broad cultural influence.

Key architectural features of these centrally located sacred spaces underscored their fusion of holiness and household, for access was carefully regulated. At the same time, however, the anchorite was clearly acknowledged as a living person inhabiting a domestic space, one sometimes even cared for by servants. Indeed, the paradox of anchorholds as pious domestic spaces is that the theoretically walled-off structure necessarily contained multiple access points, including windows, grills, and doors through which conversation, food, supplies, and waste could flow. Local supporters donated the clothing and candles necessary for an anchorite's everyday needs, and figures such as Julian of Norwich (1342–1416) became the touchstone of a kind of living sanctity at the heart of her city.

An illustration from a fifteenth-century English manuscript (Figure 17.2) depicts the enclosure of an anchoress by a bishop. In typical medieval artistic style, the bishop's authority is signified by his comparatively large size as he and the symbols of his office loom over the anchorhold and tiny woman inside. Rituals for enclosing an anchorite emphasized the transition as a kind of living death to the world; one, for example, required carrying an anchorite across the threshold in a coffin and reading prayers from the Office of the Dead as she was bricked into the space. Yet the manuscript illuminator chose to include a relatively large window in order to demonstrate visually the woman within and to reinforce her paradoxically accessible inaccessibility.

The popular thirteenth-century English *Guide for Anchorites* similarly suggests that anchorhold walls were far more porous than theoretical models would have it. Therein, an anchorite was presumed to retain domestic and therefore "housewifely" duties even as her space was the home of God from which the anchoress—"Godes chamber" herself—would never depart. A sample prayer from the guide spells out the organic relationship between home, spirit, and domestic labor: "My spirit is a narrow house for You where You come to it; may it be enlarged by You. It is broken down; rebuild it."[25] Thus employing concrete domestic terms, the anchoress is urged to ask God to enlarge, clean, and restore the heart of her house, even as she provides that same revitalizing spiritual function for the urban community around her.

Anchorholds were not the only type of purpose-built pious home. Donors to lay religious women's communities, for example, sometimes had buildings specifically constructed to contain their communities. For example, the numerous court beguinages of the southern Low Countries were entirely novel structures built specifically to purpose. Financed by donations and gifts, these specific projects of pious domesticity were also periodically supported by ecclesiastical and royal coffers. In 1251, papal legate and author of the *Doctrine of the Heart*, Hugh of St Cher, issued an indulgence to pay for a chapel and house for beguines in Aarschot. And in 1264, the

FIGURE 17.2   Bishop enclosing an anchoress (early fifteenth century). Corpus Christi College, Cambridge, Parker Library MS CCC79 fol. 96r. Thanks to the Master and Fellows of Corpus Christi College, Cambridge, for permission to reprint.

French king Louis IX established a new community of Parisian beguines in a structure built precisely for that purpose.

If anchorholds and communal buildings represent the pious domestic made public, medieval people also explored ways to reverse this equation by bringing church into the home. Wealthy families purchased and had consecrated portable altars that imparted the visible sacrality of ecclesiastical spaces to familiar domestic places. A late fourteenth-century Italian widow, for example, bequeathed to a local church "my decorated altar that I have at home."[26] Such individuals also dedicated large amounts of money to constructing entire household chapels within the home. Financed by familial wealth and usually overseen by fathers and husbands, such chapels enhanced a household's prestige and emphasized its members' elevated piety. Even as the new constructions were often requested and used by women, however, priestly authority was necessary to enshrine formally the sacred within the profane. Conversely, unauthorized or excessively popular altars could in turn draw inquisitorial scrutiny.

INDIVIDUAL TRANSCENDENCE

The late medieval construction of material pious spaces within the home was intriguingly paralleled by a move in the opposite direction: transcendence of the mundane domestic world through a range of practices including reading, contemplation, and mystical experience. Although these devotions might suggest *escape from* the walls of home, closer reading suggests a clear contemporary sense that the devotional experience specifically *emerges from* those homey images and spaces.

A large body of work on late medieval devotional images has treated the use of domestic imagery in pieces such as the Flemish artist Rogier van der Weyden's *The Magdalen Reading* (mid-fifteenth century), which depicts Mary Magdalen engrossed in pious reading amidst the household activity around her. Reading was indeed central to the pious at-home devotion of people with access to education and books. As literacy rates soared with the growth of schools and commercial culture during the later Middle Ages, the production and circulation of devotional books followed suit. Particularly popular were texts such as Jacob of Voragine's *Golden Legend* and Thomas à Kempis's *Imitation of Christ*, only two of the many contemporary vernacular guides to salvation. Hundreds of humble prayer books copied by monastic or lay hands survive from the era, containing idiosyncratic collections of psalms, saint's lives, prophecies, and other devotional material, as well as illustrations and marginalia whose inexpert execution should make them no less interesting or revealing to modern readers.

Especially popular among elite circles in northern Europe, however, were lavishly illustrated Books of Hours that put key devotional texts, calendars, and a quasi-monastic prayer cycle in the hands of the laity. Wealthy families would often commission a beautifully illuminated Book of Hours, complete with prayers, psalms, and holy images of God's creation and the saints, particularly the Virgin Mary. Volumes such as the well-known fourteenth-century *Hours of Jeanne d'Evreux*, the early fifteenth-century *Très Riches Heures* of Duke Jean de Berry, and many less expensive versions became a staple of wealthier Christian households. Such gorgeous books embodied the filaments of piety, text, and place, particularly for female devotional readers.[27]

Richly complex works such as the late fifteenth-century Book of Hours depicting Mary of Burgundy at prayer (Figure 17.3), for example, reveal some of the astonishing connections between late medieval spiritual imagination and space. Seated by a window in an oratory, Mary reads her Book of Hours in silence. Surrounded by symbolic items representing purity, faithfulness, and devotion, she slowly moves her finger down the text, the very picture of domestic devotion. This is no ordinary household space, however, for the window opens into a light-filled Gothic church in what Andrea Pearson terms a "women's viewing community"; at the altar, the Virgin and Christ child receive adoration from kneeled figures on the left, including a woman holding a devotional book who has been variously identified as Margaret of York and Mary of Burgundy herself.[28] Familiar walls are dissolved through Mary's serene contemplation, space and time itself unfolded in a moment of transcendence. In Mary of Burgundy's meditation, respite from the quotidian cares and pressures of the household awaits precisely

FIGURE 17.3 Mary of Burgundy at prayer in a Flemish book of hours (*c.*1475). Österreichische Nationalbibliothek, Vienna, Austria, Cod 1857, fol. 14v.

through devotion mediated by book, familial relationships, architecture, and objects of the home.

Books of Hours and other devotional texts also circulated among networks of readers whose complexity refuses easy division by geography, gender, or social status. When a lay-person read a book and then passed it to others, he or she extended the framework of pious domesticity beyond material walls.[29] The *Guide for Anchorites* serves as only one example of many, in which the author clearly intended the precise space of the anchorhold to reach imaginatively into others' homes, and thus to potentially create an anchorite within each reader. Such complex contemplative practices defy traditional historiographical categories of "public" and "private," "enclosed" and "unenclosed," or "secular" and "sacral."

Mental pilgrimage provides another vivid illustration of transcendent spiritual practices at home. An accessible alternative to physical pilgrimage, it allowed late medieval Christians to participate in a spiritual journey that imaginatively breached household walls. Pilgrimage was a particularly appealing, traditional, and yet difficult practice, and it is thus not surprising that devout Christians sought non-corporeal ways around it, including by proxy (sending an object) or through prayer.[30] With no risk to finances, reputation, or physical safety, mental pilgrimage allowed women in particular to undertake spiritual journeys using such texts as Felix Fabri's fifteenth-century *The Sion Pilgrims* or Francesco Suriano's *Treatise on the Holy Land*. Such guides for armchair pilgrims, whether monastic or lay, creatively transcended boundaries of time, space, and social identity.[31] They also, however, prompted new clerical concerns about *non-corporeal female mobility*, and the specter of women mentally wandering without supervision.

CONCLUSION

As western European communities slowly converted to Christianity, medieval people drew deeply upon the cultural fabric of household imagery, weaving the strands of home and the holy into a remarkable array of new meanings and patterns. Integrating piety and domesticity in a dazzling variety of practices, they creatively melded, materially constructed, and artistically represented, deployed, or employed the familiar to reach the divine, and they did so in highly gendered ways. Home was literally familiar territory in which to live out the Christian life, and its material and symbolic significance resonated particularly for women—even across region, doctrine, and social status. Combining the virtues of both Mary and Martha, pious domesticities offered medieval people multiple options for merging the active and contemplative—and in so doing, for making Christ at home.

FURTHER READING

Beattie, Cordelia, Anna Maslakovic, and Sarah Rees Jones, eds. *The Medieval Household in Christian Europe, c.850–c.1550: Managing Power, Wealth, and the Body*. Turnhout: Brepols, 2003.
Bynum, Caroline Walker. *Christian Materiality: An Essay on Religion in Late-Medieval Europe* New York: Zone Books, 2011.
Gilchrist, Roberta. *Gender and Material Culture: The Archaeology of Religious Women*. London: New York, 1994.
Kowaleski, Maryann and P. J. P Goldberg, eds. *Medieval Domesticity: Home, Housing, and Household in Medieval England*. Cambridge: Cambridge University Press, 2009.
McSheffrey, Shannon. *Gender and Heresy: Women and Men in Lollard Communities, 1420–1530*. Philadelphia: University of Pennsylvania Press, 1995.
Mulder-Bakker, Anneke. *Lives of the Anchoresses: The Rise of the Urban Recluse in Medieval Europe*. Philadelphia: University of Pennsylvania Press, 2005.
Mulder-Bakker, Anneke and Jocelyn Wogan-Browne, eds. *Household, Women, and Christianities in Late Antiquity and the Middle Ages*. Turnhout: Brepols, 2005.
Os, H. W. van. *The Art of Devotion in the Late Middle Ages in Europe, 1300–1500*. Princeton, NJ: Princeton University Press, 1994.
Simons, Walter. *Cities of Ladies: Beguine Communities in the Medieval Low Countries, 1200–1565*. Philadelphia: University of Pennsylvania Press, 2001.
Van Engen, John. *Sisters and Brothers of the Common Life: The Devotio Moderna and the World of the Later Middle Ages*. Philadelphia: University of Pennsylvania Press, 2008.
Wood, Diana. "Woman and Home: The Domestic Setting of Late-Medieval Spirituality," in W. J. Sheils and Diana Wood, eds. *Women in the Church: Papers Read at the 1989 Summer Meeting and the 1990 Winter Meeting of the Ecclesiastical History Society*. Oxford: Published for the Ecclesiastical History Society by B. Blackwell, 1990, 159–74.

NOTES

1. This chapter focuses upon Christian manifestations as particularly shaped by relationships with ecclesiastical hierarchies, but many of the intersections between gender, piety, and domesticity can be traced across Jewish and Muslim households as well.

2. On the gendering of medieval space, see Sarah Rees Jones's essay, "Public and Private Space and Gender in Medieval Europe," in this volume, Chapter 16.

3. Diana Webb's explorations of domesticity and devotion are an excellent foundation. See, for example, "Domestic Space and Devotion" in Sarah Hamilton and Andrew Spicer, eds, *Defining the Holy: Sacred Space in Medieval and Early Modern Europe* (Aldershot: Ashgate, 2005), 27–47.

4. Derek A. Rivard, *Blessing the World: Ritual and Lay Piety in Medieval Religion* (Washington, DC: Catholic University of America Press, 2008), 285.

5. The classic study is Caroline Walker Bynum, *Holy Feast, Holy Fast: The Religious Significance of Food to Medieval Women* (Berkeley: University of California Press, 1988).

6. *The Life of Saint Douceline, A Beguine of Provence*, trans. Kathleen Garay and Madeleine Jeay (Woodbridge, UK: Boydell & Brewer, 2008), 26.

7. W. A. Pantin, "Instructions for a Devout and Literate Layman," in J. J. G. Alexander and M. T. Gibson, eds, *Medieval Learning and Literature: Essays Presented to Richard William Hunt* (Oxford: Oxford University Press, 1979), 400.

8. On clerical gender, lives, and local attitudes, see Jennifer D. Thibodeaux, ed., *Negotiating Clerical Identities: Priests, Monks and Masculinity in the Middle Ages* (Basingstoke: Palgrave Macmillan, 2010).

9. *The Good Wife's Guide (Le Ménagier de Paris): A Medieval Household Book*, trans. Gina Greco and Christine M. Rose (Ithaca, NY: Cornell University Press, 2009), 55, 141.

10. Denis Renevey, "Household Chores in *The Doctrine of the Hert*: Affective Spirituality and Subjectivity," in Cordelia Beattie, Anna Maslakovic, and Sarah Rees Jones, eds, *The Medieval Household in Christian Europe, c. 850–c. 1550: Managing Power, Wealth, and the Body* (Turnhout: Brepols, 2003), 167–85.

11. Glenn Burger, "Labouring to Make the Good Wife Good in the *Journées Chrétiennes and Le Menagier de Paris*," *Florilegium*, 23 (1) (2006): 19–40, at 28.

12. Maiju Lehmijoki-Gardner, Daniel Ethan Bornstein, and E. Ann Matter, eds, *Dominican Penitent Women* (Mahwah, NJ: Paulist Press, 2005), 13, 50–51.

13. *Life of Saint Douceline*, 27.

14. Maiju Lehmijoki-Gardner, *Worldly Saints: Social Interaction of Dominican Penitent Women* (Helsinki: Finnish Literature Society, 1999), 96–98.

15. *The Good Wife's Guide*, 218.

16. Quoted in Webb, "Domestic Space and Devotion," 33.

17. Lehmijoki-Gardner, *Worldly Saints*, 15.

18. Suzanne Noffke, *The Letters of St. Catherine of Siena*, vol. 1 (Binghamton, NY: State University of New York, 1988), 41.

19. John H. Van Engen, *Sisters and Brothers of the Common Life: The Devotio Moderna and the World of the Later Middle Ages* (Philadelphia: University of Pennsylvania Press, 2008), 133.

20. For a thorough consideration of the sisters' reception across the Middle Ages, see Giles Constable, "The Interpretation of Mary and Martha," in *Three Studies of Medieval and Religious Social Thought* (Cambridge: Cambridge University Press, 1995), 1–141.

21. Anneke Mulder-Bakker, *Lives of the Anchoresses* (Philadelphia: University of Pennsylvania Press, 2005), 67.

22. Translated in Walter Simons, *Cities of Ladies: Beguine Communities in the Medieval Low Countries, 1200–1565* (Philadelphia: University of Pennsylvania Press, 2001), 119.

23. Louisa Burnham, *So Great a Light, So Great a Smoke: The Beguin Heretics of Languedoc* (Ithaca: Cornell University Press, 2008), 79.

24. Steven Justice, "Inquisition, Speech and Writing: A Case from Late-Medieval Norwich," in Rita Copeland, ed., *Criticism and Dissent in the Middle Ages* (Oxford: Oxford University Press, 1996), 315.

25. Christopher Roman, "Anchoritism and the Everyday: The Sacred-Domestic Discourse in the *Ancrene Wisse*," *Florilegium*, 23 (2) (2006): 99–122, at 114.

26. David Bornstein and Roberto Rusconi, eds, and Margery Schneider, trans., *Women and Religion in Medieval and Renaissance Italy* (Chicago: University of Chicago Press, 1996), 191.

27. See, for example, Sandra Penketh, "Women and Books of Hours," in Lesley Smith and Jane H. M. Taylor, eds, *Women and the Book: Assessing the Visual Evidence* (Toronto: University of Toronto Press, 1996), 266–81.

28. Andrea Pearson, *Envisioning Gender in Burgundian Devotional Art, 1350–1530: Experience, Authority, Resistance* (Aldershot: Ashgate, 2005).

29. See, for example, Sean Field, "Marie of St. Pol and Her Books," *The English Historical Review*, 125 (513) (2010): 255–78; and Eamon Duffy, *Marking the Hours: English People and their Prayers, 1240–1570* (New Haven: Yale University Press, 2006).

30. Leigh Ann Craig, *Wandering Women and Holy Matrons: Women as Pilgrims in the Later Middle Ages* (Leiden: Brill, 2009).

31. Kathryne Beebe, "Reading Mental Pilgrimage in Context: The Imaginary Pilgrims and Real Travels of Felix Fabri's 'Die Sionpilger,'" *Essays in Medieval Studies*, 25 (2008), 39–70.

PART IV

LAND, LABOR, ECONOMY

CHAPTER 18

....

SLAVERY

....

SALLY MCKEE

IN 1398, the merchant of Prato, Francesco Datini, finally convinced his wife, Margherita, to accept into his household the illegitimate daughter that his slave, Lucia, had borne him six years earlier. As for Lucia, he married her off to one of his servants. In 1464, Alessandra, the imposing matriarch of the noble Strozzi family in Florence, chided her son Filippo for postponing marriage. She had heard that his slave, Marina, was tending to his needs so well that he felt little urgency in finding a wife. In the last decade of the fifteenth century in the city of Valencia, a slave named Ysabel brought suit for her freedom against the heirs of her late master, Alfonso de la Barreda, a baker.[1] Ysabel claimed that, shortly after she was purchased at the age of eleven, she became her master's regular sexual partner. Indeed, since her two children were his, she had expected him to free her in his last will. To refute her claim, Alfonso's legitimate children argued that if Ysabel's children had been their father's, he would certainly have freed her, as was custom.

In one crucial respect, Lucia, Marina, and Ysabel experienced slavery in ways that were unique to women. All three women performed sexual service that was implicitly sanctioned by the Christian societies in which they lived. No Christian society of the late Middle Ages would have tolerated male slaves performing sexual services for their masters or mistresses, although undoubtedly it happened. The circumstances of these three slave women's appearances in the historical record are indicative of how commonplace, if sometimes emotionally fraught, sexual relations between masters and their enslaved women were.

The individual and collective tensions arising from sex between masters and slaves resembled the stresses created when male household members engaged in sex with free servants. Both kinds of sexual relationships, and the children that could result, raised anxieties in spouses, heirs, neighbors, and public authorities. However, the coercion a master exerted over a slave differed from the coercion of an employer over a free servant. Unlike free servants, slaves were considered property, possessed almost no legal rights, inherited their legal condition, and occupied the lowest and most shameful position in society. As David Wyatt has characterized the condition of slaves, they were the lowest of the low.[2]

These defining features of a slave's condition rendered absolute the coercion implicit in master-slave relationships. Undoubtedly, some masters and slaves felt real affection for each other, so much so in some cases that slaves could exercise agency within a limited range. There is also no question that slaves could try to ameliorate their lives by means of sexual service, either offered or conceded. Mitigating circumstances, however, could only alter the fundamental inequity between a master and a slave, if the slave were freed. Whether or not slaves found ways to exert power over their own actions, over their masters, or even over the households in which they lived, sexual relationships between masters and slaves rested on a bedrock of coercion. Coercion defined, prescribed, and fixed all relationships between slaves and their masters and mistresses.

For the sexual service of slaves to have been commonplace, the coercion had to be tacit. Although families did not broadcast to outsiders that the males in their households had or were having sex with (and had children by) slave women, neither did such behavior attract the opprobrium of anyone except the strictest moralists. Men will be men, boys will be boys, and female slaves will always be sly and crafty, so the stereotypes held. The assumptions underlying these stereotypes have evolved since the Middle Ages, but still persist. Even today the sexual services extracted from slave women strike historians as a feature of medieval slavery either too minor to linger over or too undocumented to be studied, in contrast to the better documented and more discussed phenomenon of sexual service in the slave-owning US South. As ever, silence allowed and allows us to pretend either that a phenomenon does not exist or is not as common as people fear.

Like economics and law, gender analysis is indispensable to the study of slavery. It reveals patterns in the kinds of labor slaves performed, the prices at which they were sold, the legal positions they occupied, the conditions of their enslavement, and even evolving notions of ethnic or social cohesion in the societies in which they lived. The ways in which gender shaped the experience of being enslaved lie so close to the heart of the practice that, whether or not they used the word "gender," most historians in the past half-century have had to take gender into account. The ones who ignored it altogether missed critical details of slavery's history.

Such myopia is found in the long debate over the transition from the Roman economic system based on slavery to what economic historians have traditionally called feudalism. The scholars engaged in this debate belong to a broader tradition initiated in the nineteenth century principally by Karl Marx, who held that the key means of economic production in a given society determines, to a great extent, how everything else in that society functions. One of their primary goals was to ascertain when, in the various regions of Europe, slavery ended and other forms of servitude, like serfdom, began.[3] They studied how the Roman Empire's economy, in which the laborers most crucial to its economy were enslaved, evolved into the medieval economy, in which they were semi-free, and, then from there, into the modern system dominated by wage labor. By the mid-twentieth century, a consensus had formed around the general idea that slavery in Western Europe died out by the ninth century.

So intricate did the debate become that historians eventually called into question basic assumptions and terminologies that had once been the bedrock of medieval history. The meanings and applications of once common terms, like "feudal," "fief," or "serf," required so many qualifications as to the time and place that their meanings were, by the end of the twentieth century, utterly destabilized. As the terms of the debate changed, so, too, did the economic historians who once posed the question of "When in the Middle Ages did slavery die out?" begin to question whether, in fact, it ever did.

Since the 1970s, economic historians like Chris Wickham have moved the terms of the debate along even further by drawing a distinction between the "slave mode of production"—the extensive use of slave labor in agricultural production—and the legal status of slave.[4] Slavery as a mode of production ended everywhere in the west before 400 CE, well before the shift to unfree tenant labor on estates. At no time thereafter did slaves play more than a minimal role in agriculture. The slaves who continued to be found in royal, aristocratic, and even peasant households in northern and southern Europe performed mostly domestic work.[5] Untangling the existence of slaves from the prevalence of a slave mode of production has diminished the confusion surrounding the persistence of slavery in Western Europe.

Susan Mosher Stuard has also shed critical light on slavery's supposed demise in the early Middle Ages. In her 1995 article, "Ancillary Evidence for the Decline of Slavery," perhaps still the most significant work touching on medieval slavery and gender, Stuard suggested that the end of slave labor in agricultural production did not signal the end of slavery for the simple reason that women continued to be enslaved and were put to work in other ways.[6] Using linguistic and documentary evidence, Stuard showed that, for centuries after male slaves disappeared from Europe, landowners still had slave women working on their estates.[7] They performed labor in the household that was considered appropriate for women, and they worked in small-scale industrial settings. Carolingian monastic and aristocratic sources refer to *gynaecea*, textile workshops where slave women both lived and worked. To buttress her evidence, Stuard tracked the meaning of *ancilla*, over the course of the Middle Ages. She found that the word retained a stable meaning of "enslaved woman" over the entire period, in contrast to the ever-changing meaning of *servus*, once the term for a male slave but also the source of the word, "serf" and "servant." Slavery, then, did not disappear entirely from the great estates when male slaves ceased to work on the land.

Stuard's contribution to the history of slavery lay not simply in demonstrating that slavery persisted in medieval Europe long after its supposed demise. She also made a major contribution to the gendering of medieval history. In Stuard's view, any analysis of an economy that fails to take into account its full range of labor value is incomplete. The labor of slave women might have contributed little to the economy throughout the Middle Ages. "Marginal" is how Chris Wickham characterizes male and female slave labor over the entire period.[8] But, as Stuard shows, the perceptible rise in demand for enslaved women after the Carolingian period was intimately tied to broader commercial trends.

About five years after Stuard's article appeared, economic historians started thinking about slavery in the early Middle Ages outside of the context of agricultural labor. In the twenty-first century, they are again taking an interest in early medieval slavery as part of a reassessment of trade in the Carolingian period. Michael McCormick, in his *The Origins of the European Economy* (2000), staked out the position that slaves were key goods that Christian merchants had to offer Muslim traders in the ninth and tenth centuries.[9] After an outbreak of the bubonic plague wiped out large populations in Muslim territories, the Abbasid rulers in Baghdad encouraged the importation of slave labor from Europe.[10] Consequently, Muslim merchants were in the market mainly for male slaves, although some female slaves carried higher prices.[11] Europe could offer little else that was commensurate in value and comparable in ease of portability to the luxury goods (especially spices and textiles) that aristocratic and ecclesiastical consumers desired from Muslim markets. Christian traders developed techniques of capture, confinement, transport, and sale for this slave trade, and what they learned was passed down through the centuries. To McCormick, the conclusion is clear: "The slave trade fueled the expansion of commerce between Europe and the Muslim world."[12] In other words, the export of slaves from Europe helped balance Christian—Muslim trade.

Some historians focused on the early Middle Ages, both to understand the economic changes occurring within Europe after the western Roman Empire ended and their connections to other, non-Christian regions. Other historians, mostly working in the late medieval Mediterranean, approached the subject of slavery differently and to a different purpose. These historians—the direct descendants of the generation of social historians who began to emerge in the 1970s—dealt with slaves as part of the revival and flourishing of Mediterranean trade from the twelfth century on. Looking primarily in notarial, tax, and census records in cities along the northern shore of the Mediterranean from the late twelfth to the sixteenth century, most of them did not notice that the large number of records involving slaves is misleading by its very number.

Without a gauge of the volume of the trade in slaves, it is difficult to put the thousands of notarial transactions, court, and governmental records involving slaves into meaningful perspective. One key limitation of the archival evidence is that it overwhelmingly concerns dealings between Christians in certain cities of the Italian peninsula, Iberia, southern France, and the eastern Mediterranean colonies of Italian powers. It sheds very little light on the number of slaves supplied by Christian traders to Muslim markets, where the demand for slaves was greater than it was in Europe. In other words, the greatest amount of evidence survives from the places and times where the practice of owning slaves was negligible. As we shall see further on, where it is possible to estimate the numbers of slaves in Christian cities along the Mediterranean coast—the last bastions of slave-owning in Western Europe—it becomes clear that their numbers declined sharply over the fifteenth century. By the end of that century, in Italian cities and in southern France, the slave populations were small in size, female, and old.

Despite its drawbacks, this economic scholarship remains essential reading in the historiography of slavery. In the first half of the twentieth century, the Italian historians Domenico Gioffrè and Luigi Tria extracted hundreds of wills, tax records, and contracts for slave sales, insurance, and rentals from the State Archives of Genoa, the Italian city-state most deeply implicated in the Mediterranean slave trade in the Middle Ages.[13] After Tria and Gioffrè came Charles Verlinden's two massive volumes on slavery in the Middle

Ages, which presented a large amount of unrefined data with a minimum of analysis.[14] Like those of Gioffrè, Verlinden's numbers made abundantly clear that late medieval slave traders preyed overwhelmingly on young women. Thereafter, historians of medieval and early modern Italy, like, for example, Henri Bresc and Michel Balard, built on Verlinden's foundation. They published detailed, local studies that supplied more information than ever before about the numbers, prices, and sources of slaves.[15] Their work showed that, starting in the late twelfth century, females formed a growing majority among the slaves traded by Christians in European and non-European markets. Apart from acknowledging the stark bottom lines of their calculations, however, these historians overlooked the gender implications of their findings.

Iris Origo, the Anglo-American scholar, did not. Her 1955 article, "Domestic Enemies: The Eastern Slaves in Tuscany in the Fourteenth and Fifteenth Centuries," focused directly on the presence of female slaves in Tuscan households.[16] She drew attention to the social dynamic between masters and mistresses, on the one hand, and their slaves—most of them women—on the other. For the first time, a scholar presented the experience of being an enslaved woman as being different from that of an enslaved man. Not only did Origo directly address the sexual service required of many slave women, she also pointed to the social impact of the offspring of slave—master unions on Florentine society, especially in the form of foundling hospitals. Her depiction of slaves and their owners as antagonists in the intimate arena of households was, like Stuard's later article, a milestone in historiography of slavery and gender. Origo's article stands as a perennial reminder that the principal beneficiaries of Renaissance Italy's burgeoning humanist culture, like those of ancient Athenian democracy, tended to be men with property.

After Origo, one of the only other twentieth-century historians to consider at length issues involving gender and slavery was the French historian Jacques Heers, in his study of slaves and free servants in the medieval Mediterranean world.[17] Like Origo, he judged important the sexual services imposed on many slave women, but he saw little difference in the sexual coercion of slaves and servants. Heers used numerous examples from notarial contracts and court records to show how the presence of slave women caused tensions between the husbands, wives, and their legitimate offspring. Without treating sexual service as a special form of labor that contributed to the monetary value of slave women, he explored the consequences of men engaging in sexual relations with servile women within their own households.

Since Heers's work appeared in the early 1980s, regional studies of medieval Mediterranean slavery have proliferated, particularly in the field of medieval and early modern Iberian slavery. Articles and a few books on slavery in Scandinavia, Germany, Italy, Spain, Frankish Greece, and the crusader states appeared at the turn of the twenty-first century. With the notable exception of Ruth Mazo Karras's work on slavery and concubinage in Scandinavia, relatively few scholars, however, have tackled directly the subject of slavery and gender.[18] David Wyatt's 2009 study of slavery in Britain and Ireland addresses slavery and gender, tying enslavement, abduction, and rape to the construction of masculine identity among warriors.[19]

The interest in medieval slavery has also extended eastward. Thanks primarily to Youval Rotman's study of Byzantine slavery, we can now be sure that the Christians of Western Europe by no means held a monopoly on the export of slaves to the Muslim world.[20] Rotman's work has remarkably little to say about gender and slavery, but certain trends can be inferred from his study.[21] Prior to 1000 CE, the Byzantine emperors' wars of expansion, especially those in eastern Europe, supplied many captives for markets in the empire and abroad. Slavs and Bulgars predominated among the enslaved, but, in the period before the Muslim conquests, captives from Byzantine lands in Africa were also sold in Byzantine markets. As in the western Mediterranean, starting in the second half of the ninth century, the number of women (especially from north of the Black Sea) sold in Muslim markets by Byzantine traders slowly overtook the number of male slaves. As far back as the fifth century, traders in slaves from north of the Black Sea, Africa, and other territories on the frontiers of the empire supplied the Byzantine market with boys who had already been surgically altered.[22] Because the Byzantines used slaves in domestic service, private and public construction projects, artisanal shops, and in the imperial household, the sex ratio of the slave population in the Byzantine Empire was more evenly balanced than it was in Western Europe.

In contrast to the steady demand for slaves within the Byzantine Empire and the equally steady engagement of Byzantine merchants in the Mediterranean slave trade, the practice of slavery in Western Europe was much less uniform. From the twelfth century on, slave-owning and slave-trading slowly died out in northern Europe, while at the same time it was on the rise in southern Europe. In Norway, slavery seems to have lasted until the eleventh century, in Denmark and Sweden for another hundred years at least.[23] Slaves existed in newly conquered Norman England in the eleventh century, where they might have amounted to anywhere between 10 and 25 percent of the population, but by the late twelfth century, when serfdom had become the dominant form of unfree labor, slavery had nearly disappeared.[24] War continued to provide the best pretext to capture innocents and put them to work in households or sell them on.

In the Mediterranean, the year 1204 was a pivotal moment, when a combined Frankish and Venetian army breached the walls of Constantinople and brought down the Byzantine Empire in the misadventure known as the Fourth Crusade. In the course of dismembering the eastern empire, the Frankish and Venetian conquerors captured thousands of people living mainly on the coasts of modern-day Greece and Turkey, on the Aegean Islands, and in regions north and east of the Black Sea. They then sold their captives in Muslim markets or put them to work (mostly as domestic servants or textile workers) alongside the Byzantine semi-free peasantry on their newly acquired estates. A large proportion were women and children, taken captive by Christian and Muslim pirate-traders. Over the thirteenth, fourteenth, and fifteenth centuries, the Venetian, Genoese, and Catalan merchants who sought to profit from the markets opened by the Fourth Crusade transported captives back to their home ports, where customs officials assessed and taxed their value as slaves. Most were then exported to other markets around the Mediterranean, including Venice's own colony of Crete. A smaller number were sold in the merchants' home ports—either privately or at public auction.

Certain distinct trends developed as a result of the revived Christian trade in slaves. To begin with, from the twelfth century on, Christian merchants sold more slaves to Muslims and other non-Christians outside of Europe than they sold to Christians within Europe. The desire of Christians in Western Europe to own slaves did not keep pace with the deepening involvement of Christian merchants in the Mediterranean slave trade. The relatively low demand in Europe for slaves probably had much to do with their increasingly higher prices. In mid-thirteenth century Genoa, the price of slaves—especially female slaves—rose significantly. Stephen Epstein calculated that in 1250 it took one hundred days for a skilled weaver to recoup the price of a slave, but by the end of the century, it took him nearly a year.[25] Thereafter, the price of slaves steadily climbed, and required a far greater capital outlay than most people could afford. Not surprisingly, then, very few households could afford to own more than one slave at a time.[26] The cost of slaves was so high that slave labor was not even much used to compensate for the dearth of workers after the devastations of the Black Death, starting in 1347. Although the number of slaves rose in the second half of the fourteenth century, they rarely if ever (as far as we can tell) amounted to more than 3 percent of an Italian, Aragonese, or southern French city population. The greatest concentrations of slaves in Western Europe were in the cities whose merchants were most active in the trade, namely Genoa, Barcelona, and Venice. After the mid-fifteenth century, when the Ottomans closed off the Black Sea to Venetian and Genoese traders, Italian merchants turned away from trading in slaves, and Iberian merchants turned their attention to sources of slaves from sub-Saharan Africa. In Italy, the number of slaves rose again only when Florence and Venice resorted to male slaves, taken from Turks, north Africans, and men from sub-Saharan Africa, for service on the large state-owned war galleys of the sixteenth and seventeenth centuries. But that specialized use of slaves did not lead to a rise in slave-owning in private households.

At the same time that the demand for slaves within Europe declined overall, another distinct trend emerged: most remaining demand focused on females. The fewer slaves there were, the greater a majority women formed among them. Iberian cities were perhaps the exception to this trend, where a tolerance of slave-owning lasted longer than elsewhere in Western Europe. There the sex ratio among slaves was very likely more balanced, since Iberians had access to a larger supply of slaves than had previously been available, once the sub-Saharan trade picked up in the sixteenth century. Elsewhere, the trend in the post-plague period is unequivocal. A study of approximately two thousand slave contracts from Genoa, Florence, and Venice shows that between 1360 and 1500, women represented over 80 percent of slaves purchased in Venice and Genoa, the two cities in the Italian peninsula most involved in the trade in slaves. Of those slaves, Russians figured predominantly in Genoa, and Tartars, followed at a distance by Russians, represented the largest ethnic group among slaves bought and sold in Venice. Over the fifteenth century, as the number of slave sales in Genoa and Venice declined, the average age of the slave women at the time of sale grew older.[27]

Slave women performed the most menial tasks in a household. They washed clothes, made bread, wove cloth, scrubbed floors, and performed the myriad other undesirable chores that other members of the household were too proud to perform. In households with few other servants, slaves often cooked the meals. Many slaves worked as wet nurses to the family's children, and some masters rented their slaves to others for that purpose.[28] Few slaves worked in artisanal workshops. The male slaves in Venice were usually put to work as ferrymen in the city's canals. In fact, some cities passed ordinances prohibiting slave labor in skilled trades. Thus, the work that Christians in Western Europe delegated to slaves tended to be gendered. Women's work—already considered low status and low-skilled—became slaves' work.

Why were slave women so expensive, given that they performed the most arduous, menial work of a household and tended to lead brutish lives? How do we account for the demand for female slaves when the main risk of owning a female slave—pregnancy— was potentially so costly? (Pregnancy led either to the death of the slave woman herself in childbirth or to an additional mouth to feed.) Why did the number of female slaves rise during the same period in which slave-owning in Christian Europe declined over-all? No contemporary source contains a straightforward explanation, and few historians of slavery have attempted answers. However, one hypothesis merits thought: perhaps slave women's potential for sexual service and use as status symbols played a larger part in the demand than did their value as domestic servants.

The sexual value of female slaves seems to have transcended time and place. It was not a development of the later Middle Ages. Nor was it confined to the Mediterranean; wherever slavery had been practiced earlier in northern Europe, the appeal of owning females was the same. As Bishop Wulfstan, who understood well the workings of the slave market in eleventh-century England, observed,

> For [the English] would buy men from all over England and sell them off in Ireland in the hope of profit, even putting on sale girls whom previously they had sexually abused and who were now pregnant. You could see and sigh over rows of wretches bound together with ropes, young people of both sexes whose beautiful appearance and youthful innocence might move barbarians to pity, daily exposed to prostitution, daily offered for sale. A detestable crime, wretched infamy for vindictive men, worse than beasts, to consign their lovers, even their own blood, into slavery.[29]

For Wulfstan, it could be taken for granted that female slaves would be expected to pro-vide sexual service for owners. Where slavery was practiced in northern Europe, it was also common for masters to prey on the women they held in thrall (derived from the Old English word for slave). For the most part, contemporaries in southern Europe chose not to discuss—at least, in writing—the practice of using slave women as sexual servants. Perhaps it was too obvious to comment on.

The prices of slave women provide indirect evidence that their value was linked to sexual service. Prior to the fourteenth century, the majority of slaves sold in Catalan, Genoese, and Venetian auctions came from the Greek-speaking regions and were Orthodox Christians. Within one hundred years of the Fourth Crusade, however, the city-states of Italy and Aragon grew increasingly uncomfortable owning and selling Greeks, whom they viewed increasingly as Christians like themselves and therefore protected from enslavement. By that time, the flow of slaves from the Black Sea ports of Kaffa and Tana provided a non-Christian alternative. Instead of Greeks, the slave-owning denizens of Spanish and Italian cities began to buy Tartars, Turks, Syrians, Russians, Circassians, Abkhazians, Mingrellians, Bulgarians, and others. Local slave traders marched captives, mainly women, south to the port, where they sold them to Venetian, Genoese, and Catalan merchants, who conveyed most of the captives to their home ports, and from there to other markets.

Once the Black Sea ports became the main conduits through which slaves entered Christian hands, women with light complexions were prized more than darker-skinned women. Those from Russian and Circassian regions were famously light-skinned, fair-haired women. On the whole, no matter where they came from, slave women with light complexions fetched higher prices than did darker-skinned women from the African continent. Muslim merchants displayed the same preferences for light-skinned women. The price differential between light-skinned and dark-skinned slaves, between slaves from north of the Black Sea and those from sub-Saharan Africa, make it clear that cosmetic appearance played a role in a female slave's appeal.[30] It should not be assumed, however, that only fair-skinned slave women drew the sexual attentions of the males around them. After all, then and now, compulsory sexual service is as much if not more a means of asserting a man's authority as it is an expression of desire.

It is undeniable that all serving women, including free domestic servants, were vulnerable to sexual exploitation. The historical record has as much to say about the exploitation of servants as it does about slave women. Yet the desirability of free serving-women in the eyes of potential employers did not factor into their wages, which conformed to economic norms set by the market in servants. The service performed by slave women was different. Only enslaved women's economic value was predicated, at least in part, on their physical appearance. Female slaves were not always or solely purchased for their potential use as sexual partners. Men might have found the prestige associated with owning a female slave, especially a light-skinned one from the Black Sea region, sufficient reason to purchase one. But in the eyes of traders and prospective owners, a female slave's suitability for sexual service added value to her price.

Regardless of the criteria by which they were selected at sale, slave women's sexual service was not a well-kept secret. Governments repeatedly passed ordinances banning married men from having carnal knowledge of their servants and slaves. We learn from court records and diaries about the household tensions caused by master—slave sexual relations. Wives were jealous, and some saw slaves as competing for the affections and attentions of the head of the household. Legitimate children were often just as hostile, fearing that slave offspring might make claims on the patrimony of the household.

Recognizing the prevalence of sexual service is not an end in itself, for it has significant implications for perceptions of difference in the medieval period. Here it is worth recalling that, unlike that of free serving-women, the ancestry of slave women was always understood by Christians to be different from theirs. Only people born in lands outside of the Roman communion were deemed as legitimately enslaved. This was a period, it should be remembered, when those political units loyal to the pope as the head of the Church overlapped to a considerable extent with those people who believed they shared a common ancestry. The chief characteristics of late medieval slavery—the predominance of women, the ethnic labels used to distinguish among them, the labor they were expected to perform—can be usefully correlated with the changes in the way Europeans understood religious and ethnic difference in the pre-modern era. The study of slavery and sexual service in the fourteenth and fifteenth centuries provides essential background to discussions of ethnic and religious difference in the early modern and modern era.

Ultimately, the sexual service that slaves performed points the way to thinking about the offspring of unions between free and enslaved people, who were perceived in the late Middle Ages to be a priori ancestrally distinct. How those children, or to be more precise, the ones who survived, were incorporated into society speaks to the difference they were perceived to embody, both corporeally and figuratively. Many children of slave women and free men wound up in foundling hospitals, where many of them died. It was not uncommon for families to keep the children of slave women within their households. Biological families were especially willing to accept children produced by the head of household before he married, the so-called natural children—meaning, those borne to two unmarried people with no legal impediment to their marrying each other. In the wills of Italian and Iberian citizens, many female testators left bequests to the natural children of their husbands, brothers, and sons.[31] Like Datini's natural daughter by his slave woman, the children of slave women by unmarried men stood a better chance of remaining with their mothers than the children born to slave concubines of married men.

Children of slave women were sufficiently abundant to cause legal change.[32] By Roman law, the status of a child followed that of the mother, so that any child born of an enslaved woman was also a slave. But in some city-states of Italy and in Iberia, statutory law deemed a child of a slave woman and a free father to be free, if free paternity could be proved. The change emerged partially in deference to the wishes of fathers (mostly from the upper echelons of society) to endow their natural children with their own status. When it was deemed socially beneficial, a child's legal status followed that of the father.

Most slaves were women, and they were especially valued for their sexual services. As the "slave mode of production" dwindled in the Christian Mediterranean, slavery came to resemble a form of sex-trafficking. As David Wyatt has observed, "If we recognize [slavery's] intimate association with sexual exploitation and expressions of power/masculinity then we will also notice that there has been a disturbing continuity in the existence of slavery from the medieval period and into the modern era."[33] Adjusting the frame through which we view medieval slavery should stimulate new understandings about this pernicious practice and the women, children, and occasionally men who suffered under it.

The decline of domestic slavery in Western Europe over the fifteenth century does not lessen its importance to the subsequent history of slavery. In fact, it offers a very instructive contrast. The increased involvement in the sixteenth century of Christian traders in the sub-Saharan African slave trade did not lead to a widespread resurgence of slave-owning in Europe. Why were Europeans averse to domestic slavery at home yet tolerant of slavery in their nascent overseas colonies? As explanations, Christian charity, changes to more economically efficient forms of domestic labor, and sheer hypocrisy do not tell the whole story. Could it be the case that in the fifteenth and sixteenth centuries, before enslavement was racially and biologically rationalized, slaves—most of whom were women—and the children they produced were too familiar (in all nuances of the word) for Christians in their homes and heartlands to maintain in such base conditions?

Overseas, colonial powers elaborated racial epistemologies and social structures that kept slaves in a profoundly unfamiliar state. The British, Spanish, and, later on, US authorities paid great and punitive attention to the status of children born of masters and slaves, locking them permanently into a state of slavery. Intermarriage between people understood to be of different races was banned wherever slavery was the dominant form of labor. Yet, despite the strictures, sexual service was as much a feature of early modern and modern slavery as it was of medieval slavery. The differences between the earlier and later forms lies in how those societies managed its consequences. A comparison of sexual service in the medieval period with the phenomenon in later centuries shows us that, before the concept of race emerged, slaves (regardless of ancestry) and their children resembled too closely their owners and kin in the households of Italy, southern France, and Iberia. Viewed in this way, gender relations between masters and slaves help explain why racialized slavery emerged in the western hemisphere, but not in Western Europe.

If Susan Stuard's admonition not to forget the women helped direct attention to the role of slavery in a broadly defined early medieval economy, then a similar one about slave women and their children might lead to more work on the political dimension of pre-modern Western European ethnography. The analytical lens of gender is essential to any project that seeks to understand the links between legal status, the economy, religion, and ethnicity.

FURTHER READING

Epstein, Steven A. *Speaking of Slavery: Color, Ethnicity, and Human Bondage in Italy*. Ithaca: Cornell University Press, 2001.

Gioffrè, Domenico. *Il mercato degli schiavi a Genova nel secolo XV*. Genoa: Fratelli Bozzi, 1971.

Heers, Jacques. *Esclaves et domestiques au Moyen Age dans le monde méditerranéen*. Paris: Fayard, 1981.

Karras, Ruth Mazo. *Slavery and Society in Medieval Scandinavia*. New Haven: Yale University Press, 1993.

McKee, Sally. "Inherited Status and Slavery in Late Medieval Italy and Venetian Crete," *Past & Present*, 182 (2004): 31–53.

McKee, Sally. "Domestic Slavery in Renaissance Italy," *Slavery & Abolition*, 29 (3) (2008): 305–26.

Origo, Iris. "The Domestic Enemy: The Eastern Slaves in Tuscany in the Fourteenth and Fifteenth Centuries," *Speculum*, 30 (1955): 321–61.

Stuard, Susan Mosher. "Ancillary Evidence for the Decline of Medieval Slavery," *Past & Present*, 149 (1) (1995): 3–28.

Verlinden, Charles. *L'esclavage dans l'Europe médiévale*, 2 vols. Bruges: De Tempel, 1955–77.

Wyatt, David. *Slaves and Warriors in Medieval Britain and Ireland, 800–1200*. Leiden: Brill, 2009.

NOTES

1. Iris Origo, *The Merchant of Prato, Francesco di Marco Datini* (London: Knopf, 1957), 169; *Selected Letters of Alessandra Strozzi*, trans. Heather Gregory (Berkeley: University of California Press, 1997), 111; the case of Ysabel from Debra Blumenthal's *Enemies and Familiars: Slavery and Mastery in Fifteenth-Century Valencia* (Ithaca: Cornell University Press, 2009), 169–70.

2. David Wyatt, *Slaves and Warriors in Medieval Britain and Ireland, 800–1200* (Leiden; Boston: Brill, 2009), 51–52.

3. Marc Bloch, *Slavery and Serfdom in the Middle Ages: Selected Essays*, trans. William R. Beer (Berkeley; Los Angeles: University of California Press, 1975); Pierre Dockès, *Medieval Slavery and Liberation*, trans. Arthur Goldhammer (Chicago: University of Chicago Press, 1979); Pierre Bonnassie, ed., *From Slavery to Feudalism in Southwestern Europe* (Cambridge; New York: Cambridge University Press, 1991); M. L. Bush, ed., *Serfdom and Slavery: Studies in Legal Bondage* (London; New York: Longman, 1996); Stanley L. Engerman, ed., *The Terms of Labor: Slavery, Serfdom, and Free Labor* (Palo Alto, Calif.: Stanford University Press, 1999).

4. Chris Wickham, *Framing the Middle Ages: Europe and the Mediterranean, 400–800* (Oxford: Oxford University Press, 2005), 259–63.

5. Wickham, *Framing the Middle Ages*, 560.

6. Susan Mosher Stuard, "Ancillary Evidence for the Decline of Medieval Slavery," *Past & Present*, 149 (1) (1995): 3–28.

7. Stuard, "Ancillary Evidence," 7.

8. Wickham, *Framing the Middle Ages*, 276–77.

9. Michael McCormick, *Origins of the European Economy: Communications and Commerce, A.D. 300–900* (Cambridge; New York: Cambridge University Press, 2001).

10. McCormick, *Origins*, 775.

11. McCormick, *Origins*, 248.

12. McCormick, *Origins*, 776.

13. Domenico Gioffrè, *Il mercato degli schiavi a Genova nel secolo XV* (Genoa: Fratelli Bozzi, 1971); Luigi Tria, *La schiavitù in Liguria: Atti della società ligure di storia patria* (Genoa: Società ligure de storia patria, 1947).

14. Charles Verlinden, *L'esclavage dans l'Europe médiévale*, 2 vols (Bruges: De Tempel, 1955–77).

15. Henri Bresc, *Un monde méditerranéen: Economie et société en Sicile, 1300–1450* (Rome: Ecole française de Rome, 1986); Michel Balard, "Esclavage en Crimée et sources fiscales Génoises au XVe siècles," *Byzantinische Forschungen*, 22 (1996): 9–17; Michel Balard, "Giacomo Badoer et le commerce des esclaves," in E. M. Mornet, ed., *Milieux naturels, espaces sociaux: Etudes offertes à Robert Delort* (Paris: Publications de la Sorbonne, 1997), 555–64.

16. Iris Origo, "The Domestic Enemy: The Eastern Slaves in Tuscany in the Fourteenth and Fifteenth Centuries," *Speculum*, 30 (1955): 321–61.

17. Jacques Heers, *Esclaves et domestiques au Moyen Age dans le monde méditerranéen* (Paris: Fayard, 1981).

18. Ruth Mazo Karras, "Concubinage and Slavery in the Viking Age," *Scandinavian Studies*, 62 (1990): 141–62; Wyatt, *Slaves and Warriors*; Blumenthal, *Enemies and Familiars*; Gemma Teresa Colesanti, "Las esclavas y los esclavos en los libros de cuentas de Catalina Llull (1472–1486)," in Maria Teresa Merrer i Malloi and Josefina Mutgé i Vives, eds, *De l'esclavitud a la llibertat: Esclaus i lliberts a l'Edat Mitjana. Actes de Colloqui Internacional celebrat a Barcelona del 27 al 29 de maig de 1999* (Barcelona: Consell Superior d'Investigacions Cientifiques, Institució Milà, 2000), 547–56; Coral Cuadrada Majó, "Esclaus i esclaves a la Baixa Edat Mitjana: Els diferents destins de canvi de vida," in Malloi and Vives, eds, *De l'esclavitud a la llibertat*, 325–40; Steven A. Epstein, *Speaking of Slavery: Color, Ethnicity, and Human Bondage in Italy* (Ithaca: Cornell University Press, 2001); Elizabeth S. Girsch, "Metaphorical Usage, Sexual Exploitation, and Divergence in the Old English Terminology for Male and Female Slaves," in Allen J. Frantzen and Douglas Moffat, eds, *The Work of Work: Servitude, Slavery and Labor in Medieval England* (Glasgow: Cruithne Press, 1994), 30–54; Ruth Mazo Karras, *Slavery and Society in Medieval Scandinavia* (New Haven: Yale University Press, 1993); idem, "Desire, Descendants, Dominance: Slavery, the Exchange of Women, and Masculine Power," in Frantzen and Moffat, eds, *The Work of Work*; Sally McKee, "Greek Women in Latin Households of Fourteenth-Century Venetian Crete," *Journal of Medieval History*, 19 (1993): 229–49; idem, "Households in Fourteenth-Century Venetian Crete," *Speculum*, 70 (1995): 27–67; idem, "Inherited Status and Slavery in Late Medieval Italy and Venetian Crete," *Past & Present*, 182 (2004): 31–53; idem, "Domestic Slavery in Renaissance Italy," *Slavery & Abolition*, 29 (2009): 305–26; Giulia Rainis, "Per la storia della schiavitù femminile nell'Italia longobarda: Prassi contrattuale e quadri legislative," *Studi medievali*, 48 (2) (2007): 721–52; Guy Romestan, "Femmes esclaves à Perpignan aux XIVe et XVe siècles," in *La Femme dans l'histoire et la société méridionales (IXe-XIXe s.): Actes du 66e congrès de la Fédération historique du Languedoc méditerranéen et du Roussillon organisé à Narbonne les 15 et 16 octobre 1994 à l'occasion du VIIIe centenaire de la fin du gouvernement de la vicomtesse Ermendgarde* (Montpellier: Fédération historique du Languedoc méditerranéen et du Roussillon, 1995), 187–218.

19. Wyatt, *Slaves and Warriors*, 61–171.

20. Youval Rotman, *Byzantine Slavery and the Mediterranean World*, trans. Jane Marie Todd (Cambridge, Mass.: Harvard University Press, 2009), 67.

21. See Charles M. Brand, "Slave Women in the Legislation of Alexius I," *Byzantinische Forschungen*, 23 (1996): 19–24.

22. McCormick, *Origins of the European Economy*, 591. See also Kathryn Ringrose, "The Byzantine Body," in this volume, Chapter 23.

23. Karras, *Slavery and Society in Medieval Scandinavia*, 137–38.

24. David Pelteret, *Slavery in Early Medieval England: From the Reign of Alfred until the Twelfth Century* (Woodbridge: Boydell, 1995), 232–33.

25. Steven A. Epstein, *Wage Labor and Guilds in Medieval Europe* (Chapel Hill, NC: University of North Carolina Press, 1991), 223.

26. McKee, "Domestic Slavery," 307–10.

27. McKee, "Domestic Slavery," 318.

28. Christoph Cluse suggests that the money brought to masters from the renting out of their slave women as wet nurses was an incentive to keep them pregnant. "Frauen in Sklaverei: Beobachtungen aus genuesischen Notariatsregistern des 14. und 15.

Jahrhunderts," in Frank G. Hirschmann and Gerd Mentgen, eds, *Campana pulsante convocati: Festschrift anlässlich der Emeritierung von Prof. Dr. Alfred Haverkamp* (Trier: Kliomedia, 2005), 78–86.

29. *Vita Wulfstani*, §20 (see *Vita Wulfstani of William of Malmesbury*, ed. R. R. Darlington, Camden Society, vol. 40 (London, 1928), 43); "Life of Bishop Wulfstan of Worcester," in *Three Lives of the Last Englishmen*, trans. Michael James Swanton (New York: Garland Press, 1984), 126. Partially quoted in Pelteret, *Slavery in Early Medieval England*, 77.

30. Epstein, *Speaking of Slavery*, 187–89.

31. Thomas Kuehn, *Illegitimacy in Renaissance Florence* (Ann Arbor: University of Michigan Press, 2002), 151–60; Debra Blumenthal, *Enemies and Familiars*, 149–53.

32. A point I make in "Inherited Status and Slavery."

33. Wyatt, *Slaves and Warriors*, 397.

CHAPTER 19

....

URBAN ECONOMIES

....

KATHRYN REYERSON

PANORAMA

....

URBAN women ran the gamut in the Middle Ages from rich to poor, elite to marginal, immigrant to indigenous, married to single or widowed, Christian to Muslim and Jew. Economic opportunities followed suit.

Elite women were usually active in the occupations of their husbands and sons, though not in every place or at every time. The late fourteenth-century letters exchanged between Francesco Datini da Prato, a merchant deeply involved in international trade, and his wife Margherita detail the domestic role for a woman of the urban mercantile elite; she managed a large and complex household with many servants and even some slaves. The wife of the Goodman of Paris did much the same; her husband, in the late fourteenth century, penned *Le Ménagier de Paris* to advise his young wife about household management and honorable conduct. In the first decades of the fourteenth century, the widow Agnes de Bossones was a typical wealthy rentier in Montpellier, possessed of rental properties from which her agents collected rents. In the 1330s and 1340s, Martha de Cabanis, also a Montpellier widow and guardian of her sons, invested large sums in long-distance Mediterranean trade and local industry. Amy Donat managed a successful pawn and jewelry business in London in the late fourteenth century. In fourteenth-century Bruges, the women of the Cosericghen family worked as moneylenders, generation after generation. These elite women were not idle housewives; they worked closely with their husbands and, if widowed, sons.[1]

Across Europe, female artisans of the middling classes worked most often in the textile and food trades. They produced trimmings and adornments for luxury fabrics. They worked as brewsters, bakers, or innkeepers. Some were apprenticed young in trades; on March 9, 1328 the Montpellier silversmith Johannes Rigaudi apprenticed his daughter Bonaffasia to the goldsmith Petrus Berengarii for four years to learn from his wife the trade of spinning gold. Some women worked on their own, separate from their husbands. In the late fifteenth century Alice Claver, silkwoman of London, traded as a very successful entrepreneur, making use of *femme sole* status that permitted her to conduct business, make contracts, and even plead in law courts without her husband.

Poorer women mostly worked as servants or market hucksters. Others found employment as day laborers and laundresses. Servants might be hired contractually, usually for the year, and in the Mediterranean world, domestic slaves were not uncommon. Some market hucksters, vendors who hawked or haggled merchandise, enjoyed remarkably long careers. On the central market square in Montpellier, the singlewoman Johanna Poitela rented a stall for forty years, from which she sold fruits and vegetables. Below servants and hucksters struggled vagabonds, the very poor, and the enslaved. For prostitutes, who were much maligned but usually tolerated, the sex trade provided some subsistence.

Social status and wealth matter a great deal, but so, too, did other distinctions among women. A second major distinction was marital status. Most women married if they or their families had sufficient funds to furnish a dowry. Some entered religious houses, and some remained single because of lack of fortune or opportunity. The latter were generally at a disadvantage with limited resources and without the support that family ties provided. Widows might be poor, but widowhood could free women of means from the control of husbands and male relatives.

We know about rich and poor, widowed and married, and the many other sorts of women who lived in medieval towns thanks to a wide variety of sources. Marriage contracts and wills allow us to glimpse women at crucial life-moments. Other documents let us see them at work: loan contracts, partnership agreements, procurations (mandates to serve as legal representative), sales receipts, recognizances (recognitions of debt to be repaid according to the terms of the contract), apprenticeship contracts, and work contracts. In company with their fathers, husbands, brothers, and sons, women operated at many different levels of urban finance, trade, real estate, and industry.

URBAN EUROPE

The divide between urban and rural in the Middle Ages has been overstated, but there is no doubt about the economic differences between town and country. Though towns never disappeared with the fall of the Roman Empire in the west, urban growth took off in the eleventh century, closely joined to economic expansion in agriculture, industry, and trade that continued through most of the thirteenth century. Many a town saw its population triple in this period, and there emerged major urban centers such as London, with as many as 80,000 people in 1300, or Paris with 200,000 or more. Immigration of men and women (sometimes especially women) into towns accounted for much of this population growth. Europe entered a period of contraction and crisis in the fourteenth and fifteenth centuries, with some population decline in cities such as Pistoia before the Black Death of 1348 and significant declines thereafter in most European cities (Hanseatic cities such as Lübeck represent the exception).

The particular place of a woman in her life cycle, whether as daughter, wife, mother, widow, or even longtime singlewoman, had bearing on her role in the urban economy. It may also be that the size of a town or city should be taken into account when assessing women's economic opportunities. Although historical demographers consider as "urban" some medieval agglomerations as small as 2,000 inhabitants, it is reasonable to expect that women in a small town functioned differently from women in a regional city of 25,000 or more. Some urban economies may also have been structured in such a way as to be more accommodating to women. During the Reconquest, when newly conquered towns needed immigrants, women on the Castilian frontier enjoyed very favorable legal rights. They worked in trades and crafts (often family-oriented), in inns and shops, and as sellers of goods. A woman's work was often associated with and subordinated to that of her husband. Other tasks occupied women as well; they were domestic servants—maids and housekeepers, nurses for the wealthy of the town, and washerwomen. These humbler women were mostly Christian, but one could also find Jewish and Muslim women among them, as well as Muslim slaves. In the later Middle Ages, the economic and legal situation of women in Castile deteriorated, as the frontier settled and the realm became more stable.[2]

All towns and cities had food industries, and most also produced textiles; for some, cloth production was a major export industry. Bruges attracted considerable numbers of female immigrants, perhaps because of the relatively favorable economic conditions they found there in the cloth industry. These were areas of women's specialization, though women were not, in most cases, in leadership positions. Men were active in international trade, as traders of luxury goods and bulk items, as masters in artisanal industries, as local, regional, and royal administrators, and as professionals and professors in law, medicine, the arts, theology, and philosophy. Men's work and women's work were, as a rule, very distinct in medieval cities.

THE STATE OF THE FIELD

There is considerable disagreement among scholars about women's experience in medieval urban economies. Interpretations are closely tied to understandings of patriarchy as a useful paradigm for women's economic experience in the medieval era. Judith Bennett, in a recent contribution, *History Matters*, has argued for a continuing patriarchal equilibrium across time, based on the data of wages and work.[3] Other historians, however, have sought to focus less on limits and more on possibilities for women within a patriarchal system. The gender system of the Middle Ages favored men, but with that said, women's experiences varied greatly according to time, marital status, social status, family background, and available training; all these had an impact on women's economic opportunities within the patriarchal regimes of medieval cities. Women's economic agency was also based on such intangibles as individual personality, and such factors as the nature of specific urban economies.

Late medieval England is the site of the most intense debate about the handicaps for women resulting from patriarchal structures. Marjorie McIntosh has recently summarized the state of the arguments along the following lines. One point of view, put forth by Caroline Barron and Jeremy Goldberg, maintains that women enjoyed a kind of golden age, electing *femme sole* status that gave them an identity separate from their husbands and an independent economic and legal situation, with some limitations. On the other side of this argument are Maryanne Kowaleski and Judith Bennett, who see a continuous pattern of under-rewarded work for women with little independent occupational identity. The evidence for the actual adoption of *femme sole*, to be sure, is slim. McIntosh places herself between Bennett's gloomy assessment and the rosy one of Barron and Goldberg, arguing that some women in England had opportunity and could exercise agency. Thanks to marriage and remarriage, Barbara Hanawalt also sees some late medieval women in London doing well, but she definitively puts to rest any fiction of a golden age.[4]

Many historians assume that women of the urban elites focused on household management and played only a limited role in the broader economy. Thus, according to Régine Pernoud, the rise of the mercantile bourgeoisie in France occasioned a decline in the position of women by the end of the Middle Ages. Yet documents of practice unequivocally show that elite (and lesser) urban women invested in trade and managed property holdings, including agricultural lands. Moreover, merchant letters reveal the role of wives, though at home, in the business affairs of their husbands. Elite women were, like those of more modest social strata, still subject to the strictures of a society that, in assumptions and practice, privileged men, but they were not idle. In spite of strict urban statutory prohibitions, for example, the aristocratic women of Ragusa showed a limited yet undeniable engagement in business. Women in medieval southern French cities exerted similar agency.[5]

Another issue concerns how women's economic participation might have changed in the later Middle Ages, especially after the demographic catastrophe of the Black Death. Second-wave feminism produced little agreement about the fate of women in the late medieval and early modern eras. Joan Kelly-Gadol held a dim view of women at the time of the Renaissance. Kathleen Casey seconded Kelly-Gadol in her belief that the early modern era ushered in a less desirable period for women; she offered an optimistic assessment of women's experience in late medieval Europe. Judith C. Brown and Jordan Goodman, however, argued that the fate of urban women in early modern Europe was much more favorable.[6]

In late medieval northern Europe, Martha Howell has found that women were disadvantaged by a trend away from the household as the economic center of urban artisanal industry. In a town like Cologne where women oversaw childrearing and domestic functions and were part of a household production unit, they could achieve relatively high-status employment in conjunction with their husbands, but in an urban center such as Leiden where small commodity production involving drapery among other occupations, with guild organization as a basis, tended to exclude women, their participation in the urban economy was diminished.[7] In Italy the situation had never been positive, and the later Middle Ages saw erosion in what opportunities there were. Eleanor S. Riemer has shown that already by the late thirteenth century, Sienese laws limited wives' investments of dotal funds in market activities.[8] The negative trend for women's roles in the urban economy in the transition from the Middle Ages to the early modern era needs nuance but remains the dominant paradigm.

NORTH/SOUTH DIFFERENCES IN ECONOMY AND LAW

Economic and legal differences among Europe's regions caused the experience of urban women to vary, particularly north to south. The trading systems of the North Sea/Baltic and Mediterranean worlds bore some similarities in investment and contracts, but considerable differences in the kinds of goods traded. In the north, the trade was in bulk goods and raw materials, cereals, tar, pitch, timber, furs, and wool to fuel the Flemish cloth industry. In the south, there was a luxury trade in products from South Asia and the Far East (spices, silks, drugs, exotic nuts, and fruits) and a trade in grain, sugar, and cotton. The industry par excellence in the Middle Ages was that of textiles, with wool cloth predominant. Flanders and northern France were the major cloth producers until the fourteenth century, when Italian, Languedocian, and Catalonian industries developed.

Legal differences also existed north to south, with Germanic law influential in the north, along with some Roman law, and written Roman law traditions mixed with Germanic influences predominant in southern Europe. Common law evolved separately in England and profoundly shaped urban customs and laws, as in the institution of *femme sole*. Women's access to and control over wealth—in terms of both inheritance and marital property—were fundamental to their involvement in the urban economy. This access varied with legal influences. With the recovery of Roman law, in Germany and the Low Countries, the resulting mix of custom and contract laid a very different groundwork for women's economic activities than did the urban statutes of southern European cities. In Mediterranean Europe, the experiences of Jewish women and of enslaved Muslim women were culturally and legally distinct.[9]

In order to engage in a legal contract that could create an economic investment, women in many parts of Europe needed a male guardian who assumed legal liability. In Italian cities, the Roman law legacy, co-mingled with Lombard law, stipulated guardianship for women, and it left women with many fewer options for independent action. In Ghent, women had to have guardians unless they had been emancipated or held special merchant status. In Normandy, women could not make contracts without their husbands' approval; this curtailed their ability to participate in business. In a 1270 law code of northern France, married women were denied the ability to go to court without their husbands, unless someone had beaten or abused them. However, if a woman was in a trade, she could litigate in matters related to business.[10]

In England married women did not normally engage in lawsuits without their hus-bands. There were exceptions to these negative conditions. *Femme sole* status in England permitted a married woman to operate independently of her husband and his busi-ness. In Bruges women were usually allowed to function economically without the con-straints of guardianship. James Murray comments, "Bruges, by contrast, was every bit as commercialized and 'patriarchal' as Florence, yet women were neither under the strict guardianship of men nor absent from the market place."[11]

Catalan society, in the kingdom of Majorca's continental territories, presents a differ-ent view of women's involvement in the urban economy. The city of Perpignan was influ-enced by Visigothic laws that allowed both men and women to inherit. However, after 1250, the impact of Roman law recovery ushered in new constraints for women. Widows who were guardians of their children were the only women to engage in economic activ-ities on their own. Nonetheless, married women with children made wills and were thus a means of transmission of wealth; wealth flowed through them, even if they did not actually control it. For women in Perpignan, Visigothic traditions ensured that mater-nal as well as paternal kin were important, but the gender rules of Roman law steadily limited the extent of their activity and influence. In contrast, in early fourteenth-century Languedoc, Montpellier women—married and widowed—renounced Roman law pro-tections, restrictive of women's agency, to open up contractual opportunities for inde-pendent action. Married women of Montpellier without children could not dispose of their goods through a will without their family's permission. Women with children were free to frame their wills as they chose, but were restricted in the amount they could leave their spouses.[12]

Inheritance—that all-important mechanism through which wealth is passed by one generation to the next—varied widely across Europe. In the north primogeniture was common, especially in rural areas and aristocratic milieux, and daughters and younger sons were excluded from the main patrimony. Where there were no sons, daughters did inherit. France presented a mosaic of inheritance practices running the gamut from pri-mogeniture to the admission of female heirs to an equal share in a paternal estate. For women of Bruges, partible inheritance gave them equal shares of an estate with male heirs. In the south of France, partible inheritance called both male and female offspring to inherit in the case of intestate succession. Many southern French towns excluded dowried daughters from inheritance in intestate situations; these laws assumed that the dowry represented the woman's share of an estate. Testators could designate women as heirs or leave them bequests in wills. In Italy if there were sons, daughters did not inherit from their fathers, nor did mothers inherit from sons. As in towns of southern France, in northern and central Italy, a woman's dowry came to be construed as her legitimate share of the patrimony. Only in the absence of close male agnates might she receive more.[13]

Marriage and its economic possibilities also varied widely across the cities of medi-eval Europe. Marriage brought and conveyed resources and status to women and men. Dowries were a major source of women's fortune, especially in southern Europe. In medieval Italy, the introduction of dowry and the control of the paternal family over marital gifts led to women's lack of ability to manage their resources. In Florence, the widow, her dower (the property that came to her upon the death of her husband), and her children stayed in the patrilineal family, and if she chose to remarry, she left her children and her dower in their paternal home. There was no economic agency for the woman, whether wife or widow. That said, women still were vessels of influence. Giovanni Rucellai, a member of the fifteenth-century Florentine elite, wrote that Rucellai marriages with women of prestigious families such as the Strozzi and the Medici raised the status of the Rucellai family; clearly Giovanni saw women as a powerful vehicle of social mobility, even if their agency was limited. Dowry inflation in Venice placed enormous stress on middling families, necessitating the involvement of multiple family members in constituting a bride's dowry and the opulent and expensive trousseau that afforded prestige and social stature as well as economic security to both men and women. In Italy, women's dowries were inalienable, but husbands controlled the property, whatever the source, dotal or nondotal.[14]

In medieval London, social mobility came through women and marriage. London widows could remarry multiple times, accumulating dowers that they carried with them into new marriages. Such widows were highly sought after in the London marriage market, playing a significant role in the transmission of wealth from one generation to another. Changes in the marriage practices of Flanders brought conditions less favorable to women in the course of the later Middle Ages. In Arras, marriage by contract came to replace marriage under custom, with the result that widows no longer were the proprietors of the property of their dowers, though they received the revenues.[15]

Elite Women and the Economy

To manage a large urban household, the elite wife oversaw the work of multiple servants; she delegated tasks and kept order. She might send a domestic servant to market or have her husband place orders for goods needed in the household. She might or might not have been deeply involved in the food preparation for her husband, children, and entourage. We can picture her with her wimple and a large set of keys attached to her belt, well dressed, but not so as to attract opprobrium or openly violate sumptuary laws that dictated appropriate attire. The confinement of some elite women to the home could result in a very different arena of economic activity for elite men and women, with men in the public sphere and women in the domestic. Family fortune facilitated the absence of the elite woman from the public economic scene. Her outside economic contribution was not necessary to the survival or success of the household. Social pressures also played a part. When prescriptive literature emerged in the later Middle Ages, that is, literature that laid down authoritative rules or directions for how things should be done, a domestic economic focus for married women of the urban mercantile elite was preeminent. The domestic focus for the economic activities of the elite woman was reinforced in the later Mediterranean Middle Ages, as exemplified by the writings of Leon Battista Alberti (1404–72).[16] However, not all elite women were exclusively occupied with the household.

Some elite women worked as moneychangers. In some cities like Lyon and at Bruges in Flanders, as noted above, there is evidence that women were active as moneychangers, a form of medieval banking closely associated with international trade. By contrast, though financial operations in foreign exchange and moneychanging in Montpellier were significant, there is no direct evidence of women's involvement. Urban women were also deeply involved in lending money. They often favored a female clientele, and if the lenders were elite women, debtors might be women of lesser status who were in need of funds.[17] The female poor were often the beneficiaries of credit, in networks of women, some horizontal, some vertical.

Beyond finance and lending, elite women invested in international trade. Elite widows in Montpellier were common participants in a luxury trade that demanded capital and commercial organization. Widows acted alone, but might also be present with their sons. In these commercial transactions, wives were also mentioned in large numbers; most singlewomen seem to have lacked the requisite capital for luxury trade investments. A town like Montpellier had considerable international connections in the luxury trade and in the trade in commodities across the Mediterranean world and western Europe. Its male merchants traveled far and wide. Women invested in long-distance trade as sedentary investors; men were both sedentary investors and traveling merchants. Women tended not to travel for trade for reasons extending from family responsibilities to the dangers of the highway and the high seas, though they did travel occasionally on pilgrimage. Merchant wives in Genoa served as procurators (legal representatives) in the investment of funds of their husbands. They also invested on their own, without reference to husbands, in *commenda* partnerships which involved a traveling partner and a sedentary one, a role women could assume. The sedentary partner furnished the capital in the form of money or goods, usually deriving three-fourths of the profits; the traveling partner provided his labor and received one-fourth. Genoese women of modest station also invested in *commenda* contracts, participating in that city's risk-taking and entrepreneurship. At least during the early heyday of Genoese commerce, women were engaged in the commercial expansion of the town. The later Middle Ages brought a less propitious economic environment, as Genoa's fortunes declined, and less involvement of women in investments in international trade.

MIDDLING WOMEN AND THE ECONOMY

Beyond investments, women of many economic and social backgrounds participated in sales of luxury products and agricultural commodities, in real-estate transactions, in partnerships, in apprenticeships. Their activities are distinguished from those of men by number and scale rather than type. Men engaged more frequently and in larger transactions and investments. An important segment of the medieval urban economy was in the hands of vendors, who sometimes sold retail and sometimes wholesale. Medieval transactions do not distinguish between "retail" and "wholesale" operations, and it is very difficult to separate out these two markets, save through the inadequate measure of size of the transaction. Moreover, medieval urban inhabitants, male and female, dealt in both dimensions of the market. In Montpellier, markets regularly overlapped, so that women who sold silk as mercers often had close links with women who decorated these cloths or produced the trimmings to decorate them.

Women's roles in urban artisanal industry remain a steady topic of study and debate. The last decades have witnessed an attempt to rehabilitate guilds from the rather negative interpretation of their economic impact; newer views emphasize that guilds provided useful collective economic functions, trained new recruits, offered charity to their members, and mediated trade disputes, all the while monitoring the quality of production, controlling prices, and fostering some technological innovation.[18]

Women's place in artisanal industry was often one of lesser influence than that of men, with a lack of professional recognition. The experience of women vis-à-vis guilds nonetheless varied dramatically from city to city. The later Middle Ages saw the increasing exclusion of women from activities such as brewing, which had once been the source of considerable livelihood for women in England. But new research demonstrates London daughters' ability to inherit and, by extension, exploit urban property.[19] The Montpellier food trades, textile industries, and burnishing of precious metals count the participation of women in apprenticeship and in employment, but notaries rarely noted an occupation for women, and there is no evidence they were members of the urban guilds in the trades in which they labored.

More generally, when guilds incorporated in the later Middle Ages, both men and women found that access to the career progression from apprentice to master was increasingly difficult. Women rarely participated in this hierarchy. With few exceptions, women were apprenticed in crafts that might be classified as women's work (textiles, food trades, and luxury accessories); they rarely achieved master status. There were clear sex distinctions in the artisanal industry of most large cities, and women were excluded outright from some. The prestigious trades of Montpellier, such as pepperers, apothecaries, changers, and drapers, did not accept women apprentices.[20] With few exceptions, guilds across medieval Europe did women little good.

There were always exceptional situations. In some few cases, women had their own guilds, and sometimes women were masters in them. Women served as masters (*mestrigghe*) in the cloth industry in Bruges. The compendium of guild statutes of Étienne Boileau (*c.*1270) mentions five female guilds in Paris, all associated with the silk industry. In some male-dominated guilds, widows could take over the mastership of their late husbands.[21] Within the eighty of approximately 120 Parisian guilds that admitted women (tax records of 1292 and 1313), women could sometimes achieve master status, often only by virtue of being the widow of a deceased member. In early fourteenth-century Toulouse, women participated in five lesser guilds. In Barcelona, women engaged in spinning appear to have exercised some economic agency, as they had their own shops and apprentices. Aristocratic women of Genoa ran workshops of women spinning gold. In the Florentine tax records of 1427 and 1430, only 270 of 7,000 female heads of household, in fact, had an occupation listed, though within this number there were numerous occupations, often modest, for female heads of household. Italy and England represent cases where there were no guilds exclusive to women.

On balance, women's artisanal work is hidden from our scrutiny because of its less official stature, compared to that of guildsmen. Although women may have been skilled in certain trades and crafts, even entering into apprenticeships, they were generally excluded from official recognition in tax records or guild memberships.

POOR WOMEN: SERVICE, SLAVERY, AND AN ECONOMY OF MAKESHIFTS

Although we know much more about women from noble, mercantile, and artisanal families, historians have not ignored the many poor women who made their homes in medieval towns. Scholarship of the late 1980s and early 1990s broke ground in this respect. David Herlihy in *Opera Muliebria* provided a useful synthesis of the relationship between women and work in the Middle Ages, and subsequent case studies have focused particularly on singlewomen and widows.[22] On the positive side, such women could often escape the paternal or spousal oversight that wealth invited. On the negative side, low social and economic status left women (and men) more vulnerable to life's vicissitudes. Singlewomen, widows, poor women, and female vagrants had to work at low pay to support themselves and, at times, their families.

Female domestic servants were numerous in Europe and the Mediterranean world, and their status varied. Domestic service in Florence was so low status as to be almost comparable to slavery. In Ragusa, this might have been especially true, as the servant population there included large numbers of enslaved, as well as free, women. Most slaves in Ragusa were women.[23] In Montpellier, however, domestic service was sometimes the subject of apprenticeship or work contracts, a practice that suggests it was viewed as a minor artisanal industry.

Women in wet-nursing often fared better than those in domestic service. We have evidence for this from both Florence and Perpignan. Pay was better, and wet nurses could also hope to make useful contacts in employers' homes that might assure better futures for their own children. A municipal service for foundlings in Montpellier employed wet nurses on behalf of its charges. The work was not overly onerous, as there was usually one child per wet nurse, but women often had to stop nursing their own children as a result. Wet-nursing did not have long-term stability as employment, however, as women served for the short term, with significant turnover in the occupation.

Peddling and huckstering were another common recourse of poorer women in medieval cities and towns.[24] Hucksters most often hawked fruits and vegetables, eggs, chickens, cheese, and sometimes, old clothes. Rarely were female peddlers on the open roads, unless accompanying their husbands, but in town they might carry their goods on their back or in baskets or push handcarts. Those selling in markets from stands and stalls were the most

fortunate. Hucksters in medieval cities like London and Exeter regularly irritated city officials by buying goods early in the morning and selling late in the day (forestalling), or
selling goods over market price (regrating). Hucksters made famous by Rose the Regrater
in William Langland's *Piers Plowman* were part of a transient, makeshift economy of distributive trades. As Langland stated: "Rose the retailer was her right name: She's lived the
life of a huckster eleven years," implying some continuity nonetheless.[25] Hucksters were
also active in southern Europe, where, for example, they retailed foodstuffs in late medieval Seville. In Italy, according to the poet Francesco de Barberio, women's occupations
included selling fruits, vegetables, cheese, eggs, and chickens. Female frippers (peddlers
of used clothing) were active in Bologna, Florence, and Toulouse.[26]

By the later Middle Ages, economic difficulties and poverty encouraged an increase
in hucksters. Huckstering was sometimes the only work women could get, but it gave
rise to long, venerable traditions. In Montpellier, an informal community of fourteen
women can be identified in the 1330s as hucksters on the Herbaria Square in the city
center. Through their testimonies in a lawsuit over the public status of the square, they
made reference to generations of additional women hucksters stretching back several
decades. Some of the market sellers were single, some married, and some widowed.
These women were an articulate group, with considerable collective memory of events
on the market square and a long history of rental of space for collapsible stalls.[27]

The poor and the sick, male and female, were numerous in medieval cities, and elite
women sometimes helped their poorer counterparts. The care of the poor and the sick
in hospitals was a common target of charitable donations. Urban wills, especially those
of women, often left bequests to recluses, to houses of repentant women (reformed prostitutes), and to poor girls for dowries. Such bequests created vertical ties among women,
tying rich and poor together in the obligations of Christian charity.

Where there was female poverty (and there was female poverty in all medieval cities), prostitution was rarely absent. Prostitution was not the route to riches, but it could
be remunerative for some. In London, though individual prostitutes (common women)
rarely made much money, the bawds (men and women) arranging sexual encounters
could make more. Montpellier prostitutes of the 1330s rented rooms, bought houses,
purchased chests and luxury clothing, and traveled.[28]

Medieval cities often segregated prostitutes into specific areas or brothels. In mid-
fifteenth-century Avignon, where the papal court had once provided many clients for
prostitutes, the Avignonese segregated prostitutes into red-light districts. Venetians
tried to regulate and facilitate prostitution with the creation of a public house in the
parish of St Matteo di Rialto. Bologna created a civic brothel in the 1330s, after earlier
attempts to restrict prostitution to outside the city walls failed. Florence established an
office of decency, the *Onestà*, to regulate the behavior of such women. In some parts of
the Continent, such as southern France, municipal authorities shifted from civic repression to relaxation of regulations, legalization, and even institutionalization of prostitution, with the opening of public brothels in many cities between 1350 and 1450.[29]

The presence of Jews, Muslims, and domestic slaves in Mediterranean Europe rendered the practice of prostitution even more complex. Municipalities feared the mixing

of good women and prostitutes. In Daroca Christian prostitutes were visible along the route to the river where Jewish women went to draw water. In Valladolid the brothel was located near a main road and the town fountain. Female slaves in Mediterranean Europe were vulnerable to sexual exploitation. Sally McKee thinks their high purchase price shows women were purchased for sex, as their costs could not have been recovered through their work alone.[30] In spite of efforts to prevent the prostitution of slaves, there was cross-confession sex, and there were slaves working in brothels.[31]

CONCLUSION

Whether the focus is on elite women, artisanal women, or poor and marginal women, there was a great variety of economic experience in the towns and cities of western Europe. Because of this, generalizations are difficult to sustain. The older assessments registering disagreement about women's place in the urban economy of medieval western Europe have now been joined by newer disagreements. It is likely that the future assessments of the situation of women in the urban economy will continue to vary from region to region, from city to city, and from scholar to scholar as additional case studies are produced. But it is only with examination of local cases that the depth and breadth of women's roles in the medieval urban economy can acquire sufficient nuance to do justice to their rich historical experience.

FURTHER READING

Bennett, Judith M. *Ale, Beer, and Brewsters in England: Women's Work in a Changing World, 1300 to 1600*. Oxford: Oxford University Press, 1996.

Bennett, Judith M. and Amy M. Froide, eds. *Singlewomen in the European Past, 1250–1800*. Philadelphia: University of Pennsylvania Press, 1999.

Dillard, Heath. *Daughters of the Reconquest: Women in Castilian Town Society 1100–1300*. Cambridge: Cambridge University Press, 1984.

Farmer, Sharon. *Surviving Poverty in Medieval Paris: Gender, Ideology and the Daily Lives of the Poor*. Ithaca: Cornell University Press, 2002.

Hanawalt, Barbara A. *The Wealth of Wives: Women, Law, and Economy in Late Medieval London*. Oxford: Oxford University Press, 2007.

Herlihy, David. *Opera Muliebria: Women and Work in Medieval Europe*. New York: McGraw-Hill, 1990.

Howell, Martha C. *Workers, Production, and Patriarchy in Late Medieval Cities*. Chicago: University of Chicago Press, 1986.

Karras, Ruth Mazo. *Common Women: Prostitution and Sexuality in Medieval England*. Oxford: Oxford University Press, 1996.

Klapisch-Zuber, Christiane. *Women, Family, and Ritual in Renaissance Italy*, trans. Lydia G. Cochrane. Chicago: University of Chicago Press, 1985.

McIntosh, Marjorie Keniston. *Working Women in English Society, 1300-1600.* Cambridge: Cambridge University Press, 2005.

Murray, James M. *Bruges: Cradle of Capitalism, 1280-1390.* Cambridge: Cambridge University Press, 2005.

Otis-Cour, Leah Lydia. *Prostitution in Medieval Society: The History of an Urban Institution in Languedoc.* Chicago: University of Chicago Press, 1985.

Stuard, Susan Mosher. *A State of Deference: Ragusa/Dubrovnik in the Medieval Centuries.* Philadelphia: University of Pennsylvania Press, 2002.

Winer, Rebecca Lynn. *Women, Wealth, and Community in Perpignan, c. 1250-1300: Christians, Jews, and Enslaved Muslims in a Medieval Mediterranean Town.* Aldershot: Ashgate, 2006.

NOTES

1. The Datini correspondence was edited in two works: *Le lettere di Margherita Datini a Francesco di Marco, 1384-1410*, ed. Valeria Rosati (Prato: Cassa di Risparmi, 1977); and *Le lettere di Francesco Datini alla moglie Margherita (1386-1410)*, ed. Elena Cecchi (Prato: Società pratese di Storia Patria, 1990). See also Frances Gies and Joseph Gies, *Women in the Middle Ages* (New York: Barnes & Noble, 1980), 184-209. For the Goodman of Paris, see *The Goodman of Paris: A Treatise on Moral and Domestic Economy by a Citizen of Paris (c. 1393)*, ed. Eileen Power (London: G. Routledge & Sons, 1928), and *Le Ménagier de Paris*, ed. Georgine E. Brereton and Janet M. Feinley (Oxford: Clarendon Press, 1981); and James Murray, *Bruges: Cradle of Capitalism, 1280-1390* (Cambridge; New York: Cambridge University Press, 2005).

2. Heath Dillard, *Daughters of the Reconquest: Women in Castilian Town Society 1100-1300* (Cambridge: Cambridge University Press, 1984).

3. Judith M. Bennett, *History Matters: Patriarchy and the Challenge of Feminism* (Philadelphia: University of Pennsylvania Press, 2006).

4. Marjorie K. McIntosh, "The Benefits and Drawbacks of *Femme Sole* Status in England, 1300-1630," *Journal of British Studies*, 44 (2005): 410-38; Barbara A. Hanawalt, *The Wealth of Wives: Women, Law, and Economy in Late Medieval London* (Oxford: Oxford University Press, 2007), 215.

5. On the south of France, see, for example, Francine Michaud, *Un signe des temps: Accroissement des crises familiales autour du patrimoine à Marseille à la fin du XIIIe siècle* (Toronto: Pontifical Institute of Mediaeval Studies, 1994) and Andrée Courtemanche, *La richesse des femmes: Patrimoines et gestion à Manosque au XIVe siècle* (Paris: Vrin; Montreal: Bellarmin, 1993).

6. Joan Kelly-Gadol, "Did Women Have a Renaissance?" in Renate Bridenthal, Claudia Koonz, and Susan Mosher Stuard, eds, *Becoming Visible: Women in European History*, 2nd edn (Boston: Houghton Mifflin, 1987), 174-201; Kathleen Casey, "The Cheshire Cat: Reconstructing the Experience of Medieval Women," in Berenice A. Carroll, ed., *Liberating Women's History: Theoretical and Critical Essays* (Urbana: University of Illinois Press, 1976), 224-49; Judith C. Brown and Jordan Goodman, "Women and Industry in Florence," *Journal of Economic History*, 40 (1980): 73-80.

7. Martha C. Howell, "Women, the Family Economy, and the Structures of Market Production in Cities of Northern Europe During the Late Middle Ages," in Barbara A. Hanawalt, ed., *Women and Work in Preindustrial Europe* (Bloomington: Indiana University Press, 1986),

198–222, and Martha C. Howell, *Workers, Production, and Patriarchy in Late Medieval Cities* (Chicago: Chicago University Press, 1986). See also Martha C. Howell, "Gender in the Transition to Merchant Capitalism," Chapter 35 in this volume.

8. Eleanor S. Reimer, "Women, Dowries, and Capital Investment in Thirteenth-Century Siena," in Marion A. Kaplan, ed., *The Marriage Bargain: Women and Dowries in European History* (New York: Harrington Park Press, 1985), 59–79.

9. Rebecca Lynn Winer, *Women, Wealth, and Community in Perpignan, c. 1250–1300: Christians, Jews, and Enslaved Muslims in a Medieval Mediterranean Town* (Aldershot: Ashgate, 2006) offers a case study of both Jewish and Muslim women.

10. F. R. P. Akehurst, trans., *The Etablissements de Saint Louis: Thirteenth-Century Law Texts from Tours, Orléans, and Paris* (Philadelphia: University of Pennsylvania Press, 1996).

11. James M. Murray, *Bruges, Cradle of Capitalism*, 303.

12. Winer, *Women, Wealth, and Community in Perpignan* examines inheritance, see 5, 20. For Montpellier, see Kathryn L. Reyerson, "Southern French Legal Procedure and Local Practice: Legal Traditions in Dialogue," paper presented at 40th International Congress on Medieval Studies, Western Michigan University, Kalamazoo, MI, May 2005.

13. On inheritance patterns, see Jean Yver, *Egalité entre héritiers et exclusion des enfants dotés: Essai de géographie coutumière* (Paris: Éditions Sirey, 1966). For laws and women's inheritance in southern France, see Laurent Mayali, *Droit savant et coutumes: L'Exclusion des filles dotées, XIIe–XVe siècles* (Frankfurt am Main: Vittorio Klostermann, 1987).

14. Kathryn L. Reyerson, "La mobilité sociale: Réflexions sur le rôle de la femme," in Sandro Carocci and Marilyn Nicoud, eds, *La mobilità sociale nel medioevo: Rappresentazioni, canali, protagonisti, metodi d'indagine* (Rome: École Française de Rome, 2010), 491–511. See also Anthony Molho, R. Barducci, G. Battista, and F. Donnini, "Genealogy and Marriage Alliance: Memories of Power in Late Medieval Florence," in Samuel K. Cohn and Steven A. Epstein, eds, *Portraits of Medieval and Renaissance Living: Essays in Honor of David Herlihy* (Ann Arbor: University of Michigan Press, 1996), 39–70. Donald E. Queller and Thomas F. Madden, "Father of the Bride: Fathers, Daughters, and Dowries in Late Medieval and Early Renaissance Venice," *Renaissance Quarterly*, 46 (1993): 685–711, and Stanley Chojnacki, *Women and Men in Renaissance Venice: Twelve Essays on Patrician Society* (Baltimore: Johns Hopkins University Press, 2000). See also Susan Mosher Stuard, "Brideprice, Dowry, and Other Marital Assigns," Chapter 10 in this volume.

15. On London widows, see Hanawalt, *The Wealth of Wives*. Martha C. Howell, *The Marriage Exchange: Property, Social Place, and Gender in Cities of the Low Countries 1300–1550* (Chicago: University of Chicago Press, 1998), discusses marriage and widows in Flanders.

16. Leon Battista Alberti, *I Libri della famiglia*, ed. R. Romano and A. Tenenti, with Francesco Furlan (Turin: G. Einaudi, 1994), 269.

17. William Chester Jordan, *Women and Credit in Pre-Industrial and Developing Societies* (Philadelphia: University of Pennsylvania Press, 1993), provides a detailed examination of such lending practices.

18. For background on the debate, see Stephan R. Epstein, "Craft Gilds in the Pre-Modern Economy: A Discussion," *Economic History Review*, 61 (2008): 155–74, and the reply by Sheilagh Ogilvie, "Rehabilitating the Gilds: A Reply," *Economic History Review*, 61 (2009): 175–82. See also Richard Mackenney, *Tradesmen and Traders: The World of the Gilds in Venice and Europe, c. 1250–c. 1650* (Totowa, NJ: Barnes and Noble, 1987), and Peter

Berezin, "Did Medieval Craft Gilds Do More Harm than Good?" *The Journal of European Economic History*, 12 (2003): 171–97.

19. Maryanne Kowaleski and Judith M. Bennett, "Crafts, Gilds, and Women in the Middle Ages. Fifty Years after Marian K. Dale," in Judith M. Bennett, Elizabeth A. Clark, Jean F. O'Barr, Anne Vilen, and Sarah Westphal-Wihl (eds), *Sisters and Workers in the Middle Ages* (Chicago: University of Chicago Press, 1898), 11–38. For London daughters, see Kate Kelsey Staples, *Daughters of London: Inheriting Opportunity in the Late Middle Ages* (Leiden: E. J. Brill, 2011).

20. Kathryn L. Reyerson, "The Adolescent Apprentice/Worker in Medieval Montpellier," *Journal of Family History*, 17 (1992): 353–70.

21. David Herlihy, *Opera Muliebria: Women and Work in Medieval Europe* (New York: McGraw-Hill, 1990).

22. Herlihy, *Opera Muliebria*. See, for example, Judith M. Bennett and Amy M. Froide, eds, *Singlewomen in the European Past 1250–1800* (Philadelphia: University of Pennsylvania Press, 1999).

23. Christiane Klapisch-Zuber, "Women Servants in Florence during the Fourteenth and Fifteenth Centuries," in Hanawalt, ed., *Women and Work*, 56–80. Susan Mosher Stuard, "To Town to Serve: Urban Domestic Slavery in Medieval Ragusa," in Hanawalt, ed., *Women and Work*, 39–55. See also Sally McKee, "Slavery," in this volume, Chapter 18.

24. Marjorie Keniston McIntosh, *Working Women in English Society, 1300–1620* (Cambridge: Cambridge University Press, 2005), 128–32.

25. William Langland, *Piers Plowman*, ed. Elizabeth Robertson and Stephen H. A. Shepherd, Norton Critical Edition (New York: Norton, 2006), 74–75. See also Hanawalt, *The Wealth of Wives*, 200–201, 203; Maryanne Kowaleski, "Women's Work in a Market Town: Exeter in the Late Fourteenth Century," in Hanawalt, ed., *Women and Work*, 148–49; and Merry Wiesner Wood [Hanks], "Paltry Peddlers or Essential Merchants? Women in the Distributive Trades in Early Modern Nuremberg," *The Sixteenth-Century Journal*, 12 (1981): 3.

26. Herlihy, *Opera Muliebria*, 70, 95, 155.

27. McIntosh, *Working Women*, 131–32. See also Kathryn Reyerson "Public and Private Space in Medieval Montpellier: The Bon Amic Square," *Journal of Urban History*, 24 (1997): 3–27. See also idem, "Le témoignage des femmes (à partir de quelques enquêtes montpelliéraines du XIVe siècle)," in Claude Gauvard, ed., *L'Enquête au Moyen Age* (Rome: École Française de Rome, 2008), 153–68.

28. Ruth Mazo Karras, *Common Women: Prostitution and Sexuality in Medieval England* (Oxford: Oxford University Press, 1996); idem, "Prostitution in Medieval Europe," in Vern Bullough and James A. Brundage, eds, *The Handbook of Medieval Sexuality* (New York: Garland, 1996), 243–60; Jacques Rossiaud, *Medieval Prostitution* (New York: Barnes and Noble, 1988); and Kathryn L. Reyerson, "Prostitution in Medieval Montpellier: The Ladies of Campus Polverel," *Medieval Prosopography*, 18 (1997): 209–28. See also Leah Lydia Otis-Cour, *Prostitution in Medieval Society: The History of an Urban Institution in Languedoc* (Chicago: University of Chicago Press, 1985), and idem, "Prostitution and Repentance in Late Medieval Perpignan," in Julius Kirshner and Susanne Wemple, eds, *Women of the Medieval World: Essays in Honor of John H. Mundy* (Oxford: Blackwell, 1985), 137–60.

29. Joëlle Rollo-Koster, "From Prostitutes to Brides of Christ: The Avignonese *Repenties* in the Late Middle Ages," *Journal of Medieval and Early Modern Studies*, 32 (2002): 109–44;

Elisabeth [Crouzet-] Pavan, "Police des moeurs, société, et politique à Venise à la fin du Moyen Age," *Revue historique, 264* (1980): 241–88; Carol Lansing, "Concubines, Lovers, Prostitutes: Infamy and Female Identity in Medieval Bologna," in Paula Findlein, Michelle M. Fontaine, and Duane J. Osheim, eds, *Beyond Florence: The Contours of Medieval and Early Modern Italy* (Palo Alto: Stanford University Press, 2003), 98; John Brackett, "The Florentine Onestà and the Control of Prostitution, 1403–1680," *Sixteenth Century Journal, 24* (1983): 273–300. See also Maria Serena Mazzi, *Prostitute e lenoni nella Firenze del Quatrocento* (Milan: Fine, 1991). On prostitution in southern France, see Rossiaud, *Medieval Prostitution,* and Otis-Cour, *Prostitution in Medieval Society.*

30. See Sally McKee, "Slavery."

31. David Nirenberg, *Communities of Violence: Persecution of Minorities in the Middle Ages* (Princeton: Princeton University Press, 1996), 145–46; Sally McKee, "The Implications of Slave Women's Sexual Service in Late Medieval Italy," in M. Erdem Kabadayi and Tobias Reichardt, eds, *Unfreie Arbeit: Ökonomische rechtliche und geistesgeschichte Perspektiven* (Hildesheim: Olms, 2007), 101–14; Jaume Serra Barceló and Margalida Bernat Roca, "Folles fembres bordelleres: La prostitució femenina al tombant de l'Edat Mitjana," in Maria Barceló, ed., *Al tombant de l'edat mitjana: Tradició medieval i cultura humanista* (Palma de Mallorca: Institut d'Estudis Baleàrics, 2000), 213–49.

CHAPTER 20

RURAL ECONOMIES

JANE WHITTLE

A LATE fifteenth-century English ballad offers a lively representation of women's work in the rural medieval economy. In it, the husband and wife argue over who does the most work. The man's work is described only as plowing, all day long. In contrast, the woman milks cows, makes butter and cheese, raises poultry, bakes bread, brews ale, processes flax and wool into yarn, weaves cloth, and does the housework. Despite lying "all night awake with our child," she tends to the cows and tidies the house each morning before her husband even gets up.[1] The ballad takes the woman's side, arguing that women's work involved hard labor and skill. Its moral is that the contribution of women and men to the rural economy was different but complementary: both were crucial to survival and prosperity.

Medieval Europe was overwhelmingly rural: more than 90 percent of the population lived in the countryside or small towns. With little mechanical power available, all aspects of the economy depended heavily on human labor: women and men worked hard to make a living. On the one hand, a history that ignores either women's economic role, or the role that gender played in shaping the economy, distorts our understanding of economic development and of women's lives. Women, like men, worked long and hard. On the other hand, women's position in society was not simply determined by their degree of participation in the economy. It is a modern assumption that active economic involvement and hard work translate into status and wealth. As any medieval peasant would have explained, while hard work might make the difference between survival and starvation, it did not bring wealth or power. A similar lesson can be learned about women's economic involvement. To explain why women owned less land than men, why women were excluded from certain occupations, and why they were normally paid less than men, it is necessary to look well beyond the economy at customs, laws, political institutions, and religious teachings that favored men and worked against women.

This chapter is structured around three aspects of involvement in the rural economy. The first is the ownership and tenure of land, particularly the proportion of female landholders. In an economy which was primarily agricultural, land was an essential resource. Possession of land indicates involvement in the management of agriculture, but land was also an important source of status, power, and wealth. The second aspect is the gender division of labor. Occupations, tasks, and patterns of work were all gendered in the medieval period. Some were tightly restricted to either men or women, others showed a preponderance of one gender or the other, while other activities were mixed. Nonetheless, as the fifteenth-century ballad described above shows, daily work routines in rural households were understood in gendered terms. Despite often being presented as "natural," particularly with regard to unpaid and caring work within the home, the gender division of labor did change over time. Technological innovations and commercialization had an impact. The third aspect of gendered involvement in the rural economy is paid labor and the level of wages. In the late medieval period, women were active participants in the labor market as servants and day laborers, but they were typically paid between three-quarters and one half of what men received. The discussion of women's wages crystallizes many of the issues about women's unequal participation in the economy. Were women paid less because they were less physically strong than men, worked shorter hours due to domestic duties, or were less skilled? Or was it because the gender division of labor "crowded" women into certain occupations while excluding them from others? Or was it simply that laws, customs, and social expectations dictated that women's wages should be lower? This debate spills over into a consideration of the gender division of labor: why were women excluded from some occupations? Why were women and not men assumed to be burdened with unpaid housework and childcare? Why, as Judith Bennett has noted, was "women's work characteristically low-status, low-skilled and low-paid?"[2]

Europe experienced significant economic change in the one thousand years between 500 and 1500. Indirect evidence of improved agricultural productivity is provided by population growth, with more people being supported from the same area of land, and by urbanization and increased industrial production, which indicate the ability to support a larger nonagricultural population. Over time, more agricultural and craft products were sold, and traded over long distances: the growth of towns and industry is evidence of this commercialization, as is the gradual replacement of unfree labor with wage labor. Population growth and economic growth slowed in the early fourteenth century, with famine in 1315–1318, followed by a sharp reduction in population (30–50 percent) caused by the Black Death in 1347–1351. Recovery was slow and uneven, with population levels remaining low and many towns experiencing decline or stagnation until the early sixteenth century. Nonetheless, rural society prospered: serfdom largely disappeared from Western Europe in the fourteenth and fifteenth centuries, and the agrarian economy continued to commercialize in the fifteenth century, with an increasingly prosperous peasantry, an expanding rural cloth industry, and high real wages.

How did these changes affect women's involvement in the economy? Did women's level of economic involvement and agency improve or decline across the medieval period? David Herlihy in *Opera Muliebria* argues that women's work became increasingly restricted. For instance, in the early medieval period women dominated all stages of cloth and clothing production including spinning, weaving, fulling, dyeing, and tailoring. By the fifteenth century, only spinning was still restricted to women, and the other processes were dominated by men. There was also a decline in the proportion of landholders who were women. Female peasant tenants were more common in the period before the Black Death than in the early sixteenth century. There were more aristocratic women holding land in c.800–c.1100 than afterwards. Other historians see improvements, arguing that the labor shortages after the Black Death increased employment opportunities for women and thus improved their economic fortunes and levels of independence.[3]

In a study of women's work in early modern Germany, Sheilagh Ogilvie usefully classifies explanations offered by historians, economists, and sociologists for gender inequalities in the preindustrial economy as: "technological," that is determined by the physical characteristics of the two sexes and their interaction with the existing technology of production; "cultural," that is determined by norms, mentalities, and informal customs, for instance relating to marriage, family dynamics, and education; or "institutional," that is determined by the rules or laws that govern dominant institutions such as the manorial system, guilds, or markets. Thus Elizabeth Barber's explanation that women dominated textile production in the prehistoric and ancient world because it fitted well with their home-based duties of childcare and food preparation relies on a technological explanation. Bennett's argument that women's work remained low-paid, low-skilled, and low status between c.1300 and c.1700, despite commercial and demographic change, because of a deeply ingrained patriarchy, is a cultural explanation. The arguments of Herlihy and Ogilvie that male-dominated guilds were responsible for formally excluding women from well-paid and skilled work in textile production is an institutional explanation, as is that put forward by Marjorie McIntosh that demographic and market conditions were favorable to women in the years after the Black Death.[4] Yet, while many historians tend towards one type of explanation rather than another, these explanations are not exclusive, and it is possible (and indeed likely) that more than one type is necessary. While technological and institutional changes offer convincing explanations of shifts over time, it is hard to explain the long-term persistence of gendered differences without turning to cultural explanations, particularly the existence of patriarchy, a deeply ingrained social hostility to women's independence, and an assertion of their inferiority to men.

WOMEN AND LAND

Property, and especially real property or land, was crucial to the medieval economy. Instead of relying on earning wages, most people worked the land and/or produced items in their own homes as independent manufacturers. Rights to land, tenements, and goods were essential to prosperity. Property rights were gendered: sons and daughters had different rights of inheritance, married men and women had different rights of ownership, and widowers and widows had different rights to land and goods after their spouse's death.

Aristocratic women in the early and central medieval period are rarely considered by historians as economic actors, a point also made by Joanna Drell (Chapter 21 this volume). However, like their fathers and husbands, these women owned and managed property. Husbands were often absent on matters of politics, war, administration, or pilgrimage, and women were expected to be competent managers of estates in their absence, as well as during widowhood, as Drell notes. The will of Aethelgifu, an elite woman who owned twelve estates in tenth-century England, is unusual in revealing the details of her landed and personal property. She bequeathed seventy-four oxen, thirty-four cows, 760 sheep, and three herds of swine, and she mentioned food rents rendered in malt, meal, fish, honey, and cheese. She owned not only land and livestock but also the people necessary to work the estate: in her will, she freed seventy slaves, while others were given as gifts to her family and friends. They included a miller, fuller, huntsman, dairymaid, shepherd, and swineherds. Aethelgifu listed many of her workers by name, and she knew whether they were married and how many children they had. She clearly had a thorough knowledge of her estates and workforce. According to England's *Domesday Book*, 350 elite women, mostly widows, held landed estates in 1066 accounting for 5 percent of total lands. In the more detailed *Exon Domesday* and *Little Domesday*, 10–14 percent of smaller landowners (such as "thegns" and "freemen") were women. One woman, Leofgyo, held a manor at Knook in Wiltshire and made "gold thread embroidery for the king and queen": she appears to have been granted land in return for her work.[5]

Elsewhere in early medieval Europe, many women owned land in their own right even when married, and they could alienate land by grant or sale if they wished to do so. In a study of tenth-century Christian Spain, Wendy Davies shows that while 46 percent of property transactions were carried out by men acting without women, the rest involved women—19 percent women acting without men, 29 percent married couples, and 9 percent other mixed-gender groups (such as mothers and sons). The women involved in these property transfers ranged from elite women in court circles to ordinary free peasant women. Women were still active participants in the land market of Castile in northern Spain in the late thirteenth century. Herlihy identified Spain and southern France as areas where female landholders were particularly prominent from the ninth to twelfth centuries, accounting for 8–18 percent of alienations of land. In Montpellier, many elite women owned and devised land from the tenth century onwards, although by the thirteenth century this role had declined (perhaps because women's dowries were by then usually made up of moveable goods rather than land).[6]

From the thirteenth century onwards, there is better evidence about peasant women's rights to land. These were influenced by local customs of inheritance, which varied a great deal across Europe. England was dominated by primogeniture (inheritance by the eldest son), although sons sometimes inherited jointly. Daughters only inherited land when there were no sons, and widows typically received a third of the property they had held with their husband. In medieval Scandinavia, land was divided among sons and daughters, with each daughter inheriting half the portion given to each son. Widows had rights to all the property they brought into a marriage. Late medieval Germany was also dominated by partible inheritance between sons and daughters. In France, inheritance customs differed between the north and south. In northern France, property tended to be divided among children, male and female: in the Paris region, parents had the right to favor particular children as they wished; in Brittany, property was divided with strict equality among all children. Only in Normandy was land divided between sons only, with daughters excluded. In some places in southern France, impartible inheritance favored a single heir: in the Basque region and some other localities, it was eldest child—whether male or female—who inherited, while more commonly land went to the eldest son (and to the eldest daughter if there were no sons). Throughout these regions, widows were generally given preference to inherit property before children, except in Normandy, where they were excluded from receiving land.

How did such customs translate into practice? In England, where inheritance customs favored men, lists of tenants from the early fourteenth century show that women held about one fifth of tenancies in their own right. The effects of restricted landholding percolated through women's lives. Village society in medieval England is richly documented by manorial court rolls. Manorial courts were run by feudal lords and oversaw many aspects of the village economy: the transfer of land by inheritance or sale, the payment of rent, agreements of debt and credit between villagers, brewing of ale for sale, and the marriage, place of abode, and labor services of unfree tenants. Women are less well recorded than men in court rolls: fewer women were tenants and women did not act as manorial jurors as men did, nor were they elected to the office of constable or reeve. For instance, only 20 percent of individuals appearing in the manor court of Brigstock between 1287 and 1348 were women. Nonetheless, the unfree status of serfdom affected women as well as men: the daughters of unfree tenants paid fines for permission to marry; labor services were due from female tenants as well as male tenants, and regulations might specify labor was supplied by men, women, or whole families. Women do appear frequently in court rolls as brewers of ale. Ale was the staple drink of medieval England, preferred even to water. It was sold regularly in villages and small towns, and manorial lords had the right to charge a small fine for testing its quality. Manorial court rolls list brewers, the majority of whom were either women or men appearing in right of their wives. There is also evidence that women engaged in the village economy by acting as moneylenders. This activity tended to be restricted to widows as married women could not make contracts independently of their husbands.[7]

Emmanuel Le Roy Ladurie's vivid description of village life in Montaillou in the French Pyrenees reveals that, despite a misogynistic and male-dominated culture, women could be independent economic actors following their own occupations and making contracts. In the region of Montaillou, inheritance was impartible: families were so strongly identified with a single house that the word "house" meant "family." Each house had a powerful head who ran its economy and chose his or her heir from among its members. Most heads were men, but women also took this role. In the early fourteenth century, a woman—Mengarde Clergue—headed the wealthiest and most important peasant house in Montaillou. Alazais Azema headed another, and she became a cheesemonger and pig farmer in her widowhood. Some of these women inherited the headship of a house from their parents rather than husbands. In her widowhood, Guillemette Maury left her marital house, reverted to her natal surname, and became head of her parents' house in a nearby village. She farmed a vineyard, kept a flock of sheep, and cheated her nephew (who was a shepherd). Sybille Baille inherited her mother's house, separated from her husband with whom she had two sons, and worked as a stock-raiser. Even married women who did not head houses sometimes had identifiable occupations, such as the sheep farmer Sybille Pierre.[8] The sheep-farming economy, whereby flocks owned by peasant households were moved over long distances by itinerant shepherds, placed women like her in a powerful position over their male employees, the shepherds.

While women's rights to land may have strengthened in the period up to 1000, no study of medieval female landholders after 1000 reveals an increase in the proportion of women owning or renting land over time. The situation was either one of stability or decline. Decline was often associated with commercialization and the switch to giving daughters dowries in goods and cash rather than land. Before the Black Death, 17–20 percent of peasant tenants in English manors were female; by the early sixteenth century, this had fallen to 10 percent or less. This decline occurred in a period of plentiful land and economic prosperity for the English peasantry. Yet the implications of this change are not clear-cut. Cash dowries could be worth more than a small inheritance of land, and daughters often received endowments that matched the arrangements made for younger sons. And, despite the drop in female tenancies, women continued to be active managers and cultivators of their husbands' land and became independent economic agents as widows, even as the rural economy commercialized. An example of such a woman is Avice Lombe, a wealthy peasant from early sixteenth-century Norfolk, who managed to accumulate wealth in a combination of land, livestock, and cash, increasing her property during each of her four marriages.[9] The institutional structures of law and inheritance were prejudicial against women, but they still left room for some women to prosper, especially in widowhood.

GENDER DIVISION OF LABOR

The peasant economy of medieval Europe combined agriculture with textile production. Everywhere, grain (wheat, barley, rye, and oats) was the staple diet, eaten as bread or stewed in pottage. In northern areas, grain cultivation was combined with keeping livestock, primarily cattle and sheep, which provided meat and milk for butter and cheese, while ale brewed from malted grains was the primary drink. In southern Europe, grain cultivation was supplemented with olives grown for oil and vines for wine. Everywhere, poultry, pigs, fruit, and vegetables raised on the farmstead, typically by women, provided important elements of the ordinary diet. The two main types of textile production relied on agricultural products: sheep's wool for woolen cloth, and plant fibers, primarily from flax and hemp, for linen.

The gender division of labor described in the late medieval ballad with which this chapter started was common across northwestern Europe. Illustrations from religious psalters emphasize women's participation in agriculture. Thirteenth-century psalters from southern Germany show women raking hay and harvesting wheat with a sickle; the early fourteenth-century English *Luttrell Psalter* depicts women weeding crops, harvesting wheat, milking sheep, and spinning wool; while the many psalters produced in the Dutch and Flemish workshops of the fifteenth and early sixteenth centuries illustrate women making hay and harvesting wheat, picking grapes, shearing sheep, milking cows, feeding pigs, and bundling firewood. In southern Europe, women tended vines and olive groves, but were less commonly involved in grain agriculture.[10] Everywhere, women are revealed as consistently present in the agricultural workforce.

It is often assumed that women's responsibility for childcare led them to concentrate on work that could to be done around the house and farmstead. However, there was no overriding reason why all childcare had to take place within the house, or why, other than breastfeeding, such care had to be undertaken by women. This type of argument is undermined by the clear evidence that women did agricultural work in the fields. Late medieval sources such as Fitzherbert's *Book of Husbandry* (1523) describe women's responsibility for marketing butter, cheese, poultry, ale, and other items they produced, as well as taking grain to the mill, activities that also took them well away from the house. Archaeological evidence demonstrates that rural houses even in the late medieval period were normally simple structures, typically consisting of a single main room with an open hearth at its center and smoke escaping through the thatched roof above. Furnishings and possessions were limited. An inventory of a moderately prosperous peasant in Normandy in 1401 lists all the moveable goods in his house: two furnished beds, four pairs of bed sheets, one table, one bench, two bins, three copper cooking pots, two brass bowls, and various items made of tin (six pans, two plates, two pots, and a small barrel).[11] Most medieval households owned less than this. Where evidence exists, women do seem to have been responsible for "housework," but this routine work consisted of sweeping the floor, cleaning the few cooking and eating utensils, and preparing meals, often cooked in a single pot over the fire. The really laborious work done by women around the home involved processing raw materials into useful products: grain into flour, flour into bread, barley into malt, malt into ale, milk into butter and cheese, pigs into salted meat, wool and flax into yarn and cloth. In the late medieval period, many of these products, particularly yarn, ale, and cheese, were sold for cash. Both men and women worked to provide the family's direct subsistence, and both produced goods for sale.

In the early Middle Ages, labor requirements differed and slavery was more prevalent. Among slaves, such as those mentioned in Aethelgifu's will, women worked as "hand-grinding slaves" turning grain into flour, as dairymaids, and as producers of textiles and clothing. Male slaves commonly worked as animal herders, plowmen, and craftsmen. Constance Berman has suggestively argued that the spread of water-powered mills to grind grain across France and England in the tenth and eleventh centuries transformed women's work, offering a major stimulus to the expansion of viticulture and the textile industry. Grinding grain by hand was a menial task involving long hours of hard, repetitive labor. The construction of water mills, of which there were at least 6,000 in England by 1086, freed up women's time to be used in other activities. Guy Bois notes that lords in tenth-century Burgundy instructed their female slaves or servants to take up spinning and cloth-work instead of hand-grinding, while Berman's own work on western France links the introduction of water mills to the establishment of the wine and wool trade between Bordeaux and eastern England. She argues that once freed from the necessity of hand-grinding, women first helped to establish vineyards and later turned their attention to spinning, enabling both wine and cloth production to increase.[12]

The strongest evidence for women's work in the early medieval period relates to cloth. In the ancient world and the era before c.1000, women dominated all aspects of cloth production. Christine Fell discusses archaeological and linguistic evidence from Anglo-Saxon England that indicates women's role. Finds such as thread-boxes, spindle whorls, and weaving batons occur in the graves of women but not men. Linguistically, *spinelhaelf* (or spindlehalf) was used to refer to property descending down the female side of the family, while the occupations of spinning, weaving, fulling, dyeing, and sewing were all given feminine "-ster" endings such as spinster and webster. In France and Germany, the ancient form of large-scale high-quality cloth production, in which women were gathered together in a *gynaeceum* or women's workshop, survived into the medieval period. These workshops undertook the whole process of cloth production, from preparing the fibers to finished pieces of cloth. In early medieval Bavaria, there were cloth workshops or *gynaecea* on major rural estates, staffed entirely with female slaves. Although dominated by women, cloth production was not restricted to slaves. Free peasant women undoubtedly spun yarn and wove cloth on simple upright looms. Elite women were expected to be skilled in weaving and embroidery. And in Spain in 619, a church council decreed that weaving and spinning were the only manual work suitable for nuns in female monasteries.[13]

While the years around 1000 saw the spread of water mills and an expansion of the cloth industry, they also saw the disappearance of the *gynaeceum* and the entry of men into cloth production. In Paris in the late thirteenth century, by which time extensive occupational data survive, there were many male weavers, and cloth-finishing processes such as dyeing and fulling had been taken over entirely by men. The Florentine cloth industry in northern Italy, which relied predominantly on female weavers until the late fourteenth century, turned to male weavers in the fifteenth century. In rural Normandy, all weavers were men by the fifteenth century. In England, there were still some female weavers in the period 1350–1500, but they were greatly outnumbered by men. Spinning continued to be a female monopoly but was low-paid. It took eight to ten times longer to spin the yarn than to weave it into cloth. In Normandy, the production of an ell of linen cloth required one male weaver (paid 10 d.) and a number of women who prepared and spun the wool (who received 6 d. in total). For woolen cloth, a male weaver was paid 17 s. for 24 ells of coarse woolen cloth, and the women who combed, carded, and spun the wool 25 s.[14] Although poorly paid, spinning with a distaff and drop spindle had one advantage: it was a portable occupation that could be combined with other activities such as watching over children or animals, or even walking to market.

The transfer of weaving from women's work to men's coincided with two important changes in woolen cloth production. The first was the adoption of the horizontal loom, a more complex piece of machinery than the older upright loom, and one that allowed higher-quality cloth to be produced more quickly.[15] The second was a radical reorganization in the way cloth was produced. In the early Middle Ages, ordinary cloth was produced for direct use by peasant women working at home, and high-quality fabrics (for elite use and gift exchange) were made in women's workshops on estates. In contrast, the later medieval cloth industry was based on specialist weavers (male and female) producing for sale cloth of various grades. Weaving became a full-time occupation, but one carried out at home and with the assistance of other family members. The growth of weaving as a specialist occupation correlated with the gradual decline in women's involvement.

Other industries experienced similar trends. Bennett's study of English brewing describes how in 1300 almost every village in England contained women who brewed ale commercially but on a small scale, for home consumption and for sale to neighbors. With improved standards of living after the Black Death, demand for ale increased and thus, the scale of production. The introduction of beer brewed with hops in the fifteenth century intensified this trend. Beer keeps for longer than ale, and thus can be made in larger quantities. Women rarely had the time, wealth, access to credit, or political influence within the community to run large-scale businesses; by the early sixteenth century, brewing had become a specialist male trade located in towns rather than the countryside. Women still participated in brewing, taking over the husbands' businesses as widows, working as servants for brewers, as small-scale retailers, and brewing for home consumption, but they no longer dominated the industry.[16]

Increased male participation did not occur in all growing industries, however. Dairying remained an all-female occupation in England and elsewhere despite increased cheese consumption. Enterprises could be quite large scale, such as the dairy of sixty-three cows run by head dairymaid Katherine Dowe and three other female servants for the monastery of Sibton Abbey in early sixteenth-century Suffolk; they also produced linen cloth, and raised both pigs and poultry.[17] Nor did the commercialization of the rural economy always work against women. Women found work as petty retailers and used their houses to run taverns and inns. The influx of women from rural areas into late medieval towns (evident from unequal sex ratios in urban censuses and taxes) suggests women sought work within the more commercial and industrial urban economy, even if such work was often insecure and low-paid.

McIntosh, citing evidence of market-based work, mostly in small towns, concludes women had "unusual opportunities and agency" in the 150 years after the Black Death. There was a shortage of agricultural labor, the growing cloth industry needed women to spin yarn, women carried out petty retailing and offered services to earn a cash income. However, her conclusions contradict those of Herlihy who found that women were increasingly excluded from a range of occupations, despite labor shortages.[18] In fact, it seems very unlikely that the quantity of work carried out by women either increased or decreased across the medieval period: women had always worked hard and continued to do so. The particular types of occupation women worked in did change over time, but the status of women's work changed little. When they were dominated by women, weaving and brewing were not high-status or profitable occupations. Nor were the petty marketing activities women took up in the later period. Women, with a very few exceptions, were consistently excluded from controlling high-status and profitable activities. The final section of this chapter, on wage labor, reinforces this conclusion. There is plenty of evidence of women working for wages, but rarely were they paid the same as men, and wage labor itself was a low-status occupation.

WAGE LABOR

There were two quite different forms of wage labor in the late medieval economy. First, there was labor carried out by the day or task in return for a cash wage. This is familiar from more modern economies and needs little explanation. The second is service, the work of servants. Servants were contracted for longer periods of time, often a year, and lived within their employer's household. They were paid largely with board and lodgings, but also received a cash wage. Medieval servants should not be confused with "domestic servants" of the type found in the nineteenth century. Medieval servants participated in whatever work was required by the household. In rural households, they worked in agriculture and textile production, although they also helped with any housework or childcare that needed to be done. In elite households, male servants, employed partly as a mark of status for the employer, carried out domestic work such as cooking and cleaning, and only laundry work seems to have been reserved for women.

It was common for young men and women to work as servants before marriage in northwestern Europe. The English Poll Tax returns of 1377–1381 show that around 8 percent of taxpayers were servants. In towns, female servants often outnumbered male servants; in the countryside, the proportion of females varied between half of all servants in rural Yorkshire to a third in the midland county of Rutland. Outside of England, rural servants are poorly documented, but there is plenty of evidence of young unmarried male and female servants in towns such as Nuremberg, Ypres, and Reims. Female servants in Bergen even formed their own guild in the fourteenth century. Birgit Sawyer and Peter Sawyer argue that in Scandinavia female servants were more attractive employees than men because they could undertake indoor work during the winter, such as brewing, baking, spinning, and weaving, as well as working in agriculture during the summer. In contrast, men's work was highly seasonal as a result of being conducted largely outdoors.[19]

In southern Europe, including southern France, Italy, and Spain, women tended to marry relatively young and move directly from their parental household to that of their husband. This meant that working as servants before marriage was rare. On the other hand, women in this region were often widowed young, and remarriage was less frequent for women than men. Many of these older women sought work as servants.

Otherwise, it was only the poorest girls who entered service, such as those sent from the Tuscan countryside to cities like Florence, where they worked until marriage in return for an employer paying their dowry.[20]

Records of rural wage labor provide plentiful evidence about the gender division of work. In England from the thirteenth century onwards, plowing, mowing with a scythe, and threshing grain were typically carried out by men, while weeding, haymaking, and binding sheaves and gleaning in the grain harvest were dominated by women. Harvesting grain with a sickle was a mixed activity. Women also planted beans, winnowed grain, and collected firewood. Nonetheless, it is a common feature of wage accounts that many more days were worked by men than women. In the period after the Black Death when there was a shortage of agricultural labor, occasional exceptions can be found; for example, women sometimes outnumbered men as reapers at harvest time.[21]

In fifteenth-century continental Europe, women worked for wages processing flax and wool into yarn, weeding crops, making hay, harvesting wheat, cutting grapes, and shearing sheep in Normandy, while in Languedoc, women weeded crops, picked grapes, and gathered olives. At harvest time, women bound the sheaves of wheat, and one female binder was needed for every two male reapers. In the area around Seville in the late fifteenth century, men's and women's work alternated between tending their smallholdings (devoted to viticulture) and working on the large estates for wages, following a pattern that was both seasonal and gendered. In winter and early spring, men earned wages tending estate olive groves, while women dug and hoed the vines on the smallholding. During the summer, men worked in the grain harvest in July and August before returning to harvest the grapes on their own holdings in September. Then between November and January, olives were harvested: wage-work done almost entirely by women, who left home and boarded for the duration on the large estates. Women's wages were low, perhaps half of what an unskilled male laborer earned.[22]

Women's rates of pay in late medieval England have been subject to intense debate. Scattered evidence from before the Black Death demonstrates that men and women were sometimes paid the same wages. Simon Penn considered that the labor shortage following the Black Death led to more equality, and women often received wages equal to men's. This has been disputed by Sandy Bardsley, who argued that men only received the same pay as women when they were young, old, or in some other way disabled; healthy adult men were always paid more than healthy adult women. Evidence from the seventeenth century supports this conclusion, showing that old men and boys joined women in tasks like weeding for the same pay. However, it also demonstrates that in times when the labor market was oversupplied, such as the early seventeenth century (a situation similar to the early fourteenth century), able-bodied men desperate to find work accepted women's wages to do tasks normally performed by women, such as weeding and haymaking. Bennett has noted that on average, women's wage rates remained remarkably stable over time at between one half and three-quarters those paid to men, a conclusion supported by Bardsley.[23]

Bennett's explanation for this persistent gender wage gap is that wages were determined at least in part by patriarchal prejudices that devalued women's work in comparison to men's. This conclusion has been forcefully disputed by John Hatcher, who argues that men and women *were* paid the same for piece work (work paid by the task), and only day wages (paid for time) varied. Borrowing from Joyce Burnette's discussion of the male–female wage gap in early modern England, he suggests that women's day wages were low because women were less physically strong and also may have worked shorter hours due to their "need to care for their families and to work in the house." Women's lack of strength also explains their exclusion from the best-paid agricultural work, such as mowing with a scythe. In essence, Hatcher argues that women's wage rates in agriculture were determined by the market: "systematic discrimination of this type is extremely hard to sustain in competitive markets such as those prevailing for agricultural labor in later medieval England." The debate remains unresolved. We lack conclusive evidence about piece rates or hours of work for the late medieval period. Few historians would agree that the market for labor was wholly competitive in the late fourteenth and fifteenth century. Women's total exclusion from working with the scythe, a well-paid task, cannot be explained by strength alone as some women were stronger than many men.[24]

A further, but connected, issue is whether the wage gap between men and women narrowed after the Black Death and whether women increased as a proportion of the wage labor force. For Languedoc, Le Roy Ladurie found that women's agricultural wages almost equaled men's in the immediate aftermath of the Black Death, but by the 1360s had stabilized at 50 percent of those paid to men doing similar tasks, and remained at this rate until the mid-sixteenth century, when they deteriorated further to 37 percent. Similarly, Bois found that women's wages were "less than half the level of male wages" in fifteenth-century Normandy. For England, Penn is more positive, arguing that women were more often paid the same as men after the Black Death and made up an increased proportion of the wage labor force. Recently, Tine de Moor and Jan Luiten van Zanden have suggested there was a " 'golden age for women' active in the labor market" in northwestern Europe between the late fourteenth and late fifteenth centuries, when plentiful employment opportunities meant that women delayed or eschewed marriage in order to earn wages, an argument first put forward by Jeremy Goldberg.[25]

As with the debate over wage rates, evidence remains limited. But it can be argued that positive assessments are too rosy. While real wages for agricultural laborers rose after the Black Death, wages for the type of work that women did were still low, and working for wages was a low-status activity. Higher wages might have allowed women to buy land, which was relatively cheap in this period, and secure the independence of running their own farming household. Yet the proportion of female landholders declined, particularly in the most commercialized regions where wage labor was common. Day laboring gave women their own small income, but female day laborers lived with fathers or husbands and lacked full control of the money they earned. Female servants living away from home were more financially independent, but the work of service was a demanding twenty-four-hour, seven-days-a-week occupation, which limited independence in other ways. A flexible workforce of poorly paid women benefited the wider economy, but the degree it benefited medieval women themselves is questionable.

CONCLUDING COMMENTS

"Women," "rural Europe," and "medieval" are all huge categories that mask a great deal of variation and large swathes of Europe for which evidence of everyday life is slight or nonexistent. There is no general agreement, and perhaps not enough questioning, of what an improvement or decline in women's economic position would have looked like, or what changes in women's economic position meant to their wider position within society. In this quagmire of uncertainty, some continuities stand out. Women's predominance in textile production and food processing persisted over millennia; the majority of women's wages remained fixed at between a half and three-quarters of men's from the thirteenth century to the twentieth; women never dominated high-status, profitable occupations.[26] But change is part of the story, too. Technological change and commercialization had the capacity to shake up existing modes of life and shift the gender division of labor, as with the spread of water mills, and large-scale brewing. We should also be wary of assumptions. Despite the consistent characterization of agricultural work in the fields as "male," women's participation in agriculture was widespread. It is assumed that women always were responsible for childcare and housework on the basis of very little evidence indeed, as it is also assumed that this shaped their working lives. Yet housework and childcare changed over time like other aspects of economy and society. There is no question, however, that women worked hard in medieval Europe, and made a vital contribution to the key sectors of the economy: agriculture, textile production, and food provision.

FURTHER READING

Bardsley, Sandy. "Women's Work Reconsidered: Gender and Wage Differentiation in Late Medieval England," *Past & Present*, 165 (1999): 3–29.

Bennett, Judith M. *History Matters: Patriarchy and the Challenge of Feminism*. Manchester: Manchester University Press, 2006, chapters 4 and 5.

Berman, Constance Hoffman. "Women's Work in Family, Village, and Town after 1000 CE: Contributions to Economic Growth?" *Journal of Women's History*, 19 (3) (2007): 10–32.

Emigh, Rebecca Jean. "The Gender Division of Labour: The Case of Tuscan Smallholders," *Continuity and Change*, 15 (1) (2000): 117–37.

Goldberg, P. J. P. *Women, Work, and Life Cycle in a Medieval Economy*. Oxford: Oxford University Press, 1992.

Herlihy, David. *Opera Muliebria: Women and Work in Medieval Europe*. Philadelphia: Temple University Press, 1990.

Le Roy Ladurie, Emmanuel. *Montaillou: Cathars and Catholics in a French Village 1294–1324*. Harmondsworth: Penguin Books, 1980.

Mate, Mavis. *Daughters, Wives, and Widows after the Black Death: Women in Sussex, 1350–1535*. Woodbridge: Boydell Press, 1998.

McIntosh, Marjorie Keniston. *Working Women in English Society, 1300–1620*. Cambridge; New York: Cambridge University Press, 2005.

Penn, Simon. "Female Wage-Earners in Late Fourteenth-Century England," *Agricultural History Review*, 35 (1987): 1–14.

Stone, Marilyn and Carmen Benito-Vessels, eds. *Women at Work in Spain: From the Middle Ages to Early Modern Times.* New York: Peter Lang, 1998.

Whittle, Jane "Inheritance, Marriage, Widowhood, and Remarriage: A Comparative Perspective on Women and Landholding in North-East Norfolk, 1440–1580," *Continuity and Change*, 13 (1) (1998): 33–72.

NOTES

1. P. J. P. Goldberg, ed., *Women in England c. 1275–1525: Documentary Sources* (Manchester: Manchester University Press, 1995), 169–70.

2. Judith M. Bennett, *History Matters: Patriarchy and the Challenge of Feminism* (Manchester: Manchester University Press, 2006), 106.

3. David Herlihy, *Opera Muliebria: Women and Work in Medieval Europe* (Philadelphia: Temple University Press, 1990); P. J. P. Goldberg, *Women, Work, and Life Cycle in a Medieval Economy: Women in York and Yorkshire c.1300–1520* (Oxford: Oxford University Press, 1992); Marjorie K. McIntosh, *Working Women in English Society, 1300–1620* (Cambridge; New York: Cambridge University Press, 2005).

4. Sheilagh Ogilvie, *A Bitter Living: Women, Markets, and Social Capital in Early Modern Germany* (Oxford: Oxford University Press, 2003), 7–15; Elizabeth Wayland Barber, *Women's Work: The First 20,000 Years: Women, Cloth, and Society in Early Times* (New York: Norton, 1994), 29–30; Bennett, *History Matters*, 54–81; Herlihy, *Opera Muliebria*, 188–91; Ogilvie, *Bitter Living*, 320–44; McIntosh, *Working Women*, 250–53.

5. Julia Crick, ed., *Charters of St. Albans* (Oxford: Oxford University Press, 2007), 91–100, 148–54; Peter Coss, *The Lady in Medieval England 1000–1500* (Stroud: Sutton Publishing, 1998), 17; Pauline Stafford, "Women in Domesday," in A. K. Bate and Malcolm Barber, eds, *Medieval Women in Southern England* (Reading: Graduate Centre for Medieval Studies, University of Reading, 1989), 77–82; Christine Fell, *Women in Anglo-Saxon England* (Oxford: Basil Blackwell, 1984), 42.

6. Wendy Davies, *Acts of Giving: Individual, Community, and Church in Tenth-Century Christian Spain* (Oxford: Oxford University Press, 2007), 172; Teofilo F. Ruiz, "Women, Work, and Daily Life in Late Medieval Castile," in Marilyn Stone and Carmen Benito-Vessels, eds, *Women at Work in Spain: From the Middle Ages to Early Modern Times* (New York: Peter Lang, 1998), 104–107; David Herlihy, "Land, Family, and Women in Continental Europe, 701–1200," *Traditio*, 18 (1962): 108; Elizabeth Haluska-Rausch, "Transformations in the Powers of Wives and Widows near Montpellier, 985–1213," in Robert F. Berkhofer, Alan Cooper, and Adam J. Kosto, eds, *The Experience of Power in Medieval Europe: 950–1350* (Aldershot: Ashgate, 2005).

7. Judith M. Bennett, *Women in the Medieval English Countryside: Gender and Household in Medieval Brigstock before the Plague* (Oxford: Oxford University Press, 1987), 21–23; Chris Briggs, *Credit and Village Society in Fourteenth-Century England* (Oxford: Oxford University Press, 2009), 115.

8. Emmanuel Le Roy Ladurie, *Montaillou: Cathars and Catholics in a French Village, 1294–1324* (Harmondsworth: Penguin Books, 1980), 5, 360–77.

9. Jane Whittle, "Inheritance, Marriage, Widowhood and Remarriage: A Comparative Perspective on Women and Landholding in North-East Norfolk, 1440–1580," *Continuity and Change*, 13 (1) (1998): 36–37; Jane Whittle, *The Development of Agrarian Capitalism: Land and Labour in Norfolk 1440–1580* (Oxford: Oxford University Press, 2000), 140.

10. Bridget Ann Henisch, *The Medieval Calendar Year* (Pennsylvania: Pennsylvania State University Press, 1999); Janet Backhouse, *Medieval Rural Life in the Luttrell Psalter* (London: The British Library, 2000); Rebecca Jean Emigh, "The Gender Division of Labour: The Case of Tuscan Smallholders," *Continuity and Change*, 15 (1) (2000): 124–25.

11. Goldberg, ed., *Women in England*, 167–69; Guy Bois, *The Crisis in Feudalism: Economy and Society in Eastern Normandy c. 1300–1550* (Cambridge; New York: Cambridge University Press, 1984), 181.

12. Constance Hoffman Berman, "Women's Work in Family, Village, and Town after 1000 CE: Contributions to Economic Growth?" *Journal of Women's History*, 19 (3) (2007): 24–25.

13. Fell, *Women in Anglo-Saxon England*, 39–42; Carl I. Hammer, *A Large-Scale Slave Society of the Early Middle Ages: Slaves and Their Families in Early-Medieval Bavaria* (Aldershot: Ashgate, 2002), 22; Christina Cuadra Garcia, "Religious Women in the Monasteries of Castile-Leon," in Stone and Benito-Vessels, eds, *Women at Work*, 39.

14. Berman, "Women's Work," 10; Bois, *Crisis of Feudalism*, 111.

15. John H. Munro, "Medieval Woollens: Textiles, Textile Technology and Industrial Organisation, c. 800–1500," in David Jenkins, ed., *The Cambridge History of Western Textiles*, vol. 1 (Cambridge: Cambridge University Press, 2003), 194–97.

16. Judith M. Bennett, *Ale, Beer, and Brewsters in England: Women's Work in a Changing World* (New York: Oxford University Press, 1996).

17. Jane Whittle, "Housewives and Servants in Rural England, 1440–1650," *Transactions of the Royal Historical Society*, 6th ser., 15 (2005): 69–70.

18. McIntosh, *Working Women*, 251–52; Herlihy, *Opera Muliebria*, 180.

19. Richard Smith, "Geographical Diversity in the Resort to Marriage in Late Medieval Europe," in P. J. P. Goldberg, ed., *Women in Medieval English Society* (Stroud: Sutton Publishing, 1997), 35–36; Goldberg, *Women, Work, and Life Cycle*, 165; P. J. P. Goldberg, "Marriage, Migration, and Servanthood: The York Cause Paper Evidence," in Goldberg, ed., *Women in Medieval English Society*, 2; Birgit Sawyer and Peter Sawyer, *Medieval Scandinavia: From Conversion to Reformation, circa 800–1500* (Minneapolis: University of Minnesota Press, 1993), 210–11.

20. David Herlihy and Christiane Klapisch-Zuber, *Tuscans and their Families: A Study of the Florentine Catasto of 1427* (New Haven: Yale University Press, 1985).

21. Mark Page, ed., *The Pipe Roll of the Bishopric of Winchester 1301–2* (Winchester: Hampshire County Council, 1996); Simon Penn, "Female Wage-Earners in Late Fourteenth-Century England," *Agricultural History Review*, 35 (1987): 7–11; Sandy Bardsley, "Women's Work Reconsidered: Gender and Wage Differentiation in Late Medieval England," *Past & Present*, 165 (1999): 11, 23–25.

22. Bois, *Crisis in Feudalism*, 110–14, 247–48; Emmanuel Le Roy Ladurie, *The Peasants of Languedoc* (Urbana: University of Illinois Press, 1974), 108–10; Mercedes Borrero Fernandez, "Peasant and Aristocratic Women: Their Role in the Rural Economy of Seville at the End of the Middle Ages," in Stone and Benito-Vessels, eds, *Women at Work*, 11–31.

23. Penn, "Female Wage-EarnersÂ'; Bardsley, "Women's WorkÂ'; Bennett, *History Matters*, 82–83, 101–103.

24. John Hatcher, "Women's Work Reconsidered: Gender and Wage Differentiation in Late Medieval England," *Past & Present*, 173 (2001): 194–95; Michael Roberts, "Sickles and Scythes: Women's Work and Men's Work at Harvest Time," *History Workshop*, 7 (1979): 7–12.

25. Le Roy Ladurie, *Peasants of Languedoc*, 109–11; Bois, *Crisis of Feudalism*, 114; Penn, "Female Wage-Earners," 13–14; Tine de Moor and Jan Luiten van Zanden, "Girlpower: The European Marriage Pattern and Labour Markets in the North Sea Region in the Late Medieval Period and Early Modern Period," *Economic History Review*, 63 (1) (2007): 26–27; Goldberg, *Women, Work, and Life-Cycle*.

26. Bennett, *History Matters*, 82–107.

....

CHAPTER 21

ARISTOCRATIC ECONOMIES: WOMEN AND FAMILY

....

JOANNA H. DRELL

As the nexus for arranging alliances, transmitting power across generations, and manipulating kinship connections, the family was critical for the management of the aristocratic economy in the Middle Ages. Although medieval historians rarely discuss aristocrats in the economic terms used for peasants and townspeople, especially with regard to "work," the elite engaged in a variety of economic activities. When describing how the Norman leader Robert Guiscard accumulated power in eleventh-century southern Italy, Byzantine princess Anna Comnena noted the "profitability" of the marriage alliances he made for his daughters:

> There [at Salerno] he made excellent arrangements for his daughters and then prepared for the campaign...One daughter he had pledged to Raymond, son of the count Barcino; the other he married off to Eubulus, who was himself a count of great distinction. Nor did these alliances prove unprofitable for Robert; in fact, from all sources he had consolidated and amassed power for himself—from his family, from his rule, from his inheritance rights...

Four centuries later, wealthy English landowner John Paston operated on much the same principles. He noted the "profit" he derived from his wife's proper management of his household: "I pray you to see to the good governance of my household and the guidance of other things concerning my profit." This essay examines the economic activities—the "work," if you will—of aristocratic families, c.1000–c.1400, specifically how families survived and thrived. While those in other classes brewed ale, did day labor for a wage, or tilled their plots, in contrast, aristocrats "worked" by managing estates and by acquiring more estates, sometimes through conquest but more often through marriage, inheritance, and lineage. Through the same means, they also sought to extend and amplify their social power.[1]

In advancing family wealth and power, aristocratic families relied on women as much as men. The southern Italian chronicler Gregory Malaterra, for instance, recounted count Roger of Sicily's profound distress upon the death of his heir, Jordan, in 1092, a grief in short order transformed to exultation when his wife, Adelaide of Savonna, bore another son, Simon. Parents, servants, community, even former Calabrian enemies responded joyfully to the boy's birth:

> The announcement that a boy is born brings forth new joy
> The mother hears it and rejoices, there is no need for sorrow;
> They hasten and announce the joyful news to the happy father!
> Who claps his hands, rejoicing that his prayers are answered
> [...]
> The count has an heir: a future duke is furnished for Sicily,
> The Calabrians choose for themselves to be subject to his sword.
> And since it is given to him to be a father, he fulfills his every vow.[2]

A male heir had been produced, grief tempered by a lineage preserved. There was probably no more significant "work" for a noble woman than producing an heir to ensure dynastic succession.

Malaterra's verse celebrating this birth of a male heir is hardly surprising, especially for a family seeking territorial dominance. Primogeniture, despite its familiarity in many cultures and its resonance in literature and fairy tales, was not the lone potential scenario for the aristocratic family. Marriage united the properties of two families, placing women in a unique position as conveyers of lands, goods, and cash between the households into which they were born and those into which they married. The absence of a male heir or the practice of multiple heirs could thrust a woman into the role of property holder, a circumstance that underscores the significance of knowing the practical realities of a woman's possession of property. What sorts of property was she likely to receive, moveables such as gold-trimmed silk sheets in an Apulian dowry (*corredum*) or a clearly delineated "strategic" piece of land? How secure was a woman's grasp on her dowry or inheritance? Could a woman freely manage and alienate her holdings? In short, to what degree could a woman exercise agency, and operate independently of male authority?

Aristocratic women usually married young, and had little, if any, choice in spousal selection, their marriages often arranged for political or economic purposes. Since grooms were usually much older than their brides, women might expect long widowhoods. For a classic example, we need look no further than Adela of Blois (1058–1137), youngest daughter of William the Conqueror. Adela was betrothed by age thirteen and married by age fifteen to Stephen-Henry, a man eighteen years her senior and the eldest son of Thibaut III, count of Blois, Chartres, Meaux, and Troyes. Their marriage united two powerful families in northern France, the Anglo-Normans and the Thibaudians, and it produced at least six children. As if being a wife and mother were not labor enough, Adela's activities as countess included the adjudication of disputes as well as the authorization and transmission of land grants. In effect, she ruled as the co-count, first with her husband, and later with her son, during her thirty-eight-year widowhood.

In a letter written while he was at the siege of Antioch, Stephen-Henry acknowledged her skills and responsibilities, advising her to "act well, order your land illustriously, and treat both your children and your men honorably, as befits you."[3]

Countess Adela was but one of a number of well-documented aristocratic women who worked for their families as diplomats, administrators, and managers. Women balanced the expectations of law and social custom against obligations to family, and although their world was predominantly patriarchal, daughters, wives, mothers, and widows participated actively in their family economies. Despite the many limitations imposed on women in the period—legal, customary, social—ladies, baronesses, duchesses, and countesses were crucial in transferring and preserving familial wealth, for example through marriage and inheritance. They were equally crucial in matters of household and estate management. Indeed, the wealth and labor of women was so important that aristocrats were willing, when necessary, to circumvent traditional concepts of gender. In effect, women were often at the core of the aristocratic economy.

Aristocrats were not everywhere the same, and this chapter focuses mostly on French, English, and Italian families. Drawing examples from across the continent for this broad period, it underscores regional difference as well as the constants and complexities of aristocratic families and women. We begin with a brief overview of scholarship and sources for examining the aristocratic family and women; we then consider women and possession of property through marriage, inheritance, and the law; and we conclude with a look at women's management of household property.

DUBY AND HIS CRITICS

Since the early 1950s, the contours of aristocratic kinship for different regions and periods have been extensively studied—how widely kinship bonds extended, whether they were vertical or horizontal, affinal or conjugal. Or more simply put, what was a family and whom did it include? Georges Duby pioneered the field of medieval kinship and family structure through his work on the Mâconnais region. Duby argued that a transformation of the aristocratic family took place around the first millennium when primogeniture replaced partibility as the preferred form of inheritance. As Duby told it, after 1000 and in an effort to restrict the fragmentation of family properties, fathers began to favor a patrilineage developed through one son only, the only one to whom marriage and inheritance were initially allowed. One son—frequently the eldest—succeeded to the family patrimony or lordship, while the others were left to seek their fortunes elsewhere, often through marriage or adventure. Younger sons formed a class of dispossessed and disaffected youth. In Duby's view, from these practices emerged the patrilineage in which more limited or "conjugal" families (mother–father–children) were central and kinship, once wide, was more narrowly conceived in terms of patrilineal (agnatic) descent. In Duby's view, this shift to primogeniture took several centuries, peaking in the mid-twelfth century. By the early thirteenth century, these patrilineal practices had loosened largely due to the increasing complexity of society and centralization of authority. The patrilineal model petered out by the end of the 1200s, as family dynamics shifted to recognizing patrimonial claims by younger siblings.[4]

Duby's vision was clear and compelling, but no longer stands owing to the discovery of new sources and more subtle reading of old ones. The accumulation of regional studies—ranging from the principality of Salerno and the duchy of Gaeta to the county of Champagne and the duchy of Normandy—has led to a revision of Duby's notion of a millennial turn toward patrilineal models in favor of more nuanced and flexible models for the organization of aristocratic families. Investigation of the articulation of lineage, patrimonial strategies, and expressions of affection have led many scholars—Constance Bouchard, Theodore Evergates, Amy Livingstone, and others (myself among them)—to view the organization of the aristocratic family as "situationally" or "operationally" fluid. The medieval aristocratic family was neither simple nor monolithic in its structure. It was conjugal at its core but could call on an external network of kin should the need arise. Whether a family was large or small, conjugal or extended, its internal dynamic could be as flexible as the circumstances demanded.[5]

This new emphasis on the fluid structures of aristocratic families has had a profound impact on the study of gender. Earlier generations largely ignored the study of women, save for exceptional political and religious actors, such as Eleanor of Aquitaine and Hildegard of Bingen. But in the process of challenging Duby's model of strictly agnatic kinship, historians began to appreciate the position and influence of women in the medieval family, and the result was a fraying of a once-common metaphor, the aristocratic "gender triptych"—a privileging of patriarchal–patrilineal–patrimonial interests in a predominantly male-oriented society. Sources both prescriptive and normative reveal the variety and flexibility of family dynamics. Patrilineage may have barred women's access to some types of property but did not mean that women had to be propertyless. Moreover, women's influences on their families could be exercised through avenues other than land-holding, not least as mothers raising their children. In a modification of the gender triptych metaphor, Amy Livingstone summarized: "Threads of patrilineage, primogeniture, and patriarchy were interwoven in to the tapestry of the lives of the medieval elites. They were not the dominant hues, however..."[6]

A lively conversation continues about the extent of continuity or change in women's roles and authority, not just in the family but in medieval society more broadly. The degree to which gender has entered the "master narrative" of medieval history—the standard political and institutional narrative of the Middle Ages—and fostered a reassessment of the meanings of "power" and "influence" is made evident in some of the essays in Mary C. Erler and Maryanne Kowaleski's 2003 edited collection, *Gendering the Master Narrative: Women and Power in the Middle Ages*.[7] However, new research has not altered a fundamental reality: lineage on balance favored the paternal line, male heirs were preferred in bequests, and primogeniture excluded women (as well as younger sons). Not only were women disadvantaged before the law and largely excluded from many public roles, but also, according to some scholars, their control over their own lives diminished after c.1000. Even conceding that medieval society was largely male-dominated, study of the aristocratic family has created space for a rethinking of gender and power during the Middle Ages.

PROPERTY: LANDED AND OTHERWISE

No single, newly discovered source has prompted this reevaluation of aristocratic families and genders. Instead, a new picture has been assembled from manifold and disparate pieces: documents of practice (such as wills, charters, and contracts), law codes, narratives, conduct guides, literary texts, and estate treatises. This evidence—diverse in genre and frequently fragmentary and anecdotal—has placed a premium on scholarly creativity and resourcefulness. Of all available sources and methods, perhaps none has yielded more fruit than the study of private charters. Charters, most originally (and sometimes still) preserved in monasteries and other ecclesiastical institutions across Europe, tell us how property passed from hand to hand through marriage, through inheritance, through legal cases, through donation. They also allow us to study all the people involved in these transactions: buyer and seller, donor and beneficiary, witnesses, guarantor, executor, and guardian. From these records, we can reconstruct ties of friendship, kinship, and even spiritual obligation (most surviving charters were preserved because they buttressed church claims to lands granted by pious laypeople). Charters together with legal tracts addressing alienation of land, testaments, and marriage tell us a great deal about the exchange of property and devolution of property of heirs.

Evergates's exemplary study of the county of Champagne between 1000 and 1300 reconstructed the lives of the regional aristocracy using charters in concert with comital sources (counts' letters, grants, and registers of internal administration) and letters patent (private transactions between aristocratic men, women, and their officials). According to Evergates, "The volume and detail of those practical records expose a diversity of individual lives and lineages that eludes any normative model of the medieval aristocratic family." Aristocratic women feature prominently in the material from Champagne, owning and managing property and engaging in other economic activities. Dowry and inheritance, in particular, gave women a loud and influential voice, in sharp contrast to what Jo Ann McNamara characterized as the "silence and ineffectiveness" assigned to them in Duby's interpretation.[8] We can see women's active voice in three particular areas: properties acquired at marriage; properties acquired through inheritance; and the thorny issue of the extent to which women were allowed full control of these properties.

The dowry was most often the means by which medieval aristocratic women acquired property. As Stuard has discussed (Chapter 10 of this volume), throughout our period it was customary for the bride's family to provide her with a dowry upon marriage, a potentially considerable drain on any family's resources, even for aristocrats.

Dowries usually included lands, money, and domestic goods or "moveables" (such as clothes, jewelry, linens, pots, cauldrons). For instance, in 1384 Paolo Sassetti, a wealthy Florentine merchant, provided his orphaned niece, Lena, with a generous dowry. In addition to cash, Lena received two marriage chests containing clothing and jeweled hair ornaments—one of which was "like a little tiara." Decades earlier, in the early 1300s, the trepidation of Florentine families in the face of dowries spiraling ever upward in size was famously expressed by Dante Aligheri in *Paradiso*, canto xv, through the voice of an ancestor who reflects on an earlier, simpler time when: "No daughters' birth brought fear unto her father / for age and dowry then did not imbalance."[9] Women's dowries might have often seemed an early form of "antemortem" inheritance from their parents, though as we shall see, later additional bequests were not precluded. Marital economics were not limited to women's dowries, however. A marriage agreement could require a dowry from the bride's family but also demand a dower from groom to bride, sometimes called a "reverse-dowry" or morning-gift—named for the Germanic custom of dowering the bride after the marriage was consummated, traditionally the morning after the marriage. According to place and time, a groom's dower could represent one quarter to one half of his present and future possessions. This gift was intended to provide economic security to the bride during marriage and in widowhood.

A key issue is whether women had any rights over the wealth they obtained from their marital assigns. Could women alienate this wealth freely or only with spousal consent? Practice varied across Europe, but in general, two rules prevailed: (1) the dowry belonged to the wife but the husband managed it as long as he lived and (2) dowry and dower could not be sold without the consent of both spouses. In multicultural southern Italy—where Roman law prevailed in some regions and Germanic (Lombard) law in others—the laws are clear, but actual practice is not. It is not unusual to find a conflation of the two traditions, a reflection of the practical realities of a blended culture. In theory, women living under Lombard law needed their husbands' permission to alienate dower; they were, in effect, not legally competent. The standard charter formula in Lombard areas articulates these ideas, as this charter from Montevergine, 1102, illustrates: "As a woman...I am not able, according to the law [Lombard], to act without the consent and will of my husband and guardian (*mundoald*), in whose authority (*mundium*) I recognize that the law subjects me." Clearly the gift of the dower from husband to wife came with strings attached. Contrastingly, Roman law did not require a husband's consent for a wife to alienate her dowry properties. Nonetheless, numerous charters include women consenting to the actions of their husbands, "according to the law and custom of the Romans." Such instances may indicate that husband and wife held dowry and dower jointly, with the husband taking the lead in transactions. The recognition of the wife's consent, according either to Roman or Germanic practice, potentially limited her husband's liberal power over his resources.[10]

Dowries sometimes moved from mother to daughter, a subject of increasing interest to scholars as it suggests that properties were sometimes matrilineal in practice. In Champagne, a number of aristocratic women tried to preserve their dowries to give them to their own daughters.[11] In England, the mother of Margaret, countess of Lincoln, left her daughter a significant inheritance.[12] And in Marseilles, 1248, a woman whom we know only as Maria donated parts of her dowry to her daughter, Marieta, including

> ...a hundred pounds of royal crowns which I, Maria...give and donate, constitute and consign from my dowry to you Raimund Montanee [Marieta's husband]...in the name of and to give a dowry to my daughter, Marieta, on top of the goods which my husband and I have given out of the dowry which my husband had from me and received from someone else for me.[13]

Maria was able to transmit goods from her dowry to her daughter not only through a personal donation but also by means of a gift from both parents. Overall such transactions enabled a woman to transmit her family wealth, in property or whatever form it took, to her daughter, thereby ensuring that the wealth that had supported her would support her daughter.

Another intriguing trend is quite clear: over time, less property was assigned to wives. As early as the 1090s, for example, the Genoese restricted the amount of property to be included in a husband's dower to his wife. A century later, this dower was capped at one hundred pounds of Genoese money. These measures reduced the marriage contribution by the groom/groom's family, and eventually made the dower a cash rather than landed transaction. It may have been intended to limit the amount of the wife's wealth beyond her husband's control.[14]

By this time, King William II of Sicily was also reducing the total percentage of a family's property that could be included in dowers. He specifically barred his upper nobility from endowing their wives with strategic, patrimonial properties:

> If any baron or knight marries a wife and he has three fiefs, he may legally establish one of the three fiefs as a dower for his wife. But if he has fewer, we permit him to establish a dower in money depending on the nature and number of the fiefs. However if he has more than three, he may legally establish a dower out of the part that has been determined to be greater. Moreover, a count or baron who holds castles or fortified residences (*castra*) can establish a dower from these castles or fortified residences, but he cannot establish as a dower the castle or fortified residence from which the baron or county takes its name.[15]

The common effect of this legislation in Genoa, Sicily, and elsewhere was a limiting of a wife's property, strategic or otherwise. The intent was not necessarily anti-woman, for some of these top-down measures seem aimed primarily at controlling the movement of patrimonial wealth—between families and government, men and women, and among generations. But William II's concern over patrimonial lands used as dowers portended the emergence in general of a more restrictive world for women.[16]

Despite some regional variations on specific details, children of both sexes were generally provided for by their parents through a combination of inheritance, *inter vivos* gifts, and dowry. Germanic law and Roman legal traditions, both of which encouraged the partitioning of goods among siblings (including women), influenced inheritance practice in parts of Italy and southern France. Such partitioning was not necessarily equal, however, and women were often disadvantaged in the size and quality of their legacies. Evergates has argued, for example, that women in Champagne were less likely to receive properties tied to all-important feudal obligations and more likely to receive lands known as *allods* that were owned outright with no service obligations. In other words, when girls received land from their parents, their land carried less social value. I have found an analogous situation in Salerno, where daughters were more likely to inherit cash and goods from their parents, whereas their brothers received landed properties. A will from Salerno in 1119 detailed the different bequests made to the heirs of Alfanus, son of Ademarius. The sons received 100 *tari* each, the daughter, an infant, 600 *tari*. Additional evidence suggests that the sons also received property, though no such information is provided for the daughter. The little girl's legacy provides her dowry, while not affecting the integrity of the family property. Southern Italian wills also reveal a tendency to leave bequests of moveables to daughters and land to sons.[17]

No single model of inheritance was universal, even within small regions. In the eleventh and twelfth centuries, for example, multiple inheritance practices operated among noble Salernitans. Some preferred a single heir, but others made multiple-heir bequests that recognized many different kin, including wives, sons, daughters, cousins, siblings, *nepotes* (unclear if these are nephews/nieces, grandchildren, or generic descendants), illegitimate children, and in-laws. Multiple heirs often ended up as joint owners, and joint tenure (*consorteria* or *parage*) was particularly common among the noble families of San Severino and Capaccio. In twelfth- and thirteenth-century Rome and northern Italy, Sandro Carocci has found families that were patrilineal in structure, but nevertheless avoided strict primogeniture. One son was favored over the others, but all were provided for. Amidst all this variation, the common goal was to preserve the integrity of a family holding across generations, while nevertheless providing some maintenance for all children.[18]

In fact, concern for children other than the primary heir was so developed among aristocratic families in the Loire region that Amy Livingstone has argued that an "ethos of inclusion suffused the lives of these families." In the Loire, aristocratic families sometimes used both partible and impartible inheritance; they sometimes divided interest in the land but insisted the land be shared; and they sometimes favored one heir but expected him to accept that his patrimony was collectively held by all his siblings. Both the affective and landed bonds of these families are evident in the formulae of the charters and other records that enable us to draw lines from a donation made "out of love for my kin," to the arranging of "shared impartible inheritance." For a medieval aristocracy whose familial relations have been frequently characterized as emotionally distant, the sentiment fueling such gifts and joint tenures is particularly striking. Notably, a daughter's marriage did not preclude her later claiming a part in the partible inheritance of her siblings. Wives were also not restricted in their relations with siblings and other natal kin. Property transactions among siblings, sometimes acting together with a parent, reveal the natal family continuing to play active roles in the life of married daughters/sisters/nieces. According to Livingstone, "the lives of sisters and brothers intersected from birth to death." Any Duby-esque narrowing of the patrilineal descent group is hard to discern in these families.[19]

The absence of a male heir sometimes compelled an aristocratic family to confront the competing priorities of wanting to provide for all daughters through partible inheritance while ensuring the integrity of strategically important patrimonial property (especially a castle). In an effort to codify informal arrangements from previous years, Blanche, countess palatine of Troyes, in 1212 asked a baronial council in Champagne to issue a statute concerning female succession to strategic property. The council squared the tenurial circle by ruling that each daughter could receive a portion of her father's patrimony but that the father's fortified residence should pass to his eldest daughter impartibly intact. This solution, a subtle interplay of partible inheritance and primogeniture (now better termed "*primAgeniture*"?) reconciled an aristocratic family's affective bonds with its military obligations. The practical effect was inheritance of a castle by a woman.[20]

Regardless of the origin or composition of a noblewoman's wealth—inheritance, dowry, or gift; property, cash, or other "moveables"—law and custom determined her ability to do anything with it. For wives, this limitation was usually quite clear: her husband had oversight of her and her resources. Other women, particularly widows but also sometimes heiresses, were often required to secure the permission of a guardian to alienate property. In Salerno, identifiable guardians of widows included (in descending order of frequency): sons, brothers, sons-in-law, unspecified relations, cousins, nephews, brothers-in-law, and uncles. The practical ramifications of legal guardianship are not always clear, but the institution's survival into the mid-thirteenth century and its possible abuse are evident in Frederick II's reiteration of earlier legislation to protect women "unjustly served by their guardians." Abuse is hardly surprising given the economic value of the legal power of guardianship and its potential for exploitation.[21]

Scattered evidence hints that a woman might have been able to circumvent her guardian's authority, possibly with her husband's complicity. In these examples, a woman (or her dying husband) selected as her guardian someone with no familial claim to her dowry or inheritance. This unrelated guardian pledged that the woman "would have the license to do with her possessions whatever she might want with the consent of that man whom she might choose [as her guardian]."[22] This arrangement empowered women, and it also served to prevent the extended family from meddling in plans of a dying husband and his soon-to-be widow. They could together dispose of conjugal property as they saw fit.

The burden of guardianship was more prevalent in southern Europe than farther north, and even in the south it was often circumvented. As a result, widows often enjoyed more economic freedom than other women. The thirteenth-century *Customs of Amalfi* offer an indication of the benefits and limits of widowhood in a corner of southern Italy:

> A married woman after the death of her husband is lady and mistress of the property
> of her husband, to hold and control and manage these goods on behalf of her

children and her husband's heirs for as long as she keeps the bed of her husband. That is, if she does not marry nor go to a second marriage and whilst she keeps the bed of her husband, then she must be clothed and given shoes out of the property of her husband, but she must not sell or give away even one pennyworth of her husband's property.

The *Customs* also provided for the material support of underage heirs by enabling a widow to "alienate (with the decree of the bailiff and judges) as much of her husband's property as is necessary for her life and subsistence and that of her children..."[23] In other words, a widow with underage children was able to circumvent the rule that she had usufruct only of her husband's wealth.

The economic advantages of widowhood are evident in the exclamation of an English dowager, as later reported by her grandson, Thomas of Stitney: "O good lord, how is it that widows have a greater reward than married folk? How much better and more comfortable an estate we widows have than we had in marriage!" Aristocratic widows in late medieval England could enjoy their dowers, life-interests, and the jointures (or joint purchases) formerly shared with their husbands. However, what benefited the dowager did not necessarily benefit her heir. According to Rowena Archer, "[it is] only too apparent that the mere survival of dowagers could and did cause havoc in the normal course of succession." We might recall that women married quite young, making a lengthy widowhood likely and remarriage a strong possibility. The tensions between widows and frustrated sons waiting to inherit might be further complicated by unscrupulous stepfathers who exploited their wives' dower lands. The problem is also complicated by the fact that men, too, married more than once, and often the heir was not the son of the dowager but of an earlier marriage. The Statute of Gloucester, 1278, addressed the matter, making it possible for an heir to reclaim some of the lost dower. Nonetheless, the problem persisted.[24]

Whatever the formal rules, however, many widows had to negotiate carefully between the interests of natal kin and marital (both conjugal and in-laws) family. Fathers and brothers were often eager to protect dowry from the claims by marital kin, hoping that they might eventually reclaim the properties for themselves. The parents and brothers of dead husbands had much the same concern about dowers, hoping to insulate such wealth from a widow's natal family. It was not uncommon for a young widow to return to the guardianship of her father or another male relative. Charters recording donations to the abbey of SS. Trinità of Cava de' Tirreni, outside of Salerno, detail the experience of Aloara, widow of Count Peter. In 1036, before he died, Peter returned Aloara's legal authority to her natal family, specifically to her two brothers, Counts Malfredus and John. Aloara's brothers subsequently served together as her guarantors in a series of donations. In another example, John, son of John Dauferius, preparing his will before he set off on pilgrimage to Jerusalem in 1133, bequeathed the guardianship of his wife, Altruda, to his father-in-law, Landulfus, in the event of his death. In sum, if a widow were not forced to remarry, she could enjoy a measure of independence, but the latitude could be severely limited.[25]

Aristocratic women could help transmit and safeguard their families' properties through dowry and inheritance. In some areas, the significance of their position in the family economy gave them certain protections—for example, from exploitative guardians or relations. Whether daughter, wife, or widow, the situation for women was not entirely bleak, but there were restrictions and limitations on the amount, type, and access they had to property.

PROPERTY AND HOUSEHOLD MANAGEMENT

To this point, we have seen that a medieval aristocratic woman could sometimes gain access to familial property and exercise some control over it through dowries and legacies, although significant barriers limited her roles as an independent property holder. For the medievalist, however, landowning is not the sole means to gauge a woman's function in the economic life of an aristocratic family. Evergates identifies women in the county of Champagne who "did homage and received homage; they donated the fiefs [they] held by inheritance, dowry and dower; [they] consented to the transactions of their fief holders; and [they] arbitrated disputes in which fiefs were at issue."[26] Based on his analysis of over 10,000 entries from surveys of fiefs and homage registers from 1178 to 1275, women accounted for almost 20 percent of fief-holders in 1250, peaking in 1262—a marked increase from 1178, when women were only 6 percent of fief-holders.[27] It became more common, moreover, for a woman to use a seal by the 1160s, that is, to finalize legal arguments forged by her own authority in household matters. These expressions of public authority were modest but significant, and they were supplemented by women's more private activities maintaining households, raising children, arranging marriages, creating alliances, and managing estates.

In the operation of households and the management of estates we gain the clearest idea of the diversity and breadth of a woman's involvement in the aristocratic economy. Household management was a conventional female duty, and it was no small task. Christine de Pizan explored a woman's myriad household responsibilities in her fifteenth-century conduct manual, *A Medieval Woman's Mirror of Honor* (1405). She treated the operation of several different kinds of elite households, including castles, manors, and fortified homes. Recognizing that women frequently ran households, Christine addressed the fiscal, administrative, agricultural, commercial, and managerial acumen women needed. Noblewomen had to be proficient in skills ranging from elementary mathematics to farming if they were to be effective managers. To "Princesses," Christine offers this advice:

> ...the wise princess is to supervise carefully her revenues and expenses, a habit that should be cultivated not only by the nobility, but by anyone else desiring to live wisely... She will keep careful watch on the nature and extent of her household expenses.

In reminding noblewomen of the importance of skillful household management, Christine echoes the theme of "profit" with which this chapter began:

> The excellent keeper of the household sometimes brings in more profit than derives from the rents and income of the land itself. Such was the case with that wise, prudent housekeeper, the Countess of Eu...Not ashamed to devote herself to all honest work of the household, she generated such profit from it that this income was greater than from all of the revenues of her land.[28]

The fourteenth-century household accounts and receipts of Elizabeth de Burgh further reveal the complexities of managing the noble household. Her accounts list the multitudinous expenses of a wealthy home, from the food (including swan, sheep, cod, and conger eels), to the maintenance of horses and stables, to clothing herself and the staff (shoes, furs, fabric). The accounts, moreover, record the entertainments of the household (falconry, hunting), as well as the special feasting arrangements when royalty visited, as the Black Prince did in 1358.[29]

While it is unsurprising to encounter medieval women performing the socially important tasks of organizing pantries and hosting dinner parties, it might be more surprising to find them overseeing the quotidian financial and administrative activities of a vast estate. The *Rules of Robert Grosseteste*, a comprehensive estate management treatise by the bishop of Lincoln, was prepared expressly for Margaret, countess of Lincoln, in 1241. Twice widowed, first by John de Lacy, next by Earl Walter Marshal of Pembroke, Margaret was one of the wealthiest women in England. She oversaw a large household of servants and staff, as well as estates comprising both her dower lands and maternal patrimony. The degree to which she actually followed Grosseteste's *Rules* is unclear; nonetheless, they provide a vivid picture of the activity and layers of administration within the bustling community that was a noble estate. According to the *Rules*, Margaret was expected to supervise everything from selecting personnel, to managing livestock, to entertaining on a grand scale. Although Margaret had a steward to carry out her instructions, there is little doubt regarding who was the ultimate planner and authority. The *Rules* explore "how a lord or lady shall know for each manor all the lands by their parcels, all their rents, customs, usages, bond services, franchises, fees and holdings" (Rule 1); and they teach that "...[the lord or lady] have these inquests and enrollments made to shed light on [your] rights and to know more certainly the state of affairs of [your] people and...lands to be able to decide henceforth what to do and what not to do with [your] property" (3). The *Rules* advance "how you may learn by the comparison of the accounts with the estimate the diligence or negligence of your servants and bailiffs of manors and lands" (7), and "at what times of the year you ought to make your purchases" (12). Here, the emphasis on economic/fiscal responsibility is unmistakable.[30]

The countess of Lincoln was a rich widow, managing her own estates, but wives also administered estates in the absence of their husbands. For example, Elizabeth de Burgh's accounts list her requirements for travel as she conducted manorial visitations in her husband's absence. Christine de Pizan further advises "noblewomen" that, with their husbands away,

> the ladies will have responsibilities for managing their property, their revenues, and their lands...She must know the yearly incomes from her estate...must be well informed about the rights of domain of fiefs and secondary fiefs, about contributions, the lord's rights of harvest, shared crops, and all other rights of possession, and the customs both local and foreign...The lady must be knowledgeable enough to protect her interests so that she cannot be deceived. She should know how to manage accounts and should attend to them often...

De Pizan takes the "absence" issue a step further, advising noblewomen what to do in widowhood. Noble widows should "have precise knowledge of their lords' last will and testament," in order to care for their children and the needs of the estate. Christine's concern is that a widow should protect her inheritance, her "due rights," and the rights of her children. Finally, Christine also addresses the economic role of the widowed noblewoman if war erupts: she is expected to raise necessary funds in the best interests of the realm.[31]

Medieval aristocratic women had their hands full as household and estate administrators. Based on Christine's advice and that given to Margaret and Elizabeth, we are left to marvel at the manifold skills and wealth of knowledge essential for women to manage their households effectively. Their efforts were not unappreciated. The extent of lordship that women exercised over their property and fiefs is illustrated by Domitilla, wife of Ingelbald Brito of Vendome. Domitilla's original name was Hildiard but some years after her marriage she begins to appear in charters as "domitilla" or "dometa." Livingstone speculates that "Domitilla" was a diminutive of "domina," and therefore a reflection of Hildiard's authority over property, fiefs, and retainers. Not only did Domitilla and Ingelbald jointly hold and donate lands, but Domitilla also managed possessions independently during Ingelbald's lifetime. After his death she supervised the lordship and was clearly recognized as a local lord.[32]

CONCLUSIONS

This essay has highlighted the principal ways in which a woman could participate in the aristocratic economy: property, both real and movable, and acquired by gift, inheritance, and marriage; household management; and administration of estates. The work of aristocratic women in the family economy reinforces the observation once made by family historian David Herlihy: "The great, external, dramatic events of the day, the wars and crusades, are the work of active men. But their accomplishments were matched and perhaps made possible by the work of women no less active."[33] Circumstances varied, of course, over time and place, but women were frequently the key players in the transmission and preservation of their families' patrimonies, in essence the heart of the multigenerational devolution of aristocratic family wealth. Though Margaret of Lincoln, Elizabeth de Burgh, Adela of Blois, and Domitilla of Vendome had more avenues open to them for exercise of economic influence than the nameless women whose dowries inspired legislation in Genoa or Sicily, they were also likely esteemed by their families and societies.

Our understanding of women's involvement in the aristocratic economy remains imperfect, but their roles as producers and caretakers of children—from bearing them, to educating them, to arranging prudential marriages for them—had clear economic implications. An aristocratic woman's economic role, moreover, could change profoundly as she moved from city to countryside, and it could be fundamentally altered by famine, plague, and political discord, areas that merit further study. A woman's place in the articulation of aristocratic lineage, too, could have profound implications for her family's socioeconomic standing. At this moment, historians have firmly placed women's contributions to the aristocratic economy on the scholarly agenda, and we can confidently see much flexibility in the society once considered staunchly patriarchal. New sources and historical perspectives will continue to bring us a greater understanding of the diverse "works" of the baronesses and countesses of medieval Europe.

FURTHER READING

Beattie, Cordelia, Anna Maslakovic, and Sarah Rees Jones, eds. *The Medieval Household in Christian Europe, c. 850–c.1550*. Turnhout: Brepols, 2003.

Bennett, Judith. "History that Stands Still: Women's Work in the European Past," *Feminist Studies*, 14 (1988): 269–83.

Bisson, Thomas. "Nobility and Family in Medieval France: A Review Essay," *French Historical Studies*, 16 (1990): 597–613.

Bouchard, Constance. *Strong of Body, Brave and Noble: Chivalry and Society in Medieval France*. Ithaca: Cornell University Press, 1998.

Davis, Isabel, Miriam Muler, and Sarah Rees Jones, eds. *Love, Marriage, and Family Ties in the Later Middle Ages*. Turnhout: Brepols, 2003.

Drell, Joanna. *Kinship and Conquest: Family Strategies in the Principality of Salerno during the Norman Period, 1077–1194*. Ithaca: Cornell University Press, 2002.

Duby, Georges. *The Chivalrous Society*, trans. Cynthia Postan. Berkeley: University of California Press, 1978.

Epstein, Steven. "The Family," in David Abulafia, ed., *Italy in the Central Middle Ages, 1000–1300*. Oxford; New York: Oxford University Press, 2004.

Evergates, Theodore. *The Aristocracy in the County of Champagne*. Philadelphia: University of Pennsylvania Press, 2007.

Herlihy, David. *Medieval Households*. Cambridge, Mass.: Harvard University Press, 1988.

Hughes, Diane Owen. "From Brideprice to Dowry in Mediterranean Europe," *Journal of Family History*, 3 (1978): 262–196.

Jewell, Helen M. *Women in Dark Age and Early Medieval Europe, c.500–1200*. Basingstoke; New York: Palgrave Macmillan, 2006.

Notes

1. *The Alexiad of Anna Comnena*, trans. E. R. A. Sewter (Baltimore: Penguin Books, 1969), 61. Jennifer Ward, ed., *Women of the English Nobility and Gentry: 1066–1500* (Manchester: Manchester University Press, 1995), 142.

2. Gaufredus Malaterra, *De rebus gestis Rogerii Calabriae et Siciliae comitis*, trans. G. A. Loud, in Katherine Jansen, Joanna Drell, and Frances Andrews, eds, *Medieval Italy: Texts in Translation* (Philadelphia: University of Pennsylvania Press, 2009), 430–31.

3. Kimberley A. LoPrete, "Familial Alliances and Female Lordship," in Theodore Evergates, ed., *Aristocratic Women in Medieval France* (Philadelphia: University of Pennsylvania Press, 1999), 20.

4. Georges Duby, *The Knight, the Lady, and the Priest: The Making of Modern Marriage in Medieval France*, trans. Barbara Bray (New York: Pantheon Books, 1983); idem, *The Chivalrous Society*, trans. Cynthia Postan (Berkeley: University of California Press, 1978).

5. Theodore Evergates, *The Aristocracy in the County of Champagne* (Philadelphia: University of Pennsylvania Press, 2007), 82–83. Joanna Drell, *Kinship and Conquest: Family Strategies in the Principality of Salerno During the Norman Period, 1077–1194* (Ithaca: Cornell University Press, 2002); Amy Livingstone, *Out of Love for My Kin: Aristocratic Family Life in the Lands of the Loire, 1000–1200* (Ithaca: Cornell University Press, 2010); Mark Haggar, "Kinship and Identity in Eleventh-Century Normandy: Case of Hugh de Grandmesnil, c. 1040–1098," *Journal of Medieval History*, 32 (2006): 212–30. For more on the debates in recent years, see Theodore Evergates, "Nobles and Knights in Twelfth-Century France," in Thomas N. Bisson, ed., *Cultures of Power: Lordship, Status and Process in Twelfth-Century Europe* (Philadelphia: University of Pennsylvania Press, 1995), 11–35. Also, Duby, "Lineage, Nobility, and Knighthood," in *Chivalrous Society*, 59–80; Constance Bouchard, *Strong of Body, Brave and Noble: Chivalry and Society in Medieval France* (Ithaca: Cornell University Press, 1998), 67–102.

6. Susan Stuard credits Stanley Chojnacki for the "gender triptych" turn of phrase in his work on Venetian noblemen. See Stuard, "Burdens of Matrimony: Husbanding and Gender in Medieval Italy," in Lester K. Little and Barbara Rosenwein, eds, *Debating the Middle Ages: Issues and Readings* (Malden, Mass.: Blackwell, 1998), 298 n. 31. Livingstone, *Out of Love for My Kin*, 236.

7. See Mary C. Erler and Maryanne Kowaleski, eds, *Gendering the Master Narrative: Women and Power in the Middle Ages* (Ithaca: Cornell University Press, 2003), 7–8. Helen M. Jewell, *Women in Late Medieval and Reformation Europe, 1200–1550* (Basingstoke; New York: Palgrave Macmillan, 2007), 99–103.

8. Theodore Evergates, "Aristocratic Women in the County of Champagne," in idem, ed., *Aristocratic Women*, 74–75. According to Evergates, his work is a "sociological analysis of a regional elite, its formation and evolution, and its practices" (Evergates, *Aristocracy in the County of Champagne*, 1). JoAnn McNamara, "Women and Power Through the Family Revisited," in Erler and Kowaleski, eds, *Gendering the Master Narrative*, 21.

9. Paolo Sassetti, "Marriage, Dowry, and Remarriage in the Sassetti Household (1384–97)," trans. Isabelle Chabot, in Jansen, Drell, and Andrews, eds, *Medieval Italy*, 446–47. Dante Alighieri, *Paradiso*, trans. Allen Mandelbaum (New York: Bantam Books, 2004), Canto XV, ll. 103–104.

10. Drell, *Kinship and Conquest*, 77–80; Patricia Skinner, *Women in Medieval Italian Society, 500–1200* (New York: Pearson Education, 2001), 141–47.

11. Evergates, ed., *Aristocratic Women*, 92.

12. Louise J. Wilkenson, "The *Rules* of Robert Grosseteste Reconsidered: The Lady as Estate and Household Manager in Thirteenth-Century England," in Cordelia Beattie, Anna Maslakovic, and Sarah Rees Jones, eds, *The Medieval Household in Christian Europe, c.850–c.1550* (Turnhout: Brepols, 2003), 225.

13. Patricia Skinner and Elisabeth Van Houts, trans. and eds, *Medieval Writings on Secular Women* (London: Penguin, 2011), 135.

14. Diane Owen Hughes, "From Brideprice to Dowry in Mediterranean Europe," *Journal of Family History*, 3 (1978): 277. David Herlihy, *Medieval Households* (Cambridge, Mass.: Harvard University Press, 1988), 98–99. Steven Epstein, "The Family," in David Abulafia, ed., *Italy in the Central Middle Ages, 1000–1300* (Oxford; New York: Oxford University Press, 2004), 191.

15. Drell, *Kinship and Conquest*, 118–19, nn. 130, 131.

16. Skinner, *Women in Medieval Italian Society*, 153, 196.

17. Evergates, *Aristocratic Women*, 90. Drell, *Kinship and Conquest*, 70, 100–103.

18. Drell, *Kinship and Conquest*; Sandro Carocci, *Baroni di Roma: Dominazioni signorili e lignaggi aristocratici nel Duecento e nel primo Trecento* (Rome: Ecole française de Rome, 1993), 155.

19. Amy Livingstone, *Out of Love for My Kin*, 4–6, 48, 91–94, 118. On affective ties, see Philip Grace, "Family and Familiars: The Concentric Household in Late Medieval Penitentiary Petitions," *Journal of Medieval History*, 35 (2) (2009): 189–203; Sylvia Federico, "Shifting Horizons of Expectation: The Late Medieval Family," in Isabel Davis, Miriam Müller, and Sarah Rees Jones, eds, *Love, Marriage, and Family Ties in the Later Middle Ages* (Turnhout: Brepols, 2003), 123–28. Federico suggests the aristocratic medieval family should not be "demonized" as "little more than an affect-less machine for the production of heirs," 123.

20. Theodore Evergates, trans. and ed., *Feudal Society in Medieval France: Documents from the County of Champagne* (Philadelphia: University of Pennsylvania Press, 1993), 51–52.

21. Drell, *Kinship and Conquest*, 157 nn. 43, 81; Skinner, *Women in Medieval Italian Society*, 201.

22. Drell, *Kinship and Conquest*, 88 n. 160.

23. Skinner and Van Houts, eds, *Medieval Writings*, 230–31.

24. Rowena Archer, "Rich Old Ladies: The Problem of Late Medieval Dowagers," in A. J. Pollard, ed., *Property and Politics: Essays in Later Medieval English History* (Gloucester: A. Sutton, 1984), 19, 22, 20.

25. Drell, *Kinship and Conquest*, 82–83; Francesco Brandileone, *Le cosi dette clausole al portatore e il mundio sulle vedove nei docummenti Cavensi* (Milan: Vallardi, 1907), 10–11.

26. Evergates, *Aristocracy in the County of Champagne*, 193; Evergates, *Aristocratic Women*, 3.

27. Evergates, *Aristocracy in the County of Champagne*, 53 and 205, Appendix C, Table C.1.

28. Christine de Pizan, *A Medieval Woman's Mirror of Honor*, trans. Charity Cannon Willard, ed. Madeline Pelner Cosman (New York: Persea Books, 1989), 114; 173–74.

29. Ward, *Women of the English Nobility*, 162–79, 180–81.

30. Dorothea Oschinsky, *Walter of Henley and Other Treatises on Estate Management and Accounting* (Oxford: Clarendon Press, 1971), 389–415. Wilkenson, "*Rules* of Robert Grosseteste Reconsidered," 226.

31. Christine de Pizan, *A Medieval Woman's Mirror*, 170–71, 120–21.

32. Livingstone, *Out of Love for My Kin*, 176–77.

33. David Herlihy, "Land Family and Women in Continental Europe, 701–1200," *Traditio*, 18 (1962): 113.

PART V

BODIES, PLEASURES, DESIRES

CHAPTER 22

···

CARING FOR
GENDERED BODIES

···

MONICA H. GREEN

IN differentiating "sex" and "gender," many feminist scholars have used the mantra that "sex" refers to the biological, while "gender" refers to the cultural. But where does one draw the line between biology and culture when it comes to the physical body itself? In wrestling with this question, the field of medical history has pioneered the study of bodies as sites for the creation of female and male identities.[1] Questions of health and health-seeking affected nearly every other aspect of medieval history. Pursuit of health could be a driving force in municipal regulations, religious investments, economic arrangements, and family dynamics. Women's medicine and women's medical practice played key roles in the development of literate culture throughout western Europe. This essay suggests that questions of law and religious difference are equally important in understanding health's history.

The expanding field of paleopathology (the study of human remains to determine health conditions in the past) is teaching us about how medieval women and men were differentially affected by diseases, both epidemic and chronic, as well as by accidents and daily labor.[2] Some of those bodily afflictions were tied to the sex of bodies: childbirth for women, conditions of the penis and scrotum for men. But even men might experience breast problems or what was deemed to be menstruation, and both men and women might have their gender roles imprinted on their bodies in ways we might not have predicted.

Male practitioners' involvement with female patients was widespread and normative, yet there were certain limits, a largely unspoken sense that men ought not see women's genitalia. What, then, were the exceptions to that "rule"? This essay examines how pregnancy was inspected and childbirth attended. I argue that observation and medical interventions of these maternal physiological processes were differentially gendered depending on prevailing notions of expertise and competence. Then, I look briefly at the hermaphroditic body to examine other aspects of gendering in medicine.

Bodies were veiled by clothes, but also by verbal occlusion, by shame. This occlusion was particularly pronounced with respect to female bodies and genitalia, which medieval medical texts often treated briefly and opaquely. It is no coincidence that the two most important studies on medieval childbirth to date have been done by art historians.[3] Nevertheless, some documentary sources, particularly those composed outside the experiences of the Christian majority in western Europe and outside that society's learned language, Latin, speak more clearly about how the most intimate aspects of gender were stamped on the bodies of medieval women, men, and the intersexed.

ATTENDING AND INSPECTING THE PREGNANT BODY

Given that every medieval person started life through childbirth, it is shocking how little we know about birth in the Middle Ages. Most pictorial representations are in fact nativity scenes (labor completed, new mother refreshed, and newborn bathed or swaddled), and only a handful of written documents describe birth itself. Even the large corpus of texts on women's medicine touches only briefly on pregnancy or birth. The so-called *Trotula* ensemble—a group of three texts composed in southern Italy in the twelfth century and soon combined to form the most popular book in its field—offered only limited material about birth. The second text in the group, the *Treatments for Women*, which probably reflects the practices of a famed Salernitan twelfth-century female practitioner named Trota (or Trocta), addresses birth only when expert medical intervention is needed. It never even uses the term "midwife."

Our evidence on pregnancy and birth currently suggests that by the end of the Middle Ages, these experiences were gendered in a complicated way. Consider the images in Figure 22.1. In the upper left, we see a rare image of a labor in progress: the birthing mother in bed, a rope hanging from above for her to pull, and female attendants assisting. The fetal images show the various presentations that might confront the attendants; only the first (the fetus descending head first) would not bring complications. Since the volume in which these images appear was made in London around the year 1400, we might imagine that they were drawn from the knowledge of London midwives and that they were intended for their direct use. On both counts, we would be wrong.

In fact, this manuscript participates in a millennium-old iconographic tradition of fetal images and brings together a large collection of learned surgical texts, all of them in Latin: the *Surgeries* translated from the Arabic of 'Ali ibn 'Abbas al-Majusi and the Cordoban physician al-Zahrawi, the *Surgery* of Roland of Parma, and most surprisingly, the recently retrieved surgical books of the ancient writer Celsus. This large, expensive volume spoke to the Latinate culture of elite male surgeons. If it was used by midwives, it would have been through their mediation.

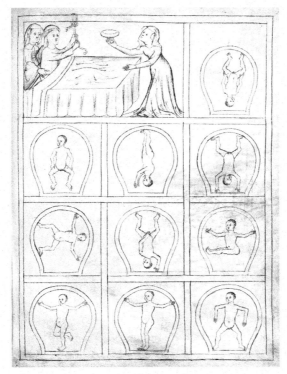

FIGURE 22.1 An all-female scene of active labor, together with the fetus-in-utero images from Muscio's *Gynecology*. Oxford, Bodleian Library, MS Laud misc. 724, *c*.1400 (London), f. 97r. Reproduced by permission.

By 1400, the involvement of male practitioners during pregnancy and childbirth did not necessarily force the exclusion of women, but it certainly compromised their work. Male physicians touted their expertise (and were duly consulted) on matters of fertility and they might supervise illnesses that arose during pregnancy; male surgeons were asked to mend lesions or abnormalities of the external genitalia and were called for emergencies such as protracted labor, extraction of the dead fetus, or retained placenta. What was true at the end of the Middle Ages, however, had not been true earlier and was not true for everyone. Midwives or other women were preferred whenever ocular or manual assessment of female reproductive organs was needed. The female-only scene of uncomplicated birth in Figure 22.1 was normative for most: with the exception of elite women, normal childbirth remained an exclusively female affair throughout the Middle Ages. How, then, did males come to have the hands-on involvement that they did?

The medieval legal tradition provides some answers. Two principles of Roman law shaped engagements with the pregnant female body and would find interesting interpretations in the medieval period. First, female midwives were accorded a special role of "inspecting the belly" (*Digest* 25.4) in cases where a divorced or widowed woman was suspected of being pregnant. Indeed, midwives were the only medical practitioners whose forensic role was explicitly acknowledged. Second, Roman law authorized cutting open the body of a dead woman, if a (supposedly) still-living fetus could thereby be extracted (*Digest* 11.8.2, also known as the *Lex regia*).

There is ample evidence for professionalized midwives in the urbanized Roman world in the centuries before the Justinian Code was compiled in the sixth century. Such women, the best of them literate and learned in medical theory, were uniquely responsible for both gynecological and obstetrical care. Males had their roles to play, it is true, sometimes choosing the midwife (and the wet nurse) and otherwise orchestrating the birth scene. Male medical practitioners might also have supervised pregnancies and intervened in emergencies. Yet various medical writers, including the Greek writer Soranus of Ephesus and his late antique Latin translators, addressed female midwives when they wrote on gynecology and obstetrics. Moreover, artwork, inscriptions, documents, and other writings amply show that women practiced both as midwives (*maiai/ obstetrices*) and as general practitioners (*iatrinai/medicae*). Women were even credited with having authored individual remedies and may occasionally have composed medical texts.[4]

With the decline of Rome, some Latin works on women's medicine from North Africa were transmitted to Italy, but they barely survived the early Middle Ages. The *Gynecology* of Muscio (composed in the fifth or sixth century) was revived in the eleventh century, largely because of its obstetrical content; but it was stripped of all indications it had once been intended specially for midwives. Little evidence for professional midwives (that is, women whose practice, based on standardized training and principles, offered both a public role and an economic livelihood) can be found until the thirteenth century and in many areas, not until much later.

In the meantime, the tasks of verifying pregnancy and virginity that had been assigned to midwives in antiquity were assigned by canonical legists in the twelfth and thirteenth centuries to "matrons," women who had no particular expertise beyond being mothers and neighbors. Ivo, bishop of Chartres (1091–1116) said that he consulted "upright and mature women" to determine the normal period of gestation. Pope Gregory IX (1227–1241) ordered that "discerning and upright matrons" or "matrons of good reputation, trustworthy and expert in marital affairs" should examine a wife's virginity, in pleas of annulment based on a husband's impotency. "Matron" did not yet mean "midwife." Gregory's immediate predecessor, Pope Honorius III (1216–1227), asserted that an assembly of matrons provided more reliable testimony than midwives:

> And because, as the canon says, *the hand and the eye of midwives are often deceived*, we wish and command that in this matter you take care to depute upright, discerning and prudent matrons to inquire whether the said girl is still a virgin.[5]

As Honorius's harsh comment suggests, when midwives again emerged in the thirteenth century, they were little respected. They were likely illiterate, and texts on women's medicine were not written for their specific use. When the Dominican Thomas of Cantimpré (d.1271) discussed birth assistance in his *On the Nature of Things*, he wrote for priests who might have to take medical action when "a midwife knowledgeable in the science of obstetrics cannot be found." There is no indication that Thomas intended midwives to read his book themselves; rather, he suggested that his (male) clerical audience might "call together some more discreet midwives and instruct them privately [from his written text], and through them others might more easily be instructed."[6]

A tiny number of female medical practitioners owned medical books. For some, these books were merely valued heirlooms from physician fathers. For others, they were surely used. The dowager queen of France, Blanche of Navarre (d.1398), for example, owned a book on surgery that she bequeathed to one of her female servants who practiced medicine in the household. Margarida Tornarona (d.1401), of the Aragonese town of Vic, surely used her Catalan and Latin medical books in her medical practice. Anne de Beaujeu (1461–1522), Duchess of Bourbon and, for a time, regent of France, owned four medical books—an herbal, a lapidary, a veterinary work, and, remarkably, a Latin book of medicine, al-Rāzī's *Book of Almansor*. But no midwives can be documented as owners of the hundreds of extant manuscripts of women's medicine. And although several medieval translations of the *Trotula* claim to have been made for female audiences, the first documentable female owners lived in the sixteenth century.[7]

This is perhaps not as odd as it at first appears, for literacy and book learning were valued differently for different levels of medical practice. With the proliferation of new medical texts from southern Italy in the twelfth century, physicians (expected to be learned in medical theory) were universally assumed to be book-learned. Surgeons lagged behind, but arguments for literacy began in the thirteenth century and there was a widespread expectation by the fourteenth that they, too, would own books, even if they were in the vernacular. For midwives, in contrast, the first text explicitly addressing them was not written until after the mid-fifteenth century.[8] Licensed midwifery (which had begun in northern France in the fourteenth century, later in other areas) did not require literacy or formal training; midwives simply had to demonstrate upstanding moral character and swear to attend all women, even the poor.

The term used in modern public health, "traditional birth attendant," might serve us better than "midwife" in surveying the informal networks of obstetrical knowledge exchange in the Middle Ages. Montserrat Cabré i Pairet has explored the often vague terminology used in several languages; words we might translate as "midwife" could also mean "godmother," "nurse," or simply "mother." In late medieval Marseille, such women were variously called matrons (*matrone*), officers (*bayla/baille*), and midwives (*obstetrices*). The advent of licensing at the end of the Middle Ages may have offered such women more formal means of knowledge transmission and firmer claims to legal rights and medical turf. To what extent licensing contributed to (or was facilitated by) increasing levels of literacy among midwives is as yet unclear. The sixteenth century brought a wave of printed midwifery publications, but we do not yet know whether midwives often owned or read these. (Lay male readers certainly did, though for decidedly nontherapeutic reasons.)[9]

Midwives' marginal engagement with literate medicine in the very centuries that midwifery was reprofessionalizing in Europe coincides with their loss of one aspect of their field that midwives in the ancient world had enjoyed: expertise over the theoretical underpinnings of reproductive medicine. In the highly professionalized medical world of Bologna in 1302, for example, we find that

> Master Bartholomeus of Varignana and Master Bertholatius Saracenus, at the order and desire of Lord Peter the judge, both went to see Gilia and diligently they examined her for signs and symptoms [of pregnancy]. And the said physicians sent two wise midwives to touch the said Gilia just as philosophers of medicine prescribe. When, on the basis of the thoroughly observed signs and symptoms which we saw and heard in her and also all those things related by the said midwives, we have reasonably judged her to be pregnant.[10]

Although these men relied on midwives for intimate examination, they considered midwives' testimony insufficient for their learned interpretation of the "signs and symptoms" of pregnancy. For legal purposes it was the testimony of men that counted most.

CAESAREAN SECTIONS

The Roman *Lex regia* enjoined that if a pregnant woman died, she should be cut open to remove the fetus lest "the hope of the living seem to perish with the dead." Since the transfer of property often hung in the balance if a new heir was born alive, this forcible extraction of fetus from dead mother had immediate legal consequences. Roman law said nothing about who was expected to perform the procedure, and medieval practices of what came to be known as Caesarean section took some surprising turns.

In 1990, Renate Blumenfeld-Kosinski noted that the depictions of Julius Caesar's birth in many French manuscripts showed a shift from female attendants performing the procedure in fourteenth-century copies to male attendants in fifteenth-century copies (see Figure 22.2), and she argued that these images documented a male takeover of obstetrics at the end of the Middle Ages.[11] As a description of the images themselves, this is accurate as far as it goes. But the images can hardly be taken as evidence of general practices. The images are meant to show the birth of a social elite (Caesar) and with one exception, the images showing male operators derive from a single artistic tradition, produced in Paris or Bruges in the late fifteenth century, usually for patrons at the Burgundian court. Nevertheless, Blumenfeld-Kosinski raised an intriguing question: did Caesarean section provide an opening wedge for male involvement in obstetrics? It may have done so, but it was only one of several. And perhaps not the earliest: male involvement with obstetrical situations can be documented as early as the thirteenth century.

Let us consider why men might be found, if not in the birthing room itself, then just outside the door. Fathers had a strong presence, of course, not only because of heirs but also because of property: under Roman law, a husband did not become the automatic heir of his wife until they had produced a child together. And priests may have

FIGURE 22.2 The birth of Caesar, showing a male who has performed the surgical procedure and female attendants attending to the child. Jean du Chesne, *Commentaires de César* (a translation of Julius Caesar, *De bello gallico*), Oxford, Bodleian Library, MS Douce 208, after 1473 (Bruges), f. 1r. Reproduced by permission.

been called in when mother or child were in imminent danger of death. The example of Thomas of Cantimpré is certainly suggestive of a close clerical awareness of birth.

But it was unlikely that priests would have been available in every situation of need; it is not surprising that emergency baptism was the only sacrament whose performance was permitted to the laity. From the thirteenth century, the developing doctrine of Limbo put new emphasis on the fate of the newborn's soul. Whereas Christians had once believed dead infants, innocent of any possible sin, went to heaven, a new emphasis on Augustine's notions of original sin taught that an unbaptized soul went to Limbo. The fate of the unbaptized child was of such pressing concern by the end of the thirteenth century that temporary resuscitation of stillborn babies (so they could be quickly baptized) was a common saintly miracle. But it was better to prevent stillbirths altogether, and towards this end, scrutiny focused on midwives and the priests who supervised them. Perpetuating Thomas of Cantimpré's concern in the latter half of the fifteenth century, an unknown cleric re-edited, rearranged, and added new material to a Dutch translation of the *Trotula* ensemble. He also shifted the book's audience away from women (the original audience for the Dutch *Trotula*) and toward male clerics and the auditor-midwives they instructed. The author's concern is grave:

> For surely, as our philosophers declare and describe for us as truth: if the woman in labour dies, helpless, under your hands; or if the innocent child expires there, helpless and defenseless, under your hands without a proper baptism, it will never see the light but will be assigned to Limbo, where there is eternal darkness. There it will call without ceasing for eternal vengeance on all those who were in attendance when it was to enter this world through birth and who let it die helpless—and on the midwife most of all, for she bears more responsibility than all the other women.[12]

These midwives, if unable to prevent disaster, needed to be able to offset it, and it was the desire to ensure that midwives knew how to administer emergency baptisms that prompted the first licenses issued by northern French bishops in the fourteenth century.[13]

Even before the doctrine of Limbo was formally elaborated, we find evidence that Caesarean section was being mulled over as a possible option in cases of maternal death. A letter from Aelfric to Wulfstan, archbishop of York, dated between 1002 and 1005, recommends the procedure not simply because it allowed infants "to escape the inferno and attain the kingdom of heaven," but also because, in some cases, it produced children known to go on to live long lives. Eudes de Sully (d.1208), bishop of Paris, echoed the ancient Roman law in support of surgical extraction, and we find increasingly regular injunctions to perform the procedure in church councils in subsequent decades.[14] The apparent normativity of the procedure by the fourteenth century is suggested by Boccaccio's *Decameron* (Day 10, novel 4), in which a pregnant woman, believed (mistakenly) to have died, is saved from evisceration only because she had stated to her female kinsfolk that the fetus had not yet reached the point of ensoulment. The women of the German town of Ebnek petitioned the pope in the fifteenth century for the right to be buried in consecrated ground even if they died with a fetus inside them, suggesting that the practice of maternal evisceration was getting out of hand.[15]

Despite the urgent need to extract a newborn to save its eternal soul, no persuasive evidence indicates that mothers were knowingly sacrificed to save their children. But as long as a fetus had developed to the point that it was recognizably human (ensoulment was associated with quickening, around the end of the third month of pregnancy) and as long as there was reason to think that it could be delivered alive, an attempt was made to provide the gift of eternal salvation—baptism—even if death quickly followed.

What no ecclesiastical pronouncement says, however, is who was expected to perform the procedure. At such moments of crisis, the midwife's usual skills were no longer required: no need to monitor dilation, provide food or drink, support the mother in bearing down, or assist the passage of fetus through birth canal. But whose skills were needed? Caesarean section is a surgical procedure and surgery as a profession was masculinizing in later medieval Europe. Trota of Salerno, one of only two female writers about women's conditions, advised only minimal surgery—use of needle and thread to repair vaginal tears and, possibly, the use of a fingernail to make an episiotomy. True, we can find female surgeons in later medieval Europe and at least one female surgeon was explicitly licensed lest female patients "fear slander of matronly modesty."[16] But such women constituted a tiny fraction of documented surgeons.

It is not surprising, therefore, that the few historical cases of Caesarean section thus far documented show considerable male involvement. Giordano of Rivalto, a Dominican friar in Florence, boasted in 1305 that he had called in physicians and midwives to perform a Caesarean section on a dead woman. The record for a planned Caesarean section in Marseille in 1331 clearly states that the midwives themselves wanted to call in a male barber, "who was experienced." In 1462, Gaspare Nadi, a master mason from Bologna, described how Master Giovanni of Navarre, a physician, extracted a male child from the body of his deceased wife. In 1473 a local official in a small town in southern France gave a male barber permission to cut a fetus from its dead mother's womb.[17]

Perhaps in some instances, these moments of crisis were the first time male practitioners involved themselves in aspects of women's reproductive medicine. But there is ample evidence that such involvement was in fact already common. The production of a living heir and a healthy mother could earn years of beneficence and patronage from wealthy clients. But better to achieve that goal by advising successfully on fertility matters or preparing the woman's vagina for conception and birth; these were far more compelling advertisements of the learned physician's or surgeon's skills. Long before we have evidence of male practitioners actually touching women's reproductive organs and genitalia, we have evidence from across Europe for male physicians' involvement in the diagnosis and treatment for infertility. Long before fourteenth-century writers like Henri de Mondeville (writing c.1310) and Guy de Chauliac (writing in 1363) would finally add obstetrical material to their works, compilers of surgical manuscripts were readily incorporating copies of the *Trotula* texts into their books, as well as the series of images of fetal mal-presentations extracted from Muscio's late antique *Gynecology*. Physicians and surgeons were particularly attracted to al-Zahrawi's *Surgery* because it offered guidelines on supervising midwives or barbers when emergency obstetrical interventions were needed. The Italian physician and surgeon, William of Saliceto (writing in 1268–1275), clearly undertook direct inspections of women's genitalia and surgical treatment of genital sores and growths. The compiler of a Middle English surgical compendium c.1470 included a series of remedies for uterine prolapse, vaginal tears, and other consequences of difficult labor alongside texts of learned surgery.[18]

Involvement in Caesarean section probably did play a role in increasing male practitioners' knowledge of female and fetal anatomy. The earliest medieval image of Caesarean section, from Paris c.1260, shows a learned male physician supervising two midwives who are extracting twin fetuses through a Caesarean cut, and it illustrates the chapter of Avicenna's *Canon* describing the anatomy of the uterus.[19] But Caesarean section may have been an intervention that male practitioners little relished, both because of its awful violence and because it put them in a position of tremendous theological and legal responsibility. It is surely no coincidence that in several of the cases documented thus far, the procedure was performed by barbers (unlearned operators more accustomed to performing phlebotomies) rather than learned practitioners. It is likely that all practitioners who could did their utmost to avoid the chaos of surgical extraction and its traumatic aftermath.

BODIES IN BETWEEN

In his *Introduction to History* (*Muqaddimah*), written in 1377, Ibn Khaldun explained why the art of midwifery was gendered female: "The craft is as a rule restricted to women, since they, as women, may see the pudenda of other women." Medical care in the Middle Ages was a function not of fixed biological constraints, but what each society permitted. Both European Christians and Muslims throughout the Mediterranean world had strong views about the need for women to inspect other women's genitals, but where Muslims empowered midwives as special legal authorities, Christians (as we have seen) diffused that authority over the body among non-specialist "matrons." Male Christian physicians in medieval Europe performed Caesarean sections because their patients had religious and legal need for it, but Muslim physicians, living in a society that had no comparable views in theology or law about fetuses and newborns fated soon to die, did not.[20] Similarly, Christian attitudes about abortion silenced virtually all medical discussion about a topic which, though still ethically charged, was more openly discussed in the Islamic world.[21] When medical writings were exchanged across such different societies, as happened in Europe from the twelfth century, gender boundaries could move in interesting ways.

During the twelfth century, three different translations were made of Arabic surgical texts into Latin, and these introduced into western Europe such surgical categories as enlarged male breasts, hypospadias (where the urethral opening appears on the underside of the shaft of the penis), inguinal hernias, softness of the testicles, castration, hermaphroditism, and various growths on the male genital organs. These conditions muddled the lines between male and female bodies, and as Christian scholars absorbed these Arabic teachings, they forged their own path. As with pregnancy inspection and extraction of the fetus from its dead mother, Roman law was a critical influence on Christian practice. Hermaphroditism had been addressed in ancient Roman law because an individual's sex had bearing on inheritance rights: "The question has been raised to which sex shall we assign an hermaphrodite? And I am of the opinion that its sex should be determined from that which predominates in it."[22] In other words, if the individual seemed to have more "male" parts than female, or if those were more prominently developed, then its legal status would be male, and vice versa. In the Islamic world, not simply inheritance was at issue, but the very fabric of religious observance. As Paula Sanders showed in her brilliant study of the question, if the hermaphroditic child did not manifest a predominant sex by the time it reached puberty, it posed a threat of *fitna*, social disruption, since it had the potential to disrupt the practices of prayer, burial rights, and any number of other circumstances. For medieval Christians, the hermaphrodite presented a different problem: the legitimacy of individual marriages.

The first Latin surgical writer to make extensive use of Arabic writings on hermaphroditism and related issues was Bruno of Longobucco, writing in Bologna in 1253. On the topic of enlarged male breasts, he follows al-Zahrawi closely in saying that nature abhors this condition, because the male breast becomes womanly. Excision of the superfluous fat was necessary. Bruno's successors in Latin Europe mentioned enlarged male breasts, too, but only in the most perfunctory way. Lanfranc of Milan (d. before 1306), for example, treated enlarged male breasts quite casually, expressing no disgust with the condition and embedding the topic in a much longer chapter that took quite seriously the range of female breast disorders, including cancer. Bruno was also one of the few Latin surgical writers to engage with his Arabic sources on the topic of eunuchs. Here, he follows 'Ali ibn al-'Abbas, explaining that he includes advice on castration solely because powerful magnates want eunuchs to guard virgins in their households. He omits his source's explicit condemnation of castration as an abominable violation of both nature and the physician's duty to preserve or restore health. Bruno's origin in southern Italy (and thus his exposure to practices in the Islamicate and Byzantine worlds) may have contributed to his tolerant attitude towards this practice of creating individuals of intermediate sex.

But artifice was one thing, "accidental" intermediacy another: "Hermaphroditism, as Haly ['Ali ibn 'Abbas al-Majusi] says, is an unnatural and most vile disease, especially in males."[23] Bruno adds nothing to al-Majusi's description or treatment, and there is no evidence that he ever encountered a case. Bruno maintains the distinctive Muslim focus on manner of urination as decisive in determining the primary sex of the hermaphrodite. Both the male and female hermaphrodite should be treated by cutting off whatever parts were "in excess." Interestingly, neither of Bruno's contemporaries, Theodoric of Cervia or William of Saliceto, mentioned hermaphrodites, even though they had been trained under the same teacher at Bologna and, like Bruno, drew on al-Zahrawi and Ibn Sina (Avicenna, whose encyclopedic *Canon* became available at the same time as al-Zahrawi's *Surgery*).

At the end of the thirteenth century, the Italian surgeon Lanfranc offered another take on hermaphroditism. Lanfranc addressed hermaphroditism within a larger chapter on removing skin-like growths that obstruct the vagina or cervix, and excising excessive growths "that hang from the vagina" with which some women were accustomed to play the part of men with other women. Surprisingly, virtually none of this new material comes verbatim from al-Zahrawi or Ibn Sina. Even though they had both addressed these topics, Lanfranc seems to be describing procedures and tools that he had employed himself. He describes methods of cutting, suturing, and cautery, with the standard surgeon's goal of cutting away excess. Notably, however, he mentions one situation where the surgeon must stay his hand: "If [the seemingly excess flesh] is firm and strong and innervated so as to seem like a male member, and especially if when touching a woman it becomes erect, in no way should you touch it with the cautery iron nor should you think to treat it with anything."[24]

This emphasis on sexual function is telling, related to shifts in canon law. When Gratian, the twelfth-century legist who made Roman law foundational to the emerging legal code of the church, addressed the question of the hermaphrodite's status as a potential witness in a legal proceeding, he used the phrase *qualitas incalescentis sexus ostendit. Incalescentis sexus* means "of the sex which is able to be heated" or, as we would put it, "sexually aroused."[25] This notion first appeared in a medical context at the monastery of Monte Cassino in the third quarter of the twelfth century. A short anatomical text describes how the sex of the child is determined by where in the womb the combined parental seed falls:

> If, on the contrary, the seed falls in neither [the right or left] but is located exactly in the middle of the uterus, that which will be born will be a hermaphrodite. For if the woman should bear five [children at a time], two will be males and two females, and the fifth will be a hermaphrodite. Although [the hermaphrodite] has both sexes, according to the decrees of the princes it has the privilege of whichever sex it uses more and in which it takes [sexual] delight.[26]

Hence, sexual functioning, and not mere appearance, was critical to how medieval Christians determined how to treat a hermaphrodite. The two known cases of medical practitioners becoming involved with evaluation or treatment of hermaphroditic bodies hinged on compromised heterosexual functioning within marriage. A woman from Bern in the early fourteenth century had her marriage to a man dissolved because she could not have sex with him as a woman; she subsequently had her penis and testicles freed by a surgeon's cut, allowing her to live the rest of her life in marriage as a man. Second, a woman in Catalonia was examined in 1331 because she "could not fulfill her conjugal debt nor conceive nor bear a child" (no "cure" was mentioned in her case). She was found, according to her husband and the surgeon's report, to have "a male penis and testicles like a man."[27]

In tackling the medical challenges of hermaphroditism, then, Christians drew on the technical expertise of Arabic sources, but forged their own path. In Christian Europe, the hermaphrodite was not problematized in the same way and was mostly of concern for complicating the legitimacy of individual marriages. Guy de Chauliac, writing in 1363, says simply that hermaphroditism is "nature doubled with respect to sex." A "cure" was possible in some cases (again, by excision), but as a medicalized category it seemed quite minor. The attention that hermaphroditism would receive in the Renaissance was of a completely different order.[28]

EMBODYING HISTORY

Despite a growing number of studies on questions in women's medicine (for example, studies of individual texts and case studies of individual midwives), medieval women's and gender history has been surprisingly slow to take up questions from the history of medicine as central to the field as a whole.[29] One reason for this reluctance may be a sense that the narratives of health have a flatness to them, that nothing ever changed in health conditions or health interventions in the Middle Ages. Yet new work on any number of questions—for instance, public health in medieval cities, new scientific methods for reconstructing the histories of plague and leprosy, infertility as a problem of monarchic rule, the history of slavery and its connections to wet-nursing—have elements of their stories that demand both gender and medical-historical analysis.

Across all the cultures and religious groups of the medieval Mediterranean and Europe, death and injury in childbirth—whether of the mother, the child, or both—must have been common. But we should not assume a uniformity of obstetrical care. Whether we will find evidence that the vigorous surgical interventions in obstructed birth documented in Greco-Roman antiquity (even in Roman Britain) were sustained in the Middle Ages remains to be seen. For the moment, we just have sad evidence of women at all social levels dying in childbirth, their fetuses often undelivered.[30] Medical interventions, even at their most efficacious, could have done little to alleviate the dangers of such common obstetrical emergencies as hemorrhages and acute infections, and it is especially essential, therefore, that charms, inscribed amulets and scrolls, prayers, and other birth paraphernalia be assessed as evidence for the very real fears of obstetric catastrophe.

Gender, an aspect of culture, is constructed on the material substrate of the biological body. As we have seen, in addition to law, language (including literacy) and religion are potent elements in that cultural construction. Work that transcends Christian world-views and experiences, or that, even when focusing on Christians, moves outside the homogenizing discourses of the shared European language of Latin has proved especially fruitful in unveiling practices surrounding reproductive medicine. In a recent survey of evidence for midwives in the medieval Islamic world, Avner Giladi has hinted that Ibn Khaldun's appreciation for the art of midwifery may stem from the time he spent in Muslim Spain, where to date we have the highest concentration of evidence for the practices of midwifery by women. In some cases, Muslim women were even the attendants of choice for elite women in Christian-dominated territories.[31] The recent discovery in Marseille of the first and only known trial of a midwife for the death of a woman in her care has raised new questions about the medical interactions of Christian and Jewish women. The earliest translations of the Latin *Trotula* and two other major texts on women's medicine were made into Hebrew, and the first Latin text devoted exclusively to pregnancy and birth was written by a recent convert to Christianity, who may conceivably have been familiar with those earlier Hebrew texts.[32]

Pregnancy and childbirth are just one aspect of women's bodily experiences, of course, and one that not all women experienced. But they, like the phenomena of andrological conditions and intersex, are not only fundamental aspects of real human lives, but also good to think with. The term "technologies of the body" has been used to capture the fact that the goals of bodily interventions have not always been the same. The medical writings of Trota of Salerno ranged from a pro-natalist emphasis on fertility testing to cosmetics to treatments for lesions on the male genitalia.[33] There is no mention of abortion in her work and little mention of alleviation of pain, though the physical demands of both heterosexual intercourse and celibacy on women's bodies are acknowledged. One of the most important lessons of the past generation of scholarship on caring for gendered bodies in the Middle Ages has been that we must be attuned to every culture's own articulation of its goals in trying to keep bodies whole and sound, or at the very least, useful.

Further Reading

Barkaï, Ron. *A History of Jewish Gynaecological Texts in the Middle Ages.* Leiden: Brill, 1998.
Flügge, Sibylla. *Hebammen und heilkundige Frauen: Recht und Rechtswirklichkeit im 15. und 16. Jahrhundert,* 2nd edn. Frankfurt am Main: Stroenfeld, 2000.
Green, Monica H., ed. and trans. *The "Trotula": A Medieval Compendium of Women's Medicine.* Philadelphia: University of Pennsylvania Press, 2001.
Green, Monica H. "Gendering the History of Women's Healthcare," *Gender & History,* 20th Anniversary Special Issue, 20 (3) (November 2008): 487–518; rpt in Alexandra Shepard and Garthine Walker, eds. *Gender and Change: Agency, Chronology and Periodisation.* Oxford: Wiley-Blackwell, 2009. 43–82.
Green, Monica H. *Making Women's Medicine Masculine: The Rise of Male Authority in Pre-Modern Gynaecology.* Oxford: Oxford University Press, 2008.
Green, Monica H. "The Sources of Eucharius Rösslin's *Rosegarden for Pregnant Women and Midwives* (1513)," *Medical History* 53, no. 2 (Spring 2009), 167–92; available *gratis* on PubMed Central at http://www.pubmedcentral.nih.gov/tocrender.fcgi?iid=178168.
Green, Monica H. "Moving from Philology to Social History: The Circulation and Uses of Albucasis's Latin *Surgery* in the Middle Ages," in Florence Eliza Glaze and Brian Nance, eds, *Between Text and Patient: The Medical Enterprise in Medieval and Early Modern Europe.* Florence: SISMEL/Edizioni del Galluzzo, 2011, 331–72.
L'Estrange, Elizabeth. *Holy Motherhood: Gender, Dynasty, and Visual Culture in the Later Middle Ages.* Manchester: Manchester University Press, 2008.
Moulinier, Laurence. "Le corps des jeunes filles dans les traités médicaux du Moyen Age," in L. Bruit Zaidman, G. Houbre, C. Klapisch-Zuber, and P. Schmitt Pantel, eds, *Le corps des jeunes filles de l'Antiquité ànos jours.* Paris: Perrin, 2001, 80–109.
Park, Katharine. *Secrets of Women: Gender, Generation, and the Origins of Human Dissection.* New York: Zone Books, 2006.
Zuccolin, Gabriella. "Gravidanza e parto nel Quattrocento: le morti parallele di Beatrice d'Este e Anna Sforza," in Luisa Giordano, ed., *Beatrice d'Este (1475–1497).* Pisa: ETS, 2008, 111–45.

Notes

1. A comprehensive list of medieval texts on women's medicine, in Latin and all vernaculars, can be found in Monica H. Green, "Medieval Gynecological Texts: A Handlist," *in Women's Healthcare in the Medieval West: Texts and Contexts* (Aldershot: Ashgate, 2000), appendix, 1–36, supplemented by Monica H. Green, "Bibliography on Medieval Women, Gender and Medicine, 1980–2009," posted for free access on *Sciència.cat,* <http://www.sciencia.cat/english/libraryenglish/publicationssc.htm>, published 2 March 2010.

2. For example, A. L. Grauer, "Where were the Women?" in A. Herring and A. Swedlund, eds, *Human Biologists in the Archives* (Cambridge: Cambridge University Press, 2002), 266–87; Sharon N. DeWitte, "The Effect of Sex on Risk of Mortality During the Black Death in London, A.D. 1349–1350," *American Journal of Physical Anthropology*, 139 (2009): 222–34.

3. Jacqueline Marie Musacchio, *The Art and Ritual of Childbirth in Renaissance Italy* (New Haven; London: Yale University Press, 1999); and Elizabeth L'Estrange, *Holy Motherhood: Gender, Dynasty, and Visual Culture in the Later Middle Ages* (Manchester: Manchester University Press, 2008).

4. See Ann Ellis Hanson and Monica H. Green, "Soranus of Ephesus: *Methodicorum princeps*," in Wolfgang Haase and Hildegard Temporini, eds, *Aufstieg und Niedergang der römischen Welt*, II, 37.2 (Berlin; New York: Walter de Gruyter, 1994), 968–1075; Rebecca Flemming, "Women, Writing and Medicine in the Classical World," *Classical Quarterly*, 57 (1) (2007): 257–79.

5. Monica H. Green, "Documenting Medieval Women's Medical Practice," in Luis García-Ballester, Roger French, Jon Arrizabalaga, and Andrew Cunningham, eds, Practical Medicine from Salerno to the Black Death (Cambridge: Cambridge University Press, 1994), 322–52; rpt. with addenda in Green, *Women's Healthcare*, essay II.

6. Monica H. Green, *Making Women's Medicine Masculine: The Rise of Male Authority in Pre-Modern Gynaecology* (Oxford: Oxford University Press, 2008), 139 and 148.

7. Monica H. Green, "The Possibilities of Literacy and the Limits of Reading: Women and the Gendering of Medical Literacy," in *Women's Healthcare in the Medieval West: Texts and Contexts* (Aldershot: Ashgate, 2000), essay VII, 1–76. For Tornarona, see Manuel Camps Surroca and Manuel Camps Clemente, "Els llibres de les biblioteques de metges i cirurgians catalans antics," *Gimbernat*, 32 (1999), at 14–15; for the Duchess of Bourbon, see "Inventaires des livres qui sont en la librairie du chasteau de Molins," in A.-M. Chazaud, ed., *Les Enseignements d'Anne de France, duchesse de Bourbonnois e d'Auvergne, à sa fille, Susanne de Bourbon* (Marseille: Laffitte Reprints, 1978), 231–58, items 45, 164, 208, and 241; for owners of the *Trotula*, see Green, *Making Women's Medicine Masculine*.

8. Green, *Making Women's Medicine Masculine*; and Green, "Sources of Eucharius Rösslin's *Rosegarden*."

9. On the fluidity of women's healing roles, see Montserrat Cabré, "Women or Healers? Household Practices and the Categories of Health Care in Late Medieval Iberia," *Bulletin of the History of Medicine*, 82 (2008): 18–51; and Carmel Ferragud Domingo, "La atención médica doméstica practicada por mujeres en la Valencia bajomedieval," *Dynamis: Acta Hispanica ad Medicinae Scientiarumque Historiam Illustrandam*, 27 (2007): 133–55. For Marseille, see Monica H. Green and Daniel Lord Smail, "The Trial of Floreta d'Ays (1403): Jews, Christians, and Obstetrics in Later Medieval Marseille," *Journal of Medieval History*, 34 (2) (June 2008), 185–211; for midwives' growing professional identities, see Tiffany D. Vann Sprecher and Ruth Mazo Karras, "The Midwife and the Church: Ecclesiastical Regulation of Midwives in Brie, 1499–1504," *Bulletin of the History of Medicine*, 85 (2011): 171–92; for audiences of midwifery texts in the sixteenth century, see Green, *Making Women's Medicine Masculine*, conclusion.

10. Alessandro Simili, "Un referto medico-legale inedito e autografo di Bartolomeo da Varignana," *Il policlinico, periodico di medicina, chirurgia e igiene*, 58 (1951): 150–56.

11. Renate Blumenfeld-Kosinski, *Not of Woman Born: Representations of Caesarean Birth in Medieval and Renaissance Culture* (Ithaca, NY: Cornell University Press, 1990).

12. Anonymous, "The Book of Albertus on the Secrets of Women," in Orlanda Lie, "What Every Midwife Needs to Know: The *Trotula*, Translation Flanders, Second Half of the Fifteenth Century," in L. van Gemert et al., eds, *Women's Writing in the Low Countries 1200–1875. A Bilingual Anthology* (Amsterdam: Amsterdam University Press, 2010), 141.

13. Kathryn Taglia, "Delivering a Christian Identity: Midwives in Northern French Synodal Legislation, c. 1200–1500," in Peter Biller and Joseph Ziegler, eds., *Religion and Medicine in the Middle Ages* (York: York Medieval Press, 2001), 77–90.

14. F. M. Powicke, C. R. Cheney, M. Brett, et al., *Councils and Synods: With Other Documents Relating to the English Church* (Oxford: Clarendon Press, 1981), I: 247–48; Odette Pontal, ed., *Les statuts synodaux Français du XIIIe siècle. Tome 1: Les Statuts de Paris et le synodal de l'ouest* (Paris: Bibliothèque Nationale, 1971), 72.

15. Ludwig Schmugge, "Im Kindbett gestorben: Ein kanonistisches Problem im Alltag des 15. Jhdts.," in Peter Landau and R. M. Helmholz, eds, *Grundlagen des Rechts: Festschrift für Peter Landau zum 65. Geburtstag* (Paderborn: F. Schöningh, 2000), 467–76.

16. Monica H. Green, trans., "Trocta (?), Obstetrical Excerpts from the Salernitan Compendium, *On the Treatment of Diseases*," and idem, "Medical Licenses from the Kingdom of Naples," in Katherine L. Jansen, Joanna Drell, and Frances Andrews, eds, *Medieval Italy: Texts in Translation* (Philadelphia: University of Pennsylvania Press, 2009), 314–15 and 324–25.

17. Steven Bednarski and Andrée Courtemanche, "Sadly and with a Bitter Heart: What the Caesarean Section Meant in the Middle Ages," *Florilegium* 28 (2011): 33–69, provides a useful summary of all historical Caesarean cases reported to date.

18. Green, *Making Women's Medicine Masculine*, 98–99; London, Wellcome Library, MS 564, c. 1470, f. 144v; Katharine Park, *Secrets of Women: Gender, Generation, and the Origins of Human Dissection* (New York: Zone Books, 2006).

19. Besançon, Bibliothèque municipale, MS 457, c.1260 (Paris), f. 260v.

20. On the legal roles of midwives in the Islamicate world, see Ron Shaham, *The Expert Witness in Islamic Courts: Medicine and Crafts in the Service of the Law* (Chicago: University of Chicago Press, 2010), chapter 3. On the lack of evidence for the practice of Caesarean section, see Emilie Savage-Smith, "The Practice of Surgery in Islamic Lands: Myth and Reality," *Social History of Medicine*, 13 (2000): 307–21, at 308; and Peter Pormann and Emilie Savage-Smith, *Medieval Islamic Medicine* (Edinburgh: University of Edinburgh Press, 2007), 134–35 and 142, n. 55.

21. Maaike van der Lugt, "L'animation de l'embryon humain dans la pensée médiévale," in Luc Brisson, Marie-Hélène Congourdeau, and Jean-Luc Solère, eds, *L'embryon: Formation et animation. Antiquité grecque et latine, traditions hébraïque, chrétienne et islamique* (Paris: Vrin, 2008), 233–54; Wolfgang P. Müller, *The Criminalization of Abortion in the West* (Ithaca, NY: Cornell University Press, 2012); Basim Musallam, *Sex and Society in Islam: Birth Control Before the Nineteenth Century* (Cambridge: Cambridge University Press, 1983).

22. *Ulpianus, on Sabinus, Book I*, Justinian's *Digest*: Dig.1.5.10, trans. S. P. Scott, *The Civil Law*, II (Cincinnati: Central Trust Company, 1932), found online at: <http://webu2.upmf-grenoble.fr/Haiti/Cours/Ak/Anglica/D1_Scott.htm#V>, accessed 8 July 2012.

23. Susan P. Hall, *The Cyrurgia Magna of Brunus Longoburgensis: A Critical Edition* (PhD dissertation, Oxford University, 1957), 290: "Hermofrodita, ut dicit Haly, est passio innaturalis et turpissima ualde uiris."

24. Lanfranc of Milan, *Cyrurgia, in Cyrurgia Guidonis de Cauliaco. et Cyrurgia Bruni, Teodorici, Rolandi, Lanfranci, Rogerii, Bertapalie* (Venice, 1519), f. 198va: "Si vero dura sit & fortis: & neruosa: ita quod virge virili assimiletur: & maxime si tangendo mulierem erigitur: illam nullo modo ferro tangas: nec cum aliquo curare cogites."

25. Gratian, *Decretum*, II, causa IV, question II and III, Item l. 15: § 22: "Hermaphroditus an ad testamentum adhiberi possit, qualitas incalescentis sexus ostendit." Oddly, this point has not been noted in previous scholarship on hermaphroditism in medieval western Europe: Cary J. Nederman and Jacqui True, "The Third Sex: The Idea of the Hermaphrodite in Twelfth-Century Europe," *Journal of the History of Sexuality*, 6 (4) (April 1996): 497–517; Maaike van der Lugt, "L'humanité des monstres et leur accès aux sacrements dans la pensée médiévale," in A. Caiozzo and A.-E. Demartini, eds, *Monstres et imaginaire social: Approches historiques* (Paris: Créaphis, 2008), 135–62; Irina Metzler, "Hermaphroditism in the Western Middle Ages: Physicians, Lawyers and the Intersexed Person," in Sally Crawford and Christina Lee, eds, *Bodies of Knowledge: Cultural Interpretations of Illness and Medicine in Medieval Europe* (Oxford: Archaeopress, 2010), 27–39.

26. Monte Cassino, Biblioteca della Badia, MS 167, s. xii$^{3/4}$, pp. 201–202.

27. Green, *Making Women's Medicine Masculine*, 106.

28. Paula Sanders, "Gendering the Ungendered Body: Hermaphrodites in Medieval Islamic Law," in Nikki R. Keddie and Beth Baron, eds, *Women in Middle Eastern History: Shifting Boundaries in Sex and Gender* (New Haven; London: Yale University Press, 1991), 74–95.

29. Monica H. Green, "Integrative Medicine: Incorporating Medicine and Health into the Canon of Medieval European History," *History Compass*, 7 (4) (June 2009): 1218–45.

30. For example, S. Mays, K. Robson-Brown, S. Vincent, J. Eyers, et al., "An Infant Femur Bearing Cut Marks from Roman Hambleden, England," *International Journal of Osteoarchaeology*, 22 (3) (2012), published online ahead of publication June 2012; Alex Werner, ed., *London Bodies: The Changing Shape of Londoners from Prehistoric Times to the Present Day* (London: Museum of London, 1998), 60–62.

31. Avner Giladi, "Liminal Craft, Exceptional Law: Preliminary Notes on Midwives in Medieval Islamic Writings," *International Journal of Middle East Studies*, 42 (2) (2010): 185–202; Jean-Pierre Molénat, "Priviligiées ou poursuivies: quatre sages-femmes musulmanes dans la Castille du XVe siècle," in Cristina de la Puente, ed., *Identidades marginales* (Madrid: Consejo Superior de Investigaciones Científicas, 2003), 413–30.

32. On the murder case, see Green and Smail, "Trial of Floreta d'Ays." On the work of the Hebrew translator, "Doeg ha-Edomi," see Carmen Caballero Navas, "Algunos 'secretos de mujeres' revelados: El *Še'ar yašub* y la recepción y transmisión del *Trotula* en hebreo [Some 'Secrets of Women' Revealed: The *She'ar yašub* and the Reception and Transmission of the *Trotula* in Hebrew]," *Miscelánea de Estudios Árabes y Hebraicos, sección Hebreo*, 55 (2006): 381–425; and Gad Freudenthal, "The Aim and Structure of Steinschneider's *Die Hebraeischen Übersetzungen des Mittelalters*: The Historiographic Underpinnings of a Masterpiece and their Untoward Consequences," *Studies on Steinschneider: Moritz Steinschneider and the Emergence of the Science of Judaism in Nineteenth-Century Germany*, ed. Reimund Leicht and Gad Freudenthal (Leiden: Brill, 2011), 191–211. The *Pomum aureum* (Golden Apple), written in 1444 by the Jewish convert, Pierre Andrée de Pulcro Visu of Perpignan, remains unedited.

33. Monica H. Green, "Bodies, Gender, Health, Disease: Recent Work on Medieval Women's Medicine," *Studies in Medieval and Renaissance History*, 3rd ser., vol. 2 (2005): 1–46, at 3–6; and idem, "Reconstructing the *Oeuvre* of Trota of Salerno," in Danielle Jacquart and Agostino Paravicini Bagliani, eds, *La Scuola medica Salernitana: Gli autori e i testi* (Florence: SISMEL/Edizioni del Galluzzo, 2007), 183–233.

CHAPTER 23

THE BYZANTINE BODY

KATHRYN M. RINGROSE

THE Byzantine world believed that the external appearance of an individual's body reflected the quality of an individual's inner soul or personality. This was especially true in elite circles, at court, and in the ecclesiastical world. It was believed that the physical body was malleable, that by changing the outward form of the body one could also change the nature of the inner person. As a result, bodily mutilations, and especially castration, an extreme form of bodily modification by western standards, were common in Byzantium. Because castration altered the way a man matured, it created persons who were perceived to lack many male traits and develop other special abilities, ranging from business and administrative skills to access to the spiritual world. These individuals occupied key roles in society while living lives filled with ambiguity. Within the Byzantine world, the boundaries between gender categories were very flexible, with the result that it is difficult today to define Byzantine men, women, and eunuchs using western terminology.

The Byzantine Empire, with its capital in Constantinople, was the eastern extension of the Later Roman Empire. For the purposes of this discussion, the Byzantine period extends from the reign of Justinian I (527–565) to the fall of Constantinople to the Turks in 1453. This culture produced rich and varied ideas about the body, ideas that differ sharply from those embraced in the West. The Byzantine body can be traced in a variety of visual and written sources which, when taken together, help us to reconstruct how people in Byzantium understood and saw the body.

SOURCES

Visual sources, primarily in the form of mosaics, frescoes, and manuscript illuminations, might seem the best place to look for ideas about external appearance. Unfortunately, as the result of the iconoclastic crisis of the eighth and ninth centuries, most figurative imagery from the heartland of the empire was destroyed. We have to rely on the famous mosaics of Ravenna and the icons preserved at the Vatican and at the monastery of St Catherine in the Sinai desert for visual images of the early centuries of the empire. After the ninth century and the end of iconoclasm, we have a much richer store of images. Manuscript illuminations also offer valuable material, although they are often small, stylized, and difficult to decode.

Written material about the body in Byzantium comes from two main traditions: aristocratic and religious. There are significant differences between these two kinds of source materials, and there is little middle ground. Meanwhile, few sources reflect the opinion of ordinary individuals. In other words, the nature of our sources can easily distort our assumptions about the body in Byzantium. Moreover, we must face the reality that all of our primary sources, with the exception of the writings of Anna Comnena, reflect a male point of view.

Byzantine historical sources are divided between monastic chronicles and historical narratives. The former catalogue current events inside and outside the monastery. Their authors had little interest in the Byzantine body. The secular historical narratives, written by members of the courtly elite, reflect aristocratic traditions and court politics. These narratives include stereotyped descriptions of idealized bodies and courtly behavior. Law codes, both civil and ecclesiastical, offer legislation regarding families, marriage, definitions of gender categories, and monetary values placed on the physical body. They allow us to explore attitudes about the value of the personal body, the importance of bodily integrity, and the nature of intermediate gender categories. We are fortunate in having a large number of personal letters from the tenth century. These contain scattered nuggets regarding the personal lives of the aristocracy. The great ceremonial book *De Ceremoniis* (Regarding Ceremonies), a tenth-century manual describing traditional court ceremonial, offers detailed information about the role of the body in traditional court ceremonial. The same is true of the ninth- and tenth-century *tactica*, lists of office holders and rules of protocol. Finally, some earlier writings from the second and third centuries remained very popular in Byzantium and continued to be cited in later writings. Important among these are the physiognomic writings of the second-century Sophist, Polemo. These writings evaluate the moral and intellectual value of individuals depending on the configuration of their bodies, especially their faces.

Byzantine sources are also heavily weighted toward religious materials. There is a large sermon literature and rich body of hagiographical material. We also have excellent documentation regarding the founding and operation of Byzantine monasteries. In all these religious sources, attitudes about the body are usually negative.

The Greek romance literature of late antiquity was known in the Byzantine world, but no new romances were written until the twelfth century. There are a few popular works like the *Timarion*, a fanciful romp that takes its hero to a kind of court in hell presided over by the last iconoclastic emperor, Theophilus. Byzantine literary sources also include the *oneirokritikon* (dream books), guidebooks for individuals who analyze dreams. These often contain valuable material about perceived gender types. Finally, we have a few books of advice for aristocratic young men.[1]

ELITE BODIES

The aristocratic Byzantine body, following traditions that date from antiquity, was cared for and perfected. Greek tradition taught that a beautiful body reflected a beautiful soul. Bodily perfection was the product of ongoing effort, of cultural conditioning and careful nurturing. Among mature men, the Byzantine aristocratic ideal favored a man whose body was well proportioned, relatively tall, with dark skin reflecting many hours spent outside in military exercise. These attributes told the observer about a person's inner being. The assumed connection between outward physical appearances and inner worth is illustrated in Michael Psellos's portrait of the great Byzantine emperor Basil II (reigned 976–1025), whom Psellos saw during his lifetime:

> As for his personal appearance, it betrayed the natural nobility of the man, for his eyes were light-blue and fiery, the eyebrows not overhanging nor sullen, nor yet extending in one straight line, like a woman's, but well-arched and indicative of his pride. The eyes were neither deep-set [a sign of knavishness and cunning] nor yet too prominent [a sign of frivolity], but they shone with a brilliance that was manly. His whole face was rounded off, as if from the center of a perfect circle, and joined to his shoulders by a neck that was firm and not too long. His chest was neither thrust out in front of him, nor hanging on him, so to speak, nor again was it concave and, as it were, cramped; rather was it the mean between two extremes, and the rest of his body was in harmony with it.
>
> As for height, he was of less than normal stature, but it was proportionate to the separate parts of his body, and he held himself upright. If you met him on foot, you would find him much like some other men, but on horseback he afforded a sight that was altogether incomparable, for in the saddle he reminded one of the statues which the great sculptors carved, with their riders adopting a similar pose. When he gave rein to his horse and rode in the assault, he was erect and firm in the saddle, riding uphill and downhill alike, and when he checked his steed, reining it in, he would leap on high as though he had wings, and he mounted or dismounted alike with equal grace. In his old age the beard under his chin went bald, but the hair from his cheeks poured down, the growth on either side being thick and very profuse, so that it wound round on both sides and made into a perfect circle so that he appeared to possess a full beard.[2]

While Psellos wrote from personal observation, he was clearly influenced by the physiognomic literature of late antiquity, best represented by the writings of the second-century Sophist, Polemo.[3] In Psellos's account Basil's personal appearance reflects his nobility, masculinity, and harmonious proportion. Psellos gives special attention to Basil's luxuriant beard. Men's beards had a very special significance in Byzantine culture, where a long, thick beard was a sign of maturity, both intellectual and sexual. It also signified that he was neither a woman nor a eunuch. If a man's beard was cut off, usually as a punishment, he was considered to have suffered a serious loss of status and masculinity.

In Byzantium, ideal male physical characteristics were defined in opposition to the physical characteristics of women. Indeed, Byzantine men were very concerned about the possibility of appearing effeminate, even to the point of undergoing cosmetic surgery. The seventh-century surgeon, Paul of Aegina, describes very clearly the surgical techniques used to reduce male mammary glands. He considers enlarged mammary glands to be an unsightly deformity and offers a detailed description of the types of incision, excision of fatty tissue, and suturing needed to correct this problem.[4]

Another important male trait that appears in the physiognomic literature and is reflected in Byzantine sources is consistency. A truly masculine man was always consistent in everything he did. In contrast, changeability was assumed to be characteristic of women and eunuchs. The physiognomic literature claims that a changeable, and therefore effeminate, nature can be read in a man's eyes. A very hostile source says that the much-hated iconoclastic emperor, Leo V the Armenian, had such a nature: "He transformed himself into various shapes like a most wicked Proteus."[5]

Within the secular literary tradition of the Byzantine elite, the body was seen as something of value that should be carefully nurtured and cared for. The ideal was a beautiful body, with symmetrical form and features that identified the individual as fully masculine or feminine, a billboard that advertised an aristocrat's social standing. At the same time, in an apparent contradiction, mature men also saw a special kind of beauty in adolescent boys who had a liminal kind of immature masculinity. Their bodies are often described as beautiful in a way that, in our culture, borders on the feminine. Their faces were smooth or covered with soft down. Their skin was soft and pale. Blond or light hair was favored. They were slim and graceful. Mature men admired these pubescent boys, but today it is difficult to know to what extent this reflects appreciation or physical desire. The sexual ambiguity of pubescent boys had an appeal that is hard for the modern observer to comprehend. Later we will see that this ambiguous beauty is one of the reasons that eunuchs were employed at the Byzantine court.

Standards of beauty for women were also well established, although they were not as clearly articulated as standards for men. While we cannot get many explicit details from this early period, we have a few intriguing insights into the standards for imperial beauty from the ninth century. These come from three legendary accounts of the Byzantine bride show. When a young prince was of age to marry (in his late teens) a group of courtiers was sent out to canvas the nearby provincial towns to look for an appropriate bride. They were charged to find an imperial bride whose body matched a certain standard of beauty and proportion. Echoing the story of Cinderella, her foot had to be the perfect size to fit the imperial shoe. The candidates came from the best of the provincial families and had to please the committee and, later, the empress, with regard to physical beauty, education, and deportment. Our best account of a bride show can be found in the *Life of Philarete* by Nicetas.[6] Set in the early ninth century, it describes the selection of Maria of Amnia as the bride of Constantine, son of the empress Irene.[7]

It is hardly surprising that when a woman was selected to wed an imperial prince, she was chosen for her external appearance, especially in a culture that believed that external beauty reflected the beauty of the soul. The *De Ceremoniis* is clear that the Byzantine court valued beauty as part of its public image. Imperial attire was elegant and luxurious. Courtiers, especially those who, in public, stood closest to the imperial family, were selected for their beauty. The beauty and dignity of the earthly court at Constantinople was meant to replicate the imagined court of heaven, with the imperial family representing the heavenly family while the esthetically distinct court eunuchs stood in for heavenly angels.

The twelfth-century writings of Anna Comnena describe the beauty of the empress Maria. The author speaks through the mouth of an aristocrat, John Ducas, as he urges Nicephoros Botaniates to marry Maria:

> He [John] spoke to him [Nicephoros] at great length of her noble birth and physical attractions; again and again he praised her. She was in fact very tall, like a cypress tree; her skin was snow-white; her face was oval, her complexion wholly reminiscent of a spring flower or a rose. As for the flash of her eyes, what mortal could describe it? Eyebrows, flame-colored, arched above eyes of light blue... [S]uch was the proportion and perfect symmetry of her body, each part in harmony with the rest, that no one till then had ever seen its like among human-kind—a living work of art, an object of desire to lovers of beauty.[8]

Clearly for aristocratic women as well as men, bodily symmetry and proportion were important. The eyes and eyebrows were judged according to traditional physiognomic standards. Pale hair, whether blond or red, was much admired. Pale skin on women, unlike men, was desirable, reflecting a life spent indoors, secluded and guarded. Today's suntanned, athletic California woman would not have been considered beautiful at the Byzantine court.

THE CLOTHED BODY

By the tenth century, the court at Constantinople had developed an elaborate structure ruled by strict codes of dress and deportment. Similar court traditions had existed in the Neo-Assyrian Empire (934–610 BC), and were subsequently adopted by Hellenistic monarchs and the later rulers of the Persian Sassanian Empire (AD 224–651). They were adopted in turn by the eastern Romans, later called the Byzantines, and soon became part of the tradition of both the eastern and western Christian churches. Our images of the imperial family and its courtiers are marked by elaborate clothing that reveals only their hands and faces. Scholars have long remarked that the bodies of these individuals are completely hidden and appear to lack shape and movement, and suggested that this reflects a kind of prudishness brought about by Christian belief. While this makes sense, it is at least as important to note that, by the middle Byzantine period, the clothed and ornamented body of the aristocratic individual had become a "billboard" that presented the viewer, whether a worshiper at Hagia Sophia or a foreign envoy being presented at court, with all the information needed regarding the person being observed.

Clothing and ornamentation reflected an individual's importance and gender status, the kind of ritual taking place, the date and time of year, and the degree to which the ceremony was secular or religious. All of this was "written" on the robes worn by the key persons of the court and their attendants and reinforced by the ceremonial objects that the courtiers carried. This is especially evident in the famous mosaic pictures of Justinian and Theodora at Ravenna and in the later pictures of emperors and empresses found in the upper gallery of Hagia Sophia.

The outer garments of courtiers differentiated their wearers' ranks according to the colors, fabrics, and the patterns woven into the silk panels set into the garments. Festal days were marked by particular colors, and even jewelry was coded. For example, only the imperial family, its eunuchs, and its horses were allowed to wear large pearls. Byzantine secular ceremonial practices were adopted by the Catholic and Orthodox churches, with the result that even today, in a formal church setting, clerical bodies support fabric "billboards" that impart information to members of the congregation. Vestments change colors with the ecclesiastical year. The draping of the stole differentiates a priest from a deacon.

THE IMPERIAL BODY

The importance of context and external appearances was magnified by the complexity of the succession process in Byzantium. Gilbert Dagron observed that "the legitimacy of the Byzantine emperor comes directly from God. It is not inherited from parent to child. There is no such thing as 'royal blood.' "[9] Sons of emperors were officially "adopted" into the imperial succession and outsiders "married into" the succession. As a result, imperial sons could be deprived of the right to rule, usually through murder or disfigurement. Like the ancient priestly body, the imperial physical body had to be perfect. The sons of aristocratic families outside the court circle could become emperors through marriage. Once an emperor, whether male or female, was crowned, his or her physical body was confirmed as "holy" through highly ritualized special treatment. The imperial body was rarely touched, and only by certain individuals under carefully regulated conditions. The changing of the imperial crown (the emperor had several for a variety of occasions) could not be seen except by the Patriarch or the eunuchs directly serving the emperor.

THE DISCIPLINED BODY

A basic tenet of Roman law stipulated that the body of a Roman citizen could not be violated in any way. The Byzantine aristocracy inherited this tradition and was generally protected from corporal punishment. Yet two important exceptions to this rule remained. The imperial body had to be perfect, and, if necessary, the body of an emperor or ambitious aristocrat could be disfigured in order to make him ineligible for public office. The physical body was believed to be inherently difficult to govern and could lead an individual into evil deeds. Therefore, it was necessary that the body be ruled by the mind, be disciplined. This was especially true of the bodies of the poor, uneducated, or servile. As a result, within the Byzantine secular tradition the physical body was often punished symbolically. If a body—and the person it defined—offended, the body needed to be disciplined. The hand that stole a loaf of bread was cut off. Noses were cut off and eyes gouged out, punishments considered to be preferable to death. Again, bodily perfection was assumed to be related to moral perfection, and the body was the logical target for punishment for the sins of the soul.

Bodily mutilation was a way of publicly displaying human failings for all to see. One of the most famous examples of mutilation we have involves two brothers, both monks and poets, Theodore and Theophanes (the Graptoi, or inscribed ones), who were supporters of the icons. Legend has it that the emperor Theophilos, the last of the iconoclastic emperors, ordered that they be beaten and then have iconoclastic verses inscribed on their foreheads—they became human advertisements for the iconoclastic cause.

HOLY BODIES

Hagiographical literature—the stories of holy men and women—offers different views about the nature of the body, the soul, and the intellect. Early in the eleventh century, Symeon the New Theologian affirmed that the body, soul, and intellect of every man and woman on earth were God's creation. Yet, he says, the body ages and changes and is vulnerable, while the soul remains unchanged. Every individual has free will to adopt either virtue or vice, and once the soul and the intellect have made this choice they remain unaltered. The body, however, is made up of corruptible matter, elements that are opposites of one another: heat and cold, dry and wet elements. The body is also subject to natural movements of its substance, movements that are otherwise irrational; here Symeon seems to be referring to male sexual desire, involuntary erections, and ejaculations. He lumps lack of sexual control with conjugal pleasure, greediness, gluttony, excessive sleep, laziness, and luxuriant habits, all of which, he says, are not the fault of the body but rather the fault of the soul. Once the soul has experienced these things through its intermediary, the body, it will continue to seek these earthly pleasures.[10]

The problem of the nature of body, soul, and intellect, as articulated by Symeon, had long been important for the eastern Christians. The Mediterranean world was well acquainted with dualistic doctrines that taught that the body (and by extension, the material world) was evil, and the soul (and by extension the spiritual world) was good. By the eleventh century, most of these dualistic doctrines had been declared heretical. As a result, the physical human body itself had been technically brought back into the fold of orthodoxy. But, like the Greek and Roman philosophers before them, Christian holy men were troubled by uncontrollable urges, by life in a male body that could inadvertently and uncontrollably have an erection or a nocturnal emission. References to the snake that lives in the belly and rears its head are common in Byzantine hagiography. These same concerns were also attributed to holy women. The male authors of hagiographical texts dealing with female saints portray them as troubled by the conflict between mind and body, by life in a female body that might suddenly long for sexual pleasure or, by its very beauty, lead men into sin. The author of the *Life of St Matrona of Perge* writes:

> She did not consider the body to be the most evil of foes, after the manner of the hateful and loathsome Manichaeans, but constrained its unreasonable urges with great wisdom, correcting it as is necessary, in obedience to the blessed Paul who says, 'Make not provision for the flesh, to fulfill the lusts thereof.'[11]

This author is careful not to take a heretical Manichaean position on these issues while retaining the discomfort with the physical body expressed in the writings of St Paul.

Most of our ecclesiastical sources come from the most conservative part of the Byzantine religious world and reflect fear and rejection of the body.[12] This contrasts with the attitudes of the secular aristocracy, which celebrate the beauty of the human body and clothe it in luxury. This contrast is striking, yet both conservative ecclesiastical authors and secular court writers were united in the underlying assumption that the outward appearance of the body reflected the quality of the inner person, the soul. Men who had adopted the ascetic life routinely starved their bodies into sexual submission. They were celebrated for the degree to which they could abstain from sustenance and bear the discomfort of a life without warmth or freedom of movement. The appearance of their bodies reflected these deprivations. Just as, among the aristocracy, the beauty, form, and appropriate physiognomic characteristics of the external body reflected the beauty of the soul, so, within the conservative religious community the wasted, abused body of the saint reflected the ascetic purity of the soul.

Byzantine hagiographical writings are filled with stories of monks whose physical desires, usually associated with demonic interventions, are healed by holy men. Father Nicetas was tormented by a demon who tried to take advantage of the fragility of his body.[13] Gregory, a monk in Nicetas's monastery, was troubled by thoughts about intercourse and sexuality, and came to Nicetas for healing. After the saint counseled him Gregory said:

> Today the saint said this prayer over me that I should no longer be tormented by this evil passion. I was amazed to find that I could have ventured, with security, to lie down with a woman. The fact is that I have become insensible and without sensual feeling. I have said goodbye to the world.[14]

For the monk Gregory, freedom from the distractions of the physical world was very important. He believed that the saint had the power, through prayer, to help him remove his inner being from the evils of the real world, in this case his desire for women.

St Stephen the Younger "restrained all his bodily urges through fasting and other forms of mortification."[15] The Patriarch Nicephoros I of Constantinople "through self-control and fasting avoided having erections."[16] St Symeon fasted "to overcome the snake in his belly."[17] The blending of secular and religious self-presentation is seen in the life of St Ioannikios, which traces the saint's evolution from soldier to ascetic:

> During his life as a soldier he performed there every military duty well, surpassing all in intellect and strength; and he appeared to everyone as a pleasant and most attractive man, not only because of the blossoming gracefulness of his youth and the splendor of his handsomeness, but also because of his steadfastness and discipline and his praiseworthy demeanor and the great asceticism of his conduct.[18]

Later, after he became an ascetic, St Ioannikios regularly drove the spirit of fornication out of women. He did so by taking the spirit into his own body and then doing battle with it. After one of these healing sessions, as he battled the spirit of fornication in his own body, he tried everything—fasting, vigils, sleeping on the ground—to force it to leave his body. Desperate, he offered his body to a large snake, hoping it would eat him and thereby destroy the demon.

Hagiography provides images of the bodies of good women as well as those of men. Women who wished to pursue the ascetic life set for themselves the same goals as men, with the added complication that society tried to protect them from the most rigorous ascetic experiences. The latter were found only in male monasteries, where men were protected from the temptation to sin that came from contact with women. This gave rise to a number of lives of women saints who altered their gendered self-presentation in order to enter monasteries as eunuchs or young men. The lives of these transvestite saints tend to be very stereotyped—these women usually were fleeing from their husbands or fathers. Transvestite saints often were accused of fathering children on local women, accusations that they did not dispute. They were punished and then vindicated at death, when the monks prepared their bodies for burial and discovered them to be women.[19]

If allowed, female ascetics aspired to the same rigorous lifestyle as male ascetics. They ate little and carefully, disciplined their bodies, and never bathed. The most graphic example of this is found in the life of St Mary of Egypt, one of many reformed prostitutes who became saints. In this particular account she was found in the desert by a monk who initially assumed she was a demon. He describes her nakedness, her skin tanned almost to blackness, and her short, sparse white hair. Initially, he did not suspect that she was a woman. He says that she is neither male nor female, but a creature. She has so deprived her body that she has lost her female nature entirely and purified her body, having "worn out her flesh for the sake of Christ our God." The same theme is found in the life of St Theoktiste of Lesbos. Those who saw her said, "skin alone kept the bones in place for there was hardly any flesh."[20]

This hagiographical literature, with its constant emphasis on the rejection of sexuality, may seem rather sterile, but Averil Cameron makes the opposite argument, suggesting that by using erotic language to describe spiritual relationships and writing about the denial of sexuality, Byzantine authors actually heightened their readers' awareness of sexuality, making this ascetic literature into erotic literature.[21]

DEMONIC BODIES

In addition to images of holy bodies, hagiography also provides standard images of evil bodies. Predictably, they are ugly and deformed, the opposite image of the bodies of holy men. The monk Cosmos had a vision of demons, little men with blackened faces that were hideous in different ways. Some were distorted, some had bloodshot eyes, some swollen lips or reddened skin. The giant guarding the gate to Tartarus had a black face, smoking nostrils, and a long tongue that hung out of his mouth. His right arm, the one on his "good" side, was paralyzed.[22] The ugliness of the demon's deformed body reflects the evil in his soul.

CASTRATED BODIES

Throughout the Christian world people were taught that the human body was created by God. The Byzantines, however, accepted the possibility of altering the physical body, creating an individual who was neither a woman nor fully a man, a person who was nevertheless very useful to society. Castrated men were key figures in Byzantine society, church, and government. Eunuchs could be found in all parts of Byzantine society, though mainly in service to the aristocracy and the church. Castration is a dramatic example of the deliberate modification of the male body, and in Byzantium it played an important role in elite, courtly, religious, cultural, and social organization. Byzantine ideas about eunuchs might have influenced the human intervention that created them, or these ideas might merely have been formulated to account for the existence of eunuchs.

The Byzantine Empire did not exist in a vacuum and its treatment of the human body had many roots in the cultures of the great civilizations of Persia and the Tigris and Euphrates river valleys. The traditions surrounding human castration are very old, probably originating among the herders of large animals in central Asia. Eunuchs are found in the historical records of China, India, Byzantium, the Middle East (though not among the Jews), Egypt, Muslim Spain, and much of Sub-Saharan and North Africa. When Muhammad was born about 570, eunuchs had been prominent figures at eastern courts for at least two and a half millennia. They appear as court servants in Mesopotamian texts from 2000 BC and in Egyptian texts from about 1300 BC. In the medieval Islamic world, eunuchs had roles in both church and state that were almost identical to those of the eunuchs in medieval Byzantium. Later, the practice of castration spread to the papal court at Rome, where eunuchs staffed the choirs from the late

Middle Ages to the nineteenth century. The use of castrates in music was especially common in Europe in the seventeenth and eighteenth centuries. In the eighteenth century, a religious castration cult appeared in Russia.

Leaving aside eunuch singers at the papal curia and in opera houses, and eunuchs who lived and worked in Muslim Spain, eunuchs were rare in Europe. This is not to say that human castration was not practiced there; it was often a punishment for sexual sin (one immediately thinks of Peter Abelard's "calamity"), and it was inflicted upon enemies defeated in war. In the Byzantine world, however, courtly sources regarded castration as a creative act that produced specialized individuals who filled important social roles. They did not see castration as an act of violence, and it rarely appears as a punishment except for sexual crimes. It could also be a profoundly political act, as witnessed by the castration of a legitimate imperial heir, Ignatios, and an illegitimate one, Basil Nothos, in both cases rendering them unable to claim the imperial throne.

On rare occasions Byzantine sources make reference to "natural" eunuchs. They were believed to be especially blessed because they never had to deal with sexual desire. It is difficult to know what kind of individuals these were, probably men with undescended testicles or individuals suffering from one of the genetic anomalies that produce ambiguous genitalia. The vast majority of eunuchs in Byzantium, however, were castrated.

Before modern drug therapy, human castration involved the removal or disabling of the testicles and, in some cultures, the removal of the penis. In China, medical technology could accomplish ablation of both the testicles and penis with a relatively low mortality rate. In the rest of the world the mortality rate following this operation was so high that, at least in Byzantium, it was rarely used and castration was accomplished by tying off or removing the testicles. The castration of adult men was especially dangerous, and it resulted in an individual who retained a male appearance and, although sterile, some limited sexual ability. If done before puberty, however, castration was a relatively safe surgery, with the added advantage that castrated children, because they never passed through puberty, developed very distinctive physical characteristics. These included unusually long limbs and necks and lack of male musculature. They had heart-shaped faces because the bones of the jaw and temple did not develop normally, fine skin, and no facial hair or body hair. The hair on their heads was luxuriant, and they were never troubled by baldness. Their voices remained at a childlike pitch. They were infertile and, unless castrated very late in puberty, could not achieve an erection. As they aged, eunuchs castrated before puberty suffered from serious cardiac and skeletal problems connected with prolonged testosterone deprivation.

This is what science tells us about eunuchs. The Byzantines were convinced that eunuchs had other special gifts. Because eunuchs could not ejaculate sperm, they were thought to retain their mental energy and develop intellectual capabilities beyond those of other men. Because they could not marry or father children, they were considered unusually loyal to those they served. Because of their physical ambiguity, they were assumed to have special powers in liminal events and activities, including rituals connected with magic, death, religion, the court, and the imperial succession. Because they were assumed to be incapable of sexual intercourse, they were trusted as guardians of women and teachers of children.

The Byzantines were quite aware that the bodies of these castrated young men had been significantly altered, and they reacted variously to the act of castration and its results. For many, the act itself was seen as a necessary evil. Eunuchs had become an integral part of the Byzantine world, but there was a certain reluctance to take responsibility for deliberate castration. Somebody had to castrate children if the society was to continue to have eunuchs. The seventh-century surgeon, Paul of Aegina, tells us that slave owners sometimes brought young male slaves to him and demanded that he castrate them. He says that he did not like to do this and then implies that he was not in a position to refuse. He has left us with a detailed description of how a castration was done.[23] Other texts claim that the Byzantines, as good Christians, did not perform castrations, but rather bought eunuchs from Muslim countries where, they assumed, castration was a routine procedure. Interestingly, Islamic texts level exactly the same charge against the Byzantines. We know that there were some areas (Paphlagonia, for example) where tribal rulers routinely selected attractive young boys and sold them off to be castrated; eunuchs were also imported from Slavic lands. By the tenth century not all eunuchs came from enslaved populations or from foreign lands. As eunuchs gained power in both the secular and ecclesiastical bureaucracies, freeborn parents began to castrate their younger sons in order to prepare them for a successful career either in the church or at court. Since the castration of a freeborn Roman (as the Byzantines considered themselves) was technically illegal, the surgery was sometimes done by a nurse in infancy or, later, the family might claim that the child suffered from a hernia or other problem that only castration could solve.[24] In the hagiographical tradition, there are many stories in which saints save children from castration. Beyond this, we have little information. Our sources rarely talk about a eunuch's birth, castration, or death. Once an individual was recognized as a eunuch, he lost his original identity and received a new name and an education that might enable him to claim aristocratic status. He was parted from his natal family but retained his ethnicity. In both the secular and ecclesiastical worlds, eunuchs were associated with angels and liminality. The youth, beauty, and purity of eunuchs were celebrated, yet it was also recognized that their beauty faded early and that they died young.

Secular aristocratic sources alternate between admiration and scorn for eunuchs. Some authors describe eunuchs as a kind of third sex, neither man nor woman. Others criticize eunuchs, claiming that they lack the qualities that define "real" men and exhibit characteristics traditionally associated with women. Like women, eunuchs were believed to eat too much, exhibit erratic behavior, enjoy money and worldly pleasures, and cry especially readily. They were assumed to be willing, passionate, passive sexual partners for men, more eager to participate in sexual activity then women were.[25] They were envied their close proximity to political power and characterized as devious and greedy.

Within religious writings, attitudes toward eunuchs are ambivalent. In these sources it is not uncommon to find monks, holy men, and even patriarchs who were eunuchs—often castrated as children so that they could more easily embrace the ascetic life. On the one hand, this was seen as praiseworthy and eunuch monks were admired for their purity. On the other hand, they were criticized because they were not tested by sexual desire. Because eunuchs were assumed to be passive partners in sexual acts and enjoy this role, their entry into monasteries was often restricted because they were believed to tempt older monks to sin. As a result, the Byzantines established monasteries specifically for eunuchs.

One of the few texts that directly deals with the sexuality of eunuchs is in the life of St Andrew the Fool. In this text there is an exceptionally graphic description and a strong condemnation of a young eunuch's perceived sexual desires:

> His [the eunuch's] face was like a rose, the skin of his body white as snow, he was well shaped, fair-haired, possessing an unusual softness, and smelling of musk from afar. As Epiphanios [the saint's young disciple] had been brought up together with this lovely young eunuch and was his friend they loved each other dearly.[26]

The saint accused the eunuch of being a sodomite and spoke very harsh words to him. He accused him of being a willing sexual partner for his master and of trying to seduce Epiphanios. Epiphanios tried to defend his friend, saying that he was a slave and required to do what his master demanded. The saint was merciless and told the eunuch that he must refuse his master and suffer martyrdom rather than lose his soul through the sin of sodomy. The author claimed that the eunuch's embarrassment proclaimed his guilt.[27] It is very unusual to find a Byzantine text that deals with sexual desire, and especially intercourse between men, as frankly and openly as this text.

By the tenth and eleventh centuries in Byzantium, eunuchs had become increasingly powerful in administrative affairs. They specialized in bookkeeping and financial matters, and served as librarians, guardians of the symbols of imperial power, doctors, and teachers. They had administrative duties in the army, and a few even achieved fame as military strategists.

Is it possible to categorize eunuchs using modern conceptions of gender? Though unable to father children, eunuchs were sexually active. Men perceived them as potential passive partners, though they also criticized eunuchs for desiring and giving pleasure to women. Byzantine sources that praise eunuchs categorize them as men, though men of a special sort. Pejorative sources compare them to women, but never actually categorize them as women. Ultimately the Byzantine eunuchs constituted a special subcategory of men, one that we would call a socially constructed gender category. The key elements in this category involved infertility and significant changes in appearance—both achieved through the intentional removal of those male sexual organs responsible for fertility and the development of male secondary sexual characteristics. This gender category, then, acquired a number of other assumed qualities: ambiguity, spirituality, liminality, and the ability to render perfect service.

Not surprisingly, there were striking similarities between the eunuchs of Islam and the eunuchs of Byzantium.[28] In both cases, eunuchs served either at court or in aristocratic homes. In both Byzantium and Islam, eunuchs were given new names after castration and their family roots were forgotten.[29] In both cases, eunuchs served in religious institutions. In the case of Islam, there is a long tradition of eunuchs guarding major religious shrines,[30] where they were believed to have special spiritual powers, a phenomenon echoed among the eunuchs of Byzantium. In both Byzantium and Islam, eunuchs played important roles in collecting and preserving historical materials, running pious foundations, sponsoring art, and funding the construction of religious buildings. They acted as guardians and teachers of women and minor children and as go-betweens, serving groups that would not usually, due to social custom, be allowed to mingle. Both Byzantine and Muslim eunuchs were valued for their faithfulness and trustworthiness and were usually put in charge of money, property, symbols of authority, and prisoners. Both served as sexual targets for men, acting as passive partners in sexual acts. In both cultures, the position and assumed abilities of eunuchs were a function of the special traits they were believed to possess because their bodies and physical maturation had been deliberately altered through castration.

There is one major difference between Byzantine and Muslim attitudes toward eunuchs and sexuality. The Byzantines, while they assiduously guarded their women, were mainly preoccupied with guaranteeing that, before marriage, a woman remained a virgin and that, after marriage, her child was the child of her husband's body and was not fathered by another. They were not excessively preoccupied with regulating women's sexual pleasure. As a result, women were guarded by eunuchs who, though unable to produce semen or a full erection, were still able to give them some degree of sexual pleasure. Islamic society felt a need to regulate both a woman's reproductive capacity and her sexual pleasure. As a result, the eunuchs who guarded Muslim women were fully castrated, with both the testicles and the penis removed. When Muhammad II the Conqueror seized Constantinople, he insisted that all partially castrated eunuchs be removed from the palace.

Conclusion

Do the ways in which the Byzantines perceived, altered, and decorated the Byzantine body answer any of our modern questions about the body? Were there gay men in Byzantium? Did women have any kind of intimate sexual experiences with one another? Do the sources available to us allow us to answer these questions?

The answer is no. In Byzantium gender was determined by the body's physical appearance, personal behavior, and assigned roles in society. It was assumed that, depending on their class, men, as active sexual partners, took their pleasure where they could find it and that women, boys, and eunuchs, were all fair game. Willing participation in a sexual act as a passive partner could damage a man's reputation, but it was unlikely to change his gender status. Eunuchs were assumed to act as passive sexual partners, and to enjoy this role, but whether this was their preference is difficult to determine.

The traditions that we find in Byzantium regarding the body combine Greco-Roman philosophical and medical teachings, traditional popular assumptions about men, women, and sexuality, and beliefs that the body is not stable, that it can be constructed and reconstructed by society in order to create individuals that fill societal needs. Christianity grew up within this social framework. In some cases, as, for example, in its rejection of dualistic notions regarding the physical body, Christianity shaped societal attitudes and rehabilitated the body. In other cases, as, for example, its support of castration traditions, Christianity shaped its teachings to social needs and turned a blind eye toward castration.

The Byzantine world regarded bodily externals as clear evidence of an individual's inner soul or personality. This was especially true in elite circles, at court, and in the ecclesiastical world. Castration, an extreme form of bodily modification by western standards, was common in Byzantium. Because castration altered the way a man matured, it created persons who were perceived to lack many male traits but who had other special abilities, ranging from business and administrative skills to access to the spiritual world. Modern gender and behavioral labels do not readily fit the Byzantine world. As historians, we must investigate the Byzantine body in terms of the Byzantine world, always remembering that our sources are limited and often misleading.

FURTHER READING

Ayalon, David. *Eunuchs, Caliphs and Sultans: A Study in Power Relationships.* Jerusalem: The Magnes Press, The Hebrew University of Jerusalem, 1999.

Brown, Peter. *The Body and Society: Men, Women, and Sexual Renunciation in Early Christianity.* New York: Columbia University Press, 2008.

Connor, Carolyn L. *Women of Byzantium.* New Haven: Yale University Press, 2004.

Garland, Lynda, ed. *Byzantine Women: Varieties of Experience AD 800–1200.* Aldershot: Ashgate Publishing, 2006.

Gleason, Maud W. *Making Men: Sophists and Self-Presentation in Ancient Rome.* Princeton: Princeton University Press, 1995.

Herrin, Judith. *Women in Purple: Rulers of Medieval Byzantium.* London: Weidenfeld & Nicolson, 2001.

James, Liz, ed. *Desire and Denial in Byzantium.* Aldershot: Ashgate Publishing 1999.

James, Liz, ed. *Women, Men and Eunuchs: Gender in Byzantium.* London: Routledge, 1997.

Marmon, Shaun. *Eunuchs and Sacred Boundaries in Islamic Society.* Oxford, Oxford University Press, 1995.

Murray, Stephen O. and Will Roscoe. *Islamic Homosexualities: Culture, History, and Literature.* New York: New York University Press, 1997.

Ringrose, Kathryn M. *The Perfect Servant: Eunuchs and the Social Construction of Gender in Byzantium.* Chicago: University of Chicago Press, 2003.

Talbot, Alice-Mary, ed. *Holy Women of Byzantium: Ten Saints' Lives in English Translation.* Washington, DC: Dumbarton Oaks, 1996.

Tougher, Shaun. *The Eunuch in Byzantine History and Society.* London: Routledge, 2008.

NOTES

1. The best known is the *Strategikon* of Kekaumenos.

2. Michael Psellus, *Fourteen Byzantine Rulers*, trans. E. R. A. Sewter (London: Penguin, 1966), 48.

3. Maud W. Gleason, *Making Men: Sophists and Self-Presentation in Ancient Rome* (Princeton: Princeton University Press, 1995).

4. Paul of Aegina, *Chirurgie* (Paris: Librairie de Victor Masson, 1855), ch. 46, 86.

5. Alice-Mary Talbot, "Life of Theodora of Thessalonika," in Alice-Mary Talbot, ed., *Holy Women of Byzantium: Ten Saints' Lives in English Translation* (Washington DC: Dumbarton Oaks, 1996), 173.

6. M. H. Fourmy and M. Leroy, "La Vie de S. Philarete," *Byzantion*, 9 (1934): 113–67.

7. Both Judith Herrin, *Women in Purple: Rulers of Medieval Byzantium* (Princeton: Princeton University Press, 2001), 136 and Gilbert Dagron, *Emperor and Priest: The Imperial Office in Byzantium* (Cambridge: Cambridge University Press, 2003), 47 believe that the bride show existed as an institution.

8. Anna Comnena, *The Alexiad*, trans. E. R. A. Sewter (London: Penguin 1969).

9. Dagron, *Empire and Priest*, 36, 40, and 181.

10. Symeon Le Nouveau Theologien, *Cateches*, trans. Joseph Paramelle, Sources Chrétiennes, 113 (Paris: Cerf, 1965), III: 63–65.

11. Jeffrey Featherstone, "Life of Matrona," in Talbot, ed., *Holy Women of Byzantium*, 20.

12. It is important to remember that in the Greek Orthodox Church, even in the Byzantine era, the lower clergy, including priests, were allowed to marry (provided they did so before ordination), father children, and raise families within the communities that they served. Only a priest who became a bishop was required to set aside his wife.

13. Denise Papachrysanthou, "Un confesseur du second iconoclasm: La vie du patrice Nicétas," *Travaux et mémoires*, 3 (1968): 309–51 and H. Delahaye, ed., *Synaxarium ecclesiae Constantinopolitinae: Propylaeum ad Acta Sanctorum Novembris* (Brussels, 1902) (= *Synaxarion CP*), 330.

14. *Synaxarion CP*, 330.

15. Alice-Mary Talbot, "Life of St. Stephen the Younger," in idem, ed., *Byzantine Defenders of the Images: Eight Saints' Lives in English Translation* (Washington, DC: Dumbarton Oaks, 1998), 1.

16. Elizabeth A. Fisher, "Life of the Patriarch Nicephoros I of Constantinople," in Talbot, ed., *Byzantine Defenders*, 56.

17. Douglas Domingo-Foraste, "Life of Sts. David, Symeon and George of Lesbos," in Talbot, ed., *Byzantine Defenders*, 167.

18. Denis F. Sullivan, "Life of St. Ioannikios," in Talbot, ed., *Byzantine Defenders*, 259.

19. "Life of Anna Euphemiana," in *Synaxarion CP*, 170; "Life of St. Matrona," in J. P. Migne, ed., *Patrologia cursus completus, series graeca* (Paris, 1857–66), 116; Nicholas Constas, "Life of St. Mary/Marinos," in Talbot, ed., *Holy Women of Byzantium*, 7.

20. Maria Kouli, "Life of St. Mary of Egypt," in Talbot, ed., *Holy Women of Byzantium*, 65–93. This same theme can be found in the life of St Theoktiste of Lesbos. Those who saw her said that "the skin alone kept the bones in place for there was hardly any flesh." Angela C. Hero, "Life of St. Theoktiste of Lesbos," in Talbot, ed., *Holy Women of Byzantium*, 20.

21. Averil Camerion, "Sacred and Profane Love: Thoughts on Byzantine Gender," in Liz James, ed., *Women, Men and Eunuchs: Gender in Byzantium* (London: Routledge, 1997), 1–23.

22. Cyril Mango, *Byzantium: The Empire of New Rome* (London: Weidenfeld and Nicolson, 1980), 152.

23. Paul of Aegina, *Chirurgie*, ch. 68, 111.

24. This is the theme of several of the miracles of St Artemios; see Virgil S. Crisafulli, *The Miracles of St. Artemios: A Collection of Miracle Stories by an Anonymous Author of Seventh Century Byzantium* (Leiden: E. J. Brill, 1997). It also is found in the life of David, Symeon, and George. See J. van den Gheyn, ed., "Acta Graeca SS. Davidis, Symeonis, et Georgi Mitylenae in insulae Lesbo," *Analecta Bollandiana*, 18 (1899): 240. See a newer translation of this life in Talbot, ed., *Byzantine Defenders*, 205.

25. *Vita Anna Euphemiana*, 173–78.

26. Nikephoros, *The Life of St. Andrew the Fool*, ed. Lennart Rydén (Uppsala: L. Rydén, 1995), 2: 83–85.

27. Ibid.

28. David Ayalon, *Eunuchs, Caliphs and Sultans: A Study in Power Relationships* (Jerusalem: Magnes Press, The Hebrew University, 1999); Stephen O. Murray and Will Roscoe, eds, *Islamic Homosexualities: Culture, History, and Literature* (New York: New York University Press, 1997), 4.

29. An important exception to this is the family of the eunuch John the Orphanotrophos, who managed to retain close ties to his family, making his siblings wealthy and powerful.

30. For a detailed study of eunuchs in Islamic religious institutions, see Shaun E. Marmon, *Eunuchs and Sacred Boundaries in Islamic Society* (Oxford: Oxford University Press, 1995).

CHAPTER 24

SAME-SEX POSSIBILITIES

HELMUT PUFF

THE following pages aim to tell a complicated story. The notion that, if only we look hard enough, we will be able to identify solid textual foundations for our understanding of same-sex eroticism in medieval times is tempting but illusory. Theology is a prime suspect for a foundational discourse, and this is why I will launch this chapter with the discussion of a religious poem against sodomitical sex. Under analytic scrutiny, it appears that religious precepts are equivocal on the matter of same-sex relations. Censorious discourses about same-sex sexual acts, including theological ones, are riddled with contradictions. In addition, their dissemination depended on conscious efforts at making prohibitions known and the institutions to enforce the prescribed sexual order—an institutional apparatus that was often lacking during the medieval period. Whether we look to religious traditions or secular precepts, there is not one single authoritative source for western Christianity's concerns about sex between men or between women. Importantly, attitudes toward homoeroticism were subject to historic change in the millennium between the decline of the Roman Empire and the Reformation. Once we acknowledge these and similar complications, we can make the move from the punitive term "sodomy" to the many same-sex possibilities that pervaded the Middle Ages.

Research into medieval same-sex sexualities has shifted dramatically in past decades. This scholarship focused initially on prescriptive literature or court records with their invariable condemnations of same-sex sexual acts. Since then, novel modes of reading and the consideration of previously neglected archives have helped to reconfigure sodomy into what, for the purpose of this essay, I have called same-sex possibilities. Prescriptive texts, rather than condemning homosexuality outright, transported complex and often contradictory messages. What is more, medieval culture accommodated uncensored, at times unquestioned, and at other times celebrated expressions of same-sex love—sexual and nonsexual.

Current research on same-sex possibilities therefore compels us to consider the manifold relations between prescriptive texts on the one hand and the erotic potential of homosocial ties on the other hand. My starting point in this exploration is not the supposed origins of homophobia or acceptance, but the late Middle Ages, a time during which theologians and believers harvested various earlier texts that regulated sex, forging ever closer and occasionally deadly connections between prescriptions and lived experience. It is this late medieval vantage point that exposes to plain view the brittleness of prohibitive discourses on same-sex ties.

SAME-SEX ACTS AS SAME-SEX SINS

The fifteenth-century poet Michel Beheim strongly warned his audience against the dangers of "unchastity" (c.1457–1464); ten of thirty-nine poems in a cycle on the seven deadly sins are devoted to this cardinal vice. Among them is a diatribe brandishing the "sin against nature" as the foremost type of lust to be shunned: "Of a sin harmful and vile, sinful, loathsome, vile, barren, severe, dissolute, filthy, sick I want to tell you…"[1] The author never describes what this sin actually is, but he prescribes horror as the appropriate Christian response to this sin. Whoever sins thus, so read the poem's concluding lines, forsakes God and his creation, degrading his or her human nature to animality. Such sinners risk not only their salvation, however; they also inflict ferocious damage on others. Examples such as the Flood, the destruction of Sodom, or the punishment of Lot's wife are introduced to illustrate God's wrathful punishment of this sin of sins. Beheim's poem marshals cascades of verbal venom in order to also mobilize his reader's wrath.

The poetic fervor in this case is calculated to teach a lesson. Broadly put, that lesson constitutes sexual activities as sins when practiced outside strictly defined parameters. Yet how can one grasp the sin that warrants no compassion for the sinner? The poet never gives the answer to this question. Instead, he shrouds the deed or deeds at its roots in darkness. One may best glean the act's definition from a declaration of what it is not, placed in the mouth of one who commits it: "You, Lord and God, created man and woman and commanded them to multiply. But I want to assiduously diminish and damage the human race on earth" (ll. 25–30). The speaker, whether a man or a woman, is said to be in the know about God's injunction to procreate and yet has nonprocreative sexual intercourse. How this is accomplished remains unsaid. The sinners in this category are simply imagined to defy human society as well as God—a willful act of rebellion that warrants their extinction. At the same time, others—the poem's audience—are at risk to rebel against God in like manner and therefore need to be shielded from the sexual knowledge alluded to here. Let us turn the poem's rhetoric on its head. Let us ask how these verses, selected from the vast archive of late medieval religious instruction in the vernacular, affected their audience: This text was written to foreclose possibilities of doing and learning. How is it possible, we may ask, to unlock what it keeps from view so assiduously and at the same time invites us to see?

In coming to terms with the hermeneutics of this sin—a sin said to be the most horrid sexual act—modern critics have long stood on the shoulders of their medieval forbears. They have, in a way, fallen prey to the siren calls of writings with regard to the "sin against nature." They have assumed that what is referred to here or elsewhere is more or less transparent. They have assumed furthermore that the poem's parts present a coherent front against the sin in question, a sin variably described as sodomy, the sin against nature, or the mute sin. Some critics have added to the terminological complexities by mapping modern terms such as homosexuality or gayness on top of medieval categories of thinking. Is Beheim's much vilified sin the same as the one(s) Peter Damian condemned 400 years earlier (c.1049)? In a treatise on the "sodomitical vice" among clergymen, this reform theologian differentiated four types of sexual acts against nature: masturbation, mutual masturbation, intercourse "between the legs," and anal intercourse.[2] In the twelfth century, Peter the Chanter equated the sodomites with the biblical figure of Onan, "who spilled his seed on the earth."[3] The thirteenth-century scholastic Albert the Great explained *sodomia* as "the sin against nature, of man with man, or woman with woman" in a passage of his summa. What is presented as one sin, *the* sin against nature, comprises in fact a multiplicity of acts and dispositions.

Whereas the poem's evocations of horror are strikingly monolithic, its textual layers are not. "Of a sin that is harmful..." is a poetic vessel for terms the poet introduces as referring to the same supposed act: "Sodomy," "heresy," "the four crying sins," and "the unspeakable sin" are among the theological themes the author invokes. In an effort to multiply the effects on the listener or reader, late medieval theologians, sermonizers, and authors heaped image on image, story on story, discourse on discourse when addressing the so-called sin against nature. Put differently, Beheim's text is above all a compilation. The poem's topics and rhetoric are predicated on other texts; its encyclopedic profile is a sign of its date of composition and the traditions on which the late medieval poet could rely. At the same time, the poem does not directly inform us about how people acted, lived, felt, or thought.

From the thirteenth century on, a marked upswing of lay devotion across Europe went hand in hand with an increased demand for religious edification in writing. In the fifteenth century, even laymen like Beheim, an itinerant minstrel known to have plied his trade at several secular courts as well as in cities, composed in this vein. Like several other fifteenth-century vernacular poets, the author forged links between the sphere of theological erudition and popular poetic forms, spreading the word on how to lead a proper Christian life through novel ways.

In the case of this cycle of poems on the cardinal vices, Beheim adapted a model text, likewise positioned at a communicative nexus, a vernacular treatise by the great theologian Henry of Langenstein (1325–1397).[4] Due to the active patronage by a ruling dynasty, the Habsburgs of Austria, Henry was instrumental in launching a center of translation, production, and dissemination of religious texts in the vernacular, most of them scholastic in origin, at the nodes of university, court, and town. This center's output transcended its local milieus in an appeal to broad audiences across central Europe; similar such centers existed in Paris, the Low Countries, and elsewhere. Beheim's poem is evidence that the Christianization of everyday life with its corollary, the vilification of behavior deemed unchristian, gained momentum by the mid-fifteenth century among the laity. This movement awarded the clerically untrained poet as well as other lay believers a considerable and active role in siding with its messages. By collecting, redacting, and editing his poetry in manuscripts, Beheim made sure his efforts would be remembered.

Scholars have recently begun to question the lucidity of the metaphors, stories, and arguments related to what Beheim and others call the sin against nature and similar terms. They have shown them to be verbal creations, coined at particular junctures in the history of Christianity, and they have linked their emergence to vicissitudes of church history such as the eleventh-century reforms, the rise of scholasticism, and the fight against so-called heresies. In the process of exploring this sin's meandering meanings throughout history, critics—queer critics above all—have expounded on its ability to generate ever new meanings.[5] In a way, the sin or sins against nature, as the poet has it, appears as the unknowable sin. As we have seen, however, unknowability results from the poet's own obfuscations. The text's opacities rest on ways of speaking with distinct historical trajectories and purposes. Like other late medieval texts destined for lay edification, "Of a sin that is harmful…" draws on centuries of religious instruction. In fact, the overt display of dread serves as the glue that covers over multiple sources at the poem's core.

Commemorating Same-Sex Love and Companionship

Let us contrast our poetic diatribe with monuments from a context that affirms same-sex intimacy. Sir John Clanvowe passed away in Constantinople in 1391, and Sir William Neville, "for whom [Clanvowe's] love was no less than for himself," died of grief for his "companion in march," the *Westminster Chronicle* tells us. One grave became the final resting place for these two English knights. Burials of same-sex couples are documented throughout the Middle Ages. Fortuitously, in the case of Clanvowe and Neville, the tomb monument survives (see Figure 24.1). It depicts a stylized kiss between the "sworn brothers," the chronicle's term to describe their tie.[6]

In a parish church in Sussex, England, one brass commemorates two women, Elizabeth Etchingham (d.1452) and Agnes Oxenbridge (d.1480), who were also buried together (see Figure 24.2). The design is suggestive of emotional intimacy between female aristocrats born to two intermarrying noble families. Whereas the two English knights were remembered in written as well as in monument form, the brass is the only record we have with regard to these women aristocrats, a reflection, among other things, of their female sex and their having been single throughout their lives. No description of them as "sworn sisters" survives. Remarkably, their relationship, whatever its exact name or nature, was remembered several decades after the death of one of them. From the vantage point of familial memory, no necessity existed to erect the tomb monument.[7]

FIGURE 24.1 Tombstone of Sir William Neville and Sir John Clanvowe, detail, late 14th c., formerly Galata, Istanbul Archeology Museums. Photo: Robert Ousterhout.

FIGURE 24.2 Memorial brass for Elizabeth Etchingham and Agnes Oxenbridge, c.1480, Etchingham (England). Photo: Judith Bennett.

In the case of the two English knights, the alignment of heraldic signs is evocative of companionship and emotional charge; their arms are impaled, that is each half of the escutcheon bears the family's crest of one of them, as was common practice with spouses or bishops and their sees. By contrast, Etchingham's and Oxenbridge's "portraits" invoke difference by rendering the latter larger than the other. It is unclear whether this discrepancy captures a facet of their bond such as their respective ages at death and the fact that Oxenbridge commissioned the monument or whether it reflects factors external to it such as financial considerations on the part of the executors. Yet the composition countervails this asymmetry in size by stressing their connection and having the two women gaze at each other.

By honoring same-sex liaisons in a church setting, the two monuments declare openly the righteousness of these relationships. Following iconographic conventions, they gesture toward the intertwined lives of the deceased while issuing a strong appeal to the viewer for aid in bringing about salvation through prayer. At the same time, these monuments leave us moderns with questions about whether their bond was sexual. After all, both the carved stone for Clanvowe and Neville as well as the epitaph for Etchingham and Oxenbridge frame same-sex ties as marriage-like bonds. As a rule, dead spouses were buried together and commemorated as couples. In sum, monuments like these constitute an area of sociocultural possibility that marshals the imagery of spouses for bonds between unrelated members of the same sex.

Whatever the nature of these same-sex bonds, evidence for them and others has long been neglected or misidentified. Only recently have medievalists begun to investigate the forms, structures, and meanings of same-sex sociality and sociability in medieval Europe. Researchers have posited that voluntary kinship and same-sex ties complemented or, as some have it, challenged the ties of blood and marriage. At the same time, historians of sexuality have moved beyond investigating sexual acts to map the vast landscape of same-sex social contacts. They have started to reconceptualize eroticism not as a practice apart but as a bond embedded in other bonds. From these critics' preliminary findings it would appear that the medieval millennium manifested itself, among other ways, through a vibrant culture of homosocial interactions.[8]

Proponents of Christian monasticism sometimes distinguished sinful "friendship and physical desire" among male and female monastics from its laudable counterpart, "spiritual brotherhood." Critics of exalted ties of friendship within monasteries notwithstanding, the English abbot Aelred of Rivaulx (1110–1167) eloquently advocated amical bonds within monasteries. He envisioned monastic communities as infused with the affections of lovers, building on the semantic kinship of love (amor) and friendship (amicitia), a formula he had culled from an ancient text, Cicero's On Friendship. Using the example of his own youthful failings, the author set his On Spiritual Friendship in an actual community: Rievaulx with its many oblates (children donated to the monastery) and its need to integrate those who had not chosen to take the vows. Thus he presented ideal notions of monastic friendship as troubled in practice. Besieged by fleshly desires, friends needed to learn how to observe the "laws and rights of friendship" and extricate themselves from the "concupiscence of the flesh." These temptations are only vaguely described, possibly because the passage invites readers to overcome their own, personal tribulations for the sake of spiritual friendship.[9]

As centers of schooling and literary production, monasteries also were spaces where erotic desires were expressed in writing. The following Latin verses, celebrating an unnamed male youth as an object of love, originated from the same monastic milieu and the same period as Aelred: "Believe me, if those former days of Jove should return, / His handservant would no longer be Ganymede / But you, carried off to heaven; by day the sweet cup / And by night your sweeter kisses you would administer to Jove."[10] The studied neopaganism evident in these lines was above all a literary code, practiced among an erudite and exclusive group of clerics who shared an erotic, emotional, and aesthetic sensibility.

Monasteries were exceptional spaces, not least for their usual—albeit not invariable—single-sex communities. But many activities outside the monastery, whether in agriculture, education, labor, or play, also separated one sex from the other. Even if married, women spent much time with other women, and men with men. Sculpted capitals from Romanesque churches in southern Europe reflect this wide spectrum of same-sex behavioral and affective possibilities. They show erotically evocative scenes of couples, among them men entwined with other men, or women with women. Some of these sculptures seem to denounce the vagaries of lust, some of them show bodily entwinements, and yet others border on the ornamental or the grotesque. Comparable figurations populate the margins of medieval manuscripts or tapestries. In such images, antagonism toward same-sex relations tangle with their eroticism.[11]

Entertaining the possibility of the erotic within the spectrum of homosocial engagements compels researchers to recognize the many emotional and (occasionally) erotic investments of medieval men and women. It unearths a link between kinds of intimacy that few people acknowledged was there, to echo a formulation once used by Alan Bray with regard to Elizabethan England.[12] Rather than ask whether particular relationships involved genital contact—a somewhat fruitless question—we need to recognize that eroticism could be present in many different ways.

In fact, modern assumptions may be a poor guide to medieval gestures of intimacy. For example, the English chronicler Roger of Howden reported that when Richard the Lionheart, then pretender to the English crown, paid a visit to the French King Philip II in 1187, they formed such an "intense love" toward one another that they ate from the same dish and slept together at night. Such displays of love between aristocrats did not reflect personal sentiment, let alone sexual predilections. These acts were part of a politically motivated set of diplomatic niceties whose main purpose was to bridge over their difference in royal status.[13]

The discourse of love was both a flexible and a fraught terrain. As a result, it has proven slippery for the certainties that modern critics seek to impose on particular passages, quotations, or terms. As Jane Burns has suggested elsewhere in this volume, love can also be thought of as a performative code. Such a perspective offers a telling window onto individual agency against a backdrop of cultural expectations. It would be erroneous, for instance, to posit the primacy of affective bonds between the sexes for the medieval period. Some critics argue that the cultivation of male–male love among aristocrats actually shaped the celebration of romantic love between a man and a woman. In the aristocratic milieu of court life, in other words, heterosexual love may not have been the primary bond from which same-sex ties departed. Rather than being distorted reflections of heterosexual love, as many critics see it, same-sex bonds may actually have been the model on which ideas of heterosexual love were based. Characteristically, courtly literary texts of the central Middle Ages eroticized not so much distinctly female or male but noble bodies whose portrayal made one sex resemble the other, as James Schultz has argued. *Fin amors* or "courtly love" was an idealized realm that did not revolve around heterosexuality, even though the love between noble men and women was a major theme. Such new understandings of same-sex social, emotional, and erotic possibilities continue to upend old certainties about social organization, often assumed to be transhistorically applicable, like the notion of homosexuality as a supposed deviation from a heterosexual norm.[14]

After 1100, the intellectual movement known as scholasticism cultivated another way of speaking about same-sex intimacy, the discourse of sodomy. Scholastics systematized earlier theological statements about same-sex eroticism. They saw both sexes as saddled with sexual lust as an irrevocable result of the Fall. Occasionally, those said to have given over their lives to material wealth and luxuries were believed to engage especially in the excesses of lust with both sexes. Furthermore, they associated same-sex eroticism with gender inversion for both men and women, though the link was not nearly as clear-cut as it is in modern sexology. But such statements never crystallized into a sodomite as a type with visual or bodily characteristics. Male effeminacy, for instance, was also—if not primarily—understood as resulting from socializing beyond all measure with women or from excessive desire for them. The sodomite's plasticity allowed for the figure's inclusion in various contexts—though wherever and whenever invectives against sodomites surfaced, they seem to have produced shockwaves.

Yet did the sodomite have a gender? In conceptual theology, the term sodomy referred to both men and women. When the figure was actualized on the level of examples, stories, and illustrations, the sodomite most often was thought to be a man. But this primary identification with men seems not to have prevented the application of the term sodomy to women, even if writings and trial records writings occasionally show evidence of confusion in the latter case.

If the confluence of discourses by the later Middle Ages increased awareness of and fears around same-sex eroticism, this does not mean that the early Middle Ages was a time free of censure or penalty for same-sex sexual acts. Toleration, let alone tolerance, is a concept ill-equipped to capture the prehistory of "the persecuting society" that emerged in the second millennium. John Boswell's seminal thesis helped us to move away from leveling Christianity's approach to "homosexuality" as unchangingly censorious and to investigate the erotic potential within Christian traditions. But his argument that homosexuality was subjected to new persecution in the central Middle Ages appears strained in light of evidence for long-standing condemnations of same-sex eroticism.[15]

SODOMY AND THE LAW

Legal discourse is a case in point. The uneven emergence of legal norms would ultimately result in occasional, though rarely systematic, enforcement of sexual orthodoxy against "heretics," "buggers," or "sodomites." Yet like other discourses thought to be foundational, the law follows a complex trajectory. Modern law can seem univocal and uncompromising, but medieval law was many-voiced and muted by the differing traditions—especially Roman and customary—from which it drew.

Claims to the contrary notwithstanding, legislation in ancient Rome had featured practically no prohibitions against sex between men; sex between women never entered the purview of lawmakers. To be sure, Romans shared with classical Athenians unease about citizens subjecting themselves to anal penetration. Accordingly, one imperial law seems to have protected freeborn male youths from being thus violated. Yet the rise of Christian ideas of the self led to much more (and more negative) attention to same-sex relations.[16] First, whether in a secular or a religious context, prohibitions ceased to distinguish strictly between penetrator and penetrated; both were said to have defiled themselves. New Testament precedent might have played a role in this shift. St Paul castigated the followers of Christ in Rome for what he called somewhat enigmatically "dishonorable passions" and "unnatural" relations practiced among men and among women (Rom. 1:26ff.).

Second, starting with Emperor Justinian's law code, strongly censorious language replete with biblical allusions became common in statutes against same-sex sexual acts. This is so even though the regulations in this same code condemned perpetrators to ecclesiastical penance only. In fact, there was a long hiatus in which no comparable legal precepts were passed. One of the first laws strongly to condemn same-sex sexual acts was promulgated in the city of Nablus, in the Latin kingdom of Jerusalem, in 1120 at a gathering of both laymen and clerics; its canons, mostly inspired by Byzantine legal precepts, received little attention at the time, and there is no evidence of enforcement. Burning at the stake was prescribed for "sodomitical depravity," unless the sinner had sought penance before being accused publicly, in which case he or she could be reintegrated into Christian society. The canon's main purpose seems to have been to assuage divine wrath in a time of calamities for the Christian Kingdom of Jerusalem. Perceptions about widespread sexual depravities in foreign, especially Muslim, cultures seem to have contributed to a greater propensity for legislating sexual behavior. In that sense, the rules (which included stipulations against adultery and other sexual sins) may have been more declarative than directive.[17] Two modes are operative, if not at odds, with one another in this case, as in the making of sexual precepts in general. On the one hand, we see a pastoral approach that encouraged penance; this is also evident in early medieval penitentials (books of penance issued between the sixth and the eleventh centuries), as well as in the later medieval "literature of confession."[18] On the other hand, the canon came packed with a punitive spirit that sought to eradicate certain sexual behaviors.

Also evident in much secular legislation on sodomy, this seemingly aimed to protect communities from what were seen as the dangerous effects of sexual unorthodoxy.

In melding customary law, Christian theology, and Roman law together, a French thirteenth-century legal code from the Orléans region spelled out penalties for both women and men who had had sex with one another: "He who has been proved to be a sodomite must lose his testicles. And if he does it a second time, he must lose his member. And if he does it a third time, he must be burned." Similarly, the female offender was said to have to lose bodily members. But unlike with men, body parts were not specified, and, what is more, they did not necessarily signify the sexual nature of the offense: "A woman who does this shall lose her member [*sic*!] each time, and on the third must be burned."[19] The parallel formulation for women thus betrays, among other things, the difficulties of addressing gender difference in legal stipulations. Although atypical in its consideration of female sodomites who were rarely mentioned in legislation until the early sixteenth century, this code is a harbinger of sodomy legislation across Europe from the thirteenth century on.

Sodomy legislation became more common, as urban authorities in Italy and elsewhere took charge of their cities' legal affairs. As early as 1308, the Italian city of Lucca declared its intent to aid ecclesiastical authorities in persecuting and punishing sodomites. In 1448, the council there followed the example of Venice (1418) and Florence (1432) and created an urban commission in order to fight sodomites in town systematically. No records survive in the case of Lucca from before the sixteenth century, when anal intercourse between men and women also fell under the commission's jurisdiction. But in nearby Florence, the so-called "Officers of the Night"—a commission entrusted with the task of fighting what was perceived to be the widespread practice of sodomy among urban men—punished a good part of its male residents during the fifteenth century for sodomy. No fewer than 4,062 individuals were implicated in sodomy investigations between 1478 and 1502, many of them more than once. Only a minority of them were severely punished they were imprisoned, exiled, and publicly humiliated, but only rarely executed. Most were merely fined. "Sex between males was a common and integral feature of daily life in this city," is Michael Rocke's assessment of this massive archive which reflects, as he argues it, how the Officers of the Night "managed" sodomy within the city. In Bruges, one of northern Europe's largest cities, no such legal apparatus existed. Citizens found guilty of sodomy were few in numbers but frequently sentenced to death; between 1490 and 1515, sixteen men and women were executed in twenty-one cases of same-sex offenses.[20]

The increased will to punish what was called sodomy coincided not only with an increased readiness of civic authorities to embrace religious tenets.[21] With and without specific sodomy laws on the books, secular authorities started to discipline and punish more actively from the thirteenth century on. The cross-fertilization of different spheres of the law, secular and religious, as well as the connections between different legal and religious traditions, created incentives to interfere in sexual lives.

LITERARY IMAGINATIONS

Vernacular literatures offer a different textual horizon. Starting in the twelfth century, poems, tales, and epics debated, among other important themes, how the sexes ought to relate to one another. Courtly narratives in various languages therefore abound with a plethora of beautiful, monstrous, or hybrid bodies and strange desires. Male warrior couples surface in this context; marriages between women are not unheard of; fantastical sexual systems raised the audience's curiosity about foreign places, such as the island whose king exiled all women. In other words, courtly texts explored social and sexual possibilities.

In Occitan poetry, Bieiris de Romans, a female author, addressed a beloved lady (*bella domna*) in a thirteenth-century poem. In Gottfried of Strasbourg's *Tristan*, King Marke of Cornwall loves the beautiful and accomplished young courtier Tristan, his "companion" (l. 3725). It was not this love that upset his vassals, however, but the king's declaration that he would not marry, making his nephew Tristan heir instead.[22]

Registering a plethora of same-sex literary phenomena is not only a question of plots, characters, and content, however. It also pertains to how mostly male poets and minstrels would have performed texts for their audiences. Ventriloquizing the voices of male and female lovers provided a wealth of opportunities to impart erotic messages through the inflections of voices, gestures, and other strategies of performance.

Contemplating sexual alternatives was especially common in linguistic-cultural borderlands. Hebrew poets in Muslim Spain, for example, emulated the theme of male–male love they knew from their Arab counterparts. The very notion of what constituted sex between women seems to have derived from cultural interstices, as Sahar Amer argues for French medieval literature. After all, much of medieval vernacular literature was translated, be it from Latin or from one vernacular language to another. Among other things, such exchanges between literatures in different languages offered opportunities to negotiate cultural codes. The twelfth-century German-language poet Heinrich von Veldeke rewrote the anonymous French *Roman d'Eneas*, for instance. In the process, he toned down the accusations of sodomy heaped on Aeneas, the mythical founder of Rome, for pursuing young men (*garçon[s]*) erotically (l. 8572).[23] With regard to the Trojan Aeneas, such a barb must have rung true. After all, the mythical object of Zeus's love, Ganymede—a figure well known in medieval literature—was from Troy. Indeed, some courtly plots feature accusations against knights said to prefer the love of men to the love of women.

At the same time, vernacular literature's permeability enabled a marked influx of religious ideas. Alan of Lille's poetically powerful *Plaint of Nature*, with its condemnations of sodomy, left a deep imprint on later versions of the *Romance of the Rose*. Short didactic texts, an innovation of thirteenth-century poets, also started to feature diatribes against male–male love. Such texts were evidently in dialogue with scholastic theology. But religious notions of sexual improprieties must also have resonated with aristocratic concerns about lineage. Dante's *Divine Comedy* and Geoffrey Chaucer's *Canterbury Tales*, arguably two of the most ambitious works of medieval literature, exhibit allusions to a sin that in other contexts went by the name of sodomy. These authors incorporated it in such evocative ways that critics have yet to come to terms with the deeper implications of these passages.[24]

THE RISE OF PHOBIA AGAINST
SAME-SEX EROTICISM

Toward the end of the Middle Ages, vilified same-sex eroticism on the one hand and appreciative representations of same-sex ties on the other hand became even more entangled. Once we place the friend, the beloved same-sex other, next to another figure, the royal favorite for instance, their uncanny similarity demonstrates some of the tensions at work in the medieval past. Above all, this was the case in political contexts where the stakes were high and our sources are relatively abundant. Favoritism at court conjures up the image of someone who rose to prominence, wealth, and a position of influence by affective ties. Such a rise in status occasionally upset social hierarchies and extant political allegiances, as it did in the case of Edward II of England and his "minions." Female lovers were a threat to political authority only rarely. But this was different with male aristocrats who boasted a special bond to their king. Only many decades after his demise did Edward's undue (according to his peers) preference for social upstarts raise writers' suspicions of erotic attachments between him and them.[25] The tussle of favoritism and friendship permeated the political realm once the figure of the sodomite became available, affording a powerful weapon of vilification.

Similar tensions were also prevalent in the religious sphere. In a sermon explicating different kinds of lust, among them sodomy, Bernardino de Bustis (c.1450–c.1513) tells the miracle story of a marriage between two men: when the ring the male "sodomite" had given to his male spouse on the occasion of their wedding could no longer be taken off, the remorseful youth went to a holy person for help. Pulling the ring off "painlessly," this cleric is said to have shown the ring thereafter while preaching as evidence for the sinner's potential redemption, even after he had committed a severe sin.[26]

Was the marital same-sex bond around which the story revolves an echo of the liturgical ceremony for "making brothers"? We have formulae from Greek-language sources suggesting that rituals existed where two men (or women) joined hands before the altar—a symbol for matrimony already in ancient times.[27] The difference in age between the two male spouses in our story may indicate otherwise, however. As a rule, sexual acts, whether same-sex or opposite-sex, invoked an imagery of asymmetrical relations, even if actual sex acts often differed from such stereotypical notions. Conversely, friendship conjured up images of men or women of the same or a similar age. Yet the history of friendship has shown that the actual ages of friends sometimes belied ancient ideals of the mirrored selves. Wherever we look, tensions arise between verbal descriptions and social practices.

Importantly, by telling such a story, the sermonizer placed the concept of sodomy within lived experience. This is so, because he invited "sodomites," especially those supposedly victimized, to extricate themselves from their sinful lives "painlessly." The gulf between the rhetoric of sodomy as presented in Beheim and everyday practices was such that innovative sermonizers such as Berthold of Regensburg, Bernardino of Siena, or Johann Geiler of Kaysersberg felt the need to make more explicit their warnings against the dangers of same-sex eroticism. They painted a portrait of "sodomites" rich in detail that resonated with the social contexts their listeners inhabited. The records document that these religious reform campaigns occasionally met resistance for offending decorum.[28]

In late medieval Europe, both church and secular authorities exercised an increasing disciplinary grip on everyday life, in the sexual realm as well as in others. We should not expect that medieval people simply accepted the sodomy harangues they were exposed to. Yet we also should not underestimate the rewards of a religiosity that involved observing one's neighbors' activities, erotic and otherwise. As celibates, clerics were especially vulnerable to charges of sexual transgressions. Responses to their wrongdoing oscillated between the humorous and calls for moral reform of the clergy. The so-called "Reformation of the Emperor Sigismund" (c.1439), a widely circulating imperial reform manifesto, used sodomy as a reason to call for clerical marriage.

Put differently, the fact that a poem like Beheim's obfuscated many aspects of same-sex eroticism may in fact have enabled a richly woven tapestry of emotions, desires, and behaviors to go largely unharmed, even at times when the warnings against same-sex sexual acts multiplied, intensified, and resulted in occasional punishments or executions. Although most of our records come from instances when authorities intruded on this social nexus, they give us glimpses of what may have been common practice.

Jehanne and Laurence, two women who worked together in the fields (farm labor was differentiated along the lines of sex) entertained an erotic liaison for which they were prosecuted before a French provincial court. We know about their bond through a 1405 appeal for a royal pardon that was filed on behalf of Laurence, a sixteen-year-old wife. Her supporters portrayed Jehanne as a sexual predator and mannish woman, while casting Laurence as an innocent victim to her advances. Theirs was not a one-time encounter, however; they had engaged in sex several times.[29]

Some individuals who had sex with members of their sex patterned their relationships in the image of social and gender conventions. Characteristically, the few judicial proceedings against women who had sex with women involved female subjects who assumed masculine prerogatives in a variety of ways. Katherina Hetzeldorfer from the German city of Nuremberg reinvented herself through cross-dressing. Without leaving her native city, her assumption of a male persona would hardly have been possible. All we know about her life comes from the investigation against her from 1477, which records that she and a woman she met while traveling migrated to the city of Speyer on the Rhine, where the two lived together. There, Katherina's sexual partner passed as her "sister." Yet this woman-as-man and supposed "brother" to the other woman did not keep her secret. In conversations with others she admitted to their erotic relationship. When Katherina's roguish sexual behavior—she had or attempted to have sex with several women in Speyer—came to the attention of the authorities, she initially protected her unnamed "sister" before court. Pressured, she confessed to having had a sexual liaison; Katherina was punished by drowning. Whereas medieval hagiographic texts praise female saints who passed as religious men as particularly saintly, cross-dressing in the countryside or cities exposed women in late medieval Europe to the risk of prosecution. A male witness in a thirteenth-century court case from Bologna called a woman "unlucky" when learning that she had fallen for a widow, "because she could not act on her desires." Yet women who committed themselves to other women strike one as savvy creators of their selves, erotic and otherwise. Hetzeldorfer, at any rate, knew how to make the "instrument" necessary to perform her desires, and so did others, we may suspect.[30]

Dressing and acting like men provided women with opportunities otherwise inaccessible to them. The reverse, men cross-dressing as women, may have been less prevalent other than when the masquerades were transparent, such as in carnival or on stage. But John Rykener sold his sexual services as Eleanor and was apprehended in London in 1394. He claimed to have learned cross-dressing from a woman. In the fifteenth century, censure was not only a question of legal prosecutions, however. We can detect urban rumbling about sexual mores in Hetzeldorfer's court investigation. In 1434, Johann von Swizo, an imperial councilor, had to flee from the city of Basel after it had transpired that he had been a "bridegroom," i.e. had sex, with a male youth.[31] Rules of sexual conduct were enforced within communities.

Links between discourses and the social environment under the heading of sodomy mattered profoundly. Toward the end of the Middle Ages, ever more agents—clerics, councilors, and many others—were engaged in forging such connections. The continuing research into links made in medieval times between texts and acts across a variety of discourses is a task that involves such diverse disciplines as the history of religion and theology, history of ideas, legal history, social history, gender history, literary history, history of art, and history of sexuality. Daringly, John Boswell once launched the search for gay life in the medieval past: "Gay People in Western Europe from the Beginning of the Christian Era to the Fourteenth Century" reads the subtitle to his monumental, interdisciplinary study.[32] In the more than thirty years since that book, differences between the present in which we research and the past that haunts us have become more apparent, and the term "gay" is rarely used by scholars of the premodern period. Yet the possibility of the impossible—connecting across the ultimate divider, time—continues to animate our search for same-sex possibilities in medieval Europe.

Further Reading

Burger, Glenn. *Chaucer's Queer Nation*. Minneapolis: University of Minnesota Press, 2003.

Burger, Glenn and Steven F. Kruger, eds. *Queering the Middle Ages*. Minneapolis: University of Minnesota Press, 2001.

Dinshaw, Carolyn. *Getting Medieval: Sexualities and Communities, Pre- and Postmodern*. Durham, NC: Duke University Press, 1999.

Frantzen, Allen J. *Before the Closet: Same-Sex Love from "Beowulf" to "Angels in America."* Chicago: University of Chicago Press, 1998.

Karras, Ruth Mazo. *Sexuality in Medieval Europe: Doing Unto Others*. New York: Routledge, 2005.

Kuefler, Mathew. *The Boswell Thesis: Essays on Christianity, Social Tolerance, and Homosexuality*. Chicago: University of Chicago Press, 2006.

Lochrie, Karma. *Heterosyncrasies: Female Sexuality When Normal Wasn't*. Minneapolis: University of Minnesota Press, 2005.

Lochrie, Karma, Peggy McCracken, and James A. Schultz, eds. *Constructing Medieval Sexuality*. Minneapolis: University of Minnesota Press, 1997.

Phillips, Kim and Barry Reay. *Sex before Sexuality: A Premodern History*. Cambridge: Polity, 2011.

Thoma, Lev Mordechai and Sven Limbeck, eds. *"Die sünde, der sich der tiuvel schamet in der helle": Homosexualität in der Kultur des Mittelalters und der frühen Neuzeit*. Ostfildern: Thorbecke, 2009.

Notes

1. Michel Beheim, *Die Gedichte des Michel Beheim*, vol. 2, ed. Ingeborg Spriewald (Berlin: Akademie-Verlag, 1970), 183.
2. Peter Damian, *Letters*, vol. 2: *31–60*, trans. Owen Blum (Washington, DC: Catholic University of America Press, 1990), 6–7.
3. Peter Cantor, *Verbum adbreviatum*, quoted in John Boswell, *Christianity, Social Tolerance, and Homosexuality: Gay People in Western Europe from the Beginning of the Christian Era to the Fourteenth Century* (Chicago: University of Chicago Press, 1980), 375–78.
4. Heinrich von Langenstein, *Erchantnuzz der sund*, ed. Rainer Rudolf (Berlin: E. Schmidt, 1969), 96–97.
5. Mark Jordan, *The Invention of Sodomy in Christian Theology* (Chicago: University of Chicago Press, 1997).
6. Alan Bray, *The Friend* (Chicago: University of Chicago Press, 2003), 13–19, quotation on 19. See also Siegrid Düll, Anthony Luttrell, and Maurice Keen, "Faithful Unto Death: The Tomb Slab of Sir William Neville and Sir John Clanvowe, Constantinople 1391," *Antiquaries Journal*, 71 (1991): 174–90, which includes a detailed description of the tombstone as well as a transcription of the inscribed text.
7. Judith Bennett, "Two Women and Their Monumental Brass, c. 1480," *Journal of the British Archaeological Association*, 161 (2008): 163–84.
8. Judith Bennett, "'Lesbian-Like' and the Social History of Lesbianisms," *Journal of the History of Sexuality*, 9 (2000): 1–24; Merry Wiesner-Hanks, "Guilds, Male Bonding, and Women's Work in Early Modern Germany," *Gender and History*, 1 (1989): 125–37 (with a discussion of changes in the medieval period).

9. Aelred of Rievaulx, *Spiritual Friendship*, trans. Lawrence C. Braceland (Collegeville, Minn.: Cistercian Publications, 2010), 91, 83.

10. Hilarius, a twelfth-century cleric and poet. Quoted in Boswell, *Christianity*, 374.

11. Glenn W. Olsen, *Of Sodomites, Hermaphrodites, and Androgynes: Sodomy in the Age of Peter Damian* (Toronto: Pontifical Institute of Medieval Studies, 2011); Ilene H. Forsyth, "The Ganymede Capital at Vézelay," *Gesta*, 15 (1976): 241–46; A. V. Kolve, "Ganymede/Son of Getron: Medieval Monasticism and the Drama of Same-Sex Desire," *Speculum*, 73 (1998): 1014–67. See also Michael Camille, *Image on the Edge: The Margins of Medieval Art* (Cambridge, Mass.: Harvard University Press, 1992).

12. Alan Bray, "Homosexuality and the Signs of Male Friendship in Elizabethan England," in Jonathan Goldberg, ed., *Queering the Renaissance* (Durham, NC: Duke University Press, 1994), 40–61.

13. Klaus van Eickels, *Vom inszenierten Konsens zum systematisierten Konflikt: Die englisch-französischen Beziehungen und ihre Wahrnehmung an der Wende vom Hoch- zum Spätmittelalter* (Stuttgart: Thorbecke, 2002), 343–93.

14. Stephen Jaeger, *Ennobling Love: In Search of a Lost Sensibility* (Philadelphia: University of Pennsylvania Press, 1999); James Schultz, *Courtly Love, the Love of Courtliness, and the History of Sexuality* (Chicago: University of Chicago Press, 2006).

15. John Boswell, *Christianity*; R. I. Moore, *The Formation of a Persecuting Society: Authority and Deviance in Western Europe 950–1250*, 2nd edn (Malden: Blackwell, 2007); Allen Frantzen, "The Disclosure of Sodomy in 'Cleanness,'" *PMLA*, 111 (1996): 451–64; Elizabeth B. Keiser, *Courtly Desire and Medieval Homophobia: The Legitimation of Sexual Pleasure in 'Cleanness' and its Contexts* (New Haven: Yale University Press, 1997).

16. Bernadette Brooten, *Love between Women: Early Christian Responses to Female Homoeroticism* (Chicago: University of Chicago Press, 1996); Craig A. Williams, *Roman Homosexuality*, 2nd edn (Oxford; New York: Oxford University Press, 2010), 130–36; Mathew Kuefler, *The Manly Eunuch: Masculinity, Gender Ambiguity, and Christian Ideology in Late Antiquity* (Chicago: University of Chicago Press, 2001).

17. Benjamin Z. Kedar, "On the Origins of the Earliest Laws of Frankish Jerusalem: The Canons of the Council of Nablus, 1120," *Speculum*, 74 (1999): 310–35.

18. Pierre J. Payer, *Sex and the Penitentials: The Development of a Sexual Code, 550–1150* (Toronto; Buffalo: University of Toronto Press, 1984); idem, *Sex and the New Medieval Literature of Confession, 1150–1300* (Toronto: Pontifical Institute of Mediaeval Studies, 2009).

19. Louis Crompton, "The Myth of Lesbian Impunity," in Salvatore Licata and Robert P. Petersen, eds, *The Gay Past: A Collection of Historical Essays* (New York: Harrington Park Press, 1985), 11–26, here 13.

20. Umberto Grassi, "L'offitia sopra l'onestà : La repressione della sodomia nella Lucca del cinquecento (1551–1580)," *Studi storici*, 48 (2007): 127–59; Michael Rocke, *Forbidden Friendships: Homosexuality and Male Culture in Renaissance Florence* (New York: Oxford University Press, 1996), 10; Marc Boone, "State Power and Illicit Sexuality," *Journal of Medieval History*, 22 (1996): 135–53.

21. James A. Brundage, *Law, Sex, and Christian Society in Medieval Europe* (Chicago: University of Chicago Press, 1987).

22. Angelica Rieger, "Was Bieiris de Romans Lesbian? Women's Relations with Each Other in the World of the Troubadours," in William D. Paden, ed., *The Voice of the Trobairitz: Perspectives on Women Troubadours* (Philadelphia: University of Pennsylvania Press, 1989), 73–94; Gottfried von Strassburg, *Tristan*, ed. Xenja von Ertzdorff (Munich: Fink, 1979).

23. Norman Roth, "'Fawn of My Delights': Boy-Love in Hebrew and Arabic Verse," in Joyce E. Salisbury, ed., *Sex in the Middle Ages: A Book of Essays* (New York: Garland, 1991), 157–72; idem, "'Fawn of My Delights': Boy-Love in Hebrew and Arabic Verse," in Salisbury, ed., *Sex in the Middle Ages,* 157–72; Sarah Amer, *Crossing Borders: Love Between Women in Medieval French and Arabic Literatures* (Phildelphia: University of Pennsylvania Press, 2008); *Le Roman d'Eneas,* ed. Monica Schöler-Beinhauer (Munich: Fink, 1972).

24. Carolyn Dinshaw, *Getting Medieval: Sexualities and Communities, Pre- and Postmodern* (Durham, NC: Duke University Press, 1999); Glenn Burger and Steven F. Kruger, eds, *Queering the Middle Ages* (Minneapolis: University of Minnesota Press, 2001); Glenn Burger, *Chaucer's Queer Nation* (Minneapolis: University of Minnesota Press, 2003).

25. Claire Sponsler, "The King's Boyfriend: Froissart's Political Theater of 1326," in Burger and Kruger, eds, *Queering the Middle Ages,* 143–67.

26. Bernardino de Bustis, *Rosarium sermonum predicabilium* (Hagenau, 1513), 135r.

27. John Boswell, *Same-Sex Unions in Premodern Europe* (New York: Villard Books, 1994).

28. Franco Mormando, *The Preacher's Demons: Bernardino of Siena and the Social Underworld of Early Renaissance Italy* (Chicago: University of Chicago Press, 1999); Helmut Puff, *Sodomy in Reformation Germany and Switzerland, 1400–1600* (Chicago: University of Chicago Press, 2003).

29. Joan Cadden, *Meanings of Sex Difference in the Middle Ages: Medicine, Science, and Culture* (Cambridge; New York: Cambridge University Press, 1993), 224.

30. Carol Lansing, "*Donna con Donna?* A 1295 Inquest into Female Sodomy," in Philip M. Soergel, ed., *Sexuality and Culture in Medieval and Renaissance Europe* (New York: AMS Press, 2005), 109–22, here 115; Helmut Puff, "Female Sodomy: The Trial of Katherina Hetzeldorfer (1477)," *Journal of Medieval and Early Modern Studies,* 30 (2000): 41–61.

31. David Lorenzo Boyd and Ruth Mazo Karras, "The Interrogation of a Male Transvestite Prostitute in Fourteenth-Century London," *GLQ: A Journal of Lesbian and Gay Studies,* 1 (1995): 459–65; Georg Steinhausen, *Deutsche Privatbriefe des Mittelalters,* vol. 2 (Berlin, 1907), 138.

32. Boswell, *Christianity.* See also Matthew Kuefler, ed., *The Boswell Thesis: Essays on Christianity, Social Tolerance, and Homosexuality* (Chicago: University of Chicago Press, 2006).

CHAPTER 25

PERFORMING COURTLINESS

E. JANE BURNS

MEDIEVAL courtly traditions are typically understood to include two highly gendered phenomena: chivalry, the exclusive domain of fighting men, and courtly love, a torturous amorous ritual undertaken by knights courting aristocratic ladies. Historians have often understood medieval chivalry to be the practice of a dominant stratum of lay society governed by an ethical code of behavior, a framework for regulating how the male aristocracy should live, love, govern, fight, and practice piety, especially in the thirteenth century when chivalry was at its peak. If the chivalric code underwrites violence, it also limits it, we are told, while the code of amorous conduct teaches fighting men restraint in civil and social encounters.[1] This ethos of knighthood practiced by a company of men is amply reflected in twelfth- and thirteenth-century literary articulations of King Arthur's Round Table, where chivalry allows knights to engage in various forms of combat designed to display their prowess and secure honor and renown.[2]

CHIVALRY AND LOVE SERVICE

Literary texts complicate the chivalric paradigm, however, by emphasizing the crucial role of love service, which requires knights to venture outside the comfortable company of men into the lesser known, unpredictable, and potentially dangerous domain of women. The dilemma is first glimpsed in troubadour love lyric when poet-lovers, who are not knights, deploy a single-voiced love song to gain the favor of women whom they cast as the all-powerful lady-lord, the Provençal or Occitan *domna*. She is said to have the ability to heal and cure their lovesickness or, alternately, to inflict pain, imprisonment, and even death. The ostensibly submissive suitors attempt to convince and seduce a seemingly haughty beloved whom they configure as unjustly refusing their suit. In longer Old French narrative accounts known as romances, the love dynamic shifts significantly because knights on horseback can attempt to prove their love to the resisting lady by accomplishing physical deeds of valor. They struggle to win her over not by singing, pleading, or convincing her with words as the Occitan poets do, but through chivalric action.

And yet, the very ladylove who is posited as necessary for inspiring knightly feats in courtly romances is also often shown to compromise chivalric success. In the twelfth-century Arthurian romance *Erec et Enide*, for example, the narrator explains that private lovemaking has seriously disrupted the public practice of chivalry because the previously incomparable hero Erec has neglected jousting with his male companions in favor of jousting in bed.[3] Lancelot may be declared the "best knight" because he is inspired to perform stunning feats by his love for Guenevere, but he also performs as the "worst knight," losing miserably in combat under her influence. Even Perceval is so distracted by thoughts of Blanchfleur that he appears to be asleep. In courtly romance narratives, then, the practice of chivalry often stages female protagonists as both necessary for chivalric success and an obstacle in its path.

However, this dominant literary paradigm, which pits heterosexual male subjects against female objects of desire, does not fully represent the gender relations lying at the heart of medieval practices of chivalry and love.[4] If we take medieval French and Occitan literature alone, we find, for example, that the desires expressed by courtly protagonists range far beyond the limited models offered by amorous knights and troubadours. We learn of the desire of female singers to court male lovers; the desire of men to love other men and women to love other women; the desire of women to choose their marriage partners, not to marry at all, or even to kill their boorish or abusive husbands. In addition to a knight's desire for political influence or protection on crusade, a minstrel's desire to be paid, or a troubadour's desire to escape from courtly sloth, we hear of a lady's desire to defend herself in court, a woman's desire to avoid pregnancy, a shepherdess's desire to escape the lord who has raped her, and even the desire of imprisoned female silk workers to be free from exploitation. None of this material conforms to the scenarios of desiring knights and desired ladies outlined above, and yet courtly literature is replete with these stories. If courtly codes of chivalry and love often attempt to control and regulate desiring bodies while also marginalizing and standardizing their pleasures beneath a canopy of imposed heteronormativity, as feminist analyses and studies of masculinity and sexuality have amply demonstrated, the full spectrum of courtly literary texts also records the many ways in which those regulatory efforts fall short.[5] A closer look at the widest range of courtly practices reveals in fact that knights function in a world of disparate behaviors and conflicting meanings where chivalric ideals are often advanced only to be challenged and amorous rules proposed but soon contested.

COURTS AS PERFORMANCE SPACES

To understand courtly practices as complex articulations of bodies, pleasures, and desires within both historical and fictive frameworks, we might begin by situating medieval chivalry and the practice of love within the larger cultural frame that ultimately defines them both: the medieval court. The many and diverse medieval courts in the European Middle Ages provided performance spaces in which courtly players, both historical composer-performers and their fictional characters, enacted complex and contradictory configurations of gender and power.

The term "performance" is used in this essay to refer to a broad spectrum of literary and historical practices. While "performance" here includes music, song, and narrative literary works presented at historical courts, it also encompasses a wide range of courtly practices enacted by historical individuals including rituals of homage, tournaments, hunts, feasts, and festivals, all of which are deliberately framed and enacted as distinctive chivalric and courtly events. Equally important, the term "performance" here includes fictive representations of those same rituals, festivals, and everyday practices of court life that are imagined and presented to us in lyric and romance.[6] For our purposes, the performance model is especially useful in rethinking gender within courtly traditions because it allows us to see women, as well as men, functioning in varied roles on all sides of the courtly stage: as musicians, singers, composers, as members of the courtly audience, and as literary characters who assume a wide array of cultural functions in the stories told at court.

To view the courtly traditions of chivalry and love as taking place within the performance spaces of medieval courts does not make these practices any less historical, less real, or less meaningful. Neither does it make them mere fantasy. In fact, studies focusing on medieval performance practices have shown that musical and theatrical performances provide the most tangible evidence of a direct relationship between courtly texts and the historical institutions of the societies that produced them. Medieval musicologists, literary scholars, and historians have all discussed the different ways in which games of love and chivalry were played out in competitive environments where political and poetic favors were conferred by powerful lord-patrons who hosted elaborate festivities to display their abundant generosity across a spectrum of social classes. All of those assembled at court depended on the lord (or lady) for patronage, promotion, or remuneration in some form, whether as food and housing, clothing, goods, horses, land, or income.[7] All benefited from courtly entertainments.

Medieval literary texts document the literal use of court space for a wide range of performances: musical entertainment, dances, performances of troubadour song in the Occitan tradition and of *trouvères* in the north, romances read aloud or actually enacted, sometimes with musical interludes, and epic narratives composed and sung at court. Old French romance tales include scenes of private reading aloud, especially between young lovers, public reading, and other forms of storytelling that range from improvised retellings to full dramatic enactment of individual scenes by professional performers.[8]

From the time of Geoffrey of Monmouth's *History of the Kings of Britain* (1136), King Arthur's court was praised as a locus of superlative splendor and exemplary generosity featuring fashionable knights, beautiful ladies, and entertainment of the highest quality (IX, 11). A few decades later, the Anglo-Norman poet Wace glorified what he called "courtly life" in his *Roman de Brut* (1155), describing a world of musical performances, singing, storytelling, chess, and other games that are praised in romance narratives generally. This same life of luxury, however, drew the ire of John of Salisbury (*Policraticus*, 1159) and other clerics at the court of Henry II (Walter Map, Peter of Blois, Girard of Barri), who denounced the Plantagenet court for the very excesses extolled in fictive versions of it. The court, they claimed, was a site of pleasurable indulgence rather than moral teaching. The *Policraticus* warned more specifically that court life thrived on falsehood and frivolity while promoting the pleasures of the flesh rather than spiritual virtues. Thus was the very soul of any cleric working for secular authorities gravely threatened. Walter Map further decried the degenerate English court as too much like courts in Byzantium or Sicily, which were overrun with riches, precious gems, and silks in stark contrast to the austere French court of Louis VII, governed only by bread, wine, and the simple joys of life.[9]

Whereas clerical voices condemned court life while romance authors extolled it, they agree that medieval courts were important staging grounds for competing cultural and political interests. In the north, Old French tales of love and adventure often pit the interests of knights against those of the clerical class, while Occitan poets in southern France use elaborate sexual/poetic flirtations to vie for social positioning at court. Frequent allusion to an amorous rival called a "slanderer" (*lausengier*) may encode political as well as poetic or amorous rivalry, possibly representing members of the lower or middle knightly classes and legal bureaucrats vying with troubadours for administrative positions.[10] As they traveled between courts, or in some cases resided within them, medieval musicians and performers of many kinds entertained court inhabitants in a range of regional and poetic languages. They did so with songs of love and tales of adventure that often commented on social and political concerns. Their compositions also often critiqued the practice of courtliness itself, exposing at times the drawbacks of both chivalry and courtly love while also promoting them.

Despite important regional differences, medieval courts functioned to varying degrees as centers of legal, economic, and social transactions between competing groups and individuals, not the least of whom were paid dramatic performers. Courts fostered by the Occitan, French, and Anglo-Norman aristocracy from the later eleventh through the thirteenth century were highly diverse, and courtly traditions practiced within them changed significantly over the course of the central Middle Ages. The heterogeneity of courtly performance spaces only increases when we consider court life in German-speaking lands, such as the great court held by the Emperor Frederick Barbarossa in Mainz in 1184 that drew attendees from France, Italy, Greece, Spain, and England, or courts in the kingdoms of Aragon and Castile, such as Alfonso II's in Aragon in the 1170s, which pointedly adopted courtly values to legitimize the region's claims to Provence.[11] The potential scope of the medieval court expands further when we consider courtly practices in Italy, the courts of the Norman kings of Sicily, European-style courts in Muslim Spain, and the substantial network of western-derived medieval courts in the Levantine Crusader states.

From the end of the eleventh century in southern France, troubadour songs and their brief fictional biographies (called *vidas*) refer to specific historical courts as the staging ground for Occitan love lyrics and political songs: the courts of Duke William

IX of Aquitaine and his granddaughter Eleanor of Aquitaine, counts Raymond V and VI of Toulouse, Ermengard of Narbonne, and many lesser lords in Occitania, northern Italy, and Spain. Within a generation, the male and female troubadours were imitated by male and female French-speaking singer-composers in the north known as *trouvère* poets. As we leave the world of lyric compositions, whether written by troubadours and *trobairitz* (women troubadours) in the south of France or *trouveres* in the north, and shift into the imagined worlds created in Old French romance narratives, "the court" becomes a site of knightly endeavor as well as a locus for expressing a wide range of amorous desires. The historical courts at which these romances were produced were particularly those of Count Henry the Liberal and Marie of Champagne in Troyes, the court of Count Philip of Flanders, and courts of King Henry II of England and Queen Eleanor along with those of their sons young Henry and Richard the Lionheart.[12]

In romance narratives generally, the "court," whether it is the court of the iconic King Arthur or the prestigious King Marc of the Tristan legends, or the domain of lesser counts and lords, is defined less by physical location or architectural structure than by the people who comprise it: the assembled knights and ladies, seneschals, squires, retainers, clerks, and servants. One of their key functions is to provide the audience for court entertainment and the authentication for deeds of valor undertaken by competing knights. In these tales the "court" itself often moves regularly, as did many historical courts.[13] King Arthur travels from Camelot to Caerleon or Cardigan to Winchester, moving from castle to castle or from a fortified residence to tented encampments in the forest. Regardless of location, the court provides the locus for legal transactions performed publicly such as trial by combat or ordeal, ceremonies of homage and dubbing, or procedures to settle land and inheritance disputes. It is also the performance space in which chivalric deeds are recounted and recorded.

GENDERED COURTLY PERFORMANCES: HISTORICAL AND FICTIVE

By the thirteenth century, the important role that performance played in court culture is made particularly apparent in a text called the *Roman du Hem*, one of the earliest known registries of court festivals in France; it is also one of the earliest extended accounts of French chivalric activity in which women's participation is key but not scripted according to predictable or conventionally codified courtly behavior. As Nancy Freeman Regalado has shown, this "tournament book" from 1278 stages historical men and women who attended the festivities at Le Hem as participants in an elaborate cultural "theater" of courtliness.[14] The duke of Lorraine, along with members of the royal family of France—Robert the count of Clermont and sixth son of Louis IX, and Robert II, count of Artois and cousin to King Philippe III—engage in a series of jousts, while also taking up roles in dramatic interludes. As they play the parts of well-known Arthurian figures from twelfth-century romances by Chrétien de Troyes and from the thirteenth-century *Prose Lancelot*, an allegorical figure named "Dame Courtliness" praises the historical Edward I using motifs from Arthurian tales about Merlin, Lancelot, and Gawain. A figure named Queen Guenevere, accompanied by her seneschal Sir Kay, presides over every event. Indeed, it is her seamless performance that transforms the elaborate historical festivities into an enactment of romance, casting participants in this historical tournament as members of her own courtly retinue. At one point, one hundred knights at the banquet rise to play a part in one of the five romance interludes. Even the physical world of the court at Le Hem easily replicates the fictional world of King Arthur's court, as Regalado points out, since everyday material objects such as the high table, torches, a canopy, or crown become sets, costumes, and props in the Arthurian segments. In the end, the tournament's feasts and jousts and Arthurian sequences, all enacted by named historical men, work together to emphasize an ideal chivalric performance. But that performance takes place within a courtly setting inaugurated and sustained by the work of historical women performing the roles of Dame Courtliness and Queen Guenevere along with a series of unnamed courtly maidens.

We can read this tournament book as the account of a historical tournament in which participants enacted scenarios from Arthurian romance, or we can read it as a literary "chronicle" that describes a historical event by enfolding it within Arthurian courtly motifs of chivalry and love. Either way, the actions and activities of fighting men in this hybrid world are orchestrated and directed by female protagonists who play the leading roles in all five interludes enacted on this complex stage of courtliness.

Taking the *Roman du Hem* as a point of departure, we might understand medieval courts as porous cultural zones in which diverse protagonists in scenarios of chivalry and courtly love migrated with relative ease between the realms of history and fiction. On this stage of cultural interactions, the Arthurian Queen Guenevere can speak with historical counts and dukes as if she lived among them much as the historical queen Eleanor of Aquitaine can take on a fictional persona. Indeed, she does just that in one of the earliest texts often invoked by literary scholars to define the phenomenon of courtly love: Andreas Capellanus' Latin treatise called *The Art of Courtly Love*. In Book II, Chapter 7, the court in question is a court of law where love cases are heard by protagonists whose historical affiliations are only slightly veiled: Queen Eleanor (Eleanor of Aquitaine), the countess of Champagne (Marie of Champagne), and Lady Ermengard of Narbonne.[15] These authoritative female figures, who dispense pseudo-legal decisions in cases brought by distressed male lovers, appear in a text that also puts forward fictional Rules of Love (Book II, Chapter 8). The brief narrative segment recounting the discovery and dispersal of these "rules," whose precise role and function scholars have long debated, tells us that a written account of the Rules was found at King Arthur's lavish palace by an aspiring knight attempting to prove through combat that he had the love of a woman more beautiful than any at that incomparable court.

Perhaps most important, however, the elaborate process of obtaining the Rules of Love described in Andreas' treatise is defined and determined by a character named specifically and only as a "courtly damsel." It is she who sets the terms for the knight's protracted performance of chivalry and love service, much as the allegorical protagonist Dame Courtliness and the fictive queen Guenevere set the stage for knightly encounters in the *Roman du Hem*. These female players who orchestrate, direct, and oversee court life play a very different role from the adored ladylove of lyric and romance. So, too, do the women exerting legal authority in love cases in Andreas' treatise.

The *Roman du Hem* and the *Art of Courtly Love*, then, allow us to consider the phenomenon of courtliness as a kind of stage for competing cultural values rather than a means of enforcing a strict code of male conduct or an ideal model for male aristocratic behavior. From this perspective, medieval courts might best be understood as highly charged sites of cultural negotiation between a number of competing stakeholders who extend far beyond accomplished knights and beloved ladies. They include a fuller spectrum of members of the upper and lower nobility, clerics, individual poetic and amorous competitors, literary patrons, minstrels and other court performers, and a retinue of squires, servants, and others who lived and worked at court.[16] In this setting, courtliness includes and often highlights important modes of resistance to the idealized patterns of conduct often claimed to define it. The fault lines in the system, apparent from the earliest troubadour, William IX, are often articulated by or around female characters in a world where gender is often ambiguous, at play, and subject to prolonged public debate.

Women as Courtly Players

We know that noble women in Occitania and northern France alike exercised considerable influence and authority. Documents from the south of France indicate that women made marriage contracts, and, as executors of their husbands' estates, they commanded castles, ruled cities, traveled the land, received oaths of fealty, negotiated treatises, settled disputes, and participated in local military sieges and more distant crusades. Even though civil law may have disqualified women from judging and ruling, customary law allowed such practices. In the county of Champagne in northern France between 1152 and 1284, aristocratic women inherited land and goods and even received vows of homage from men officially in their service.[17]

What of women in courtly literary scenarios? If we are to consider courtly traditions beyond their articulation in strict social codes governing the behavior of male suitors and knights, we will need to look beyond the standard catalog of courtly literary texts (typically focused on the troubadour *canso*, classic twelfth-century romance, and Andreas Capellanus' *Art of Courtly Love*), beyond heterosexuality, beyond the upper classes, and beyond the confines of the western court. We will need to consider "outlying" phenomena, such as women's sewing songs that feature mothers, daughters, and servant girls sewing in elite settings, or the same-sex affection of female businesswomen in Old French narratives like *Escoufle*. These texts were performed at court, although the world they represent is only partially courtly. They tell of ladies in noble households much more humble than princely, or of ladies engaged with mercantile pursuits in urban settings. Equally important is the hybrid literary phenomenon of "courtly mysticism" developed by beguine women in the thirteenth century. And within more traditional literary genres performed at court, we will need to consider songs of women who challenge and critique the troubadour love traditions along with female protagonists disguised sometimes as male minstrel-performers who retell and recast key features of chivalric narratives. We will also want to consider heroines who deploy unexpected forms of speech, such as legal or learned discourses. And we should look at forms of self-expression beyond speech: the use of clothing and textiles as tools for communicating and negotiating social and political relations. Finally, we will need to account for courtly "ladies" in romance narratives who take up the roles of unauthorized chivalric questers, cross-dressed knights, inventive escape artists, entrepreneurs, or readers. Many—though not all—of these female protagonists fall into the category of autonomous women who are not defined in relation to a father, brother, suitor, or knight-protector.[18] All of them exist within the literary world of courtliness.

GENDERED CHALLENGES TO COURTLINESS

Indeed, when we examine the many ways in which female protagonists function in the performance spaces of courtly literary texts we can see that relations of gender and power implicit in courtly traditions are constantly discussed publicly, negotiated, and reformulated. Time and again, the courtly performances of female protagonists challenge received definitions of masculinity and femininity, complicating the very categories of knights and ladies. Arthurian literature is replete with scenes of the arming, disarming, and rearming of fighting knights in a constant—if partial—reenactment of the initial dubbing ceremony, along with the repeated dressing and undressing of questing knights as they seek lodging during their travels. In the lyric tradition, troubadour and *trouvère* songs have been understood by scholars as constant rhetorical and musical reenactments of a single love scenario through formulaic variations on a repeating theme. And yet when female protagonists in romance or female poet-singers invoke, reiterate, or restate proposed norms of chivalry and courtly love, they often interact with those cultural paradigms by refashioning and replaying them with a difference. In lyric, because the lady cannot retain her status as a putatively all-powerful "lord" and also play the traditionally male role of powerless suitor-supplicant, an entirely new set of power dynamics emerges when ladies court men. In romance, perhaps the most obvious difference for women questers is that there is no "company of women" equivalent to King Arthur's company of knights for female protagonists to join. Once dislodged, however slightly, from their expected position as the adored ladylove in romance narratives, noble women, even though typically protected, defended, and accompanied by a qualified knight, are quite literally "on their own," forging new cultural spaces within existing courtly traditions. One thinks, for example, of the character known only as "Meleagant's sister," an unlikely quester and undaunted adventurer in Chrétien de Troyes's classic twelfth-century romance, *The Knight of the Cart*, who singlehandedly frees "the world's best knight," Lancelot, from imprisonment in a tower.[19] Female protagonists like this lady/knight have no built-in audience to hear stories of their exploits at court. Indeed, the few literary examples we have of women telling stories are not set in courtly venues but in more private spaces, such as the household settings of "sewing songs" or through "off-stage" deliveries we witness only rarely; for example, the gathering of ladies who tell a tale of female genitalia in the brief narrative *Lai du Lecheor*. These female protagonists offer stories of courtly events that directly and purposefully counter the glorification of knightly pursuits.[20]

From this perspective, courtly literature's constant reiteration of the established rules of love or codes of chivalric behavior might suggest not that those conventions are firmly in place but, on the contrary, that courtly literary texts assert a message of idealized and codified conduct that was actively resisted, challenged, and often altered. Those alternative or resistant courtly practices are often enacted by women. This is true for actual performance practices on the part of historical women singer-composers, authors, and patrons and for a wide range of inscribed performances delivered by female characters in courtly texts.

Literary challenges to the male love song in the Occitan tradition come in many forms. Musicologist Susan Boynton has shown that historical women from a wide range of social classes, including rustic women, urban women, aristocratic girls and women, professional female minstrels, servant musicians, courtesans, and slaves, scattered across medieval Europe and the Arab world, created, transformed, and transmitted medieval lyric poetry. Outside the Arab courts, where women were especially prominent as musicians during the Abbasid period (750–1258 CE), the lyric compositions of the Occitan *trobairitz* in the thirteenth century are exemplary in providing a range of female voices which engage and negotiate with existing poetic traditions by mimicking, critiquing, and reinventing them. Their songs, most often taking the form of musico-literary debates, play actively with both cultural and rhetorical definitions of masculinity and femininity, love and love service. Songs by women *trouvères* in the northern French tradition engage many established genres of poetic composition but are perhaps most distinctive in the often caustic laments of unhappily married women (*mal mariées*) and in the sewing songs (*chanson de toile*) in feminocentric romances where young women plot love, elopement, and marriage most often in defiance of their families' wishes.[21] The female-voiced sewing songs also complicate the question of authorship significantly because they appear as lyric insertions within male-authored romance narratives, that is, moments when female protagonists in those texts stop speaking and break into song.

Here again the performance model proves useful in helping us understand the possibility of hybrid "authorship" or interactive literary creation, while also enabling us to consider these songs as a kind of "female performance" no matter the gender of the romance author. Indeed, the concept of performance is just as crucial here as it is in helping us to understand anonymous compositions found in the Occitan corpus, which editors have termed "female performances" even though they may not bear the name or mark of a known *trobairitz*.[22] Although there is no equivalent to the *trobairitz*

composer-performers in the Italian, Spanish, or German traditions, we do find significant inscribed women's voices in these male-authored lyric compositions. In Gallego-
Portuguese *cantigas de amigo* from the Iberian peninsula, for example, poems authored
by male "troubadours" are delivered to the audience in the voice of a woman, suggesting
at least the possibility of imagining or staging females as the singers of these compositions. In the German lyric tradition, we hear otherwise highly limited female protagonists sometimes imagined and presented surprisingly as agents of reason who take
ethical stands regarding courtly culture. The English ballad tradition features accounts
of maidens raped, pregnant, and abandoned talking back as they disrupt conventions of
sexuality and courtship.[23]

Although some *trobairitz* speak openly of the difficulties of being a female singer-
composer and "courting men," and a number of Old French romance heroines, such
as Nicolette in the anonymous thirteenth-century *Aucassin and Nicolette* or Silence
in Heldris de Cornuaille's *Romance of Silence*, take up the role of minstrel-singer only
when cross-dressed, at least one text from the later Middle Ages, *Ysaie le Triste* (dated
to the fourteenth or early fifteenth century) features a heroine, Marthe, who composes
in verse and prose, orally and in writing, acting as both an amateur author in her private chambers and a professional performer at court in female dress. Over a dozen literary compositions, presented alternately as read, recited, or sung, and sometimes with
musical accompaniment, are attributed to this remarkable character over the course of
the romance. Similarly, the Occitan heroine Flamenca, in a romance by the same name,
comes into her own when she escapes from imprisonment and enters the public sphere
of the court, cross-dressed and speaking from the position of a male troubadour, only to
critique the typical helplessness in that tradition of the female love object.[24]

In all these instances, female voices are in debate and negotiation with established
courtly traditions of love and chivalry, as they are at times in the manuscript tradition.
In one thirteenth-century *chansonnier* (manuscript collection of troubadour lyric), for
example, we find texts of songs from the first troubadour William IX interspersed with
songs of the *trobairitz*, thus creating the effect of a debate among competing voices.
Indeed, the manuscript tradition offers perhaps the most compelling evidence for reading courtly traditions as instances of historico-literary performances. What we find
recorded there, especially for Occitan lyric, is a lively tradition of improvisation, songs
that change either slightly or substantially with each delivery, songs whose very "authorship" depends to a degree on an interactive process between composer-performer
and audience participants. That interactive process is clearly documented at times in
romance narrative where we see characters like Tristan, for example, in Gottfried of
Strassbourg's thirteenth-century version of the tale, performing as a court musician
before an audience. In this case, members of the historical audience who listened to this
tale had an opportunity to see a representation of their very situation, as viewers of a
courtly performance.[25]

It might be helpful in addition to remember that in troubadour lyric, the earliest literary formulation of courtliness, gender itself is presented as highly volatile and subject to
change. Most obvious in this regard is the troubadour poet's frequent use of a *senhal* or

male code name for the beloved lady whom the singer positions as his lord or overlord, thus staging women as men. While troubadour lyric provides a highly complex system of male desire often thwarted and unsatisfied in its rhetorical formulations, it also advances, poetically, the possibility of privileging same-sex social relations between lord and vassal, while showing how ideally positioned "ladies" can potentially (mis)behave as lords and as resistant "women." Troubadour poet Bernart de Ventadorn (1150–80) famously explains the problem with his noncompliant beloved who acts "like a woman instead of a lady" as follows: "She does not want what one ought to want, and what she is forbidden to do, she does."[26] This commonplace scenario in which the "lady" can be a "lady," a "lord," a "woman," or all three at once, launches the courtly literary tradition with the possibility of subjects that can move metaphorically, to some degree at least, across divisions of gender and also class.

In the romance tradition, a compelling example is provided by the quintessential courtly lover, Lancelot, who often openly defies the model of chivalric excellence he is said to represent, substantially challenging the gendered status quo of knights and ladies. Known in the courtly world as "the world's best knight," even though he is often unhorsed and dangerously distracted, Lancelot appears in the thirteenth-century *Prose Lancelot* as possessing "the neck and hands of a lady," and he openly plays the lady/lord to his chivalric companion Galehaut's love suit. Similarly complex homosocial relations bind male protagonists in *Sir Gawain and the Green Knight*.[27]

Any number of cross-dressed courtly heroines, though often embedded in tales that end by reinforcing the status quo, demonstrate through their cross-dressed singing, courting, seducing, or display of chivalric prowess on horseback that gender in the courtly world is far from fixed or immutable. We see this played out in courtly narrative, for example, in Nicolette in the thirteenth-century *Aucassin and Nicolette* who plays the competent knight to her beloved's "damsel in distress." While he sighs and laments plaintively from a tower enclosure, she plots and engineers his rescue. If the role reversal in this text is, in some sense, a parodic send-up of courtly traditions, it also throws into stronger relief the courtly practices of heroines cast in nonparodic settings where female rescuers liberate helpless or captive knights. In Marie de France's brief narrative (*lai*) "Lanval," the somewhat magical courtly ladylove breaks with a strictly prescribed "courtly" role to seek out the beloved Lanval and court him on her terms. She reappears later during Lanval's trial at King Arthur's court to defend this knight successfully against Arthur's false charges and literally sweeps the helpless knight off his feet onto her horse. In fourteenth-century texts, other female characters actually take up arms and fight in what is known as the "tournament of ladies."[28]

Still other courtly heroines in romance narratives ably orchestrate and manipulate trial proceedings to prove their own innocence rather than that of a beleaguered knight. Iseut, in Béroul's version of the *Romance of Tristan*, stages an elaborate trial of her own devising, with King Arthur and her husband King Marc as prime witnesses, and disproves charges of adultery against her by deftly reformulating the very terms of guilt and innocence. The heroine Lienor, in Jean Renart's *Romance of the Rose or Guillaume de Dole*, successfully defends herself against a false charge of adultery using, along with deft speech, the highly charged material objects of a belt and silk purse, a brooch, and a ring. All three performances take place in a courtly setting, before an assembled courtly audience, but in each case the lady is shown to engage courtly traditions in ways that far exceed her prescribed role as the properly silent beauty, devoted queen, or young and naïve demoiselle.

When women move into the subject position and start playing roles of troubadour/ lover/singer, mounted quester/liberator, or legal defender, the very definitions of these courtly practices, traditionally undertaken by male protagonists, expand signifi- cantly. And what of allegorical figures such as Raison and La Vieille in Jean de Meun's *Romance of the Rose*, whose modes of speech mimic and replay the style and authority of scholastic learning? Or the voice of the "lady" who critiques the standard catalog of love's attributes in Richard of Fournival's *Bestiary of Love*? What are we to make of the array of female protagonists in Marie de France's *lais* and other Old French romances who exhibit substantial skill in medicinal healing? Or the enigmatic heroine Niniane (Vivien), seduced initially by the rhetorical arts of the learned clerical figure, Merlin, until she becomes a sage in her own right by acquiring the skills of the "master," taking her place alongside other knowledgeable fairy figures such as Morgan, La Reine Sebile, and the Lady of the Lake? Perhaps even more audacious is the courtly heroine Sibeline in the little-known thirteenth-century French romance *L'Empereur Constant*, who engi- neers her own marriage scenario by declaring, in a forged document enclosed in a silk purse, that she is the Emperor of Constantinople. No love service or deeds of valor are undertaken for her by a chivalric suitor. Rather, this courtly demoiselle rises metaphori- cally from the status of young noble woman to that of emperor, while shedding her pre- scribed role as a marriageable daughter to act instead as the courtly father/emperor who brokers the marriage deal.[29]

Still other female protagonists are joined in same-sex relations, whether homosocial, homoerotic, homoaffective, or mystical. In the love song addressed by *trobairitz* Bieris de Romans to her lady friend, for example, and in the lesbian-like relations between key female protagonists in Jean Renart's *Escoufle*, we see heroines coming together in love and work. Thirteenth-century female mystics like Hadewijch, Mechthild of Magedeburg, and Marguerite Porete forge a specifically "courtly" mystical discourse, creating a brand of erotic expression that often confers dual gender on both the lover and beloved. Other forms of female mystical discourse engage the rhetorical traditions of courtly love directly, but use them ultimately to describe overpowering and even debilitating amorous unions between Christ and the woman lover.[30]

In other cases, the practice of courtly love has the potential of significantly trou- bling distinctions of sex and gender as female protagonists in lyric and romance deploy clothes to counter misogynist paradigms of woman's nature. Although the ideology of courtly love seeks to regulate sexual practice through compulsory heterosexuality by dressing bodies in gender-specific clothing, that same clothing often produces gender identities that fall beyond the sex-based binary terms of male and female. These bodies are, above all, sartorial bodies for which gender is subject to change and debate.[31]

Conclusion

Whether as historical composer-singers, historical personages turned "actor" as in the *Roman du Hem*, or inscribed speaker-actors in literary texts, "performers" of courtly traditions stage complex relations of desire and pleasure around bodies that are variably gendered across a spectrum of possibilities. Indeed, courtly traditions record the availability of a range of subject positions for both knights and ladies, not as predictably sexed bodies, but as spacings on a continuum that can produce, at different moments, "different densities of sexed being."[32] Agency in the courtly world, then, is not something wielded by dominant protagonists of either gender. Rather, agency functions as a relational dynamic between individual protagonists and the cultural formations that both surround and create them. In many ways, courtly traditions allow gender to shed its binary moorings in rigidly matched pairs of masculinity and femininity, providing instead a series of discursive sites where competing cultural forces produce political and literary subjects of mutable genders. What we see, then, across a wide variety of historical and literary versions of courtliness, are the tensions, questions, and debates about gendered identities posed by a system that challenges and critiques courtly traditions even as it enacts them.

Further Reading

Amer, Sahar. *Crossing Borders: Love between Women in Medieval French and Arabic Literatures*. Philadelphia: University of Pennsylvania Press, 2008.

Bennett, Judith M. and Amy Froide, eds. *Singlewomen in the European Past 1250–1800*. Philadelphia: University of Pennsylvania Press, 1999.

Burns, E. Jane. *Courtly Love Undressed: Reading Through Clothes in Medieval French Culture*. Philadelphia: University of Pennsylvania Press, 2002.

Gaunt, Simon and Sarah Kay, eds. *The Troubadours: An Introduction*. Cambridge: Cambridge University Press, 1999.

Karras, Ruth Mazo. *From Boys to Men: Formations of Masculinity in Late Medieval Europe*. Philadelphia: University of Pennsylvania Press, 2003.

Kay, Sarah. *Courtly Contradictions: The Emergence of the Literary Object in the Twelfth Century*. Stanford: Stanford University Press, 2001.

Klinck, Anne and Ann Marie Rasmussen, eds. *Medieval Woman's Song: Cross-cultural Approaches*. Philadelphia: University of Pennsylvania Press, 2002.

Krueger, Roberta L., ed. *The Cambridge Companion to Medieval Romance*. Cambridge; New York: Cambridge University Press, 2000.

Lochrie, Karma, Peggy McCracken, and James A. Schultz, eds. *Constructing Medieval Sexuality*. Minneapolis: University of Minnesota Press, 1997.

Vitz, Evelyn Birge, Nancy Freeman Regalado, and Marilyn Mawrence, eds. *Performing Medieval Narrative*. Cambridge; D. S. Brewer, 2005.

Notes

1. Jean Flori, *Eleanor of Aquitaine: Queen and Rebel*, trans. Olive Classe (Edinburgh: Edinburgh University Press, 2007), 22. Constance Bouchard, *Strong of Body, Brave and Noble: Chivalry and Society in Medieval France* (Ithaca: Cornell University Press, 1998); Richard Kaeuper, "The Societal Role of Chivalry in Romance: Northwestern Europe," in Roberta L. Krueger, ed., *The Cambridge Companion to Medieval Romance* (Cambridge; New York: Cambridge University Press, 2000), 97–114; C. Stephen Jaeger, *The Origins of Courtliness: Civilizing Trends and the Formation of Courtly Ideals 939–1210* (Philadelphia: University of Pennsylvania Press, 1985); and idem, *Ennobling Love: In Search of a Lost Sensibility* (Philadelphia: University of Pennsylvania Press, 1999).
2. Of course, the institution of knighthood, or armed combat as deployed in war, has its own codes and rules of engagement, which differ from depictions of chivalry in literary texts.
3. *The Complete Romances of Chrétien de Troyes*, trans. David Staines (Bloomington: Indiana University Press, 1990), 31.
4. E. Jane Burns, "Courtly Love, Who Needs It? Recent Feminist Work in the Medieval French Tradition," *Signs*, 27 (1) (2001): 23–57.
5. E. Jane Burns, *Bodytalk: When Women Speak in Old French Literature* (Philadelphia: University of Pennsylvania Press, 1993); Roberta L. Krueger, *Women Readers and the Ideology of Gender* (Cambridge: Cambridge University Press, 1993); idem, "Questions of Gender in Old French Courtly Romance," in Krueger, ed., *The Cambridge Companion*, 132–49; Helen Solterer, *The Master and Minerva: Disputing Women in French Medieval Literature* (Berkeley: University of California Press, 1995); Simon Gaunt, *Gender and Genre in Medieval French Literature* (Cambridge: Cambridge University Press, 1995); Peggy McCracken, *The Romance of Adultery: Queenship and Sexual Transgression in Old French Literature* (Philadelphia: University of Pennsylvania Press, 1998); Sarah Kay, "Desire and Subjectivity," in Simon Gaunt and Sarah Kay, eds, *The Troubadours: An Introduction* (Cambridge: Cambridge University Press, 1999), 212–27; Matilda Tomaryn Bruckner, "Fictions of the Female Voice: The Women Troubadours," in Anne Klinck and Ann Marie Rasmussen, eds, *Medieval Woman's Song: Cross-cultural Approaches* (Philadelphia: University of Pennsylvania Press, 2002), 127–51; Karma Lochrie, Peggy McCracken, and James A. Schultz, eds, *Constructing Medieval Sexuality* (Minneapolis: University of Minnesota Press, 1997); Sahar Amer, *Crossing Borders: Love between Women in Medieval French and Arabic Literatures* (Philadelphia: University of Pennsylvania Press, 2008); William Burgwinkle, *Sodomy, Masculinity, and Law in Medieval Literature: England and France 1050–1230* (Cambridge: Cambridge University Press, 2009); James A. Schultz, *Courtly Love, the Love of Courtliness, and the History of Sexuality* (Chicago: University of Chicago Press, 2006); Ruth Mazo Karras, *From Boys to Men: Formations of Masculinity in Late Medieval Europe* (Philadelphia: University of Pennsylvania Press, 2003); and idem, *Sexuality in Medieval Europe: Doing Unto Others* (New York: Routledge, 2005).
6. See Peter Burke, "Performing History: The Importance of Occasions," *Rethinking History*, 9 (1) (2005): 35–52; Susan Crane, *Performance of Self: Ritual, Clothing, and Identity During the Hundred Years War* (Philadelphia: University of Pennsylvania Press, 2002).
7. Linda M. Paterson, *The World of the Troubadours: Medieval Occitan Society, c.1100–c.1300* (Cambridge: Cambridge University Press, 1993), 100–14; Frederic Cheyette, *Ermengard of Narbonne and the World of the Troubadours* (Ithaca: Cornell University Press, 2001).

8. See Evelyn Birge Vitz, *Orality and Performance in Early French Romance* (Suffolk, UK: D. S. Brewer, 1999); and idem, "Erotic Reading in the Middle Ages: Performance and the Re-performance of Romance," in Evelyn Birge Vitz, Nancy Freeman Regalado, and Marilyn Lawrence, eds, *Performing Medieval Narrative* (Cambridge: D. S. Brewer, 2005), 73–88; Joyce Coleman, *Public Reading and the Reading Public in Late Medieval England and France* (Cambridge: Cambridge University Press, 1996).

9. Laurence Harf-Lancner, "Les Malheurs des intellectuels à la cour: Les clercs curiaux d'Henri II Plantagenêt," in Christoph Huber and Hendrike Lähnemann, eds, *Courtly Literature and Clerical Culture* (Tübingen: Attempto, 2002), 4–7.

10. Sarah Kay, *Courtly Contradictions: The Emergence of the Literary Object in the Twelfth Century* (Stanford: Stanford University Press, 2001); Simon Gaunt, *The Troubadours and Irony* (Cambridge: Cambridge University Press, 1989); Paterson, *The World of the Troubadours*, 107.

11. Paterson, *The World of the Troubadours*, 115–16.

12. Sarah Kay, "Courts, Clerks, and Courtly Love," in Krueger, ed., *The Cambridge Companion*, 81–96.

13. Paterson, *The World of the Troubadours*, 90.

14. Nancy Freeman Regalado, "Performing Romance: Arthurian Interludes in Sarrasin's *Le Roman du Hem* (1278)," in Vitz et al., eds, *Performing Medieval Narrative*, 103–22.

15. *The Art of Courtly Love by Andreas Capellanus*, trans. John J. Parry (New York: Columbia University Press, 1941), 184–86.

16. Paterson, *The World of the Troubadours*, 90–119; Ruth Harvey, "Courtly Culture in Medieval Occitania," in Gaunt and Kay, eds, *The Troubadours*, 8–27; Vitz, *Orality and Performance*.

17. Cheyette, *Ermengard of Narbonne*, 13; Susan B. Edgington and Sarah Lambert, eds, *Gendering the Crusades* (Cardiff: University of Wales Press, 2001); Amy Livingstone, *Out of Love for My Kin: Aristocratic Family Life in the Lands of the Loire: 1000–1200* (Ithaca: Cornell University Press, 2010); Paterson, *The World of the Troubadours*, 222–23; Theodore Evergates, *The Aristocracy in the County of Champagne 1100–1300* (Philadelphia: University of Pennsylvania Press, 2007); Kimberly LoPrete, *Adela of Blois: Countess and Lord* (Dublin: Four Courts Press, 2007).

18. Burns, "Sewing like a Girl: Working Women in the *chanson de toile*," in Klinck and Rasmussen, eds, *Medieval Woman's Song*, 99–126; Amer, *Crossing Borders*; Barbara Newman, *From Virile Woman to WomanChrist: Studies in Medieval Religion and Literature* (Philadelphia: University of Pennsylvania Press, 1995), 137–67; Matilda Bruckner, "Fictions of Female Voice: The Trobairitz," in Klinck and Rasmussen, eds, *Medieval Woman's Song*, 127–51; Solterer, *The Master and Minerva*; E. Jane Burns, *Courtly Love Undressed: Reading Through Clothes in Medieval French Culture* (Philadelphia: University of Pennsylvania Press, 2002), 59–87; Roberta L. Krueger, "Transforming Maidens: Single Women's Stories in Marie de France's *lais* and Later French Courtly Romances," in Judith M. Bennett and Amy Froide, eds, *Singlewomen in the European Past 1250–1800* (Philadelphia: University of Pennsylvania Press, 1999), 146–91.

19. *The Complete Romances*, trans. Staines, 249–51.

20. Burns, *Bodytalk*, 151–57.

21. Susan Boynton, "Women's Performance in the Lyric before 1500," in Klinck and Rasmussen, eds, *Medieval Woman's Song*, 47–65; Bruckner, "Fictions of Female Voice"; Nancy Jones, "The Uses of Embroidery in the Romances of Jean Renart: Gender, History, and Textuality," in Nancy Vine Durling, ed., *Jean Renart and the Art of Romance* (Gainesville, Fla.: University of Florida Press, 1997), 13–44.

22. Matilda Tomaryn Bruckner, Laurie Shepard, and Sarah Melhado, eds and trans., *Songs of the Women Troubadours* (New York: Garland, 1995), xxxix–xlvii. Eglal Doss-Quinby, ed., *Songs of the Women Trouvères* (New Haven: Yale University Press, 2001).

23. Esther Corral, "Feminine Voices in the Galician-Portuguese *cantigas de amigo*," in Klinck and Rasmussen, eds, *Medieval Woman's Song*, 81–98; Ingrid Kasten, "The Conception of Female Roles in the Woman's Song of Reinmar and the Contessa de Dia," in Klinck and Rasmussen, eds, *Medieval Woman's Song*, 165–67; Ann Marie Rasmussen, "Reason and Female Voice in Walter Von der Wogelweide's Poetry," in Klinck and Rasmussen, eds, *Medieval Woman's Song*, 168–86; Judith M. Bennett, "Ventriloquisms: When Maidens Speak in English Songs, c. 1300–1550," in Klinck and Rasmussen, eds, *Medieval Woman's Song*, 187–204.

24. Marilyn Lawrence, "Oral Performance and Written Narrative in the Medieval French Romance *Ysaye le Triste*," in Vitz et al., eds, *Performing Medieval Narrative*, 89–102; Karen A. Grossweiner, "Implications of the Female Poetic Voice in *Le Roman de Flamenca*," in Barbara K. Altmann and Carleton W. Carroll, eds, *The Court Reconvenes: Courtly Literature across the Disciplines* (Cambridge: D. S. Brewer, 2003), 133–40.

25. Stephen G. Nichols, "The Early Troubadours: From Guilhem IX to Bernart de Ventadorn," in Gaunt and Kay, eds, *The Troubadours*, 66–82; Alexandra Hillenbrand, "Music and Performance in Courtly Culture," in Keith Busby and Christopher Kleinhenz, eds, *Courtly Arts and the Art of Courtliness* (Cambridge: D. S. Brewer, 2006), 642–48.

26. *Lyrics of the Troubadours and Trouvères: An Anthology and a History*, trans. Frederick Goldin (Garden City, NY: Anchor Books, 1973), 147.

27. E. Jane Burns, "Refashioning Courtly Love: Lancelot as Lady's Man or Ladyman," in Lochrie, McCracken, and Schultz, eds, *Constructing Medieval Sexuality*, 111–34.

28. *Aucassin et Nicolette*, trans. Eugene Mason (London, 1973); *The Lais of Marie de France*, ed. and trans. Glynn Burgess (Harmondsworth: Penguin Books, 1986); Helen Solterer, "Figures of Female Militancy in Medieval France," *Signs*, 16 (3) (1991): 522–49.

29. Sarah Kay, "Women's Body of Knowledge: Epistemology and Misogyny in the *Romance of the Rose*," in Sarah Kay and Miri Rubin, eds, *Framing Medieval Bodies* (Manchester; New York: Manchester University Press, 1994), 211–35; Solterer, *The Master and Minerva*, 97–130; Peggy McCracken, "Women and Medicine in Medieval French Narrative," *Exemplaria*, 5 (2) (1993): 239–62; Laine E. Doggett, *Love Cures: Healing and Love Magic in Old French Romance* (University Park: Pennsylvania State University Press, 2009); E. Jane Burns, *Sea of Silk: A Textile Geography of Women's Work in Medieval French Literature* (Philadelphia: University of Pennsylvania Press, 2009), 70–83.

30. Jacqueline Murray, "Twice Marginal and Twice Invisible: Lesbians in the Middle Ages," in Vern L. Bullough and James A. Brundage, eds, *Handbook of Medieval Sexuality* (New York: Garland Publishing, 1996), 191–222; Amer, *Crossing Borders*, 88–120; Newman, *From Virile Woman*, 137–67; Karma Lochrie, "Mystical Acts, Queer Tendencies," in Lochrie, McCracken, and Schultz, eds, *Constructing Medieval Sexuality*, 180–200.

31. Burns, *Courtly Love Undressed*, 24–26.

32. Leslie Rabine, "A Feminist Politics of Non-identity," *Feminist Studies*, 14 (1) (1988): 11–31; Denise Riley, *"Am I that Name?" Feminism and the Category of "Women" in History* (Minneapolis: University of Minnesota Press, 1988), 6; Joan Wallach Scott, *Only Paradoxes to Offer: French Feminism and the Rights of Man* (Cambridge, Mass.: Harvard University Press, 1996), 14–15.

PART VI

··

ENGENDERING CHRISTIAN HOLINESS

··

CHAPTER 26

GENDER AND THE INITIAL CHRISTIANIZATION OF NORTHERN EUROPE (TO 1000 CE)

LISA M. BITEL

SOMETIME in the 670s, the Irish bishop Tírechán wrote how, some two hundred years previously, two sweet daughters of King Lóegaire Ua Néill had gone to bathe—"as women are wont to do"—at the well of Clébach near the hill fort of Connacht's kings. There, fair-haired Ethne and redheaded Fedelm encountered a band of loitering men. "Who are you and where have you come from?" the royal ladies demanded. One man snapped back: "It would be better for you to profess our true God than to ask questions about our background." He was Patricius, the British slave who had later become the missionary bishop Pátraic—and by the time Tírechán wrote, Saint Patrick.

"Who is God?" asked the elder sister. "Where is God and whose God is he and where is his dwelling place?" Patrick responded eloquently, "Our God is the God of all men. God above heaven and in heaven and under heaven." Ethne and Fedelm forthwith agreed to convert. Patrick baptized them, clothed them in white, and administered the Eucharist, and they then immediately died. They were buried in a mound near the well.[1] The symbolic sacrifice of two women from Ireland's most powerful royal dynasty was a small price to pay for the Christianization of the entire island.

Throughout the medieval period, learned churchmen like Tírechán rehearsed similar conversion narratives about brave priests and willing converts. They created a shared history of missionary men advancing northward through Europe like a crack Roman legion, barking Gospel verses at simple-minded pagans and performing the occasional miracle. Their histories strove to insert local kings, saints, and homelands into the triumphalist timeline of Christianization, first created by Eusebius of Caesarea (d.339). Non-Christians in these narratives either succumbed to the irresistible logic of Christian salvation or were damned for their stubborn resistance.

Religious change was never as quick as medieval authors made it out to be. Christianization took many generations, varied profoundly by region, and involved more than just preaching and baptism. This essay retells the history of the initial Christianization of Europe north of Rome during the first millennium CE, using the lens of gender and new kinds of textual and material evidence to move beyond the comfortable clichés of conversion narratives. Uncovering daily encounters, exchanges, and frictions, it seeks to understand how now-lost Christianities operated on the ground. It also traces how some historical moments opened opportunities for female religious leadership, even as Christian institutions worked to limit women's roles and restrain new gender ideologies.

BUILDING CHRISTIANITY

"And all Gaul, Britain, Africa, Persia, the East and India, all barbarian peoples adore one Christ," Saint Jerome boasted sometime around 380 CE. Jerome was almost correct. Frankish kings and queens would not begin to convert to Roman (as opposed to Arian) Christianity until the second half of the fifth century. British bishops were attending major synods and councils by the early fourth century, but Christians seem to have disappeared from most of that island for the entire sixth century. The new Anglo-Saxon rulers of England began to convert just before 700. The peoples of the Rhineland waited until the eighth century to turn Christian, the Saxons a few generations later, and the Slavs in the tenth century. Magyars, Poles, and Bohemians followed shortly after, as did the Danes. Norway and Sweden only began to have bishops—which suggests congregations of Christians—in the mid-eleventh century.

Religious change required more than energetic missionizing, as depicted in Tírechán's story of Patrick and his princesses. All sorts of travelers and immigrants, both male and female, carried, crafted, and shared new religion. Before 400 CE, the bearers of Christianity were often soldiers, government officials, merchants, laborers, tourists, or slaves who moved—with or without families, friends, or armies—along military highways and trade routes. Moreover, even if the occasional missionary like Patrick *did* baptize thousands of pagans in a day (which is doubtful), communities responded to Christianity in specifically local ways, adapting religion to existing practices, relationships, social structures, polities, and landscapes. Whenever and however Christianity reached new believers, men and women collaborated in producing yet another instance of what the historian Peter Brown has labeled "micro-Christianities."[2] North of the Loire, a preposterously rich variety of beliefs, practices, and rituals flourished under the name of Christianity between about 300 and 1000 CE.

As long as Christianity remained illegal, believers who lived in distant provinces of the Roman Empire purposely kept a low profile. They worshipped at home, used ambiguous symbols (such as doves and shepherds) to mark their faith on silver and crockery, and treasured everyday items imbued with hidden religious meaning—bits of fabric from a saint's cloak, a lump of rock salt blessed by a holy woman, a thin strip of silver inscribed with a misspelled Bible verse. Christians also revealed themselves, when they wanted, in their dress and demeanor, the configuration of their households, their friendships, traffic patterns, and conversation. For example, young women who stayed home and refused wine, as well as widows who declined a second wedding, performed the Christian virtue of chastity. Unusual household arrangements, such as a woman living alone, or women living together without kinsmen, also suggested the presence of Jesus followers. During rare official persecutions, most Christians kept sensibly quiet. When arrested and punished, Christian martyrs taught lessons in gendered religious behavior. The *Passio* (or death story) of the Carthaginian matron Perpetua (d.203) and her unnamed, pregnant slave, and the legend of Saint Blandina of Lyon (discussed below) taught both women and men how their sacrifices ensured the collective salvation of all Christians.

After the Emperor Constantine legalized Christianity in 313 and Emperor Theodosius declared it the imperial religion in 380, Christian leaders did not, or still could not, impose a single central religious authority. The Bishop of Rome had little influence outside of clerical circles until after about 800 and was usually more interested in Roman politics than Christianizing Europe. Nonetheless, believers throughout the dwindling Empire publicly organized themselves for collective worship, behaving just like Jesus followers everywhere, or so they imagined.

Bishops began to warn their flocks against fraternizing with pagans. Believers were to avoid climbing into bed or sitting down to eat with those of other faiths. Beginning in the early fourth century and continuing throughout the long process of conversion, church councils repeatedly prohibited marital and other sexual relations between Christian women and non-Christian men. Wherever Christians and non-Christians met in a borderland, or new converts mingled with believers in older religions, church officials used both the negative propaganda of prohibitive rules and the positive lessons of saintly role models to protect women—whom they considered the most vulnerable believers—from the lure of apostasy.

In any newly Christian territory, its first bishops trained priests, dealt with local rulers, and communicated with Christian leaders elsewhere, as Saint Martin did for the people of Tours and Saint Germanus for the citizens of Auxerre. The next stage of Christianization, at least after the fourth-century legalization, saw the building of baptisteries, churches, and then monasteries. Previously, small congregations had probably gathered at rural estates where wealthy landowners hosted religious rituals in spare rooms and garden shrines. If no priest lived nearby, they awaited an itinerant one armed with a traveling altar. In colonial cities, aristocrats sometimes converted homes into places of worship, as did Genovefa of Paris (d.509), who used her house to shelter other vowed women. Newly confident, Christians walked from their homes to their meeting places, redecorated rooms with religious murals, and carried their dead to new cemeteries.

In Gaul, Ireland, and Britain, Christians reclaimed previously sacred sites, converting public buildings and ancient shrines into churches and rebuilding on abandoned sites. For instance, the Irish missionary Saint Columbanus supposedly stumbled across an undisturbed pagan site in Haute-Saône during the sixth century and promptly built a monastery on it.[3] Elsewhere, Christians copied familiar architectural models for their places of worship; the basilica, with its single nave and semi-circular apse, used by Roman administrators as civic centers and courts in every city they built, became the preferred shape of Christian churches, too. In such ways, despite the variety of micro-Christianities across the former Empire, all Jesus followers spoke in a vocabulary of *romanitas*, Roman-ness.

Gendered Models of Sanctity

Long before bishops and basilicas appeared in northern Europe, Christian theologians had established many of the religion's gendered doctrines and practices. Most Christian communities had decided before 300 CE that women should not preach or administer sacraments.[4] Saint Paul's advice to Corinthian Christians promoted such policies, and so, too, did patristic teachings. Saint Augustine (d.430) insisted, for example, that women were physically and mentally weaker than men.[5] This gender bias in Christianity meshed well with existing legal systems and social practices, and also shaped the earliest historical notices of Christian heroism in the north.

When a correspondent of Eusebius of Caesarea (or perhaps Eusebius himself) wrote in the fourth century about the cruel deaths of Christians in Lyons almost two hundred years earlier, he laid special emphasis on the innocent purity of female victims, especially the slave girl Blandina. She was, like the other condemned prisoners, "mangled and broken" by numerous tortures, but she endured bravely, "like a noble athlete." When she was exposed to wild beasts in the arena and then hung on a cross, her comrades "beheld with their outward eyes, in the form of their sister, him who was crucified for them." Blandina was later scourged, exposed again to hungry animals, strapped to a "roasting seat," and eventually—when nothing else could kill her—bound up and gored by a bull.[6] The trope of the silent female martyr who overcame her femininity—equated in Blandina's tale with servility, illiteracy, and bodily weakness—pervaded Christian literature of both east and west. However, since very few women were literate in the early medieval period, they must have learned about such pious exemplars from preachers.

In Ireland, where medieval writers later lamented their lack of early martyrs, some Christian women of the fifth century were persecuted but not executed. Pátraic, writing to British bishops toward the end of the fifth century, boasted of his particular success with female converts, including his baptism of one "blessed lady of native Irish birth." Christian missionaries had different relationships with male and female converts. However, Pátraic recognized the special challenges of female converts and sympathized with women who wished to vow lifelong celibacy; they endured "persecution and their own parents' unfair reproaches," he noted, adding that slave women especially endured "constant threats and terrorization."[7] For Pátraic, as for Eusebius and the letter-writer of Lyon who reported Blandina's martyrdom, persecuted vowesses signaled the highest degree of religious conviction. Assuming that women were by nature weaker in mind and body, the missionaries especially admired female dedication.

Pátraic did not comment on whether more women than men chose chastity, nor did he explain why women's vows so angered their kin. Even Christian families had practical reasons for opposing women's religious vocations. Vowesses deprived their families and masters of able workers, the income of bride-gifts, the political support of future offspring, and the alliances made through sexual unions. Yet families still had to support these "unproductive" women, who, whether they lived at home or on their own, required income and armed protection. When Caesarius, bishop of Arles, wrote some of the first guidelines for communities of vowesses in the early sixth century, he did not neglect such mundane concerns. Although the sisters spun, wove, and sewed, they were not self-supporting; Caesarius noted that all gifts from parents and other donors should be inspected by the abbess.[8]

The virgin martyrs and suffering slave girls of the European north were certainly not the clever and long-lived patrician ladies, such as Melania and Paula, who had once hobnobbed with theologians and bishops in more southerly cities. Saint Genovefa (now Geneviève, patron saint of Paris, d.509) was one of the few northern saints who behaved like an aristocrat. When famine struck besieged Parisians around 480, she used her privileges as a Gallo-Roman landowner to commandeer government boats, collect imperial taxes in the form of grain from regional farms, and feed the city. Genovefa's hagiographer, who wrote around 529, praised her feminine humility but also admired her administrative talents, her constant travel around her territory, and the great honors bestowed upon her by bishops, saints, and royalty. When she arrived in other cities, for instance, their citizens greeted her with a traditional ceremony of welcome normally reserved for emperors and bishops. She also organized the building of a church in honor of Saint Denis. In short, the writer represented Genovefa as a surrogate bishop of Paris. She was eventually buried next to King Clovis, in a church and royal mausoleum built by Queen Clothild, so that she might continue to protect Paris and its rulers after death.[9]

By 500 or so, however, patrician saints and virgin martyrs faced new competition as Christian role models. Hagiographers and cult-keepers in northern Europe began searching eagerly for the earliest signs of Christianization in their respective homelands, aiming to establish their respective communities and kingdoms in the grander European narrative of conversion. They found what they needed in a new group of male heroes: bishops. Merovingians, for example, celebrated a cadre of seven second-century bishop-martyrs, "rediscovering" their tombs, cherishing their relics, and building new shrines in their honor. Genovefa's cult was soon overshadowed by that of Saint Denis, whose burial place Genovefa had herself discovered. Later generations of French kings went to rest in Saint Denis, and it was he, not Genovefa, who became the patron saint of all France.

CHRISTIANS ON THE GROUND

The construction of Christianity varied by region, demography, and cultural context. Christians had reached Britain by the third century, if not earlier, but had little time to build new places of worship before the Germanic invasions beginning in the fifth century. No buried foundations, early naves, or baptisteries survive from the period of initial conversions, as they still do in Trier, Bourges, or Fréjus (near Cannes). The most obvious remains of British Christianization from before 500 are large lead tubs adorned with Christian symbols, found at Icklingham (Suffolk) and elsewhere around the southern half of the island. The tubs were probably used as baptismal cisterns or lavers for washing before worship, but it remains unclear where that worship took place. However, the poorly organized British Christians may well have allowed women to participate more visibly in liturgies than they did in churches on the continent. When some aristocratic British families converted to Christianity, they remodeled their estates to create spaces for worship (as at Lullingstone in Kent, where rooms were adorned with Christian iconography). Unlike churches, whose holiest spaces were reserved for male clergy, in private homes both men and women trod upon Christian mosaics and gazed at the murals. When neighbors gathered on feast days or a traveling preacher stopped to visit and pray, houses became sites of public worship. When a century of invasion and displacement ended, and Anglo-Saxon rulers began converting to Christianity, official worship no longer took place in domestic space.

Across the waters, where substantial Christian communities had been building religious monuments for at least 250 years, Gregory of Tours and other sixth-century writers already could mention ancient churches. Between the legalization of Christianity and the disappearance of Roman government in the mid-fifth century, urban dwellers had gradually shifted their city centers and major public spaces from forums, always at the cross of major north–south and east–west roads, to the urban edges, nearer the cemeteries and earliest Christian shrines. Beyond city walls, they built proper cathedrals. By Gregory's time, though, Christian leaders had forgotten who had built the first shrines and who the first converts had been. Gregory repeated the legend of Saint Denis and his missionary colleagues, sent from Rome to evangelize seven cities in Gaul, but had little to say about Denis' shrine, which was still fairly new; Genovefa's hagiographer claimed that she had found the saint's remains in a neglected graveyard outside Paris. The oldest church in the city, according to Gregory, stood outside the southeastern city gate, near the tomb of an unidentifiable woman. "Here lies Crescentia, dedicated to God," read her stone. Yet, Gregory mournfully noted, no one "could tell what her merit had been or what she had done in life."[10]

Despite the notable exception of Genovefa, men were typically the organizers and long-distance, transregional couriers of religion. Women more often moved Christianity from house to house, across the generations, and from fathers to husbands. A few Christian women crossed longer distances to wed, of course, bringing new religion with them. Clothild, who came from Burgundy, helped convert the first king of all the Franks, Clovis, to Christianity; Bertha, her great-granddaughter, married the pagan Aethelberht of Kent in the late sixth century, who subsequently became a Christian. Both Clovis and Aethelberht may have been considering conversion long before they married, but the motif of the missionary queen became popular in hagiography and history. Proselytization was a Christian queen's duty. When Bishop Nicetius of Trier wrote in 563 to the princess Clodosinda, who had married an Arian Lombard king, he instructed her on orthodox doctrine and suggested that she point out her husband's doctrinal errors; Nicetius directly linked orthodoxy to Clodosinda's honor and goals as queen, wife, and mother.[11]

Throughout the period of Christianization, men and women, already accustomed to gender-segregated foot traffic and labor patterns, used holy places and spaces in different ways. Women across northern Europe had long tended to distinctive deities and feminine holy places; they also kept the hearth gods and household shrines, and attended to mother-goddesses' holy springs.[12] Newly Christian women who had once tossed offerings into springs now handed their gifts directly to saints who specialized in the care of women and children. Hagiographers encouraged women's donations with stories of saints who miraculously cured blindness, paralysis, infertility, and threatening illnesses. They prayed to saints who might help them successfully bear and raise their children. Some converts played it safe by appealing to both old gods and new, but church councils forbade the easy mix of religions. In the later sixth century, the diocesan council of Auxerre prohibited prayers or offerings at springs, sacred trees, or in household shrines—the three types of sacred sites most frequented by Gallo-Roman and Germanic women.[13]

Women's innocence and ignorance featured regularly in stories of such interactions between females and their saints. Thus, for example, Gregory of Tours told how a pious old lady, putting out the lights in a church crypt, was accidentally locked in. Settling down to wait until dawn, she was surprised by a troop of chanting clerics, including one latecomer who arrived dripping wet. She mopped up the mess, and reported it to the bishop the next morning. He realized that her naiveté had allowed her to witness a congregation of saints, including Saint Stephen, martyred by drowning. The bishop seized the damp rag from the holy woman, and it became part of his liturgical equipment. Gregory, who was himself a relic collector, approved. Sacred objects, as his histories made clear, belonged in the hands of churchmen educated to use them—although Gregory admired Queen Radegund, wife of the Frankish King Chlothar, who was also a notable collector of relics.[14]

In fact, Radegund presents an excellent corrective to Gregory's depictions of naïve women and his bias toward male role models for Christians. Radegund (d.586) was a Thuringian princess captured and forced to marry Clovis' son Chlotar in the 530s. Radegund played queen by day but rose every night for secret devotions in the privy. She washed the feet of beggars, fed them from the royal table, and gave them her robes and jewelry. Eventually, she fled her husband in order to become a nun. When the Bishop of Noyon refused to veil her without her husband's permission, Radegund consecrated herself. She founded a monastery for women at Poitiers and later became a saint, celebrated by three contemporary biographers—one, Baudonivia, was a nun in Radegund's convent.[15]

Missionary Invasions

By the sixth century, bishops in long-established southerly dioceses felt secure enough to consider sending organized missions to pagan kingdoms. Pope Gregory I (d.602) has been much celebrated for organizing a mission to the kingdom of Kent in the 590s. He may have been inspired by earlier proselytizers, such as Denis and Genovefa, or by Gildas's lament about lost British missionaries, or the story of Saint Germanus's visit to fifth-century Britain. Gregory initially urged his chief representative, known now as Saint Augustine of Canterbury, to impose strict Christianity: tolerate no pagan sacrifices; accept no pagan burial customs; condemn unchristian sexual habits such as polygamy, concubinage, or serial marriage. Faced with English resistance, though, Pope Gregory later advised more flexibility, allowing Christian practice to blend with local custom. Do not nag chieftains about multiple wives and concubines, he wrote; allow menstruating and post-parturient women, deemed unclean in biblical law, to attend church. Gregory even advised Augustine to remodel traditional sites of devotion and rededicate them as Christian churches.[16]

Augustine's job was, in short, to Christianize the culture, landscapes, sexualities, and the gender system of the English. Persuading an individual or a community to accept baptism was easy compared with closing a forest shrine, imposing a calendar of holy days, or coaxing patriarchs to give up polygyny. In a dispersed rural population, adulteries and idolatries were easy to hide. And kings were of little help, refusing to enforce new moral codes and often tolerating the continued presence of non-Christians. Churchmen who gathered at regional synods and councils in Britain, and across Christendom, had even less success in regulating gender relations and sexual behavior in newly Christian communities. Preachers exhorted converts about the sins of fornication, adultery, homosexual acts, incest, and bestiality. But kings and chieftains needed heirs and valued their warriors, herds, slaves, and women.

In these political and social circumstances, clerics struggled to answer questions about how typical Christians should live their religion. Could soldiers become monks? The answer was yes (but only in western Europe, not in Byzantium). Could priests take money for administering sacraments? As Pátraic knew, the answer was no. Could Christians do business with pagans? Only if they avoided touching anything tainted with heathen religion. Could women participate as fully and conscientiously as men in Christian rituals? To a limited extent, if they were nuns; but not at all if they were ordinary married women struggling to live as wives, lovers, daughters, and kinswomen in typical communities of northern Europe.

The gendering of religious space was a special concern, and bishops steadily reduced women's access to the most important ritual moments of Christianity. Theologians equated masculinity with celibacy and sexual purity, and femininity with embodiment, senses, and sin. At the Council of Orange in 441, clerics officially prohibited deaconesses from performing major sacraments, fearing pollution and inefficacy. In 567, the Council of Tours decreed that bishops' wives could no longer cohabit with their spouses, effectively ending the ecclesiastical role of the *episcopa*. Not long after, at Auxerre, churchmen forbade women from touching communion bread; contact with female flesh endangered the miracle of the Eucharist. Other clerical councils prohibited women from approaching church altars too closely or keeping night vigils.[17] The most sacred spaces of Christian communities became reserved for the exclusively male ordained clergy, who alone could perform the sacrament of the Eucharist and preach the Bible.

The general thrust of all church writings—conciliar rulings, hagiographies, penitentials, episcopal letters—blamed women for sexual sin. Women were to be punished more harshly for adultery and fornication. They were often blamed for rape, along with male perpetrators, on the grounds that victims could prevent their violation with fierce and noisy struggling. Even women's incest was deemed especially heinous; penitentialists of the seventh century ranked the incest between a mother and son as far worse than between a father and daughter. Nonetheless, Christian laymen and women routinely disregarded their pastors, bishops, and lawmakers in such matters. The keepers of secular laws only took action when illicit sex undermined a reproductive marriage or cast doubt on an heir's legitimacy. Adultery and the despoiling of virgins were generally unacceptable, but concubinage and a widower's remarriage remained common.[18] The basic need for heirs and laborers continued to contradict ecclesiastical efforts to control marriage and reproduction. In Ireland, for instance, early medieval jurists maintained the ancient privilege of divorce, whether initiated by husband or wife. Elsewhere, the Christian nobility became adept at annulling or simply ignoring their marriages when necessary. When religious doctrine threatened royalty's practice of resource polygyny, the reproduction of viable male heirs, and the serial monogamy so crucial to medieval politics, kings and queens alike sometimes forgot how to be good Christians.

VOWED WOMEN, GENDERED SPACES

Gendered limits on women's participation in religion applied also to vowed women. Devout women and men had already begun to live in hermitages and single-sex households by the late fourth century. Sulpicius Severus mentioned a hermitess living in Gaul in the 390s. A decade later, Victricius, bishop of Rouen, reported admiringly on the public roles of virgins, chaste widows, and celibate wives who paraded through the city to welcome some saints' relics to his diocese. Victricius was enthusiastic about his Christian sisters who, as they marched to meet the saints, appeared "resplendent, radiant with the intoxication of chastity."[19] Vowed women, including widows, lived in a wide variety of situations unrecognized as religious vocations by both medieval documents and modern scholars. In other words, some convents might have been, to most folks, little more than a farm inhabited by a few pious kinswomen.[20]

Vowed women supported themselves by farming or producing goods for sale in local markets. Clothmaking and needlework were their constant occupations, and only vowed women seem to have produced vestments and liturgical textiles (at least one early medieval nun won sainthood for her embroidery).[21] Still, while some monasteries prospered, many women's settlements apparently lacked resources to survive more than a generation or two, probably because their wealth reverted to kinsmen at the death of their founders. Hagiographers often stressed the poverty of holy women, but this alleged poverty might be more spiritual trope than historical reality, especially given the immense wealth of some royal nunneries in early medieval England and Francia. And some communities of nuns mentioned only once or twice in documents may not actually have dissolved, but merely faded from written history.

Generosity to vowed women—from parents, foster-relations, and neighbors, as well as churchmen and strangers—was strongly encouraged. Hagiographers taught that refusal to support religious women was sinful and potentially perilous. A certain murderous pagan named Thunor, for example, was supposedly swallowed by the earth for objecting to land grants to the nuns of Thanet.[22] Women also solved the problem of funding their vocations—as well as providing themselves with resident clergy, farm laborers, and protectors—by joining with men to form mixed-sex monastic communities. Historians used to call these "double" monasteries, but the term implies more gender segregation than was probably customary. Tírechán mentioned several Irish women who founded ecclesiastical settlements—not by dying, as the Uí Néill princesses allegedly did, but by joining with male kinsmen to build family churches on their shared properties.

Mixed-sex monasteries were common in the European north (and remained so, it seems, throughout the Middle Ages).[23] At major communities, such as Coldingham in Northumbria or Kildare in Leinster, women and men collaborated to maintain buildings, conduct regular public rituals, and offer religious instruction. Abbesses of these mixed settlements, like abbots of other monasteries, arbitrated between feuding lords and offered safe spaces for political and ecclesiastical negotiations. Hild, abbess of Whitby (d. c.680) hosted a major ecclesiastical debate about Easter at her monastery. Yet only a few women's communities and mixed-sex monasteries, such as Whitby, Radegund's Sainte Croix, or Brigit's community of Kildare, acquired transregional political prestige.

WOMEN IN THE MISSION FIELDS

By 800, self-identified Christians dwelt everywhere from the eastern limits of the Frankish kingdoms to the Portuguese coast, and from Sicily to Scotland's northern islands. Christianity had infiltrated every corner of western Europe except Scandinavia.

After Arianism had disappeared in the 670s, varieties of belief and practices among Christians became more subtle, and gendered religious practices grew more uniform across regions. Political and religious leaders had learned how to work together for mutual benefit, and churchmen had even begun to Christianize the very institution of kingship with religious rituals of royal ordination, first for kings, and eventually for their queens.²⁴ However, clerics also interfered in royal politics by prohibiting certain forms of political violence, particularly harm to women and children. In 697, for instance, Adomnán, a nobly born abbot of the island monastery of Iona off the coast of western Scotland, forbade injury to noncombatants during wartime; warriors, he declared, should compensate any injured women, children, and clergy. His policy, recorded as *Cáin Adomnáin*, was announced throughout Ireland with little immediate effect, but church leaders continued their struggle to protect noncombatants.

For their part, kings, queens, and nobles contributed vast wealth to religious foundations, especially royal mausoleums or houses for chaste royal women. Hagiographers cherished the memories of royal abbesses who humbly submitted to clerical authority. These women were "living sermons," as the historian Jo Ann McNamara called them, despite the church's teaching that women should not proselytize, preach, or otherwise imitate their savior.²⁵ From the mid-seventh century, wealthy Frankish and Bavarian women advertised their Christianity with jewelry and embroidered garments. Archaeologists continue to turn up burials of Christian women wearing precious gold and garnet brooches and pendants shaped like crosses. In the eighth century, when Irish and English missionaries headed beyond the expanded eastern borders of the Frankish Empire, women there began to follow the same fashion.

In this second wave of missionizing, some women were exceptionally active. Several English abbesses kept in close contact with Saint Boniface (d.754) as he proselytized in war-torn Saxony. Some wealthy vowesses provided resources as well as encouragement; Eadberga, a West Saxon princess and abbess of Minster on the Isle of Thanet, sent Boniface priestly vestments and books. "I have been unable to obtain a copy of *The Sufferings of the Martyrs* which you asked me to send you," she wrote to him in 720, "but I shall send it to you as soon as I can…By this same messenger I am sending you fifty shillings and an altar cloth, because I was unable to get for you a more precious gift. Small as they are, they are sent with great love."²⁶

Boniface asked all his colleagues in England—nuns as well as monks—for help in developing a monastic infrastructure for his converts. He wished, as one ninth-century writer put it, "that the people would be attracted to the church not only by the beauty of its religion but also by the communities of monks and nuns."²⁷ One of those who heeded his summons was a West Saxon noblewoman named Leoba (d.779), who settled in the diocese of Mainz, where Boniface eventually became archbishop. She was highly educated and well suited as abbess of the women's monastery at Bischofsheim; her nuns became leaders of their own religious communities throughout Germany.

Leoba's story, written by Rudolf of Fulda almost sixty years after her death, reveals some of the gender-tinged issues—as well as class and ethnic tensions—that confronted Christians in the eastern mission fields. When the body of a newborn child was found in a mill stream near Bischofsheim, villagers immediately blamed the nuns, shouting insults about false virgins and the poisoning of their water. Leoba handled the affair with theatrical aplomb. Her nuns undertook an extraordinary and highly visible (and audible) regime of nonstop prayers and processions. This dramatic liturgy brought quick results. A beggar girl confessed to fornication, pregnancy, and the infanticide. "Then a great shout rose to heaven," explained Rudolf. "The vast crowd was astounded at the miracle, the nuns began to weep with joy, and all of them with one voice gave expression to the merits of Leoba and of Christ our Saviour."[28] The beggar remained possessed by the devil for the rest of her life.

No wonder the aging Boniface supposedly summoned Leoba before departing for his final mission in Frisia and begged that she expand her work to new regions. He promised that her bones would lie in his own tomb at Fulda. Leoba became a frequent traveler to the courts of Pepin the Short and his son, Charlemagne, and a close confidant of Charlemagne's queen, Hildegard. She also advised bishops on matters of religious discipline and policy. Most of all, though, Leoba liked visiting the new convents she helped establish. When she died, she was buried at Fulda, but Boniface's monks insisted that she have her own tomb rather than sharing his.

Leoba's biography provided a role model for later generations of Christian women, along with earlier and equally popular saints' lives, such as the legends of Radegund, Brigit, and virgin martyrs from late antiquity. The process of Christianization continued after the tenth century, as Europeans expanded the boundaries of western Christendom to include Scandinavia, eastern Europe, and eventually the Holy Land. However, as religious leaders labored to regularize, centralize, and formalize the variety of ideas, rites, and customs that eventually became Christianity, and as the majority of Europeans came to identify as Christians, the goals and tactics of missionaries also changed. There was no place for a humbly literate preacher like Pátraic or a confident female aristocrat such as Genovefa in the borderlands of tenth- or eleventh-century Europe.

CHRISTIANIZATION ON THE
EDGE OF EUROPE

The final episodes in northern European Christianization lack even a single Radegund or Leoba. Medieval chroniclers wrote mostly about monumental events such as the baptism of kings and the establishment of episcopal dioceses in Denmark, Norway, Sweden, and Iceland. King Harald Bluetooth of Denmark accepted Christianity in 965, the Norwegian King Olav Tryggvason in 995, and the Swedish King Olaf Skötkonung around 1000, when the Icelandic Althing also voted for collective conversion. Bishops from Germany and England competed to convert Danes and Norwegians during the tenth and eleventh centuries. The trade entrepôt of Birka, on the island of Björkö in Lake Mälaren, about 30 kilometers from Stockholm, hosted two early missions by Saint Anskar, who came from Germany in 829 and 850. Its graveyards have since yielded burials of both men and women who were probably Christians (along with some possible Muslims and many dedicated devotees of Thor). But in Birka and Scandinavia generally, Christianity's progress depended partly on the current ruler and his religious preferences.[29]

Anskar's biographer Rimbert mentioned only two women among the Birka converts, a "pious matron" named Frideborg and her daughter, Catla. When misfortunes befell Frideborg, she refused to sacrifice to the local deities, arguing that she had promised her faith to Jesus. Nonetheless, she lacked a firm grasp of Christian ritual and doctrine, perhaps because Birka lacked a priest. When Frideborg fell ill and believed herself to be dying, she and her daughter tried to create a quasi-Eucharist.

> She then asked her daughter, who was also a woman devout in the faith, to drop some wine into her mouth when her last moments came, since she could not receive the sacrament, so that she might at least in this way commend her departure from this world to the mercy of the Lord.[30]

Frideborg and her daughter had heard of the Eucharist but apparently never even seen the ceremony. Frideborg bequeathed her possessions to the beggars of Dorestadt, where she had heard there were many churches, priests, and hungry Christians. Catla made the trip with the help of devout women who took her to the holy places in the town and advised her on doling out charitable gifts. Apparently, enough information flowed in and out of Birka that Frideborg knew where to send her daughter with the goods, and Catla could easily find clerics and women to help her.

Beyond this kind of rare, incidental reference, little textual evidence is available about Scandinavian women's responses to Christianization. The archaeological evidence is just as meager and hard to interpret. Eleventh-century inscriptions, culled from about 2,500 Swedish runestones, have yielded some women's names carved with explicitly Christian symbols. In the region of Uppland, more than a third of all such inscriptions mention women.[31] One small survey of late tenth- and eleventh-century Christian burials across Scandinavia found that twenty-five out of thirty burials were definitely female. This hints that women advertised their Christian identity more frequently than men, but women were more often buried with pagan symbols, too, such as pendants shaped like the god Thor's hammer.[32]

Some modern scholars have argued from similar material evidence, including ceramic jugs decorated with crosses, that women were primarily responsible for religious practice in medieval Scandinavia and, further, that non-Christian cults offered them far more spiritual authority than Christianity. Norse sagas featured plenty of female seers and shamans, and also depicted women of the pre-Christian period as more sexually active and socially prominent than in later centuries. However, historians further argue, Christianity's moral code had both benefits and drawbacks for women: it limited women's sexual practice to heterosexual marriage, but also prevented the tradition of paternal infanticide. Women may have been attracted to the emotional, supportive nature of Christian spirituality, which emphasized individual salvation as opposed to kin-based corporate identities; they happily traded in the goddess Freya for the Virgin Mary. Yet such arguments assume that thirteenth-century and later sagas offer reliable information about earlier gender relations. Further, the arguments also depend on reductive views of religion, defining Christianity as a set of doctrines, beliefs, and rules, and paganism as a set of practices and objects. Men as well as women participated in the sacrifices and rites of local Scandinavian cults, and both genders accepted baptism—both in sagas and in real life. Women did not necessarily have any greater interest or responsibility for religion generally, nor were they necessarily more emotionally needy than men. Christian objects buried with women are simply some of our best evidence for religious change.

The mini-Christianities that reached Scandinavia beginning in the tenth century were not the same as those that had traveled in the baggage of Romanized Europeans during late antiquity or, indeed, with the English princess Leoba in the eighth century. Still, among the countless versions of Christianity that flourished in northern Europe during the premodern period, some religious habits endured over centuries and across political boundaries. One of the most damaging to women was the gendering of barbarianism and related paganism as female. When the armies of Caesar first penetrated the Germanic forests and Celtic Britain, Tacitus wrote of mysterious priestesses perched high in the trees, fierce goddesses, and warrior queens. Early bishops used the same tropes when blaming women for resistance to Christianization, a charge that persisted well into the second millennium of Christian history. Later medieval chroniclers and storytellers recast ancient beliefs as women's magic; as the great master of sagas, Snorri Sturluson, wrote around 1225, the all-knowing Norse God Odin had once taught humans how to make powerful spells, but "it was not thought respectable for men to practice it; and therefore the priestesses were brought up in this art."[33]

CONCLUSION

The Christianization of Europe was never completed, nor will it ever be. Believers continue to spread new kinds of Christianity which, they are convinced, perfect the earlier kinds. Throughout the Middle Ages, Christian thinkers and organizers strove constantly to bind all Christians together in a single religious system and to regularize Christian practice and doctrine. Meanwhile, men and women carried their own varieties of Christianity across the European continent, disregarding their preachers and building their religion from the habits and objects of everyday life. The only rituals shared by all Christians in early medieval Europe were baptism and the Eucharist, and the only concept they agreed upon was an afterlife made possible by Jesus' crucifixion. One other habit common to all Christians was the gendered quality of religious experience. Christ accepted both male and female as his followers, according to the New Testament, but a thousand years ago, according to European preachers and leaders then, God also endorsed gendered Christianities.

FURTHER READING

Bitel, Lisa. *Landscape with Two Saints: How Genovefa of Paris and Brigit of Kildare Built Christianity in Barbarian Europe.* Oxford: Oxford University Press, 2009.

Brown, Peter. *The Rise of Western Christendom: Triumph and Diversity, A.D. 200–1000.* Cambridge, Mass.: Blackwell, 1996.

Carver, M. O. H., ed. *The Cross Goes North: Processes of Conversion in Northern Europe, AD 300–1300.* Woodbridge, Suffolk: York Medieval Press, 2003.

Foot, Sarah. *Veiled Women,* 2 vols. Aldershot: Ashgate, 2000.

McNamara, Jo Ann. *Sisters in Arms: Catholic Nuns Through Two Millennia.* Cambridge, Mass.: Harvard University Press, 1996.

Muldoon, James, ed. *Varieties of Religious Conversion in the Middle Ages.* Gainesville: University Press of Florida, 1997.

Sawyer, Birgit. "Faith, Family, and Fortune: The Effect of Conversion on Women in Scandinavia," in Anneke B. Mulder-Bakker and Jocelyn Wogan-Browne, eds, *Household, Women, and Christianities in Late Antiquity and the Middle Ages* (Turnhout, Belgium: Brepols, 2005): 110–23.

Thomas, Charles. *Christianity in Roman Britain to AD 500.* Berkeley: University of California Press, 1981.

NOTES

1. Tírechán, "Collectanea" or "Itinerary," in Ludwig Bieler and Fergus Kelly, eds, *The Patrician Texts in the Book of Armagh* (Dublin: The Dublin Institute for Advanced Studies, 1979), sec. 26: 142–45; see also introduction, 35–43. Translations are by Bieler with my emendations. See also Catherine Swift, "Tírechán's Motives in Compiling the 'Collectanea': An Alternative Interpretation," *Ériu* 45 (1994): 53–82.

2. Peter Brown, *The Rise of Western Christendom: Triumph and Diversity, A.D. 200–1000* (Oxford: Blackwell Publishers, 2003), 13–17.

3. Jonas of Bobbio, *Vita S. Columbani,* 60; Dana C. Munro, trans., *Life of St. Columban* (Philadelphia: Department of History of the University of Pennsylvania, 1895). Cf. Sulpicius Severus, *Dialogi* 3.8; Davide Fiocco, ed., *Lettere e dialoghi* (Roma: Città nuova, 2007). Gregory the Great, *Dialogi* 2.8; Myra L. Uhlfelder, trans., *The Dialogues of Gregory the Great: Book Two: Saint Benedict* (Indianapolis: Bobbs-Merrill, 1967).

4. But see Gary Macy, *The Hidden History of Women's Ordination: Female Clergy in the Medieval West* (Oxford: Oxford University Press, 2008).

5. Augustine, *De Nuptiis,* esp. 1.10, 27.

6. Eusebius, *Church History,* 5.1.

7. Tírechán, "Collectanea," sec. 26.

8. J. P. Migne, ed., *Patrologiae cursus completus* (Paris, 1844–92), 67: 1103–21. Online at <http://pld.chadwyck.com/>.

9. *Vita S. Genovefae,* in Bruno Krusch, ed., *Monumenta Germanicae Historiae Scriptores rerum Mervingocarum* (Hannover and Berlin, 1826–), 3 (1896), ch. 50 (hereafter *MGH SRM*); Gregory of Tours, *Histories, MGH SRM,* 1, ch. 4.1; L. Thorpe, ed. and trans., *Gregory of Tours: The History of the Franks* (Harmondsworth: Penguin, 1974); May Vieillard-Troïekouroff, *Les monuments religieux de la Gaule d'après les oeuvres de Grégoire de Tours* (Lille: Service de reproduction des thèses de l'Université, 1977), 215–16.

10. Gregory of Tours, *Glory of the Confessors*, trans. Raymond Van Dam (Liverpool: Liverpool University Press, 1988), 103.

11. Bede, *Ecclesiastical History*, 1.25; Thomas Stapleton and J. E. King, eds and trans., *Baedae Opera historica: With an English Translation* (London: W. Heinemann, 1930). Gregory of Tours, *Histories*, 2.30–31; Nicetius, in Migne, ed., *Patrologia*, 68: 375–380.

12. Simone Deyts, *Un people de pélerins: Offrandes de pierre et de bronze des Sources de la Seine* (Dijon: Revue Archéologique de l'Est et du Centre-Est, supp. 13, 1994), esp. 13–16.

13. Giovan Domenico Mansi, ed., *Sacrorum conciliorum nova et amplissima collectio…* (Paris: H. Welter, 1901–27), 9: 911; 12: 107; 14: 786.

14. Baudonivia, *Vita S. Radegundae, Acta sanctorum quotquot toto orbe colluntu* (Antwerp: Johann Mersius, 1643–) Aug. 13, chs 13–16 (hereafter *AASS*); also found in Jo Ann McNamara, John E. Halborg, and E. Gordon Whatley, eds and trans., *Sainted Women of the Dark Ages* (Durham: Duke University Press, 1992), 86–105.

15. Venantius Fortunatus, *Vita S. Radegundae, AASS* Aug. 13 and McNamara, Halborg, and Whatley, *Sainted Women*, 70–86.

16. Bede, *History of the English Church*, I.25–27; Gregory I, *Register Gregors, VII, MGH Epistolae selectae*, ed. Erich Caspar, 11.29; Ephraim Emerton, trans., *Correspondence of Pope Gregory VII, Selected Letters from the Registrum* (New York: Columbia University Press, 1990).

17. *Vita S. Genovefae*, 22.

18. Julie Coleman, "Rape in Anglo-Saxon England," in Guy Halsall, ed., *Violence and Society in the Early Medieval West* (Woodbridge, Suffolk: Boydell & Brewer, 1998), 193–204; Thomas Kuehn, "Remarriage," in Margaret Schaus, ed., *Women and Gender in Medieval Europe: An Encyclopedia* (New York: Routledge, 2006), 706–707.

19. Jo Ann McNamara, *Sisters in Arms: Catholic Nuns Through Two Millennia* (Cambridge, Mass.: Harvard University Press, 1996), 67–68; Victricius of Rouen, *De laude sanctorum*, ed. R Demeulenaere (Turnhout: Brepols, 1991); Gillian Clark, "Victricius of Rouen: Praising the Saints," *Journal of Early Christian Studies*, 7 (3) (1999): 378–79.

20. Sarah Foot, *Veiled Women* (Aldershot: Ashgate, 2000), 1: 64–65; Roberta Gilchrist, *Gender and Material Culture: The Archaeology of Religious Women* (London; New York: Routledge, 1994), esp. 63–91.

21. Kathleen Mulchrone, ed., *Bethu Phátraic; The Tripartite Life of Patrick* (Dublin: Hodges Figgis, 1939), 252, 266. Whitley Stokes, ed., *Félire Oengusso Céli Dé: The Martyrology of Oengus the Culdee* (Woodbridge, Suffolk: Boydell Press for the Henry Bradshaw Society, 1905), 42.

22. Felix Liebermann, ed., *Die Heiligen Englands* (Hannover, 1889), 11–12. R A. B. Mynors, Rodney M. Thomson, and Michael Winterbottom, eds, *Gesta regum anglorum: The History of the English Kings* (Oxford: Clarendon Press, 1998), 4: 181.2–4.

23. Foot, *Veiled Women*, vol. 1, 49–56; Roberta Gilchrist, *Gender and Material Culture: The Archaeology of Religious Women* (London: Routledge, 1994), 28–29. See also articles in Alison I. Beach, ed., *Manuscripts and Monastic Culture: Reform and Renewal in Twelfth Century Germany* (Turnhout: Brepols, 2007). Katherine Sykes, "'Canonici albi et moniales': Perceptions of the Twelfth-Century Double House," *Journal of Ecclesiastical History*, 60 (2009): 217–32.

24. *Cain Adamnain: An Old-Irish Treatise on the Law of Adamnan* [based on an earlier edition by Kuno Meyer] in Paul Halsall, ed., *Internet Medieval Sourcebook* (New York: Fordham

University, 2001) at <http://www.fordham.edu/halsall/source/CainAdamnain.asp> (last accessed March 3, 2012). Máirín Ní Dhonnchadha, "The Lex innocentium: Adomnán's Law for Women, Clerics and Youths, 697 A.D.," in Mary O'Dowd and Sabine Wichert, eds, *Chattel, Servant or Citizen: Women's Status in Church, State and Society* (Belfast: Institute of Irish Studies, Queen's University of Belfast, 1995), 58–69.

25. Jo Ann McNamara, "Living Sermons: Consecrated Women and the Conversion of Gaul," in John Nichols, ed., *Peace Weavers* (Kalamazoo, MI: Cistercian Publications, 1987), 19–38.

26. Michael Tangl, ed., *Die Briefe des heiligen Bonifatius und Lullus: Epistolae Selectae* (Munster: MGH, 1989), 15.

27. Rudolf, *Vita Leobae abbatissae Biscofesheimensis*, in *MGH Scriptores*, 15: 118–31; trans. C. H. Talbot in Thomas F. X. Noble and Thomas Head, eds, *Soldiers of Christ: Saints and Saints' Lives from Late Antiquity and the Early Middle Ages* (University Park, PA: Pennsylvania State Press, 1995), 254–77: cap. 10.

28. Ibid., 12.

29. Ruth Mazo Karras, "God and Man in Medieval Scandinavia: Writing—and Gendering—the Conversion," in James Muldoon, ed., *Varieties of Religious Conversion in the Middle Ages* (Gainesville: University Press of Florida, 1997), 100–14. Anders Winroth, *The Conversion of Scandinavia: Vikings, Merchants, and Missionaries in the Remaking of Northern Europe* (New Haven: Yale University Press, 2012), 89–90, 134.

30. Rimbert, *Vita Anskarii*, 20; Charles H. Robinson, trans., *Anskar, The Apostle of the North, 801–865* (London: Society for the Propagation of the Gospel in Foreign Parts, 1921).

31. Anne-Sofie Gräslund, "The Role of Scandinavian Women in Christianisation: The Neglected Evidence," in M. O. H. Carver, ed., *The Cross Goes North: Processes of Conversion in Northern Europe, AD 300–1300* (Woodbridge, Suffolk: York Medieval Press, 2003), 490–91.

32. Jörn Staecker, "The Cross Goes North: Christian Symbols and Scandinavian Women," in Carver, ed., *The Cross Goes North*, 478.

33. Cornelius Tacitus, *Germania*, 8; H. Mattingly, trans., *The Agricola and the Germania* (Harmondsworth: Penguin Books, 1970); Snorri Sturluson, *Heimskringla, or the Chronicle of the Kings of Norway*, Project Gutenberg at <http://www.archive.org/stream/heimskringlaorth00598gut/hmskr10.txt> (last accessed March 3, 2012), 7.

CHAPTER 27

THE GENDER OF THE RELIGIOUS: WO/MEN AND THE INVENTION OF MONASTICISM

ALBRECHT DIEM

THERE is something odd about the historiography of Christian monasticism. Historians tend to focus either on female monasticism as a separate field of research or on the *differences* between male and female monastic life, and those talking about monasticism in general often dutifully squeeze the obligatory "fifteen pages on women" into their books. All this makes us overlook that medieval monastic life emerged as a sequence of "unisex" models. The long-lasting experiment of shaping ideal religious communities and stable monastic institutions created forms of monastic life that were largely applicable to *both* genders (albeit usually in strict separation). Throughout the Middle Ages, male and female monastic communities largely used a shared corpus of authoritative texts and a common repertoire of practices.[1] Instead of taking for granted that both men *and* women had similar options for living a monastic life, we may ask why and how monasticisms (there was never *one* monasticism) offered relatively nongendered ways of life within societies that were otherwise profoundly shaped by gender differences.

The history of female martyrs, holy virgins and widows, nuns, and anchoresses (I use the term "religious women" as reference to all of them) is usually told as a narrative that links islands of knowledge. Compared to the amount of historical evidence on religious life in general, these islands of knowledge are scarce. Nevertheless, we know much more about the female *gender* of the religious than about the male. Men made history; they were the frames of reference but, as such, they were rarely an object of reflection. Ubiquitous as they were, religious men were rather invisible as far as their gender is concerned.[2]

The history of monasticism, like all histories, needs structures and narratives as ground to stand on. Yet good chronological syntheses must be questioned in detail, unmasked in their anachronisms, and challenged in their generalizations. When, for example, do prohibitions and sanctions in monastic rules reveal a problem? When do they mark its solution? When do our sources on women's monasticisms tell us something about women, and when about monasticisms? Quite often, the unintentional background information—the stage décor rather than the play itself—provides the most reliable insights.

In this essay I will step away from the attempt to give a chronological overview on the gender of the religious in the Middle Ages. Great scholars have done this, and no summary would do justice to their work.[3] Instead, I shall try to undertake the task of "gendering" religious life (particularly in its monastic variants) by starting out with its nongendered aspects: how were these nongendered ways of life established—in discourse and in practice—and how were the genders of the religious constructed in our sources? I will focus mostly on the formative—or experimental—phase of medieval monastic life (which ends with the Carolingian monastic reforms), and I intend to formulate questions for future research rather than give answers or clear-cut models.

CHRISTIAN GENDERS?

Let me start with the (in many respects) revolutionary Pauline statement in Gal. 3:28 that "there is neither Jew nor Greek, there is neither slave nor free, there is no male and female, for you are all one in Christ Jesus." To my knowledge, no one has yet done systematic research on how this biblical verse traveled through Christian Antiquity and the Middle Ages, how it has been used, understood, contextualized, and submitted to exegesis. For women, this "all one in Christ Jesus" message offered a curious sort of parity. One the one hand, women became excluded from holding offices already in the early Church. There is still debate as to how far this was the case in the beginning and what roles women played in the varied Jesus movements that diverged from the current that happened to evolve into Christianity.[4] On the other hand, even within the millstream that successfully claimed orthodoxy, women were not excluded from partaking in the Christian community—from baptism, participation in the Eucharist, the hope for eternal salvation and divine grace—nor from the triumph of martyrdom or living a life of ascetic rigor. Women and men were equally welcome in heaven (and hell); in principle, salvation and sin had no gender.

Nevertheless, we have to ask whether those women who excelled as Christians—by enduring martyrdom, by mortification of the body, or by ascetic withdrawal—were allowed to retain their female gender and to what extent their achievements were either caused by or led to a change of gender. Many of the great martyrs and ascetics (both legendary and historical) who would become role models for later religious women either became masculine or, at least, were perceived to have overcome the supposed weakness of their female sex.[5] We read this not only in the report of the passion of Perpetua, who was slaughtered at the beginning of the third century under Emperor Septimius Severus (she may have been a historical figure), but also in the lives written about the repenting prostitute Pelagia, the desert mother Sarah, and Melania, the Roman matron who gave away one of the greatest fortunes ever accumulated in the Roman Empire. All of them (and many others) are described as surrendering their own gender for the greater good. This shows us, on the one hand, how permeable gender boundaries could be. On the other hand, it raises the suspicion that there was a powerful Christian discourse that accepted only one (masculine) gender of the holy, which may have been applicable both to those who were born male and to anyone who is willing to abandon "his" womanhood.

Rich matrons, noble ladies, and members of royal houses are those whose names and stories we know today. Hardly anyone else could afford to live a life of chastity, virginity, and seclusion or to follow the rules written for medieval monasteries. What we tend to call religious *women* refers, in fact, to a tiny minority within ancient and medieval societies. Theirs was a very "classy" gender—probably more than that of religious men.

These women were well educated as well as well born. Some holy men were acclaimed for their lack of worldly knowledge, but holy simplicity was not an aspiration of holy women. Most were praised for their education, learning, and knowledge of biblical texts and the works of the "holy fathers." None of the works of biblical exegesis or moral exhortation that addressed a female audience or were commissioned by women was "dumbed down." Religious women may have needed to turn themselves into men in order to endure martyrdom or suffer through a life in the desert, but none of them had to overcome the weakness of her sex in order to gain wisdom and knowledge.

That said, our sources often seem to lack appreciation for women's intellectual contributions. For example, *On Illustrious Men*, the bio-bibliography of Christian theologians, historians, and hagiographers compiled by Jerome (d.420) and continued by the priest Gennadius of Marseille (d. *c*.495), speaks exclusively about illustrious *men*; women are mentioned only as observers. The most notorious examples of women as learned but supposedly unproductive participants in Christian intellectual life are Paula (d.404) and Julia Eustochium (d.420), two aristocratic Roman ladies. They probably should be credited, along with Jerome for producing the Vulgate (the Latin translation of the Hebrew Bible and the Greek New Testament that became widely used throughout the Middle Ages). Paula and Eustochium were, after all, at least as proficient in the biblical languages as was Jerome himself.

A slightly later example of silencing female authorship is the *Regula Caesarii ad virgines* (*Caesarius's Rule for Virgins*), the "mother" of all monastic rules for nuns and a highly ambivalent manifesto of female enclosure and male exclusion. Was it really Bishop Caesarius of Arles (d.542) who wrote and constantly revised this text, or was it a product of collaboration first with his sister and later with his niece, the first two abbesses of his monastic foundation?[6] We can ask that question more generally: in which forms did women partake in the production of texts about women? Katrinette Bodarwé and Rosamond McKitterick have weaned us from the assumption that the "Anonymous" or "Pseudo-," who was by far the most prolific Christian writer, was by default a man.[7] There is, to conclude, no need for modern scholarship to defend or prove the intelligence and learnedness of religious women.

A HISTORY OF ONE'S OWN

Christianity has long struggled with a tension between the spiritual equality of women and men and the general practice of excluding women from official roles in the Christian cult. But there is also another tension: between reality and its perception, between the history of religious women and men as it manifests itself in the "unintentional stage décor" mentioned above and the ways in which religious men and women imagined their roots and constructed their identities.

One of the most persistent (but also misleading) *topoi* in monastic origin myths is that of the "little sister," or sometimes niece or cousin. Almost every important monastic founder is described as having a female relative following in his footsteps. Pachomius (d.346), the father of Egyptian monasticism, organized a female community for his sister Maria, as did Ambrose (d.397), Augustine (d.430), Shenoute of Atrippe (d. c.450), Romanus and Lupicinus (the founders of the Jura monasteries), and Leander of Seville (d. 601) for their sisters. Caesarius had his two Caesarias (his sister and his niece), Boniface (d.754) his Leoba (not his sister but probably a relative); it would be easy to continue this line far into the Middle Ages. If a great monastic founder did not have a "little sister," tradition needed to invent one. This is the case for Honoratus (d.492), the founder of Lérins, John Cassian (d.435), and Benedict of Nursia (d. c.550). "Big sisters" are less common, but they exist as well; after all, Anthony (d.356) became the father of monasticism *after* he had placed his sister (who may have been older, but we do not know) into some sort of a convent,[8] and the great Basil (d.379) followed the footsteps of his sister Macrina (d.379) when he fulfilled his monastic aspirations.[9]

The "big brothers," most of our sources suggest, created a variant of their own monastic project that was adjusted to the supposedly weaker condition of women and to their different social place: the nuns' spiritual handicap of being unable to perform the sacraments, the special precautions that were necessary to safeguard their virginity and reputation (usually by applying stricter modes of separation and enclosure) and the need to find others to work in the fields or to oversee the economic functions of female monasteries. This "big brother" motif shaped how monks and nuns generally understood their own history: female monastic institutions grew like ribs from a male monastic backbone. Women's monasticisms may, at times, have been almost equal in status, but they were seen as mere variants of a current male monastic mainstream, basically sharing its history, traditions, and origin myths. In the beginning were the named and unnamed, historical and legendary holy *fathers*: Anthony, Paul the Hermit, Benedict, Columbanus, Macharius, Pachomius, among others. It would be worthwhile to reread late antique and medieval sources on female monasticism, inclining one's ear to the voices claiming that nuns, female ascetics, and anchorites have a history of their own—maybe one in which "founding mothers" such as Thecla, Perpetua, Melania, or the ever-patient Julia Eustochium held a place along with the ubiquitous "holy fathers."

Distinct female monastic voices might also wait to be heard in the transmission and arrangement of texts in manuscripts. For example, several collections of monastic rules and ascetic treatises organize their content in male and female sections, implying that there was a gendered monastic identity.[10] Some collections of saints' lives and other monastic narrative texts are arranged along gender lines as well; others adopt different ordering criteria. In all cases, the arrangements of texts in these manuscripts tell gendered stories, and historians have just begun to listen.[11]

The Traps of Narratives

If we are really interested in the invention of monasticism, the myth of the "desert fathers" and their little sisters have little historical value. The "desert we came from" is—to a large extent—a desert in the mind of monastic reformers of the beginning of the ninth century or a desert imagined by nervous seventeenth-century Benedictine monks who reshaped their institutional past to fend off the challenges of Protestantism and Counter-Reformation. The achievements of Carolingian monks in preserving most of the Latin sources on the origins of monasticism and the merits of scholars such as Jean Mabillon (d.1707) for shaping the modern historian's craft are appreciable, but the "story" they evoke remains a story told from an exclusively male perspective with an agenda rooted in their own world. As such, these stories eventually tell more about the Carolingian monastic reforms or about post-Reformation Catholicism than about the subject matter itself.

Still, Mabillon and other scholars of the seventeenth and eighteenth centuries, such as Herribert Rosweyde (d.1629), Lucas Holstenius (d.1661), Jean Bolland (d.1665), or Bernhard Pez (d.1735), are the giants on whose shoulders we stand—not only because they provided the narrative that is still in our heads and textbooks, but also because they created the textual canon, as well as its genres, on which we still rely today. Rosweyde published in 1629 a collection of Latin monastic short narratives and aphorisms of desert fathers (*verba seniorum*), and saints' lives under the title *Liber vitae patrum* (*The Book of the Lives of the Fathers*), following the arrangements that can be found in Carolingian manuscripts; reprinted in Migne's *Patrologia Latina*, it has not yet entirely been replaced by modern editions. In this collection, most prominent among the few depictions of female ascetic life is a series of lives of Mary of Egypt, Pelagia, and Thaïs. All of them are repenting "harlots."[12] A woman's path to religious life seems to have been more arduous and prone to scandal. Is this Rosweyde's view, the view of Carolingian reformers, or something approaching the authentic experiences of early Christian women? A gendered view of early monasticism and the emergence of religious life needs to take note of these veils and to learn to look behind them. It belongs to the achievements of feminist, postmodern and queer scholarship, literary criticism, and new historicism to have taken the power out of these old paradigms and created new frames of reference.[13] Yet occasionally these new approaches shape new curtains tightly woven by impenetrable fanciful jargon.

THREE WAYS OF GIVING RELIGIOUS WOMEN A PLACE (IN THE MARGIN)

One starting point for lifting the curtains that may be blurring our view of "the gender of the religious" is to look closer at the discursive methods that determine the place of female religious life. I suggest that medieval monastic sources deploy three principal techniques of defining the relation between male and female religious life. These discursive techniques emerged quite early and developed a life of their own throughout the Middle Ages. For all three of them, Gennadius of Marseilles' *On Illustrious Men* provides suitable examples. This text includes short biographical sketches of three fathers of monasticism: Pachomius (d.346), Evagrius Ponticus (d.399), and John Cassian (d.435), and each of these sketches can serve as case study.

First, monastic discipline was regarded as in principle applicable to communities of men and women alike, even though it is still the male theme with female variations. Gennadius describes Pachomius as the "founder of the monasteries of Egypt" and adds that "he wrote a Rule suitable for both sorts of monks."[14] Other texts about Pachomius corroborate that "both sorts of monks" refers to male and female monks.[15] There are several later instances of applying one rule to both male and female communities. Bishop Aurelian of Arles (d.545), for example, wrote one rule that is preserved in versions for both genders. These two versions show minor differences, for example with regard to priestly duties (only applicable to monks) or with regard to preventing occasions of sexual contact between members of the community (also omitted in the version for nuns). The *Rule of Benedict*, which in the ninth century became the legal basis for monastic life, was then applied to women as well and is preserved in several different female versions.[16]

Second, some took a different approach to male and female religious life. Gennadius reports that Evagrius Ponticus wrote, among other works, a "teaching text for cenobites and monks in groups that was suitable for communal life, and for a sacred woman a little book adjusted to her piety and sex."[17] This is one of the rare instances of one author writing different treatises for religious women and men. His *Sayings for Monks* (*Proverbia ad monachos*), a collection of 137 sayings modeled after the collections of Proverbs in the Bible, describe monastic life as a continuous striving for "wisdom," "knowledge," and "prudence" (*sapientia, scientia*, and *prudentia*) and as a neverending battle against sinful thoughts and temptations. The monk's weapons are ascetic discipline and abstinence. It is an individual battle for which the community provides the most suitable framework.

The other text, his *Instructions for a Virgin*, has an entirely different emphasis. Wisdom and knowledge hardly play a role, and the individual battle for perfection is replaced by the requirement to follow precepts, especially on segregation from the sinful world, and on acting in moderation. Protecting virginity and chastity (both of the body and the mind) play, according to Evagrius, a crucial role in a religious woman's life.[18] It would be a crude oversimplification to assume that Evagrius's monks were supposed to become smart (his notion of *scientia* and *sapientia* has little to do with our notion of knowledge and wisdom) while nuns were simply supposed to be obedient and enclosed and to protect their virginity, but it is clear that Evagrius handled two different frameworks for male and female ascetics. For him, there was no "unisex monasticism."

Evagrius's *Sayings for Monks* appear relatively often in medieval manuscripts (about twenty are known), while his *Instruction for a Virgin* is preserved only in four copies. Yet if we look at the impact of the ideas expressed in these texts, we get the reverse impression. Individual striving for wisdom through ascetic discipline did not become the ground from which medieval monasticism emerged, but Evagrius's exhortations to women found many echoes in later ideas directed at and adopted by both sexes, of: performative virginity, seclusion, clear-cut boundaries, and controlled contact with the outside world. If we would establish a genealogy of monastic discipline, Evagrius's letter to a veiled virgin would figure more prominently than the treatise he wrote for monks.[19]

Third, John Cassian exemplifies an approach so centered on men that women almost disappear. Cassian was a student of Evagrius and belonged to the last ascetic theologians who understood monastic life as an individual striving for perfection. The author of two all-important monastic treatises, the *Conferences* (*Collationes*) and the *Institutions*, he claims to offer the authoritative adaptation of the Egyptian monastic ideal to local circumstances of Gaul. In his works, women's monastic life is not addressed at all. His ascetic world was truly male-only and did not even give access to those who were willing to give up their female gender.

Cassian was not alone. Benedict, the father of Western monasticism, may have had a younger sister, but the author of the *Rule of Benedict* wrote an ascetic program that did not have anything to say to religious women, even though it was later adapted for nuns. None of the rules, letters, or sermons written by the Irish monastic reformer Columbanus (d.614) contains references to the religious women. For these three monastic founding fathers religious women were of no concern, despite all their claims to formulate universal monastic ideals.

The fact that women did *not* exist in the minds of some of the monastic founding fathers (aside from constituting a danger and causing anxiety) is less remarkable than the observation that none of them got away with it. The *Rule of Benedict* had already been rewritten twice in the seventh century as a rule of nuns, once by Bishop Donatus of Besançon (d. *c.*660), and once by an anonymous author (whose gender we do not know). These two female rules are actually the oldest witnesses for the existence of Benedict's Rule, much older than the first preserved manuscripts of the supposedly original text. Columbanus founded three monasteries for monks and none for nuns, but his successors (including the author of his *Life*) were all too eager to turn his monastic ideal into one that appealed to the entire audience of Frankish nobility, male and female. They founded such important Merovingian female monasteries as Remiremont, Chelles, and Faremoutiers.

It is not difficult to find medieval monastic founders who shaped monastic models for monks only, and to tell monastic history as an exclusively male history, ignoring "the other sort of monks," if we speak in Gennadius's terms. But those who aimed at applying their ideas and bringing them into practice usually regarded this exclusion as an error to be corrected quietly. It would be worthwhile to write a history focusing only on the specific constellations in which monastic ideals *went* unisex. Some of these constellations are discussed in the next section.

Was the First Medieval Monk a Woman?

Pachomius, Aurelian, and those revising Benedict or Columbanus may stand for different ways of "gendering" monastic discourse and creating the notion of "unisex" monasticism built upon male models. What happens if we question their shared assumption of a "male monastic backbone" and go back to the sources? Does the notion that "we (monks) are coming from the desert and you (nuns) just do it our way" hold, or is it possible to tell the story in a different way? Medieval monasticism not only emerged in a process of constant give-and-take between female and male monastic models (and their textual representations) but also, in many regards, owed more to the tradition of sacred virgins and widows than to the desert fathers. Medieval monks and nuns have, to put it metaphorically, more in common with Jerome's friend, the virgin Paula, than with the "first hermit," Paul of Thebes, one of Jerome's hagiographic creations.

We would expect that female monastic texts were generally revisions and adaptations of those written by monks (such as in the case of the *Rules of Pachomius, Aurelian,* and *Benedict*), but sometimes it happened the other way around. Aside from the *Regula Benedicti*, the most influential programmatic monastic text was the *Rule for Virgins* for which Caesarius of Arles claimed authorship.[20] This text blends the tradition and experiences of urban sacred virgins and widows with Augustine's monastic rules and Caesarius's own rather ambivalent monastic experience as a monk in the monastery Lérins (one of the first monastic communities in Gaul, founded as an attempt to emulate the ideal of Egyptian desert monasticism). Caesarius had begun his career as an overly zealous monk who left Lérins after his ascetic standards had caused trouble—an experience that made him consider whether there were options for a monastic life that was not determined by ascetic rigor. The monastery for women that he founded in Arles served as a sort of laboratory for finding such alternatives. The *Rule for Virgins*, which was extended and rewritten over a period of almost thirty years, can be read as a laboratory report for his monastic experiment. It is likely that he regarded its results as suitable for male monastic communities as well. His successor, Aurelian (d.551), used this text as the basis for his *Rule* for monks and nuns. Another bishop, Ferriolus of Uzès (d.581), inserted parts of Caesarius's *Rule* into his *Rule for Monks*. The *Regula Tarnatensis*, an anonymous rule from the same period, also closely follows the structure and often the wording of Caesarius's text. All three of these rules for monks did not acknowledge that they were, at least partly, inspired by female monastic practice.[21]

Before Caesarius (and possibly his sister and niece) composed the *Rule for Virgins*, Caesarius had written a "proto-rule," a lengthy exhortatory letter addressed to Caesaria and her community. This letter was an admonition to preserve the nuns' virginity (of the body and the mind) and avoid any uncontrolled contact with men outside the monastery. It can be placed in one line with other admonitions to virgins, such as the aforementioned *Instruction for a Virgin* by Evagrius Ponticus or some of the grumpy letters of Jerome to his female friends. Yet the vast majority of manuscripts in which Caesarius's letter is preserved provide a version that addressed monks instead of nuns. This male adaptation of a praise of virginity and constant mutual supervision changed only the grammatical gender of the original addressed to nuns.[22]

Reusing texts is important; even more important is adapting ideas. Turning Caesarius's letter into a letter to monks reflects how a female monastic ideal, that of protected virginity under careful custody, entered a general monastic discourse. It eventually replaced the ideal of the battle for chastity by a more convenient ideal: monasteries populated by male (or female) virgins who performed their lifelong chastity by observing their rules, by mutual control, and by separation from the outside world. John Cassian was among the last monastic theologians to describe ascetic life in the old terms of monasteries as communities of monks engaged in a battle against their unceasing sexual desire, tormented by erotic dreams and ashamed of nocturnal pollutions and spontaneous erections.[23] After him, this discourse faded away, and sexuality transformed from an attribute of human sinfulness to a manageable opposite of virginity, which could be protected through monastic discipline. John Cassian, with his *Conferences* and his *Institutes*, represents the past, and Caesarius, with his *Rule for Virgins*, the future. Virginity was in a way "hijacked" by monks.[24]

Caesarius's *Rule for Virgins* contains three other fundamental innovations. It was the first monastic program to impose a strict enclosure on its community. After having entered the monastery, a nun was not allowed to leave the monastic confines under any circumstances, and any access from outsiders (especially men) had to be reduced to a minimum. It secondly created the idea of a monastery as a holy community—*congregatio sancta* or *grex sancta* (holy congregation or holy flock)—capable of collectively performing intercessory prayer for the outside world. And third, the Rule itself became an unchangeable holy text with a legal function, a *regula sancta* (holy rule). All three innovations percolated far beyond female communities alone.

Caesarius's ideal of total enclosure (instead of simply keeping one's monastic vows) mostly affected female monastic life. When female monasticism was addressed in the context of monastic reforms, it was often in an attempt to reinforce enclosure according to Caesarius's model.[25] Yet I would argue that Caesarius's concept of enclosure did have an impact beyond the realm of female monasticism.[26] Almost every monastery prescribes some degree of enclosure, and we tend to take the sacredness of monastic confines for granted. The notion of the monastery as sacred and inaccessible space, however, entered monastic tradition at a relatively late stage, and was not rooted in its desert origins. Desert monasteries had walls for their protection, but there is no indication that their founders regarded monastic space as particularly holy. Lérins, the island outpost of Egyptian monasticism in Southern Gaul, was described as the "Island of Saints" but rarely as a "Holy Island." The *Rule of Benedict* pays some attention to organizing and ordering monastic space, but there is no indication that this space carried spiritual meaning in itself. For Western monasticism, one of the turning points in developing the notion of the monastery as a sacred space was the monastic reform movement instigated by the followers of Columbanus in the first half of the seventh century. It is arguable that Caesarius's experiment served as one of the sources of inspiration, since his concept of enclosure and Columbanus's notion of the *septa secreta* (separated space) show striking similarities—and Columbanian monks did know Caesarius's *Rule*.

A crucial function of monasteries throughout the Middle Ages was the production of intercessory prayer, that is, prayer for the remission of sins and the eternal salvation of donors and their families as well as for political stability, prosperity, and the protection of rulers and their dynasties. Medieval monasteries did not sustain themselves by producing beer and honey, but by prolifically manufacturing prayer. Despite the nuns' inability to perform votive masses by themselves, their virginal prayer was by no means regarded as less valuable than that of monks. The quality of prayer was largely determined by the purity of those praying. For this reason alone it was necessary to "reconceptualize" monks and nuns as virgins, or at least as bearers of an undisputed chastity, instead of individuals who willingly admitted that by default they were *not* chaste, because they understood true chastity as a goal that could only be approached in a lifelong battle, but never fully achieved.

Collective intercessory prayer did not emerge from the desert. There, individual "holy men" may have served as intercessors between earthly disputants and also between God and the sinful Christian individual.[27] The intercession was personal and charismatic. Nothing about the desert fathers suggests that an entire group of monks assume such intercessory service. One of the earliest references to a monastic community supporting the outside world through prayer appears in the context of Caesarius's community of virgins. The *Life of Caesarius* tells how the besieged city of Arles was defended by the prayer of Caesarius's nuns, and Caesarius begs the nuns several times in his Rule to pray for him, a sinner polluted by the world the nuns had left for good.[28] A community of women thus started what would become the daily bread of monks and nuns throughout the Middle Ages.

Third, female monastic practice might undergird the basic economic frameworks of monastic life. A community of desert dwellers living by humble labor is a far cry from medieval monastic houses sustained by the possession of fields, vineyards, villages, and serfs, not to mention episcopal privileges and royal immunities. An informal desert community is also very different from one governed under a rule understood as a legal text. If we believe Athanasius's *Life of Saint Antony*, his hero gave away all his possessions and withdrew to the desert while placing his sister in a well-established female religious community. One could say that medieval monasteries stand in the tradition of Anthony's sister rather than Anthony himself.

Caesarius of Arles' main concerns, aside from ensuring enclosure, were physical protection and discipline in his female community and safeguarding the legal and economic situation of his foundation. After all, its survival depended on an outside world that respected boundaries, as well as on a steady stream of material support. Both aspects were, to a large extent, legal matters. After several futile attempts, Caesarius succeeded in the year 515 in obtaining a privilege from Pope Hormisdas that protected the monastery's independence and property.[29] This charter—for a female monastery—was the first of its sort and inspired later grants of privileges for other monasteries, male as well as female.

A last example: Benedict of Aniane (d.821), the great Carolingian monastic reformer, wrote a commentary on the *Rule of Benedict*, the *Concordia Regularum* (*Concordance of Rules*).[30] Following along the *Rule of Benedict*, Benedict of Aniane groups together fragments on the same topic from other monastic rules, both male and female. In recasting these excerpts, Benedict of Aniane turned every section from rules for nuns into the male grammatical form. Benedict was not very passionate about reforming female monasticism, but he was very interested in what the female monastic tradition had to say, and he had no problem applying the experience of female communities to monks. He was especially fascinated with an anonymous seventh-century revision of the *Rule of Benedict*, the *Regula cuiusdam ad virgines* (*Someone's Rule for Virgins*) This text is almost entirely incorporated in his *Concordance of Rules*.

These appropriations of female monastic experience show that it is necessary to scrutinize the traditions of monastic practices as they are proclaimed in medieval sources and to contrast them with evidence found outside the established narratives. It would be fruitful to write the history of religious life as a genealogy of concepts and ideals, one that is open to finding their roots in unexpected places, and more often than not, in female monastic tradition.

Diversity and Unification

Almost every attempt to organize monastic life produced something new and different, despite all the rhetoric of forming part of a tradition, restoring the old, and following a the texts of the "holy fathers." Therefore, the abstract term *monasticism* should be used, if ever, in the plural, certainly for the period before the ninth century, when the *Rule of Benedict* became promoted as the standard for all monasteries. Medieval authors were probably more aware of this diversity than modern scholars. The adjective "monastic" (*monasticus/a/um*) and expressions such as "monastic life" (*vita monastica*) or "monastic discipline" (*disciplina monastica*) rarely appear in medieval texts. In the *Patrologia Latina Database*, the most important repository of theological texts written before the thirteenth century, the expression "life according to the rule" (*vita regularis*) and the label "Benedictine" (*benedictinus/a/um*) appear only in the comments written by the modern editors, not in the sources themselves. Modern scholars of medieval monasticism usually apply these expressions as if they had stable and clear meanings. They might know what these expressions mean, but I do not.

Historians of our time have been, however, not entirely alone in their attempts to create (in their case, retrospectively) a unity within the diversity of monastic life. The history of Christian religious life swings like a pendulum between a unifying urge for reform and a tendency toward diversification, radicalization, or supposed "decline." Pursuing a purer religious life often became a subversive activity, setting standards higher than those required—and lived—by priests and bishops; these more radical forms of religious life had to be rendered unthreatening to ecclesiastical institutions and incorporated into them. For monks, the Council of Chalcedon held in 451 was critical, as it placed monasteries under the control of local bishops, made monastic vows irreversible, and bound the foundation of new monasteries to episcopal consent.[31] Much of what the fathers of Chalcedon imposed on monks had been applied to religious women since biblical times. Controlling, supervising, and sustaining religious women always belonged to the core responsibilities of bishops, and turning monks and ascetics into "nuns" appeared to be an effective way to rid them of their seditious potential.

Later attempts to standardize and regulate the life of the religious did not necessarily take place at the same time for men and for women, and they were not equally successful. When Caesarius tried to submit the religious women of his city to a life in enclosure under the "Holy Rule," he may have produced an immensely influential prototype of monastic life, but he did not succeed in his primary objective. To his dismay, some religious women in Arles chose not to enter his monastery, and this is not only the case for sixth-century Arles. There was throughout the Middle Ages a steady undercurrent of female religious life outside the structures of monastic institutions: in domestic settings, in chaste marriages, as recluses, hermits, canonesses, etc.[32] Women (or rather the "classy gender" mentioned in the beginning of this essay) had less influence but more choices, and the two are closely interrelated.

The holy men who lived in caves and cages, or as secret monks with coarse hair shirts under courtly garments, or as unwashed desert dwellers, had become by the eighth century a matter of the past and a literary topos not to be emulated. For religious men, thereafter, the choice was reduced to either entering a clerical career or joining a proper monastery. To eliminate everything apart from these two options was the first major objective of the Carolingian monastic reforms. People who chose not to fit in, such as the wandering apostles Aldebert and Clemens (active in the mid-eighth century) or the fugitive monk Gottschalk (d. c.860), might in previous centuries have had a chance of sainthood and fame, but Carolingians regarded them as outlaws and heretics.

Carolingian monastic reformers, who to a large extent shaped the prevalent monastic institutions of the Middle Ages, could—and probably did—learn a lot from what Caesarius of Arles had begun 250 years earlier. But they were not very interested in female monastic life. What an individual religious woman did and how a community of religious women organized itself concerned them less than the project of controlling and unifying those (mostly male) monastic institutions that were supposed to be multifunctional, supporting pillars of the Carolingian state.

CONCLUSION

The monastic reforms conducted under Charlemagne and his son Louis the Pious in the first half of the ninth century can be regarded as a turning point. In bringing to a close the formative or experimental phase of Western monasticism, they introduced much more defined roles for religious women and men. I propose that we avoid projecting these more solidifying post-Carolingian notions of the "gender of the religious"—or maybe even notions of gender and gender roles in general—back into this "experimental" phase.

This does not mean, however, that the story told here ends with the Carolingians. Pastoral care and religious authority had become an exclusively male domain (certainly after the Fourth Lateran Council in 1215), but its object remained nongendered, as were the norms and concepts of morality. Neither virtues nor vices and sins have a gender. The strict requirement that every Christian individual had to confess and receive the Eucharist at least once a year, which formed the basis for the "pastoral revolution" of the thirteenth and fourteenth centuries, began with the words "To every faithful person of either sex" (*Omnis utriusque sexus fidelis*).

FURTHER READING

Bodarwé, Katrinette. *Sanctimoniales litteratae: Schriftlichkeit und Bildung in den ottonischen Frauenkommunitäten Gandersheim, Essen und Quedlinburg*. Münster: Aschendorff, 2004.

Brown, Peter. *The Body and Society: Men, Women, and Sexual Renunciation in Early Christianity*, 2nd edn. New York: Columbia University Press, 2008.

Coon, Lynda L. *Dark Age Bodies: Gender and Monastic Practice in the Early Medieval West*. Philadelphia, PA: University of Pennsylvania Press, 2011.

Diem, Albrecht. *Das monastische Experiment: Die Rolle der Keuschheit bei der Entstehung des westlichen Klosterwesens*. Münster: LIT-Verlag, 2005.

Elm, Susanna. *"Virgins of God": The Making of Asceticism in Late Antiquity*. Oxford: Clarendon Press, 1994.

Hamburger, Jeffrey and Susan Marti, eds. *Crown and Veil: Female Monasticism from the Fifth to the Fifteenth Centuries*. New York: Columbia University Press, 2008.

Müller, Anne and Gert Melville, eds. *Female vita religiosa between Late Antiquity and the High Middle Ages. Structures, Developments and Spatial Contexts*. Münster; Berlin: LIT-Verlag, 2011.

McKitterick, Rosamond. "Nuns' Scriptoria in England and Francia in the Eighth Century," *Francia*, 19 (1) (1992): 1–35.

McNamara, Jo Ann. *Sisters in Arms: Catholic Nuns through Two Millennia*. Cambridge, Mass.; London: Harvard University Press, 1996.

Rapp, Claudia. "Figures of Female Sanctity: Byzantine Edifying Manuscripts and their Audience," *Dumbarton Oaks Papers*, 50 (1996): 313–44.

Schulenburg, Jane Tibbets. *Forgetful of their Sex: Female Sanctity and Society, ca. 500–1100*. Chicago: Chicago University Press, 1998.

NOTES

1. An exception is Nira Pancer, "Au delà du sex et du genre: L'indiffération des sexes en milieu monastique (VIᵉ–VIIᵉ siècles)," *Revue de l'histoire des religions*, 219 (3) (2002), 299–323.

2. Lynda L. Coon, *Dark Age Bodies: Gender and Monastic Practice in the Early Medieval West* (Philadelphia; Oxford: University of Pennsylvania Press, 2011), provides a thought-provoking study of the male body of the religious.

3. On the history of religious women, see especially Jo Ann McNamara, *Sisters in Arms: Catholic Nuns through Two Millennia* (Cambridge, Mass.; London: Harvard University Press, 1996); Jane Tibbetts Schulenburg, *Forgetful of Their Sex: Female Sanctity and Society, ca. 500–1100* (Chicago: University of Chicago Press, 1998).

4. Peter Brown, *The Body and Society: Men, Women, and Sexual Renunciation in Early Christianity*, 2nd edn (New York: Columbia University Press, 2008).

5. Gilian Cloke, *This Female Man of God: Women and Spiritual Power in the Patristic Age, AD 350–450* (London; New York: Routledge, 1995).

6. Lindsay Rudge discusses this idea in her PhD thesis *Texts and Contexts: Women's Dedicated Life from Caesarius to Benedict*, University of St Andrews, 2007. Her thesis is not yet published but it is available online.

7. Katrinette Bodarwé, *Sanctimoniales litteratae: Schriftlichkeit und Bildung in den ottonischen Frauenkommunitäten Gandersheim, Essen und Quedlinburg*, Quellen und Studien, 10 (Münster: Aschendorff, 2004); Rosamond McKitterick, "Nuns' Scriptoria in England and Francia in the Eight Century," *Francia*, 19 (1) (1992): 1–35.

8. Athanasius, *Life of Anthony*, ch. 3 (Greek version), trans. Tim Vivian and Apostolos N. Athanassaki (Kalamazoo MI: Cistercian Publications, 2003), 61: "His sister he entrusted to well-known and faithful virgins, giving her to them to be raised in virginity…"

9. Susanna Elm, *"Virgins of God": The Making of Asceticism in Late Antiquity* (Oxford: Clarendon Press, 1994), 25–105.

10. Three examples: Munich, Bayerische Staatsbibliothek Clm 28118, saec. IXⁱⁿ; Vatican, Biblioteca Apostolica Vaticana, Reg. lat. 140, saec. VIIIᵉˣ; El Escorial, I.III.13, saec. IX/X; Bamberg, Staatsbibliothek 142, saec. Xᵉˣ. Only the manuscript containing Benedict of Aniane's *Codex Regularum* has been studied thoroughly.

11. Claudia Rapp provides a pioneer study on Byzantine hagiographic manuscripts: "Figures of Female Sanctity: Byzantine Edifying Manuscripts and Their Audience," *Dumbarton Oaks Papers*, 50 (1996): 313–44.

12. The Latin expression *meretrix* has a much broader meaning than what we would consider a "sex worker" today. See also Patricia Cox Miller, "Is There a Harlot in This Text? Hagiography and the Grotesque," in Dale B. Martin and Patricia Cox Miller, eds, *The Cultural Turn in Late Ancient Studies: Gender, Asceticism and Hagiography* (Raleigh, NC: Duke University Press, 2005), 87–102.

13. See, for example, Virginia Burrus, *The Sex Life of Saints: An Erotics of Ancient Hagiography* (Philadelphia: University of Pennsylvania Press, 2004); John Kitchen, *Saint's Lives and the Rhetoric of Gender: Male and Female in Merovingian Hagiography* (Oxford: Oxford University Press, 1998).

14. Gennadius of Marseille, *De viris inlustribus*, in Carl Albrecht Bernoulli, ed., *Hieronymus und Gennadius: De viris inlustribus* (Freiburg: Mohr/Paul Siebeck, 1895), 63, no. VII.

15. On Pachomius's female foundations living under the same rule, see Palladius, *Lausiac History*, ch. 33.1, trans. Armand Veilleux, in idem, *Pachomian Koinonia* (Kalamazoo,

Mich.: Cistercian Publications, 1981), 2: 129: "They also have a monastery of about four hundred women, with the same constitution and the same way of life, except for the goat skin."

16. Katrinette Bodarwé, "Eine Männerregel für Frauen: Die Adaption der Benediktsregel vom 9. bis 10. Jahrhundert," in Anne Müller and Gert Melville, eds, *Female vita religiosa between Late Antiquity and the High Middle Ages: Structures, Developments and Spatial Contexts* (Münster; Berlin: LIT-Verlag, 2011), 235–72.

17. Gennadius of Marseille, *De viris inlustirbus*, 64–65, no. XI.

18. Evagrius's *Sayings for Monks* are available in an English translation by Jeremy Driscoll, *Evagrius Ponticus: ad monachos* (New York: Newman Press, 2003). There is no English translation of *Instruction for a Virgin*. The text is edited by André Wilmart, "Les versions latines des sentences d'Evagre pour les vierges," *Revue Bénédictine*, 28 (1911): 143–53.

19. Albrecht Diem, *Das monastische Experiment: Die Rolle der Keuschheit bei der Entstehung des westlichen Klosterwesens* (Münster: LIT-Verlag, 2005), 54–62; Susanna Elm, "Evagrius Ponticus' *Sententiae ad Virginem*," *Dumbarton Oaks Papers*, 45 (1991): 97–120.

20. This seminal text is available in an excellent English translation by Maria Caritas McCarthy, *The Rule for Nuns of St. Caesarius of Arles: A Translation with a Critical Introduction* (Washington, DC: Catholic University of America Press, 1960).

21. For an overview of monastic rules, see Adalbert de Vogüé, *Les règles monastiques anciennes (400–700)* (Turnhout: Brepols Publishers, 1985).

22. For a translation, see William E. Klingshirn, *Caesarius of Arles: Life, Testament, Letters* (Liverpool: Liverpool University Press, 1994), 129–39.

23. On this topic, see David Brakke, "The Problematization of Nocturnal Emissions in Early Christian Syria, Egypt, and Gaul," *Journal of Early Christian Studies*, 3 (1995): 419–60; Jacqueline Murray, "Men's Bodies, Men's Minds: Seminal Emissions and Sexual Anxiety in the Middle Ages," *Annual Review of Sex Research*, 8 (1997): 1–26.

24. This idea is discussed in depth in Diem, *Das monastische Experiment*.

25. Jane Tibbetts Schulenburg, "Strict Active Enclosure and its Effects on the Female Monastic Experience (c. 500–1100)," in John A. Nichols and Lillian Thomas Shank, eds, *Medieval Religious Women*, vol. 1: *Distant Echoes* (Kalamazoo: Cistercian Publications, 1984), 51–86.

26. Pancer, "Au delà du sex et du genre," 302–307.

27. Peter Brown, "The Rise and the Function of the Holy Man," *Journal of Roman Studies*, 61 (1971): 80–101.

28. *Life of Caesarius*, book 1, ch. 28, trans. Klingshirn, *Caesarius of Arles*, 22: "The man of God formulated the idea by divine inspiration from the ever-reigning Lord that the church of Arles should be adorned and the city protected not only with countless troops of clergy but also by choirs of virgins."

29. Klingshirn, trans., *Caesarius of Arles*, 120–22.

30. Benedict of Aniane, *Concordia Regularum*, ed. Pierre Bonnerue, *Corpus Christianorum Series Latina*, 168/168a (Turnhout: Brepols, 1999).

31. Canons of the Council of Chalcedon, chs 4, 7, 8, 16, 24, trans. Richard Price and Michael Gaddis, *The Acts of the Council of Chalcedon* (Liverpool: Liverpool University Press, 2005), 3: 95–102.

32. As Anneke Mulder-Bakker notes in this volume, Chapter 29, and in her *Lives of the Anchoresses: The Rise of the Urban Recluse in Medieval Europe* (Philadelphia: University of Pennsylvania Press, 2005).

....

CHAPTER 28

WOMEN AND REFORM IN THE
CENTRAL MIDDLE AGES

....

FIONA J. GRIFFITHS

IN his early twelfth-century biography of Pope Gregory VII—the pope most closely identified with reform of the church during the central Middle Ages—the German priest Paul of Bernried highlighted the visions of a little-known laywoman, Herluca of Epfach. Described by Paul as a "virgin dedicated to God," Herluca appeared in his account as an ardent supporter of Gregory's efforts to purify the church, a visionary who "did much to encourage Gregorian obedience." Paul depicted Herluca as a particular advocate of Gregory's campaign against clerical marriage. Reporting one vision in which a bloodied Christ appeared to Herluca, Paul presented her interpretation that Christ's sufferings had been brought on by clerical immorality. Herluca subsequently refused consecrated bread offered by unchaste priests (among them Richard, the priest at Epfach) and was divinely rewarded for her public fidelity to the Gregorian reform: in lieu of the consecrated bread, Herluca received a sweet taste in her mouth, a spiritual gift granted to her, as Paul notes, through the "wonderful generosity" of God.[1]

Paul's reference to Herluca's visions was not incidental: shortly after he had completed his now-famous biography of Gregory, Paul began work on a life of Herluca herself (composed *c.* 1130/1). Paul knew Herluca well and clearly admired her; he reported that he had visited her several times at Epfach, the informal community of religious women that grew up around her. The two were also reunited some years later, at Bernried, a newly founded house of regular canons in the diocese of Augsburg. When Herluca was forced to leave Epfach ("by the madness of wicked peasants," as Paul wrote), she retired to Bernried, where Paul, a reformer who had fled Regensburg at about the same time, found temporary refuge. Paul's biography of Herluca was dedicated to the canons at Bernried, where Herluca died sometime around 1127.[2]

Paul's biography of Gregory is a central text of the church reform movement, a document that provides important information concerning Gregory himself and that highlights the efforts of reformers to purge the church, and its priests, of immorality. His biography of Herluca, though less well known to contemporary audiences, is no less significant: it hints at the important role played by women within the reformed religious life of the period. As Paul's account suggests, women's religious enthusiasm was characteristic of reform—even intrinsic to it. Quite apart from his emphasis on Herluca's reforming visions and his efforts to promote her sanctity, Paul included women in his discussion of the monastic revival that swept Europe in his time. As he told it, religious life thrived among Gregory's supporters: women (nuns and anchoresses) equally with men (monks and lay brothers) received God's grace in return for their obedience to Gregorian teaching.

Yet Paul's emphasis on the involvement of women in reform is notably at odds with traditional scholarship on the subject, which has tended to privilege the actions of men—the "popes and kings" whose dominance of the historical record (and whose quarrels) struck Catherine Morland in Jane Austen's *Northanger Abbey* as "very tiresome." Although women were active in medieval reform movements, and their activity was often recorded in the medieval sources, they have been largely absent from scholarly interpretations of reform. This chapter seeks to redress this imbalance by focusing on women's involvement in the various reform movements of the central Middle Ages. Two caveats are in order. First, the surviving sources shape, to a large extent, what it is possible for us to know about women's experience of reform. These sources are richest for nuns, less so for holy laywomen, and largely silent concerning the experiences of priests' wives, who were branded "concubines" by reform. Second, we inevitably know more about what men thought of these women than we do about their own response to reform (this is true, for example, of Herluca: all we know of her is filtered through Paul's account). Since nuns were more likely to be literate than laywomen, their responses to reform are the most accessible to us.

In what follows, I trace the various approaches that have dominated the subject of women and reform and propose some new directions. Recent scholarship has constructed reform as having either opposed women (associating all women with threats to priestly chastity and unleashing a powerful clerical misogyny) or largely ignored them (concerning itself chiefly with masculinity and engaging "woman" primarily on the level of discourse). Drawing important insights from both approaches, I argue for a synthesis that joins considerations of women's experience of reform to men's perceptions of women and sexuality within the context of reform. Paul's respect for Herluca, his clear sense of her as a spiritual figure alongside prominent churchmen, and his presentation of her visions as validating reforming ideas provide a useful touchstone for a reconsideration of women and reform. Women were neither absent from reform, nor were they necessarily rejected by it: within a spiritual climate that privileged male celibacy and male spiritual power, women could function as guarantors of both. Indeed, appropriate spiritual involvement with a holy woman (or with a community of religious women) may have been as much a marker of male commitment to reform as was the rhetorical, and often public, rejection of the potentially polluting influences of "women."

TRADITIONAL HISTORIOGRAPHIES

Scholarship on women and reform has been inflected both by developments in women's history and by shifting understandings of "reform." On one level, scholarship on the topic has simply mirrored the trajectory of women's history. Early scholarship on reform largely ignored women, judging reform (defined by the interests and concerns of ordained men) as irrelevant to women; although the reforming activities of such women as Matilda of Tuscany were sometimes recognized, they were noted for achievements that were traditionally gendered "male" and were described in terms of their "virility." The advent of women's history, while legitimizing the study of women *qua* women, cast doubts on the relevance of traditional chronologies for women, unsettling the entire concept of a reform for women; indeed, Joan Kelly's famous question—"Did women have a Renaissance?"—implied a separate history for women that was logically irreconcilable with the "master narrative" (and, in fact, posited decline for women in periods generally recognized as progressive or culturally productive). More recently, scholars have recognized that reform had important implications for women, although in this they have often been motivated by a version of what Merry Wiesner-Hanks has called the "Glinda question" ("are you a good or bad witch?")—was reform good or bad for women?—a question that presumes women's passivity, and their status as *objects* of reform, rather than as potential supporters and even initiators of it.[3]

Scholarship on women and reform has also been shaped by evolving perceptions of what reform in eleventh- and twelfth-century Europe actually was.[4] Indeed, reform was a complex phenomenon that resists neat definitions: there was no single universally recognized program for reform, and so-called reformers disagreed among themselves regarding reform objectives and methods. In modern historiography, reform has been used as a catch-all term to describe the many attempts to reorganize medieval religious life, whether ecclesiastical or monastic, in the period from about 1050–1200 (although "reforms" also took place earlier and later). Yet, in almost whatever way the term has been understood—whether to refer to a papacy embroiled in conflict with secular powers over investiture (the appointment of church officials), a church occupied with the moral reform of the priesthood and the enforcement of clerical celibacy, or a popular spiritual movement that revitalized monastic life during the period—historians have typically constituted reform as having either excluded or opposed women.[5]

Traditional scholarship simply ignored the possibility of reform's relevance to women (or women's relevance to reform), judging them largely extraneous to the institutional concerns of ordained men. More recent scholarship has argued that matters of sexuality and sexual boundaries—and so, also, women—were in fact central to the restructuring of the church. Attempts to reform the clergy during the latter part of the eleventh century rested to a large degree on the separation of priests from their wives, a campaign with significant implications for those women. Rejected and vilified, priests' wives were famously attacked by Peter Damian as "hoopoes, screech owls, nighthawks, she-wolves, leeches...strumpets,

(and) prostitutes." Paul of Bernried reported certain extreme responses to such vilification, reporting that some priests' wives "went mad and threw themselves into the fire,"
while others "went to bed quite well but were found dead in the morning."[6]

Attention to the rhetoric of church reform has suggested that the reforming imperative to establish and maintain sexual boundaries extended beyond the wives of priests to
affect women broadly: both laywomen and, ultimately, nuns. Indeed, opponents of clerical marriage spoke from long-standing and broad-ranging clerical anxieties concerning
purity and pollution, anxieties that centered on the bodies of women, and their sexual
potential. Thus, reform involved not simply the separation of priests from their wives,
but also the separation (rhetorically, at least) of religious men from *all* women, who
were increasingly associated with physical filth, sexuality, and sin. For the tenth-century reforming abbot Odo of Cluny, woman was quite literally a *saccus stercoris*, a bag of
excrement. According to Jo Ann McNamara, the enforcement of clerical celibacy during
the reform period prompted a crisis of masculinity that was averted only through the
radical reinstatement of sexual difference, which was made manifest through the strict
separation of the sexes within the religious life and what she describes as the "fanatic
claustration" of nuns. As she put it, powerfully asserting a model of reform's opposition
to women: "The Gregorian revolution aimed at a church virtually free of women at every
level but the lowest stratum of the married laity."[7]

Crucially, the taint of sexuality was not limited to laywomen. Even nuns, women
who had given themselves to the heavenly bridegroom and were theoretically sexually unavailable, were depicted as potential sources of temptation to priests and monks.
Within the monastic sphere, then, reform is thought to have sharpened long-standing
ambivalences concerning women and sexuality. Indeed, Bernard, the famous abbot of
Clairvaux, warned monks against *any* close contact with women, which he argued could
never be pure. As he cautioned:

> To be always in a woman's company without having carnal knowledge of her—is this
> not a greater miracle than raising the dead? You cannot perform the lesser feat; do
> you expect me to believe that you can do the greater?[8]

The assumption that reform rejected *all* women (including monastic women), and
even that it actively *opposed* them, became almost automatic in the closing years of the
twentieth century. McNamara, whose ambitious study *Sisters in Arms* traces women's
involvement in the religious life across two millennia, characterized the eleventh and
twelfth centuries as a time when nuns were progressively excluded from the liturgy
and denied even self-governance. Early medieval abbesses had ruled over communities of nuns, many of them noblewomen, who enjoyed social and spiritual prestige. In
McNamara's view, the prominence and relative autonomy of nuns came to an end with
reform, a feminist assessment that did not, in the end, differ much from the traditional
one. Richard Southern's view of women's experience of monastic revival was summed
up by his stark title: "Decline." As he commented, the reform period was marked by a
rightmindedness that made clear the "necessity for male dominance."[9]

If we accept that the drive to abolish clerical marriage was inspired by and productive of revulsion toward sexuality, and thus women, as many scholars have argued, then "woman" became quite literally the antithesis of reform—a symbol, as Pauline Stafford has argued for the earlier period, of everything "that the male cleric was to reject." Within the monastic context, many echoed Bernard in railing against the dangers of too-close association of the sexes. The bishop Marbode of Rennes, for example, invoked Eve to urge monks to avoid women: "the beginning of sin was caused by a woman and through her we all die, so if we want to avoid sin, we must cut the cause of sin away from us."[10]

WOMEN AND REFORM: A REASSESSMENT

These downbeat interpretations of women and reform are strikingly at odds with Paul of Bernried's celebration of Herluca's visionary support for clerical celibacy in particular, and church reform in general. Although Paul acknowledged the dire effects of reform particularly on priests' wives, he nevertheless presented Herluca, a woman, and a laywoman at that, as a central figure of reform. Paul's Herluca was, moreover, explicitly critical of the priesthood: she was rewarded by God for her avoidance of immoral priests and was empowered to deliver her criticisms of the priesthood publicly. Indeed, she was credited with having prompted the conversion of the priest Richard through her "constant rebukes and reproaches," saving him from sharing in the grim fate of the married priest Adalbert of Rott, whose soul she saw in a vision being dragged off to hell.[11]

In light of reform's presumed misogyny, even more curious are Herluca's reported friendships with male religious, not just Paul himself but also the monk Adelbero, whom she "deeply loved...in Christ." Throughout the biography, Paul invoked the support that Herluca received from male religious. In addition to Paul and Adelbero, both William of Hirsau, a central figure of the south German reform movement, and his disciple Theoger of St Georgen supported Herluca in her religious life. Their support is all the more striking given that she never took monastic vows. Herluca remained, until her death, a laywoman. Yet, anxieties about sexual scandal are conspicuously absent from Paul's account of her relationships with religious men.

Connections between church reform, clerical misogyny, and assumed "decline" for religious women were clearly complicated. Two underlying assumptions repay closer examination, the first one briefly and the second at greater length. First, we might too readily assume that reformers' vitriolic opposition to clerical marriage was necessarily and primarily about *women*. According to R. I. Moore, reform was at heart concerned with sharpening the distinction between the spiritual and the secular, and with exalting clergy over laity. Although relations to women provided one way to distinguish between laymen and priests, women were significant not primarily as symbols of sexuality (as scholars such as McNamara have assumed), but as indices of men's relations to property. In Moore's view, the central issue for reformers in their struggle against clerical marriage was not simply ensuring the cultic purity of ordained men through their separation from women, but also more prosaic concerns regarding the ownership and transmission of property, from which, of course, churchmen were meant to abstain.[12] Money, not sex, was at issue here (although the implications for the erstwhile wives of priests were the same: denunciation and rejection).

Other scholars have argued that the reform movement was primarily about men and the distribution of power among them (although not in the reflexive way in which traditional histories have always been "about men"). In this view, reform was, at heart, a contest between men in which women figured symbolically as indices of male virtue. In this contest, constructions of masculinity, not misogyny, took center stage. Focusing on the pollution language of reform, Conrad Leyser called into question the assumption that the women who appear in reform era sources signify real historical actors. Instead, he argued that "woman" served a rhetorical function for reformers, providing a means for elite men to discuss and negotiate power among themselves. According to Leyser, reform was not intentionally misogynist: it did not deliberately exclude or vilify women, although exclusion and vilification may have been one result. Maureen Miller has similarly questioned the impact of reform on women, demonstrating that reformers were more concerned with notions of masculinity, and its gradations among ordained and secular men, than with vilifying women. In her view, it was laymen—and not women— who bore the brunt of the negative rhetoric of reform. Acknowledging the gendered language of reform, yet deflecting attention away from the misogyny so often associated with it, Miller concluded that "The movement was about *men*."[13]

A second assumption concerning women and reform is equally ripe for revision: namely, that reform resulted in decline for nuns, who were reduced to dependency on male provosts and spiritual advisors, and whose traditional autonomy was winnowed away under a constant rhetoric about female monastic abuses in need of correction. As we have seen, scholars as different as McNamara and Southern have agreed on this point: as male monastic communities were revitalized from the eleventh century, and as new communities were founded in response to unprecedented spiritual enthusiasm, women were systematically excluded. Indeed, Southern's discussion of women's religious experiences during the eleventh and twelfth centuries appears in a chapter entitled "fringe orders and anti-orders." Subsequent accounts of women and monastic reform have tended to reproduce this schema, presenting women's religious lives as distinct from orthodox monasticism (exemplified in the newly founded reforming orders of the period, chiefly the Cistercians), which is implicitly defined as male.

On the face of it, the judgment that women were marginal to monastic reform may seem fair. The communities that have been seen to exemplify reform—Cluny in the tenth and eleventh century, and Cîteaux in the twelfth—had ambivalent relationships with women. Although Cluny founded a women's house at Marcigny in 1055 (almost a century and a half after the foundation of Cluny itself and after the establishment of dozens of Cluniac priories for men), this house was intended for the wives of men who had entered Cluny. Women's houses were never more than marginal to the order.

The Cistercian situation was more complex. Traditional accounts have presented Cistercian growth as an exclusively male phenomenon, echoing and even channeling medieval anxieties about the presence of women. Apart from the women's foundations of Jully (which may have had its origins in a "double" community, a community of women and men, at Molesmes) and Tart l'Abbaye, women have been understood as absent from the early Cistercians. As Constance Berman has noted, medieval accounts of the order deny the involvement of women in the early years, while modern accounts have tended to reinforce an exclusively male image of Cistercian monasticism, positing an early "golden age" during which Cistercian monks kept themselves entirely separate from women.[14]

Writing in the 1930s, the German historian Herbert Grundmann attributed Cistercian opposition to the incorporation of women's houses during the thirteenth century to men's unwillingness to provide for women's spiritual and material care, which he characterized as a "trouble and responsibility." Since women could not be ordained, nuns relied on men as priests to administer the sacraments, celebrate the divine office, and hear their confessions, services that were known from the thirteenth century as the *cura monialium*, the care of nuns. The *cura* was an inescapable fact of the religious life for women's houses, which could never be spiritually self-sufficient like male monasteries. According to Grundmann, the *cura monialium* was a distraction and a financial burden, which he believed male orders preferred to avoid. McNamara and other recent scholars have added pollution anxieties concerning sexuality and women to the disincentives of male monastic involvement with nuns that were identified by Grundmann; they agree generally on women's spiritual marginalization and the decline for religious women during the period.[15]

Male monastic statements of anxiety and even antipathy towards women are certainly not hard to find. Bernard of Clairvaux's warning that it is easier to raise the dead than to have a pure friendship with a woman neatly epitomizes the anxiety of monks about the pollution associated with women. Often repeated, too, is the misogynist declaration attributed in a sixteenth-century text to the Premonstratensian abbot, Conrad of Marchthal:

> Since nothing in this world resembles the evil of women and since the venom of the viper or the dragon is less harmful to men than their proximity, we hereby declare that for the good of our souls, our bodies, and our worldly goods we will no longer accept sisters into our order and we will avoid them as we do mad dogs.

Anxieties about sexuality were clearly at the root of some men's desire to avoid involvement with nuns (though Conrad implied that women were also a financial drain). The twelfth-century Rule of Grandmont prohibited admission to women, warning: "If the most mild David, the most wise Solomon, and the most strong Samson, were captured by feminine snares, who will not fall to their charms?" Stories of a scandal at the Gilbertine community of Watton in England confirmed the potential dangers of contact between the sexes within the religious life: a sister had been made pregnant by one of the lay brothers (he was castrated; she was miraculously delivered of the pregnancy).[16]

And yet, for all of the anxiety evident in the medieval record, for all the monastic rules that legislate against the incorporation of women, and for all the warnings against contact between the sexes, it is not clear that women were excluded from monastic reform during the central Middle Ages. Warnings against women are striking and quotable, but more numerous are records of women's attraction to the religious life, approving reports of men's involvement with them, and evidence of a tremendous expansion of female monasticism. Indeed, Bruce Venarde has shown that between 1070 and 1170 (the key decades of reform) the number of monasteries for women in France and England quadrupled, with some decades witnessing as many as fifty new foundations. This was a stunning increase. Moreover, as Sharon Elkins has observed, a significant number of houses founded for women in England during the twelfth century actually housed women *and* men, a phenomenon similar to that which Constance Berman has noted at Obazine and Nonenques, where women adopted the religious life alongside men.[17] These examples significantly undercut assumptions of monastic misogyny and avoidance of women.

Like Paul's reports about Herluca, contemporary accounts emphasize the reform enthusiasm of both women and men. In his chronicle entry for the year 1091, the reformer Bernold of Constance highlighted the involvement of women in the monastic upsurge of the age:

> An innumerable multitude not only of men but also of women flocked at this time to this form of life, to live communally under the obedience of clerics or monks... Many daughters of farmers strove to renounce marriage and the world so as to live under the obedience of some priest. Even married women did not cease to live religiously and to obey religious men with greatest devotion.

The emphasis on women's spiritual involvement alongside men is echoed in the *Little Book on the Various Orders and Callings that Exist in the Church*, a mid-twelfth century polemical text advocating for reform. A section of the *Book* commented on the existence of women who "sweetly take up Christ's yoke with holy men or under their guidance," highlighting, once again, the spiritual partnership of women and men within the context of reform.[18]

Holy men were, moreover, praised for their attention to the spiritual lives of women. As Gaucher of Aureil's biographer put it, the saint "sought to build the heavenly Jerusalem with walls of both sexes and therefore built a convent of the sisters a stone's throw from his own cell, sharing his poverty with men and women alike." In the same way, Hermann of Tournai commented that the reformer Norbert of Xanten received both men and women at his foundation at Prémontré. Presenting Norbert's ministry to women as especially virtuous, Herman asked: "if... Norbert had done nothing else... but attract so many women to God's service by his exhortation, would he not have been worthy of the greatest praise?"[19]

As these accounts suggest, the presence of women was not simply incidental to certain reformers, but central to their spiritual mission. For the men of the southern German Hirsau reform movement (themselves staunch supporters of the reformed papacy), concern for religious women formed such an essential part of the apostolic life that, in most cases, involvement with women followed fast on the heels of monastic reform. Many, if not most, Hirsau houses during the reform period included women in some capacity, as at Disibodenberg, where the famous abbess and theologian Hildegard of Bingen was enclosed as a young girl, and at Schönau, where Elisabeth of Schönau received and began to record her visions (aided by her brother, the monk Ekbert). Among Hirsau reform houses, the presence of both sexes was seen as spiritually advantageous, an idea reflected in the twelfth-century chronicle of Petershausen, which observed that it is "not blameworthy, but greatly worthy of praise, if women are received in monasteries as nuns in the service of God, so that each sex, although separated one from the other, may be saved in one place."[20]

Like Hirsau, the communities of Fontevrault and the Paraclete in France and Sempringham in England incorporated women, formalizing men's involvement in the *cura monialium* and even—as at Fontevraud—placing women's spiritual lives at their center. At Fontevraud, the monks served the women, providing for their spiritual and material care and vowing obedience to a female authority figure: ultimate power over men and women was vested in the hands of an abbess and not, as elsewhere, an abbot. Men's service to women was, moreover, depicted as spiritually beneficial to them. As the biography of Robert of Arbrissel reports, the men agreed to "obey the command of Christ's handmaids," for the salvation of their souls. In his proposed Rule for the Paraclete, Abelard proposed that male and female monasteries should be paired geographically and bound in a "mutual affection." In his view, men had a "duty" to provide care for religious women, whom he characterized as brides of Christ, and therefore as the lords (*dominae*) of monastic men (who were merely Christ's servants). At Sempringham, men's care for women was understood in biblical terms, as paralleling the care provided by John for the Virgin Mary after the crucifixion. The early thirteenth-century *Book of St Gilbert* commented that: "Just as he [John] received our Lord's mother into his home, so this man [Gilbert] took into his charge those women who followed her example."[21]

Male commitment to women at Fontevraud, the Paraclete, and Sempringham, though well known, is nevertheless often seen as exceptional and temporary, rather than broadly indicative of reform. As many scholars have noted, communities that initially accepted both women and men (so-called "double monasteries") tended after a generation or so to separate, seemingly confirming the model of decline for monastic women.[22] Prémontré is often cited as the outstanding example of this tendency, perhaps because of Conrad of Marchthal's picaresque likening of women to vipers and dragons.

However, recent work, particularly in Germany and the United States, has begun to call into question the assumption that male monastic reformers ultimately rejected women. New sources and methods are revealing men's continued involvement with women even after the initial flush of reform enthusiasm. Through close attention to charters from Premonstratensian monasteries in northwestern Germany, for instance, Shelley Wolbrink revealed what she terms a "culture of cooperation" among men and women during the early thirteenth century.[23] As she showed, at the women's monastery of Füssenich in northwestern Germany, Premonstratensian men continued to serve

alongside women, sometimes for decades at a time, and certainly long after the supposed separation of the sexes within the Premonstratensian order.

Working from monastic necrologies (lists of deaths), Elsanne Gilomen-Schenkel similarly revealed the spiritual cooperation of men and women well after the supposed separation of double houses.[24] Although some double communities were short-lived, others
continued into the fifteenth century and beyond: the women's communities of Engelberg
and Interlaken, for instance, reached their height in the first half of the fourteenth century. The women at Engelberg were not relocated until 1603. Moreover, even when men's
and women's houses did physically separate, they sometimes continued to function as a
single spiritual community. After the relocation of the women's community from Muri
to Hermetschwil in 1200, for instance, a shared necrology continued to report the deaths
of both monks and nuns: 117 monks and 144 nuns appear in the post-separation years,
between 1200 and 1260. Similarly, at Marbach, the men continued to provide spiritual
care for the women of the community, even after the women's move to Schwartzenthann
(a move prompted by a gift of land to the women, and not by the men's rejection).

As these examples suggest, attention to documents of practice (charters and necrologies) in addition to prescriptive texts (rules and monastic legislation) is yielding a more
nuanced picture of women's experience of reform monasticism. Although some orders
did place restrictions on the incorporation of women, these restrictions were not always
prompted primarily by misogyny. In the Cistercian case, for example, limitations on
women's incorporation may have been a pragmatic response to the increasing demands
for pastoral care that the expansion of women's houses represented, rather than an indication of growing monastic antipathy towards women, per se. Indeed, individual Cistercian
abbots (the abbots of Villers and Salem, for instance) supported women's monasteries
and continued to provide pastoral care for them throughout the thirteenth century.

RELIGIOUS WOMEN AS REFORMERS

Thus far, I have depicted reform as a movement for spiritual renewal in which women
were clearly involved and which allowed certain opportunities for spiritual contact
between the sexes. Much of my discussion has centered on how male reformers viewed
and interacted with women. But what of women's own experience of reform? What
of the reform of individual female monasteries? And how might we best characterize women as reformers? If reform was "about men" (a conclusion that may be true of
reform in an institutional but not a spiritual sense), then were women who embraced
reform unwitting instruments of male clerical interests?

One strain of scholarship, inspired by the assumption that reform opposed women,
has tended to valorize women's resistance to reform, delighting in stories of women's
rebellion against clerical authority, as at Markyate where the nuns threw a copy of
Periculoso (1298), the hated papal decree requiring strict enclosure of all nuns, at the
back of their departing bishop.[25] Of course, some religious women did resist reforms

that challenged their existing way of life and sometimes their autonomy. The imposition of reform could also be clearly gendered, and nuns knew this. Church officers often justified reforms by asserting that a women's house was degenerate, corrupt, and financially mismanaged. So, for instance, criticisms of Judith, abbess of Kemnade, combined accusations of economic mismanagement with sexual immorality; reform at Kemnade (as at certain other women's houses) resulted in the ejection of the women and their replacement by monks.

Yet, despite the sometimes drastic effects of reform, particularly for aristocratic communities of canonesses in Germany, whose way of life was condemned at the Second Lateran Council (1139), women's responses to reform were not universally negative. Although some canonesses resisted the imposition of a monastic rule through reform (as at Regensburg and Überwasser), others embraced it (as at Villers and Hohenbourg). Individual women were active reformers: Relinde of Admont, who was sent from the Hirsau-affiliated double house at Admont to Bergen to initiate reform; Matilda of Diessen, who reformed her community against the opposition of her fellow canonesses; and Bertha de Bardi, a nun who was chosen to reform and head the community at Cavriligia. Some women also founded their own reform-minded communities: Hildegard at Bingen, Hildeburg at Pontoise, Paulina at Zell, and Herluca (briefly) at Epfach.

Many religious women directly promoted reformist goals, championing papal authority and urging the moral reform of the clergy. Herrad of Hohenbourg highlighted reform in her *Garden of Delights*, a richly illuminated compilation of theology, biblical history, and canon law that she designed for canonesses at the recently reformed community she headed.[26] Herrad was particularly concerned with the moral standing of the clergy, but she did not dwell on the sexual transgressions of priests, perhaps because this subject tended to demonize women. Instead, she warned forcefully against clerical corruption, using images that vividly depicted the results of clerical hypocrisy and greed: a monk in hell, weighed down by his illicit moneybag; corrupt churchmen condemned at the Judgment; and Avarice associated with grasping priests.

Hildegard of Bingen and Elisabeth of Schönau were equally critical of corrupt churchmen. Presenting herself as a visionary inspired by God, Hildegard railed against the failings of the clergy whose inadequacies had resulted in what she called an "effeminate age." In Hildegard's view, the clergy had polluted the church with their avarice, lechery, and evil living. She presented the grotesque image of *Ecclesia* (the church) apparently giving birth to antichrist, suggesting that the church itself would harbor its own greatest enemy. Elisabeth directed her attention similarly, launching pointed attacks on both church and clergy in *The Book of the Ways of God*. As she wrote, in a visionary voice: "The head of the Church has languished and its members are dead, for the apostolic seat is filled with pride, avarice is cultivated, and it is full of iniquity and impiety."[27]

For these women, support for reform was not blind obedience to male clerical authority, but rather the opposite: the opportunity to criticize—openly and apparently quite legitimately—perceived male clerical degeneracy and excess. Although they could not be ordained, these women placed themselves in judgment over ordained men, and they were able to do so by adopting the language of reform. Like Herluca, their efforts on behalf of reform suggest that women's exclusion from the ecclesiastical hierarchy might actually have *increased* their investment in reform issues. Women's interest in the integrity of the priesthood may have been sharpened by their distancing from it.

Quite apart from the reform activities of these admittedly exceptional women, it is clear that reform offered certain opportunities to religious women. First, it increased access to monastic life, as Tengswich of Andernach noted when she questioned Hildegard of Bingen's practice of accepting only noble women into the monastery. "The Lord himself brought into the primitive Church humble fishermen and poor people," Tengswich reminded Hildegard.[28] Second, fidelity to papal authority sometimes shielded women from censure, enabling them to comment critically on unreformed clergymen, and even in certain cases to bypass priests as spiritual guides and ministers of the sacraments, as Herluca reportedly did. Third, reform coincided with a period of tremendous intellectual and artistic vitality within monastic life, for women as well as men. As Alison Beach has shown, female scribes and artists were active in the production of books, sometimes alongside male collaborators, and extant catalogues record the richness of women's library holdings; as we have seen, some women were also active in the composition of their own texts, producing visionary texts, biographies, letters, commentaries, and even sermons.[29]

CONCLUSION

The study of women and reform resists easy conclusions. Just as there was no one reform movement, there was no universal and essential female experience of it. Benedictine nuns, canonesses, priests' wives, saints, recluses, laywomen, and self-proclaimed visionaries: each of these groups had a distinctive experience of reform. Within each group, too, there was variation: some canonesses embraced reform, for instance, while others resisted it. Recent scholarship on women and reform has acknowledged these variations, yielding a rich picture of women's reforming activities and enthusiasm that challenges earlier presumptions of clerical misogyny and women's decline. Of course, we know most about nuns like Herrad, Hildegard, and Elisabeth, women who left substantial written legacies. Our knowledge of laywomen like Herluca, who left no writings of her own, is much less detailed. The circumstances of Herluca's religious life, her relations with priests (both those who supported her and those whom she rebuked), and her friendships with other women, are subjects about which we would like to know more. Dyan Elliott has drawn our attention to the deleterious effects of reform for priests' wives, but we need to know much more about how such women responded to the imposition of clerical celibacy.[30] Paul of Bernried reported the story of one clerical wife, who, "spiteful because of her separation from her husband," avenged herself by poisoning the wife of the reforming count in whose lands her priest-husband held his benefice.[31] Surely many clerical wives resented the degradation and public vilification attendant upon enforced separation from their husbands. How did they respond?

Other topics are ripe for further consideration. Attention to the local circumstances of reform, to the small, informal, and sometimes ephemeral religious communities—like that which grew up around Herluca at Epfach—is likely to add significantly to a picture of monasticism that has typically focused on large and ultimately successful male houses. Augustinian communities (like Bernried) remain understudied; examining these may yield a more nuanced picture of reform for women, especially because Augustinian canons (unlike monks) embraced the active life and the care of souls (the gender-neutral *cura animarum*). Finally, attention to biographies of female saints from the reform period (most of which remain unavailable in modern editions) will likely provide rich new evidence for women's involvement in reform monasticism and their response to reforming ideologies. Paul of Bernried clearly saw Herluca as a central figure of reform. What more might we learn about reform were we to adopt his vantage point?

These new histories matter to more than historians of women and gender. Berman's focus on the experience of Cistercian nuns, for example, has revised the early history of the Cistercian order as a whole, challenging traditional accounts of the order's origins and expansion. In the same way, consideration of gender and sexuality in the political discourse of reform led Megan McLaughlin to argue for perceptions of "public" and "private" during the period quite different from those that have typically been assumed. Right order in the church, she argued, was characterized by right order within the household, hence the prevalence of marriage metaphors among reformers and the emphasis on marital legitimacy within society broadly.[32]

Women were omnipresent within reform, as reformers themselves, as supporters of reform, as its opponents, and as its objects. They were also, importantly, omnipresent in the rhetoric of reform. When reformers (male and female) talked about the church imperiled by secular encroachments or clerical immorality, they turned to the language of sexuality and pollution, presenting *Ecclesia* as a bride abandoned, a woman raped, or a queen cast down. Women were central, too, to men's experience of reform. Between churchmen, women served as markers of male self-mastery and spiritual control. Although church reformers rejected clerical marriage, urging clergy to avoid contact with women, many nevertheless maintained close spiritual relations with women, pioneering a model of what Elliott called as "heteroasceticism."[33] Even Peter Damian, the most radical opponent of clerical marriage, engaged in a long-standing spiritual relationship with Agnes of Poitou, the widow of Henry III. Gregory VII, too, was famously close with Matilda of Tuscany, who was often at his side, traveling with him throughout Italy "like another Martha."

Such openness to women among even the most radical reformers demands explanation. One solution is simply to recognize that there was a significant gap between reform rhetoric and practice. The gendered language of reform, and even the denunciation of clerical marriage by which it was often accompanied, may have had less of an impact on women in general than scholars have tended to assume. Another solution is more speculative. If we allow that "woman" functioned rhetorically as a measure of a man's character, as Leyser has suggested, it is possible that contact with women could be both licit and illicit. That is to say, instead of assuming that separation from women became the sole marker of reform—with the clergy defined by their absolute separation from women and laymen defined by their total involvement with them—it may be the case that reformers could further differentiate themselves by the nature of their involvement with women, hence the eager defense of relations with women as being both legitimate and spiritually motivated. In this case, reform for religious men may have had less to do with accepting or rejecting women than with learning how to use them and the symbols associated with femininity.

Although tentative, this explanation allows for the continued and self-conscious presence of women among certain monastic reform communities that historians have treated as male. While the mixing of the sexes within the religious life was never uncomplicated, the presence of spiritual women could be defended by men who established a model of reform that included both sexes and in which, importantly, women could be accorded priority. Their examples argue against a vision of reform that either opposed women or ignored them, suggesting instead a culture in which men's involvement with women was seen as legitimate, and indeed spiritually rewarding.

FURTHER READING

Barstow, Anne Llewellyn. *Married Priests and the Reforming Papacy: The Eleventh-Century Debates*. New York: E. Mellen Press, 1982.

Beach, Alison I. *Women as Scribes: Book Production and Monastic Reform in Twelfth-Century Bavaria*. Cambridge; New York: Cambridge University Press, 2004.

Berman, Constance H. *The Cistercian Evolution: The Invention of a Religious Order in Twelfth-Century Europe*. Philadelphia: University of Pennsylvania Press, 2000.

Constable, Giles. *The Reformation of the Twelfth Century*. Cambridge; New York: Cambridge University Press, 1996.

Cowdrey, H. E. J. *Pope Gregory VII, 1073–1085*. New York: Oxford University Press, 1998.

Cushing, Kathleen G. *Reform and the Papacy in the Eleventh Century: Spirituality and Social Change*. Manchester: Manchester University Press, 2005.

Griffiths, Fiona J. *The Garden of Delights: Reform and Renaissance for Women in the Twelfth Century*. Philadelphia: University of Pennsylvania Press, 2007.

Griffiths, Fiona J. and Julie Hotchin, eds. *Partners in Spirit: Men, Women, and Religious Life in Germany, 1100–1500*. Turnhout: Brepols, 2014.

McLaughlin, Megan, *Sex, Gender, and Episcopal Authority in an Age of Reform, 1000–1122*. Cambridge: Cambridge University Press, 2010.

Parish, Helen L. *Clerical Celibacy in the West, c.1100–1700*. Burlington, Vt.: Ashgate, 2010.

Robinson, I. S. "Reform and the Church, 1073–1122," in David Luscombe and Jonathan Riley-Smith, eds, *The New Cambridge Medieval History*, volume IV: *c. 1024–c. 1198*. Cambridge; New York: Cambridge University Press, 2004, part 2, 268–334.

Venarde, Bruce L. *Women's Monasticism and Medieval Society: Nunneries in France and England, 890–1215*. Ithaca: Cornell University Press, 1997.

Wilms, Beatrix. *"Amatrices ecclesiarum": Untersuchung zur Rolle und Funktion der Frauen in der Kirchenreform des 12. Jahrhunderts*. Bochum: Studienverlag Brockmeyer, 1987.

Winston-Allen, Anne. *Convent Chronicles: Women Writing about Women and Reform in the Late Middle Ages*. University Park, Pa.: Pennsylvania State University Press, 2004.

Notes

1. Paul of Bernried, *Vita Gregorii*, 122, 114, trans. in I. S. Robinson, *The Papal Reform of the Eleventh Century: Lives of Pope Leo IX and Pope Gregory VII* (Manchester: Manchester University Press, 2004), at 362–63, 358.

2. Paul of Bernried, *Vita Herlucae*, 44, in *Acta Sanctorum* (hereafter AASS) Apr II, 556.

3. Joan Kelly-Gadol, "Did Women Have a Renaissance?" in Renate Bridenthal and Claudia Koonz, eds, *Becoming Visible: Women in European History* (Boston: Houghton Mifflin, 1977), 137–64. Merry E. Wiesner-Hanks, "Women, Gender, and Church History," *Church History*, 71 (3) (September 2002): 600–620, 609.

4. Gerd Tellenbach, *The Church in Western Europe from the Tenth to the Early Twelfth Century*, trans. Timothy Reuter (Cambridge: Cambridge University Press, 1993), 157–84; Julia Barrow, "Ideas and Applications of Reform," in Thomas F. X. Noble and Julia M. H. Smith, eds, *Early Medieval Christianities, c. 600–c. 1100* (Cambridge: Cambridge University Press, 2008), 345–62; I. S. Robinson, "Reform and the Church, 1073–1122," in David Luscombe and Jonathan Riley-Smith, eds, *The New Cambridge Medieval History*, vol. 4: *c. 1024–c. 1198* (Cambridge; New York: Cambridge University Press, 2004), part 1, 268–334.

5. A notable exception is Beatrix Wilms, *"Amatrices ecclesiarum": Untersuchung zur Rolle und Funktion der Frauen in der Kirchenreform des 12. Jahrhunderts* (Bochum: Studienverlag Brockmeyer, 1987).

6. Michael Frassetto, ed., *Medieval Purity and Piety: Essays on Medieval Clerical Celibacy and Religious Reform* (New York: Garland, 1998). Peter Damian, Epist. 112, 34, in Kurt Reindel, ed., *Die Briefe des Petrus Damiani* (Munich: Monumenta Germaniae Historica, 1983–93), 3: 278; *The Letters of Peter Damian*, trans. Owen J. Blum (Washington, DC: Catholic University of America Press, 1989–2005), 4: 276. *Vita Gregorii*, 116, in Robinson, *Papal Reform*, 359.

7. Frassetto, ed., *Medieval Purity and Piety*; Dyan Elliott, *Fallen Bodies: Pollution, Sexuality, and Demonology in the Middle Ages* (Philadelphia: University of Pennsylvania Press, 1999). Jo Ann McNamara, "The *Herrenfrage*: The Restructuring of the Gender System, 1050–1150," in Clare A. Lees, ed., *Medieval Masculinities: Regarding Men in the Middle Ages* (Minneapolis: University of Minnesota Press, 1994), 3–29, 18, 7. See also Dyan Elliott, *Spiritual Marriage: Sexual Abstinence in Medieval Wedlock* (Princeton, NJ: Princeton University Press, 1993), 102.

8. Bernard of Clairvaux, Sermon 65, 4, in J. Leclercq, C. H. Talbot, and H. M. Rochais, eds, *Opera*, 8 vols (Rome: Editiones Cistercienses, 1957–77), 2: 175; trans. Kilian Walsh and Irene M. Edmonds, *On the Song of Songs*, 4 vols (Kalamazoo, MI: Cistercian Publications, 1971–80), 3: 184.

9. Jo Ann Kay McNamara, *Sisters in Arms: Catholic Nuns Through Two Millennia* (Cambridge, Mass.: Harvard University Press, 1996). R. W. Southern, *Western Society and the Church in the Middle Ages* (Harmondsworth: Penguin, 1970), 310–12.

10. Pauline Stafford, "Queens, Nunneries and Reforming Churchmen: Gender, Religious Status and Reform in Tenth- and Eleventh-Century England," *Past & Present*, 163 (1) (May 1999): 3–35, 8. Marbode, Epist. 8–9, trans. in *Les deux vies de Robert d'Arbrissel, fondateur de Fontevraud: légendes, écrits et témoignages*, ed. Jacques Dalarun et al. (Turnhout: Brepols, 2006), 532–33.

11. *Vita Herlucae*, 23, in AASS Apr II, 554. *Vita Gregorii*, 115, in Robinson, *Papal Reform*, 359.

12. R. I. Moore, *The First European Revolution, c. 970–1215* (Oxford: Blackwell, 2000), 11; idem, "Property, Marriage, and the Eleventh-Century Revolution: A Context for Early Medieval Communism," in Frassetto, ed., *Medieval Purity and Piety*, 179–208.

13. Conrad Leyser, "Custom, Truth, and Gender in Eleventh-Century Reform," in R. N. Swanson, ed., *Gender and Christian Religion* (Woodbridge, Suffolk: Boydell and Brewer, 1998), 75–91. Maureen C. Miller, "Masculinity, Reform, and Clerical Culture: Narratives of Episcopal Holiness in the Gregorian Era," *Church History*, 72 (1) (March 2003): 25–52, 27.

14. Constance Hoffman Berman, *The Cistercian Evolution: The Invention of a Religious Order in Twelfth-Century Europe* (Philadelphia: University of Pennsylvania Press, 2000), 39–45.

15. Herbert Grundmann, *Religious Movements in the Middle Ages: The Historical Links Between Heresy, the Mendicant Orders, and the Women's Religious Movement in the Twelfth and Thirteenth Century, with the Historical Foundations of German Mysticism*, trans. Steven Rowan (Notre Dame, Ind.: University of Notre Dame Press, 1995), 91. McNamara, *Sisters in Arms*, 220.

16. Conrad of Marchthal cited in Southern, *Western Society and the Church*, 314. *Regula sancti Stephani*, 39, in *Patrologiae cursus completus: Series latina*, ed. J.-P. Migne (Paris: Migne, 1841–64), 204: 1152. Giles Constable, "Aelred of Rievaulx and the Nun of Watton: An Episode in the Early History of the Gilbertine Order," in Derek Baker, ed., *Medieval Women* (Oxford: Basil Blackwell, 1978), 205–226.

17. Bruce L. Venarde, *Women's Monasticism and Medieval Society: Nunneries in France and England, 890–1215* (Ithaca: Cornell University Press, 1997), 54. Sharon K. Elkins, *Holy Women of Twelfth-Century England* (Chapel Hill: University of North Carolina Press, 1988), xvii; Berman, *Cistercian Revolution*, 40.

18. Bernold, *Chronicon*, ed. G. H. Pertz, *Monumenta Germaniae historica. Scriptores* [hereafter MGH SS] (Hannover, 1844), 5: 453. Giles Constable and Bernard Smith, eds and trans., *Libellus de diversis ordinibus et professionibus qui sunt in aecclesia* (Oxford: Clarendon Press, 1972), 4–5.

19. Biography of Gaucher of Aureil cited in Henrietta Leyser, *Hermits and the New Monasticism: A Study of Religious Communities in Western Europe, 1000–1150* (New York: St. Martin's Press, 1984), 50. Theodore J. Antry and Carol Neel, eds, *Norbert and Early Norbertine Spirituality* (New York: Paulist Press, 2007), 80.

20. *Casus monasterii Petrishusensis*, 9, in MGH SS 20: 625. Urban Küsters, "Formen und Modelle religiöser Frauengemeinschaften im Umkreis der Hirsauer Reform des 11. und 12. Jahrhunderts," in Klaus Schreiner, ed., *Hirsau, St. Peter und Paul, 1091–1991* (Stuttgart: Kommissionsverlag, K. Theiss, 1991), 1: 195–220.

21. *Deux vies*, 192–95. Betty Radice and M. T. Clanchy, trans., *The Letters of Abelard and Heloise* (London: Penguin, 2003), 157. Raymonde Foreville and Gillian Keir, eds, *The Book of St Gilbert* (Oxford: Oxford University Press, 1987), 124–25.

22. Penny Schine Gold, *The Lady and the Virgin: Image, Attitude, and Experience in Twelfth-Century France* (Chicago: University of Chicago Press, 1985), 86–89; C. H. Lawrence, *Medieval Monasticism: Forms of Religious Life in Western Europe in the Middle Ages* (New York: Longman, 1984), 169–72; Giles Constable, *The Reformation of the Twelfth Century* (Cambridge; New York: Cambridge University Press, 1996), 73; McNamara, *Sisters in Arms*, 296.

23. Shelley Amiste Wolbrink, "Women in the Premonstratensian Order of Northwestern Germany, 1120–1250," *Catholic Historical Review*, 89 (3) (July 2003): 387–408.

24. Elsanne Gilomen-Schenkel, "Das Doppelkloster—eine verschwiegene Institution: Engelberg und andere Beispiele aus dem Umkreis der Helvetia Sacra," *Studien und Mitteilungen zur Geschichte des Benediktiner-Ordens und seiner Zweige*, 101 (1990): 197–211.

25. Elizabeth M. Makowski, *Canon Law and Cloistered Women: Periculoso and its Commentators, 1298–1545* (Washington, DC: Catholic University of America Press, 1997), 115–16.
26. Fiona J. Griffiths, *The Garden of Delights: Reform and Renaissance for Women in the Twelfth Century* (Philadelphia: University of Pennsylvania Press, 2007).
27. Hildegard, *Scivias* III, 11, 25; ed. Aldegundis Führkötter, with Angela Carlevaris, *Corpus Christianorum Continuatio Medievalis* (Turnhout: Brepols, 1978) 43A, 2: 589–90; trans. Mother Columba Hart and Jane Bishop (New York: Paulist Press, 1990), 501–502. Elizabeth of Schönau, *Liber viarum Dei*, 15, in F. W. E. Roth, ed., *Die Visionen der hl. Elisabeth und die Schriften der Aebte Ekbert und Emecho von Schönau* (Brünn: Verlag der Studien aus dem Benediktiner- und Cistercienser-Orden, 1884), 113; Anne L. Clark, trans., *Elisabeth of Schönau: The Complete Works* (New York: Paulist Press, 2000), 195.
28. Hildegard of Bingen, Ep. 52, trans. in Joseph L. Baird and Radd K. Ehrman, *The Letters of Hildegard of Bingen*, 3 vols (New York: Oxford University Press, 1994–2004), 1: 127.
29. Alison I. Beach, *Women as Scribes: Book Production and Monastic Reform in Twelfth-Century Bavaria* (Cambridge; New York: Cambridge University Press, 2004).
30. Elliott, *Fallen Bodies*, 81–106.
31. *Vita Gregorii*, 91, in Robinson, *Papal Reform*, 333.
32. Megan McLaughlin, *Sex, Gender, and Episcopal Authority in an Age of Reform, 1000–1122* (Cambridge: Cambridge University Press, 2010).
33. Dyan Elliott, *The Bride of Christ Goes to Hell: Metaphor and Embodiment in the Lives of Pious Women, 200–1500* (Philadelphia: University of Pennsylvania Press, 2012), 150.

CHAPTER 29

···

DEVOTED HOLINESS IN THE
LAY WORLD

···

ANNEKE B. MULDER-BAKKER

In the later Middle Ages, hundreds of women lived as lay recluses and anchorites, secluded in the midst of cities. Thousands of women lived a religious life in the private households of beguines and adherents of the Modern Devotion. Unknown numbers practiced pious asceticism in the privacy of their homes. As noted by André Vauchez, the renowned expert on sainthood, the most prominent saintly people in this period—particularly prophets and mystics—were to be found among such laypeople.[1] Several dozen of these holy laywomen, and a few laymen, have left to us life stories (many only recently discovered), written by themselves or by spiritual biographers. This chapter is based on about twenty of these texts.

From the eleventh century onward, a profound transformation reshaped the countries of Latin Christendom. Spurred by new agricultural methods that enabled the cultivation of sea and river clay, northern Europe began to rival the ancient centers of civilization to its south. The emergence of trade and industry in the southern Netherlands, the Rhineland, and Bavaria encouraged urban development. City dwellers began not only to accumulate political and economic power but also to engage actively in religion, which slowly ceased to be the exclusive domain of professionals (clergy and monastics). Paris emerged as a spiritual center, which Pope Innocent III celebrated as "Paris, the paradise of the world." Northern Europe became an identifiable region with its own distinctive culture.[2]

In this distinctive region, a number of religious initiatives would change the face of Christianity: new religious orders (Cistercians and Premonstratensians); beguines; (informal) networks of lay faithful; urban recluses; and, in the fifteenth century, the religious households of the sisters and brothers of the Modern Devotion. Religiously gifted women felt encouraged here to cultivate their devotion in a lay context, and the growing cities of the north offered them exciting and challenging contexts in which to devote themselves fully to religion. While the new mendicant movements from the south gave men the opportunity to follow God in an urban context, laywomen from the north provided inspiring examples for men *and* women. Clare of Assisi (d.1253) had yearned for a mendicant life, but in her native Italy, she was vigorously pushed back behind cloister walls. The *mulieres religiosae* (women religious) of the north developed a new urban religiosity that offered laypeople new choices for piety, alternatives to the stark options of mendicant life or the convent. It is on these holy laywomen in northern Europe—roughly, the lands between the Seine and Elbe plus England and Scandinavia—that this chapter focuses.

Substantial information on the lived experience of religion and the religious creativity of ordinary people is scarce. Thanks to recent research, especially in England, we have begun to learn about lay practices at parochial levels—for example from items donated to churches by aristocrats, city administrators, and ordinary parishioners. However, although donations for the liturgical celebration of certain festivals (especially, Corpus Christi) and the particular iconographies of donated altar panels (especially those focused on Holy Kinship) reflect the piety of patrons, they were predominantly displays of status and reveal little about individual beliefs, especially those of women.[3]

Other recent research, mostly in Germany, has shown us what theologians—especially Jean Gerson (the first "public intellectual"), Marquand of Lindau, and the theologians at the University of Vienna who, in the fifteenth century, developed a new *Frömmigkeitstheologie* (theology of piety)—contrived for the lay faithful. Popular preachers offered advice in sermons, and devotional treatises written in the vernacular did the same. Such German scholars as Arnold Angenendt, Klaus Schreiner, and Berndt Hamm use these sources to integrate abstract theology with the lived devotion of clergy, laywomen, and laymen in their studies.[4] But it remains to be seen how much these sources say about the piety of the laymen and particularly laywomen. Although many of the tracts were specifically written for a female audience, the women that the authors had in mind were, for the most part, cloistered nuns. Katherine French's studies on England are, in this respect, more useful because they include documents of practice and secular women. She contrasts the results of archival research with prescriptive sources to determine how real women behaved, as opposed to how didactic works interpreted this behavior. For French and other scholars working on English sources, the extraordinary autobiography of Margery Kempe (d. *c*.1438) provides a rich source of information.

Research on lay piety would benefit greatly from focusing strictly on the writings of and about holy laypeople in northern Europe, from the spiritual biography of Gertrude of Ortenberg (d.1335) in Germany to the autobiography of Kempe in England. If we are searching for the involvement of laypeople in religious culture and the lay practices of religion, these texts provide us with illuminating evidence, particularly if we focus on contemporary biographies. Many such texts on holy laywomen (and some holy laymen)—as distinct from the vowed religious in cloisters—have not yet been studied either collectively or systematically. Unlike traditional lives of saints, these texts were usually not written with a view to canonization; they were designed as exemplary narratives of devoted holiness, narratives filled with appealing anecdotes. These texts certainly sought to shape and praise models of lay piety, but by incorporating a great deal of basic information about the religious practices of the heroine and the religious culture in which she lived, they also provide us today with discreet and unguarded glimpses of laywomen's piety. They offer unprecedented detail about the interwoven textures of daily life and personal piety. The richest of these texts were written by authors who were (more or less) contemporaries of their subjects; these are least touched by sermonizing as well as *Frömmigkeitstheologie*. To tap into this treasury of detail on laywomen's piety, I will begin with a brief outline of the socio-economic developments in northern Europe, discuss some of the biographies in detail, and then explore a few aspects of the shared spirituality of holy laypeople and the faithful.

Socio-Economic Background

By the thirteenth century, urban society in northern Europe became focused on the household as the basic unit of society. The house became the main stage on which the householder and his wife acted as the two main protagonists.[5] A couple, with their children and often a few servants, ran the household and adjoining workshop or business. Well-known holy laywomen such as Mary of Oignies (d.1213), Yvette of Huy (d.1228), Elisabeth of Thuringia (d.1231), Bridget of Sweden (d.1373), and Dorothy of Montau (d.1394) governed such households, along with their husbands. Margery Kempe did the same, though she lived on her own after she turned forty. After the death of their husbands, widows could maintain their independence as long as they had sufficient financial resources, and the holy women studied here all had this advantage.[6]

Children usually left home at relatively young ages to train in other households. They often obtained a solid education, girls included. As future wives, they would come to play vital roles in the household and workshop. It is therefore not surprising that many holy laywomen could read, both in the vernacular and in Latin. In northern Europe, couples married relatively late, and many people never married. For scholars such as Mary Hartmann and Katherine Lynn, this pattern of late marriage was, in fact, the most fundamental difference between northern Europe and the rest of the world.[7] Women already had years of self-support behind them when they married, and had grown accustomed to a certain independence. Moreover, they had a shorter time to bear children and cared for correspondingly smaller families. Women's independence continued after marriage, with some wives even taking up their own occupations. Margery Kempe, for example, founded a brewery and later a mill. Since urban children in the north shared in their parents' inheritance whether they were married or not, it was relatively easy for girls to acquire independent livelihoods and survive, for example, as beguines or urban recluses. Christina the Astonishing (d.1223) and her two sisters in Brabant constituted an independent household after the death of their parents. Ida of Louvain (*fl.* 1250) left her parental home as a young adult and lived in a private (ascetic) household in the city. Agnes Blannbekin (d.1315) moved from the countryside to Vienna, where she established herself as an independent religious woman. Others allowed themselves to be enclosed in cells, such as Eve of Liège (d. after 1264) and Lame Margaret of Magdeburg (d. *c.*1250).[8]

The availability of such life choices created differences in women's piety in northern and southern Europe. In southern regions, where women had fewer opportunities for personal independence, female piety was directed toward convents. Only in the cities of Lombardy and Tuscany did some women pursue pious lives out of convents. After her father's death, Catherine of Siena (d.1380), for example, lived in an ascetic household together with her mother and sister. Even some holy laymen, such as Homobonus of Cremona (d.1197), emerged in Italian cities.[9] But for most women in Italy and southern France, the primary site for a religious life was the monastery, not the household.

In the north, townspeople formulated new pieties that suited their life experiences, drawing on individual and ethical interpretations of Christian faith. They also developed new rituals to bind believers together. Though long undervalued, women's roles in these changes were substantial. The anchoress Lame Margaret became a binding force among the citizens of Magdeburg. The widow Gertrude of Ortenberg created an appropriate religious routine for craftsmen, who could not go to church to pray seven times a day. The learned woman Juliana of Cornillon (d.1258) conceived a major new feast for the Eucharist, the festival of Corpus Christi, for which she fashioned the Latin liturgy. This festival, with its procession through the city and its pageant play, evolved into a central celebration of urban identity throughout Europe. Juliana and her companion, the recluse Eve of Liège, are the most striking examples of holy laywomen who understood the needs of the urban community and provided appropriate rituals.[10]

RELIGION OF THE LAY

While, in canon law, *religio* is a technical term for holy orders, the term *religiosus* became increasingly elastic from the thirteenth century onward; it came to signify any exemplary religious person, not just vowed monastics. According to the canonist Hostiensis (d.1271), it was not permanent vows and monastic life that made someone into a truly religious person, but devotion, piety, and striving for Christian perfection.[11] Initially, such exemplary lay religiosity was mostly embodied by beguines and female recluses, the *mulieres religiosae*. In the fourteenth century, laymen in addition to laywomen began to focus on a consecrated life in the world, this especially in the Upper Rhine; they called themselves Friends of God. In Strasbourg, a banker named Rulman Merswin (d.1382) and his wife inspired a large group of devout individuals, and in Basel, a woman we know only as Margaretha was, in her house *Zum Goldenen Ring* (of the Golden Ring), the hub of another group.[12]

In the fifteenth century, reformist Dominican John Nyder enumerated eight types of consecrated laypeople in what he describes as the "German countries" (by which he meant much of northern Europe). In his *De secularium religionibus* (*Practicing Religion in the World*), he posits that these eight types "devoted themselves to divine service more devoutly than other lay persons," even more devoutly than the professional "religious" in the monasteries.[13] He distinguishes hermits, the virtuosos who lived in total isolation far from the civilized world; beguines and beghards; male and female recluses; and secular canonesses, a specifically German phenomenon dating from Carolingian times. These categories included believers who had stepped out of their ordinary lives in order to devote themselves full-time to God, though not in a monastic context. Religious women often lived in small groups together in one house, he writes, a *domus animarum* (house of souls). Indeed, we find many such houses, called in the vernacular *Gotzhusen* (houses of God) or *Seelshusen* (houses of souls) in urban charters; some were, for example, the ascetic domestic households of widows. Nyder then identifies other people who, in their daily existence at work and with their family, led strictly religious lives. They might be tertiaries living according to the Third Rule of St Francis or St Dominic (these were, it should be noted, distinct from those tertiaries who lived in monasteries). They might be *donati*, that is, lay believers who lived in a spiritual brotherhood with monks.[14] Nyder's work was sometimes coolly received by clerics and monastics, but it was usually cautiously accepted, and his categories fit well the holy laypeople discussed here.

Holy laywomen were religious leaders and much more. As André Vauchez has shown, pious laypeople, in particular independent laywomen, found newly prominent voices during the crisis of the papal schism in the fourteenth and fifteenth centuries. And, as John Van Engen has demonstrated, new religious initiatives then came from churchmen such as Geert Grote *and* from inspired women.[15] These women were not just charismatic leaders but also exponents of new ideals in their communities of belief. Raised in the great cities of northern Europe, they dedicated their entire lives to God in the secular world, and in so doing, they gave expression to still unarticulated aspirations of their fellow citizens. They developed a religious lifestyle that was independent of the old monastic existence, and they assumed leadership roles in their informal communities of knowing and believing. They became the visible exponents of a broad religious renewal that swept up men and women in its wake. As Henry Mayr-Harting once astutely stated at a conference on Christina of Markyate, these women provided "the electricity of spiritual power to administrators and church prelates."

The noble lady Gertrude of Ortenberg (*c.*1275–1335) was such a leader, a widow of great authority in Strasbourg and the neighboring Offenburg. Her epitaph reads, "she protected the city from many dangers," and her protection is elucidated by many anecdotes in a spiritual biography written by a younger adherent.[16] After the death of her husband, Gertrude, pregnant with her fourth child, moved to the city of Offenburg, situated across the Rhine from Strasbourg. There she converted to the religious life without ever entering an order or a convent, and she settled down as an independent religious widow amidst other devout women. Heilke of Staufenberg, a young woman also from noble stock, soon joined her. While Gertrude developed into the spiritual mother and mystic, Heilke revealed herself to be the master and mistress; she managed the household and molded an intellectual network of poor women and learned mendicants. Later, the (anonymous) female biographer also joined them. The homes of the poor sisters were close to the Convent of the Franciscans, where the women performed their daily prayers. Devout brothers and *hohe lesemeister* (readers) acted as private teachers and confessors; they regularly visited Gertrude at home. Gertrude and Heilke also travelled to Strasbourg, where they heard famous mendicant preachers. One of the sermons so strikingly evoked Gertrude's own aspirations that she asked Heilke to "repreach" it at home. Apparently the women held "preaching sessions" at home, where they listened to Heilke, discussed the sermons (and, I suppose, other texts), and accommodated the learning into their own spirituality. Toward the end of Gertrude's biography, the biographer included a summary of the above-mentioned sermon and gave it her own interpretation. She modeled the entire biography along the lines of this sermon and showed that Gertrude lived the ideal of the detached woman in the world, the ideal about which the mendicants, in particular Meister Eckhart (d.1328), the famous Dominican scholar who worked in Strasbourg in those years, were preaching.

Gertrude's biographer reports that, in the first period of her religious life, Gertrude focused on penance, asceticism, and spiritual growth. After sixteen years, when she was about forty, she experienced a decisive life change, after which she became more engaged in public life. She and Heilke then moved for several years to Strasbourg, where Gertrude continued her exemplary asceticism, while providing pastoral guidance to the rich and assisting the poor at the same time. She helped organize processions, mediated feuds, assisted exiles, and devoted herself to peace. "God revealed the sins of fellow citizens to her, whom she then reminded of their responsibility. The words that she spoke to people struck right to the heart. In her salvific agency she even outdid the mendicants" (fol. 233v).

A SELECTION OF TEXTS

We have recently gained access to many more texts that, like the biography of Gertrude, tell us about the lives of holy laywomen. For instance, Gertrude felt inspired by Elisabeth of Hungary, Lantgravina of Thuringia, a lay saint about whom detailed information is available through the testimonies of her ladies-in-waiting. Elisabeth became the icon of the holy laywoman on the continent of Europe. According to her ladies, Elisabeth traveled around the country with her husband, striving to build a strong Christian government. In an intimate love relationship with him, she bore him three children. While she exercised strict asceticism (she often slipped from the marital bed in the middle of the night to continue sleeping on the floor), she subjected herself to a harsh confessor. When, after the death of her husband, that confessor inquired whether she wished to enter a monastery (as previous princesses had done) or opt for an anchorhold (as became then the fashion), she resolutely dismissed both options. She wanted to remain in the world as a devout laywoman living in the city. In Marburg, she set up a private household, founded a hospital for the poor, and worked herself into such a state of emaciation that she died three years later.

In turn, Elisabeth was perhaps aware of the first *mulieres religiosae* in the Low Countries, Yvette of Huy and Mary of Oignies. As a young widow, Yvette cared for lepers and gathered around her men and women who shared her ideal of apostolic living. At the age of thirty-three, she had herself enclosed in an anchorhold, from whence she kept watch over the city and its faithful. An intimate friend of hers wrote a theologically elaborate Latin life that testified to a deep, personal love for the *sapientissima mater* (wisest of mothers). Mary of Oignies, married and living with her family in a religious community near Nivelles, spent the last years of her life as a recluse in Oignies, while working closely with Jacques de Vitry, the later cardinal. Jacques wrote a life with touching detail (he criticized the endless tears of Mary, but was himself irresistibly brought to tears while celebrating mass). He modeled the laywoman into a saint incarnate: anyone could be a saint under his or her own conditions of existence. The noble widow Jutta of Sangerhausen (d.1260) was inspired by Elisabeth of Thuringia and did missionary work from her anchorhold in East Germany. She, like Elisabeth, was called *soror in seculo*, a religious laywoman in the world, by Mechthild of Magdeburg (d. c.1282) who wrote about her.[17]

The Life of Mary of Oignies was distributed in England, where Margery Kempe was encouraged by her example (Mary's crying suited her well). It also was known in Italy, where first Pope Gregory IX and later Catherine of Siena would be inspired by Mary's example. Just as Elisabeth was a model on the continent, Bridget of Sweden had a similar role in Scandinavia and England. After Bridget and her husband took a spiritual "gap year" to prepare for the last phase of their lives, and after her husband died shortly afterwards, Bridget became a prophet in her native Sweden and the conscience of the church in Rome. Catherine of Siena would later emulate her in Italy and Rome.[18]

Kempe, Bridget, and Catherine were authors themselves, just as Hadewijch of Brabant (*fl.* thirteenth century) and Mechthild of Magdeburg composed devotional texts in the vernacular. Juliana of Cornillon created a Latin liturgy of the Corpus Christi festival. Eve of Liège, Julian of Norwich (d. after 1416), and Katharina Tucher (d. c.1440) also authored religious texts. Agnes Blannbekin elaborated a religious doctrine in Vienna, which she had a Franciscan transcribe in Latin.[19]

Alongside these well-documented holy laywomen were many others unknown to us today. We know about these women only if contemporaries regarded them as living saints and wrote about them. These contemporary accounts were sometimes blurred in later times, as the church sought to adapt these women's profiles to prevailing ecclesiastical standards. Viewed through this clerical filter, Elisabeth of Thuringia displays many of the characteristics of a Franciscan, and Catherine of Siena a Dominican. Only since Gabriella Zarri's study, *Le sante vive*, have holy women been properly placed in their primary locations: court circles, households, parishes, and confraternities. Only since such studies as Thomas Luongo's work on Catherine has appropriate emphasis been placed on the historical agency of these women. As a result, we can now see them as innovative pioneers of lay spirituality.[20]

THEMES

As a rule, laypeople in the Middle Ages were good Christians; they believed what the church instructed them. They lived out the history of salvation in their own devotions, celebrated the Eucharist, venerated the saints, and went on pilgrimages. In so doing, they made choices—from a vast array of options—about how to express their faith, and their choices reflected both context and personality. They respected the limits set by the church but were also led by holy laypeople, who aspired to extend the boundaries of lay piety. They experienced their faith outside the monastery and often even outside the church building, in places and circles in which they were familiar. While the church sought to monopolize the sacral in the clerical body and keep ritual in church, holy lay-women and the faithful were hardly deterred. For them, the sacred was immanent to the entire community of the faithful. Despite canonical and clerical opposition, but in concord with sympathetic mendicants and confessors, the pious found niches in which they could express their faith. These niches included ascetic, devotional households; personal networks and confraternities; intellectual work; and the claiming, by some women, of religious authority.

First, holy households were both a model and a practice. When, in 1509, the confraternity of the humble porters in Lübeck wanted an altar panel for their chapel, they commissioned a painting on a topic much favored by other guilds: holy kinship. The panel showed St Anne and her three daughters, all called Mary, with their husbands and their children (according to legend, John the Baptist and the leading apostles all belonged to the extended family of Anne). But unlike other more famous holy kinship panels, the porters did not have Anne dwelling in the midst of her "clan" as the central figure in the family; instead, they had four separate panels painted, each with a nuclear family: mother and father, sometimes a grandmother, and one or two children at play. The composition shows four conjugal households in a row, and the message was clear: faith was to be experienced in the nuclear family.[21]

By the later Middle Ages, some households functioned as religious centers, with the mistress in charge: "mother knows best."[22] Sometimes these were ascetic domestic households, like that of the widow Gertrude of Ortenberg. Her biographer describes in detail how Gertrude was a rich, noble lady, knowledgeable about such matters as estate income, autumn slaughtering, and purchases of bread and wine. At the same time, the biographer highlights how utterly ascetic and deprived was Gertrude's daily routine. In her own devotional practice Gertrude followed the Third Rule of St Francis. Her house was a place where poor women, fellow citizens, and mendicants met. The house of Catherine of Siena and her mother also seems to have been an ascetic domestic household, where a network of religious (older) women and mendicants met each other. In fifteenth-century Rome, Francesca Romana's house was the center of a group of penitent women. Even the Cathar Arnauda de Lamothe operated for a time from a manor in Massac.[23] There she preached, bestowed blessings on people, and engaged regularly with the Cathar "laywomen" and "laymen."[24]

Beguines and sisters of the Modern Devotion also lived in private religious households that were neither convents nor monasteries. These women made no monastic vows and did not enter cloistered life. They did not renounce their right to self-determination, and they did not sever ties with their urban neighbors. According to Katherine Lynch, what many women sought from such communities was "an existence that had real continuity with their everyday lives and tasks, a more flexible sort of affiliation."[25] Just as the Roman family headed by the paterfamilias was St Benedict's model for monks governed by a father abbot, the medieval urban household managed by the lady of the house was the model for the ascetic religious household. Of course, it must be noted, in the fourteenth and fifteenth centuries, many private households of beguines and the devout were transformed into convents and even monasteries. Whether under external pressure or not, these women (and men) eventually accepted vows and a rule.

To date, little attention has been paid to these pious households and their significance for religious life. When, in the twelfth and thirteenth centuries, *mulieres religiosae* in the southern Netherlands were looking for appropriate modes of life in the city, they were urged by Jacques de Vitry to constitute religious households. He obtained permission for this way of life from Pope Honorius III, so that "religious women, not only in the diocese of Liège but also in France and the Empire, [were] permitted to live in the same house and to incite each other toward the good by mutual exhortation." In 1233, an episcopal synod in Mainz decreed that women who did not want to follow a recognized rule, but practiced chastity and wore special clothing, should live from their own manual labor in privately owned houses. As implicitly acknowledged in this decree, the ascetic domestic household was part of the landscape of late medieval German towns.[26]

In short, the household, especially the ascetic domestic household run by a widow, became an appropriate place for women to cultivate their faith in a manner that was comfortable for themselves, reliable for their fellow citizens, and acceptable even to critical clerics. From such homes, they were able to fulfill a spiritual role in their neighborhoods and the surrounding world. Some acquired the status of living saints. What Kim Bowes noted about late antiquity—that the household was the place where female holiness could flourish—appears to have applied to the later Middle Ages as well.[27]

In medieval legend, Martha, the hard-working sister of the more contemplative Mary (considered to be Mary Magdalene by the faithful in northern Europe), came to epitomize the ideal of the holy woman in the world. For Meister Eckhart, Martha was a matron "of wise understanding" who was free and unfettered in life. From her own home where she lived with her sister Mary, she practiced the spirituality of active life, or as Eckhart put it, "dear Martha stands in the midst of things, but not in things" (Sermon 86). This is exactly what the holy laywomen did: they combined the ideal of the contemplative life with active charity. In previous centuries, monks had always regarded their contemplative way of life as the ultimate expression of faith and viewed charitable laypeople as second-class believers. Monks acted charitably, but only at the monastic doors that separated their withdrawn life from the world outside. In the thirteenth century, townsfolk practiced charity in more active, inner-worldly forms and strove for contemplation in—not away from—the bustle of everyday life. *Mulieres religiosae* combined work in hospitals with their life of prayer and meditation. They claimed, along with Eckhart, the spirituality of active life as the highest form of perfection. Martha was their icon; the mother of a beguine house, by consequence, was often called *Maerte* or Martha.[28]

Second, in addition to ascetic domestic households, holy women operated within informal and formal networks based on these households. Ida of Louvain, for instance, welcomed townspeople, who came for good conversation or spiritual instruction, to her house. Beguines then stayed for the night; in the evening, they would sit on the balcony, gaze at the sky, and talk about heavenly things. Clerics, monks, and mendicants also came to visit her, constituting an informal religious network centered on the women. Peter of Dacia, on his visits to Christina of Stommeln (d.1312), always encountered a stable group of believers at her house.[29] These inspiring and informal networks were elaborately detailed in the autobiography of Margery Kempe, who presented herself as someone who flourished in such groups. At home, her husband helped realize her eccentric wishes and went along on local pilgrimages (though not on the longer trips abroad). She dined with him once a week, on Friday evenings. But she also dined away from home, with those who asked her to eat with them, as such occasions professed togetherness and a community of faith. She found her religious identity and sense of belonging in these little communities. She also took spiritual sustenance from a reading group in which she, a priest, and others read devotional texts and lives of such figures as Mary of Oignies and Bridget of Sweden.

Books were important to Margery and women like her; they were the carriers of relationships, the conveyors of the spiritual bonds both among readers, and the forgers of a spirituality that linked readers to the holy folk about whom they read.[30] These holy examples inspired and authorized them; in Margery's view, for example, the tears of Mary and Jacques de Vitry legitimized her own weeping and fit her own experiences into the history of salvation. Three-fourths of the surviving medieval manuscripts from the Low and German countries contain devotional texts, often a whole range of different texts in a single volume. Could such miscellanies have been composed for pious reading groups? The research on this subject—that is, the use of an entire manuscript, rather than of an individual text found in many manuscripts—has only just begun.[31]

As to more formal networks, the thirteenth century was also the moment when confraternities and parish guilds appeared all over northern Europe. Apart from various socio-economic and political functions these groups had first and foremost a religious purpose. They took care of masses, processions, and funerals; they encouraged the instruction of group members; and they strove to ensure peace, concord, and amity. Gilles Gerard Meersseman has assembled a large quantity of source material on this subject and paved the way for further investigation—which is still to be done. Katherine French has discovered a large number of all-female groups existing in fifteenth-century England. These parish guilds, as she calls them, gave women the opportunity to support their religious communities with money-raising, gifts, and labor. Did such groups also exist on the continent? Anne Winston-Allen points to the emergence of the rosary and rosary fraternities. What these types of associations meant for laypeople's piety is still to be determined.[32]

Third, the holy laypeople of the later Middle Ages claimed intellectual power, even taking their places alongside church theologians. In the fifteenth century, German countries experienced an explosion of devotional texts written in the vernacular. In England Kempe read new devotional tracts in English. But the faithful were not satisfied with such devout instruction; they wanted more. They commissioned translations of biblical texts (e.g. the Bible translated in Brussels in 1360), biblical commentaries, and theological treatises. Some clerics thought difficult theological texts were not suitable for lay reading, but this did not deter the Friends of God in Basel from commissioning a copy of the *Summa theologica* of Thomas Aquinas. The group also took great pains to acquire a manuscript—revised into their local dialect—of Mechthild of Magdeburg's *The Flowing Light of the Godhead*. In authoring her liturgy for the festival of Corpus Christi, Juliana of Cornillon demonstrated that she was a theologian of international stature, just as Julian of Norwich would do in the next century with her *Revelations of Divine Love*. Heilke of Staufenberg was another theologically astute laywoman who instructed Gertrude of Ortenberg and others. The Latin *vita* of Lame Margaret of Magdeburg contains the lessons that she offered her study circle, lessons that she expressly sought to be preserved for posterity. Yvette of Huy personally gave her son a cleric's basic education. Christina the Astonishing interpreted Latin texts to her visitors. In Nuremberg, the merchant's widow Katharina Tucher set herself to study after her husband's death. She compiled a library of manuscripts, partly consisting of contemporary devotional tracts (sometimes copied in her own handwriting) as well as saints' lives, and partly comprising liturgical texts, bible commentaries, and writings of the church fathers and theologians. She personally wrote a diary in dialogue form, relating conversations between her and Christ. The booklet tells of Katharina's spiritual struggle to organize her life and to hear the voice of Christ in her heart. She contemplated life in a convent, and admired an anchoress living in a cell for thirty years, but she recognized that she could, along with Mary Magdalene, wash Jesus's feet and serve God in the world.[33]

Agnes Blannbekin might have had a similar library at her disposal in Vienna when she created her *Offenbarungen* (*Revelations*), in which she unveiled a complete doctrine, also in the form of mystical dialogues, written down in Latin by a helpful Franciscan priest. As I have argued elsewhere, Agnes, Katharina, and the others did not allow the clergy to prevent them from studying theological issues. They confidently developed their own visions, but—and here is where the limit lay—they did not put these to writing in scholastic form or write them in Latin. They recorded what Christ "revealed" to them (sometimes after years of study), or they worked with established theologians. This collaboration had an unexpected effect: it brought the lived spirituality of women together with the book-learning of men. Together they developed a new genre, what I have called *the Book of Life*.[34]

Fourth, these holy laywomen sometimes claimed public authority within their communities. They did not, of course, attain official ministries within the power structures of the church. Nor did they acquire equal rights with pious laymen. But they were much more than (merely) charismatic phenomena, as traditional scholarship has so often assumed. I would argue that the holy women, and the laypeople in their wake, were respected as authoritative religious leaders. Their authority is best imagined through the metaphor of society as a woolen cloth—that is, a fabric with warp and weft. Each community needs warp threads of laws and institutions, but it also requires connecting threads of conventions and traditions; these threads are not enforced by coercive power but rather by persuasive individuals. Without warp threads, society has no solidity; without weft, it has no social dignity. Administrators and clergy provided most of the warp threads of medieval society. But within the living community of believers, holy women wove the weft. Gary Macy's incisive study of clerical ordination provides an apposite example.[35] Macy argues that true ordination as a priest and deacon (in the sense that we understand it) did not exist prior to the Fourth Lateran Council in 1215; rather, it was the vocation of a holy person that mattered to the community and the special ministry that person performed. An anchoress or a holy widow could have a vocation just like a priest (though for different kinds of ministry). After 1215 the new sacramental ordination of a priest was detached from any particular church or community, and it became a generic, all-decisive, and exclusive moment, which granted a universal, sacred power. The priest's authority became tied to the service at the altar and not to a particular vocation. It was given to trained clerics. Thereafter, only ordained clerics could exert spiritual power, and, as a consequence, all others—including holy women—became lay outsiders. Macy's argument is compelling, but it might see too sharp a break in 1215. Perhaps the faithful in fourteenth-century Offenburg and Strasbourg still accepted Gertrude's vocation in the community and thus, her spiritual power. The weft threads in the social fabric still maintained these communities as much as did the warp threads. Due to Gertrude's spiritual power, she commanded a non-institutional form of authority, a gravitas that did not depend on the institutional powers of church and city.

Laywomen forged, then, the horizontal bonds of piety in late medieval Europe. In their households and among their circles of neighbors and fellow citizens, they confidently and discreetly wielded power, a power quite different from that of monastery or pulpit. These holy laywomen strove for religious perfection in the world, and they acquired reputations of living sanctity. Were they just marginal and enigmatic figures? No. They acted in the heart of society. With their local authority they provided the social dignity and offered the support to the emerging offices and institutions of the later Middle Ages. These holy laywomen were resolute in their faith, confident in their worship, and influential in their world.

Translation Robert Olsen

FURTHER READING

Angenendt, Arnold. *Geschichte der Religiosität im Mittelalter*. Darmstadt: Wissenschaftliche Buchgesellschaft, 1997.

Blume, Dieter and Matthias Werner, eds. *Elisabeth von Thüringen—eine europäische Heilige*, 2 vols. Petersberg: Imhof, 2007.

French, Katherine L. *The Good Women of the Parish: Gender and Religion after the Black Death*. Philadelphia: University of Pennsylvania Press, 2008.

Luongo, F. Thomas. *The Saintly Politics of Catherine of Siena*. Ithaca: Cornell, 2006.

Lynch, Katherine. *Individuals, Families, and Communities in Europe, 1200–1800*. Cambridge; New York: Cambridge University Press, 2003.

Macy, Gary. *The Hidden History of Women's Ordination: Female Clergy in the Medieval West*. Oxford; New York: Oxford University Press, 2008.

Mulder-Bakker, Anneke B. *Lives of the Anchoresses: The Rise of the Urban Recluse in Medieval Europe*. Philadelphia: University of Pennsylvania Press, 2005.

Mulder-Bakker, Anneke B. and Liz Herbert McAvoy, eds. *Women and Experience in Later Medieval Writing: Reading the Book of Life*. New York: Palgrave MacMillan, 2009.

Simons, Walter. *Cities of Ladies: Beguine Communities in the Medieval Low Countries*. Philadelphia: University of Pennsylvania Press, 2001.

Van Engen, John. "Friar Johannes Nyder on Laypeople Living as Religious in the World," in Frans J. Felten, Nikolas Jaspert, and Stephanie Haarländer, eds, *Vita Religiosa im Mittelalter: Festschrift für Kaspar Elm*. Berlin: Duncker & Humblot, 2004, 583–615.

NOTES

1. André Vauchez, "Le charisma et l'institution," in idem, ed., *Histoire des saints et de la sainteté chrétienne* (Paris: Hachette, 1986), VII: 38–41.
2. David Nicholas, *The Northern Lands: Germanic Europe, c. 1270–c. 1500* (Oxford: Blackwell, 2009). He pays no attention to culture and religion.
3. Katherine L. French, *The Good Women of the Parish: Gender and Religion after the Black Death* (Philadelphia: University of Pennsylvania Press, 2008). Civic religion: André Vauchez, ed., *La Religion civique à l'époque médiévale et moderne (Chrétienté et Islam)* (Rome: École française de Rome, 1995).
4. Daniel Hobbins, "The Schoolman as Public Intellectual: Jean Gerson and the Late Medieval Tract," *American Historical Review*, 108 (2003): 1308–37. *Frömmigkeitstheologie* was coined by Berndt Hamm: Robert Bast, ed. and trans., *The Reformation of Faith in the Context of Late Medieval Theology and Piety: Essays by Berndt Hamm* (Leiden: Brill, 2004). Arnold Angenendt, *Geschichte der Religiosität im Mittelalter* (Darmstadt: Wissenschaftliche Buchgesellschaft, 1997); Klaus Schneider, ed., *Laienfrömmigkeit im späten Mittelalter: Formen, Funktionen, politisch-soziale Zusammenhänge* (Munich: Oldenbourg, 1992). A critical view by John Van Engen, "Multiple Options: The World of the Fifteenth-Century Church," *Church History*, 77 (2008): 257–84.
5. Peter Blickle, *Kommunalismus: Skizzen einer gesellschaftlichen Organisationsform*, 2 vols (Munich: Oldenbourg, 2000) and *Das Alte Europa: Vom Hochmittelalter bis zur Moderne* (Munich: Beck, 2008). Older studies such as David Herlihy's *Medieval Households* (Cambridge, Mass.: Harvard University Press, 1985) are mostly economically oriented

and focus on southern Europe. Household and domesticity have now become booming topics; see Jennifer Kolpacoff Deane, "Pious Domesticities," Chapter 17 in this volume.

6. Anneke B. Mulder-Bakker, ed., *Mary of Oignies: Mother of Salvation* (Turnhout: Brepols, 2006) with English translation of *vita* and studies. Yvette: Anneke B. Mulder-Bakker, ed., *Living Saints of the Thirteenth Century* (Turnhout: Brepols, 2011), 47–141 also with English translation of *vita*. Dieter Blume and Matthias Werner, eds, *Elisabeth von Thüringen— eine europäische Heilige*, 2 vols (Petersberg: Imhof, 2007). Claire L. Sahlin, *Birgitta of Sweden and the Voice of Prophecy* (Woodbridge: Boydell, 2001). Ute Stargardt, "Dorothy of Montau," in Alastair Minnis and Rosalynn Voaden, eds, *Medieval Holy Women in the Christian Tradition c. 1100–c. 1500* (Turnhout: Brepols, 2010), 475–96. Barry Windeatt, ed., *The Book of Margery Kempe* (Harlow: Longman, 2000).

7. Mary S. Hartmann, *The Household and the Making of History: A Subversive View of the Western Past* (Cambridge; New York: Cambridge University Press, 2004); Katherine Lynch, *Individuals, Families, and Communities in Europe, 1200–1800* (Cambridge; New York: Cambridge University Press, 2003); Martha C. Howell, "From Land to Love: Commerce and Marriage in Northern Europe during the Late Middle Ages," *Jaarboek voor Middeleeuwse Geschiedenis*, 10 (2007): 217–53.

8. Christina: Barbara Newman, ed. and trans., *Thomas of Cantimpré: The Collected Saints' Lives* (Turnhout: Brepols, 2008), 125–57. Herman Vekeman, ed. and trans., *Ida van Leuven, c. 1211–1290* (Budel: Damon, 2006). Ulrike Wiethaus, trans., *Agnes Blannbekin, Viennese Beguine: Life and Revelations* (Woodbridge: Brewer, 2002). Eve of Liège and Lame Margaret: Mulder-Bakker, ed., *Living Saints*, 143–396. General: Walter Simons, *Cities of Ladies: Beguine Communities in the Medieval Low Countries* (Philadelphia: University of Pennsylvania Press, 2001); Anneke B. Mulder-Bakker, *Lives of the Anchoresses: The Rise of the Urban Recluse in Medieval Europe* (Philadelphia: University of Pennsylvania Press, 2005); Minnis and Voaden, eds, *Medieval Holy Women*.

9. Catherine of Siena: Maiju Lehmijoki-Gardner, *Worldly Saints: Social Interactions of Dominican Penitent Women in Italy, 1200–1500* (Helsinki: Suomen Historiallinen Seura, 1999) and see note 20. Homobonus: André Vauchez, *Les laïcs au Moyen Age* (Paris: Cerf, 1987), 77–82. For France, see Renate Blumenfeld-Kosinski, "The Strange Case of Ermine de Reims (c.1347–1396)," *Speculum*, 85 (2010): 321–56.

10. For Gertrude of Ortenberg, see note 16. Lame Margaret and Juliana of Cornillon: Mulder-Bakker, ed., *Living Saints*, 143–396.

11. Elizabeth Makowski, "*Mulieres religiosae*, Strictly Speaking: Some Fourteenth-Century Canonical Opinions," *Catholic Historical Review*, 85 (1999): 1–14 and idem, "*A Pernicious Sort of Woman*": *Quasi-Religious Women and Canon Lawyers in the Later Middle Ages* (Washington, DC: Catholic University of America Press, 2005). Centre européen de recherches sur les congregations et ordres religieux and Centre international d'études romanes (CERCOR), ed., *Les mouvances laïques des ordres religieux* (Saint-Étienne: Université de Sainte-Étienne, 1996) contains initial surveys of religious ways of life between the monastery and the world. No in-depth study has yet been made, which represents a great deficiency in our knowledge of lay piety.

12. Bernard McGinn, *The Presence of God: A History of Western Christian Mysticism*, vol. IV: *The Harvest of Mysticism in Medieval Germany* (New York: Crossroad, 2005), 407–32.

13. John Van Engen, "Friar Johannes Nyder on Laypeople Living as Religious in the World," in Frans J. Felten, Nikolas Jaspert, and Stephanie Haarländer, eds, *Vita Religiosa im Mittelalter: Festschrift für Kaspar Elm* (Berlin: Duncker & Humblot, 2004), 583–615.

14. Cf. Charles de Miramon, *Les "donnés" au Moyen Age: Une forme de vie religieuse laïque (1180–1500)* (Paris: Cerf, 1999).

15. Vauchez, "Le charisma et l'institution," 38–41; Van Engen, "Multiple Options," 263.

16. The fourteenth-century Middle High German text is preserved in a fifteenth-century manuscript in the Royal Library in Brussels, MS 8507-09. It is not yet edited nor extensively studied. See Eugen Hillenbrand, "Heiligenleben und Alltag: Offenburger Stadtgeschichte im Spiegel eines spätmittelalterlichen Beginenlebens," *Die Ortenau*, 90 (2010): 157–76. My own *Lives of Their Own: The Dedicated Spiritual Life of Upper Rhine Women*, which deals with Gertrude of Ortenberg and Heilke of Staufenberg, is forthcoming.

17. Balazs J. Nemes, "Jutta von Sangerhausen (13. Jahrhundert): Eine 'neue Heilige' im Gefolge der heiligen Elisabeth von Thüringen?" *Zeitschrift für Thüringische Geschichte*, 63 (2009): 39–73.

18. On the other side of forty: Anneke B. Mulder-Bakker and Renée Nip, eds, *The Prime of Their Lives: Wise Old Women in Pre-industrial Europe* (Louvain: Peters, 2004).

19. Columba Hart, trans., *Hadewijch: The Complete Works* (New York: Paulist Press, 1980). Sara S. Poor, *Mechthild of Magdeburg and Her Book: Gender and the Making of Textual Authority* (Philadelphia: University of Pennsylvania Press, 2004). Nicholas Watson and Jacqueline Jenkins, eds, *The Writings of Julian of Norwich: "A Vision Showed to a Devout Woman" and "A Revelation of Love"* (Turnhout: Brepols, 2006). Juliana and Eve: see notes 10 and 8; Agnes Blannbekin: see note 8; Katharina Tucher: see note 33.

20. For Elisabeth of Thuringia, see note 6. Gabriella Zarri, *Le sante vive: Profezie di corte e devozione femminile tra '400 e '500* (Turin: Rosenberg & Sellier, 1990). F. Thomas Luongo, *The Saintly Politics of Catherine of Siena* (Ithaca: Cornell, 2006).

21. Lübeck, 1509; Sankt-Annen Museum, Inv. 125.

22. Inspiring studies by Felicity Riddy, "Women Talking About the Things of God: A Late Medieval Subculture," in Carol M. Meale, ed., *Women and Literature in Britain, 1150–1500* (Cambridge; New York: Cambridge University Press, 1993), 104–27; idem, "Mother Knows Best: Reading Social Change in a Courtesy Text," *Speculum*, 71 (1996): 66–86; Christine Peters, *Women, Gender and Religion in Late Medieval and Reformation England* (New York: Cambridge University Press, 2003).

23. Discussed by John Arnold, "Heresy and Gender in the Middle Ages," Chapter 31 in this volume.

24. Anna Esposito, "St. Francesca and the Female Religious Communities of Fifteenth-Century Rome," in Daniel Bornstein and Roberto Rusconi, eds, *Women and Religion in Medieval and Renaissance Italy* (Chicago: University of Chicago Press, 1996), 197–218. On women in the neighborhood: Karen Scott, "Urban Spaces, Women's Networks, and the Lay Apostolate in the Siena of Catherine Benincasa," in E. Ann Matter and John Wayland Coakley, eds, *Creative Women in Medieval and Early Modern Italy: A Religious and Artistic Renaissance* (Philadelphia: University of Pennsylvania Press, 1994), 105–19.

25. Lynch, *Individuals*, 86.

26. R. B. C. Huygens, ed., *Lettres de Jacques de Vitry (1160/1170–1240), évêque de Saint-Jean d'Acre* (Leiden: Brill, 1960), 74, no.1; written evidence of this papal privilege has not been preserved. Frank-Michael Reichstein, *Das Beginenwesen in Deutschland* (Berlin: Köster,

2001), 301. The Council of Vienne (1311) also made an exception for pious women living in households.

27. Kim Bowes, *Private Worship, Public Values, and Religious Change in Late Antiquity* (Cambridge; New York: Cambridge University Press, 2008).

28. On Martha, see also Deane, "Pious Domesticities." Brian Stock, "Activity, Contemplation, Work and Leisure between the 11th and 13th Century," in Brian Vickers, ed., *Arbeit, Musse, Meditation: Studies in the* vita activa *and* vita contemplativa (Stuttgart: Teubner, 1991), 87–108; François-Olivier Touati, "Les groupes de laïcs dans les hôpitaux et les léproseries au Moyen Age," in CERCOR, ed., *Les mouvances laïques*, 137–62.

29. On Ida, see note 8. Christine Ruhrberg, *Der literarische Körper der Heiligen: Leben und Viten der Christina von Stommeln (1242–1312)* (Tübingen: Francke, 1995).

30. Patricia Zimmerman Beckman, "The Power of Books and the Practice of Mysticism in the Fourteenth Century: Heinrich of Nördlingen and Margaret Ebner on Mechthild's *Flowing Light of the Godhead*," *Church History, 76* (2007): 61–83; Rebecca L. R. Garber, *Feminine Figurae: Representations of Gender in Religious Texts by Medieval German Women Writers, 1100–1375* (London: Routledge, 2003); Mary C. Erler, *Women, Reading, and Piety in Late Medieval England* (Cambridge; New York: Cambridge University Press, 2002); D. H. Green, *Women Readers in the Middle Ages* (Cambridge; New York: Cambridge University Press, 2007).

31. Anneke B. Mulder-Bakker, "The Household as a Site of Civic and Religious Instruction: Two Household Books from Late Medieval Brabant," in idem and Jocelyn Wogan-Browne, eds, *Household, Women, and Christianities in Late Antiquity and the Middle Ages* (Turnhout: Brepols, 2005), 191–214. Cf. Alexandra Barrat, *Anne Bulkeley and Her Book: Fashioning Female Piety in Early Tudor England: A Study of London, British Library, Ms Harley 494* (Turnhout: Brepols, 2009), a book of a mother and a daughter in a monastic context.

32. Gilles Gerard Meersseman, *Ordo fraternitatis: Confraternite e pietà dei laici nel Medioevo*, 3 vols (Rome: Herder, 1977); Vauchez, *Les laïcs*, 95–122; very illuminating, Caroline M. Barron, "The Parish Fraternities of Medieval London," in idem and Christopher Harper-Bill, eds, *The Church in Pre-Reformation Society* (Woodbridge: Boydell, 1985), 13–37; French, *The Good Women of the Parish*; Anne Winston-Allen, *Stories of the Rose: The Making of the Rosary in the Middle Ages* (University Park, Penn.: Penn State University Press, 1998).

33. McGinn, *The Harvest*; Ulla Williams and Werner Williams-Krapp, *Die "Offenbarungen" der Katharina Tucher* (Tübingen: Niemeyer, 1998).

34. Anneke B. Mulder-Bakker, "Two Women of Experience, Two Men of Letters, and the Book of Life," in idem and Liz Herbert McAvoy, eds, *Women and Experience in Later Medieval Writing: Reading the Book of Life* (New York: Palgrave MacMillan, 2009), 83–101.

35. Gary Macy, *The Hidden History of Women's Ordination: Female Clergy in the Medieval West* (Oxford; New York: Oxford University Press, 2008), 106.

CHAPTER 30

....

CULTS OF SAINTS

....

MIRI RUBIN

THE operation of gender affected all aspects of the cult of saints, from who was considered a saint to who could approach relics and shrines. While early Christians revered martyrs, early medieval Europeans respected greatly the virtues of bishops and monks. After 1200, the cult of the Virgin Mary was preeminent, and this meant that a woman's faith, love, and suffering inhabited the center of European devotional lives. The business of canonizing saints, building shrines, and recording the miracles of saints was dominated by men and associated with education, clerical authority, and freedom of movement. But the later medieval centuries saw a broadening of the range of holy lifestyles. Living saints had their followings in cities as well as in stark secluded places. With the intensification of travel, exchange, commerce, and cultural production, new genres and languages described and commemorated lives deemed holy. Many cults flourished without formal recognition—canonization, as it came to be known by the twelfth century—and some were the subject of disapproval from the church hierarchy. Ecclesiastical officials sought to contain emergent cults of holy women, since women—lay women in particular—were more suspect as examples of spiritual authority. Yet there was also a countervailing trend—bolstered by traditions of holy virgins and martyrs, nourished by the ever-present perfection of the Virgin Mary—that embraced female saints and their cults throughout the Middle Ages.

The historical study of cults of saints tells us more about collective perceptions of sanctity than about the personalities of the saints themselves. Our emphasis on the cult of saints—that is, on communication with the remains and virtues of saints—requires that we study the narratives and rituals through which such contact was made possible. We will discuss the cults of saints in the Middle Ages through three interlocking approaches, all attuned to the operation of gender. First, we will establish *who saints were and how they were made*; next, how *hagiography* in its many genres made saints known; and finally, we will consider how people *experienced saints*, in liturgies, on pilgrimages, and through mementoes from shrines.

WHO WERE THE SAINTS AND HOW WERE THEY MADE?

The veneration of saints commemorates a holy person's merits through the actions of a devotee—pilgrim, offerer of gifts, reciter of prayers. A saint's virtue was the source of blessing, cure, and protection. Issues of authority and power abound here: who authorized a person's sanctity? who managed the shrine? who approached it, touched its precious holdings? Though attachment to a saintly figure can be highly personal, the veneration of saints is a social practice that borrows freely from familial, communal, and political customs. Choosing a favored saint is an act of identification, worn like a badge.

Early Christian communities established modes of respect for exemplary followers of Jesus, taken from the idioms of Roman cults for both men and women. Christians faced waves of persecution, and accounts of death in profession of Christian faith produced a type of holy person, the martyr. Martyrs defied pagan emperors and judges, and they even seemed to vanquish death, in imitation of Jesus. The first known martyr's cult— that of St Polycarp of Smyrna—developed in the middle of the second century. A letter published by the church of Smyrna spread word of his death and encouraged its readers to remember that, like him, they too were sojourners on the way to a better world. When Emperor Constantine (272–337) embraced Christianity and allowed it to flourish publicly, he was baptized in a *martyrion*, a chapel dedicated to the memory of a martyr. He enriched his capital of Constantinople with many other such memorials. In the catacombs of the Empire's other great city, Rome, saints Peter and Paul were remembered as martyrs, too.

While in most areas of civic life women were unwelcome, martyrdom narratives told of impressive female martyrs. Some were among the most beloved medieval saints. Catherine of Alexandria is a good example, a most popular saint in the Middle Ages. The daughter of King Costus of Alexandria, she refused to marry Emperor Maxentius. She triumphantly disputed religion with pagan philosophers, and with her intuitive understanding, reversed hierarchies of gender and of knowledge, too. Ultimately she suffered death, her body tortured on a wheel. By the fourth century, there was a robust understanding of the power of relics, especially those from martyrs. Victricius, bishop of Rouen (d.410) imagined the power of sacred bodily remains, like "blood, after martyrdom, is on fire with the reward of divinity."[1]

As Christianity spread, martyrdom declined, and forms of Christian life multiplied, sanctity was associated with missionaries active in uprooting pagan practices. Cult practices are hard to discern in these early centuries. Burials *ad sanctos* (close to saints) were clearly important to believers who sought such proximity. A funerary church discovered in Marseille in 2004 contains dozens of burials—of women, men, and children—in the apse near the altar and its saint.[2] Some such saints were local community leaders, generally men, responsible for the spiritual well-being of their flocks in a time of uncertainty and upheaval; communities of Christians had to be fed, cities defended against invaders, churches built, sermons preached, and new Christians brought into the fold. The responsibility of nurturing Christian communities in these ways fell to bishops; some gained meritorious sanctity through this route, and thus continued in their function as protectors even after death. The bishops of Rome claimed special dignity due to the foundation of their see by St Peter. In the sixth and seventh centuries, they attempted to enhance their influence through the creation of Roman saints and liturgies.

The best example of the saintly bishop is probably Ambrose, archbishop of Milan (339–397), in whom learning, political authority, charisma, and office combined. He crafted a liturgy for Milan, confronted the emperor, and extolled chastity for elite Roman women. Ambrose understood the cult of saints as history in the making. He envisioned a Christian world linked by cultic activity, not only of local saints, but also of more distant ones. To that end, he distributed Milanese relics into Gaul and North Africa.

Further north, St Martin of Tours, a soldier turned ascetic and bishop, offered a focus for local liturgical and political cohesion. Martin's vision created a diocese of not only the city and its churches, but also the villages around it, all bound together in a shared cult of saints. His life inspired many sites and memories: among others, the monastery of Marmoutiers, the church of St Martin of Tours where he was buried, and the monastery of Ligugé in the neighboring diocese of Poitiers. Two centuries later, historian and hagiographer Gregory, bishop of Tours (538/9–593/4), promoted St Martin by writing about his life anew. He turned Martin into the most celebrated Frankish saint, a position Martin would later share with St Denis, the favorite of the Frankish kings.[3]

Alongside saintly bishops in fifth-century Gaul emerged an itinerant female saint who rarely settled or dealt with administrative responsibilities, St Genovefa (420–509). Her life and activities exemplify the saintliness women radiated without holding ecclesiastical office, and sometimes in conflict with men who did. She traveled the Parisian basin, transforming the pagan landscape—with its holy trees and springs—into a Christian one, much as Helena (died c.330)—mother of Emperor Constantine—had done a century earlier in the Holy Land. Genovefa's cult also provides a lesson in the power of popular participation: Parisians flocked to her burial site even before it was covered by a suitable edifice.[4]

Freer than women to choose from many possibilities of pious perfection, some men were drawn to seclusion in the desert, others to extravagant works of charity, and others still to the dangerous work of missions and conversion of pagans. The accounts of the elusive St Patrick (fifth century) and of St Boniface (c.672–754) illustrate how the merits of apostles and martyrs were later emulated by northern Europeans who spread Christianity to pagan peoples. Local communities remembered their founders and protectors, as with San Vitale of Ravenna, or the martyrs Protasius and Gervasius in Milan. Many such saints and their cults were little known beyond their localities.

By the late sixth century, another form of holy perfection became institutionalized: monasticism. Monks and nuns worshipped communally in lives of poverty, chastity, and obedience. Powerful abbesses sometimes ruled over joint communities of men and women, though this became less common as time passed. While monks and nuns were only a minority of the European population, they touched everyone through economic, political, and kinship relations, as well as by religious example. It is not surprising, therefore, that the monastic orders provided saints; they also systematically coordinated the ideas and practices of their cults. Benefactors of religious houses sought to enjoy the prayers and prestige that such communities generated and even to benefit from access to the relics they stored.

The monastic tradition continued to be central as a launching pad for sanctity. The eleventh and twelfth centuries saw a great deal of innovation and reform, with emphasis in some orders on simplicity of life and poverty. Alongside exemplary monastic living there were saintly hermits. For example, Wulfric of Haselbury (c.1080–1154) was a priest turned solitary. He worked at bookbinding for his local church, and when he died, he was found dressed in a hair shirt and a mail vest. Women were not as free to choose such a life. Unlike male hermits who were allowed to live in forests or on mountaintops, bishops sought to regulate and enclose women's solitude. Local saints were sometimes identified by monks among meritorious children, whose cults were then fostered in monasteries. At St Benet-at-Holm in Norfolk, a cult formed around Margaret, a young virgin killed and found in a wood, the causes of her death unknown. Another pious young woman, Oda, received hagiographical treatment by the Premonstratensian monk Philip of Harvengt (c.1100–1180), who even cut off her nose to collect her blood as a relic.[5]

The new monastic orders of the eleventh and twelfth centuries emphasized poverty, physical labor, and meditation over elaborate liturgical discipline. The Cistercian congregation, founded in 1098 at Cîteaux (near Dijon), aimed to retain its group identity through cults of Cistercian saints, shared from Yorkshire to Bohemia. A good example is the cult of Bernard, Abbot of Clairvaux (1090–1153), twelfth-century Europe's foremost preacher and ecclesiastical activist. Cistercian houses gathered and disseminated news of St Bernard's lifetime healings, post mortem miracles, and occasions of exemplary prayer. While their attitude toward women was ambivalent, they also recognized the exemplary quality of women, and sometimes of those who lived in proximity to them.

As new forms of settlement, work, and religious life developed in eleventh- and twelfth-century Europe, ideas about saints and sanctity also changed. Urbanization and commercialization raised new moral anxieties—and opportunities. As cities grew in wealth and influence, they produced distinctive religious cultures suited to the lives of artisans and merchants. In the city of Cologne, a powerful ecclesiastical and mercantile center, the relics of its saintly bishop, Anno II (1056–1075) were distributed to all its churches, which were further bound tightly together by liturgical processions. New forms of holiness emerged in cities, and these new cults of saints often only arose among ordinary people. They included many women, and children too, including boys—like William of Norwich—allegedly killed by Jews.

At roughly the same time, kingdoms began to foster national saints. St Stephen of Hungary (c.1000) symbolized the new Christian order as well as sacred kingship.[6] Since dynasties favored their mothers and daughters too, Bohemia promoted its St Ludmilla and Hungary its St Elizabeth. Kingdoms developed unique cultic centers like the embellished Westminster of Henry III, Louis IX's Sainte-Chapelle, and St Vitus' cathedral in

Charles IV's Prague. Italian republics and principalities—Milan, Siena, Genoa, Venice—developed their own civic religious cultures with an important saint's cult at its heart. These were not new cults, but ones buoyed by the enhancements of wealth, ritual, and works of art, like the tabernacle of Orsanmichele in Florence or Siena's Duomo.

The Franciscan movement emerged from this urban world, reformulating the perfect Christian life as an itinerant ministry of preaching lived in "apostolic" poverty. While he came perilously close to being considered a heretic, Francis of Assisi (1181–1226) was eventually embraced by Pope Innocent III. The response to Francis was strong, and women, too, were inspired by his urban apostolate. When Clare of Assisi (1194–1253) attempted to follow his example, she was denied the freedom to do so. Instead, she created an order of nuns who lived in rigorous enclosed poverty; sainthood was hers in the end, but by a very different route than that of Francis. Similarly, women who wished to join the Dominican order had to live as enclosed nuns, not as mendicant religious. For other women, sainthood came not through monasticism or mendicancy but through lay piety. Lay women joined religious associations attached to the friars and followed active devotional lives, often associated with charitable works.[7] In the Low Countries and parts of the Holy Roman Empire, women gathered in communities of beguines and constituted parishes of prayer, labor, and devotion. Their saintly lives were appreciated by leading churchmen and hagiographers; women like Elizabeth of Spaalbeck, whose meditation led to levitation, became exemplars of the sanctity of northern urban women.[8]

Some of these holy townswomen were treated as saints even in their lifetimes, but more often after death. The case of Margherita of Cortona (c.1247–1297) is highly edifying. She left her rural home in her twenties, accompanied by a son, the fruit of an illegitimate liaison with a man of some standing. In Cortona, she gained the patronage of two religious women, who guided her toward a life of penance. By 1275 she was able to join the Order of Penance, an association of lay people allied with the Franciscan order. Margherita's pious life of ascetic privation, attempted seclusion, and prayer far outstripped the rigors undertaken by other lay people. Fra Giusta Bevegnati wrote a hagiographical account of Margherita's life, in imitation of Christ's. Like Margherita, urban saints were often ordinary townspeople. Matteo di Termini, son of a Sicilian family, had studied in Bologna and served King Manfred of Sicily, and joined the Augustinian Order as a lay brother, as Agostino Novello. The 1324 altarpiece painted by Simone Martini (1283–1344) depicts his miracles—particularly the saving of children—embedded within distinctly urban settings.[9]

The cult of St Bridget of Sweden reflects another later medieval trend, that of sainthood associated with domestic, local, and familiar settings. The emergence of the Holy Family as a popular theme in visual representations and pastoral care worked to interweave sanctity into the spheres of family and work. In Mary and her mother Anne, Brigittine nuns saw models of labor and spirituality, and these were appreciated by lay folk, too. The carved groups of the multigenerational holy kindred, placed in most German parish churches in the course of the fifteenth century, demonstrate clearly how far ideas of sanctity had traveled over the medieval centuries: from desert to city streets, from stigmata to the prick of the spinning distaff, from single-sex environments to the spirituality of family life.

Alongside the exemplary figure of poverty of St Francis, a living commentary on the spiritual dangers of immersion in the world, the cult of the Virgin Mary—and of her family—flourished. For all her uniqueness, Mary was imagined in these centuries as very much a member of a family. Though very ancient in origins, medieval Mary was a recent European creation, as was the Holy Family. In these cults the ordinary was made fascinating: mundane work in home and workshop was like the labor of Mary and Joseph; family time—meals, prayer, reading—was sanctified; so, too, were relationships with kin, like Jesus' grandmother, aunts, and cousins. While late medieval Europe maintained a lively interest in pilgrimage, it also produced family-based, neighborhood-bounded cultic possibilities, facilitated by devotional reading, invigorated by images, and enhanced through lay initiatives in vernacular piety.

Texts: Getting to Know the Saints

Early Christian writers intent on commemorating the lives of martyrs and saints took their models from classical tales of great men and heroes. Saints' lives were valued for the examples they offered and the hope that one martyr's passion (stories of their deaths) might inspire other martyrs. The seventh-century passion of St Eulalia described her "strengthened in ardor" by the reading of the life of the Blessed Thyrsus. Saints' lives were also written to attract and delight their audiences. By 700, a hagiographer from Whitby appealed to the reader:

> So, if any reader should know more about all the miracles of this kindly man or how they happened, we pray him for Christ's sake, not to nibble with critical teeth at this work of ours which has been diligently twisted into shape by love rather than by knowledge.[10]

The hagiographical genre began with the early lives of martyrs, tales of good defying evil; in these tales, even young women could be heroes. Hagiographers described martyrs as living in heavenly communities, with a new kinship that was born at martyrdom. Yet even in heroism, gendered roles emerged: the slave Blandina, a martyr of Lyon who was roasted to death and whose feats are described in *The Letter of the Churches of Lyons and Vienne* (c.177), comforted the others "like a mother caring for her children."[11] Perpetua and Felicitas suffered their martyrdoms in Carthage, and their deaths had inspired, by c.203, an account that combined—in two equal parts—autobiography and holy biography. This account of the deaths of a young matron (Perpetua), her two young children, and her maid (Felicitas) deeply influenced later mystical writings by medieval holy women. The imagined diary of Perpetua was tender, and it inspired her hagiographer to deviate from well-trodden rhetorical paths. Here is no encomiastic praise, but attention to emotion: a mother imprisoned, her children abandoned. This is a new type of heroism, in imitation of Christ and renunciation of the world. In turn, the female martyr became the bride of Christ.

A robust model of male sanctity was also developing in fourth-century Egypt, and Athanasius (c.293–373), Patriarch of Alexandria, captured it in his *Life of St Antony*. Athanasius invented the monastic mode of saintly perfection: religious life lived in a community, discernment of the devil and his tricks, and a strong sense of moral rectitude. St Antony was presented as a "beacon of orthodoxy," even as that orthodoxy was still struggling to emerge. The ascetic ideal he represented came to dominate the Christian imagination, particularly in the Mediterranean. Those inspired by him were often violent polemicists against Christians who adhered to the old ways, who visited oracles, engaged in pagan athletics, and dabbled in magical cures. In their hands, hagiography became a site for arguing about sanctity and virtue.

In western regions of the Empire, above all in Gaul, similar zeal was captured in *The Life of St Martin of Tours* by Sulpicius Severus (c.363–c.425) and in *The Life of Ambrose* by his friend, Paulinus, bishop of Nola (c.353–431). These stories provided models of bishopsaints. The *Life of St Martin* showed the bishop caring for his flock and providing for the needy, while Ambrose's life cast as high virtue his struggles against emperors and heretics.

Hagiography—writing the exemplary lives of saints—was probably the most creative and plentiful genre of the early Middle Ages. Together with the liturgy of saints, the genre circulated around the Mediterranean and beyond. An educated male clerical elite remembered saints in written tales and also provided liturgies for them. In the hub of religious enthusiasm that was seventh- and eighth-century Francia, aristocrats and bishops cooperated in hagiographical efforts. The life of a saint or a martyr's passion was a powerful tool of knowledge and representation. At the shrine of St Gall and at the tomb of St Remi in Reims, saints' lives were read out to crowds of pilgrims.[12] The lives of saints often served as the reading matter of the office for the saints' feast days. They incorporated existing genres into the telling of exemplary lives.

Gender affected the writing inspired by saints, and some of the finest literature of the early Middle Ages was in the hagiographic mood. It is said that the scholar and diplomat Venantius Fortunatus (c.530–c.600/9) was prompted to travel to Gaul after being cured of an eye disease by the intervention of St Martin. He used his gift of poetry in the service of rulers and most passionately in praise of aristocratic and royal religious women. Most influential was his vivid *Life of St Radegund* (c.520–586). Radegund was a latter-day Martin, a capable provider of well-being and safety for the church of Holy Cross in Poitiers. A later version of Radegund's life, written by her fellow nun Baudonivia, agrees in all essentials with Fortunatus: Radegund was an active, political abbess, indefatigable in resolving conflict and securing protection for her house. Yet their voices were different. Fortunatus used the language of Roman love poetry to describe his spiritual yearning for her, as in "To Radegund, When She Returned:"

> Whence has this countenance returned to me with its radiant light? What delay held you, too long absent? You have taken my happiness with you, with your return you restore it, and you make Easter doubly a day of celebration.

Baudonivia describes herself as "weak-minded" and with "but few interesting things to say."[13]

The veneration of particular saints at cult sites gave rise to the custom of pilgrimage, and to a genre, the travelogue. This recorded a personal pilgrimage with the view of sharing it with those back home. Precise and pedantic, such texts described holy places in detail, seeing in them the unfolding of scripture. The seventh-century bishop from Gaul, Arculf, recounted his pilgrimage to the Holy Land to Abbot Adomnán of Iona, whom he visited on his journey back to Europe. Adomnan, in turn, wrote up the account, *On the Holy Places* (*De Locis sanctis*). At Mount Tabor Arculf had reported:

> Mount Thabor is three miles from the lake of Cinereth, and is gathered into a wondrous roundness on every side ... The level top of the mountain is not barrowed to a point, but spread to a width of 23 stades, and it stands at an altitude of 30 stades ...

> One of the party was moved to say to the Lord:

> "It is good for us to be here, and let us make three tabernacles, one for thee and one for Moses and one for Elias."[14]

In the next century, the abbot Willibald of Eichstätt (700–787) reported a detailed network of saints' shrines and related liturgies in his itinerary of the Holy Land.

At approximately this time (and first in England according to Michael Lapidge), a powerful new form of cultic performance emerged, dedicated to the invocation of saints: the litany. Early litanies invoked the Trinity, the Virgin Mary, and—by the late seventh century—saints, too. They soon became poetic in form, and poets like Hrabanus Maurus (c.776–856) or Ratpert of St Gallen (died c.890) composed devotional litanies that were adopted into the liturgy and used for centuries to come. Litanies presented saints by order of merit: apostles, evangelists, martyrs, saints. Holy women were listed in the category *virgo* (virgin). Martyrs were placed alongside repentant prostitutes, nuns alongside saintly royals—the specific circumstances of these women were effaced by the category *virgo*. Men increasingly inhabited the category *virgo* too. Aldhelm of Canterbury (c.639–c.709) wrote on virginity for the monks and nuns under the care of Abbess of Barking; he described virginity as Christ's "eternal gift," beginning with Elijah and then prophets, apostles, martyrs, and saints. After "blessed men" came the Virgin Mary, since "the time is now at hand to make known holy women," followed by virgin martyrs.[15] Virginity—associated so strongly with that unique woman, the Mother of God—had become a marker of male virtue, too.

Apart from their power to edify and their role in liturgy, by the twelfth century, saints' lives were central to the process of canonization, which was increasingly organized by the papal administration. Criteria laid down by canon law for the recognition of a saint appeared frequently and prominently in lives of saints. Evidence of miracles associated with a holy life was necessary for canonization, and the inquisitorial method was later applied in order to probe and test rumors and reports of miracles. In the case of Hildegard of Bingen, the distinguished theologian William of Auxerre (d.1231) was employed to determine whether her visions were divinely inspired or heretical. Later, Jean Gerson (1363–1429) was summoned to judge as to whether Ermine de Reims was a deluded lay woman or an inspired saint. The scrutiny of women was strict, and the boundary between female heresy and sanctity was blurred. Yet sometimes the person who was sent to investigate suspicious female behavior came away her devoted admirer.

The impulse to edit and compile, revisit and rewrite the lives of saintly persons was evident early in the Christian tradition. The canoness Hrotsvit (c.935–c.1102) rewrote legends of the life of the Virgin Mary, St Agnes, and others, in dramatic pieces.[16] Within monastic orders, lives of saintly members were written and rewritten, and their miracles and their exemplary actions collected. The new religious orders fostered exemplary figures to be shared, and thus enhanced the sense of solidarity within the order. Hagiographical writing by a monk about another often employed a familiar, intimate tone. The Cistercian order also produced lives of women, especially from the areas of the southern Low Countries.

Records of miraculous healings at shrines also contributed to the cults of saints. These were assembled by the guardians of their shrines—like those of St Foy of Conques or the Virgin Mary at Rocamadour. They confirmed the value, for pilgrims, of visiting shrines; they also provided material for processes of canonization. Cult centers also produced entertaining and informative texts—in both poetry and prose—created for the edification of visiting pilgrims. For example, the Castilian poet Gonzalo de Berceo (c.1190–1264), from the Benedictine monastery of San Millán de la Cogolla in Rioja, collected Marian miracles for the benefit of his own fellow monks and pilgrims.

By the thirteenth century, friars were particularly active in collecting cultic materials relevant for edification and preaching throughout the Christian calendar. The Dominican Bartholomew of Trent created the *Epilogus*, a digest of saints' lives, and this was heavily used by the Franciscan Jacob de Voragine (c.1229–1298), who authored the most influential of all collection of saints' lives, the *Golden Legend (Legenda Aurea)*.[17] The *Golden Legend* summarized a thousand years of writings of saints and martyrs, and it did so in lively, engaging narrative. Eventually translated into all European languages, it became a standard reference book for preachers and artists.

The life of a saint was a lived narrative, and its writing and rewriting could transform it beyond recognition. Mary Magdalene was thought by the sixth century to have been a prostitute who converted in Jesus' presence. She was also believed to have lived and sought penance in Gaul. Yet by the late thirteenth century, Margherita of Cortona heard Jesus say in a vision that apart from the Virgin Mary and St Katherine, there was no greater virgin in Heaven than the Magdalene. Women religious saw in her a vessel containing Christ, himself so much desired by late medieval religious women. For those who lived in the world, Mary Magdalene represented the rewards of true penance. In the hands of preachers who understood well the desires of their female audiences, here was a saint to be emulated.[18]

Caroline Bynum has influentially explored the gendered nature of religious experience, as expressed in late medieval lives of female saints.[19] These holy women identified with the humanity and suffering of Jesus, they were attracted to the role of mother exemplified by the Virgin Mary, and they used food or its rejection as part of a language of piety. In observing the gendered traits of their religious lives, we confront a difficult question: whose sanctity is this, whose piety? These women's lives were mostly written by men—relatives, admirers, or confessors—who were always in search of the exemplary and always attuned to gender differences. The few versions we have written by women about themselves are rich with evocations of powerful bodily experiences, overwhelming states of rapture.

By the later Middle Ages, hagiography provided a widely used and appreciated reading matter for the laity as well as the religious. The sisters in communities of Modern Devotion—a spiritual movement for devout lay people—composed lives of their sisters who had resisted marriage and striven for perfection; their stories recast for late medieval use a genre long dominated by virgin martyrs. The Order's ruling Chapter intervened and forbade such publications; these writings seemed to suggest women were in charge of the determination of sanctity. Hagiography was commissioned according to personal interest; the Augustinian friar Osbern of Bokenham (1393–1447), for example, wrote a life of St Mary Magdalene at the request of Lady Isabel Bourchier, and a life of St Margaret at the desire of "dear friend."[20] Such writings were used for moral improvement and enjoyment; they followed not the liturgical calendar, but the poetical model of Chaucer's *Legend of Good Women*. Such lives were used by women of the gentry to educate their children toward the constancy that martyrs demonstrated so well.

EXPERIENCING THE SAINTS: PLACE, MATTER, AND GESTURE

Commemorating saints formed an integral and familiar part of medieval experiences. Most people were named after saints—Mary, Catherine, Margaret, Peter, John, James—in all their linguistic variations. The calendar was marked by saints' days, and documents were dated by reference to them (for example, "on the Wednesday after the feast of St Michael"); liturgies were punctuated by saints' days; civic and church buildings were adorned with paintings and sculptures of saints. Saints were also invoked in more humble and quotidian ways. When a woman lost a household object, she could invoke St Zita, a sainted maidservant famed for her help in finding lost objects. The Virgin Mary was remembered in the daily recitation of the Ave Maria, and by the end of our period she accompanied many Europeans through their daily use of the rosary. By the later fifteenth century, prints circulated cheaply and widely, offering images of saints even to humble households in liturgies, on pilgrimages, and through mementoes from shrines.

From very early on, Christians traveled in search of places and objects associated with the life of Christ, the apostles, and the ever-growing cohorts of saints and martyrs. Women under the care of Athanasius of Alexandria were already visiting those places in the Holy Land where Jesus had lived. As Christianity spread and became the official religion of the Roman Empire, well-to-do matrons and widows ventured there. When Paula (347–404), guided by St Jerome, visited Bethlehem c.385, she saw "with the eye of faith" the child Jesus alongside Mary, Joseph, and the shepherds. The first known pilgrimage account is by a Spanish pilgrim, Egeria, who visited the Holy Land in the 380s. She described an elaborate liturgy in the churches of Jerusalem, in spaces adorned with sumptuous hangings and echoing with liturgical music.[21]

Reliquaries inspired some of the finest works of medieval craft and imagination. Their owners—religious houses, cathedrals, or wealthy individuals—invested in the most precious materials. Transparency turned a reliquary into a monstrance, through which a relic could be viewed, and chunks of crystal and beryl from ancient sources were worked into containers. While some were made into the shape of a body part—a head or an arm—even these usually contained varied relic fragments. Hand reliquaries were particularly popular, since they represented the power of the saint to bless and to act in the world. The reliquary arm of St Peter of *c.*1230 from the Collegiate Church of St Ursmer in Binche in fact contained a leg bone.[22]

Attraction to the Holy Land reflects two central trends that shaped the cult of saints: the Christianization of Jewish and pagan sites, and the commemoration of virtuous men and women. The identification of the holy sites associated with the life of Jesus was promoted vigorously by St Helena with the support of her son, Emperor Constantine. In the funeral oration delivered in her honor in 395, Ambrose, archbishop of Milan, described her work—the finding and identification of the Holy Cross and Nails—as the true beginning of the Christian Empire.[23]

As to commemoration, relics spread throughout Christendom—given as gifts, traded, and sold, and preserved in altars, religious houses, and purpose-built, often portable containers or reliquaries. From around the year 500 silver reliquaries of great beauty survive from Italy, Gaul, and North Africa. These were decorated with scenes of the saint's deeds, but also with apocalyptic emblems rich in hope and expectation. Contact relics—materials which had touched the holy body or had been dipped in its liquids—were treasured by devotees. Those who knew a saint hoped to capture forever their moment of contact, as did the woman healed by St Simeon Stylites, who—according to Simeon's life of the late sixth century—went away with a portrait of him. The cult of saints may well have prompted that distinctive form of Christian art, the holy portrait, the icon.[24]

Gender affected access to relics and to the shrines of saints. With the rise of monastic hegemony in religious life, institutions of men were associated with more numerous and more prominent cults. While the liturgies of saints and martyrs unfolded in earlier centuries in the suburban churches near cemeteries and outside the walls of Roman *civitates*, by the sixth and seventh centuries, holy people were most likely to die within monastic communities. They were remembered there, their remains cherished, their feast days celebrated. Access to such spaces, usually male religious houses, was increasingly forbidden to women and in some cases even to laymen.

Nuns and abbesses tried to create collections of relics for their own houses. For example, Baudonivia tells of Radegund's commitment to acquiring relics; she sent a priest to procure remains of St Andrew, and her own chaplain to Jerusalem for a finger of St Mammas. The early medieval centuries saw a significant number of women heading important religious—even mixed—institutions, and these women traveled, went on pilgrimage, and studied abroad. They used these opportunities to learn about saints and acquire their relics: after a period of study in the monastery of Chelles, east of Paris, for example, Mildred (c.660–c.725) brought a nail of the cross back home to her monastery at Thanet-upon-Thames.

After 1100, cults multiplied in cities and their churches too. Most encounters with saints operated through relics, but images were increasingly favored for their power to invoke the portrayed saint. This is particularly true of the Virgin Mary. By the thirteenth century, pilgrims along the Via Francigena in Siena could see Duccio's magnificent window in the Duomo depicting the life of Mary, as well as the miracle-working image there, the Madonna of the Large Eyes. Some images were endowed with indulgences—the promise of remission of punishment for sins already confessed—only sparingly in the eleventh century, but much more readily by the thirteenth. The little chapel outside Assisi, the Portiuncula, where St Francis died, drew many pilgrims, attracted "to the indulgence of Assisi on the feast of the Portiuncula." In thirteenth-century Acre, an itinerary for pilgrims around the city's churches listed the indulgence earned for each stop.[25]

Indulgences increased pious yearnings to encounter saints and their holy sites personally. From such yearnings developed networks of pilgrimage all over Europe, some attracting only local attention and others drawing visitors from hundreds of miles away. Medieval people developed strategies for preserving their experiences as pilgrims: some wrote travelogues to be shared with friends and colleagues after their return, others modeled buildings in imitation of those they had seen abroad, and yet others brought back keepsakes and souvenirs. News of cults and pilgrimage sites traveled in the stories of merchants and soldiers, through preaching, and through the evidence of returning pilgrims. Pilgrimage was available differently to men and women. The displacement, cost, and danger of travel limited female pilgrimage, but did not proscribe it. A wife and daughter of merchants, Margery Kempe (c.1373–1438), from the English town of King's Lynn, was aware of the cult of the bleeding hosts in the town of Wilsnack in Mecklenburg. A devotee of the Eucharist, she traveled to Germany with her widowed daughter-in-law, as travel in pairs was safer for women, and the companionship of a native speaker of German was helpful, too. But Margery was obliged to travel to the shrine on her own and her autobiography colorfully described the hazards of pilgrimage. Being ill and somewhat disabled, she depended on the support of men. The sight of her piety, often accompanied with tears, drew attention and derision from onlookers. In Konstanz, the *Book of Margery Kempe* reports:

> ... for they did her much shame... They cut her gown so short that it came but little beneath her knee, and made her wear a white canvas like a coarse sackcloth, so she was taken for a fool so no one would have regard for her nor hold her in esteem.[26]

Privileged women traveled in greater comfort to a wide array of shrines. Kinship and marriage networks affected adherence to shrines: Mary of Burgundy, duchess of Cleves, chose the site of a Marian shrine—Marienbaum in the Duchy of Cleves in the Rhineland—for the foundation of a Bridgettine convent in 1460.[27]

Women who could not undertake pilgrimages compensated for this absence in various ways. Those dedicated to the religious life were discouraged from leaving their convents and so they went on spiritual pilgrimage, "virtual" journeys through meditative reading and with the aid of images. Such women imagined saints as constant companions: Joanna Sewell, a nun of the Bridgettine house of Syon, was depicted on her *ex libris* plate as if enclosed by a protective wall made of the figures of St Saviour, Brigitta, Augustine, and Mary.[28] Ordinary women (and men, too) could encounter saints without leaving home, through the intimacy of prayer and invocation or reading vernacular versions of their lives. Some members of the laity, especially in cities, founded devotional associations, known as confraternities, dedicated to a saint; in Italy, this was most frequently the Virgin Mary. In England, confraternities (also known as parish guilds) were more modest affairs, often with the parish as their base. Women sometimes chose to create their own associations within the parish, with their own groupings and rituals.

Privileged women were able to promote cults of saints through commissions of important cultic objects. Elizabeth Kotromanić (*c*.1340–1387), wife of King Louis of Hungary, commissioned a gilt silver tomb shrine in 1377 for the body of St Simeon (the priest said to have witnessed the presentation of Christ at the Temple and to have prophesied the Crucifixion); his body was buried in the Dalmatian city of Zadar. The chest's carved panels depict the dramatic history of St Simeon's relics: their arrival at Zadar, their miraculous power, and thwarted attempts to steal them. One panel commemorates Elizabeth's act of piety, in fulfillment of her vow.[29] All the roles of a late medieval saint are present here: patron of the city and punisher of heretics. St Simeon was proclaimed as Zadar's own, against those powerful cultic centers—St Denis and Venice—that claimed him, too.

Most people engaged with saints in the intimacy of prayer and invocation, in front of an image in a parish church, or while visiting local shrines. While accounts of long-distance pilgrimage captured the imagination then as they still do now, most pilgrims visited local sites, and most experiences of saints were similarly embedded within the rhythms of domestic life, work, and sociability.

Although sanctity is elusive and immaterial, the cult of saints in the Middle Ages was grounded in material practices involving relics, images, candles, and fragments chipped off tombs; it was also experienced powerfully through the body and its senses. The reciprocal nature of cultic devotion meant that devotees brought as well as took away. They offered garments and jewelry to adorn saints' statues, precious cloth for the making of hangings, wax for the making of candles. Visitors to shrines offered their prayers, prostrated their ailing bodies, and even, in the case of women, presented children they had brought with them. Therefore, women often appeared as witnesses to miracles in the course of canonization inquiries.

The cult of saints was marked by the materialization of memory, in gestures that symbolized ineffable hope and gratitude for aid and protection. Widespread and deeply embedded, the cult of saints could never be firmly regulated and it was always vulnerable to appropriation and misappropriation. It attracted, not surprisingly, its fair share of criticism. The late medieval English movement disparagingly known as Lollardy was persecuted as heretical. In a trial for heresy in 1429, for example, the English "Lollard" John Kynget renounced his previously held opinion "that prayer should be made to God, and to no other saint."[30] Such criticism was heard increasingly loudly in the later Middle Ages, and became the hallmark of Protestant reform. Yet, the attachment to virtue was not easily dissolved in Lutheran communities. Even during his lifetime, Luther's signatures were treated as holy relics, and after his death his portraits were believed to work miracles.[31] The cult of saints depended on and nurtured states of mind. It was shaped by gender and embedded in local identities. Its resilient forms still inform contemporary public practices that commemorate and reward virtue.

FURTHER READING

Elliott, Dyan. *Proving Woman: Female Spirituality and Inquisitional Culture in the Later Middle Ages*. Princeton: Princeton University Press, 2004.

Finucane, Ronald C. *Miracles and Pilgrims: Popular Beliefs in Medieval England*. Basingstoke: Macmillan, 1995.

Freeman, Charles. *Holy Bones, Holy Dust: How Relics Shaped the History of Medieval Europe*. New Haven: Yale University Press, 2011.

Goodich, Michael. *Miracles and Wonders: the Development of the Concept of Miracle, 1150–1350*. Aldershot: Ashgate, 2007.

Head, Thomas. *Hagiography and the Cult of Saints: The Diocese of Orleans, 800–1200*. Cambridge: Cambridge University Press, 1990.

Head, Thomas, ed. *Medieval Hagiography: An Anthology*. New York: Garland, 2000.

de Voragine, Jacobus. *The Golden Legend: Readings on the Saints*, trans. William Granger Ryan. Princeton: Princeton University Press, 2012.

NOTES

1. Patricia Cox Miller, *The Corporeal Imagination: Signifying the Holy in Late Ancient Christianity* (Philadelphia: Pennsylvania University Press, 2009), 37.
2. Manuel Moliner, "La basilique funéraire de la rue Malaval à Marseille (Bouches-du-Rhône)," *Gallia*, 63 (2006): 131–36.
3. Sharon Farmer, *Communities of St. Martin: Legend and Ritual in Medieval Tours* (Ithaca; London: Cornell University Press, 1991), esp. 13–29; Julia M. H. Smith, "Women at the Tomb: Access to Relic Shrines in the Early Middle Ages," in Kathleen Mitchell and Ian Wood, eds, *The World of Gregory of Tours* (Leiden: Brill, 2002), 163–80, at 164; Raymond Van Dam, *Saints and Their Miracles in Late Antique Gaul* (Princeton: Princeton University Press, 1993), 11–49.
4. Lisa M. Bitel, *Landscape with Two Saints: How Genovefa of Paris and Brigit of Kildare Built Christianity in Barbarian Europe* (Oxford: Oxford University Press, 2009), esp. 78–79.
5. Julian M. Luxford, "Saint Margaret of Holm: New Evidence Concerning a Norfolk Benedictine Cult," *Norfolk Archaeology*, 44 (2002): 111–19.
6. Gábor Klaniczay, *Holy Rulers and Blessed Princesses: Dynastic Cults in Medieval Central Europe* (Cambridge: Cambridge University Press, 2002), esp. 134–36.

7. As Anneke Mulder-Bakker discusses in this volume, Chapter 29.

8. Catherine M. Mooney, "*Imitatio Christi* or *Imitatio Mariae?* Clare of Assisi and her Interpreters," in idem, ed., *Gendered Voices: Medieval Saints and Their Interpreters* (Philadelphia: University of Pennsylvania Press, 1999), 52–77, esp. 58–67; Walter Simons, *Cities of Ladies: Beguine Communities in the Medieval Low Countries, 1200–1565* (Philadelphia: University of Pennsylvania Press, 2001), 130.

9. Joanna Cannon and André Vauchez, *Margherita of Cortona and the Lorenzetti: Sienese Art and the Cult of a Holy Woman in Medieval Tuscany* (University Park, Pa.: Pennsylvania State University Press, 1999), esp. 1–8, 21–36; Andrew Martindale, *Simone Martini: Complete Edition* (Oxford: Phaidon, 1988), catalog no. 41, figures 75–81.

10. Anonymous Monk of Whitby, *The Earliest Life of Gregory the Great*, trans. Bertram Colgrave (Lawrence: University of Kansas Press, 1968), 129–33.

11. Herbert Musurillo, ed. and trans., *The Acts of the Christian Martyrs* (Oxford: Clarendon Press, 1972), 78–79; Alison Goddard Elliott, *Roads to Paradise: Reading the Lives of Early Saints* (Hanover, NH: University Press of New England for Brown University Press, 1987), 20.

12. Yitzak Hen, *Roman Barbarians: The Royal Court and Culture in the Early Medieval West* (New York: Palgrave Macmillan, 2007), 110; Paul Fouracre, "Merovingian History and Merovingian Hagiography," *Past & Present*, 127 (1990): 3–38; Baudoin de Gaiffier, "La lecture des Actes des martyrs dans la prière liturgique en Occident: A propos du passionnaire hispanique," *Analecta Bollandiana*, 72 (1954): 134–66, 141–43, 153.

13. Judith W. George, *Venantius Fortunatus: A Latin Poet in Merovingian Gaul* (Oxford: Oxford University Press, 1992), 161–63, and poem 8.10, 196–97, lines 1–4; Jo Ann McNamara and John E. Halborg, eds and trans., with E. Gordon Whatley, *Sainted Women of the Dark Ages* (Durham, NC: Duke University Press, 1992), 86.

14. *Adamnan's De locis sanctis*, ed. Denis Meehan, Scriptores Latini Hiberniae 3 (Dublin: Dublin Institute for Advanced Studies, 1958), 97.

15. Michael Lapidge, ed., *Anglo-Saxon Litanies of the Saints* (Woodbridge, Suffolk; Rochester, NY: Boydell Press for the Henry Bradshaw Society, 1991), esp. 54–57; Felice Lifshitz, "Priestly Women, Virginal Men: Litanies and Their Discontents," in Lisa M. Bitel and Felice Lifshitz, eds, *Gender and Christianity in Medieval Europe: New Perspectives* (Philadelphia: University of Pennsylvania Press, 2008), 86–102; Aldhelm, *The Poetic Works*, trans. Michael Lapidge and James Rosier (Cambridge: D. S. Brewer, 2009), 107, 139.

16. Peter Dronke, *Women Writers of the Middle Ages* (Cambridge; New York: Cambridge University Press, 1984), 57–65.

17. Alain Boureau, "Barthélémy de Trente et l'invention de la 'Legenada aurea'," in Sofia Boesch Gajano, ed., *Raccolte di vite di santi dal XIII al XVIII secolo: Strutture, messaggi, fruizioni* (Fasano di Brindisi: Schena, 1990), 23–39, esp. 23–25; Jacobus de Voragine, *The Golden Legend: Readings on the Saints*, trans. William Granger Ryan (Princeton, NJ: Princeton University Press, 1993).

18. Katherine L. Jansen, "Like a Virgin: The Meaning of the Magdalen for Female Penitents of Later Medieval Italy," *Memoirs of the American Academy in Rome*, 45 (2000): 132–52.

19. Caroline Walker Bynum, *Holy Feats and Holy Fast: The Religious Significance of Food to Medieval Women* (Berkeley: University of California Press, 1987).

20. Mathilde van Dijk, "Miracles and Visions in *Devotio Moderna* Biographies," *Studies in Church History*, 41 (2005): 239–48; Osbern Bokenham, *Legends of Holy Women*, trans. Sheila Delany (Notre Dame, Ind.: University of Notre Dame Press, 1992).

21. David Brakke, *Athanasius and the Politics of Asceticism* (Oxford: Clarendon Press; New York: Oxford University Press, 1995), 292–302; Georgia Frank, *The Memory of the Eyes: Pilgrims to Living Saints in Christian Late Antiquity* (Berkeley: University of California Press, 2000), 106.

22. Cynthia Hahn, "The Voices of the Saints: Speaking Reliquaries," *Studies in Iconography*, 36 (1997): 20–31, see figure 1.

23. Barbara Baert, *A Heritage of Holy Wood: The Legend of the True Cross in Text and Image*, trans. Lee Preedy (Leiden; Boston: Brill, 2004), 26–29.

24. Galit Noga-Banai, *The Trophies of Martyrs: An Art-Historical Study of Early Christian Silver Reliquaries* (Oxford: Oxford University Press, 2008), 1–4, 155–63; Miller, *The Corporeal Imagination*, 167.

25. David Jacoby, "Pilgrimage in Crusader Acre: The *Pardouns dAcre*," in Yitzhak Hen, ed., *De Sion exibit lex et verbum domini de Hierusalem: Essays on Medieval Law, Liturgy, and Literature in Honour of Amnon Linder* (Turnhout: Brepols, 2001), 112–13.

26. *The Book of Margery Kempe*, ed. Barry Windeatt (Harlow: Longman, 2000), 152–53.

27. Virginia R. Bainbridge, "Women and the Transmission of Religious Culture: Benefactresses of Three Bridgettine Convents *c.*1400–1600," *Birgittiana*, 3 (1997): 55–76, at 66–67.

28. Kathryn Rudy, *Virtual Pilgrimages in the Convent: Imagining Jerusalem in the Late Middle Ages* (Turnhout: Brepols, 2011); Claire M. Waters, "Holy Familiars: Work, Enclosure, and the Saints at Syon," *Philological Quarterly*, 87 (2008): 135–62, at 143.

29. Marina Vidas, "Elizabeth of Bosnia, Queen of Hungary, and the Tomb Shrine of St. Simeon in Zadar: Power and Relics in Fourteenth-Century Dalmatia," *Studies in Iconography*, 29 (2008): 136–75, esp. 142–43.

30. Norman P. Tanner, ed., *Heresy Trials in the Diocese of Norwich, 1428–31* (London: Royal Historical Society, 1977), 57, 81.

31. R. W. Scribner, "Incombustible Luther: the Image of the Reformer in Early Modern Germany," *Past & Present*, 110 (1986): 38–68; Ulinka Rublack, "Grapho-Relics: Lutheranism and the Materialization of the Word," in Alexandra Walsham, ed., *Relics and Remains* (Oxford: Oxford University Press, 2010), 144–66.

CHAPTER 31

··

HERESY AND GENDER IN THE MIDDLE AGES

··

JOHN H. ARNOLD

IN 1494, after a brief spell in prison to loosen her tongue, Peyronette, widow of Pierre Beraud from the town of Beauregard in the diocese of Valence (in what is now south-east France), told the inquisitors what she knew of the Waldensian heresy. She had, she confessed, first met Waldensians some twenty-five years previously, when two of them, dressed in grey clothes and speaking Italian, arrived at her home. They had read from a little book of the Gospels, and had explained that they were sent by God to reform the Catholic faith, following in the example of the apostles. Peyronette reported various elements of their beliefs to the inquisitors: that oblations were voluntary and not to be required; that one should pay reverence only to God and should not take oaths; that good works done while alive were more important than any done for one after one's death; that saints could not intervene in the affairs of the world; that only Sunday was sacred; and that all feast days were invented by the Church (apart from the feast of the apostles). They spoke against the sinful clergy, who kept concubines and committed other sins; they spoke vehemently against the pope; they did not believe in purgatory, nor in prayers for the dead. They said that God had blessed all water at the Creation, and hence that clerical blessing of water was to no purpose; that priests had invented purgatory in order to get alms; that it was better to give to lepers or the poor; that God was everywhere, so there was no need to pray only in church; that images of saints were inert and powerless objects; that one should not go on pilgrimage nor undertake fasts; and that Waldensian preachers such as themselves were very much better than Catholic priests. Under further questioning, Peyronette admitted having given the Waldensians some needles as a gift (her husband also gave some money); and that also present when these Waldensians preached were her daughter Francisca and her son-in-law Simeon.[1]

Here, then, is a medieval woman engaged in heresy: receiving heretics, providing them with alms, and hearing and then repeating a radical theology. Earlier evidence tells us that there were female preachers active in Waldensianism in the thirteenth century, possibly still by the end of the fourteenth, and even at the Reformation, there were

Waldensian "Sisters" (though living a contemplative rather than active life) reported in Piedmont.[2] Some earlier strands of Waldensianism, and some other kinds of heresy, had expressed even more radical thoughts, explicitly in regard to gender: for example, that women could preach and could perform the sacraments; and even (in the case of the Guglielmites, to whom we shall return below) that women might hold the office of cardinal or pope.

There has long been a tradition in modern historiography of seeing heresy as holding a particular attraction for medieval women. The argument largely arises from a comparison of the religious opportunities afforded women in orthodox and heterodox faiths. Given that orthodox Catholicism allowed no hierarchical positions to women and heavily circumscribed female participation, surely heresy must have been attractive since it provided some equality of role? And since the principal gender tenets of orthodox Catholic theology—Eve the sinner, Mary Magdalene the reformed whore, Mary the inimitable Virgin—underwrote the oppression of women in a patriarchal society, surely the radical theologies of heretics, with their emphasis upon equality, must have furthered that attraction at a more spiritual level? In the case of Catharism, a key exemplar within this tradition, the specific context of southern France has further import. In the central Middle Ages, southern French society arguably afforded greater respect and legal standing to women than was the case in northern Europe. Furthermore, the Catholic church was slow to provide orthodox opportunities in the region, convents in particular, for women who wanted to pursue a religious life. Certainly Jacques de Vitry, writing the *Life* of the early beguine Mary of Oignies in the early thirteenth century, thought that this would provide a much-needed orthodox female competitor to the Cathar heresy.

The equation at one time seemed obvious. But now, in fact, no longer: there is good reason to argue that heresy had no particular or notable attraction to women, and moreover that some particular heresies may, in fact, have been notably unattractive. The study of both medieval orthodoxy and heterodoxy has moved on, and thinking about "gender" in regard to heresy is still in the process of catching up with these changes. In this chapter, the contours of the more traditional position—and its more recent refutations—will be examined. The chapter will, in one sense, attempt to put a seal upon any further discussion of "women and heresy" in these terms. But I shall also suggest that the nature of the question, and how it is framed, is worth revisiting; that is, that while it is no longer useful to suggest that women were particularly attracted to heresy, "gender and heresy" as entwined categories of historical analysis are still worth some future thought.

Medieval orthodox writers certainly thought that women and heresy went together. First and most importantly, women were easy converts, because of their nature. In the New Testament, in Paul's second letter to Timothy (II Tim. 3:2–7), clerics would read of wicked men who appeared pious but were not in fact orthodox ("false piety" being a common topos for heresy), and who were to be avoided: "For of these sort are those who creep into houses and lead captive weak little women [*mulierculas*] burdened with sin, who are led off by various desires." This text, with its echoes of seduction, provided some later writers with a template through which they could imagine and condemn the otherwise rather bewildering process of heretical conversion. The council of Rheims in 1157 directly alludes to the biblical text in its opening canon, which condemns "Manichaeans" of feigned piety, who "by most abject weavers (who often travel from place to place and alter their names), lead captive weak little women burdened with sin."[3] A letter from the Canons of Utrecht to the archbishop of Cologne, c.1112, supplies the latter with "evidence" against a heretic called Tanchelm. Tanchelm had been preaching against the church hierarchy, condemning the sacraments and telling people that they need not pay tithes:

> First, in the coastal places, he mixed the venom of his wickedness among ignorant people and the infirm in faith. Gradually he began to spread his errors by way of matrons and weak little women, whose intimacies, confidential conversation, and private couches he was most willing to enjoy. Thereafter, through the wives he also entrapped the husbands... Afterwards he no longer preached in dark places and in bed chambers, but upon the rooftops and delivered his sermons in the open fields to a multitude...

Later Tanchelm allegedly "married" himself to a statue of the Virgin Mary and called for wedding gifts, and "the women cast in earrings and necklaces."[4]

Several things can be noted about this gendered stereotype, which slightly complicate the simple connection between women and heresy. The "weak little women" in Paul's letter and in the Tanchelm text are not simply there in their own right, as it were: they are not simply women, but *weak* and *sinful* women who are being used to position and condemn a wider set of processes. Misogyny is in play, but its target is broader than women only; in particular, as is clear in the letter from Utrecht, there is a progression and association between uneducated coastal folk, women, their husbands, and (eventually) a wider public stage. Imagining the predilections of "weak little women" helps to explain how outrageous beliefs can find an initial audience, but as importantly, it associates the eventually rather broader audience with this mocking stereotype, and the further connotations it might bring. In medieval culture, women are frequently depicted as more associated with the body, and hence with a lack of will and reason, and they are also seen (particularly in terms of humoral medical theory) as more permeable. Again, this renders them more susceptible to heretical conversion, but also associates those men who are similarly involved in heresy with a kind of feminine weakness.

Another strand of gendered stereotyping reverses the process of "seduction," and draws upon another familiar element in medieval misogyny, where women bring the sexual, and thence spiritual, downfall of men. Early antiheresy treatises established this topos. Irenaeus of Lyons, whose second-century CE *Adversus Hereses* is perhaps the earliest antiheresy manual, discusses Simon Magus (positioned as the first Christian heretic in various late antique treatises) and his wife Helen. Helen's soul could transmigrate, and in former lives she had been, Irenaeus said, both a prostitute and the Helen who caused the Trojan War. Their followers "are constantly occupied with love-potions, love-magic" and "other abstruse matters."[5] In a somewhat similar vein, Augustine of Hippo, discussing Manichaeans in his *De heresibus* (c.428), adapted sexually slanderous tales which had earlier been told against Christians. He alleged that they held secret orgies at which they ate a "kind of Eucharist sprinkled with human seed," alleging in support evidence from two women of the sect, Margaret and Eusebia, who had been tried at Carthage.[6] A number of medieval writers further adapted the story, most notably Guibert de Nogent in his early twelfth-century account of heretics in Laon, who, he alleged, held wild orgies, and baked any resulting human offspring into a demonic viaticum which would, if consumed, keep someone permanently converted to their sect.[7] More prosaically, a hostile account of the Cathar-turned-inquisitor Robert le Bougre describes how "when previously he was a man of apparently great (but not real) religion, he apostatized around the time of the great council [Fourth Lateran, 1215], and followed a little Manichean woman from Milan, and made himself part of her evil sect for more than twenty years."[8] In these accounts, heresy is implicitly a kind of sexually transmitted disease, holding a particular association with women. In short, while it is true commentators had long seen women as intimately connected to heresy, their rhetorical purposes in emphasizing such a connection are extremely clear, and are connected to issues of gender in a wider ideological sense, rather than deriving in any substantial way from an observed sociological reality.

The modern idea that women were particularly attracted to heresy has a number of roots. One is Marxist, leading on from Friedrich Engels's argument that, in a period of religious hegemony, heresy was the only vehicle for sociopolitical dissent. For later writers (most notably the East German historian Gottfried Koch, writing in 1962), heresy was also the vehicle for gender equality; similar arguments have continued to inform some modern popular ideas of medieval "dissent." Another root is the conjunction of late nineteenth-century nationalism and religious identity, which saw early "Protestant" movements, such as the Hussite heretics in fifteenth-century Bohemia, as avatars of a kind of national modernity, freed from "papist" influence, and held that a particular marker of this "modernity" was the recognition of certain rights in regard to women. In addition, historiography from the 1970s and '80s drew upon the collective project of women's history, seeking to recover from history the previously marginalized. In this sense, heresy held—and continues to hold—a double attraction: as one of a number of "marginal" categories, it holds a potential political interest, and the dissenting women sometimes visible within heresy (or rather, for the most part, the sources created by the prosecution of heresy, such as the trial of Peyronette) provide particularly exciting opportunities for recovering "lost" voices and experiences. A particular subset of this area is writing on women's *religious* history, which is often invested with a modern desire for gender equality within contemporary churches (supporting the ordination of female clergy for example), which with varying degrees of sophistication looks back to earlier times for precedent and inspiration.

All these perspectives can still prompt important questions about the relationship between, for example, religious heterodoxy and political dissent, or between female roles and dominant ideologies. But scholarly work produced since 1979 has steadily worn away at the assumption that women and heresy naturally went together, first by demonstrating that, far from being equal or a majority, women were almost always underrepresented in heretical sects; second, by looking more critically at the roles which women played when they were visible in heresy; and third, by reconsidering both heterodox and orthodox theologies and religious practices in regard to gendered ideas. These findings are worth rehearsing in some detail.

First, the proportion of women. In a landmark article from 1979, Richard Abels and Ellen Harrison demonstrated that the assumed prominence of women within Catharism in southern France was, if anything, the reverse.[9] Working from a very large source base (primarily a mid-thirteenth-century inquisitorial register of nearly 6,000 deponents, supplemented with comparative materials documenting several hundred further witnesses), they compiled a statistical analysis of gendered participation in the heresy. The analysis and arguments were nuanced—both in terms of statistical method, and historical interpretation—but their main findings were very clear. For the spiritual elite of the sect (the Cathar "perfects" in Abels and Harrison's terms, more often called "goodmen" and "goodwomen" in subsequent literature), about 45 percent were women—a slight, albeit not insubstantial, minority. However, those female perfects were very much less active and less visible than their male counterparts. When witnesses mentioned a Cathar perfect to an inquisitor, it was predominantly a male perfect; only every fifth mention was of a woman. Of all the women perfects named in the main manuscript, only eleven are ever mentioned as having preached, whereas almost all the men did at some point perform this element of Cathar ministry; a similarly vast disparity is also true in regard to the "sacramental" elements within Catharism, such as the bestowal of the *consolamentum* (a ritual which freed the soul of a believer from its corporeal prison, bestowed either at the deathbed, or, more rarely, in order to transform someone from a believer into a "perfect"). Moreover, women were never members of what one might call the Cathar "upper clergy" (those termed "bishop," "deacon," "older son," "younger son"). All of these figures relate to the information provided by witnesses against others; perhaps even more striking is the pattern which emerges from what those witnesses had to say about themselves. From the various registers studied by Abels and Harrison, of those witnesses—predominantly the Cathar "laity," as it were—who admitted to the inquisitors that they had formerly believed in the heresy, only between a fifth and a quarter were women. By every count, both Cathar perfects and Cathar believers were very much more likely to be men; and when they were women, their roles appeared to be very considerably constrained.

Shannon McSheffrey has performed a roughly parallel analysis for the late medieval English heresy of Lollardy. Assessing those named in the major investigations into Lollardy in the fifteenth and early sixteenth century (a total of slightly less than 1,000 people), she finds that women comprised only 28 percent of the total; and those women were very likely to be involved in the heresy through a family connection (most often via a husband or father), whereas only about one third of the men mentioned had a familial relationship with another Lollard. Although earlier historiography had played with the idea of women holding a clerical role within Lollardy—and it is certainly true that some Lollards voiced ideas about women being able to preach, for example—there is no clear evidence to support this in actual fact. And whereas 19 percent of the men mentioned appear to have been literate (and thus to have had direct access to scripture, which was at the heart of Lollard devotion and proselytization), the same was true of only 3 percent of the women. Female participation in this heresy was limited, McSheffrey suggests, by the wider social constraints upon women, which rarely allowed them public recognition or a public voice.[10]

In these and other studies, women's roles within heresy have been noted as similar to women's roles in medieval social life: denied any formal status or public voice; given some degree of autonomy and power within the domestic sphere, but even there liable to become "invisible" behind mention of the male householder; predominantly playing a supporting or enabling role, rather than being active agents within a group. There are individual exceptions—we shall look at some below—but the overall picture is familiar from other kinds of social history. It is true that statistics do not tell the whole story about any kind of situation, nor should one abandon the project of considering heresy in regard to gender. But the patterns and proportions are essentially undeniable: women were never predominant in heresy, and in regard to issues of activity and visibility, were usually strongly in the minority—as one might similarly find with orthodox religion.

It is here that our third area of reconsideration, namely issues of theology, comes into play. Stereotypes in orthodox polemic can make "women" appear much more present and active than may in fact have been the case. Grado Merlo has persuasively made this point with regard to early Waldensianism. While there is evidence for the existence of Waldensian "Sisters," some of whom did preach their faith, from the beginning of the sect, a careful reading of the early sources makes plain that the Sisters were never involved in any of the public, formal occasions during which Waldes and his later followers defended their faith. Moreover, hostile accounts of early Waldensians were strongly inflected by the image of those "weak little women" (*mulierculas*) from the biblical text, the orthodox writers being outraged by the *idea* of female preaching; an idea that, Merlo suggests, did not in fact find nearly as much opportunity for practice as earlier historians have assumed.[11]

In a similar vein, suggestions that women might perform the sacraments appear to come as a further logical extension of the Waldensian idea that laymen could act as priests, though whether this extension was primarily made by Waldensians themselves is again less clear: the mid-thirteenth-century *summa* against heresy written by Rainerius Sacconi notes that "they affirm that a simple layman can consecrate the body of the Lord. I believe, also, that as to women they say the same thing, since they have not denied it before me."[12] Sacconi appears to be extrapolating from what he did know about Waldensians to what he thought he might further negatively assume about Waldensians, signaling, however, a slight degree of uncertainty. One can similarly argue in the case of Lollardy that the abstract notion of female preaching or female ministry loomed much larger than actual practice.

When condemning something as a heresy, orthodox writers had a number of received literary tropes available to them: similarity to heresy in late antiquity, the sin of pride, images of disease and poison, parallels with "Jewish blindness" and stupidity. Among these, and recurrently deployed, was the monstrous notion of allowing women to act as priests. The point is twofold: we are sometimes misled by the stereotypical condemnations of hostile sources, and the misogynist elements within those condemnations are part of a wider package of hostile representational strategies, rather than an indication that "gender" was the, or even a, primary battleground between heresy and orthodoxy.

Some heretical theology did have positive things to say about women (as did some orthodox theologies, of course). A late twelfth-century treatise directed against Waldensian tenets includes a chapter "Against the assertion that women may preach," and appears to originate from actual theological debates, rather than the ascription of a stereotype.[13] In fifteenth-century Bohemia, a period for which we have much greater access to materials produced *by* heretics rather than *about* heretics, both Jan Hus and Peter Chelčický (radical Hussite preachers) thought that women had the right to talk about religion, and possibly therefore to preach—though it is worth noting the full context in which this belief was asserted:

> Today's prelates, masters and priests boast in their offices, saying that God has placed them into their offices and they have all the knowledge of God! And they forbid women, lay people and the peasants to read the scriptures, and to speak about God because they are not priests! However, scriptures say, the Lord has looked on the humility of his handmaiden, not on the priestly office.[14]

This is pro-women, but more clearly anticlerical; and pro-women as part of a wider spectrum of lay access to the Bible, rather than as a specific aim in and of itself. This was an ideal shared, of course, with Lollardy, and to some degree also with Waldensianism. In all three cases, the principle of equal access to scripture does seem to have encompassed, as an abstract ideal at least, female use of the Bible, sometimes including public reading or preaching by women. In the case of Hussitism, however, evidence for actual female preaching comes only from hostile texts; there is a question, once again, as to what degree the principle translated into reality.

Other elements of heretical theology could be less attractive. Cathars believed in two gods, a good one who created the spirit, and a bad one who created all corporeal matter; from this view of creation flowed their other beliefs (transmigration of souls, sexual abstinence, abhorrence of killing, vegetarianism, and so forth). Peter Biller has argued that the Cathar rejection of the material world was strongly inflected with misogyny, perhaps because women were generally associated with "the body" in medieval culture, and perhaps particularly because of childbirth, which continued the reproduction of the bad god's evil world. Overall, Biller suggests, women had good reason to shun Catharism; both Waldensianism and orthodoxy were more amenable faiths.[15]

Cathar theology is rather unusual—no other medieval heresy had such a hatred for the material world—but there are other issues with regard to heretical theology which bear some further reflection. McSheffrey notes that various key aspects to Lollard theology—particularly the vehement mockery of saints' shrines, the denial of Christ's corporeality in the eucharist, and the rejection of ascetic practices such as fasting—were attacks upon areas of religious devotion which other historians have seen as holding particular interest or attraction for orthodox women. In the somewhat parallel context of Hussitism, we see something similar in July 1421, when a substantial group of women in Prague produced a letter (which they successfully demanded be read publicly to the city) denouncing the more radical Taborite wing of the heresy, rejecting the extreme, apocalyptically tinged violence of that subgroup, and calling for a more moderate religious approach. The radicalism of dissent in that particular context was specifically repellent to those particular women, perhaps because of its perceived link with social violence, perhaps because of its denial of social hierarchy.[16] One may question whether the rejection of marriage—a feature found in various medieval heresies—was attractive or dismaying to some women. The Waldensians did not reject marriage, and indeed when Peyronette, with whom we began, was asked about their beliefs in that area, she particularly emphasized their position: "that the sacrament of marriage should be guarded faithfully and firmly." At the same time, however, Peyronette's experience of Waldensianism was marked at its very inception by a wider, antifemale sentiment. After Peyronette had recounted the tenets of Waldensian belief that she learned from the visiting Italian Brothers, the inquisitor asked her how this meeting had come about. She admitted that she had been told about the heretics by one Telmon Paschal, who had arranged for them to visit her. "However, she said that the said Telmon doubted her, that she should not reveal or detect these things mentioned, given that it is the habit of a woman to talk too much," and he made her swear an oath of secrecy. Whatever degree of female emancipation was still present in late fifteenth-century Waldensianism, it did not mean that Waldensian supporters were freed from the cultural assumptions of their times.

I am not trying to suggest that heresy was uniformly a negative for women; rather, it was not a clear positive, and attitudes somewhat varied between heresies. Both Catharism and Waldensianism had a clear "elect" within the sect, who held priest-like positions; elements of those positions were available to both men and women, though their contexts, duties, and theological implications differed somewhat. Hussitism involved Catholic priests (radicalized by Hus's reformist theology); its very radical Taborite wing claimed to do away with all hierarchy, which included clerical/lay distinctions. Lollardy similarly involved some existing clergy, but made no formal distinction between lay and clerical in its reformist, dissenting faith. Each group existed in specific sociopolitical contexts: an increasingly quiet and clandestine existence for the Waldensians in the fourteenth and fifteenth centuries, open national warfare in the case of the Hussites, the aftermath of the Lancastrian usurpation for the later Lollards. Gender roles and gender ideas thus vary across and within these various "heresies," even when they shared similar theological perspectives.

There is one group for whom female roles were absolutely central: the Guglielmites. These were followers of a holy woman, Guglielma, who died in northern Italy in about 1281. She was believed to be (and possibly in reality actually was) the daughter of the king of Bohemia, thus a relative to several other very famous holy women (Elizabeth of Hungary, Agnes of Bohemia, and Margaret of Hungary). Following her death, it appears that those close to her—particularly a woman called Maifreda da Pirovano and a man called Andreas Saramita—came to believe that Guglielma had been the incarnation of the Holy Spirit, sent to the world in order to establish a new Church led by a female pope, and that following her death Guglielma would have a Second Coming, which would lead to the conversion of all non-Christians.[17] Here, alone of all the medieval heresies, an idea about specifically female spirituality stands center stage. The cult of Guglielma was in some respects much like other cults directed toward a local saint; Guglielma's body was buried in the local monastery, for example. But Maifreda appears to have played a particularly central, and possibly quasi-sacerdotal, role in its devotions: distributing consecrated hosts, bestowing blessings, and having various people (including local lords and ladies) genuflect before her and kiss her hand. Lady Sibilla Malconzato, very much involved in the sect, eventually reported to inquisitors that:

> at Easter last past, Sister Maifreda da Pirovano made herself in the manner of a priest, and Sister Fiordebellina and Sister Agnesina and Andreas Saramita and Franceschino Malconzato had vestments, and Albertone da Novate and Felicino Carentano and Ottorino da Garbagnate had white mantles, and they prepared a table in the manner of an altar, and they had a chalice and other necessary things for saying mass; and the said Sister Maifreda said mass and held the Host and raised it up, and did all things around that mass in the manner done by other priests; and the said Andreas spoke the Gospel and the said Albertone spoke the Epistles.[18]

This is perhaps the most direct account of a woman acting as a priest to be found anywhere in the medieval sources; it is interesting to note that even while Maifreda prepared the Eucharist, it was her male assistants who preached. The sect was, however, very small and secretive, and did not attract much wider participation (though it may have held some continuing attraction to the Visconti dukes of Milan, as part of their antipapal strategy).[19]

It is impossible to say what, beyond a very particular devotion to Guglielma, prompted Maifreda and Andreas to confect this woman-centered heretical piety. But the Guglielmites become, in one aspect, somewhat more comprehensible if looked at not purely in terms of "heresy," but as part of the wider swathe of pious enthusiasm found in the central and later Middle Ages. As already noted, Guglielma came (or was believed to have come) from a royal context well known for the production of female saints. Elements of the cult are essentially similar to the pious devotions directed toward other holy women. And this can remind us of a wider point. An early exploration of the possible link between women and heresy was made by the German historian Herbert Grundmann in his foundational study *Religious Movements in the Middle Ages* (written originally in 1935, revised in 1955, and translated into English in 1995). Grundmann's main point was that "heresy" did not stand alone and apart from orthodoxy. Rather, the religious phenomena labelled "heretical," particularly in the twelfth and thirteenth centuries, were part of a wider shift in religious practice and affect—notable particularly for its greater lay involvement, and its development of specifically female spiritual roles—that also included orthodoxy. "Heresy" and "orthodoxy" are but labels; as Grundmann realized, they share much more than they differ. Even where one finds a substantially different theology, as is arguably the case with Cathar dualism for example, the practices and accoutrements of the "heresy" overlap considerably with the orthodoxy to which they are opposed.

This perspective opens up a different way of approaching the question of heresy and gender. Recent work on orthodox piety has explored a variety of ways in which women enjoyed a degree of agency and could find active roles within the church. As I have been arguing, we should relinquish the question of whether heresy held a particular attraction for "women" in general; but we can certainly ask how, and in what ways, particular women were involved in heretical piety, and how, through their involvement, they may have challenged or renegotiated the constraints of gender. Once we have the richer sources of inquisitorial evidence, women's activity as both supporters of and participants in heretical sects becomes more clearly visible. For example, over the course of a number of days in 1244, a Cathar "good woman" called Arnauda de Lamothe gave a very lengthy confession to an inquisitor about her activities as an elite member of that sect. Through this material we can see more detail about her "heretical" life: entering an all-female house of heretics as a kind of Cathar "novice," then receiving the *consolamentum* and becoming a fully fledged Cathar perfect. When the northern crusaders came to Languedoc (1209–1229), Arnauda moved around to evade capture, initially moving between various all-female houses, but latterly traveling around the countryside, staying in cottages and barns. In 1212 she and her sister, "through very great fear of persecution, returned to Montauban, and left the heretical sect and ate meat, and were reconciled by the Bishop of Cahors." But in 1224 they both remade contact with the heretics, initially via another group of female Cathars who were living at Linars, pretending to be nuns. We see various different people, men and women, coming to visit Arnauda, to "adore" her (as the inquisitors put it, perhaps encoding a particular form of respectful greeting); when living in the manor of Massac, she said that "she often preached," and she frequently bestowed blessings on people's food when they sat to eat with her. On one occasion, following the death of her sister, we find her bestowing the *consolamentum* on another woman, who became her new companion.[20]

There were things which Arnauda did not get to do: she was not a member of the Cathar hierarchy, and she was notably dependent upon the support of male protectors throughout her travels. But her experience of Catharism certainly permitted her an active role, engaging regularly with the Cathar "laity," and hence probably more active than that of a Catholic nun (though the Cathar women at Linars could appear much like nuns). As a Cathar perfect, Arnauda was often the recipient of gifts from supporters. The opportunity to give spiritual gifts and alms is a recurrent feature in heresy, as much as in orthodoxy, and perhaps provided a particular form of spiritual involvement for the female laity. As we have already seen, Peyronette, the Waldensian supporter, gave some needles; various further examples of gifts by women—food, money, clothing, candles, and the like—can be found in other times and places. Whether heresy provided any greater opportunity than orthodoxy for women to bestow this kind of pious gift is unclear; but we need not think of the two in mutual opposition if we are interested in getting at the gendered experience of lived religion.

Scholars have focused on women participating collectively—through formal guilds or informal almsgiving—in orthodox lay piety, and again there is an echo in the source material for heresy. In the mid-thirteenth century, a Languedocian noblewoman called Sedeira admitted that she had received "two Waldensian women in her house many times, and heard their admonitions. Item, she ate with two Waldensians elsewhere, and used to believe they were good men." There is the occasional mention of what may be all-women audiences for some Cathar preaching from the same period. I mentioned above a sizeable group of Prague women who collectively intervened on the side of moderate Hussitism in fifteenth-century Bohemia; there is some (perhaps questionable) evidence for women fighting within Hussite armies, and certainly good evidence for noblewomen playing a key role, individually and collectively, in materially supporting Hussitism in its early years.[21] In those latter cases, the specific contexts and demands of a dissenting religion perhaps do provide participatory opportunities for some women, which would not have been available within Catholicism.

This may also be the case—though it is actually harder to argue than one might first think—with regard to some more interior aspects of heretical faith. In 1319, a man admitted to the inquisitor Jacques Fournier that he had been taught Waldensian beliefs concerning the creed and the sacraments by a woman innkeeper called Jacoba, who was then (he said) about forty years old and knew how to read. In 1521, "John Mastal detected the daughter of John Phip, of Hichenden, for saying that she was as well-learned as was the parish priest, in all things except only in saying of mass." From the same Lollard trials we hear that Alice Colins

> was a famous woman among them, and had a good memory, and could recite much of the Scriptures and other good books; and therefore when any conventicle of these men did meet at Burford, commonly she was sent for, to recite unto them the declaration of the Ten Commandments, and the Epistles of Peter and James.[22]

This "intellectual" side to heresy—teaching, learning, reciting, debating—is found among male deponents as well, of course; but might we see heresy as again providing a particular opportunity for women here? Possibly so, particularly when we move down the social scale from the late medieval gentry and urban elite, where pious orthodox women commonly had access to books of vernacular instruction and the like. But it may be that this is still part of the spectrum of lay belief and practice more broadly, and its "heretical" aspect is primarily its visibility to us, through the medium of inquisitorial trial registers.

Given that the earlier idea of female predominance in heresy has been conclusively exploded, what exactly is it that we are now hoping to find when considering heresy and gender? Areas little explored are the masculinity of male heretics, which might profitably be read alongside recent work on the masculinity of the medieval clergy, and the focus on purity and virginity within some heresies, again in parallel with orthodox strands of theology. But "heresy" continues to hold interest and excitement in part, I would suggest, because of the particular focus upon female *agency* that is associated with the project of third-wave feminism and subsequent gender studies. Heresy holds two particular attractions here. The most obvious is that we see heresy as a form of deliberate dissent, and hence agency within heresy comes to us coded as particularly active, disruptive, and daring: an agency which challenges rather than knuckles down and conforms. Those who were prosecuted for heresy tend always to prompt our sympathy, and sometimes our admiration; it is very hard to feel other than inspired by Joan of Arc (prosecuted for heresy, in part because of her claim that she could speak directly with saints), despite the fact that the specifics of both her actions and her faith may be miles away from any modern notion of progressive gender politics.

It is perhaps thus necessary to reflect further on both the differing tactics of those who found themselves pursued by authority, and our investment in their struggle. As noted above, at one point Arnauda of Lamothe and her sister decided to leave Catharism for the safety of conformity, but then reconverted; Arnauda was almost certainly executed as having "relapsed" from a previous reconciliation with the Church. Both conversions—from Catharism to Catholicism, and back again—required agency; which one does one applaud the more? The mystical writer Marguerite Porete was prosecuted and executed for heresies allegedly contained in her book *The Mirror of Simple Souls*; she appears simply to have ignored the inquisitorial prosecution launched against her, exercising a kind of negative agency (also fatal in the end).

Sometimes we find women involved on the other side of the table. In both Cathar and Lollard trials, there are a few occasions when women were held suspect in their beliefs because of what they cried out, or failed to cry out, during childbirth (for example, failing to call upon the Virgin Mary); those reporting them for this suspicious activity were other women. Those informers too were exercising agency, as were, presumably, many others who were active in their support for orthodoxy and had nothing to do with heresy.

Even if one wishes to keep hold of the assumption that resistance to or divergence from orthodoxy clearly displays greater agency than if one conforms, there are wider realms of possibility to be explored than the purely and clearly "heretical." Social history in the twenty-first century has tended to question whether the received ecclesiastical view of matters such as gender and sexuality wielded automatic hegemony in all times and places. Religious ideals about virginity and chastity were not universally upheld, nor even necessarily internalized as automatically as earlier historiographies tended to assume. Thus, for example, unmarried female sexuality could, in some contexts, be more or less tolerated, and marriage was not an automatic choice for all adult women. At the same time, aspects of religious ideology that had positive potential for women—for example, the clear canon law principle that marriage should be entered into willingly and by free choice—did not necessarily play out that way in social reality. Within the field of religious practice itself, there are possibilities for glimpsing female choice and agency that do not necessarily fall into the category of "heresy" (legally or historiographically), but which are part of the divergences from the norm that in fact permeate lay religion. The less detailed, but still intriguing, evidence of diocesan visitation records is of particular use here. At the furthest pole of heterodoxy would be women using healing charms and prayers, as can be found in various parts of Europe; disapproved of, but in fact an element in parochial religion for much of the Middle Ages. Less radical, but still intriguing, are moments when female involvement in what is assumed to be a default realm of male activity becomes visible: for example, occasional mentions of women ringing parish church bells, sometimes regularly and sometimes on a specific occasion (for instance, in order to embarrass the priest, who also happened to be the bell-ringing woman's lover, and with whom she had had an argument). Just occasionally we see some very personal negotiation or interpretation of religious practice: the woman who did not attend mass, as she feared to encounter the man who had previously raped her; the "little old woman" reported (but not named) by her parish priest for failing to attend annual confession—because she "said that she had not committed any sins."[23] Other issues of female agency and "dissent" in a broader form are found here, though less illuminated by our sources than aspects of Catharism, Waldensianism, and Lollardy.

This leads to the second and final point about the continuing historiographical allure of heresy: it is simply more *visible* than orthodoxy. Or rather, it more often allows us to see something at an individual level than orthodox sources permit. Wills, guild records, parish accounts, and the like do not provide the level of detail about belief, behavior, and everyday life that we can find in inquisitorial registers. In some instances—most particularly Jacques Fournier's investigations in Languedoc, from whence Emmanuel Le Roy Ladurie wrote his famous *Montaillou*—the texture of human life is present in unparalleled detail, including very personal aspects of gender and sexuality. Even in less exciting registers, the sense of a voice is alluringly present. What we are perhaps responding to above all here are women under threat, women negotiating tactically with the full force of ecclesiastical authority. Here the issues of agency become particularly subtle, and perhaps refuse analytical closure. Peyronette, with whom we began, recounted to the inquisitor a sexist trope of female garrulity in the context of her first encounter with the Waldensian preachers. Toward the end of her deposition, she made further use of a gendered stereotype:

> Asked if she believed or otherwise gave faith to the aforesaid [Waldensian] preachers or masters, and their texts and doctrines, she said and spontaneously confessed that just as a woman is foolish and innocent and easily deceived, she believed and gave faith to the same preachers... believing this to be acting well and wholesomely; and on this account did not believe herself to have erred in any way. When however she saw or understood she had erred in some way, she submitted herself to the benign correction of the Holy Mother Church.

It is tempting to see this as a very self-conscious tactic on Peyronette's part, and indeed perhaps it was.[24] But perhaps, equally, she had internalized the idea of being a weak little woman who is easily led. Or perhaps both: she certainly had reason to regret her involvement with the Waldensians at the point she came to speak these words, since she was under threat of execution, and maybe in those circumstances she felt herself to have acted stupidly and to have been easily led. Agency exists in all of these possibilities; what is at stake is not simply women's role within heresy, but how we conceive of the "voice" that we seek to recover from a distant past.

Further Reading

Abels, Richard and Ellen Harrison. "The Participation of Women in Languedocian Catharism,"
   Mediaeval Studies, 41 (1979): 215–51.
Biller, Peter. "Women and Dissent," in A. J. Minnis and R. Voaden, eds, *Medieval Holy Women
   in the Christian Tradition, 1100–1500*. Turnhout: Brepols, 2010.
Brenon, Anne. *Les femmes cathares*. Paris: Perrin, 1992.
Burrus, Virginia. *The Making of a Heretic: Gender, Authority, and the Priscillianist Controversy*.
   Berkeley: University of California Press, 1995.
Klassen, John M. *Warring Maidens, Captive Wives, and Hussite Queens*. Boulder: East European
   Monographs, 1999.
McSheffrey, Shannon. *Gender and Heresy: Women and Men in Lollard Communities, 1420–1530*.
   Philadelphia: University of Pennsylvania Press, 1995.
Peterson, Janine Larmon. "Social Roles, Gender Inversion, and the Heretical Sect: The Case of
   the Guglielmites," *Viator*, 35 (2004): 203–20.
Shahar, Shulamith. *Women in a Medieval Heretical Sect: Agnes and Huguette the Waldensians*.
   Woodbridge: Boydell, 2001.
Sullivan, Karen. *The Interrogation of Joan of Arc*. Minneapolis: University of Minnesota
   Press, 1999.
Wakefield, Walter L. and Austin P. Evans, eds. *Heresies of the High Middle Ages*, 2nd edn.
   New York: Columbia University Press, 1992.

Notes

1. Peyronette's trial edited in Peter Allix, *Some Remarks upon the Ecclesiastical History of the
   Ancient Churches of Piedmont* (1690; repr. Oxford: Clarendon Press, 1821), 347–61.
2. Peter Biller, "The Preaching of the Waldensian Sisters," in Peter Biller *The Waldenses, 1170–
   1530* (Aldershot: Variorum, 2001).
3. Council of Rheims, 1157, J. D. Mansi, *Sacrorum conciliorum* (Venice, 1776), 21, col. 843.
4. *Codex Udalrici*, in P. Jaffé, ed., *Monumenta Bambergensia* (Berlin, 1869), No. 168.
5. Irenaeus, *Adversus hereses*, 1.23, in *Against the Heresies*, trans. D. J. Unger (Mahwah,
   NJ: Newman Press, 1992).
6. St Augustine, *The De Haeresibus of Saint Augustine*, ed. and trans. L. G. Müller (Washington,
   DC: Catholic University of America, 1956).
7. Paul J. Archambault, *A Monk's Confession: The Memoirs of Guibert de Nogent* (University
   Park, PA: Pennsylvania State University Press, 1996), 196.
8. Alberic de Trois Fontaines, *Chronica Albrichi monachi trium fontium*, ed. P. Scheffer-
   Boichorst, Monumenta Germaniae Historica, Scriptores 23 (Berlin, 1874), 940.
9. Richard Abels and Ellen Harrison, "The Participation of Women in Languedocian
   Catharism," *Mediaeval Studies*, 41 (1979): 215–51.
10. Shannon McSheffrey, *Gender and Heresy: Women and Men in Lollard Communities, 1420–
    1530* (Philadelphia: University of Pennsylvania Press, 1995), 165–66.
11. Grado G. Merlo, "Sulle 'Misere donnicciuole' che predicavano," in *Valdesi e valdismi
    medievali*, vol. II: *Identità valdesi nella storia e storiografia: Studi e discussioni*
    (Turin: Claudiana, 1991), 93–112.

12. Walter L. Wakefield and Austin P. Evans, eds and trans., *Heresies of the High Middle Ages*, 2nd edn (New York: Columbia University Press, 1992), 345.

13. Wakefield and Evans, *Heresies*, 213.

14. John M. Klassen, *Warring Maidens, Captive Wives, and Hussite Queens* (Boulder: East European Monographs, 1999), 169.

15. Peter Biller, "The Common Woman in the Western Church in the Thirteenth and Fourteenth Centuries," *Studies in Church History*, 27 (1990): 127–57; Peter Biller, "Cathars and Material Women," in Peter Biller and Alastair J. Minnis, eds, *Medieval Theology and the Natural Body* (Woodbridge: Boydell, 1997), 61–107.

16. Klassen, *Warring Maidens*, 199.

17. Marina Benedetti, *Io non sono Dio: Guglielma di Milano e i Figli dello Spirito Santo* (Milan: Biblioteca Francescana, 1998); Janine Larmon Peterson, "Social Roles, Gender Inversion, and the Heretical Sect: The Case of the Guglielmites," *Viator*, 35 (2004): 203–20.

18. Marina Benedetti, ed., *Milano 1300: I processi inquisitoriali contro le devote e i devoti di santa Guglielma* (Milan: Scheiwiller, 1999), 214.

19. Barbara Newman, "The Heretic Saint: Guglielma of Bohemia, Milan and Brunate," *Church History*, 74 (2005): 1–38.

20. Bibliothèque nationale de France, Paris, MS Doat 23, fols 2v–49r.

21. Doat 21, fol. 248v; John H. Arnold, "The Preaching of the Cathars," in Carolyn Muessig, ed., *Medieval Monastic Preaching* (Leiden: Brill, 1998); Thomas A. Fudge, ed. and trans., *The Crusade against Heretics in Bohemia, 1418–37* (Aldershot: Ashgate, 2002), 73.

22. Biller, "Waldensian Sisters," 138; John Foxe, *Acts and Monuments* (London, 1837), IV, 231, 238.

23. E. M. Elvey, ed., "The Courts of the Archdeaconry of Buckingham, 1483–1525," *Buckinghamshire Record Society*, 19 (1975): 161; P. Gios, ed., *Vita religiosa e sociale a Padova: La visita pastorale di Diotisalvi da Foligno alle parochie cittadine (1452–1458)* (Padua: Libraria Padovana, 1997), 65.

24. Peter Biller, "Medieval Waldensian Followers' Construction of History: Jaqueta, Peroneta, the Old One zum Hirtze, and Peyronette," in M. Benedetti and B. L. Betri, eds, *Una strana gioia di vivere: a Grado Giovanni Merlo* (Milan: Biblioteca Francescana, 2010), 181–98.

CHAPTER 32

CULTURES OF DEVOTION

KATHLEEN ASHLEY

INTRODUCTION

A DOLL'S cradle from a German convent, the Virgin's girdle in Prato, the sites of Christ's Passion in Jerusalem, the pilgrimage route to Santiago de Compostela, Florentine confraternity hymns, devotional texts such as the *Revelations* of Bridget of Sweden—each of these was central to a culture of devotion in western Europe during the Middle Ages.

In the past forty years, scholars have dismantled the trope of a monolithic "age of faith." We now see a radically more complex portrait of religious activities and their meanings in the many societies of medieval Europe. We recognize the imbrication of religion with political power and social institutions. We also have a fuller picture of the multiple competing religious ideologies and normative discourses articulated in the vast literature produced by those powerful institutions and authority figures. However, we often lack documentation about the reception of these ideologies and discourses, especially the devotional responses of both individuals and groups. The full analysis of medieval cultures of devotion requires that we pay attention both to the overt practices and value systems of a "culture" and to the more hidden thoughts and feelings of devotion.

In pursuit of this more nuanced and historically specific understanding of medieval devotional cultures, issues of gender have become an important focus of investigation. While the older narrative of the "age of faith" may have given little explicit consideration to gender, its unarticulated corollary was that men were historically important and worth studying, while women were not. Attention to medieval devotional cultures over the past forty years has generated a wealth of exciting new information about female religious experiences and has opened the door to gender-informed reconsiderations of the male experience. In particular, it has required scholars to avoid broad generalizations about medieval religion (based only on ecclesiastical gender models and proscriptions) in favor of close examinations of historically situated "cultures of devotion." There was a rich diversity of devotional texts, objects, and practices during the medieval period, and this richness justifies the renewed attention to the myriad of devotional cultures. Given their centrality to medieval lives, cultures of devotion were also prime (and often contentious) arenas for defining and negotiating gender issues—and they remain open sites for continued scholarly exploration and critical debate about gender.

DEVOTION IN POPULAR RELIGION

From the early Middle Ages, locations regarded as holy—such as the tombs of martyrs and saints—drew people wanting access to the powers of the sacred. Over the centuries, the relics of such holy bodies were dispersed and enshrined in churches across Catholic Europe, where groups of worshippers and pilgrims of both sexes could visit them. Although church or shrine authorities might attempt to control access to their relics, the pressure of popular interest created uncounted opportunities for devotional activities at these sites. In this sense, therefore, we can speak of a generalized culture of devotion as one of the characteristics of the entire Middle Ages, with the understanding that it was a culture in which all could participate and whose impulse was as much popular as clerically inspired and controlled.

Accounts of such popular devotion include mention of both men and women who flocked to places like the abbey church of St Denis outside Paris, which exhibited the nails and crown of thorns from Christ's crucifixion each year to a mob of pilgrims. Recounting the intolerable congestion on the feast day, Abbot Suger in the twelfth century describes the distress of the women pilgrims who, "squeezed in by the mass of men as in a winepress, . . . cried out horribly as if in labor" and finally had to be "lifted by the pious assistance of men above the heads of the crowd," to end up gasping for breath in the cloisters of the brethren.[1]

The major pilgrimages to Santiago de Compostela in Galicia, to Rome, and even to Jerusalem also attracted women pilgrims like Margery Kempe, the fifteenth-century townswoman who wrote about her intensely emotional spiritual experiences. In Jerusalem, she joined a tour of the Passion sites led by Franciscans carrying a cross, who "led the pilgrims about from one place to another where our Lord had suffered his pains and his passions, every man and woman bearing a wax candle in their hand." As the friars told what Christ had suffered in each place, Margery began the noisy crying that would mark her devotional career from then on:

> [She] wept and sobbed so plenteously as though she had seen our Lord with her bodily eye suffering his Passion at that time. Before her in her soul she saw him verily by contemplation, and that caused her to have compassion. And when they came up on to the Mount of Calvary, she fell down so that she might not stand or kneel but wallowed and twisted with her body, spreading her arms abroad, and cried with a loud voice as though her heart should have burst asunder, for in the city of her soul she saw verily and freshly how our Lord was crucified.[2]

Margery's conspicuous weeping seems to have marked her even more than her gender; men outnumbered women on pilgrimages, but women were accepted as pilgrims to both regional and international shrines.

Local churches were also equal-opportunity devotional sites for parishioners, who might pray before altars featuring a statue of the Virgin and Child, a painting of a sacred scene, or the image of a locally revered saint. As Richard Marks in his study *Image and Devotion in Late Medieval England* points out, "For the laity as a whole, the devotional images in their parish church remained the principal focus of affective piety until the Reformation," straddling public and private as well as social and spiritual divides.[3] We might add that parish devotion also bridged any gender divide. In the later Middle Ages, when affluent lay families used their significant material and political resources to build their own private chapels onto the local church, the opportunity for female family members to shape the devotional space was greatly increased. Heiress Anne Harling, for example, gave stained glass windows featuring the Joys and Sorrows of the Virgin to the East Harling church.[4] Indeed, the subject of women as donors and patrons continues to be one of the growth industries of medieval studies.

The appeal of popular ritualized activities—such as pilgrimages, processions, or drama—and the ubiquity of devotional images in public ecclesiastical spaces drew both men and women, although not always in equal numbers. Confraternities (associations of pious laity, called "parish guilds" in England) usually had more male than female members. Christopher Black traces the lay confraternity phenomenon from the thirteenth century onward, noting both the proliferation and variety of kinds of confraternities. Flagellants (*disciplinati*) accepted only men, but there were many mixed-sex groups dedicated to death rituals and charity, and research is revealing more and more women-only confraternities in central Italy. In Zamora (Spain), almost all the confraternities admitted women, according to Maureen Flynn, and the same was true in Bury St Edmunds (England).[5] As with other pious activities, few gender generalizations can be made about confraternities in any country, let alone all of Europe—except perhaps the existence of a diversity of arrangements that were always in flux.

COMMUNITIES OF WOMEN

Among the most exciting research to come out of the last forty years has been the rediscovery of individual female religious leaders and reconstruction of the communities they lived in, the texts they read and wrote, and the art they created. Hrotsvit of Gandersheim, Hildegard of Bingen, Christina of Markyate, Hadewijch, Mechthild of Magdeburg, Clare of Assisi, Marguerite Porete, Bridget of Sweden, Catherine of Siena, Julian of Norwich, and the nuns of Helfta and Syon have all now begun to get the scholarly attention they deserve. As the lives and writings of influential women have been recuperated and brought into the historical narrative, the previous view of women's subordination and powerlessness relative to men has been rightly revised.

These women operated in varied institutional contexts, including beguinages and other female households. Although women expressed an interest equal to men in pursuing the monastic life, by the thirteenth century many religious orders were closing off new opportunities to women, and women's convents in general were receiving less economic and political support. Especially in northern European towns, women were active both economically and religiously, notably in the Low Countries, where communities of women known as "beguines" proliferated. Walter Simons identifies at least 298 beguine communities in 111 urban sites of the region.[6] The beguinages offered a mixed life combining an active apostolate of practical or charitable work in the town with a dedication to voluntary poverty and contemplation, but without the claustration of a regular convent setting. Their popularity not just in northern Europe can be judged by the existence of similar communities in France and Lombardy.

Beguine devotions were intuitive, personal, and based on a direct gift of the divine, as opposed to the clerical preference for learned, professional, ecclesiastically mediated knowledge. The two contrasting kinds of knowledge were therefore implicitly gendered. A late thirteenth-century dialogue between a Parisian master of theology and a beguine—who speaks here—exemplifies the woman's confidence in the superior outcomes of her devotional practices:

> You talk, we act.
> You learn, we seize.
> You inspect, we choose.
> You chew, we swallow.
> You bargain, we buy.
> You glow, we take fire.
> You assume, we know.
> You ask, we take.
> You search, we find.
> You love, we languish.
> You languish, we die.
> You sow, we reap.
> You work, we rest.
> You grow thin, we grow fat.
> You ring, we sing.
> You sing, we dance.
> You blossom, we bear fruit.
> You taste, we savor.[7]

Beguine mysticism is typically characterized as being based in somatic visionary experience, but Amy Hollywood and other scholars have been challenging that stereotype by close examination of the writings of mystics such as Mechthild of Magdeburg and Marguerite Porete. Hollywood makes the convincing case that their theological writings—which influenced a male mystic, Meister Eckhart—avoid privileging the body as the vehicle for mystical experience.[8]

A second wave of intense female devotion occurred in the late fourteenth century in the Netherlands with the *devotio moderna*, in which new houses of women outnumbered those of men by four or five to one.[9] Like the beguines before them, the Sisters of the Common Life promoted a "mixed life" of social service in their urban communities along with cultivation of inner spirituality. In the fifteenth century, Margery Kempe—who forged her own individual devotional route and generated the first autobiography in English—similarly combined public ministry and mysticism following a widespread European model of "urban devotion."[10]

The barring of women from the most sacred core of ecclesiastical service—administering the sacraments and preaching—created a structural relationship between intensely pious women and the men who performed those functions for them. Called the *cura monialium* (care of nuns) or the *cura laicorum* (care of the laity), that relationship has long been a crux of interpretive interest, especially in the case of women visionaries whose devotional experiences were so exceptional and private. How to weigh the influence of the male advisor on female spirituality has been debated in studies of early medieval monasticism as well as late medieval lay piety. Mixed-sex monasteries with an abbess at the helm were not uncommon in the High Middle Ages, with Fontevrault as a twelfth-century example. According to Penny Schine Gold, at Fontevrault women held organizational power; men conducted religious services but "the women, in their lives of contemplation, were the focus of the community. The men were there to serve the nuns, both spiritually and materially."[11] It is generally agreed that this monastic model of male/female relations failed after the twelfth century. However, whether in or out of the monastery, the question of male influence on women's spirituality remains.

For women's visionary writings, "textual mediaries"—the scribe or the spiritual director who wrote down a woman's vision—were a constant presence, as Jennifer Summit comments with reference to Hildegard's scribe Volmar, Bridget of Sweden's spiritual director and editor Alfonso of Jaén, and of course the multiple scribes and clerical advisors of Margery Kempe.[12] In Margery's *Book*, we are told that a priest newly arrived in Lynn decided—with the encouragement of his mother!—to read Margery some of the most important books of "high contemplation": St Bride's [Bridget's] book, Hilton's book, Bonaventure, *The Goad of Love*, *The Fire of Love*, etc. The priest continued his reading to Margery for seven or eight years. Although most scholarly discussion of Margery Kempe focuses on her illiteracy and need to establish the orthodoxy of her devotional experiences, the actual text says he "found great ghostly comfort in her" and acknowledged that he would not have examined these devotional works if not for her.[13] In other words, Margery's autobiography emphasizes *her* spiritual influence on *him* and concludes that his subsequent acquisition of a populous benefice was a result of this deep study of meditational treatises with her. Modern scholars are still debating her claim in their efforts to reassess the agency of exceptional women.

THE PLACE OF IMAGES AND OBJECTS

One of the most controversial subjects within discussions of devotional culture is the role of images as the necessary instigators of mystical experiences for women. The theological origin for connecting images with devotion was articulated early by Gregory the Great and reiterated by Thomas Aquinas and Bonaventure in the thirteenth century.[14] They taught that the Incarnation justified the use of matter as a route to salvation, especially for those of a less developed spiritual capacity—the illiterate, lay people, and women—who could use physical images to stimulate their imaginations visually and enable them to achieve spiritual insight.

After the twelfth century—when the earthly lives of Christ, his mother Mary, and other sacred figures became the focus of devotion in imagery and texts—the relevance of their human physicality (Christ's manhood and Mary's maternal body) became a more pressing issue. The devotional images of Christ and Mary that proliferated in the later Middle Ages tended to show their physicality and their suffering, with which the viewer was invited to empathize as a means of achieving spiritual insight and, ultimately, mystical union. Images of the Virgin Mary with the Christ child were especially prevalent, and they included the Virgin, one breast exposed, feeding either her infant or a worshipper (the *Madonna lactans*), as well as statues of the Virgin that opened to reveal figures of the Trinity in her womb (the *Vierge ouvrante*). The Pietà—Mary holding the body of a dead Christ on her lap—was another ubiquitous devotional image, as were scenes of the Passion including Christ on the cross or standing before it as the Man of Sorrows, often with the instruments of the Passion. In the thirteenth-century convent at Helfta in Saxony, writings of visionary nuns gave rise to the cult of the Sacred Heart, in which the bleeding side wound of Christ was a particularly potent image for mystical devotions. The fourteenth-century anchoress Julian of Norwich developed the image of Jesus as a kind and loving Mother who brings the hungry child/meditator into his breast through his open side.[15]

By studying the devotional cultures of female monasticism, art historians have deconstructed the old master narrative in which art produced by women had no place. In *Nuns as Artists: The Visual Culture of a Medieval Convent*, for example, Jeffrey Hamburger analyzed the twelve late medieval devotional drawings surviving from St Walburg abbey, a female convent in Germany. The drawings use the *Song of Songs* as the primary script for the devotions of the nuns. Many images develop the "bridal mysticism" of the nun's spiritual marriage to Christ through scenes of the Passion. In one Crucifixion, the upper body of Christ is replaced by a heart on a cross with figures of the nun and Christ inside; there is a scene of the Eucharistic banquet, the nun kneeling at table with Christ and the Father; and there is the Heart as a House, the nun communing with Christ and the Trinity. Through the wound in Christ's side, the nun "enters a metaphorical as well as physical interior; she passes from imitation to identification and from petition to contemplative union. The heart in which the nun embraces Christ and the Trinity is the seat of her own soul, a place where she can take her spiritual bridegroom into the core of her being."[16] Hamburger, however, has been critiqued for assuming that the *anima*, the female persona of the *Song of Songs*, must imply female readers for this manuscript; in other words, he does not consider what other scholars suggest—that male readers could assume the *anima* role.

Although it is impossible to be sure in many cases how an image or object might have been appropriated and by whom, there are some instances where the legend of the figure or a relic provided the basis for explicitly gendered identification by worshippers. Relics of the Virgin Mary—her tunic at Chartres, her veil at Aachen, or her girdle at Prato—had special meaning for women seeking assistance in conceiving a child or surviving the ordeals of childbirth. St Margaret of Antioch, too, was considered the patron saint of childbirth based on the story of her painless escape from the dragon that had swallowed her. Margaret's belt relic was ritually venerated by pregnant women, and images of the saint were frequent in Italian domestic settings. Childbirth prayers addressed to the Virgin or to St Margaret were sometimes written on a parchment roll by a priest and lent out to function as a birth-girdle for a pregnant woman, the manuscript thus functioning doubly as both devotional reading and apotropaic protection.[17]

The use of some medieval objects has been located primarily in female devotional contexts, whether the convent or the lay household. Nuns and beguines in German and Netherlandish houses owned miniature cradles and dolls identified as the infant Jesus that were destined for devotional play. The immensely influential Franciscan text, the *Meditations on the Life of Christ*, might have been describing the kinds of contemplative manipulation of the Jesus doll undertaken by the female religious:

> You too, who lingered so long, kneel and adore your Lord God, and then His mother, and reverently greet the saintly old Joseph. Kiss the beautiful little feet of the infant Jesus who lies in the manger and beg His mother to offer to let you hold Him a while. Pick Him up and hold Him in your arms. Gaze on His face with devotion and reverently kiss Him and delight in Him.[18]

The *bambino* or holy doll was also popular in Italy, whether for girls entering a convent, young brides in their trousseau, or parents cultivating devotional play in their children.

However, Christiane Klapisch-Zuber, who has written on the blurred border between "devotional practices and play activities," calls attention to the ungendered ritual uses of such dolls by religious confraternities and monasteries in their processions and liturgical festivities, in which such infant Jesus figures were adored, handled, and kissed by women and men alike. In fact, one crucial source of this image of a devotee holding the baby Jesus who has been taken from a cradle was the thirteenth-century cult of St Francis of Assisi. Several lives of the saint describe how, as part of a Nativity celebration, a scene with a manger was constructed, and miracles occurring during the service included a vision of Francis lifting the Christ child to cradle him in his arms.[19] Images, objects, and actions that a modern scholar would assign to one gender thus appear to have been a focus of a much broader population that included both genders during the Middle Ages, particularly in the realm of lay piety where the separation of men and women was not the usual rule.

DEVOTIONAL TEXTS

One of the much-commented-on but undertheorized areas in our study of medieval cultures is the predominance of monitory works, especially devotional texts, addressed to women and containing explicitly gendered advice. English works include those written for enclosed women, nuns and anchoresses, such as the thirteenth-century "Katherine

Group" of texts written for English anchoresses (*Sawles Warde, Hali Maidenhede*, and three female saints' lives), the "Wooing Group" (also thirteenth century, including *The Wohunge of Ure Lauerd* and several other pieces), the *Ancrene Wisse* (thirteenth century), the fourteenth-century *Chastising of God's Children*, Richard Rolle's *Form of Living* (*c.*1348) addressed to Margaret Kirkby, Walter Hilton's late fourteenth-century *Scale of Perfection*, and the works written for Brigittine nuns at Syon in the fifteenth century.

Sometimes the work of devotion was adopted by a broader lay readership that simply ignored its original address to women religious, for example, the widely popular *Meditations on the Life of Christ* that Nicholas Love translated into English as the *Mirror of the Blessed Lyf of Jesu Crist*. Love's directions to his male and female readers invited participation *as a female* in the events of Christ's life. Likewise, the Venetian *Garden of Prayer* (1454) that advised lay women to imagine the sacred scenes in familiar contemporary settings was widely read, not just by women. As Jennifer Bryan points out, many texts addressed to women readers circulated to a wide readership of both genders, religious and lay, in diverse social classes. The inscriptions in manuscripts of *The Contemplations of the Dread and Love of God* indicate that this imitation of a Rolle devotional text was read not only by Cistercian and Benedictine nuns and laywomen—including a countess and "Agnette Dawn"—but also by a sixteenth-century friar, a London pewterer named Alin Kyes, "master governor" Robert Cuttyng, and "Peter Pungyarnar."[20] The inscribed female reader, therefore, was not necessarily the actual user of such devotional texts.

Even the Carthusians, despite their male-gendered seclusion, seem to have been fascinated with the experience and writings of female mystics. The order was based on monastic asceticism and the cultivation of solitary text-inspired contemplation. Their strong association with devotional texts of all kinds may account for the survival of Margery Kempe's *Book*, Marguerite Porete's *Mirror of Simple Souls*, and the short text of Julian of Norwich's *Showings* in Carthusian manuscripts.[21]

One conclusion of recent scholarship has been that devotional discourse often moved from religious women to religious men, despite assumptions to the contrary. Devotional texts and practices then flowed from religious institutions to the households of the laity, giving female monastics a prominent role in disseminating devotional texts to lay readers. Monastic boundaries were relatively permeable; nuns often maintained close ties with their families and surrounding communities, and the laity had reciprocal access to religious institutions through their patronage. The incorporation of monastic models of worship and devotional reading into the lives of laywomen is exemplified in the often-referenced daily schedule of Cicely, Duchess of York (mother of Edward IV and Richard III):

> When she rose at seven in the morning, the account tells us, her chaplain was ready to say Matins of the day and Matins from the Little Office of Our Lady with her, followed by various other services throughout the day. He also read to her during her dinner, and among the works of "holy matter" which she liked to hear were Hilton's *Mixed Life*, St. Bonaventure, the *de infancia Salvatoris*, the Golden Legend, and the visions of St. Maud (i.e. St. Mechthid of Hackeborn, a figure frequently mentioned in *The Myroure of oure Ladye*) and St. Katherine of Siena, as well as the *Revelations* of St. Bridget.[22]

Women were the preferred addressees in devotional manuals intended for the laity, even if such texts suggest the difficulty of melding a life of contemplation with the work of running a household. In the *Decor puellarum (Conduct of Young Women)*, written by John the Carthusian, a fifteenth-century Venetian, the young woman is instructed to

> [r]ise early and, upon waking, bless God and meditate on the mystery of the Trinity…; having dressed, coarsely but decently, and put on your shoes, wash your hands and face and comb your hair while praying, with your heart remaining in Heaven, meditating on the creation of the angels, the fall of the bad, and the confirmation of the good angels. Immediately thereafter, turn your attention to the housework: wake up the servants, light the fire, sweep, start breakfast, dress the children, make the beds, do the laundry, take care of the chickens, etc., while meditating on the celestial hierarchies, the reasons for the damnation of Lucifer, the creation of the world in six days, etc.

At dinnertime, the meditational juggling act reached its climax:

> When you sit down at table, meditate on the Nativity; say the Benedicte and make the sign of the cross on the table; while eating the first course, think of the Circumcision; while eating the second, of the Adoration of the Magi; and when you have had enough to eat, meditate on the Massacre of the Innocents and Flight into Egypt.[23]

In his gender-informed analysis of late medieval lay devotion, Robert Clark argues that the very intrusiveness of the spiritual director's program requires the woman to undertake complex negotiations in which she does have independent agency as she combines domestic and devotional tasks.

As an important marker for the world of late medieval lay devotion, the book of hours has received sustained attention, and its popularity with lay women is well known. Simultaneously demonstrating the lay appropriation of the clerical liturgy, the privatization of religion, female devotional tastes, and the active consumerism of the period, the book of hours testifies to female agency. A majority of the owners of such devotional books were women, and women patrons apparently controlled the female images that predominated in the owner portraits and sacred scenes, as social and art historians have shown. In the *Hours of Margaret of Cleves*, for example—as in many other books of hours belonging to aristocratic women—the owner/donor is shown kneeling before the Virgin and Child in the opening miniature. The miniature conveys a "high degree of reciprocity" between Margaret of Cleves and the holy figures to whom she prays, according to art historian James Marrow, who has analyzed this Dutch manuscript. The figure of the kneeling female donor overlaps the separately framed space occupied by the Virgin and Child, and the Virgin Mary's throne and robe also exit the frame into the area occupied by the donor. Unusually, both the human and the divine woman are the same size. Communication between them is emphasized by their gaze at each other, and a scroll above the Duchess Margaret's hands represents the prayer she addresses to the Virgin and Child, both of whom reach out to touch the scroll, with the Christ child writing its final word. This and the other illuminations in the book suggest the efficacy of Duchess Margaret's prayers and her power as a devotional agent. Recently, Andrea Pearson has revisited this established argument about the female gendering of books of hours, noting that within a century of the development of the genre around 1300 there was a "regendering" as men began to appropriate books designed for women and to insert their own identity into them. Pearson also argues that men promoted a rival male-gendered art form, the devotional portrait diptych.[24]

GENDER IDENTITIES AND SUBJECT POSITIONS IN DEVOTION

The first stage of scholarship emphasized the centrality of mysticism and visionary experiences to female spirituality. Caroline Walker Bynum, whose work was seminal, summarized what she believed to be the "different patterns in male and female spirituality":

> Mysticism was more central in female religiosity and in female claims to sanctity than men's, and paramystical phenomena (trances, levitation, stigmata, miraculous *inedia*, etc.) were far more common in women's mysticism. Women's reputations for holiness were more often based on supernatural, charismatic authority, especially visions and supernatural signs. Women's devotion was more marked by penitential asceticism, particularly self-inflicted suffering, extreme fasting, and illness borne with patience... And certain devotional emphases, particularly devotion to Christ's suffering humanity and to the Eucharist (although not, as is often said, to the Virgin) were characteristic of women's practices and women's words.[25]

Bynum's work revealed women religious acting with purpose, intelligence, and creativity within the specific constraints of their historical context, and her claim that certain forms of female spirituality could be distinguished from those of males during the Middle Ages was widely influential.

However, her strong case for a gendered spirituality was challenged by a second stage of feminist theorizing based on the belief that gender as a category of analysis means different things in different contexts. David Aers and Lynn Staley insist that we cannot understand the feminine "without reference to what types of associations the feminine had *and* in which contexts." This less literal, more semiotic approach to gender scrutinized the language of devotion that spoke of the physical body, of desire, of marriage and childbirth. The post-structuralists questioned whether such metaphors and such images spoke only to women, challenging the assumption that "woman" is a "transhistorical, transcultural category."[26]

A related approach to the female implications of much devotional literature has been through French feminist theories of mystical writing. The argument, based on Hélène Cixous' model of feminine writing and Julia Kristeva's "abjection," is that "the nature of the mystical experience—a loss of subjectivity and self through a union with a divine Other—requires what might be called a feminization of the mystic, whether the mystic is male or female" and "mystical writing itself may be seen as feminine."[27] According to these theorists, the femininity of mysticism was an empowered femininity, one taken on also by the figure of the Beloved, Christ.

In matters of devotional identity, gender can be a shifting concept. One result of the recent theorizing about gender has been a recognition that men are gendered, too. Once assumed to be the medieval norm, men now occupy a "marked" gendered category just as women do—which has given rise to new studies of medieval "masculinities." A prime devotional focus of both visual and textual images—that of Christ the lover-bride-groom desired by the soul—exemplifies the slipperiness of gender affiliation. Medieval exegesis of the *Song of Songs* directed the reader—male or female—to identify with the *Sponsa*, the Bride, whose affective qualities lead her to contemplative union with God. In the same mystical exegesis, the figure of Christ himself could be represented as either masculine or feminine, which also destabilized the gender identity of the worshipper. Heteronormativity is comfortably in place where the woman devotee sees Christ as a male in sexually laden language—as when, in her autobiography, Margery Kempe is told by Jesus that her sins are forgiven and their spiritual relationship will resemble that of a husband and wife:

> Daughter, you desire greatly to see me, and you may boldly, when you are in your bed, take me to you as your wedded husband, as your most worthy darling...and will that you love me, daughter, as a good wife ought to love her husband. And therefore you may boldly take me in the arms of your soul, and kiss my mouth, my head, and my feet as sweetly as you will.

However, when Christ is the feminized sufferer—a maternal figure who will suckle the worshipper from his bleeding body—then devotional subject positions slip. The Dominican friar that Margery is told by Jesus to visit affirms the divine source of her visionary gift using a feminine image: "Daughter, you suck even on Christ's breast."[28]

The destabilization of gender is even more radical in some Italian confraternity *laude*, which are songs in the desiring voice of the devotee wanting union with Christ: "Carried in his arms, I swoon / from these great pains, / which I suffer, languishing in Christ; / then I am helped; / I rise to heights; / and I give birth to a son of love." As Jennifer Rondeau comments, the singer appears to be speaking from a female subject position—the erotic voice, giving birth. However, in the Italian the singer is grammatically gendered male, and the *lauda* comes from a confraternity of flagellants, which had only male members. The singer then addresses brides, lovers, and blessed virgins, and includes himself in the female grouping! Gender identifications are also blurred when the *lauda* (always sung by a man) takes Mary's voice as the suffering mother wanting union with her son. The postmodern turn insists on the possibility of multiple interpretations depending upon the recipient's subject position, implying that all devotional images, objects, and concepts were polysemic.[29]

NEW DIRECTIONS

Whereas the first (recuperative) stage of gender and religion studies emphasized the exceptional female or focused on only one kind of devotion—for example, the mystical vision—that set some women apart from ordinary women in their communities, there has been a trend recently toward embedding devotional practices within a "thick description" of the monastic life. Corine Schleif and Volker Schier's data-packed study of the devotional life of one Birgittine nun illustrates how much we can still learn from microhistorical approaches. Katerina Lemmel, born in the mid-fifteenth century to an affluent bourgeois Nuremberg family, entered the Birgittine order at Maria Mai when her husband died. Her personal letters as well as many other supporting documents from the family, the convent, and Nuremberg show how Katerina, far from being cut off from the outside world, played a pastoral role of spiritual care for her friends, relatives, and other needy people—a role that was in theory proscribed by the Birgittine rule. Katerina and her fellow nuns fostered affective piety by recommending reading and giving texts as gifts. The devotional experiences of Katerina's convent were primarily liturgically based, multisensory, and communal, very different from the traditional view of female devotion as always visually dependent and private.[30]

Another significant development in scholarship of the twenty-first century has been a definitive breaching of the medieval/early modern wall by numerous medievalists, who argue continuities in cultures of devotion from the late medieval period into the seventeenth and even the eighteenth centuries. Although this endeavor now involves many scholars, one recent book may represent it: Nancy Bradley Warren's *The Embodied Word: Female Spiritualities, Contested Orthodoxies, and English Religious Cultures, 1350–1700*. Warren's book relies on notions of "woman" and "female" uninfluenced by postmodernism, but her study challenges traditional periodizations and traditional distinctions of public and private. "At the heart of this project," Warren writes, "is a desire to reconsider the binaries of medieval and early modern, Catholic and Protestant, domestic and foreign, orthodox and heterodox, that have obscured important aspects of English religious cultures."[31] This study of female devotional writers of the Middle Ages in relation to postmedieval women makes a persuasive case for persistence of modes of incarnational piety in individuals and religious communities, both Catholic and Protestant, across national boundaries.

Warren also wants to disrupt the presumed boundary between private affective devotion and public actions. She vigorously argues that women's imitation of Christ in both the medieval and the early modern periods should not be interpreted as victimization, passivity, or withdrawal from the active life. Identification with Christ's crucified body in fact becomes the means of entry into "very public participation in political affairs" for St Catherine and the other women whose writings and lives she analyzes.

A literary approach to representations of female devotional culture suggests other ways that such representations could function. In *Her Life Historical*, Catherine Sanok argues that Osbern Bokenham's compendium of female saints' lives, the *Legends of Holy Women*, should not be read simply as a guide to female patronage and literary tastes. Rather, she sees it as a political "fable," creating a "feminine devotional community formed through a shared interest in female saints' lives as an alternative to the factional politics of mid-fifteenth-century England." This female devotional culture is a gendered "imagined community" to pose critically against medieval communities constituted through other fictions (for example, those of inherited identity). While Sanok acknowledges that hagiography is not the only genre that represents a gendered response or a "feminine interpretive community" (pointing to courtly allegory, conduct literature, and books of hours), she insists that none was "as widely available to a broad range of lay and religious audiences," and "no other genre makes gender identity a constitutive part of its hermeneutics."[32] For Sanok, therefore, as for other literary and cultural critics, a particular culture of devotion can be deployed for political critique.

Indeed, a "gendered lens" is now challenging the very landscape of religious history, urging us to reevaluate histories once deemed resolutely male. Sherry Lindquist, for example, has recently shown female influence within the Carthusian order which based its male-only identity on contemplative prayer and intensive, silent, private reading and writing.[33] The Carthusians' elite identity—understood as rigor and purity of practice—earned the order the approval of the theologian Jean Gerson, and it also attracted the Burgundian dukes, who founded the Carthusian monastery or charterhouse (*chartreuse*) at Champmol on the edge of Dijon. One might speculate that Gerson's approval was based on the Carthusian ban of women from the precincts of their monastery, but what Lindquist asks us to notice is that, despite explicit antifeminist rules, at the Chartreuse de Champmol the Duchess Margaret of Flanders was as important a patron and decision-maker as her husband Philip the Bold, a status reflected in imagery of the couple as well as in arrangements for aristocratic female patrons to have access to the Chartreuse on special occasions in life as well as death. Evidently, in the late (as in the early) Middle Ages noble status could trump gender, even in such an ascetic devotional community as a charterhouse; in this culture of devotion there was a gap between ideology and praxis.

We have moved in the past forty years from an "age of piety" to cultures of devotion and from female spirituality to complexly gendered experiences. In the process, feminist scholars have transformed—and will continue to transform—what has been perhaps the most traditional area of medieval studies into its cutting edge.

FURTHER READING

Bynum, Caroline. *Fragmentation and Redemption: Essays on Gender and the Human Body in Medieval Religion*. New York: Zone Books, 1991.
Duffey, Eamon. *The Stripping of the Altars: Traditional Religion in England, c. 1400–c. 1580*. New Haven: Yale University Press, 1992.
Matter, E. Ann and John Coakley, eds. *Creative Women in Medieval and Early Modern Italy*. Philadelphia: University of Pennsylvania Press, 1994.

Minnis, Alistair and Rosalyn Voaden, eds. *Medieval Holy Women in the Christian Tradition, c. 1100–c. 1500*. Turnhout: Brepols, 2010.

Newman, Barbara. *God and the Goddesses: Vision, Poetry, and Belief in the Middle Ages*. Philadelphia: University of Pennsylvania Press, 2003.

Swanson, R. N. *Religion and Devotion in Europe, c. 1215–c. 1515*. Cambridge: Cambridge University Press, 1995.

Notes

1. For popular religion on the Santiago pilgrimage, see Kathleen Ashley and Marilyn Deegan, *Being a Pilgrim: Art and Ritual on the Medieval Routes to Santiago* (Farnham, Surrey: Lund Humphries, 2009); the Suger quote is on p. 37.
2. Lynn Staley, trans. and ed., *The Book of Margery Kempe* (New York: W. W. Norton, 2001), 50.
3. Richard Marks, *Image and Devotion in Late Medieval England* (Stroud, UK: Sutton Publishing, 2004), 16.
4. Gail McMurray Gibson, *The Theater of Devotion: East Anglian Drama and Society in the Late Middle Ages* (Chicago: University of Chicago Press, 1989), 96–106. See also Katherine L. French, *The Good Women of the Parish: Gender and Religion After the Black Death* (Philadelphia: University of Pennsylvania Press), 2008.
5. Christopher Black, *Italian Confraternities in the Sixteenth Century* (Cambridge: Cambridge University Press, 1989), 34–38; Maureen Flynn, *Sacred Charity: Confraternities and Social Welfare in Spain, 1400–1700* (Ithaca: Cornell University Press, 1989), 23; Robert S. Gottfried, *Bury St. Edmunds and the Urban Crisis, 1290–1539* (Princeton: Princeton University Press, 1982), 180–92.
6. Walter Simons, *Cities of Ladies: Beguine Communities in the Medieval Low Countries, 1200–1565* (Philadephia: University of Pennsylvania, 2001), 48–49.
7. From the *Compilatio singularis exemplorum*, c.1270–97, cited by Walter Simons, *Cities of Ladies*, 131.
8. Amy Hollywood, *The Soul as Virgin Wife: Mechthild of Magdeburg, Marguerite Porete, and Meister Eckhart* (Notre Dame: University of Notre Dame Press, 2001).
9. John Van Engen, *Sisters and Brothers of the Common Life: The Devotio Moderna and the World of the Later Middle Ages* (Philadelphia: University of Pennsylvania, 2008), 56.
10. Kathryn Kerby-Fulton, *Books Under Suspicion: Censorship and Tolerance of Revelatory Writing in Late Medieval England* (Notre Dame: University of Notre Dame Press, 2006), 247–71; also Anthony Goodman, *Margery Kempe and Her World* (London: Longman, 2002), 112–20.
11. Penny Schine Gold, "Male/Female Cooperation: The Example of Fontevrault," in John A. Nichols and Lillian Thomas Shank, eds, *Distant Echoes: Medieval Religious Women*, vol. I (Kalamazoo, MI: Cistercian Publications, 1984), 156.
12. Jennifer Summit, "Women and Authorship," in Carolyn Dinshaw and David Wallace, eds, *Medieval Women's Writing* (Cambridge: Cambridge University Press, 2003), 97–98.
13. Staley, *Book of Margery Kempe*, 106.
14. Herbert L. Kessler, "Gregory the Great and Image Theory in Northern Europe During the Twelfth and Thirteenth Centuries," in Conrad Rudolph, ed., *A Companion to Medieval Art: Romanesque and Gothic in Northern Europe* (London: Blackwell, 2006), 151–72.
15. For a survey of devotional images in the visual arts, see Henk van Os, *The Art of Devotion in the Late Middle Ages, 1300–1500* (Amsterdam: Rijksmuseum, 1994).

16. Jeffrey Hamburger, *Nuns as Artists: The Visual Culture of a Medieval Convent* (Berkeley: University of California Press, 1997), 218, 138.

17. Leanne Gilbertson, "Imaging St. Margaret: *Imitatio Christi* and *Imitatio Mariae* in the Vanni Altarpiece," in Sally J. Cornelison and Scott B. Montgomery, eds, *Images, Relics, and Devotional Practices in Medieval and Renaissance Italy* (Tucson: Arizona Center for Medieval and Renaissance Studies, 2006), 115–38. Also, Jacqueline Marie Musacchio, *The Art and Ritual of Childbirth in Renaissance Italy* (New Haven: Yale University Press, 1999), 141–44. Joseph A. Gwara and Mary Morse, "A Birth Girdle Printed by Wynkyn de Worde," *The Library*, 13 (2012): 33–63.

18. Isa Ragusa and Rosalie B. Green, trans., *Meditations on the Life of Christ: An Illustrated Manuscript of the Fourteenth Century* (Princeton: Princeton University Press, 1961), 38. Annette LeZotte, "Cradling Power: Female Devotions and Early Netherlandish Jésueaux," in Sarah Blick and Laura D. Gelfand, eds, *Push Me, Pull You: Physical and Spatial Interaction in Late Medieval and Renaisance Art*, vol. II (Leiden: Brill, 2011), 59–84.

19. Christiane Klapisch-Zuber, "Holy Dolls: Play and Piety in Florence in the Quattrocento," in *Women, Family, and Ritual in Renaissance Italy*, trans. Lydia G. Cochrane (Chicago: University of Chicago Press, 1985), 310–29.

20. Jennifer Bryan, *Looking Inward: Devotional Reading and the Private Self in Late Medieval England* (Philadelphia: University of Pennsylvania Press, 2008), 21. Mary Erler has also discussed the broad cross-gender culture of devotional reading, "Devotional Literature," in Lotte Hellinga and J. B. Trapp, eds, *The Cambridge History of the Book in England*, volume III: *1400–1557* (Cambridge: Cambridge University Press, 1999), 495–525. Carol Meale, "'oft sithis with grete devotion I thought what I might do pleysyng to God': The Early Ownership and Readership of Love's *Mirror*, with Special Reference to its Female Audience," in Shoichi Oguro, Richard Beadle, and Michael G. Sargent, eds, *Nicholas Love at Waseda: Proceedings of the International Conference 20–22 July, 1995* (Cambridge; Rochester, NY: D. S. Brewer, 1997), 19–46.

21. Jessica Brantley, *Reading in the Wilderness: Private Devotion and Public Performance in Late Medieval England* (Chicago: University of Chicago Press, 2007), 28–77.

22. "Orders and Rules of the House of Princess Cecill, Mother of King Edward IV," in *A Collection of Ordinances and Regulations for the Government of the Royal Household* (London: Society of Antiquaries, 1790), 37–39, cited by Ann M. Hutchinson, "Devotional Reading in the Monastery and in the Late Medieval Household," in Michael G. Sargent, ed., *De Cella in Seculum: Religious and Secular Life and Devotion in Late Medieval England* (Cambridge; Wolfboro, NH: D. S. Brewer, 1989), 225.

23. Cited by Robert L. A. Clark, "Constructing the Female Subject in Late Medieval Devotion," in Kathleen Ashley and Robert L. A. Clark, eds, *Medieval Conduct* (Minneapolis: University of Minnesota, 2001), 170–71.

24. See Roger S. Wieck, *Time Sanctified: The Book of Hours in Medieval Art and Life* (New York: George Braziller, 1988), 33–44. James H. Marrow, *As Horas de Margarida de Cleves / The Hours of Margaret of Cleves* (Lisboa: Museu Calouste Gulbenkian, 1995), 28–29. Andrea Pearson, *Envisioning Gender in Burgundian Devotional Art, 1350–1530* (Aldershot: Ashgate, 2005), especially 61–89.

25. Caroline Walker Bynum, "Religious Women in the Later Middle Ages," in Jill Raitt, ed., *Christian Spirituality: High Middle Ages and Reformation* (New York: Crossroad Publishing, 1987), 131.

26. David Aers and Lynn Staley, *The Powers of the Holy: Religion, Politics, and Gender in Late Medieval English Culture* (College Park: Penn State University Press, 1996), 268. Diane Watt,

"Introduction," in idem, ed., *Medieval Women in Their Communities* (Toronto: University of Toronto Press, 1997), 6.

27. Susannah Mary Chewning, "Mysticism and the Anchoritic Community," in Watt, ed., *Medieval Women in Their Communities*, 129.

28. Staley, *Book of Margery Kempe*, 66, 14. See also Caroline Bynum, *Jesus as Mother: Studies in the Spirituality of the High Middle Ages* (Berkeley: University of California Press, 1982); Ann W. Astell, *The Song of Songs in the Middle Ages* (Ithaca: Cornell University Press, 1990); Jacqueline Murray, ed., *Conflicted Identities and Multiple Masculinities: Men in the Medieval West* (New York and London: Garland Publishing, 1999).

29. Jennifer Fisk Rondeau, "Conducting Gender: Theories and Practices in Italian Confraternity Literature," in Ashley and Clark, eds, *Medieval Conduct*, 199. Madeline Harrison Caviness, "Reception of Images by Medieval Viewers," in Conrad Rudolph, ed., *A Companion to Medieval Art*, 65–85. For "homoerotic" devotional scenes, see Robert Mills, "Ecce Homo," in Samantha J. E. Riches and Sarah Salih, eds, *Gender and Holiness: Men, Women, and Saints in Late Medieval Europe* (London: Routledge, 2002), 152–73.

30. Corine Schleif and Volker Schier, *Katerina's Windows: Donation and Devotion, Art and Music, As Heard and Seen Through the Writings of a Birgittine Nun* (University Park: Pennsylvania University Press, 2009).

31. Nancy Bradley Warren, *The Embodied Word: Female Spiritualities, Contested Orthodoxies, and English Religious Cultures, 1350–1700* (Notre Dame: University of Notre Dame Press, 2010), 8.

32. Catherine Sanok, *Her Life Historical: Exemplarity and Female Saints' Lives in Late Medieval England* (Philadelphia: University of Pennsylvania, 2007), 53–54, 41–42.

33. Sherry C. M. Lindquist, *Agency, Visuality, and Society at the Chartreuse de Champmol* (Aldershot: Ashgate, 2008), 190–91.

PART VII

TURNING POINTS AND PLACES

CHAPTER 33

....

THE BRIDE OF CHRIST, THE "MALE WOMAN," AND THE FEMALE READER IN LATE ANTIQUITY

....

KATE COOPER

CHRISTIANITY was in the throes of a cultural revolution during the fourth century, and young women were at the front line. In October of 312, the Emperor Constantine had captured Rome from his rival Maxentius at the Battle of the Milvian Bridge, giving credit for his success to the God of the Christians. But reinventing a minority faith as a religion of empire was a complex process, and the war for hearts and minds was a more-drawn-out affair than victory on the battle-field. Ties to the imperial establishment brought grace and favor to the church, but they also gave rise to a sense of moral malaise. In this environment, the ethical decisions of members of the Christian community took on a new urgency, and sexual ethics became a matter of fierce debate. By the late fourth century, renouncing the prospect of marriage and children had begun to be seen as a heroic gesture, a bold rejection of the compromises made by prosperous Christian household-ers. Women and children played an important role: the virginal ideal was spreading like wildfire, and Christian writers were competing to reach a female readership.

The idea of virginity had not always been accepted so warmly. Support for widows and virgins had begun as a form of organized charity in the first-century church, and in the second and third centuries, the unmarried maiden is visible in Christian literature as an icon of purity. But if she remained unmarried by choice rather than necessity, a virgin's rejection of expectations could pose a threat to the social order.

Yet by the late fourth century, the ascetic revolution had come to stay. The ascetic movement was among other things a youth movement, and it was not universally accepted as respectable. A frisson of suspicion surrounding sexual asceticism was still in the air, and the "silent majority" of Christians often found the shock tactics of the ascetics alarming. Many Christian parents suspected that the young were being steered by older "handlers" who could not be trusted. In the cities, groups of virgins would sometimes be found in a bishop's entourage, their visible innocence an advertisement of their leader's moral purity, their otherworldly virtue a proof of his ability to mobilize the power of prayer. More disturbingly, it was not unknown for groups of male ascetics to play an unsavory role in the cities, as catalysts for religious violence.

One of the important questions—which our sources do not allow us to answer fully—is how women themselves felt about the increasing emphasis on virginity in the fourth-century church. A vigorous thread of argument since the 1970s has seen virginity as the banner under which women who wanted to claim independence from male control could find an autonomous social space.[1] Normally, on reaching puberty a young woman would face an early marriage, often with a man twice her age or older. A community of virgins could offer a welcome alternative, a chance to sidestep not only direct male control but the dangers of continuous pregnancy and childbirth. In a society where women's reproductive capacity was crucial to the survival of the community, the ideal of a life freed from the burden of sexuality was strangely attractive.

Early Christianity had always carried an ambivalent legacy about women's relations to men. Women were powerful, but their power was dangerous. The story of Adam and Eve captured the problem: the Achilles' heel of male rationality was men's willingness to be charmed and persuaded by the fairer sex.[2] It was the genius of Christian virginity to break the link between feminine charm and male weakness in the ancient imagination. During the second and third centuries, the virgins and widows of the church began to be seen as a source of the church's spiritual power. Virgins could live as "Brides of Christ."(The title was inspired by the New Testament letter to the Ephesians, which had compared the obedient love of the church for Christ to that of a wife for her husband.) The great second-century African writer Tertullian drew a connection between the fertility of Eve and that of Mary. Eve had brought death into the world by encouraging Adam to eat the fruit of the Tree of Knowledge, but Mary had brought life by giving birth to the Son of God.[3] Since Mary had conceived her son Jesus without carnal knowledge of a human man, her fertility could be claimed for the "cultural package" of virginity.

A different vision of the spiritual power of women celebrated the figure of the "male woman." The apocryphal *Gospel of Thomas* captures the idea in an enigmatic saying of Jesus. When he finds the disciples quarreling over whether Mary's status as a woman should bar her from holding authority, Jesus himself takes her side: "I myself shall lead her in order to make her male," he proclaims.[4] Kerstin Aspergen's *The Male Woman: A Feminine Ideal in the Early Church* (1990) argued that androgyny was a source of spiritual power for the early Christians, and the "male woman" complemented the bride of Christ as an alternative feminine ideal in early Christian literature.[5]

The place of the feminine in Christianity has been a subject of debate for modern scholars. In the 1950s, the depth psychologist Carl Jung argued that the divine feminine is a necessary element of a balanced theology, and that the presence of the Virgin Mary was necessary to balance an over-emphasis on the masculine in Christianity.[6] Feminist theologians and historians of Gnosticism built on Jung's insight, searching for theological resources in the Christian tradition that could be used to give legitimacy to women's authority and validity to women's experience.

Some years later, Elaine Pagels suggested that early Gnostic literature represented a lost tradition within Christianity which had honored the feminine more fully. Divine-feminine figures such as Sophia (divine wisdom) had been more responsive to women's concerns, she argued, than had the texts that came to represent "orthodoxy."[7] Yet at the same time Marina Warner was arguing that a female figurehead was not always an unequivocal boon to women.[8] With her infinite capacity to rise above self-interest and to empathize with the sufferings of others, the Virgin Mary offered an ideal against which real historical women could only be found wanting.

A woman could measure herself—or be measured against—ideals of sanctity as seen by the eyes of others. But she could also reflect on ideals privately, to try to make sense of her own experience. Narratives that celebrated self-denial and self-sacrifice could be threatening or empowering depending on the situation. Identifying with the struggles and triumphs of a heroine could offer a woman a way to perceive the logic of her own situation even when external pressures forced her to contradict herself. In the hands of a female reader or listener, a story was a tool for making sense of the ambiguities of women's position in the world.

Influential narratives from the end of antiquity addressed the perceived problem of the female reader in different ways. The second-century *Acts of Paul and Thecla* figures sexual renunciation as a rejection of female identity altogether, styling its heroine as an androgynous "male woman." A letter written by the great fourth-century biblical scholar Saint Jerome, by contrast, pulls away from the emphasis on androgyny, eroticizing virginity and emphasizing the feminine qualities of the Christian virgin as the bride of Christ. Finally, the anonymous *Passion of Eugenia*, written probably in the fifth or sixth century, self-consciously returns to the inspiration of Thecla's androgyny, presenting its own heroine, Eugenia, as a reader of Thecla's story.

READING VIRGINITY: THECLA OF ICONIUM AND THE IDEAL OF THE CHRISTIAN VIRGIN

Often when a daughter yearns to strive after higher things, the mother—concerned for her children or misled by their imagined temporal beauty, or perhaps consumed by jealousy—tries to make her daughter a child of this age and not the one espoused to God. All wicked things imaginable set traps, but do not flinch in fear my child! Lift your eyes upward to where your Beloved is; follow in the footsteps of that famous one who has gone before you and of whom you have heard, Thecla...let nothing extinguish your love.[9]

The passage here, from a fourth-century sermon addressed to young women, captures vividly the situation of one who had chosen to vow herself a Christian virgin, thus joining an elite group celebrated as icons of purity and singleness of heart. To choose such a future, a young woman had to persuade her parents that such a life had sufficient merit to outweigh the opportunity of marrying their daughter into an influential family. In the sermon, the virgin is invited to imagine herself as following in the footsteps of Thecla of Iconium, protagonist of the picaresque *Acts of Paul and Thecla*.

Thecla was the most controversial of the early Christian heroines, and the one with the most remarkable staying power in later periods. According to tradition, Thecla was the sole named woman among the group of disciples who joined the apostle Paul in his travels. She had abandoned her fiancé after hearing the preaching of Paul as he travelled through Iconium, and had followed him, with her hair cropped close, disguised as a boy.

Thecla's story was beloved in part because of its folkloric panache. According to the legend, she had stood trial before two different Roman provincial governors as a Christian and sorceress. The first time, her disappointed fiancé had colluded with her mother to bring her before Castellius, governor of Galatia, and when she was thrown to the beasts, she rose miraculously in a pillar of flame. The second time, in Pisidia, a rich suitor brought her before the governor when she refused his advances. When she was condemned to the beasts in the arena at Antioch of Pisidia, a lioness recognized her as a kindred spirit and refused to do her harm.

As the sermon indicates, by the fourth century Thecla had gained the unanimous sanction of the churches. But in the second century she had been a controversial figure. At the end of the *Acts of Paul and Thecla* the apostle had enjoined her to "Go and preach the word of God." A second-century order of women priests had seen the commission to preach as a confirmation of Paul's support for female leadership, and had taken the story as a precedent authorizing their own ability to preach and baptize. But it seemed to contradict Paul's own instruction, in the first letter to the Corinthians (14:34), that women should remain silent in the churches.

Stories of early Christian heroines often follow a shape very similar to the ancient romances, novel-like narratives that begin with a young couple who wish to be married, and end, after a series of adventures, when they are finally reunited. Like those of the romances, the heroines of the early saints' lives tend to be beautiful, young, and rich, which means that many of the issues that interest a historian, such as poverty or old age, are kept out of the spotlight.

But if the romances are stylized, they foreground questions about identity that were of real interest to Christian writers. The nubile heroines of the romances are routinely torn from their position in the household of their parents and cast out into the world alone. They are shipwrecked, kidnapped, sold into slavery by pirates, exposed as infants to be raised by shepherds. They must work through a series of displacements and adventures before being restored to their rightful place in society and to their relationships with parents, friends, and husbands.[10] Early Christian literature drew on these heroines of romance in remembering the women of the apostolic age. Yet rather than striving to be reunited with her beloved, the heroine of Christian romance often rejected her suitor and marriage altogether. For a woman, a marriage proposal posed a kind of identity crisis, and this was fertile ground for the imagination. Christian writers turned the "marriage plot" upside down as a way of exploring the refusal of expectations required by religious conversion.

One of the distinctive features of early Christian writers was their interest in the reader's experience. Many of the early Christian sources invite the reader to project herself into the narrative, claiming a place within the text as a shadow protagonist. In the early years, this interest in identity strategies reflected the sometimes perilous position of Christians as representatives of a minority faith.

In the 1980s, the story of Thecla was seen as a product of early Christian women's struggle for autonomy. Dennis MacDonald and Virginia Burrus suggested that the story of Thecla may have been told by women.[11] Meanwhile, Elizabeth Clark explored the paradox of authority and humility which allowed women to cultivate spiritual power by signaling their distance from worldly concerns.[12] But it is possible that the *Acts of Paul and Thecla* were not written with women readers in mind. An alternative reading sees their heroines as a literary figure of attentiveness to the apostle's preaching, a device constructed by male authors to mobilize the sympathy of a reader of either sex.[13] Of course, an author cannot always control or even foresee the meanings a reader will extract from a text—readers often find things that the writer did not know were there.

At the end of the second century, Tertullian claimed that the *Acts of Paul and Thecla* had been composed by a male presbyter who was shocked when he found that his story had been put to an unexpected use. But by the fourth century, the threat of female priests had waned. The memory of Thecla was celebrated, and yet, somehow, tamed and domesticated. An ordinary child could be urged to contemplate her example and follow in her footsteps, with the expectation that even if she did not marry, she would remain a dutiful daughter.

THE "BRIDE OF CHRIST" IN JEROME'S *LETTER 22 TO EUSTOCHIUM*: READING AS SELF-INTERPRETATION

Among the letters of Saint Jerome, the best-known is the charming and provocative *Letter to Eustochium concerning Virginity* which he addressed to a young friend as a present for her thirteenth birthday. The recipient was the third of four daughters born to Paula, Jerome's friend and financial backer. Paula's house on the Aventine Hill in Rome was the center of a circle of aristocratic virgins and widows in the early 380s—Paula herself had lost her husband some years earlier. Her third daughter Julia, nicknamed Eustochium—"little stag"—perhaps after the bounding creature of the Song of Songs, was a beloved protégée of Jerome. Written in 383 or 384, his letter to the child was to become one of the monuments of late Latin literature and one of the patristic writings most often cited and copied by medieval readers.

It is easy to see why. The extraordinary text allows us to read alongside Eustochium as she enters the biblical landscape of the Song of Songs, a cycle of love poems from the Hebrew Bible, finding a place in the text by imagining herself as the Bride of the song. In his letter, Jerome invites Eustochium to take the love poetry as a guide to what her life as a virgin will be if she accepts Christ as her Beloved.[14]

Eustochium's sisters were doing well, marriage-wise, when the letter was written, so her choice of virginity was a departure. Blaesilla had made a good marriage, and Paulina was set to marry the brilliant young senator Pammachius: the wedding would take place in 385. So in 383 and 384 all eyes were on Eustochium, the next of the sisters to make her debut in Roman society.

The ascetic movement was certainly not new to the family when Jerome arrived in Rome in 382. A family friend, Marcella, had professed virginity decades earlier, when the Egyptian bishop Athanasius of Alexandria had lived in Rome for a time, bringing with him stories of the heroic battles that were taking place in the Egyptian desert against the demons of hunger, thirst, fatigue, and sexual desire. Church tradition frowned upon women taking a vow of virginity before the age of forty. Bishops were well aware that the Christian communities needed to produce children and grandchildren in order to survive, and in a world where girls in their early to mid-teens often married older husbands, there was every chance that a girl who married early could enjoy a long widowhood after her husband's death. So the choice not to marry in the first place was seen by some as wrongheaded and in any case unnecessary. We have no way of knowing whether the child Eustochium had already begun to model herself on the widows and virgins of her mother's company by the time Jerome arrived in Rome.

In his letter to Eustochium, Jerome is clearly worried that his is not the only influence in the child's life. There is a pressing danger that friends and relatives will try to dissuade her from her choice of the life of virginity. "Do not court the company of married ladies," he says, "or visit the houses of the high-born. Do not look too often on the life which you despised to become a virgin" (22:16).[15]

Jerome knows only too well that the real problem is not Eustochium's interest in the older women, but theirs in her, of which she seems to be blissfully unaware. He is worried that her relatives will want to put her charm to work in an advantageous marriage alliance. And then, there are the ladies of other families, almost all of whom have a son or other male protégée whom they would like to steer toward a chaste, respectable, and innocent bride. Jerome shows awareness and distaste, in other letters, for a married aunt, Praetextata, who has been trying to adopt Eustochium as a protégée. (This Praetextata may have been the sister of the leader of the pagan minority in the Roman senate, which would help to explain Jerome's hostility.) Jerome knows all too well that the radiant virginal piety of a girl like Eustochium is the ideal credential for a daughter-in-law.

So Jerome distracts the girl from his real concern, and plays on her sense of loyalty. "Women of the world, you know, plume themselves because their husbands are on

the bench or in other high positions. And the wife of the emperor always has an eager throng of visitors at her door" (22:16). Holding herself aloof from these people is a matter of defending the position of Jesus, in the same way that an ambitious wife might try to support a human husband's position in the sharply ranked hierarchy of Roman senatorial culture.

Jerome is deft enough, here, to flatter Eustochium's emerging ability to hold her ground in social situations of competition for prestige. "Why do you, then, wrong your husband? Why do you, God's bride, hasten to visit the wife of a mere man? Learn in this respect a holy pride; know that you are better than they" (22:16). It is the pomp of the women "in their capacious litters, with red cloaks and plump bodies, a row of eunuchs walking in front of them" (22:16) that is his best target. Jerome and his protégée can share, here, a comfortable sense that whatever its other virtues, Christian austerity is far less ridiculous than the self-important posturing of the Roman senatorial classes. Jerome has the good sense to see that being impish rather than shrill will better capture the imagination of the child.

Even pious Christian widows are not immune to parody:

> Their houses are filled with flatterers and with guests. The very clergy, who ought to inspire them with respect by their teaching and authority, kiss these ladies on the forehead, and putting forth their hands (so that, if you knew no better, you might suppose them in the act of blessing), take wages for their visits (22:16).

Jerome is well aware that he himself has been criticized for paying court to rich ladies—indeed, his relationship with Paula and her daughters is the most conspicuous evidence against him in this respect. He is almost certainly thinking of other women among their acquaintance whose company he finds less spiritually uplifting. But his own position as a dependent of the wealthy Paula adds a certain acuity to his criticism of the wealthy ladies who act as patronesses of the Roman Church.

In Jerome's day, the city of Rome was host to vast Christian building projects, many of them paid for by aristocratic women. Thanks to their generosity—and perhaps also to their craving for display—the pagan character of the capital's built environment had begun to be supplemented by visible signs of Christian presence. Most noticeably, in the cemeteries that clustered near the city gates along the principal roads leading out of Rome, vast basilicas decorated with dazzling mosaics and colored marble commemorated the piety of these women and their families. In the eyes of a child on the verge of womanhood, such as Eustochium, the Christian heiresses who played such an important role in this transformation must have seemed glamorous and powerful.

But to capture the imagination of a virgin of rank, a different kind of glamor comes into play. In Jerome's telling, a Christian virgin becomes a person whose spiritual pedigree reaches back to the beginning of history. So she needs to gird herself with study. Even as he encourages Eustochium to stay at home, Jerome offers her an open horizon: the thrilling and often bizarre landscape of the Bible and its ancient commentaries. For this landscape, of course, there was no more competent guide than Jerome. "Read often," he tells her, "learn all that you can. Let sleep overcome you, the volume still in your hands; when your head falls, let it be on the sacred page" (22:17).

So much of this sacred history, he tells her, is directly relevant to her own enterprise as a Christian virgin. To begin with, there is the Virgin Mary: "And thus the gift of virginity has been bestowed most richly upon women, seeing that it has had its beginning from a woman" (22:21). Here Jerome moves on a tangent that tells us something about how he sees the little world of the Aventine. Having celebrated the birth of Jesus, he turns to talk of his unusual way of life: "As soon as the Son of God set foot upon the earth, He formed for Himself a new household there; that, as He was adored by angels in heaven, angels might serve Him also on earth" (22:21). He seems to want to make the connection, here, between the story of Jesus and Mary in Bethlehem and the fact that the ascetic women of his own day have begun to build a different kind of life for themselves.

Jerome wants, too, to give richness to the virgin's sense of her own privileged role in the Christian story. Referring to Luke 10:41, he tells Eustochium to "Read the gospel and see how Mary sitting at the feet of the Lord is set before the zealous Martha" (22:24). Jerome is quite dismissive of Martha's role as the host in Luke's story—the episode takes place in her own house—but his reason is clear. He wants Eustochium to focus on the second sister: "Be then like Mary; prefer the food of the soul to that of the body. Leave it to your sisters to run to and fro and to seek how they may fitly welcome Christ" (22:24). Eustochium's own older sisters, who had made brilliant marriages, were to die young— as did so many women who followed the grueling regimen of constant pregnancy—but at the time, the fuss made over them must have been great. Jerome may well suspect that Eustochium has set an envious eye on their new status.

So Jerome throws his imagination into a higher gear. He can offer something more glamorous still. Jerome had an intimate knowledge of the great biblical scholar Origen of Caesarea, whose brilliant writings on virginity, written in Greek in the third century, were only known in the Latin-speaking west through men who had travelled in the east and immersed themselves in Greek intellectual culture.

Origen celebrated the bodily purity of Christian virgins as both a metaphor for and a path to the spiritual purity of the soul. His towering achievement was in his reading of the ancient Hebrew love poetry of the Song of Songs. It is a text whose charm rests in large part on its evocative—and sexually suggestive—nuptial imagery. Origen proposed that it could be read as an allegory of the soul's love for God, which made it possible to reconcile its imagery to the austere sensibilities of Christian asceticism.

Jerome draws on Origen to make Eustochium think of herself not only as Martha's sister Mary, the one who chooses to sit at the feet of Jesus, but also, at the same time, as the Bride of the Song of Songs. "But do you, having once for all cast away the burden of the world, sit at the Lord's feet and say: 'I have found him whom my soul loveth; I will hold him, I will not let him go'" (Song of Songs 3:4) (22:24).

Eustochium will recognize instantly that the words are not Mary's but the Bride's, and she will love Jerome's audacity in making the switch. At the same time, the element of sibling rivalry has found its fulfillment: the troublesome sister has vanished, and the

Bride stands alone, ready to be adored single-mindedly by her Bridegroom, and as "the only one of her mother."

Now the idea of the virgin as bride of Christ takes on a rapturous aspect. The language is so lush that one almost forgets that Jerome is encouraging her to do something entirely harmless. Essentially, he is asking her to stay at home rather than going out, and to spend her time in Bible study when she is at home. It is *how* he asks her that is somewhat disturbing.

> Ever let the privacy of your chamber guard you; ever let the Bridegroom sport with you within. [Gen 26:8] Do you pray? You speak to the Bridegroom. Do you read? He speaks to you. When sleep overtakes you He will come behind and put His hand through the hole of the door, and your heart shall be moved for Him; and you will awake and rise up and say: "I am sick with love." [Song of Songs 5:2, 4, 8]

The modern reader may be nearly as disturbed as were some of the Roman matrons of the day by this way of addressing a widow's nubile daughter. At the same time, Jerome's letter carries the atmosphere of a heady moment in the history of biblical interpretation. A generation of women who hailed from the ancient pagan families of the Roman senate found themselves asking, as they read the stirring poetry of ancient Israel, both what it meant to be Christian and what it meant to be women.

The letter breathes humor and charm, but it is difficult to know how Eustochium would have responded to its strong erotic undercurrent, or how Jerome meant it. She may have been too innocent to be shocked, but it is also possible that she simply did not find it shocking. We know that men Jerome's age—in his early forties if he was born in 340, as scholars believe—and even older often took brides as young as Eustochium, and even in Christian ascetic circles, a certain Roman bawdiness may still have held sway. Neither Paula nor her daughter was heir, as readers in later centuries would be, to a vision of sexuality colored by centuries of ascetic imagining. And Jerome himself may have felt that by encouraging Eustochium to bind herself to her Bridegroom with bonds of erotic intensity, he could instill in her a fierce protectiveness about her vocation as a virgin of the church. This would stand her in good stead should senior relatives try to marry her off. He knew that as a titled heiress Eustochium's right to withhold herself from the marriage market was dependent on the good intentions of a single person, her mother Paula. And Paula, like any ancient person, was always only a fever away from death. Should Paula die unexpectedly, Eustochium would have to fight tooth and nail to protect her choice.

Jerome's letter survives in hundreds of medieval manuscripts from women's and men's monasteries all across Europe, so there is reason to think that both monks and nuns found the letter uplifting. It would be one of the most frequently copied texts across the medieval period, often extracted from the larger collection of Jerome's letters into *florilegia*, miscellaneous collections of texts around a given theme.

Eustochium herself is presented in the text as a reader, which invites an intimate identification with the heroine by her flesh-and-blood counterpart. The evidence suggests that the letter was popular among male readers, since the lion's share of surviving manuscripts bearing the text derive from male monasteries. We can imagine that male and female ascetics would have read the text differently, but it is not necessarily the case that men would have imagined themselves as Jerome rather than Eustochium as they read. Work on the medieval schoolroom suggests that schoolboys were often encouraged to identify with heroines rather than heroes in certain circumstances, depending on the pedagogic aims that were in view.[16] So a male ascetic could easily have embraced the feminized subjectivity of Eustochium as a guide to how the columns of the biblical text could lead him to union with Christ.

The "Male Woman:" Reading and Self-Reinvention

We turn now to a martyr romance preserved in both Greek and Latin, which was written roughly a century after Jerome's letter to Eustochium. Our narrative, the *Passion of Eugenia*, uses the motif of the male woman to explore how stories could influence the way female readers actually chose to live. It is one of the many hagiographical narratives spun around the memory of the early Christian martyrs at the end of antiquity, merging the genres of the ancient novel and the *Apocryphal Acts of the Apostles* into a genre that would become a staple of the libraries of medieval and Byzantine monasteries.

Eugenia is the daughter of a Roman governor of Egypt, who reads the letters of Paul and comes under their spell. The conversion itself is swift, immediate, and not at all troubled. Yet it leads to a long and twisted series of adventures that explore questions about the identity of the young woman disguised as a man, but a man who has distanced himself from the norms of male sexual identity.

It is while deciding whether or not to accept a likely suitor proposed to her by her father that Eugenia first comes into contact with Christian books. The effect is decisive, though it is almost invisible at first.

> Then, while she struggled with these and other entreaties, with a chaste heart, the letters of the Apostle Paul and the history of the virgin Thecla fell into her hands. Reading them secretly she wept every day, and although she lived under the most pagan of parents, in her heart she began to be a Christian.[17]

Eugenia's first contact with a Christian tradition of writing about heroic virgins has far-reaching results.

Seeking a pretext for getting away from her family to think about what she has read, Eugenia asks her parents for permission to retire to the family's country villa with her eunuch attendants, Protus and Hyacinth. The book is her travelling companion: "Reading in her litter during the journey, she turned the experiences of the virgin Thecla over in her heart."[18] The *Passion of Eugenia* shows a deep interest in the fact that its heroine is a reader of texts. The example of Thecla plays an ongoing role in her conversion.

Our heroine's transition from daughter to disciple is thus marked off spatially. The governor's daughter departs the city for the country villa. Her status as a person in transition is made vivid by the portable library: carried by eunuch servants from one world to another, the reader and book move together. The book in her hands becomes a window into a parallel universe. As she reads, she is transformed: when she descends from the litter she is no longer the same person. Her two eunuch slaves, marked as fitting companions by their ambiguous gender, join Eugenia in both the physical and the metaphysical journey. If conversion is about leaving one community, it is also about building another.

Eugenia's retirement leads to the chain of adventures that make up the narrative. First, Eugenia dresses as a young man and joins a monastery; eventually she becomes its abbot. Her attractiveness causes trouble, however: a rich lady falls in love with her, and when she refuses the lady's proposal of marriage, the lady brings an accusation of seduction against her. Eugenia's identity is revealed at the trial, where she is reunited with her father, the governor, and converts her family to Christianity. In the last act, they are all martyred for their faith.

From the fourth century onwards, the lives of the saints served as schoolroom literature. It is to medieval monasteries that we owe the preservation of early Christian hagiography, and in some cases we can see the pastoral concerns of the monasteries reflected in the narratives themselves. I have suggested elsewhere that the episodes of parent–child conflict in Roman saints' lives from the end of antiquity, such as the *Passion of Sebastian* and the *Passion of Anastasia* (fifth–sixth century), reflect the tension in monasteries about weaning child oblates away from their parents, while at the same time attempting to avoid conflict with the parents, who also served as patrons of the monasteries. Intertextual parallels between the Roman martyr narratives and the south Italian *Rule of the Master*, which seems to have been written in the second quarter of the sixth century, drive home the point.[19]

John Anson argued some years ago that the hagiographies about women who dress as men, of which Eugenia is an example, were not really about women at all. The reason a character like Eugenia could change her clothes and be accepted into a monastery as a boy, Anson argued, was that real boys were constantly streaming into monasteries. It was the job of the older monks to avoid lusting for them, or at least to avoid acting on their lust.[20] On this reading, Eugenia's encounter with a false accusation of seducing women was a humorous but also deadly serious reminder that not only propriety, but also the appearance of propriety, was important in a monk's dealings with boys as well as women.

Anson assumed that monks were the intended readers of the transvestite stories. There is every reason to think that a heroine like Eugenia found a female audience as well, since we can draw on other sources for evidence that women in late antiquity were interested in imitating female saints. The classic example of this is the women of the imperial family, who supported the cult of the Virgin Mary as a way of communicating their own close relationship to the Queen of Heaven.[21]

Martyr heroines like Eugenia seem to have been especially popular, serving as a mirror within which women could look for meaning in their own lives. Women readers of other contemporary martyr romances, such as the *Passion of Anastasia*, were invited explicitly to compare the struggle of early Christian martyrs to their own struggles in daily life.[22] For example, a sixth-century devotional handbook for married women, *To Gregoria in the Palace*, encourages a matron of the senatorial class to compare the small trials and humiliations of life with a difficult husband to the far more threatening circumstances of a martyr whose angry pagan husband had cast her into prison as a sorceress.

But the violence of martyr narratives was clearly magnetic for both male and female readers.[23] Younger monks or women might have read a narrative like the *Passion of Eugenia* differently than did older monks, since each reader would project a different subject position into the narrative. If female characters served as erotic objects within the stories themselves, they may also have served as erotic objects for a reader. Yet a creator of narrative cannot control how a reader will read or a viewer will view, and there is no reason that a protagonist cannot serve as both object and subject in the imagination. Modern work on how readers respond to texts has opened up the possibility that a text's meaning is fluid and changeable, even for the same reader. Jonathan Culler's 1981 essay "On Reading as a Woman" undermined the idea of the reader straightjacketed to a response "required" by a text,[24] while fieldwork on readers of twentieth-century romance novels suggests that a text can be alternately controlling or empowering, depending on the attitudes and needs the reader brings to the act of reading.[25]

So we can imagine a female reader for the *Passion of Eugenia* looking for a mirror. She might find herself reflected in the heroine Eugenia, and identify with Eugenia's own attempt to respond to the challenge posed by a shared heroine, Thecla. Whether or not this was a reader whom the author of the text had in mind as she or he wrote, she was a reader to whom the text made sense. By stripping away the parameters and constraints imposed on real historical women and creating a world in which a heroine could retreat from the household of her parents to consider her own future and choose her own fate, the *Passion of Eugenia* offered its female reader a space within which to imagine a self freed of the parameters and constraints imposed by her own position in a specific family.

That this self could act with the comparative freedom of a man made the exercise all the more evocative. Imagining herself as a "male woman" did not change the pressures faced by a young woman at the end of antiquity, but it may have changed her ability to meet them. How is an open question: to some, it may have offered the measure of their own weakness, and to others, an imaginative space within which to develop a more proactive approach to the pressures they faced.

AFTER THE ROMANS

The marriage between ascetic culture and imperial power would continue in Byzantium for a thousand years, but in the Latin west, Christian culture provided a thread of stability as the empire began to disintegrate. Christian identity was a concept with staying power, one that could bind communities together even as the world was falling apart. Even as the Roman order began to crumble and the east and west to go their separate ways, women readers would remain central to the imagination of religious writers.

The bride of Christ and the male woman were evocative figures: each seems to have been, if not all things to all people, at least rich enough to serve a diversity of readers and to allow for a diversity of readings. The female reader was an invaluable muse, and the effort by writers to imagine her needs added value to the literary legacy that late antiquity would leave to the Middle Ages. Women's need to find an interpretive strategy that could help them to face a difficult lot had inspired writers to reach beyond themselves, and the resulting texts were an inspiration to both women and men as they faced an unpredictable future.

And just as the female reader held her place in the Christian literary imagination, so the woman of letters continued to play a role at the end of antiquity. During the sixth century, when the social order was repeatedly threatened by civil war and barbarian invasion, women's contribution as icons of kinship, civility, and religious allegiance was more necessary than ever, even if it was not powerful enough to hold back the tide of violence. Women of rank collaborated with bishops in the care of the Christian people. For example, Pope Gregory the Great (d.604) maintained a lively correspondence with women across Italy and in Constantinople, both professed ascetics and aristocratic wives, consoling one another in the face of the Lombard invasion, sending blankets, relics, and other gifts to be useful in both practical and spiritual ways. His correspondence with Theodelinda, queen of the Lombards, is a case in point. Theodelinda was among the sixth-century barbarian princesses who were exchanged as foreign queens between competing barbarian royal families as they sought to maintain lines of diplomacy across the now fragmented Roman Empire.

Across the early medieval period princesses would be exchanged as pledges of peaceable relations between kings—"peace-weavers" in the phrase of the *Beowulf* poet. And as before, married women were encouraged to bring their husbands to the true faith. In the seventh century, for example, Pope Boniface V wrote to the Kentish princess Aethelburh, urging her to bring about the conversion of her husband, the pagan Edwin of Northumbria. The baptism of Edwin and his court on Easter day of 627 was perhaps no surprise to Boniface: the papal chancery held copies of similar letters to noblewomen and queens dating back to the days of the pagan Senate.

The prayers of virgins continued to be valued as a source of spiritual power rooted in purity. Yet in the early medieval period, virginity was no longer seen as a countercultural alternative. It had been integrated into the fabric of society, and ascetic writers no longer claimed that bodily purity was the only route to spiritual purity. Aldhelm's treatise *On Virginity*, addressed *c.*680 to Hildelith, abbess of the double monastery of Barking, stresses the value of each of the three female estates—virginity, marriage, and widowhood—reminding his reader that it is spiritual fortitude, not bodily virginity, that distinguishes the truly holy.

FURTHER READING

Brown, Peter. *The Body and Society: Men, Women, and Sexual Renunciation in Early Christianity*. New York: Columbia University Press, 1988.

Clark, Gillian. *Women in Late Antiquity: Pagan and Christian Life-styles*. Oxford: Clarendon, 1993.

Coon, Lynda L. *Sacred Fictions: Holy Women and Hagiography in Late Antiquity*. Philadelphia: University of Pennsylvania Press, 1997.

Cooper, Kate. *The Virgin and the Bride: Idealized Womanhood in Late Antiquity*. Cambridge, Mass.; London: Harvard University Press, 1996.

Cooper, Kate. *Band of Angels: A History of Early Christian Women*. London: Atlantic Press, 2013.

Elm, Susanna. *Virgins of God: The Making of Asceticism in Late Antiquity*. Oxford: Oxford University Press, 1994.

Limberis, Vasiliki. *Divine Heiress: The Virgin Mary and the Creation of Christian Constantinople*. London; New York: Routledge, 1994.

Van't Spijker, Ineke. "Family Ties: Mothers and Virgins in the Ninth Century," in Anneke B. Mulder-Bakker, ed., *Sanctity and Motherhood: Essays on Holy Mothers in the Middle Ages*. New York; London: Garland, 1995.

Wimbush, Vincent and Richard Valantasis. *Ascetic Behavior in Greco-Roman Antiquity: A Sourcebook*. Minneapolis: Fortress Press, 1990.

NOTES

1. The starting-point for modern debate on this theme can be found in Rosemary Ruether and Eleanor McLaughlin, eds., *Women of Spirit: Female Leaders in the Jewish and Christian Traditions* (New York: Simon and Schuster, 1979).

2. Kate Cooper, "Insinuations of Womanly Influence: An Aspect of the Christianization of the Roman Aristocracy," *Journal of Roman Studies*, 82 (1992): 113–27.

3. Elizabeth A. Clark, "Devil's Gateway and Bride of Christ: Women in the Early Christian World," in Jean O'Barr, ed., *Women and a New Academy: Gender and Cultural Contexts* (Madison: University of Wisconsin Press, 1989), 81–102; Dyan Elliott, "Tertullian, the Angelic Life, and the Bride of Christ," in Lisa Bitel and Felice Lifshitz, eds, *Gender and Christianity in Medieval Europe: New Perspectives* (Philadelphia: University of Pennsylvania Press, 2008), 15–33; eadem, *The Bride of Christ Goes to Hell: Metaphor and Embodiment in the Lives of Pious Women, 200–1500* (Philadelphia: University of Pennsylvania Press, 2012).

4. The *Gospel of Thomas* Logion 114 states, "Simon Peter said to him, 'Let Mary leave us, for women are not worthy of life.' Jesus said, 'I myself shall lead her in order to make her male, so that she too may become a living spirit resembling you males. For every woman who will make herself male will enter the kingdom of heaven.'" See M. Meyer, "Making Mary Male: The Categories 'Male' and 'Female' in the Gospel of Thomas," *New Testament Studies*, 31 (1985): 554–70; Elizabeth Castelli, "'I Will Make Mary Male': Pieties of the Body and Gender Transformation of Early Christian Women in Late Antiquity," in Julia Epstein and Kristina Straub, eds, *Body Guards: The Cultural Politics of Gender Ambiguity* (New York: Routledge, 1991).

5. Kerstin Aspegren, *The Male Woman: A Feminine Ideal in the Early Church* (Uppsala: Acta Universitatis Uppsaliensis, 1990).

6. Carl Gustav Jung's reaction to the encyclical *Munificentissimus Deus* proclaiming the dogma of the Assumption of the Virgin Mary, promulgated by Pope Pius XII in 1951, was published in his "Answer to Job," first published in German in 1953 and translated into English by R. F. C. Hull, in *Psychology and Religion*, v.11, Collected Works of C. G. Jung (Princeton University Press, 1973).

7. Elaine Pagels, *The Gnostic Gospels* (New York: Vintage Books, 1979).

8. Marina Warner, *Alone of All Her Sex: The Myth and Cult of the Virgin Mary* (London: Weidenfeld and Nicholson, 1976).

9. "Homily: On Virginity," trans. Teresa Shaw, in Vincent Wimbush and Richard Valantasis, eds, *Ascetic Behavior in Greco-Roman Antiquity: A Sourcebook* (Minneapolis: Fortress Press, 1990), 29–44, based on the edition of Amand and Moons.

10. On early Christian literature and the Roman novel, see Susan A. Calef, "Thecla 'Tried and True' and the Inversion of Romance," in Amy-Jill Levine, ed., *A Feminist Companion to the New Testament Apocrypha* (London: T & T Clark, 2006), 163–85; Kate Cooper, *The Virgin and the Bride: Idealized Womanhood in Late Antiquity* (Cambridge, Mass.: Harvard University Press, 1996); and Judith Perkins, *The Suffering Self: Pain and Pain and Narrative Representation in the Early Christian Era* (London: Routledge, 1995). David Konstan, *Sexual Symmetry: Love in the Ancient Novel and Related Genres* (Princeton: Princeton University Press, 1994) and Tim Whitmarsh, *The Cambridge Companion to the Greek and Roman Novel* (Cambridge: Cambridge University Press, 2008) offer an introduction to the novel itself.

11. Dennis Ronald MacDonald, *The Legend and the Apostle: The Battle for Paul in Story and Canon* (Philadelphia: Westminster Press, 1983), and Virginia Burrus, "Chastity as Autonomy: Women in the Stories of the Apocryphal Acts," *Semeia* 38 (1986), 108–117.

12. Elizabeth A. Clark, "Ascetic Renunciation and Feminine Advancement: A Paradox of Late Ancient Christianity," *Anglican Theological Review*, 63 (1981): 240–57, rpt. in eadem, *Ascetic Piety and Women's Faith: Essays on Late Ancient Christianity* (Lewiston, NY: Edwin Mellen Press, 1986).

13. This is the position argued in Cooper, *The Virgin and the Bride*, although I have reconsidered the role of women's oral traditions in *Band of Angels: A History of Early Christian Women* (London: Atlantic Press, 2013).

14. For an alternative, influential reading of the letter, see Patricia Cox Miller, "The Blazing Body: Ascetic Desire in Jerome's *Letter* to Eustochium," *Journal of Early Christian Studies*, 1 (1993): 21–45.

15. Translations from Jerome's *Letter* 22 are taken from Philip Schaff, ed., *Nicene and Post-Nicene Fathers*, Series II, volume 6. Available online at <http://www.ccel.org/ccel/schaff/npnf206.html>.

16. Marjorie Curry Woods, "Rape and the Pedagogic Rhetoric of Sexual Violence," in Rita Copeland, ed., *Criticism and Dissent in the Middle Ages* (Cambridge; New York: Cambridge University Press, 1996), 56–86.

17. *Passion of Eugenia*, ed. Mombritius, *Sanctuarium* II, 391, lines 41–44, trans. Hannah Isis Jones, in *The Desert and Desire: Virginity, City and Family in the Roman Martyr-legends of Agnes and Eugenia*, MA dissertation, University of Manchester (1998).

18. *Passion of Eugenia*, lines 46–47.

19. Kate Cooper, "Family, Dynasty, and Conversion in the Roman *Gesta Martyrum*," in Maximilian Diesenberger, ed., *Zwischen Niederschrift und Wiederschrift: Frühmittelalterliche Hagiographie und Historiographie im Spannungsfeld von Kompendienüberlieferung und Editionstechnik* (Vienna: Verlag der ÖNewsterreichischen Akademie der Wissenschaften, 2010), 273–81.

20. John Anson, "The Female Transvestite in Early Monasticism: The Origin and Development of a Motif," *Viator*, 5 (1974): 1–32.

21. Kate Cooper, "Contesting the Nativity: Wives, Virgins, and Pulcheria's *imitatio Mariae*," *Scottish Journal of Religious Studies*, 19 (1) (1998): 31–43.

22. Kate Cooper, *The Fall of the Roman Household* (Cambridge: Cambridge University Press, 2007), ch. 5: "The Invisible Enemy."

23. Kate Cooper, "The Voice of the Victim: Gender, Representation, and Early Christian Martyrdom," *Bulletin of the John Rylands Library*, 80 (3) (1998): 147–57.

24. Jonathan Culler, "Reading as a Woman," in idem, *On Deconstruction: Theory and Criticism after Structuralism*, 2nd edn (Ithaca: Cornell University Press, 2007), 43–64.

25. Janice Radway, *Reading the Romance: Women, Patriarchy, and Popular Literature* (Chapel Hill, NC: University of North Carolina Press, 1984).

CHAPTER 34

....

GENDER AT THE MEDIEVAL
MILLENNIUM

....

CONSTANCE H. BERMAN

OUR understanding of the relationship of the genders in the central part of later medieval western Europe, and our assessment of the relative power and authority of women
has changed considerably over the last generation of scholarship. In 1973, when Jo Ann
McNamara and Suzanne Wemple argued for a golden age of women's power and authority in the early Middle Ages, their study implied that the central and later Middle Ages
did not see again such widespread female prominence.[1] Their conclusion appeared to
be supported by Joan Kelly-Gadol's proposal that there had been a precipitous decline
in women's power and authority beginning in the twelfth century, continuing right
down to the Renaissance. Kelly's work has come under attack, however, extrapolating
such decline as it did from David Herlihy's "Land, Family, and Women in Continental
Europe, 701–1200," a study in which he counted percentages of women's appearances in
the charter and cartulary evidence up to 1200, and from an article by Marion C. Facinger
[Meade] that looked at how often French queens appeared along with French kings in
French royal documents from the tenth century up to 1237. In fact, neither article had
anything to say for the period after *circa* 1200. Moreover, not all French queens' documents up to 1237 were included in the published collections that Facinger had used.[2]

Such conclusions about changes in women's power and authority, however, seemed
to fit well the periodization of medieval history supported by prominent medieval historians like Georges Duby, who saw female access to power diminished by changes in
marriage and inheritance strategies in the central Middle Ages.[3] Such conclusions about
later medieval women were also based on a misunderstanding about how much documentation survived over the medieval centuries—a misunderstanding based on the
uneven chronological distribution of published documents. Thus, while Wemple and
McNamara had worked from the relatively sparse early medieval documents almost
wholly available in published form, many documents concerning women from the later
Middle Ages had not yet been consulted and many of them still remained unpublished.

THE THIRD GENDER

One of the changes in focus that we see in the work of Jo Ann McNamara was her decision to look at how institutional changes in the eleventh century had effects not just on women, but men. In looking at those changes, she contributed to the creation of a new field of study for the Middle Ages and beyond, that of men's studies.[4] McNamara explained that as the population grew and the economy expanded after the year AD 1000, the church had more opportunities to influence Christian lives, but also more problems maintaining its control over church properties and its power vis-à-vis kings and emperors. This was a moment when clerical power was challenged—in its control of the greatest amounts of wealth in the west, in its ability to dictate matters of faith, but perhaps mostly in its monopoly over writing and the bureaucratic power associated with writing and written documents. Also, while challenges to church property came from secular lords, challenges to its sexual purity came from monastics—the latter were particularly concerned about the purity of the sacraments produced by married priests. So the secular clergy came to change its own image as it asserted its hegemony over the rest of society.

Thus, in the Peace and Truce of God movements, clerics began to argue that they did not share the masculine qualities of violence, but like women and children should be included in the list of those not to be attacked by violent knights. In asserting their new hegemony, a superior status for themselves, clerics began describing themselves as part of what McNamara called "a third gender," that of celibate men superior to all others. Even some kings, like the English King Edward the Confessor, who left no sons, appear to have toyed with this idea of celibacy.

McNamara regarded all these changes in clerical ideology about its celibate superiority as a third gender, as detrimental to women. She viewed them as further support for her hypothesis that women's power and authority had declined after the eleventh century. Moreover, McNamara's reading of that period made considerable sense of some of the most vitriolic diatribes of the Gregorian reformers and of what she viewed as a significant loss of power by queens and empresses in comparison to their access to authority and power over property seen only slightly earlier. Certainly whatever else happened in these centuries, as the Eucharist became more important, the clergy used its power over the performance of the Mass as an argument for its superiority not only over secular men and women, but over nuns and other religious women. The eleventh century is a period in which the numbers of religious communities of women had suffered a decline. Meanwhile, secular women, even queens, were isolated from the centers of real power as bureaucracies and their use of written documents were introduced and separate households for queens were established. Women did not have the same access to the education provided to those bureaucrats by the budding universities, and indeed the new knowledge associated with cathedral schools and universities appears to have been prohibited for almost all women.

Indeed, the poignant story of Abelard and Heloise may be read on one level as a morality play arguing against the education of women.

But all this is over the short run. Relegating royal women to their own households, introducing bureaucrats into royal administration, and excluding women from clerical university training were obstacles that women very quickly overcame. Indeed over the course of the twelfth century, western European society found it necessary that women overcome any implied disability for authority and rule. In this age of Crusades with extended absences of menfolk from their realms, and the loss of many men on crusade and reconquest, it was women who maintained the structures of social authority. That women ruled the castle while men were away on crusade has long been a cliché of medieval history, but the social reality consequent on men's urge to prove their masculinity as well as their religiosity by going on crusade, which meant that women not only ruled at home, but ruled well, has not been explored until recently. At the top of society at least, noblewomen and queens came back to authority as regents when the men were away and sometimes as heiresses when fathers and brothers were dead. In asserting their authority, moreover, women appropriated for their rulership some of the new sources of authority that have traditionally been seen as associated with males—like written documents, as we see below with regard to the countesses of Champagne or Auxerre.

There were also other new relationships deriving from the reforms of the Gregorians and the argument for the superiority of clerical celibates, for instance for women who had been part of the Church as priests' wives. The attack on clerical marriage in the eleventh and twelfth centuries may have separated priests from the wives who had kept house, fed, and sometimes supported them—as well as providing sexual and reproductive services—but that attack had unexpected consequences. Rather than abandon their wives and families, some married clergy apparently founded tiny hermitages or monasteries and took vows of celibacy along with their families; this allowed them to maintain the affective ties of family life. Indeed, the documents of new religious groups like the followers of Stephen of Obazine or Cistercian houses like Valmagne or Silvanès in southern France include records of the incorporation of many such tiny family monasteries. Many reformers founding new houses of hermits, monks and nuns, and regular canons and canonesses incorporated such tiny women's communities into larger foundations. Moreover, the social services once undertaken by priests' wives began to be undertaken by more specialized religious groups like hospitals and military-religious orders.

Whereas once the power of writing was held most closely by clerics, by the twelfth century the control of writing, education, and bureaucracies was beginning to spread more widely. It is true that access to the new scholasticism was closely controlled by a clerical guild of priests only, and the training of monastic women like Heloise, Hildegard, and Herrad of Hohenbourg in the twelfth century would not be replicated thereafter, but those great abbesses did import some of that university method into the education of their communities of nuns. Trained lawyers, who did not have to be clerics, entered both church and secular administration. The use of written documents as dispositive contracts and the recording of acts in royal archives allowed permanent records to be made. The use of seals by both men and women to grant authenticity to their acts, and the use by bureaucrats of charter collections and written records, allowed women as well as men to replace the rule by sword alone with the rule of written precedent.[5] Although it was once common to view it as a loss of power when new bureaucrats led to queens and countesses being divorced from earlier joint rule, those women soon turned that development on its head, using those very bureaucrats and their written tools to promote women's authority in the absence or minorities of their menfolk. This is particularly apparent by the mid-thirteenth century, but there is evidence for that change even earlier.

Women and Rule

Although Facinger's early study had posited a permanent decline in women's authority and rulership, more recent appraisals of queens and royal women show well-born women ruling effectively, both before 1200 and after. The Empress Matilda (1102–1167) and Adela of Blois (c.1067–1137)—both powerful, haughty, impressive women—do not represent the last gasps of a lost golden age of early medieval women's power and authority. Many other titled noblewomen too ruled as lady/lords, and continued in later centuries to control castles, assemble armies, and rule territories, both in their own right and as stand-ins for absent husbands or sons. One thinks, for example, of Ermengard of Narbonne (r. 1134–1192), or Eleanor of Saint-Quentin, countess of the Vermandois (1183–1214), or Eleanor of Aquitaine's great granddaughters, the successive countesses of Flanders, Jeanne (1212–1244) and Margaret (1244–1278), who ruled one of the wealthiest parts of western Europe for much of the thirteenth century.[6] In France, moreover, when male heirs died on crusade, the preservation of property for direct heirs through women's regencies appears to have been more important than uninterrupted male control, even of fiefs. Indeed, rulers like Philip Augustus and his successors appear to have supported the rule of heiresses in their own right. They allowed women holding fiefs to provide their service through proxies in preference, it seems, to having whatever power and authority was inherited by a woman carried to a new husband who might consolidate her property with his own.[7]

Sometimes it was women's inheritance that was at stake in their assertion of power and authority using bureaucratic structures to their own advantage, as in the case of Matilda the Great of Courtenay (1188–1257) and her counties of Auxerre, Nevers, and Tonnerre, east of Paris. Matilda's history is a dramatic one. She rose to power and authority as a powerful heiress, the sole child of Louis VII's younger brother. She married twice, but at least from the death of her second husband on crusade in 1241, and probably from the death of her first in 1223, she ruled in her own right. She did so in part by using written documents and paid bureaucrats, whereas men may have been able to rule with force alone. Matilda is described as circulating through her counties like a knight, providing feudal service through proxy, endowing monastic communities, issuing privileges to her towns, and minting feudal coins bearing her own name, sending her grandson as her representative when vassals were called for military service, and arranging marriages for her great-granddaughters, who inherited successively, sharing rule of the counties with their husbands.[8]

Women who did not necessarily inherit could also use their power and authority as regents for husbands or sons. They too ruled very effectively using written documents as a tool. In eastern France, the political independence and economic growth of the province of Champagne and its great international fairs was established by two countesses of Champagne holding a series of regencies between the 1170s and the 1220s. Between them, Marie of Champagne, daughter of Eleanor of Aquitaine and Louis VII of France, and Blanche of Navarre, wife of Marie's son Thibaut III, ruled in forty of forty-four years, from 1179 to 1222, thirty-seven of those years as regents for minors. It was in these years of nearly continuous female governance that a strong comital government was established in Champagne. Particularly in Blanche of Navarre's case, the recourse to written records rather than the use of the sword was particularly apparent. Indeed Blanche upon her retirement to religious life commissioned a cartulary of her own and related acts. These show that this was accomplished by the countesses' purchasing of castles and fortified houses, by their demand of liege homage from all castle owners, and by their granting money-fiefs using income derived from international fairs selling local and imported cloth. Countess Blanche protected the local woolen industry against the encroachments of foreign merchants and encouraged local monastic groups in their raising of sheep for wool. Such support of the growing textile industry in this period had considerable indirect effects on the activities of women in the countryside, who were turning to more and more of the production of yarn for that industry.

Such support of industry and commerce in their towns included the countesses' protection of merchants and issuing of privileges for a series of international fairs at their towns of Troyes, Provins, Bar-sur-Aube, and Lagny. These towns moved beyond sale of cloth to become the great clearing-houses for completing contracts and redemption of bills of exchange among merchants from north and south. Such bills of exchange and other new commercial instruments were the written contracts that allowed money to flow from individuals in one place to others elsewhere without actually carrying weighty amounts of coin, but Champagne was also centrally located between north and south.

The fairs of Champagne, first referenced in the 1130s, came to international prominence during the regencies of Marie and Blanche, when their effective rulership and protection of merchants allowed such commerce to thrive. Not only were written documents important in the actual commercial business of the fairs, but charters from the countesses to the towns holding those fairs provided permanent town privileges, including protection of the silver coinage of Provins on which so much of the activity was based. Such protection allowed the Champagne fairs to thrive, and as a consequence they provided the countesses with considerable rents used to promote their own rule. Those towns were the center of "the commercial revolution" of the central Middle Ages. That they were protected and promoted primarily by countesses Marie and Blanche as regents while their husbands were away on crusade or sons too young to rule is an instance of how women used new written instruments to enhance their own authority and the economic well-being of their realms.[9]

CHANGES IN THE COUNTRYSIDE

McNamara and Wemple were much less interested in how changes in the economy might affect village women than in the power and wealth of queens and abbesses, in part because the evidence for the former was and remains so spotty. We know a good deal more about the later Middle Ages, especially in England, where scholars debate a number of issues but generally agree that women earned less than men and owned less land, but that they were active in local markets.[10] Although much has been said about the women's workshops or gynaecea of the early medieval west—where women of the lowest social status produced textiles for royal or monastic use—most historians now agree that the evidence for such women's workshops is far from representative of the early medieval economy. Indeed the evidence of a handful of polyptychs for the great monastic estates and from royal decrees is not representative of the early medieval countryside and its economic practices. Thus the gynaecaea, while one aspect of early medieval cloth production, represent only a minor part of that production. Instead, a largely silent domestic production, a literal "cottage industry" of textile production provided for most early medieval domestic use. Such domestic production of textiles, undertaken in the interstices of other everyday tasks, was probably the norm for early medieval woman.

Yet there were enormous changes in village women's situations after the turn of the first millennium. For instance, whereas it was once thought that monastic missionaries and colonists spurred much of the expansion of settlement on western Europe's internal and external frontiers, the credit for such activities is now assigned to independent and anonymous men and women in isolated farmsteads and hamlets. During the late eleventh and twelfth centuries, anonymous peasants created new fields in what had once been waste. As yields increased and profits for lords (male, female, and institutional) appeared possible, it was such lords who often first promoted the gathering of peasants into nucleated villages, drawing them away from isolated farmsteads and hamlets into the vicinity of churches, castles, and mills—amenities often offered by lords intent upon attracting tenants. Recent studies have begun to suggest that rural women began to produce for the local markets, like those documented in the Cluny records, which began appearing after *circa* AD 1000.[11] Perhaps most beneficial for peasants and rural production alike was a new era of relative peace and improved climate that allowed a rural growth; that growth was also aided by new tools and technologies like water-powered mills. The last, in particular, would have considerable effects on women's work.

Much of the change is associated with knights establishing themselves in new fortifications or castles and attempting to reap for themselves some of the benefits of a burgeoning rural population and improved rural production. Knights in their castles, however, were a mixed blessing, for they often terrorized the surrounding countryside, as we see in the series of peasant complaints found in Thomas Bisson's account of a series of such complaints from Catalonia. Violence was driven in part by higher demand for luxuries, spurring lords' efforts to drain away newly found rural wealth.

Some castle-holders concentrated on advancing their own wealth by a medieval spe-cies of the "protection racket," which we see reflected in the life of the knight Pons de Léras, who eventually reformed his life and became a Cistercian. This is indeed the era in which there was a necessity for sworn associations of Peace and Truce of God; women were to be protected, along with children and priests, but men also began to establish rules for warfare.[12]

While the church attempted to curb violence in the Peace and Truce movements, it too was investing in its estates. Churchmen and women alike invested long-held treas-ure (silk cloth, books, chalices, and other cash substitutes) in the establishment of such new villages. Documents for nuns of the Roman monastery of Santa-Maria-in-Via-Lata in Rome show efforts to improve land-holdings, including contracts with tenants to rebuild houses and replant vineyards, olive trees, and gardens, even in places like the interior of the Roman Colosseum.[13]

The possibility of profit led to investment by lords of all kinds—abbots, abbesses, lords, and lady-lords—in making land and villages more productive. Such lords actively developed vineyard plantations by granting plots to peasants in contracts that allowed full ownership to be divided between lord and peasant after a number of years. They promoted the recruiting or training of blacksmiths, millers, and other specialists to their villages, and encouraged peasants to plant orchards. They helped create new fields to be used in a new three-field/three-year rotation, and to organize shared plow teams, possibly even providing the new heavier-wheeled plows needed to bring rich, but often waterlogged, soils into use. They may have encouraged local systems of transhumance for the grazing of sheep and cattle, and introduced their own breeding animals into village herds.

It was for rural women that this process of village foundation and the introduction of amenities like water-powered mills and communal ovens had the most profound effects; water- and wind-powered mills provided considerable time-savings in food prepara-tion. Introducing water-powered (occasionally wind-powered) mills for grinding grain into flour, whatever the consequences for the revenue of lords, would change consid-erably the distribution of work within the household, lightening the heaviest labor of women, children, and slaves, who were those to whom grinding had traditionally been assigned. Indeed, the change in this aspect of medieval women's work would be so complete that one twelfth-century chronicler of the Crusades reported that European women camp-followers traversing the plains of Asia, where they had no access to water or wind-powered milling, complained bitterly when forced to grind by hand, because such work reduced them to slavery.[14] Replacing hours of hand grinding by the use of water power allowed free women and even those who were less than free, to take up or be assigned to new activities, including providing new surpluses for market sale by themselves or their lords.

While women had probably always raised chickens and eggs for payments to lords, and butchered, dried, and salted meat and fish, they now had time to do more of those activities that would bring in a little cash. Moreover, in the expanding economy of the twelfth century, demand for such foodstuffs in nearby towns or by religious institutions must have increased. Changes in women's work differed somewhat from region to region. In more mountainous areas, it may have been dairying activities that took up more female labor. Along the sea, it was probably women who were involved in the production of salt while their menfolk were fishing.[15] In Burgundy and Gascony, some of that female labor would have been devoted to the many newly established vineyards that required intensive manual labor at certain seasons. But in the latter case we can see that trade between Gascony and Britain also brought in English wool in exchange for wine—raw wool that could be spun into yarn in the off-season, when women were not busy in the vineyards. In fact, whatever other new tasks rural women were turning to in different regions of western Europe, almost all of them appear to have been devoting somewhat more of their time in preparation of wool and flax, cotton, and silk to fuel the growing urban textile industry of later medieval Europe, and this activity, particularly for the production of warp threads, was primarily hand-spinning with distaff and spindle.

Indeed, it was this activity in preparing raw materials into thread and yarn for a burgeoning textile industry that, more than anything else, would become medieval village women's principal "by-work"—the activity to be taken up and put down and taken up again during the interstices between other activities in a peasant woman's busy day. When women were waiting for the pot to boil, or minding young children, or watching over flocks, indeed even when village women waited at the new water-mills for their grain to be ground, they would have employed their time at spinning yarn. Particularly given how much more time had to be devoted to spinning yarn than to weaving it into cloth (between six and eight times the hours of work), the coincidence between the widespread introduction of new water-powered mills in villages across Europe and the takeoff of the medieval cloth industry in nearby towns suggests that the use of water and wind power for grinding grain was central to the takeoff of the medieval cloth industry, through the intermediary of changes in village women's work.

URBAN WORKING WOMEN

With the growth of towns from the eleventh century, young village women (often seeking to earn some cash before marrying) sometimes migrated to towns to assist in such labor as grinding flour. This changed as towns too began to turn to water-powered milling. We know, for instance, that in the southern French city of Toulouse multiple grinding mills were established on the Garonne by the twelfth century. The girls sought new occupations: often employment as general household servants, often industrial work such as cleaning and spinning yarn, or in warping and otherwise preparing the new horizontal looms for weaving. As the textile industry took off, the labor of young girls, widows, or religious women in the preparation of yarn and thread became essential to many urban economies. Single women in the towns, unlike village women for whom spinning was by-work, could often work full time at spinning; this allowed wool to pass more quickly from sheep to loom; and this, in turn, allowed capital investments in sheep and wool to be recouped more quickly. From at least the mid-twelfth century, some working girls and widows found safety in religious houses of nuns or in beguinages, extra-regular houses for pious women. For some of these women, the intention was to stay in a city only long enough to amass a dowry before returning to the native village for marriage. For other women, a beguinage or nunnery would constitute a permanent home in which they could live pious lives while supporting themselves wholly or in part by the labor of their own hands. In places like Flanders, such beguinages were promoted by political authorities like the Countesses Jeanne and Margaret—and appear to have been favored by the bourgeoisie who found the labor of these women important to the textile industry. Only much later, in the fourteenth and later centuries when economic times were bad and production down did medieval city governments begin to be less tolerant of such religious women, who had earlier been so important in cloth production. The same is probably true in Italy, where women of new mendicant religious orders often participated in some sort of textile work.[16]

Women's role in this textile industry has been very much problematized in the literature on towns, industry, and work in the later Middle Ages, which has tended to see a gender shift towards male dominance in production, using new and more expensive technologies—like the boat shuttle or the table loom. In fact, however, such shifts to male-only laborers were limited to the high-end of textile production, such as in the production of certain broadcloths for export that had the names of their producing towns associated with them.[17]

The increased industrialization of textile production did bring about a series of new tools, which had as much effect on women's as on men's work. Many are hard to date precisely, but it is likely that the newly invented spinning wheel was adopted in the central Middle Ages, probably first in new urban religious institutions where the spinning wheel (so much more stationary than the distaff and spindle) suited the lifestyles of nuns and beguines. But that was the major problem with the spinning wheel—that it required one's work to be confined to one place. In contrast, for village women, for whom spinning was "by-work," the spinning wheel, given the expense and the space it required, was not advantageous over spinning by hand. A second problem with the wheel for spinning was that the quality of yarn spun by wheel was not as high as that spun by hand and hand-spun yarn remained the preferred thread for warping. Still the increase in production speed caused by the spinning wheel lowered the price of spun wool—indeed lowered the price paid for all spinning whether by hand or wheel.[18]

A second new invention, possibly made first by Flemish weavers in the vicinity of Saint-Trond *circa* 1135, was the boat shuttle or *navette* (Latin: *navicula*), whose use appears to be documented for both women and men. This shuttle is the size of a hand and the shape of a small boat or canoe. It has a cavity carved out of its insides and a bobbin is inserted on a metal rod inside the shuttle. This pseudo-wheel then unwinds the thread automatically as the shuttle is thrown from one edge to the other across the field of cloth being made. The bobbin could be wound using a tiny mechanical device very much like a spinning wheel, and a weaver could alternate different colors of yarn in a variety of patterns by using two or more shuttles. Replacing as it did a wooden stick wound with thread that constantly had to be unwound by hand, or rewrapped with new thread, this boat shuttle considerably hastened the work of the weaver—whether of a huge broadcloth on a two-person heavy horizontal loom, or even on a smaller ribbon- or belt-making horizontal loom.[19] It was this shuttle, in combination with the horizontal loom that would lead to the power loom with flying shuttle of the Industrial Revolution. In the Middle Ages, however, the boat shuttle's time-saving capacity was useful for any sort of table or horizontal loom—worked by either men or women.

Probably sometime in the twelfth century (but the evidence remains quite unclear) the third invention, the heavy or horizontal loom, began to replace the earlier vertical looms (often folding ones that could be easily stored away) for most urban cloth produc-tion, although vertical looms would remain for production of tapestries. Such looms eventually had levers or pedals that could move up and down a series of sheds, which allowed the weaving of everything from plain twills to elaborate patterns with rosettes. The appearance of the horizontal loom was once thought to mark the replacement of women as weavers by men, but women remained the mainstay in the urban textile industries in the later Middle Ages. Although the usual story—the introduction of heav-ier horizontal table looms, used to produce broader and longer cloths, led to their being worked by two men sitting side by side on a long bench in front of the loom and pitch-ing or throwing the boat shuttle back and forth between—may be true of specialized circumstances, we know that often the male weaver's sole assistant was a woman. She did the warping of the loom, the mending of broken threads, and other finishing tasks, but probably also soon learned to work at the loom itself. Moreover, there is no validity to the argument that the work had become so heavy that women could no longer do it, given that it was women who took the heavy, wet, washed finished cloth out into the meadows to hang to dry. If weavers sometimes attempted to prevent women from weav-ing, it was almost entirely because of their own depressed economic condition, as the entrepreneurial drapers who engaged in the international trade in cloth came to control the entire process of cloth production by a "putting out" system, in which the laborers eventually did not even own their materials or tools.[20] Women continued to weave for domestic use throughout the Middle Ages, and women did not lose their weaving skills to men with the introduction of the new horizontal loom.

RELIGIOUS WOMEN

If women could no longer marry priests after the twelfth century, many more could marry Jesus—be brides of Christ—as nuns often living in considerable comfort in new communities of monastic women. The most important thing about religious women in the years after the end of the first millennium is that the number of houses of nuns expanded extraordinarily in the later Middle Ages. Though they cannot yet be counted, altogether we now know that for the Cistercians, numbers of women's houses would reach and probably slightly exceed those for men by the mid- to late thirteenth century. This is not to say that those communities of nuns had the same population capacity that the monks' houses had, but in fact most houses of Cistercian nuns were at capacity, whereas houses of monks had declined in size so much that there was considerable discussion of a failure of recruitment caused by the rise of the new mendicant orders.[21] Religious communities for women expanded and with them so did documentation for their female patrons (much of it still lying unpublished in the archives).[22] This trend has something to do with gender imbalances in a world where women were surviving childbirth more often and men were dying on crusades. Moreover, while men could become either priests or monks, women could only become nuns. Still, medieval donors did not hesitate to make bequests to houses of nuns for anniversary prayers, and the women themselves participated actively in such commemoration, with the mass itself performed by a hired priest. Indeed, in the early thirteenth century, even members of the famed theological faculty of the University of Paris made gifts for such prayers to the newly founded abbey of Cistercian nuns at Saint-Antoine-des-Champs outside Paris.[23] Society in the central Middle Ages was wealthy enough (and had begun to reproduce sufficiently) that it could support these female specialists in prayer (who provided many other social services as well). Unlike in the early Middle Ages, society no longer needed nearly every woman to devote herself to child-bearing simply to reproduce itself.

Young girls, like the twelfth-century Christina of Markyate, might refuse marriage and choose instead to fulfill religious ambitions, but not all nuns had never been married. Widows, like the countesses of Champagne, Marie of Champagne and Blanche of Navarre, whose heirs eventually came of age, could retire to monastic houses rather than remarry. It was often such widows, who had a certain amount of worldly experience, who were chosen as abbesses and administrators because of their skills—as we see in the case of Petronilla of Chémilly, the widow appointed to be abbess at Fontevrault by its founder, Robert of Arbrissel.[24] Their skills as widows managing their own property and as monastic administrators were quite similar—skills that do not quite count as manual labor, but which were essential to their own well-being or to that of their religious community.

Such management of property by abbesses of such religious houses was paralleled by the careful administration of property by widows and other regents; indeed the evidence for nuns' good management of property may contribute to what we can infer about secular women in positions of power—and vice versa. We see the nuns of the abbey of Saint-Antoine outside Paris acquiring street upon street of rental houses that provided them a substantial annual income (more than 600 *livres* annually). Some of the latter houses may be traced to gifts made to the abbey, but the concentration of houses in particular locales suggests that the nuns were also working hard to establish a base of rental properties for their own support by building up series of houses on a particular street. Similarly, the account book for the building and establishment of endowment for the nuns of Maubuisson reveals not only Queen Blanche of Castile buying and consolidating properties for her community of nuns, but the continuation of that activity by later abbesses of that community.[25] Whereas in the early Middle Ages, it had been more likely that property would be given to nuns temporarily only to be taken back by family members, in the later Middle Ages women's religious communities established endowments that would often support them for the next half millennium. As so many new houses of nuns and other religious women were established, moreover, it became apparent that women had not entirely been excluded from the church. The well-known growth of misogyny, primarily a clerical misogyny, in the later Middle Ages may be a sort of backlash against both lay and religious women's successful acquisition and control of property.

CONCLUSION

The expanding economy of the central Middle Ages allowed nearly every member of society to have a higher standard of living than had been enjoyed by even the elites of the early medieval ages. Whereas it is possible that the situation of most women in the later Middle Ages was not as similar vis-à-vis men as it had been in the early Middle Ages, women—even religious women vowed to poverty and obedience—had a considerably higher living standard than before the year AD 1000. That women were contributors to that economic growth, to that commercial revolution, to that "takeoff" of western society, however, has rarely been noted.

As we have seen in these pages, peasant women and the young girls of the semi-religious urban houses like the beguines, both contributed to providing the raw materials to a burgeoning textile industry, and their participation in that textile production would continue to be essential. Peasant women were heavily involved in rural development such as the planting of vineyards and gardens and raising animals for sale in new urban markets, and nuns often encouraged their tenants to undertake improvement of rural holdings. While we have long seen women ruling the castles while men were away on crusade, we are only beginning to see the means by which they ruled—whether because developing castle structures were more easily defended by a lady/lord and a few knights or because those heiresses and regents resorted to the use of written records as a proxy for brute force.

While women may have been kept away from the growing universities, that is not to say that they did not profit from the plethora of clerics being trained in those schools or the preaching and argumentation that they were developing. Thus, nuns of Saint-Antoine were regularly preached to by the university masters of Paris, and those masters probably found employment in the many chapels established for the souls of donors in the churches of Saint-Antoine and other communities of nuns in their cities. The notions of law and reason that those clerics developed, moreover, could be used to the benefit of communities of religious women. Thus, the abbess of Saint-Antoine successfully evoked the principle of the just price in her dealings with the Premonstratensians who had earlier rented her a tract of forest land for what she had decided was too high a price. Similarly the nuns of le Lys near Melun argued that royal servants should continue to pay rents to the nuns in kind, not cash, from royal granaries, because that was what had been given by Blanche of Castile and her son Louis IX. Finally, women like Marie of Champagne and Blanche of Navarre and Eleanor of Vermandois and Blanche of Castile promoted the economic growth of their realms by granting privileges to towns and villages under their control and by promoting the construction of churches and monastic communities.[26]

Unlike their menfolk who carried the treasure of their realms off to wars in the East, such women invested in the well-being of their own souls by construction and reconstruction of churches and other monuments at home and by promoting economic growth in such industries as textile or tapestry production. Such management of resources by aristocratic or wealthy women in cities and countryside was much more frequent from the twelfth century on. That we are beginning to discover this, then, calls into question older models like that first posited by McNamara and Wemple. Such revisionist thinking about women in the central Middle Ages, is based on considerable work in the archives, where much more remains to be uncovered. But recent work continues to nuance our understanding, for instance of the Premonstratensians.[27]

Further Reading

Berman, Constance Hoffman. "Women's Work in Family, Village, and Town after AD 1000: Contributions to Economic Growth?" *The Journal of Women's History*, 19 (2007): 10–32.

Berman, Constance Hoffman. "Two Medieval Women's Control of Property and Religious Benefactions: Eleanor of Vermandois and Blanche of Castile." *Viator*, 41 (2010): 151–82.

Cardon, Dominique. *La draperie au Moyen Age: Essor d'une grande industrie européene.* Paris: CNRS, 1999.

Evergates, Theodore. *The Aristocracy in the County of Champagne, 1100–1300.* Philadelphia: University of Pennsylvania Press, 2007.

Jordan, Erin. "Gender Concerns: Monks, Nuns, and Patronage of the Cistercian Order in Thirteenth-Century Flanders and Hainaut." *Speculum*, 87 (2012): 62–94.

Langdon, John. "Lordship and Peasant Consumerism in the Milling Industry of Early Fourteenth-Century England." *Past & Present*, 145 (1) (1994): 3–46.

McNamara, Jo Ann. "The Herrenfrage: The Restructuring of the Gender System, 1050–1150," in Clare A. Lees, ed., *Medieval Masculinities: Regarding Men in the Middle Ages.* Minneapolis: University of Minnesota Press, 1994, 3–29.

McNamara, Jo Ann. "Canossa and the Ungendering of the Public Man," in Sabrina Petra Ramet and Donald W. Treadgold, eds, *Render Unto Caesar: The Religious Sphere in World Politics.* Washington, DC: American University Press, 1995, 131–50.

McNamara, Jo Ann and Suzanne Wemple. "The Power of Women Through the Family in Medieval Europe: 500–1100." *Feminist Studies*, 1 (1973): 126–41.

Shadis, Miriam. "Blanche of Castile and Facinger's 'Medieval Queenship': Reassessing the Argument," in Kathleen Nolan, ed., *Capetian Women.* New York: Palgrave, 2003, 137–61.

Wemple, Suzanne. *Women in Frankish Society: Marriage and the Cloister 500–900.* Philadelphia: University of Pennsylvania Press, 1981.

Notes

1. Jo Ann McNamara and Suzanne Wemple, "The Power of Women Through the Family in Medieval Europe: 500–1100," *Feminist Studies*, 1 (1973): 126–41; cf. Jo Ann McNamara, "Women and Power Through the Family Revisited," in Mary C. Erler and Maryanne Kowaleski, eds, *Gendering the Master Narrative: Women and Power in the Middle Ages* (Ithaca: Cornell University Press, 2003), 17–30.

2. Joan Kelly-Gadol, "Did Women Have a Renaissance?" in Renate Bridenthal and Claudia Koonz, eds, *Becoming Visible. Women in European History* (Boston: Houghton Mifflin, 1977), 148–52. David Herlihy, "Land, Family, and Women in Continental Europe, 701–1200," *Traditio*, 1 (1962): 89–120, but see Constance H. Berman, "Land, Family, and Women in Medieval Rome: Reassessing a Mentor's Classic Article," *Medieval Feminist Forum*, 41 (2006): 64–74. Marion Facinger, "A Study of Medieval Queenship: Capetian France 987–1237," *Studies in Medieval and Renaissance History*, 5 (1968): 3–48; cf. Miriam Shadis, "Blanche of Castile and Facinger's 'Medieval Queenship': Reassessing the Argument," in Kathleen Nolan, ed., *Capetian Women* (New York: Palgrave, 2003): 137–61.

3. Duby's pronouncement: "*Potestas*, the power to command and to punish, the duty of preserving peace and justice, was exercised by the sword...A woman could not take sword in hand," Georges Duby, "Women and Power," in Thomas Bisson, ed., *Cultures of Power: Lordship, Status and Process in Twelfth-Century Europe* (Philadelphia: University of Pennsylvania Press, 1995), 73, is only one part of his model of medieval society that has been challenged. See more generally Georges Duby, *The Early Growth of the European Economy: Warriors and Peasants from the Seventh to the Twelfth Century* (Ithaca: Cornell University Press, 1974). On families, see Amy Livingstone, *Out of Love for My Kin: Aristocratic Family Life in the Lands of the Loire, 1000–1200* (Ithaca: Cornell University Press, 2010).

4. Jo Ann McNamara, "The Herrenfrage: The Restructuring of the Gender System, 1050–1150," in Clare A. Lees, ed., *Medieval Masculinities: Regarding Men in the Middle Ages* (Minneapolis: University of Minnesota Press, 1994), 3–29; idem, "Canossa and the Ungendering of the Public Man," in Sabrina Petra Ramet and Donald W. Treadgold, eds, *Render Unto Caesar: The Religious Sphere in World Politics* (Washington, DC: American University Press, 1995), 131–50.

5. For instance, see James Brundage, "The Managerial Revolution in the English Church," in Janet S. Loengard, ed., *Magna Carta and the England of King John* (Woodbridge: Boydell, 2010), 83–98.

6. Marjorie Chibnall, *The Empress Matilda: Queen Consort, Queen Mother, and Lady of the English* (Oxford: Blackwell, 1991); Kimberly A. LoPrete, *Adela of Blois: Countess and Lord (c. 1067–1137)* (Dublin: Four Courts Press, 2007); Miriam Shadis, *Berenguela of Castile (1180–1246) and Political Women in the High Middle Ages* (New York: Palgrave Macmillan, 2009). Fredric Cheyette, *Ermengard of Narbonne and the World of the Troubadours* (Ithaca: Cornell University Press, 2001); Constance H. Berman, "Two Medieval Women's Control of Property and Religious Benefactions: Eleanor of Vermandois and Blanche of Castile," *Viator*, 41 (2010): 151–82; Erin Jordan, *Women, Power, and Religious Patronage in the Middle Ages* (New York: Palgrave, 2006).

7. John W. Baldwin, *The Government of Philip Augustus: Foundations of French Royal Power in the Middle Ages* (Berkeley: University of California Press, 1986).

8. Much of this is drawn from an honors thesis presented at the University of Iowa by Susan Cray, who drew on René de Lespinasse, *Le Nivernais et Les Comtes de Nevers* (Paris: H.

Champion, 1909), with my thanks to Cray; Constance H. Berman, "A Thirteenth-Century Coin Hoard Found in the Collection of the American Numismatic Society and a Penny from the Cluniac Priory of Souvigny," *Trésors monétaires (Paris)*, 8 (1986): 115–27 and plate 41.

9. Rosalind Kent Berlow, "The Development of Business Techniques Used at the Fairs of Champagne from the End of the Twelfth Century to the Middle of the Thirteenth Century," *Studies in Medieval and Renaissance History* (Lincoln: University of Nebraska Press, 1971), vol. 8: 3–31, but see also Elizabeth Chapin, *Les villes de foires de Champagne, des origines au déNewbut du XIVe sièNewcle* (Geneva: Slatkin reprints, 1976), and Theodore Evergates, *The Aristocracy in the County of Champagne, 1100–1300* (Philadelphia: University of Pennsylvania Press, 2007), and idem, ed., *Feudal Society in Medieval France: Documents from the County of Champagne* (Philadelphia: University of Pennsylvania Press, 1993).

10. Judith M. Bennett, *Women in the Medieval English Countryside: Gender and Household in Brigstock Before the Plague* (New York: Oxford University Press, 1987); Katherine L. French, *The People of the Parish: Community Life in a Late Medieval English Diocese* (Philadelphia: University of Pennsylvania Press, 2001); Mavis E. Mate, *Daughters, Wives, and Widows After the Black Death: Women in Sussex, 1350–1535* (Woodbridge, Suffolk; Rochester, NY: Boydell Press, 1998).

11. Guy Bois, *The Transformation of the Year One Thousand: The Village of Lournand from Antiquity to Feudalism* (Manchester; New York: Manchester University Press, 1992). As for gynaecaea, see Constance Hoffman Berman, "Women's Work in Family, Village, and Town after AD 1000: Contributions to Economic Growth?" *The Journal of Women's History*, 19 (2007): 10–32.

12. Thomas N. Bisson, *Tormented Voices: Power, Crisis, and Humanity in Rural Catalonia, 1140–1200* (Cambridge, Mass.; London: Harvard University Press, 1998). Beverly Kienzle, "The Tract on the Conversion of Pons of Léras and the True Account of the Beginning of the Monastery of Silvanès," *Cistercian Studies Quarterly*, 309 (1995): 219–43; cf. Constance H. Berman, "The Life of Pons de Léras: Knights and Conversion to the Religious Life in the Central Middle Ages," *Church History and Religious Culture*, 88 (2008): 119–37. Thomas Head and Richard Allen Landes, eds, *The Peace of God: Social Violence and Religious Response in France Around the Year 1000* (Ithaca: Cornell University Press, 1992).

13. David Herlihy, "Treasure Hoards in the Italian Economy, 960–1139," *The Economic History Review*, 10 (1957–1958): 1–14; *S. Mariae in Vita Lata Tabularium*, ed. L. Hartmann (Vienna, 1895–1912).

14. Foucher of Chartres (1058–c.1127) in Edward Peters, ed., *The First Crusade: The Chronicle of Fulcher of Chartres and Other Source Materials* (Philadelphia: University of Pennsylvania Press, 1971).

15. Robert Fossier, *The Axe and the Oath: Ordinary Life in the Middle Ages* (Princeton: Princeton University Press, 2010).

16. Ernest W. McDonnell, *The Beguines and Beghards in Medieval Culture, with Special Emphasis on the Belgian Scene* (New Brunswick, NJ: Rutgers University Press, 1954); Erin L. Jordan, *Women, Power, and Religious Patronage in the Middle Ages* (New York: Palgrave Macmillan, 2006); Maiju Lehmijoki-Gardner, *Worldly Saints: Social Interaction of Dominican Penitent Women in Italy, 1200–1500* (Helsinki: Suomen Historiallinen Seura, 1999). Walter Simons, *Cities of Ladies: Beguine Communities in the Medieval Low Countries* (Philadelphia: University of Pennsylvania Press, 2001), describes beguines doing textile work. Even for impoverished women outside the religious institutions, demand in the cloth industry kept them in work, like the poor woman in Paris spinning with the distaff to

earn extra cash—perhaps for a pilgrimage with a sick child. See Sharon Farmer, *Surviving Poverty in Medieval Paris: Gender, Ideology, and the Daily Lives of the Poor* (Ithaca: Cornell University Press, 2002).

17. John H. A. Munro, *Textiles, Towns and Trade: Essays in the Economic History of Late-Medieval England and the Low Countries* (Aldershot, Hants; Brookfield, Vt.: Variorum, 1994).

18. Dominique Cardon, *La draperie au Moyen Age: Essor d'une grande industrie européNewene* (Paris: CNRS, 1999), and Marjorie Keniston McIntosh, *Working Women in English Society, 1300–1620* (Cambridge; New York: Cambridge University Press, 2005).

19. Giselbertus Trudonensis; Folcardus Trudonensis, *Gesta abbatum Trudonensium (continuatio prima)* (Turnhout: Brepols Publishers, 2010), online source: Brepolis Library of Latin Texts; Cardon, *La draperie*, 553 ff.

20. Samuel K. Cohn, *The Laboring Classes in Renaissance Florence* (New York: Academic Press, 1980).

21. Bernadette Barrière and Marie-Élizabeth Henneau, eds, *Cîteaux et les femmes: Actes des Rencontres de Royaumont, 1998* (Paris: Editions Créaphis, 2001).

22. See Penelope D. Johnson, *Equal in Monastic Profession: Religious Women in Medieval France* (Chicago: University of Chicago Press, 1991); Marilyn Oliva, *The Convent and the Community in Late Medieval England: Female Monasteries in the Diocese of Norwich, 1350–1540* (Woodbridge: Boydell, 1998); and Sharon T. Strocchia, *Nuns and Nunneries in Renaissance Florence* (Baltimore: Johns Hopkins University Press, 2009).

23. Constance H. Berman, "Cistercian Nuns and the Development of the Order: The Abbey of Saint-Antoine-des-Champs outside Paris," *The Joy of Learning and the Love of God. Essays in Honor of Jean Leclercq, OSB*, ed. E. Rozanne Elder, pp. 121–56 (Kalamazoo: Cistercian Publications, 1995).

24. Bruce L. Venarde, ed., *Robert of Arbrissel: A Medieval Religious Life* (Washington, DC: Catholic University of America Press, 2003).

25. On Saint-Antoine, see reference in note 23. The account book is Pontoise, A.D. Val d'Oise, 72H12, "Achatz d'héritages de Maubuisson."

26. Berman, "Two Medieval Women," *passim*.

27. See two 2016 PhD dissertations from the University of Iowa: Yvonne Seale, '"Ten Thousand Women": Gender, Affinity, and the Development of the Premonstratensian Order in Medieval France,' and Heather Wacha, 'La Puissance du Choix: Women's Economic Activity in Twelfth- and Thirteenth-Century Picardy, France.'

CHAPTER 35

....

GENDER IN THE TRANSITION TO MERCHANT CAPITALISM

....

MARTHA C. HOWELL

HISTORIANS have long recognized that the commercial economy of early modern Europe, and the larger society itself, were transformed by what scholars have labeled merchant capitalism, but they have tended to treat the transformation as though it had no particular implications for the history of gender. For their part, historians of gender in premodern Europe, even those concentrating on women's economic roles, have by and large made no clear distinction between the medieval market economy and merchant capitalism.[1] Yet there was a difference between these economic systems, and the slow transition from one to the other produced significant changes in gender roles and gender meanings for women and men from the middle and upper ranks of cities where commerce was most firmly rooted.

The changes in gender that came with merchant capitalism were filtered through a public/private divide that had been taking shape in such cities over several preceding centuries. In the end, the men and women from mercantile families, including those from artisanal trades positioned near the top of the urban social hierarchy, would adopt social practices and assign cultural meaning to those practices that would set the terms of bourgeois identity in modern Europe. For men, the process unrolled in the context of a centuries-long struggle over status that was played out on the field of honor and involved the traditional aristocracy as well as urban commoners. For women, the immediate context was medieval Europe's patriarchal system, which subordinated women's work to a family economy that was imagined—and largely functioned—as a male-headed enterprise. The increasing social and political power of entrepreneurs that came with the transition to merchant capitalism threatened this system by potentially freeing women from the patriarchal structure. As a result, women gradually lost the limited access they had had to independent entrepreneurial and managerial roles in the market economy, but, as though in compensation, they gained new status in a reconstituted private realm.

The Late Medieval Market Economy and Merchant Capitalism

Limited forms of market exchange had existed throughout the Middle Ages, even during the so-called Dark Ages, but it was only after about 1200 or 1300—much later in many areas—that a developed market economy emerged in western Europe. By then, the tripartite social order of "workers," "prayers," and "fighters," which could once be invoked to describe medieval society, was no more. Although this model had never accurately described the medieval economy, for "workers" were by no means a homogeneous group and "fighters" could occasionally also be producers and traders, the model nevertheless had captured the essence of medieval Europe's status system. Its military aristocracy claimed exclusive rights to rule, and even if in competition with ecclesiastical leaders, the aristocracy made, judged, and executed law in their individual domains. Workers obeyed.

By the late Middle Ages, however, this tripartite scheme no longer even approximated sociopolitical reality because commerce was further eroding the imagined boundaries between workers and fighters and simultaneously creating a more complex social hierarchy. In the countryside, some traditional landholders now systematically produced for the market, as did, for example, great monasteries in England that exported wool to the Low Countries and Italy. Some peasants and tenants had become market farmers. In contrast, many of their land-poor neighbors took in piecework to supplement their meager harvests; others, less lucky still, had lost their land to aggrandizing lords or entrepreneurial neighbors and found themselves an itinerant laboring class. By the fifteenth century, aristocrats consumed Asian- and European-made luxuries at rates unheard of 200 years earlier. Some courts were even direct participants in the commercial economy, not just its consumers. They employed highly skilled artisans to transform silks and fine woolens into elegant dress or precious stones into decorative jewels, or hired masons and carpenters on urban labor markets. They turned urban businessmen or their sons into financial officers and administrators of their courts, their estates, and their tax systems.

Powerful cities like Bruges, London, Cologne, Antwerp, Montpellier, Florence, Genoa, and Venice were the nodes of this commercial economy, and their long-distance traders and bankers governed their cities, albeit usually in tense competition with their overlords. Meanwhile, the burgeoning industrial economies of such cities were creating "new men" (*novi homines*), typically artisan-merchants, who were demanding—and winning—a place in city government. The artisan population from which these new men had sprung was itself now decidedly stratified, with men in elite trades at the top; brewers, butchers and furriers just below; carpenters and tailors below them; and unskilled workers at the bottom.

Because merchant capitalism gradually grew out of this fertile matrix, it is difficult to draw a clear line between merchant capitalism and the late medieval market economy, especially in the advanced form it acquired in the major commercial cities. There is, however, an analytical distinction, which has to do with the extraordinary power that merchant capitalists gained from their monopoly of certain markets. In effect, like later agrarian and industrial capitalists, they were in a position to arrange matters socially and politically, sometimes even acquiring quasi-state powers, so that they continuously accumulated riches. But merchant capitalists were not yet the capitalists of modernity, for they did not amass profits from the systematic exploitation of labor in the production of agricultural and industrial goods intended for sale. Merchant capitalists concentrated on trade, not production, even if in some of the great textile cities they also sought control of workers. As Fernand Braudel described merchant capitalists, such men turned money into more money not only by arbitrage, as had generations of traders before them, but also by controlling information, credit, and the flow of goods among far-flung and mysteriously exotic markets.[2] They were thus able to manipulate prices and supplies for their benefit.

Historians consider the post-1500 period the age of merchant capitalism because only then were merchant adventurers formally or informally backed by the state. Only then, for example, did Portuguese and Spanish states send heavily armed ships to trade in Asian and Atlantic markets; only then did the state and the merchant community join to establish private corporations, such as the Dutch East India Company (VOC) or the English East India Company (EIC).[3] Still, even in 1300 or 1400, in some cities there were men whose expertise in long-distance trade had given them quasi-monopolistic control of certain markets and credit systems—men like Peruzzi in Italy, Coeur in France, Boinebroke in the southern Low Countries. These were the ancestors of early modern Europe's age of merchant capitalism, and their success in trade was already transforming the society of cities where they operated. Their success also changed gender roles and gender meanings, for them and their wives.

CLASS AND MALE HONOR

The transformation to the age of merchant capital was thus a sociopolitical history as well as an economic one, and it produced centuries of struggle over social status. For men, the struggle centered around honor. This was a charged cultural category throughout the late medieval and early modern period because status was importantly constituted and expressed through honor, understood as the way one was regarded by peers and non-peers alike. Aristocrats had long defined themselves and legitimated their rule by asserting (and seeking to exhibit) knightly virtues like military exploits, heroism, lineage, and strong will, and by the munificence and generosity made possible by seigneurial rents, honorific dues, and the spoils of war.[4] Although this code was obsessively enacted in rituals of the late Middle Ages, narrated in the romances that circulated in noble and bourgeois circles alike, and earnestly reiterated in the mirror of princes literature then so beloved, by the late medieval centuries, it was more a nostalgic (and largely imaginary) evocation of a time long gone than a description of reality. Indeed, the courts of the day had been so transformed by merchant wealth—the treasures it brought, the expertise required to negotiate its terms, the people admitted to courtly circles on the basis of their skill in these markets—that in many settings courtiers of the day needed to display elegance and sophistication as well as the traditional "knightly" virtues. Thus we have the courtier who would be famously depicted by Castiglione in his 1528 *Book of the Courtier*, a man skilled with the sword and the horse but also well dressed, well adorned, and well spoken, *au courant* with the latest fashions in food, literature, music, and dress.[5]

As charged a category as honor was in aristocratic circles, it was no less an issue among those commoners who owed their new wealth and status to commerce. For these merchants and "new men," however, honor was an even more elusive concept, because according to medieval Europe's moral code, trade or the search for monetary profit was not just suspect, it was condemned. In fact, as some merchants amassed fortunes large enough to challenge the magnates of church and state alike, and even as ordinary craftsmen and retailers managed to climb into the ranks of the economic elite, a centuries-old discourse treating material wealth as a spiritual threat and a manifestation of temporal evils gained new force. Indeed, Dante put usurers in the seventh circle of hell, just below blasphemers and sodomites. It was not just the merchant's greed that condemned him; to judge from popular tales of the age, commerce led directly to sin. In the fifteenth-century *Croxton Play of the Sacrament*, for example, a Christian merchant agrees to sell the host to a Jew. Although the play resolves with the triumph of the host, commerce itself is figured as a force that was powerful enough to entice Christians to commit medieval Europe's greatest sin: pride.

In this narrative of condemnation, producers were just as bad as merchants. Bread might be made with spelt, not wheat, or sold at short weights. A silver coin might be clipped or debased with mere copper. A clever artisan might even fake a holy relic. Cloth bearing the honored seal of Ghent or Ypres might, in fact, be a cheaper copy made in some unknown village with Spanish, not Cotswold, wool. As a thirteenth-century teacher of Latin grammar explained in a text depicting daily life in Paris, drapers were "driven by greed, [they] sell false white and black cloths, camelins and blues and imitation burnets, greens, imitation scarlets, striped cloths and stamforts...they defraud buyers by measuring the cloths badly with a short ell and a false thumb."[6]

To counter such attacks, merchants—indeed all sellers of their wares—needed a discourse about mercantile honor, or at least one that acknowledged the virtue of men who lived from trade. Several different versions circulated throughout these centuries; although each was directed at or described a slightly different group of commercial men, all asserted that managerial competence (or simply success) in the commercial economy granted honor and, with it, the right to rule. One version attributed what Howard Kaminsky has called "noble estate" to men of property—property originally won in commerce but increasingly invested in land and title—whose honor was embodied by manners, an air of probity, and more than a touch of arrogance, and whose worthiness was demonstrated by "preferences" such as public office, privileges of various kinds, or acceptance in certain social circles.[7] Lavish hospitality could be added to this mix, another sign both of property and good will and a direct evocation of the medieval ideal of the munificence and generosity expected of elites.[8] Another hybrid version was better suited to the kind of men whose stories were told in Richard Hakluyt's famous collection of travel narratives, published in various editions between 1589 and 1600.[9] The English merchants who roamed the world for adventure and gain in these tales are recognizable descendants of the brave and curious knight-errant of medieval romance; they admire and seek elegance like the courtiers of their day. They are also, however, clever and materially ambitious, qualities that bespeak their immersion in trade and fit them for leadership. Thomas Heywood's 1605 play, *If You Know Not Me, You Know Nobody*, features exactly such a man, Thomas Gresham. A London guildsman, Gresham is represented as a merchant adventurer who takes huge risks, uses his wealth to build a civic monument (the Royal Exchange, a source of great personal profit), and winds up entertaining the Queen and royal ambassadors, thus managing to embody both old and new discourses—aristocratic prerogatives, commercial skill, nonchalant recklessness, civic-mindedness, and access to the highest ranks of politics.

Artisans and artisan-entrepreneurs in cities like Ghent, Nuremburg, London, Florence, or Lyon would also claim rights to govern by asserting that practical acumen, business skill, and civic-mindedness were qualification for government. Success in managing a workshop, the local wine trade, a putting-out system for cloth-making, or some other urban enterprise went hand and hand, the logic seemed to go, with the ability to govern. In these circles, a man of honor was above all hardworking, financially independent, responsible, and smart; he headed and provided for a well-run household; because he was a good businessman and good householder, he had earned the right to help govern his guild, confraternity, neighborhood, or city.[10] Although this was still a marginal discourse about male honor in late medieval centuries, what would be called "bourgeois honor" as the early modern period went on was founded on exactly these virtues.[11] Such men worked and they were proud to work; they were good businessmen; and because they could govern the economy, themselves, and their households, they were fit to govern others.

THE PATRIARCHAL NEXUS OF MEDIEVAL URBAN HOUSEHOLDS

What we see, then, during the long transition to merchant capitalism is the increasing ability of commercial men (the mere "buyers and sellers" of medieval invective) to participate in or influence politics, in effect to control public space—a subject to which I will return—as well as their private business affairs. This development would have a profound effect on women from the same propertied commercial classes although for them it would mean a partial retreat from public life and new status in an enhanced private space, not new power in public space. The story played out so differently for such women because their social status was imagined to derive from their association with a man, whether a father or husband, or even a lineage (almost by definition, the patriline), not from their roles in the market or other arenas outside the household. To be sure, women subject to such patriarchal control were by no means without rights and privileges; depending on their position in the household, they could be granted rights in the market as agents of the household, rights inside the household as its mistress, rights as joint owners of—or as successors to—marital or parental property.

As members of such households, women worked to sustain them, and as commerce became ever more a way of life in cities during the late Middle Ages, they combined work for subsistence with work for the market, making little distinction between them. In addition to performing duties we consider domestic, including keeping kitchen gardens and perhaps chickens, a pig, or a cow, spinning wool, and weaving, women—whether married, widowed, or single—also sold their surplus cheese or ale, their wool, or cloth to help provision their household. Some did more. They devoted most of their productive labor to the market, and a number of them gained guild rights as mistresses of shops. Usually they entered guilds as wives, widows, or daughters of masters, initially serving as support or substitute but nevertheless with independent rights to the craft. In some places, as in Paris, Rouen, and Cologne, there were all-female guilds.[12] Other women stood in for absent merchant husbands or managed the retail operation of a workshop run by a husband or son; the many women who never married did the same kind of work, often as members of a relative's household and thus under its authority, but sometimes as heads of their own. Some women of the artisan and artisan-merchant class were literate and numerate, products of the lay schools that had been established, for example, in many commercial cities of the Low Countries.[13]

Women's visibility in market production was a direct result of their role in the patriarchal system: they acted for a household that was imagined to be male, even if the male was dead, making a household headed by a never-married woman a cultural anomaly if nevertheless a material reality. Law underwrote the patriarchal system by enclosing married women in male space. In much of the north of Europe—exactly the area where women seem to have been most active in late medieval market production—a married woman bought and sold goods and services under male control.[14] Her debts were her husband's, and her earnings his as well, unless the husband had agreed that she could trade as a singlewoman under the label "femme sole," a status granted in order to protect the husband from her debts. Even widows who traded on their own were only placeholders for the now deceased male head, and in the north most of them remarried in stunningly short periods of time, thus repositioning themselves under direct male authority. In the south, where Roman law prevailed, a propertied woman retained titular ownership of her dowry during marriage, but unless a contract provided that it be managed by her male kin, her husband had lifetime control of the assets, and at his death the dowry often returned to her male kin, not to her.[15]

Still more telling, during the later Middle Ages women could not participate in other activities outside the household as independently as they could in the market. Women did have roles in parish charities and the like, but the institutions were under the supervision of men; women sometimes marched in religious or civic processions, but the processions were dominated by men; women often took active parts in neighbor-hood affairs, but to my knowledge never with formal authority as ward bosses or the like. The few actresses who traveled with theater companies were at real risk of being called prostitutes; even the prostitutes who worked in city brothels were forbidden to solicit on the streets (although some did). In most places, taverns were male spaces, and after dark so were the streets. In fact, if a woman was raped outside her home at night, it was her fault for, as the judge might say, what was she doing on the street after dark?[16]

The most convincing evidence about the limits to women's status in public was their exclusion from formal political institutions. They did not even govern the few guilds that were exclusively female; men made and executed the laws of those organizations. At best, they were appointed matrons of charitable organizations run by the city, but the organizations were under the authority of municipal governors and although women surely gave advice, it was men who formally made the rules, not women. Perhaps more telling still, in cities of the Low Countries and environs, immigrant women were inscribed as new citizens only where citizenship granted no independent political rights, but was required for operation of a workshop or retail establishment.[17] In short, medie-val urban women, no matter how frequently in public and no matter how essential their work in market production, did not become ungendered as they exited the household. The fully respectable among them remained within the patriarchal nexus.

WOMEN, PUBLIC SPACE, AND HIGH-STATUS WORK

This patriarchal system would survive the transition to merchant capitalism, but for women from merchant, artisan-merchant, and elite artisan families, it survived by drawing a firmer line between the public and the private, assuring that these women's forays into the public were limited or closely supervised. By the early modern period, a robust conception of public space had emerged, understood not just as the antithesis of the "secret" and not just as space accessible to all.[18] Rather, the concept of public space relevant here implies politics—governance—in effect, the existence of a space regu-lated on behalf of a commonality. In that specific sense, before about 1100 there was only a vague concept of public space, and in fact there were few truly public spaces, not in material fact and not in ideology, not in cities and not in the countryside.[19] Of course, feudal elites made claims to power over others, but they did not make claims to space itself, rather to people and their deeds. People of all ranks were linked to one another by their relation to personal spaces—the households of the greats (kings included) and the hovels of peasants, churches, monasteries, and manors.

This arrangement was expressed—and in fact constituted—materially. Residences of the greats were large, but they were more fortresses than what we think of as homes, and they were not divided between domestic and nondomestic activities, between nuclear family and kin group, or even between kin and retainers. Chapels and monasteries were closed to outsiders, and although churches and cathedrals were more accessible, their interiors were not freely or consistently available to the laity. While the spaces around churches did meet the definition of public space in that they were governed by ecclesiastical authorities for the benefit of the laity, these spaces did not extend far beyond the churchyard and its cemeteries.

Although almost no settlement worthy of being called a city was without some spaces defined as "common," it would take a couple of centuries before a robust conception of public space developed in cities, whether as a concept or as a material reality. In most cities, streets were narrow and dark, overhung with the second stories of private dwellings, and their wells and drainage systems were often privately owned by individuals or institutions; market places were not centralized but were scattered around town and sometimes effectively under the control of individual families or institutions. In the early days of commercialization, even the houses of rich burghers reflected this logic. Like the castles of the nobility, their residences were more fortresses than homes: they were closed to the street and internally blockaded with doors and bars; windows were sparse; light was rare. The Italian tower houses exemplify the model, but such buildings were also to be found in Ghent or Liège, Cologne or Lyon.

The absence of a robust public space in city or countryside alike meant that the activities that today we consider public existed in spaces we think of as private. Rooms with beds were also places for receptions of visitors and gathering places for household members; people slept in groups, often in the same bed, in a room which was alternately, even simultaneously, the hall, the dining room, the kitchen. Members of the nuclear family lived among others—sometimes kin, typically employees, retainers, and miscellaneous hangers-on. Solitude was rare, and there was little personal privacy as we understand the term; everyone was on view most of the time. In a world where the public, in a legal and political sense, was not yet fully instantiated and the private was the default position, what we consider the public and private were conflated in a cultural and social sense.

Hence, although women were assigned specific roles and were associated with the tools and places used to perform their tasks—the distaff, the hearth, the kitchen garden—there were few spaces consistently reserved for women except in the estates of the rich. Rather, for almost all lay women, urban and rural alike, patriarchal control was a legal, cultural, and social umbrella, so to speak, that traveled with women as they passed through the interior spaces of their residences, as they exited the domicile to do their work in markets, fields, or hospitals, or even as the aristocratic among them acceded to rule in place of the men of their lineage. In an urban world where neighbors knew neighbors and where, in all but the largest cities, everyone knew who everyone was, where married women announced their status by head coverings, and where gossip was a powerful means of social control, patriarchal authority could be clearly expressed (and enforced) without being spatial. This was the social world that had given women access to the market economy.

As the Middle Ages drew to a close, however, the rather inchoate mix of what we consider public and private was being disaggregated so that a new kind of public was being clearly demarcated from a reconstituted private. The process had begun during the central and later Middle Ages as princes defined their sovereignty territorially, but there is a distinctly urban version of the story as well. It began about 1200 or 1300, when municipal authorities, alone or with their princes, took control of and expanded physical spaces like streets and squares, monuments and walls, moats and bridges, gates and wells. They simultaneously issued reams of regulations about maintenance of streets, about clean water, about sewage, about use of open places, about governance of gates and walls, about behavior in public, about protection from fire. It was then as well that violence among individuals became the concern of municipal leaders, not simply a matter to be settled between the parties involved. Expressing and reinforcing the material changes was a discourse about the community and its communal good. Those who governed deployed terms like *gemeente, Gemeinde, commune,* even *public,* that ambiguously referred to the "whole" community and its interests in order to legitimate their claims to these spaces and the people in them. In effect, by claiming to police themselves on behalf of the "public good," cities created a material and ideological space that challenged lordship and could trump the independent power of urban enclaves like monasteries, hospitals—and households themselves.

None of the public spaces embodying the communal good were exclusively the sites of politics or commerce, festival or worship, and the conflation of functions and symbolic resonance magnified the power of urban space itself.[20] Central market squares were simultaneously sites where political pageantry was enacted and laws were promulgated; the courtyards of churches or the alleyways that ran next to them could house the stalls of moneychangers, cloth retailers, or leatherworkers. Theater was a public event, viewed by all urban classes, and usually was performed in the market squares. Religious processions such as the Corpus Christi celebrations that were held in public constituted perhaps the most significant occasion for collective worship by the laity, and the enactment itself—the solemn march through iconic sites, circling images laden with meaning, past civic buildings—linked the authority of the sacred with the power of the commune, multiplying the force of each. During the late Middle Ages, women from established artisan and merchant families were no strangers to these spaces, excepting perhaps the most elite patrician women in Italian cities like Florence.[21] They watched the plays and processions, and some even took a small part in them; in marketplaces, boutiques, and stalls they sold goods they had made and bought others for the household; they strolled and gossiped. But slowly and very unevenly, women who would later be styled bourgeois followed Florence's patricians and went home.

This retreat occurred, I have concluded, for several reasons, one being the new emphasis on women's roles in private, domestic space, a subject to which I will return. But there was another reason as well: entrepreneurial status was becoming too closely allied with sociopolitical importance, thus presaging one of the defining features of the early modern merchant capitalist: access to rule. And it was not just the richest merchants who were able to link economic with political status; elite artisan-entrepreneurs were making the same bid. Now, and at very different rates throughout Europe, management of public space, the putative locus of the good of the collective whole, was being claimed by entrepreneurs like goldsmiths, furriers, butchers, and drapers as well as by the financiers and long-distance merchants who had long held power in cities and were now even extending their political influence outside cities themselves, into the courts and countinghouses of the princes. As a result, a woman who was styled mistress in a guild, who ran the import–export business in her husband's absence or took over after his death, or who set up a money-changing bench in the city was not just in public view but also positioned as though she had a claim to occupy, even to govern, public space. She was thus, potentially at least, free of direct supervision (and purported protection) by her husband, father, or male kin. Now that her economic status offered, or could seem to offer, such independence, even such political authority, her "work," if located in the increasingly abstracted market economy, no longer seemed securely bound to the household or to the men who putatively governed it.

The shift in meaning was subtle, and women's retreat came slowly, so slowly and unevenly that it would not be visible in a few big cities for more than a century. And in some places it is hard to find evidence that during the late Middle Ages women ever had much access to independent entrepreneurial positions near the top of the economic hierarchy.[22] But by 1600 in some places, everywhere by 1700 or 1800, a change was unmistakable, even if recorded more clearly in some parts of Europe than others. The women's guilds in Cologne, Paris, or Rouen had disappeared or were on their way out. In the places where women's guild membership had come to widows or daughters of masters, widows' rights had been steadily written out of ordinances and sometimes specifically revoked, daughters' claims to practice the trade had been successfully contested by journeymen who felt the women usurped their own rights, and as time went on the guild registers and regulations had ceased even to make a *pro forma* reference to "sisters."[23] A woman less often took over her deceased husband's shop or stayed on to supervise his journeymen except in partnership with a new husband or an adult son; relatively fewer women now kept the books and handled local sales for itinerant merchant husbands; we find fewer references to female moneylenders. The women who remained as producers and sellers of commercial goods in relatively high-status enterprises worked with their husbands or fathers in their shops, safely under the patriarchal wing; the few who emerged into the limelight were rare, and getting rarer. Those who had no such secure base and worked alone found themselves—more or less as they had always been—relegated to the margins of commercial society as pieceworkers, peddlers, purveyors of hats and ribbons they had made, operators of small boutiques, wage workers, or servants.

This change came at different times in different places. Take, for example, fourteenth-century Ghent, a commercial and political giant of the century, second in size in the north only to Paris. Ghent was then run by a cabal of old patricians (born of finance and trade), newly rich merchants, and upwardly mobile artisan-merchants. Although these men were not yet what historians would call merchant capitalists, they already exhibited many of the traits that define the type—they not only grew rich from commerce, they also sought to control markets and they acquired political power to be sure they succeeded. Although women in Ghent were at this time still active in the market economy, buying and selling, borrowing and lending, just as women elsewhere in urban Europe still were, the women of Ghent were systematically excluded from key markets in this mighty commercial city. Women were, for example, denied access to the city's prestigious Meat Hall as well as the even more important Corn Hall, where regional grain trade was managed. In Ghent's celebrated Cloth Hall, women did have stalls, but they were relegated to the lower floors where textiles were sold by the piece; men reserved the upper floors and the wholesale trade for themselves, a pattern repeated in other Low Countries textile towns. Only in Ghent's Friday Market, where locals provisioned their households, could women freely enter both to buy and to sell, a clear indication of the link between their market rights and their roles as provisioners of the household.[24]

THE PRIVATE SPACES OF DOMESTICITY AND EUROPE'S EMERGING BOURGEOISIE

Although such women's retreat from market production can be seen as a loss—indeed, it would be the twentieth century before European women would make a bid for equal access to the modern capitalist economy or win independent political rights—these same women gained authority and status in a newly constituted space, the space of the private. The material manifestations of this process were the elaborately subdivided residences, private family quarters, special-purpose rooms, and elegant decorations that rich urbanites constructed in the late medieval centuries. Although the architectural shift in England was enabled by technological changes in building, this was not typically the case elsewhere, and my point is that it was only in the late centuries of the Middle Ages that urbanites came to imagine, and to construct, such edifices.[25] Although the private dwelling was formally under male governance, women were to manage it, and their role as consumer acquired new importance. They were not only expected to prepare food and clothing, take care of children, and occasionally sell things they had made at home, as had long been their chores, they also were expected to consume "tastefully" and wisely so that the home became the repository of riches won in trade, a display not just of wealth but also of social and cultural values.[26]

By cultivating the virtues necessary for effective household management, women could enact the lessons imparted by the conduct books and housekeeping manuals of the period. There they were monotonously instructed that a woman's job was to manage consumption in her husband's interests, carefully choosing and wisely using the treasures he brought home. In 1580, the Italian moralist Torquato Tasso put it this way:

> It is well ordered that...the office of acquiring should be attributed to the man and that of preserving to the woman. The man struggles to acquire and carries out farming or operates in commerce in the city.... But the woman looks after that which has been acquired and her virtues are employed inside the house, just as the man demonstrates his outside.[27]

Nowhere was such rhetoric better circulated than in the Low Countries, where the cozy domestic interior and the industrious housewife would serve as the antidote to what Simon Schama has memorably called "the embarrassment of riches."[28] As Heide Wunder has explained, it was the same in early modern German-speaking cities. There patrician and upper-middle-class women "began to limit themselves to organizational tasks in the household and devoted more time to decorating the living spaces in a stately manner and enjoying a 'homey' life with their children and husbands," and even the wives of middling artisans followed suit, so that "a woman's position as mistress of a household with authority over children and domestics became much more important."[29] England was no different, as an early seventeenth-century text almost repeating the Italian language of a generation earlier reminds us:

> The dutie of the Husband is to get goods; and of the Wife to gather them together, and save them. The dutie of the Husband is to travel abroad, to seeke [a] living; and the Wives dutie is to keep the house. The dutie of the Husband is to get money and provision; and of Wives, not vainly to spend it.[30]

Although the moralist tracts and conduct books of the period did not accurately describe the lives of women, not even those of the privileged women to whom they were addressed, they implicitly conferred status on such women, distinguishing them from women "in public," and it is perhaps that function that made them so attractive a model for behavior. These "good housewives"—a group that ideologically could include the shopkeeper's or dyer's wife, the alderman's widow, and the merchant's daughter—would never spend wastefully or wantonly; they would leave it to the aristocrats to dress fancifully and to the poor to try to copy that flamboyance with second- and third-hand goods. In this way, such women could be shielded from the venom that had long been hurled at women. These dutiful consumers, no matter how costly their wardrobes or how elaborately decorated their homes, were not the voracious, undisciplined consumers depicted in contemporary sumptuary legislation or comic literature. If this was not yet the ideology of separate spheres that would be enthroned as a model for bourgeois life in the modern west—women safely in a home where no "real" work took place, men in the market and in control of the state—it was the beginning.

CONCLUSION

Patriarchy was thus preserved, in fact solidified, but its terms slightly shifted: the women described here remained under male control and defined by the household in which they served, but just what the household meant and just what their tasks in life were meant to be were not quite what they had been.[31] Yet, it was not only women who were changed. If the narrative that excluded proper women from active participation in market production tamed consumption by taming the female consumer and tamed the female entrepreneur by assuring that she did not have much opportunity to be entrepreneurial, it also tamed men, helping them become the "men of credit" that justified their immersion in trade and fit them for rule.[32] In truth, a merchant might be the adventurer that Hakluyt often portrayed and a decidedly irresponsible householder, or he might need his wife's dowry to fund his business, require her assistance in his shop, or depend on her to keep his books.[33] The emergent discourse about the man of "credit" denied that possibility, however, making him a trustworthy businessman, a responsible householder fully in control of his family, and an honored participant in governance of his community. His wife was none of those things.

FURTHER READING

Braudel, Fernand. *The Wheels of Commerce*, vol. 2: *Civilization and Capitalism*, trans. Siân Reynolds. London: Collins, 1982.

Chartier, Roger, ed. *A History of Private Life*, vol. III: *Passions of the Renaissance*. Cambridge, Mass.: Harvard University Press, 1989.

Davidoff, Leonore and Catherine Hall. *Family Fortunes: Men and Women of the English Middle Class*. Chicago: University of Chicago Press, 1987.

Duby, Georges, ed. *A History of Private Life*, vol. II: *Revelations of the Medieval World*. Cambridge, Mass.: Harvard University Press, 1988.

Hanawalt, Barbara, ed. *Women and Work in Preindustrial Europe*. Bloomington, Ind.: Indiana University Press, 1986.

Howell, Martha C. *Women, Production, and Patriarchy in Late Medieval Cities*. Chicago: University of Chicago Press, 1986.

Hunt, Margaret. *The Middling Sort: Commerce, Gender, and the Family in England, 1680–1780*. Berkeley and Los Angeles: University of California Press, 1996.

Klapisch-Zuber, Christiane. *Women, Family, and Ritual in Renaissance Italy*. Chicago: University of Chicago Press, 1985.

Korda, Natasha. *Shakespeare's Domestic Economies: Gender and Property in Early Modern England*. Philadelphia: University of Pennsylvania Press, 2002.

Kowaleski, Maryanne and P. J. P. Goldberg, eds. *Medieval Domesticity: Home, Housing and Household in Medieval England*. Cambridge: Cambridge University Press, 2008.

Schama, Simon. *The Embarrassment of Riches: An Interpretation of Dutch Culture in the Golden Age*. London: Collins, 1987.

Wunder, Heide. *He is the Sun, She is the Moon: Women in Early Modern Germany*. Cambridge, Mass: Harvard University Press, 1998.

NOTES

1. I include myself in that charge. My *Women, Production, and Patriarchy in Late Medieval Cities* (Chicago: University of Chicago Press, 1986) made no clear distinction between these economies.

2. Fernand Braudel, *The Wheels of Commerce*, vol. 2: *Civilization and Capitalism*, trans. Siân Reynolds (London: Collins, 1982).

3. Useful literature includes John Day, *Money and Finance in the Age of Merchant Capitalism* (London: Blackwell, 1999); Jan Luiten van Zanden, *The Rise and Decline of Holland's Economy: Merchant Capitalism and the Labour Market* (Manchester: Manchester University Press, 1993); Michel Beaud, *A History of Capitalism, 1500–2000* (New York: Monthly Review Press, 2001); Immanuel Wallerstein, *The Modern World System: Capitalist Agriculture and the Origins of the European World Economy in the Sixteenth Century* (New York: Academic Press, 1976); Andre Gunder Frank, *World Accumulation, 1492–1789* (New York: Monthly Review Press, 1978).

4. For general discussions of honor, see Julian Pitt-Rivers, "Honor," in David Sills, ed., *International Encyclopedia of the Social Sciences*, 18 vols (New York: Macmillan, 1968), 6: 503–11; idem, "Honor and Social Status," in J. G. Peristiany, ed., *Honour and Shame: The Values of Mediterranean Society* (Chicago: University of Chicago Press, 1966); also Friedrich Zunkel, "Ehre," in Werner Conze, Otto Brunner, and Reinhard Koselleck, eds, *Geschichtliche Grundbegriffe: Historisches Lexikon zur politisch-sozialen Sprache in Deutschland*, 8 vols (Stuttgart: E. Klett, 1972–97), 2: 1–63.

5. First published in 1528 but begun in 1508: Baldassarre Castiglione, *The Book of the Courtier* (New York: W. W. Norton, 2002).

6. Cited in Martha Carlin, "Shops and Shopping in the Thirteenth Century: Three Texts," in Lawrin Armstrong, Ivana Elbl, and Martin M. Elbl, eds, *Money, Markets and Trade in Late Medieval Europe* (Leiden; Boston: Brill, 2007), 513.

7. Howard Kaminsky, "Estate, Nobility, and the Exhibition of Estate in the Later Middle Ages," *Speculum*, 68 (3) (July 1993): 684–709.

8. Felicity Heal, "The Idea of Hospitality in Early Modern England," *Past & Present*, 102 (February 1984): 66–93.

9. For a convenient modern abridged edition, see Richard Hakluyt, *Voyages and Discoveries: The Principal Navigations, Voyages, Traffiques and Discoveries of the English Nation*, ed. Jack Beeching (Harmondsworth: Penguin Books, 1972).

10. For this typology, see Zunkel, "Ehre"; Merry E. Wiesner, "Wandervogels and Women: Journeymen's Concepts of Masculinity in Early Modern Germany," *Journal of Social History*, 24 (4) (Summer 1991): 767–82; Ruth Mazo Karras, *From Boys to Men: Formations of Masculinity in Late Medieval Europe* (Philadelphia: University of Pennsylvania Press, 2003), especially chapter 4. For literary expressions of this code, see Herman Pleij, "Restyling Wisdom, Remodeling the Nobility, and Caricaturing the Peasant: Urban Literature in the Late Medieval Low Countries," *Journal of Interdisciplinary History*, 32 (4) (Spring 2002): 689–704.

11. For a discussion of "bourgeois" honor and its emergence in early modern England, see Reta A. Terry, "'Vows to the Blackest Devil': Hamlet and the Evolving Code of Honor in Early Modern England," *Renaissance Quarterly*, 52 (4) (Winter 1999): 1070–86; Richard Cust, "Honor and Politics in Early Stuart England," *Past & Present*, 27 (149) (February 1995): 57–94.

12. For representative empirical studies, see Margaret Wensky, *Die Stellung der Frau in der stadtkölnischen Wirtschaft im Spätmittelalter* (Cologne: Böhlau, 1980); Barbara Hanawalt, ed., *Women and Work in Preindustrial Europe* (Bloomington, Ind.: Indiana University Press, 1986). For an analysis of the empirical and interpretative literature on women and guilds in the late Middle Ages, see Maryanne Kowaleski and Judith M. Bennett, "Crafts, Gilds, and Women in the Middle Ages: Fifty Years after Marian K. Dale," *Signs*, 14 (2) (Winter 1989): 474–501.

13. For the literature on lay learning in the Low Countries, see Hilde De Ridder-Symoens, "The Changing Face of Centers of Learning, 1400–1700," in Alasdair A. MacDonald and Michael W. Twomey, eds, *Schooling and Society: The Ordering and Reordering of Knowledge in the Western Middle Ages* (Leuven: Peeters, 2004), 115–38.

14. For an explanation of such legal customs, see Martha C. Howell, *The Marriage Exchange* (Chicago: University of Chicago Press, 1986).

15. See, for example, Christiane Klapisch-Zuber, *Women, Family, and Ritual in Renaissance Italy* (Chicago: University of Chicago Press, 1985) on Florence, and Anna Bellavitis, *Famille, genre, transmission à Venise au XVIe siècle* (Rome: Ecole Française de Rome, 2008) on Venice.

16. See, for an example of such a case, the article by Walter Prevenier, "Violence against Women in a Medieval Metropolis: Paris around 1400," in Bernard S. Bachrach and David Nicholas, eds, *Law, Custom, and the Social Fabric in Medieval Europe: Essays in Honor of Bryce Lyon* (Kalamazoo, Mich.: Medieval Institute Publications, 1990), 262–84.

17. For this evidence, see Martha C. Howell, "Citizenship and Gender: The Problem of Women's Political Status in Late Medieval Cities of Northern Europe," in Mary Erler and Maryanne Kowaleski, eds, *Women and Power in the Middle Ages* (Athens: University of Georgia Press, 1987), 37–60.

18. See Sarah Rees-Jones's essay "Public and Private Space and Gender in Medieval Europe," in this volume for a definition that puts more emphasis on accessibility than governance. Understood as sites "open to all without restriction," there were "public spaces" during much of the Middle Ages. In that sense, public space always existed; the issue here, however, is how the space is governed, for the benefit of whom, and how that governance is justified. It is that ordering function that "produces" public space as I have defined it.

19. For this argument see in particular Georges Duby, ed., *A History of Private Life*, vol. II: *Revelations of the Medieval World* (Cambridge, Mass.: Harvard University Press, 1988), especially the introduction by Georges Duby, 1–33.

20. For a study of the multifunctionality of the medieval marketplace, see James Masschaele, "The Public Space of the Marketplace in Medieval England," *Speculum*, 77 (2002): 383–421.

21. See, for the relative claustration of patrician Italian women, Richard A. Goldthwaite, "The Florentine Palace as Domestic Architecture," *The American Historical Review*, 77 (4) (October 1972): 977–1012, and Roger Chartier, ed., *A History of Private Life*, vol. III: *Passions of the Renaissance* (Cambridge, Mass.: Harvard University Press, 1989).

22. See Kathryn Reyerson's "Urban Economies," in this volume. In my view, part of the problem is the dearth of adequately comparable sources and insufficient attention to the political and economic histories of the various cities.

23. For representative evidence, see Howell, *Women, Production and Patriarchy* and Heide Wunder, *He is the Sun, She is the Moon: Women in Early Modern Germany* (Cambridge, Mass: Harvard University Press, 1998).

24. Shennon Hutton, "Women, Men, and Markets: The Gendering of Market Space in Late Medieval Ghent," in Albrecht Classen, ed., *Urban Space in the Middle Ages and Early Modern Age* (Berlin; New York: Walter de Gruyter, 2009). More generally see Shennon Hutton, *Women and Economic Activities in Late Medieval Ghent* (New York: Palgrave Macmillan, 2011).

25. Sarah Rees Jones's "Public and Private Space and Gender in Medieval Europe" provides excellent evidence concerning these developments in late medieval England.

26. For a useful development of a similar argument, see Felicity Riddy, "'Burgeis' Domesticity in Late-Medieval England," in Maryanne Kowaleski and P. J. P. Goldberg, eds, *Medieval Domesticity: Home, Housing and Household in Medieval England* (Cambridge: Cambridge University Press, 2008), 14–37.

27. Torquato Tasso, *Discorso della virtùfeminile e donnesca*, ed. Maria Luisa Doglio (Palermo: Sellerio, 1997), 56–57, quoted in Evelyn Welch, *Shopping in the Renaissance: Consumer Cultures in Italy 1400–1600* (New Haven: Yale University Press, 2005), 221–22.

28. Simon Schama, *The Embarrassment of Riches: An Interpretation of Dutch Culture in the Golden Age* (London: Collins, 1987).

29. Wunder, *He is the Sun*, 81.

30. Robert Cleaver, *A Godlie Forme of Householde Government: For the Ordering of Private Families, According to the Direction of Gods Word* (London, 1612), 167–68, quoted in Alexandra Shepard, "Manhood, Credit and Patriarchy in Early Modern England, c. 1580–1640," *Past & Present*, 167 (2000): 75–106. For the way these tropes were endlessly reproduced in drama, see Natasha Korda, *Shakespeare's Domestic Economies: Gender and Property in Early Modern England* (Philadelphia: University of Pennsylvania Press, 2002).

31. For an argument about the fundamentally enduring quality of patriarchy, see Judith M. Bennett, *History Matters: Patriarchy and the Challenge of Feminism* (Philadelphia: University of Pennsylvania Press, 2006), 54–81.

32. For a discussion of the importance of credit in the late medieval/early modern commercial economy, see Craig Muldrew, *Economy of Obligation: The Culture of Credit and Social Relations in Early Modern England* (New York: St. Martin's Press, 1998); Martha C. Howell, *Commerce before Capitalism in Europe, 1300–1600* (New York: Cambridge University Press, 2010); and the sources they cite.

33. Studies of the later early modern period have amply demonstrated the role that women actually played in building and preserving familial capital, but they have also revealed how invisible women's contributions were made to seem. See, for example, Leonore Davidoff and Catherine Hall, *Family Fortunes: Men and Women of the English Middle Class, 1780–1850* (Chicago: University of Chicago Press, 1987); Margaret R. Hunt, *The Middling Sort: Commerce, Gender, and the Family in England, 1680–1780* (Berkeley; Los Angeles: University of California Press, 1996).

....

CHAPTER 36

TOWARD THE WITCH CRAZE

....

LAURA STOKES

In May 1589 the inhabitants were holding a carnival at Lützen…A man named Claude Choteau was returning at nightfall from there to a neighboring village called Wisembach, and had climbed the better part of the hill which stands between the two places, when he was suddenly pulled up by a violent whirlwind. He looked about in astonishment and could see no reason for such an unusual happening, for everywhere else it was perfectly calm. Then he observed in a retired corner…six masked women dancing around a table laid with much gold and silver, tossing their heads like mad women; and near them was a man sitting upon a black bull watching them as if he were some casual passer-by. He stood still for a little, therefore, to collect himself and observe it all more closely; but they instantly disappeared and vanished from his sight. So, recovering from his fright, he resumed his journey and had passed the top of the hill when behold! those women were following him behind, tossing their heads about as before, and preserving as if by agreement a profound silence. Before them went a man with a black face and hands curved like hooks.

Nicolas Remy, *Demonolatry* (1595)[1]

THE strange bacchanal that Remy described is the witches' sabbath, the centerpiece of the imaginative and deadly early modern concept of the diabolic witch. Contained within this stereotyped image of the witches' dance were the conceptual prerequisites for the early modern witch craze that claimed tens of thousands of lives: the narrative context for denunciations and the profile of the predominantly female ideal suspect. The witch craze was an early modern phenomenon, but the stereotype that formed its underpinnings was a product of the late Middle Ages, with its descriptive capstone in the late fifteenth-century *Malleus maleficarum* (*Hammer of the Witches*) of the Dominican inquisitor Heinrich Kramer.

Theologians and canon lawyers of the early Middle Ages had laid the groundwork for a skeptical attitude toward sorcery, labeling as superstition a wide swath of both common and elite magical practices. One of the responses to the influx of Arabic learning during the central Middle Ages was a renewed interest in magic among literate men in Europe, creating tension with the skeptical tradition, and by the late fourteenth and early fifteenth centuries this interest in magic had sparked concern, condemnation, and a wider scholarly belief in the efficacy and danger of magic. Ordinary people had always believed in magic and, at times, feared its practitioners. By the mid-fifteenth century, the educated men who presided over criminal courts were ready to hear them.

This history was to have profound ramifications during the early modern period, as the concern over magic in the fifteenth century forged a new concept of the sorcerous malefactor who was both distinctly gendered female and ornately diabolical: the early modern witch. As the idea of the diabolical witch spread throughout Europe, so did the persecution of the imagined legions of the devil's allies. During the early modern witch hunts as many as 60,000 people died, over 70 percent of them women. Scholars of the witch hunts generally agree that although the predominance of women among the accused demands explanation, witch hunting was not "woman hunting." In fact, the demonological stereotype of the witch was far more sharply gendered than were the persecutions. The gender profile of the victims of witch hunts varied greatly. In some regions, such as Normandy, the majority of the accused were actually male.

The focus of concern regarding magic during the late Middle Ages depended greatly on one's social status. The powerful—kings and popes—feared assassination by learned, male magicians. The concerns of ordinary people were more quotidian. Our evidence points to a long tradition of village magic, with both benign and malicious aims. The gender of these popular magicians (both real and imagined) varied regionally. One particular regional stereotype, the Alpine witch of what is today northern Switzerland, played an important role in the development of the witchcraft concept that was to be so influential in the sixteenth and seventeenth centuries. The Alpine witch, strongly gendered female and terrifying to the core, was the dominant popular witch stereotype in the region where the theological conception of the diabolic witch was refined during the fifteenth century.

THE TURNING POINT

In examining the question of why the diabolic stereotype and the persecution of witches developed in the Alpine region during the first half of the fifteenth century, scholars have long focused on the relationship between witchcraft and heresy. The importance of this connection received an early, fraudulent impetus in the form of documents forged by a nineteenth-century anti-Catholic polemicist, the Baron de Lamothe-Langon. The forgeries purported to show that the first witch hunts took place under the auspices of the inquisition of Toulouse, as an outgrowth of the persecution of Cathars in thirteenth-century Languedoc. The forged documents were good enough to convince scholars for nearly a century, and lent credence to the predominant explanation: that it was inquisitors who first fused sorcery and heresy into the new crime of witchcraft, laying the groundwork for three centuries of witch hunting.[2]

When the forgeries were unmasked in the 1970s, the role of inquisitors naturally required reassessment. The picture that has emerged in the subsequent scholarship, while pointing to early secular trials and downplaying the causal nature of inquisitorial involvement, reveals nonetheless that inquisitors played a crucial role in the development of the diabolic witch concept. It was not in the persecution of Cathars in thirteenth-century Toulouse, but in the persecution of Waldensians in Fribourg in 1429 and 1430, that interrogations of suspected heretics produced confessions of sorcery. The fact that Fribourg sat at a linguistic boundary, with the accused Waldensians mostly speaking German and their judges speaking French, may have contributed to a crucial linguistic slippage that took place there. The French term *vaudois*, which originally meant Waldensian, came during the fifteenth century to refer to both heretics and witches. This in turn may have contributed to the shift around 1430, whereby judges questioning Waldensians began to seek out confessions of witchcraft.[3] The ambiguity between Waldensians and witches persisted to the end of the fifteenth century, when the Dominican inquisitor Heinrich Kramer put his pen to the work of eradicating it.[4]

The persecution of Waldensians in Fribourg, however, is only one of several interwoven events that contributed to the development of the idea of the diabolic witch. The inquisitor in the Fribourg trials was Ulric de Torrenté, who worked under the authority of the bishop of Lausanne. One of the key demonological texts written during the 1430s, the anonymous *Errores gazariorum* (*Errors of the Cathars*), seems to have been written within the circle of Lausannois clerics between 1431 and 1437. The *Errores* described not the titular Cathars, but instead a new sect of the witches, conceived explicitly as a heretical, diabolic sect bound to the execution of harmful magic. The tract describes the witches' gathering as a synagogue, or congregation, under a demonic master, thereby offering the first clear description of the witches' sabbath. It should be noted that the references to Judaism in "synagogue" and "sabbath" were not at all coincidental, but the product of a parallel demonization of European Jews.[5]

Although recent scholarship has demonstrated that Ulric de Torrenté was probably not the original composer of the *Errores* (Ponce Feugeyron of Savoy is more likely), a later version of the manuscript contains details from a witch trial Ulric conducted in Vevey in 1438. Clearly, the new "crime" of diabolic witchcraft was a subject of discussion and concern in the diocese. The persistence of this concern was demonstrated over the following generation in a series of early witch trials conducted under the bishop of Lausanne, Georges de Saluces. These trials are remarkably well documented and provide an important source for the study of early witch trials. They are notable also for the predominance of men among the accused. Although there is evidence that the female gendering of witchcraft was already emerging in the demonological literature of the 1430s, in these trials, magicians (whether explicitly diabolic or not) were still predominantly men.[6]

Although the events in the diocese of Lausanne demonstrate both the active interest and early involvement of inquisitors, other key contributors to the development of the witchcraft concept during the early fifteenth century worked in different contexts. Johannes Nider, whose *Formicarius* (*The Ant Hill*, c.1436) included a lengthy discussion of witchcraft, was a Dominican reformer and a university theologian.[7] Claude Tholosan, a lay magistrate and judge, described his experience overseeing a massive witch hunt in Dauphiné in his 1436 treatise *Ut magorum et maleficiorum errores* (*As the Errors of Magicians and Witches*).[8] Not only was Tholosan a secular judge, the trials he oversaw were both earlier (beginning in 1426) and far more extensive (with a reported 258 accused) than anything the Lausanne inquisitors are known to have conducted. The argument that the inquisition created the crime of witchcraft can be relegated to the dustbin of history, as the product of nineteenth-century anti-Catholic polemic. The involvement of inquisitors is undeniable, but their contribution was only one part of a more complex puzzle.

THREE KEY TRANSFORMATIONS

The turning point of the 1430s required three key transformations. The first was the emergence of a specific demonological discourse emphasizing the importance of apostasy, and hence of heresy, to the crime of witchcraft. The second was the transformation of secular criminal justice such that its prosecutorial tools included all the necessary mechanisms. The third was an important change in the conception of magic itself, which enabled learned men to imagine illiterate women as agents of sorcery.

Through the first transformation, witchcraft came to be viewed as Satanism and apostasy. The idea that magic required the adulation of demons stretched back all the way to Augustine, but in the early Middle Ages claims of magical power were often viewed as fraud or superstition. With the growing interest in magic that emerged among elite men in the thirteenth century, belief in the efficacy of magic grew. Certain methods of divination and prognostication, such as astrology, were deemed legitimate readings of the book of nature. Most magic, however, was soundly condemned by the theological consensus that emerged in the fourteenth century. Magic, including specifically the learned and often clerical art of necromancy, was deemed diabolical in origin. This condemnation was confirmed and codified by the theological faculty of Paris in 1398. The faculty declared as errors and blasphemies a list of the various claims that magical arts were not diabolical in origin or possibly even rooted in divine revelation. The University of Paris decision is often pointed to as a crucial moment in the demonization of magic, as it provided a definitive argument against the learned defenders of magic.[9]

The theological position that magic required the adulation of demons meant that all magic bordered on apostasy. But the description of witchcraft that emerged in the demonological literature of the early fifteenth century went further. The writers of the 1430s attached the simple if diabolic practice of magic to a chthonic nexus of evil, an amalgamation of dark stereotypes that had been applied to the early Christians by their persecutors in ancient Rome. The essential elements of this nexus were the most disturbing perversions: child murder, cannibalism, deviant sex, and the worship of evil. The stereotype as it was applied to one group of religious outsiders after another was heavily overdetermined with the inversion of social norms and the violation of taboos.[10] Medieval heretics, especially the Cathars, were accused of actually worshiping the devil. They were thought to engage in sexual perversions and licentious living under the guise of piety. Heretical groups were said to use cannibalistic rites of initiation and seduce or trick new members into their ranks. The early fifteenth-century text *Errores gazariorum* attached all of these elements to the newly imagined sect of the witches.

> When the devil has heard and accepted the oath of fidelity from the seduced person...the poor seduced person adores the presiding devil and pays homage to him; and as a sign of homage kisses the devil...on the anus...These things having been done, that pestiferous sect rejoices together and dines at the reception of the new heretic...and murdered children are devoured by them.... The presiding devil cries out that the lights be extinguished...They join themselves carnally...and the natural order is little observed. When the unspeakable abominations are over and the lights are relit they eat and drink for the journey home.[11]

The chief difference between the *Errores gazariorum* and any of the overwrought descriptions of heretical antinomianism that emerged from the pens of medieval polemicists was the addition of sorcery. The sect was said to exist for the purpose of plaguing humankind with magical harm, and the new initiate's oath supposedly included the explicit promise to practice harmful magic (*maleficia*).

The second crucial transformation of the late Middle Ages was a central European revolution in secular criminal justice that completely reoriented the aims and methods of prosecution. In essence, the personal mode of accusatory process was replaced by the official mode of inquisitorial process, and the logic of proving innocence through divine intervention was replaced with that of proving guilt through human agency. The impact of these transformations in facilitating witch hunts was profound, and although the completeness of the revolution has at times been overstated, its details bear close examination.

The basis of the old accusatory process was the principle that all court cases, criminal as well as civil, were essentially private grievances of one party against another. Criminal cases were initiated by the aggrieved party, and the accuser played the role of prosecutor. Within accusatory process, ideally the accuser was held in equal jeopardy with the defendant. If the truth of the accusation was not proved to the satisfaction of the judge, the accuser could be subject to the penalty that would have been imposed on the defendant. The first consistent records of criminal justice from the Alpine region (where the stereotype of diabolic witchcraft finally coalesced in the fifteenth century) date to the late fourteenth century. On the one hand, they provide little evidence that such harsh penalties were imposed on accusers. On the other hand, they reveal a culture of slander prosecution against frivolous accusers, with financial penalties and at times even temporary banishment. Although it does not seem that the full weight of the theoretical risk of accusation was brought to bear, frivolous criminal suits were clearly discouraged.

In the inquisitorial process that was gradually adopted into central European practice, the burdens and risks of prosecution were lifted from the accuser and became the particular responsibilities of specific officials. The etymological kinship of secular inquisitorial process and the inquisitions of the medieval church is no accident. The two legal forms shared much in their structure and theory. In particular, both made use of the inquest, or top-down, ex officio investigation. They were not identical, however. While inquisitorial process was an ideal type, reflected only poorly in a messy and mixed reality, religious inquisition was an institutional structure of the hierarchical and relatively well-organized church.[12] What had originally been ad hoc investigations under the authority of the pope or of individual bishops came to be fairly consistent in practice during the late Middle Ages, under the influence of generations of manual-writing inquisitors and the authority of canon law. The early modern inquisitions, in particular the Roman Inquisition, enjoyed the reputation of fair and reasonable courts and were even preferred over the less predictable, harsher secular courts.[13] Yet the modern reputation of the inquisition as an oppressive institution is not undeserved. The medieval inquisitors pioneered the very aspects of procedure that made early modern inquisitorial process so dreadful: long imprisonment during investigations, torture, secret witnesses and accusers, and the unimpeachable unity of investigator, prosecutor, and judge. The medieval inquisitions were effective tools of persecution, and when secular courts adopted many of their techniques, without the limits and safeguards imposed by canon law and inquisitional practice, the resulting system was ideal for witch hunting.

One method of inquisition practice that was to have particular relevance for the witch hunts was torture. As a technique, torture had always been available in at least some cases, but it appears to have been rarely used in ordinary medieval criminal process. Legal theorists have argued that this was because the logic of proof in the Middle Ages demanded a different kind of evidence.[14] As a means of proof, oaths relied on honor and reputation, but also on divine intervention. To break an oath or swear falsely explicitly invited divine retribution on the oath-breaker. While the oath persisted in early modern legal procedure, it took on a secondary role in the matter of proof. The evidence sought under inquisitorial process was not that which would be demonstrated through divine agency, but that which could be perceived through human agency. The beginnings of forensic science grew out of this impetus by the seventeenth century. So too did an increasing reliance on torture, as the tool of choice to elicit the queen of proofs, a confession.

There were substantial barriers to the widespread use of torture, however, which had to be overcome before it could take a central place in the process of criminal investigation. Free men and women were protected from torture within common legal practice, as were (with increasing force with the ascendance of social rank) burghers, patricians, and the entire nobility. This left few people who were clearly vulnerable to torture: slaves, serfs, and outlaws. Unlike slaves or serfs, the status and identity of outlaws was rarely clear. In theory, an outlaw had been declared such by a judicial proclamation. In practice, however, outlawry was more often defined by outsider status. *Schädliche Leute* (dangerous people) was a legal catch-all category in medieval Germany that bundled together whole groups of strangers as potential outlaws and perennial suspects. These "dangerous people" were nonresidents, vagrants, and wanderers—some actual outlaws and career criminals, others simple outsiders. As men and women without local reputation, their word was nearly worthless. If arrested they could not swear believably to their own innocence, and no one was likely to swear for them. Without the honor and reputation sufficient to use the protection of oaths, outsiders were subjected to much harsher criminal justice, including torture and a much higher incidence of mutilation and execution. In the late fourteenth and early fifteenth centuries, in the wake of the recovery following the Black Death, communities became less cohesive under the pressure of migration and resettlement. As strangers took up residence in new communities, insider protections began to erode. Where the history of torture can be closely observed, we can see how first newly settled free residents, then burghers, then patricians, and finally even the nobility came to be potential subjects of torture.[15] Although higher status continued to provide some protection from torture, no one was truly immune any longer.

Gendering Witchcraft

The third transformation that was crucial to laying the groundwork for the early modern witch hunts was the one that, in the end, is also most important to explaining the gender shift in the conception of magical crime: the transformation of the idea of magic from a learned art to a by-product of carnally sealed diabolism. The first part of this process was the acceptance of magic as efficacious rather than as mere superstition, which was one effect of the clerical enthusiasm for necromancy. The second step was the slow conflation of elite magic, necromancy in particular, with popular sorcery. Third was the decisive demonization of magic at the end of the fourteenth century. Finally came the shift of inquisitorial and judicial concern from the self-interested magic of necromancers to the socially destructive magic feared by ordinary people, a development remarkably well-suited to the emerging idea of a diabolical conspiracy.

The acceptance of the power of magic was promoted by the respect accorded the authority of Arabic, Hebrew, and classical texts in the renaissance of the twelfth century. The systems of magic described in occult texts were highly learned, and they generated substantial interest among western clerics. In particular, enthusiasm began to circulate for the potentially powerful art of invoking demons: necromancy. Elite understandings of necromancy, the relationship of the magician and demon within it, and the belief that the art was efficacious, were all crucial to the later development of the diabolic witch.[16]

The conflation of necromancy and popular sorcery can be traced in medieval inquisitors' manuals. In his *Practica inquisitionis heretice pravitatis* (*The Conduct of Inquisitions into Heretical Depravity*) of the 1320s, Bernard Gui described a variety of magical elements that were far more characteristic of popular sorcery than of necromancy, specifically the use of ordinary and base objects as magical implements, and the focus of magic on either healing or harm. From this it is clear that at least some inquisitors were encountering reports of popular sorcery in their investigations. But the modes of magic

with which inquisitors were most familiar would have been necromancy and invocation, not barnyard curses and blessings. In bringing together the distinct magical practices of popular magic and learned necromancy, Gui laid the conceptual foundation for
diabolic witchcraft. In the 1370s, Nicolas Eymeric took this a step further, arguing that
all magic had demonic power at its basis and necessarily involved some form of diabolism. The metaphysics of demonic magic had been extended to cover all forms of magic,
concretizing the concept of the fundamental dependence of magic on heresy.[17]

The convergence of popular concepts of sorcery and clerical understandings of necromancy reached its apotheosis in the fifteenth century. Two of the key contributors to the
cumulative concept of the diabolic witch, Johannes Nider and Heinrich Kramer, both
lived and worked in the region of upper Germany that abutted the Alps. Along with the
received material of the developing demonological tradition, both of them, and especially Kramer, were also grappling with the details of the indigenous witch concept, the
Alpine witch. It was in the Alpine witch that Kramer found popular confirmation for his
strict female gendering of the witch cult.

One of the reasons that the early modern witches were predominantly women can
be traced to the fact that the Germanic popular concept of the Alpine witch, which predated the concept of the diabolic witch and helped to determine the details of demonology, was strictly female. *Die Hexe* (witch) was clearly gendered female before any of
the elements of diabolism entered into early witch trials. Not all of the important early
witch trials were trials of women. The Lausannois trials that gave rise to the demonological contribution of the *Errores gazariorum* were mainly trials of men. Nonetheless,
the image of the diabolic witch that emerged by the end of the fifteenth century was
unequivocally gendered female. One reason for this was that as the cumulative witch
concept was being completed by Heinrich Kramer in the late fifteenth century, he drew
his empirical data mostly from popular ideas of the Alpine witch.

Village magic, as practiced throughout premodern Europe, had both beneficial and
harmful aims. Properly speaking, village magic and witchcraft are categorically different things: village magic was a varied set of practices, while witchcraft was an idea, a
category of imagining. The Alpine witch was conceived as a powerful malicious entity,
possibly even supernatural and inhuman in her mythic origins, but conceived of as
human by the fifteenth century.[18] Even before demonologists recast village magic and
popular witch fears in a demonological light, the Alpine witch was purely evil. To villagers living in the valleys beneath the Alps, witchcraft was one possible explanation
for a whole array of domestic and agricultural woes. The sudden sickness of a child, the
death of a husband, a cow that gave bloody milk, a horse that foundered, the creeping
blight in a kitchen garden, and the sudden hailstorm that destroyed a harvest—all of
these were otherwise inexplicable devastations. Men of the clergy might explain such
sufferings as the work of Providence, especially after the Reformation,[19] but to ordinary
people it made more sense to believe that such evils were the result of a malicious will.

The Alpine witch was the incarnation of malice. Originally, she was conceived entirely
independently of the devil, allied instead with the destructive forces of nature. In

particular, the Alpine witch was conceived as a wolf-rider. In 1433, in Basel, a man testified about an encounter with such a witch:

> He saw … Gerin Kolerin of Buckten riding toward him on a wolf. The wolf went its
> own way and she sat on its back holding its fur in her hand. …. He was so frightened
> that he trembled … and wanted to hide.[20]

Although such eyewitness accounts are relatively rare, wolves appear in other testimonies against suspected witches. In 1486, testimony sent from a rural village to the court
in Lucerne included a description of an eerie utterance by the suspected witch's child. At
play with other village children, the child reportedly said, "We have baby foxes and baby
wolves, and when my father is away, my mother feeds them on the barn floor." The same
suspected witch was supposedly seen riding a wolf on the equinox.[21]

Beyond her affinity for wolves, the other primary identifying characteristic of the
Alpine witch was her capacity, in some cases even a compulsion, to raise hailstorms.
This tendency to wreak widespread natural destruction was well-suited to the demonological concept of the witch as a member of a secret sect dedicated to the destruction of
Christian society. Hail-raising became a stock element of demonological descriptions of
witchcraft, and hail appeared frequently in early modern depictions of witchcraft. Some
scholars have gone so far as to argue that the collective nature of the damage wrought by
hailstorms was an important conceptual mirror of the collective nature of the imagined
sect of the witches during the early modern period.[22]

The figure of the wolf, however, was not exported from the Alpine region in demonological descriptions. Instead, the wolf was slowly replaced with the figure he represented in the medieval bestiaries: the devil. The process by which the devil supplanted
the wolf was a subtle one, and for a while the two figures coexisted. A case from early
sixteenth-century Basel demonstrates this nicely. Three women were arrested on
accusations of witchcraft and confessed. Two offered details of their seduction into
witchcraft by the devil in the form of a man. The third, however, testified instead about
her companion wolf, whom she had met under a willow tree and always rode to the
witches' meetings. A postscript to her confession reveals what seems to have been
an effort by her interrogators to reconcile her wolf with the devil they expected. In
a different hand, it mentions "her lover, the devil."[23] The analogic equivalence of wolf
and devil facilitated the accommodation of the Alpine witch to the emerging diabolic
witch concept.[24]

Written after Kramer's experience searching for witches around Lake Constance,
Heinrich Kramer's infamous witch-hunting manual, *Malleus maleficarum*, drew
directly on the regional concept of the Alpine witch. It was in Kramer's *Malleus* that
the feminization of witchcraft reached its apotheosis. Nowhere else is the female gender of witches as decisive and explicit as in the *Malleus maleficarum*, from the feminine
plural in its title that grammatically excluded men, to the assertions that witches were
generally women and that women were substantially more prone to becoming witches.

Kramer's explanation of why women are prone to witchcraft reads like standard scholastic misogyny:

> The wickedness of women is spoken of in Ecclesiasticus xxv: There is no head above the head of a serpent: and there is no wrath above the wrath of a woman...All wickedness is but little to the wickedness of a woman...What else is woman but a foe to friendship, an unescapable punishment, a necessary evil, a natural temptation, a desirable calamity, a domestic danger, a delectable detriment, an evil of nature, painted with fair colours!...When a woman thinks alone, she thinks evil...A wicked woman is by her nature quicker to waver in her faith, and consequently quicker to abjure the faith, which is the root of witchcraft...Just as through the first defect in their intelligence [women] are more prone to abjure the faith; so through their second defect of inordinate affections and passions they search for, brood over, and inflict various vengeances, either by witchcraft, or by some other means. Wherefore it is no wonder that so great a number of witches exist in this sex.[25]

There is nothing in the litany of the evils of women that was original to Kramer. He had, in the manner common to scholastic writing, borrowed widely and copiously from earlier authors, adding the weight of past authority to the substance of his work. However, the assertion that the inherent weaknesses of woman meant that she was more prone to commit magical crimes was an innovation of fifteenth-century demonology. Kramer adopted this assertion from Johannes Nider's treatment of witchcraft and gender in his *Formicarius*.

Scholastic misogynistic assumptions about the capacities of women had long excluded them from being likely magicians in the eyes of educated men. While Kramer presented the evils of women as straightforward evidence of their propensity for witchcraft, Nider had recognized and directly addressed the problem posed by the proposal that women were more likely to become witches. In Nider's *Formicarius*, structured as a dialogue between a student and a doctor of theology, the student-interlocutor expresses incredulity at the thought that women, with their inferior intellects, could be the agents of magic. In response, the theologian presents the new diabolic explanation of women's propensity for witchcraft that later played such a crucial role in Kramer's *Malleus*. The foundation of magic is spiritual submission to the devil, as opposed to the necromantic assertion of intellectual control over demonic forces. One result of this emphasis on diabolism as its basis was the feminization of magic.[26]

The feminization of magic, however, did not imply the exclusion of men from witchcraft. Instead, within fifteenth-century demonology, women appear both as the archetypical witches and as the specific agents of the seduction of particular men into the sect. A story that Nider related and Kramer later repeated exemplifies this. The tale came from one of Nider's informants, a judge who had presided over a series of witch trials. Two of the accused witches were a married couple, man and wife. The husband, a young man, broke under questioning in prison and not only confessed his witchcraft, but repented. He described how his wife had first become a witch, and then (in contrast to his socially expected role as her master) he had let her draw him into the sect. The sect of witches was dominated by women, and this inversion of the proper social order carried with it chaos, disorder, and destruction.

The heresy of the witches, sealed with the body, was conceived by Kramer as an explicitly gendered counterpart of the male-dominated heresy of the Waldensians.[27] Kramer's "Waldensians" were actually Utraquists, heretical Bohemian followers of Jan Hus. The witches and his "Waldensians," he argued, were the spearheads of a diabolic, apocalyptic attack on humanity. As such, the two sects were fundamentally linked in his eyes. The role of the witches in the conspiracy was unique. While heretics, "Waldensians" in particular, were evil by virtue of their doctrines, the witches were evil by virtue of their cruel deeds. This contrast between ideas and acts was highly gendered, drawing on the same logic that Nider had used to defend the proposition that witches could be women. The physicality of the witches' heresy was reflected in the highly carnal nature of their pact with devil. This emphasis on the witches' deeds was new to the demonological assessment of witchcraft. It was an innovation of Kramer's that was reflected in his repeated, detailed descriptions of the evils of witches, which he in turn had drawn from the reports of people who lived around Lake Constance and whose nightmares were haunted by the Alpine witch.

TOWARD THE WITCH CRAZE

Kramer's apocalyptic vision of the witches' sect was to prove well-suited to the fears of the post-Reformation era, providing the conceptual basis for the mass witch hunts of the late sixteenth and seventeenth centuries. The prerequisites for the witch craze had been forged in the fifteenth century: the concept of the diabolic sect, the fantasy of the witches' sabbath, the procedural tools of secular inquisitorial process, and the feminization of the witch. Once these prerequisites were in place, the stage was set for the European witch craze.

FURTHER READING

Bailey, Michael. "From Sorcery to Witchcraft: Clerical Conceptions of Magic in the Later Middle Ages," *Speculum*, 76 (4) (2001): 960–90.

Bailey, Michael. "The Feminization of Magic and the Emerging Idea of the Female Witch in the Late Middle Ages," *Essays in Medieval Studies*, 19 (2002): 120–34.

Cohn, Norman. *Europe's Inner Demons: The Demonization of Christians in Medieval Christendom*. Chicago: Chicago University Press, 2000.

Herzig, Tamar. "Flies, Heretics, and the Gendering of Witchcraft," *Magic, Ritual, and Witchcraft*, 5 (1) (Summer 2010): 51–80.

Kieckhefer, Richard. *Magic in the Middle Ages*. Cambridge: Cambridge University Press, 1989.

Modestin, Georg and Katrin Utz Tremp, eds. "Hexen, Herren und Richter: Les sorcières, les seigneurs et les juges," *Schweizerische Zeitschrift für Geschichte*, 52 (2) (2002): 103–62.

Ostorero, Martine, Agostino Paravicini Bagliani, Kathrin Utz Tremp, and Catherine Chène, eds. *L'imaginaire du sabbat: Édition critique des textes les plus anciens (1430 c.–1440 c.).* Lausanne: Université de Lausanne, 1999.

Stokes, Laura. *Demons of Urban Reform: Early European Witch Trials and Criminal Justice, 1430–1530.* Houndmills, Basingstoke: Palgrave Macmillan, 2011.

Utz Tremp, Kathrin. *Von der Häresie zur Hexerei: "Wirkliche" und imaginäre Sekten im Spätmittelalter.* Hannover: Hahnsche Buchhandlung, 2008.

Notes

1. Nicolas Remy, *Demonolatry* (Secaucus: University Books, 1974), book I, chapter XIV, 48–49.
2. On the forgeries, see Norman Cohn, *Europe's Inner Demons: An Enquiry Inspired by the Great Witch-Hunt* (New York: Basic Books, 1975), 126–46, and Richard Kieckhefer, *European Witch Trials* (Berkeley: University of California Press, 1976), especially 17. The old standard interpretation can be found in Joseph Hansen, *Zauberwahn* (Munich: R. Oldenbourg, 1900).
3. Kathrin Utz Tremp, *Von der Häresie zur Hexerei: "Wirkliche" und imaginäre Sekten im Spätmittelalter* (Hannover: Hahn, 2008).
4. Tamar Herzig "Flies, Heretics, and the Gendering of Witchcraft," *Magic, Ritual, and Witchcraft*, 5 (1) (Summer, 2010), 51–80.
5. Cohn, *Europe's Inner Demons*. For general reference see the more recent, updated edition: Norman Cohn, *Europe's Inner Demons: The Demonization of Christians in Medieval Christendom* (Chicago: University of Chicago Press, 2000).
6. Georg Modestin and Kathrin Utz Tremp, "Hexen, Herren, und Richter," *Schweizerische Zeitschrift für Geschichte*, 52 (2) (2002), 103–104. Martine Ostorero, "Les chasses aux sorciers dans la Pays du Vaud (1430–1530)," *Schweizerische Zeitschrift für Geschichte*, 52 (2) (2002), 109–14. On Feugeyron see Ostorero, "Itinéraire d'un inquisiteur gâté: Ponce Feugeyron, les juifs et le sabbat des sorciers," *Médiévales*, 43 (2002), 103–17.
7. Michael Bailey, *Battling Demons* (University Park, Pa.: Pennsylvania State University Press, 2003).
8. Pierette Paravy, "Zur Genesis der Hexenverfolgungen im Mittelalter: Der Traktat des Claude Tholosan," in Andreas Blauert, ed., *Frühe Hexenverfolgungen: Ketzer-, Zauberei- und Hexenprozesse des 15. Jahrhunderts* (Frankfurt am Main: Suhrkamp, 1990), 118–59.
9. Richard Kieckhefer, *Magic in the Middle Ages* (Cambridge: Cambridge University Press, 1989).
10. Cohn, *Europe's Inner Demons*.
11. Alan Kors and Edward Peters, "The *Errores Gazariorum* (1437)," in *Witchcraft in Europe, 400–1700* (Philadelphia: University of Pennsylvania Press, 2001), 160–61.
12. On inquisitorial process see Günter Jerouschek, "Die Herausbildung des peinlichen Inquisitionsprozesses im Spätmittelalter und in der frühen Neuzeit," *Zeitschrift für die gesamte Strafrechtswissenschaft*, 104 (1992), 328–60. On the medieval inquisitions see Bernard Hamilton, *The Medieval Inquisition* (New York: Holmes & Meier, 1981). On canon law, which also employed inquisitorial process, see James A. Brundage, *Medieval Canon Law* (New York: Longman, 1995).
13. Gustav Henningsen and John Tedeschi, eds, *The Inquisition in Early Modern Europe* (Dekalb, Ill.: Northern Illinois University Press, 1986).

14. This is the argument of John Langbein, *Torture and the Law of Proof: Europe and England in the Ancien Régime* (Chicago: University of Chicago Press, 2006).

15. Laura Stokes, "Experiments in Pain," in Marjorie Elizabeth Plummer and Robin Barnes, eds, *Ideas and Cultural Margins in Early Modern Germany: Essays in Honor of H. C. Erik Midelfort* (Burlington, Vt.: Ashgate, 2009), 239–54.

16. Michael Bailey, "The Feminization of Magic and the Emerging Idea of the Female Witch in the Late Middle Ages," *Essays in Medieval Studies*, 19 (2002), 120–34.

17. Michael Bailey, "From Sorcery to Witchcraft: Clerical Conceptions of Magic in the Later Middle Ages," *Speculum*, 76 (2001), 960–90.

18. On the Alpine witch generally, see Laura Stokes, *Demons of Urban Reform: Early European Witch Trials and Criminal Justice, 1430–1530* (Houndmills, Basingstoke: Palgrave Macmillan, 2011), 16ff.

19. H. C. Erik Midelfort, *Witch Hunting in Southwestern Germany 1562–1684: The Social and Intellectual Foundations* (Stanford, Calif.: Stanford University Press, 1972).

20. Staatsarchive Basel-Stadt, Leistungsbuch II, fol. 111r.

21. Eduard Hoffmann-Krayer, *Luzerner Akten zum Hexen- und Zauberwesen* (Zurich: [s. n.], 1900), 19–23. Translation in Stokes, *Demons of Urban Reform*, 182–85, here 183.

22. Wolfgang Behringer, "Climatic Change and Witch-Hunting: The Impact of the Little Ice Age on Mentalities," *Climatic Change*, 43 (1999): 335–51.

23. Staatsarchiv Basel-Stadt, Criminalia, 4, 3, fol. 12r.

24. Stokes, *Demons of Urban Reform*, especially 10–33.

25. Heinrich Institoris and Jakob Sprenger, *Malleus maleficarum* (London: J. Rodker, 1928), 43. In the last thirty years it has been definitively established that Heinrich Kramer (alias Institoris) was the sole author of the book.

26. Bailey, "Feminization of Magic."

27. On Kramer's take on Waldensians and witches, see Herzig, "Flies, Heretics, and the Gendering of Witchcraft."

CHAPTER 37

TOWARDS FEMINISM: CHRISTINE DE PIZAN, FEMALE ADVOCACY, AND WOMEN'S TEXTUAL COMMUNITIES IN THE LATE MIDDLE AGES AND BEYOND

ROBERTA L. KRUEGER

TANGLED ROOTS: THE ORIGINS OF FEMINISM IN MEDIEVAL FRANCE

WOMEN'S full legal and political enfranchisement, equal access to employment, and equity in compensation are ideals of modernity whose enactment as social realities remains imperfect even today. In western European history, it was many centuries before arguments for women's emancipation rose prominently to the surface: Olympe de Gouge's and Mary Wollstonecraft's treatises on the rights of woman date from 1791 and 1792 respectively. It was even longer before concrete political gains were realized. In France, for example, girls' elementary education was not universal and mandatory until the Ferry Laws of 1881–1882; the first public high schools for girls date from 1880. French women did not have the right to vote until 1944. Women in Europe, and indeed, the rest of the world, have yet to gain parity of political representation or equity of compensation and position in the workplace.

According to historian Christine Bard, the term "feminism" in France was first associated with the emancipation of women in the 1880s.[1] If we define feminism as the active struggle for women's legal and political equal rights, then this phenomenon was non-existent in medieval Europe. Yet if we shift our perspective to look for evidence of the promotion of women's intellectual activity, the defense of female moral equality, and the affirmation of women's contributions to their families and communities, then the record becomes far richer. Despite strictures against women learning to write or even to read and women's lack of equal access to education throughout the Middle Ages, literate women left an impressive record. Early writings by medieval women, often undertaken despite considerable opposition and within a climate that was hostile to women's learning, even if they do not make radical claims for female emancipation, must be considered as essential first steps in the very long road to women's universal education, a *sine qua non* of gender equality.

The early history of feminism in medieval culture is marked by paradox and contradiction. As Alcuin Blamires has shown, the misogynist tradition was accompanied by a distinct "case for women" throughout the medieval period: blatant misogyny called forth professions of female worth in arguments that attacked the authority of the misogynists, poking holes in their logic and questioning the validity of their claims.[2] Similarly, there was a remarkable gap between the political disenfranchisement that determined the lives of most women and strong examples of female rule, women's cultural patronage, and other forms of social influence and enterprise within elite households.[3] The elevation of woman as an imperious *domna* (lady) in troubadour lyric may mask masculine attempts to control her, and yet there were poems written in a female voice that subverted lyric conventions, as well as courtly romances that explored the confusion and instability of gender roles.[4] These roles may not have been as starkly divided in the cultural imagination as some moralists would have wished. Mordant satirical portraits of clever women who dupe their husbands in the fabliaux (short tales originating in the thirteenth century in which men's and women's appetites come into comic conflict) may have masked anxiety about women's power in the home and increasing presence in the workplace. Conduct books that attempted to prescribe limited social roles for women, principally in the home, and to counsel wives to be chaste and submissive may have been, for some readers, useful resources through which women could increase their social well-being and cultural capital.

If educational opportunities were scarce, and women's writing discouraged by churchmen and husbands, vibrant examples of women's literary creation have come down to us nonetheless in a variety of genres, from lyric poetry to mystical visions and didactic treatises. These were produced in royal and elite courts, bourgeois households, and religious communities, and they created female literary traditions that are particularly rich in the French vernacular.[5] In other words, throughout this period, cultural discourses about gender and the social realities of men's and women's lives were fraught with contradictions and inconsistencies. From such tangled roots, feminist thought gradually emerged in the writings of a number of notable women and men in France, England, and Italy from the late Middle Ages onward.[6]

As female literacy spread from convents to royal courts and noble domains and then to bourgeois households, from the tenth through the fifteenth centuries, women writers throughout Europe demonstrated their intellectual capacities, articulated moral and social values from a feminine perspective, and often expressed a sense of female agency while promoting the cause of women. Among the many writers throughout Europe whose expression of female subjectivity or female solidarity have commanded scholarly attention are the canoness Hrotsvit of Gandersheim (c.935–c.1002), who has been called the first woman historian of Germany; the talented Latinist and abbess Heloise (c.1101–1164), who wrote moving and persuasive letters to her estranged husband, the philosopher Peter Abelard, in twelfth-century France; Clemence of Barking (late 1100s), whose *Life of Saint Catherine* recounts the tale of an erudite maiden in Alexandria who debated pagan philosophers and was martyred for resisting the advances of the emperor; Marie de France (*fl.* 1160s–1190s), who portrayed women's constricted lives in courtly fictions at the court of Henry II Plantagenet and penned the first vernacular collection of Aesopic fables; twelfth- and thirteenth-century female troubadours from southern France and women *trouvères* from northern French courts; female mystics such as Hildegard of Bingen (1098–1179), Saint Bridget of Sweden (1303–1373), and the beguine Marguerite Porete, who was burned at the stake in 1310 for refusing to recant her *Mirror of Simple Souls*; Saint Catherine of Siena (1347–1380); Julian of Norwich (c.1342–c.1416) and Margery Kempe (c.1373–1438) in England—and many others. Modern scholarship continues to examine and expand the archives of learned women whose writings laid the groundwork for women's universal education and subsequent emancipation.[7] Many male writers also championed the cause of women, of course; many of the first "defenses of women" were penned by men who debated the woman question with evident rhetorical flourish and zest.[8] But women's written contributions to the debate, if rarer, are arguably more poignant, as they are informed by the speaker's own lived experience. For her role as a champion of women's moral and intellectual capacity and her remarkable literary activity, we will focus particularly on the late medieval author who was France's first professional woman of letters and has been hailed by some as the Western tradition's "first feminist," Christine de Pizan (1364–1430?).

Christine de Pizan was a prolific, esteemed writer in her time. Between 1399 and 1430, she composed an abundance of lyric and narrative poetry, allegorical treatises, autobiographical dream visions, and prose treatises for men and women of the French royal family and for the dukes of Burgundy. Circulating widely, first in manuscript and then in printed books, Christine's writings reached readers well beyond these courts. As was the case with much medieval literature, Christine's works fell out of favor after the Renaissance. Later, Christine was unjustly overlooked and in one case explicitly disparaged during the late nineteenth-century revival of medieval texts. In 1894, Gustave Lanson scathingly characterized Christine as "the first in that line of insufferable blue-stockings whose indefatigable facility was equaled only by her universal mediocrity."[9] But over the past century, thanks to the collective efforts of an international team of editors and critics, many of them female scholars, Christine's work has finally achieved recognition as a highly significant body of late medieval writing.

CHRISTINE DE PIZAN AND THE DEBATE ABOUT WOMEN

Christine de Pizan deserves a prominent position in any history of gender and women in the Middle Ages, for she embodies in many ways the contradictions and cultural transitions of her era. Poised at the threshold of the early modern period, sometimes seen as an early humanist for her debt to Italian forebears and for her learning, well versed in the ancient and contemporary texts that permeated medieval culture, Christine engaged in the creative recasting of medieval courtly conventions and in the bold critique of prevailing antifeminist discourse. As a self-taught intellectual who was not a cleric, an astrologer's daughter with proximity to the royal family who was herself non-noble, a young widow who turned to her pen to support her family, comprised of three young children, her mother, and a niece, Christine occupied a marginal and yet privileged position from which to observe late medieval mores and social and political life.

Written after her husband's untimely death in 1390, Christine's first literary compositions were rather conventional lyric poems on well-rehearsed themes related to love, some of them poignantly marked by her perspective as a widow who lamented her solitude and loss of a beloved spouse. Other courtly *dits* (short narrative poems) and love debates soon followed. In several of her early pieces, Christine shows a penchant for debunking antifeminist discourse in a rhetorically engaging, clever manner. For example, in "The Letter of the God of Love" (composed in 1399), speaking on behalf of defamed women everywhere, the God of Love himself complains about clerks and authors who portray women as fickle and loose; if this were so, he asks, why would men need to resort to such subterfuge to seduce them, as they do in Ovid's *The Art of Love* or Jean de Meun's *Romance of the Rose*?[10] Matters would be presented quite differently if women had written those books, the narrator claims ("Letter of the God of Love," ll. 407–423). In "The Tale of the Rose" (from 1402), the allegorical figure Lady Loyalty is sent by the God of Love to establish a chivalric order overseen by virtuous women who confer membership only on those men who honor women and defend them against base slander—surely a woman's fantasy of what chivalry might entail.[11] But Christine achieved visibility, indeed notoriety, as a champion of women's sensibilities when she penned an argumentative letter to a cleric, Jean de Montreuil, who had written an earlier treatise defending one of the most popular works of medieval literature, the *Romance of the Rose*.[12]

The *Romance of the Rose* is a two-part narrative poem recounting a courtly male lover's quest for the Lady, portrayed as a budding rose in a garden protected by allegorical figures who attempt to protect her chastity.[13] If the first 4,000 verses, composed by Guillaume de Lorris, present love in a courtly fashion, Jean de Meun's much longer continuation (more than 17,000 verses) conveys a more worldly view, fleshed out by a new cast of personifications, extended philosophical arguments, and sporadic antifeminist slurs. Often depicting a rather cynical view of relations between the sexes, Jean de Meun's narrative concludes with the lover's conquest of the Rose, an act tantamount to rape. Christine claimed among other things, here and in subsequent epistles, that Jean de Meun's use of language was vulgar, that several of the allegorical figures unjustly defamed women, blaming all of them for sins that only a few commit, that the conclusion was "horrible and shameful" (*Debate*, 60), and that despite some admirable moments, the work overall was an offense to moral decency, failing to be useful for the common good.[14]

Christine's letter prompted written responses from several prominent clerics, both pro- and anti-*Rose*. In the context of medieval disputation, such debate was perhaps nothing extraordinary. Yet not only did Christine—in her words a "woman of untrained intellect" (*Debate*, 50)—dare to confront established male intellectuals who were often condescending, she also collected several of the letters—not only her own but also those of a detractor—and bound these in a manuscript that she sent to the queen, Isabeau de Bavière, in 1402.[15] In so doing, Christine helped foster the first major literary debate in French history and inaugurated what Renaissance writers and subsequent historians would call the *querelle des femmes*, "the debate about women."[16]

Christine's role in the *Rose* debate seems to have secured her reputation as an articulate spokesperson for moral rectitude and the writer's social responsibility. Important works produced for the royal family and the Dukes of Burgundy followed suit, such as *The Path of Long Study* (1403), the *Book of Fortune's Transformation* (1403), dedicated to the king and prepared for the dukes of Berry, Burgundy, and Orleans, and a biography of King Charles V (1404). Breaking out of the mold of lyric poetry, Christine increasingly adopted prose for her moral treatises or, as in the case of *The Book of the Duke of True Lovers*, a mix of verse and prose.[17] She claimed that the latter work, a short romance recounting an unhappy love affair between a married woman and a besotted duke, was undertaken reluctantly; indeed, the story is told not in Christine's voice but in that of the Duke himself. Yet, ever the resourceful manipulator of courtly discourse for her own ends, Christine the author managed to portray the pitfalls of such amorous arrangements for women.

The Book of the Duke of True Lovers (written at some point between 1403 and 1405) represents an important turning point in Christine's literary career. From this point forward, she wrote primarily in prose and in her own voice, albeit sometimes filtered through female allegorical figures, on behalf of moral and political causes. She adopted what Helen Solterer has called a "sapiental mode" of writing, one that conveys wisdom.[18] Yet Christine did not easily take up the mantle of woman writer or teacher. Many of the works produced in 1403–1405 portray Christine's self-conscious struggle to define her gender identity and her problems as a teacher who would impart moral wisdom to often recalcitrant pupils.[19] In *The Book of Fortune's Transformation* (1403), Christine describes how her education as a girl prevented her from entering the "haute escole" (advanced school) of men, and how she was only able to steal "scraps and flakes, small coins and bits of change" from her father's great treasure of learning.[20] Yet she also recounts how Lady Fortune gave her fortitude after her husband's death, strengthening her limbs and lowering her voice such that Christine "felt that [she] had become a true man" (107); for thirteen years, Christine tells us, her male gender identity allowed her to surmount the hardships of widowhood. And in *Christine's Vision*, the masculine image of the hammer striking the anvil and the female metaphor of childbirth are both used to convey Christine's fertile production of fifteen literary works between 1399 and 1405.[21] The autobiographic passages embedded within the larger themes of these works provide fragments of a complex self-portrait that embodies the contradictions of Christine's gendered self. Finally, in the *City of Ladies*, Christine's problematic gender identity and her conflicted role as a writer come to the fore in a crisis of self-doubt that is strikingly portrayed in the opening lines.

Written in 1405, the *City of Ladies* is in many respects typical of late medieval didactic literature.[22] It is a compilation of over one hundred exemplary tales, stories about virtuous women, drawn primarily from antiquity and the Bible, but also including more recent examples. Christine recasts Boccaccio's *Concerning Famous Women*, often correcting the Italian author's unfavorable presentation of certain heroines and adding stories from other sources. With her forceful narrative voice and her critical eye, she makes these famous women her own and uses them to advance a powerful argument.

Countering one antifeminist slur after another, like a lawyer refuting false charges with superior evidence, Christine progressively constructs a defense of women's intellectual and artistic capacities, women's constancy and resourcefulness, and their fortitude as rulers, wives, mothers, and martyr saints. Debunking centuries of misogynist slander, refuting the notion propagated by Aristotle and elaborated by church fathers and clerics that women are mentally deficient, "soft," more prone to pleasure, vice, chatter, and a host of other annoying and destructive traits, Christine cites renowned female rulers, inventors, warriors, and learned ladies to argue in no uncertain terms for women's intellectual capacity and their moral equality, if not superiority, in many respects.

Although many of the *City of Ladies'* pro-feminine arguments are found in other texts, the way in which Christine frames these ideas within a woman-made city and the depth and breadth of her vision of women's history are bold and new. Furthermore, if many of the arguments advanced earlier and later in the "case for women" engage in polemics that sometimes seem purely rhetorical, like a classroom drill or a social game, *The City of Ladies* is anything but an empty academic exercise. Christine's book springs rather from a personal dilemma in which her female identity and the honor of her sex are at stake. In the *City's* famous Prologue—surely one of the most remarkable expressions of a woman's crisis of conscience in French literature—the author sits dejectedly in her study after reading the shockingly misogynistic *Lamentations* of Matheolus, an antimarriage diatribe. Christine's narrator reasons that since all the greatest philosophers have said such negative things about women, they must therefore be true. As a result, she is filled with such self-loathing that she wishes she were a man: "Oh God, why wasn't I born a male so that my every desire would be to serve you, to do right in all things, and to be as perfect a creature as man claims to be?" (*City of Ladies*, 7). It is at this point that Lady Reason, Lady Rectitude, and Lady Justice appear as crowned queens before Christine, urging her to defend women against lies and slander for the sake of all womankind. So damaged by pervasive cultural misogyny that she would deny her identity as a woman, Christine is thus saved by raising her voice on behalf of other women and by engaging in female advocacy at the behest of feminine wisdom. Although her book does not propose a dismantling of existing social and political hierarchies or make claims for women's legal or political rights, Christine's pro-feminine revision of women's place in history explicitly seeks to create a female textual community that valorizes women's intellectual and moral worth. Whether this constitutes "feminism" in the modern sense and whether Christine's sociopolitical vision is as progressive as we might like are subject to debate.[23] But such disputes do little to diminish the significance of Christine's achievement. As evidenced by Christine's inclusion in numerous histories of French feminism, *The City of Ladies* is a landmark text in the *querelle des femmes* and a monument of early feminist thought.

CHRISTINE'S ANALYSIS OF MARRIAGE AND THE FAMILY

Yet another way in which Christine foreshadows later feminist thinking is in her sober assessment of marriage and the family. Christine's status as a widow, who for thirteen years fought off claims levied on her husband's estate, forced her to become autonomous and to plumb her reserves of wit and resourcefulness in ways that may not have been necessary had she remained married. As we have seen, Christine's commentary about herself, scattered throughout her works, provides fragmentary evidence of a woman seeking to fulfill her family responsibilities through writing and allows us to glimpse her struggle to balance the demands of family life with her desire for learning.

In *The City of Ladies* (1405), Christine presents the family as central to women's social existence and portrays women as key to the family's well-being; most of the women characters are presented in relation to their husbands, fathers, siblings, or children. Yet Christine's portrait of family life often deviates from the traditional Aristotelian patriarchal ideal as outlined by Giles of Rome, among other medieval political theorists. For Giles, the "natural" family consists of husband and wife, and the "complete" family includes heirs, presumably male.[24] By contrast, the Amazon women who appear among the *City of Ladies'* first exempla are described as visiting men only for the purposes of procreation; they retain baby girls in their female domain and leave the boys with their fathers. At the end of the book, Christine celebrates female martyr saints. Whether virgins or married, they remain fiercely loyal to families in extraordinary ways: Saint Felicity was martyred along with her seven children; Saint Marina lived disguised as a young monk with her father in a monastery and then acquiesced to a false claim that she had fathered a child rather than divulge her identity; Saint Nathalia disguised herself as a man to offer comfort to her husband during his martyrdom. Beginning and ending her book with such unconventional female lives, from the Amazons to the female saints, Christine subtly undermines the patriarchal family as the universal norm for women's social existence. In both *The City of Ladies* and the accompanying *Treasure of the City of Ladies*, she pays particular attention to widows.

Christine places married women at the core of her treatise, in Book II, where she attacks directly one of most commonplace themes of medieval misogyny, that women make married life hell for their husbands. In response to Christine's query about the validity of this claim, Lady Rectitude replies that such ideas were certainly never written by women (*City of Ladies*, 109). She then offers a counter-narrative of family life told from the women's view. Rectitude hastens to say that many women are happily married, just as Christine in her own marriage was extremely fortunate. She also concedes that some women are willful and unreasonable. Yet, as Rectitude insists, there are nonetheless many women who are abused by cruel or unfaithful husbands and must suffer in silence. Christine offers a chilling portrait of domestic violence in these times, where "there are so many wives who lead a wretched existence bound in marriage to a brutish husband who makes them suffer greater penance than if they were enslaved by Saracens" (*City of Ladies*, 109). When Rectitude asks if she is lying, the narrator provides an eyewitness response: "Yes, my lady, I've seen many women treated like this and I felt sorry for them" (*City of Ladies*, 109). Christine describes women (who prefer to remain anonymous) whose "husbands are so despicable and degenerate in their ways that the wives' parents wish that [their sons-in-law] were dead..." (*City of Ladies*, 121). These wives prefer "to be beaten and badly fed, to go penniless and be treated like drudges by them, saying to their family, 'Since you chose him for me, I intend to live and die at his side'" (*City of Ladies*, 121–122). Such scenarios occur frequently, Christine maintains, yet go unnoticed: "Such things are everyday occurrences, but no one remarks upon it" (*City of Ladies*, 122).

Although Christine laments such cruelty, she stops short of advocating that women leave their abusers. She instead advises patient resignation, an approach that may offend our sensibilities today. But Christine's advice on how to survive a bad marriage was prudent counsel at a time when separation, annulment, or divorce were rare. What is significant is that Christine portrays marriage in frank, realistic terms as a burden to many wives, thus correcting antifeminist commonplaces that depicted wives as incessant nags, faithless flirts, and extravagant spendthrifts. She presents instead numerous exempla of loving, faithful wives who offer good counsel, keep secrets prudently, and display touching devotion to aging spouses. In numerous exempla that depict the family torn apart by strife and conflict and suffering the vicissitudes of history, women hold the social fabric together. Christine's assessment of the real woes of marriage from the woman's perspective is a first step in a feminist critique of marriage that will recur throughout modern European history.

The Treasure of the City of Ladies, also known as *The Book of Three Virtues*, was written in 1405 as a companion text to the *City*. It was dedicated to the twelve-year-old princess Margaret of Burgundy who had married Louis of Guyenne, heir to the French throne, the previous year. Unlike the *City*, the *Treasure* is almost devoid of heroic exempla. Christine focuses rather on real-life situations in her present, where women's spheres are almost exclusively conjugal and domestic. Christine addresses the book not only to the princess (whose activities are outlined in Book I), but also to women of all social classes, from ladies-in-waiting at court or in manor houses (in Book II), to bourgeois wives of merchants, peasants, and laborers, and even prostitutes, who may redeem themselves by doing laundry (in Book III). Accepting the restrictions placed on women of all classes, Christine advises her female compatriots not only to cultivate virtue, preserve chastity, and perform acts of charity, but also to behave as social agents in a wide variety of capacities. High-born women may counsel their husbands to seek peace with enemies and avoid conflict. Ladies in manor houses must be able to take charge of the estate during their husbands' prolonged absences, and thus should be expert on matters ranging from legal customs and property laws to defense, weaponry, and financial management. A baroness should have "the heart of a man" (*Treasure*, 110). Bourgeois women should be resourceful managers, understanding and overseeing household finances, food purchases and preparation, the discipline and instruction of children, laundry and wardrobe maintenance, and supervision of the domestic staff, who should be treated firmly but with kindness. While all women are expected to hold themselves to the same high standard of moral integrity, Christine tailors her practical advice for each class, describing how royal women, noblewomen, and commoners can use textiles in different ways to display their status by appropriate dress or increase their household coffers by making clothes; she shows that women of all ranks can manage their assets not only to maintain but also to increase moral stature and material well-being.[25]

Christine's valorization of women's role in the family and her assessment of women's economic contributions to the household may not seem like radical positions by the standards of twenty-first-century feminism, in which many women seek to define themselves apart from their roles as wife and mother. Yet Christine's straightforward assessment of women's contribution to their families and her encouragement of women to work to increase the honor as well as the financial resources of the household show remarkable prescience about the role that women play in the formation of early modern households. The critical analysis of women's social roles would become a hallmark of developing feminist theory, and Christine's perceptions about the condition of women's lives are astute and unflinching.

After her two books for women, Christine wrote other important didactic works, including *The Book of the Body Politic*, *The Book of Peace*, and a manual of chivalry. Her last extant work, written in July 1429, celebrates the miraculous intercession of Joan of Arc, the maiden warrior, who helped Charles VII lift the siege of Orleans and restore the throne to France during the Hundred Years' War. It seems appropriate that Christine's last heroine be a contemporary woman whose courage and fortitude equal or surpass those of worthy women in the *City of Ladies* and who proves that a woman can defend her fortress—in this case, her country—with weapons and well-organized military forces, as Christine advises the baroness to do in *The Treasure* (*Treasure*, 110).

FEMALE LITERACY, WOMEN'S EDUCATION, AND CHRISTINE'S LEGACY

In both the *City of Ladies* and the *Treasure*, Christine seems to accept as God-given women's place in the medieval gender hierarchy. Men have bold voices and physical strength, Lady Reason explains, so that they may better enforce the laws they uphold (*City of Ladies*, I, 11); most women do not need to know all that men do, for their domestic duties don't require it (*City of Ladies*, I, 27). At the same time, Christine maintains that, despite women's physical weakness, their intellectual capacities are at least as strong as men's. In answer to the question whether women have an aptitude for learning, Christine replies that if women had the same educational opportunities as boys, they would excel, for "their minds are in fact sharper and more receptive when they do apply themselves" (*City of Ladies*, I, 27). A gallery of learned ladies in ancient history, from Carmentis, inventor of the Roman alphabet, to the poet Sappho, whose work Plato kept under his pillow, and the goddess Minerva, who invented metal armor, attests to women's intellectual gifts and accomplishments (*City of Ladies*, I, 28–42).

As we have seen, Christine describes her own limited access to formal education in *The Book of Fortune's Transformation*. In the *City of Ladies*, she reports that although her father encouraged her studies, her mother attempted to promote the more feminine pursuit of needlework (*City of Ladies*, II, 36). Yet Christine's "natural inclination" for learning could not be thwarted, since "What is in our nature cannot be taken away" (*City of Ladies*, 141). This autobiographical fragment proves what Christine has said elsewhere about women's education: even if girls are dissuaded from learning and are given unequal opportunities compared to their brothers, at least some of them have a "natural" intelligence that can be nurtured by parental encouragement or that can flourish in spite of it. Deploying the traditional opposition between textile work, often represented by a spindle and gendered as female, and learning, which may be represented by the pen or the book and gendered as male, Christine demonstrates that apparently "natural" categories of difference are in fact cultural norms that can be overturned by a woman's innate intellectual inclinations.

Christine never promotes her own "path of long study" as an autodidact and high-profile lay intellectual as a route that other women should follow.[26] She does assume that high-born women will learn to read, and she advises the princess to monitor her children's education carefully (*Treasure*, I, 15, 41–43). But the program of readings recommended for the young princess is a conservative one, consisting of "books of devotion and contemplation or ones dealing with good behavior." Books "containing any vain things, follies or dissipation" are to be avoided (*Treasure*, 43). Nowhere does Christine suggest that girls and women cast their sights beyond the distaff to take up the pen, as will the French poet Louise Labé in the mid-sixteenth century.

Nonetheless, it can be argued that Christine, through the variety and complexity of works that she offers to female readers, actively promotes women's self-improvement through learning. *The City of Ladies*, which was presented in a luxuriously illustrated manuscript to the queen of France and remains extant in twenty-five manuscripts, is by no means an "easy" book. It contains hundreds of classical, biblical, and historical examples, as well as citations from canonical literature of the day, set within a sophisticated, often witty allegorical frame. Viewed as an anthology of women's history, it constitutes a demanding program of instruction that provides its readers with a critical sense of women's contributions to the past. Using historical exempla and firsthand observations to critique men's complaints about female nature, Christine encourages her readers to reflect critically on their own lives.

As an author who participated in the production of her works and oversaw their circulation, Christine was aware that her manuscripts would reach audiences far beyond their original dedicatee. Writing *The Treasure of the City of Ladies* for Margaret of Burgundy, Christine also includes women of all social classes, and she tells us in the epilogue that she wants it to reach "the whole world of women, present and future, wherever this book can reach and be seen" (*Treasure*, 167). *The Treasure* is extant in twenty-one manuscripts, including seven paper manuscripts, many produced after Christine's death. There are three early printed editions, as well as a Portuguese translation in manuscript and print. The book was evidently prized in royal households well beyond the reign of Isabeau de Bavière. Antoine Vérard produced a luxuriously illustrated hybrid print edition for Anne of Brittany.[27] Anne de Beaujeu, sister of Charles VIII and regent during his childhood, had several copies of Christine's works in her library; in 1504, Anne herself wrote an instructional manual for her daughter that seems at least partly inspired by *The Treasure of the City of Ladies*.[28] Marguerite de Navarre, sister of King Francis I and queen of Navarre by her second marriage, was also familiar with Christine's work. Her debate poem *The Coach*, which advances arguments about the perils of passionate love for women, borrows much from Christine's own debate poems, and the *Heptaméron*, her celebrated collection of short stories published posthumously, recasts the frame story of Boccaccio's *Decameron* from the perspective of male and female storytellers, offering pointed critiques of gender relations that are often reminiscent of Christine's views.[29] Anne-Marie Legaré has noted that Christine was "the most frequently represented fifteenth-century author in women's libraries at the end of the Middle Ages."[30]

Christine expressly sought such broad circulation among women, as she tells us in the final lines of *The Treasure of the City of Ladies*:

> [And I thought] to myself that I would distribute many copies of this work throughout the world whatever the cost, and it would be presented in various places to queens, princesses and great ladies, so that it might be more honored and exalted, for it is worthy of it, and it might be spread among other women…It will endure in many copies all over the world without falling into disuse, and many valiant ladies and women of authority will see it and hear it now and in time to come (*Treasure*, 168).

In 1405, Christine had no way of anticipating the advent of printing, yet her words in the *Treasure*'s Epilogue about the broad circulation of her book seem almost prophetic about the great transformations in literacy that would soon occur. Indeed, her works figure among the earliest books in print. *The City of Ladies*, translated into English by Brian Ansley, was printed in London in 1521. French editions of *The Treasure of the City of Ladies* were printed in 1497, 1503, and 1536.

BEYOND THE MIDDLE AGES

By the mid-sixteenth century, female literacy extended well beyond royal and elite noblewomen to encompass bourgeois households, where women took up the pen and ushered their works into print in increasing numbers—this despite the persistence of prejudice against women's learning. In Lyon, a major publishing center, poets Pernette de Guillet and Louise Labé, the latter a daughter of a rope-maker, left jewel-like collections of poetry that recast Petrarchan conceits from the perspective of a female subject. In the Prologue to the female dedicatee of her collected sonnets, Louise Labé advised that women adorn themselves with the glory of learning rather than with sumptuous dress and that they look up from their distaffs to engage in study, which alone can provide a "unique inner satisfaction."[31] In Poitiers, Madeline des Roches and her daughter Catherine established an informal salon dedicated to literary exchange in their bourgeois household, and they published numerous poems and treatises. Marie de Romieu, a baker's daughter, composed clever occasional verse as well as a trenchant, witty poem that argued for the "excellence" of women over men.[32] Whether or not Marie knew Christine's earlier work, she carried the torch for the defense of women that would be rekindled in the early modern period in works by writers such as Marie le Jars de Gournay, Marguerite de Valois, and Gabrielle Suchon, among others.

Other women, including Gabrielle de Coignard and Anne de Marquets, wrote spiritual verse during a period of intense religious conflict. Marguerite de Navarre, mentioned earlier, composed a mystical work inspired by Marguerite Porete that was condemned by the Sorbonne. Women formed receptive audiences for the burgeoning literature of the Reformation and Counter-Reformation; women's promotion and defense of spiritual values and support of religious causes, although not specifically feminist in nature, were nonetheless forms of advocacy and political engagement that can be seen as harbingers of later kinds of social activism.

But it was in Italy, birthplace of humanism, where women's learning and literary production flourished most spectacularly in the fifteenth and sixteenth centuries. Girls of wealthy Italian families received an education at home that was often the same as that of their brothers. The learned Isotta Nogarola (1418–1466), rejecting both marriage and the convent to live as a solitary intellectual with her mother, circulated the Latin letters she exchanged with family members and prominent male scholars. She also published a dialogue with Ludovico Foscarini, governor of Venice, about the relative culpability of Adam and Eve.[33]

Later in the fifteenth century, Laura Cereta (1469–1499) left a letter book containing epistles exchanged with prominent humanists and family members; the manuscript was not published until the seventeenth century. Many of the themes introduced by Christine de Pizan resonate in her writing: the defense of woman's positive contributions to marriage; women's intellectual equality; and, in even stronger terms than Christine's, women's inherent right to an education: "Nature imparts one freedom to all human beings equally—to learn."[34]

Nogarola and Cereta wrote learned treatises in Latin. By the mid-sixteenth century, when print publication and Petrarchism were in vogue, noblewomen and bourgeois women turned their hand to writing in the vernacular, producing prose and particularly poetry in astounding quantity. In one estimate, between the time of Vittoria Colonna's first publication of poetry in 1538 and the end of the sixteenth century, "no fewer than two hundred books were authored by women or were anthologies of men's works that included women."[35] Some of these poets have become well-known in contemporary literary and feminist studies, admired for their forthright expression of female sensuality or for their clever transformation of poetic conventions: Gaspara Stampa, Vittoria Colonna, Veronica Franco, and Laura Battiferra are among the most prominent. There are many more whose works are emerging from oblivion in new editions; we cannot possibly do justice to the richness of this tradition here. Despite persistent attacks on learned ladies, literate women continued to find writing an activity to be valued in itself, for the sense of fulfillment and self-worth it brings and as a means to form bonds with other women. In the late sixteenth century, the Counter-Reformation in Europe resulted in censorship of men's and women's writings and brought about a new resurgence in antifeminism, which in turn fueled the debate about women in new pro-feminine treatises.[36]

By the late sixteenth century and early seventeenth century, in France, England, and Italy the literary traditions of female advocacy, arguments for women's education, and the feminist critique of marriage had become well entrenched. Marie le Jars de Gournay in France, Mary Astell in England, and Moderata Fonte in Italy are but a few of the outspoken women who penned eloquent defenses of women's interests in a variety of forms. These writers may not have known Christine's works, but they repeat her themes, with a stronger insistence on injustice or an even more pointed contestation of women's rights.

The traditions of female advocacy continued through the seventeenth and eighteenth centuries up to the French Revolution, reaching new heights in the late nineteenth century, when modern militancy and the word "feminist" first made their mark. Feminist hopes were raised in France, only to be dashed by the advent of the Great War. Modern historians and literary critics have explored these complex developments and their rich literary legacy in depth. Our brief and necessarily selective account of premodern female advocacy must end with Christine and her immediate successors.

The emergence of a climate in which women's worth was staunchly defended and in which women's social, political, and legal autonomy would be recognized did not occur in linear progression or as a stepwise evolution. The early history of feminism is a complicated and variegated story, accompanied by currents of discontent, resistance, and resourcefulness that ran deep for centuries, occasionally breaking dramatically into flashpoints or erupting into debates that would shape the cultural climate. But well before Enlightenment treatises proclaimed women's emancipation, social and cultural developments in the Middle Ages gave rise to the conditions in which modern feminism would take root. Not surprisingly, medieval and early modern women themselves were the most important contributors and participants in those phenomena that set the stage for European women's eventual emancipation. Although many of these women wrote as single voices in isolation or with limited circulation and although none of these women were connected to anything resembling an organized political movement, Christine de Pizan and her female forebears and successors often appealed to what Christine called a "women's community" or Laura Cereta termed a "republic of women." As they recounted their own life experiences and described contemporary women's social conditions within the context of the *longue durée* of women's history, medieval and early modern women writers helped to construct and promote textual communities of women who would be empowered by their learning.

FURTHER READING

Altmann, Barbara K. and Deborah L. McGrady, eds. *Christine de Pizan: A Casebook*. New York: Routledge, 2003.

Blumenfeld-Kosinski, Renate and Kevin Brownlee, trans. *The Selected Writings of Christine de Pizan: New Translations, Criticism*. New York: W. W. Norton & Co., 1997.

Broad, Jacqueline and Karen Green. *A History of Women's Political Thought in Europe, 1400–1700*. Cambridge; New York: Cambridge University Press, 2009.

Brown-Grant, Rosalind. *Christine de Pizan and the Moral Defence of Women: Reading Beyond Gender*. Cambridge; New York: Cambridge University Press, 1999.

Desmond, Marilyn, ed. *Christine de Pizan and the Categories of Difference*. Minneapolis: University of Minnesota Press, 1998.

Dinshaw, Carolyn and David Wallace, eds. *The Cambridge Companion to Medieval Women's Writing*. Cambridge; New York: Cambridge University Press, 2003.

Margolis, Nadia. *An Introduction to Christine de Pizan*. Gainesville: University Press of Florida, 2011.

Solterer, Helen. *The Master and Minerva: Disputing Women in Medieval French Culture*. Berkeley: University of California Press, 1995.

Willard, Charity Cannon. *Christine de Pizan: Her Life and Works*. New York: Persea, 1984.

NOTES

1. According to Bard, Hubertine Auclert was the first French woman to declare herself a feminist; Christine Bard, *Les filles de Marianne: Histoire des féminismes 1914–1940* (Paris: Fayard, 1995), 12.
2. Alcuin Blamires, *The Case for Women in Medieval Culture* (Oxford: Clarendon Press; New York: Oxford University Press, 1997); for an overview of the corpus of pro-feminine texts, 19–49, and for rhetorical strategies, 50–69. Selected texts from both traditions

are offered in Alcuin Blamires, Karen Pratt, and C. W. Marx, eds, *Woman Defamed and Woman Defended* (Oxford: Clarendon Press; New York: Oxford University Press, 1992).

3. Among the many works emphasizing women's positive agency, see June Hall McCash, ed., *The Cultural Patronage of Medieval Women* (Athens, GA: University of Georgia Press, 1996).

4. As E. Jane Burns discusses in "Performing Courtliness," Chapter 25 in this volume.

5. For an overview, see my "Female Voices in Convents, Courts and Households: The French Middle Ages," in Sonya Stephens, ed., *A History of Women's Writing in France* (Cambridge; New York: Cambridge University Press, 2000), 10–40.

6. For an excellent synthesis of developments in women's political thought with particular emphasis on emerging strains of feminism, see Jacqueline Broad and Karen Green, *A History of Women's Political Thought in Europe, 1400–1700* (Cambridge; New York: Cambridge University Press, 2009).

7. Among the first to recognize the rich literary traditions of medieval women were Peter Dronke, *Women Writers of the Middle Ages: A Critical Study of Texts from Perpetua (+203) to Marguerite Porete (+1310)* (Cambridge: Cambridge University Press, 1984) and Katharina Wilson, *Medieval Women Writers* (Athens, GA: University of Georgia Press, 1984). Almost thirty years later, critical studies of medieval European women writers and editions and translations of their work are far too abundant to enumerate here. A more recent survey of the field is provided by Carolyn Dinshaw and David Wallace, eds, *The Cambridge Companion to Medieval Women's Writing* (Cambridge; New York: Cambridge University Press, 2003).

8. For an astute analysis of the sophisticated literary strategies of these texts, see Helen J. Swift, *Gender, Writing, and Performance: Men Defending Women in Late Medieval France, 1440–1538* (Oxford: Clarendon Press; New York: Oxford University Press, 2008).

9. As quoted by Charity Cannon Willard, *Christine de Pizan: Her Life and Works* (New York: Persea, 1984), 222.

10. Christine de Pizan, "Letter of the God of Love," in Thelma S. Fenster and Mary Carpenter Erler, eds and trans., *Poems of Cupid, God of Love: Christine de Pizan's "Epistre au dieu d'Amours" and "Dit de la Rose," Thomas Hoccleve's "The Letter of Cupid"* (Leiden; New York: E. J. Brill, 1990), 51–53, ll. 342–406.

11. "Tale of the Rose," in Fenster and Erler, eds, *Poems of Cupid*, 92–125.

12. Christine de Pizan, *Le Débat sur "Le Roman de la Rose,"* ed. Eric Hicks (Paris: Champion, 1977). For an English translation of Christine's letters and other documents in the dispute, see David F. Hult, ed. and trans., *Debate of the Romance of the Rose* (Chicago: University of Chicago Press, 2010). On the debate's chronology, see Hult, *Debate*, 19–24.

13. Guillaume de Lorris and Jean de Meung, *The Romance of the Rose*, transl. Charles Dahlberg (Princeton: Princeton University Press, 1971).

14. On the stakes of the debate and Christine's position in it, see Hult, *Debate*, 11–19 and Rosalind Brown-Grant, *Christine de Pizan and the Moral Defence of Women: Reading Beyond Gender* (Cambridge; New York: Cambridge University Press, 1999), 7–51.

15. The documents that form the core of what we call today the "debate of the *Rose*" were never gathered together in one manuscript, as Hult reminds us (*Debate*, 20). Nonetheless, Christine's presentation of a few of these letters to the queen certainly helped to promote a sense of civic dispute, thus drawing attention to all those who entered the fray.

16. For Christine's role in inaugurating the "querelle," see Joan Kelly, "Early Feminist Theory and the *querelle des femmes*, 1400–1789," *Signs*, 8 (1982): 4–28.

17. Christine de Pizan, *The Book of the Duke of True Lovers*, ed. Thelma S. Fenster and Nadia Margolis (New York: Persea, 1991).

18. Helen Solterer, *The Master and Minerva: Disputing Women in French Medieval Culture* (Berkeley: University of California Press, 1995), 171–74.

19. See my "Christine's Anxious Lessons: Gender, Morality, and the Social Order from the *Enseignemens* to the *Avision*," in Marilyn Desmond, ed., *Christine de Pizan and the Categories of Difference* (Minneapolis: University of Minnesota Press, 1998), 16–40.

20. Christine de Pizan, *The Book of Fortune's Transformation*, in Renate Blumenfeld-Kosinski and Kevin Brownlee, trans., *The Selected Writings of Christine de Pizan: New Translations, Criticism* (New York: W. W. Norton & Co., 1997), 95.

21. Christine de Pizan, *Christine's Vision*, in Blumenfeld-Kosinki and Brownlee, trans., *Selected Writings*, 195–96.

22. Christine de Pizan, *The Book of the City of Ladies*, trans. Rosalind Brown-Grant (New York: Penguin, 2005).

23. For opposing views, see Sheila Delany, "'Mothers to Think Back Through': Who Are They? The Ambiguous Example of Christine de Pizan," in *Medieval Literary Politics: Shapes of Ideology* (Manchester: Manchester University Press, 1990), 88–103 and Christine M. Reno, "Christine de Pizan: 'At Best a Contradictory Figure,'" in Margaret Brabant, ed., *Politics, Gender and Genre: The Political Theory of Christine de Pizan* (Boulder, CO: Westview Press, 1992), 171–92. For a summary of the debate that casts Christine as a universal moralist, see Brown-Grant, *Christine de Pizan*, 7–10.

24. As described in Henri de Gauchi's French translation of Giles, *Li Livres du Gouvernement des Rois: A XIIIth Century French Version of Egidio Colonna's Treatise* De regimine principum, ed. Samuel Paul Molenaer (New York; London: Macmillan, 1899), 148–50.

25. As detailed in my "Christine's Treasure: Women's Honor and Household Economies in the *Livre des trois vertus*," in Barbara K. Altmann and Deborah L. McGrady, eds, *Christine de Pizan: A Casebook* (New York: Routledge, 2003), 101–14.

26. Susan Groag Bell, "Christine de Pizan (1364–1430): Humanism and the Problem of a Studious Woman," *Feminist Studies*, 3 (1976): 173–84.

27. See Cynthia Brown, *The Queen's Library: Image-Making at the Court of Anne of Brittany* (Philadelphia: University of Pennsylvania Press, 2011), 138–41.

28. Anne of France, *Lessons for my Daughter*, trans. Sharon L. Jansen (Woodbridge, Suffolk; Rochester, NY: D. S. Brewer, 2004).

29. For a translation of *The Coach* and selections from the *Heptaméron,* see Marguerite de Navarre, *Selected Writings: A Bilingual Edition*, trans. Rouben Charles Cholakian and Mary Skemp (Chicago: University of Chicago Press, 2008), 151–231 and 371–95.

30. Anne-Marie Legaré, "Charlotte de Savoie's Library and Illuminators," *Journal of the Early Book Society* (2001), p. 42, cited by Broad and Green, *A History of Women's Political Thought*, 64, note 13.

31. The French reads "un contentement de soy," more literally translated as "self-contentment"; Louis Labé, "Dedicatory Letter," in Deborah Lesko Baker, ed. and trans., *Complete Poetry and Prose: A Bilingual Edition* (Chicago: University of Chicago Press, 2006), 42–45.

32. Marie de Romieu, "Brief Discours: que l'excellence de la femme surpasse celle de l'homme, autant recreatif que plein de beaux exemples (1581)," trans. Marian Rothstein, in Anne R. Larsen and Colette H. Winn, eds, *Writings by Pre-Revolutionary French Women: From Marie de France to Elizabeth Vigée –Le Brun* (New York: Garland Publishing, 2000), 137–50.

33. Isotta Nogarola, *Complete Writings: Letterbook, Dialogue on Adam and Eve, Orations*, Margaret L. King and Diana Robin, eds and trans., (Chicago: University of Chicago Press, 2004).

34. Laura Cereta, *Collected Letters of a Renaissance Feminist*, ed. and trans. Diana Robin (Chicago: University of Chicago Press, 1997), 74.

35. Rinaldina Russell, as cited by Laura Anna Stortoni, ed., *Women Poets of the Italian Renaissance: Courtly Ladies and Courtesans* (New York: Italica Press, 1997), xv–xvi.

36. Stortoni, *Women Poets*, xii–xv.

INDEX

Lightning Source UK Ltd.
Milton Keynes UK
UKOW04f1925071016

284695UK00002B/2/P